Bilingual Education

Edited by
HERNAN LaFONTAINE
BARRY PERSKY
LEONARD H. GOLUBCHICK

A National Doctorate Association Series

AVERY PUBLISHING GROUP INC.
Wayne, New Jersey

Other Titles in the Doctorate Association Series

- URBAN, SOCIAL, AND EDUCATIONAL ISSUES, SECOND EDITION
  Golubchick-Persky
- EARLY CHILDHOOD EDUCATION
  Persky-Golubchick-American Federation of Teachers
- INNOVATIONS IN EDUCATION
  Golubchick-Persky
- CONTEMPORARY ISSUES IN ABNORMAL PSYCHOLOGY AND MENTAL ILLNESS
  Burke
- TOPICS IN HUMAN BEHAVIOR SERIES
  Belkin-Belkin

Front Cover Design By George Szekely

Back Cover Photo By Peter Garfield, Courtesy of A.F.T.

This book is dedicated to the memory of Gladys LaFontaine Correa whose life-long career as an educator influenced so many of us in bilingual education.

Contents

Prefix, xi

Section I. Overview, 1

Introduction by Joseph Fitzpatrick
A. National Policy

Chapter 1. Language Policy in the United States, *3*
Arnold H. Leibowitz

The author details in depth the historical development of language policy in the United States.

2. National Policy on Bilingual Education: An Historical View of the Federal Role, *16*
John C. Molina

The author describes the status of federal legislation during the past decade in supporting bilingual programs throughout the United States.

3. Bilingual Education: Ideologies of the Last Decade, *24*
Josue M. Gonzalez

An analysis of the different ideologies which currently exist in bilingual education as to goals, clienteles and perceptions of the significance of home language and language diversity.

4. Bilingual Education: Central Questions and Concerns, *33*
A. Bruce Gaarder

Program goals determine the meaning of bilingual education, but no less a determinant are the social and political dynamics of the bilingualism that exists in the learners and their parents.

5. Bilingual Education: A Mosaic of Controversy, *39*
Larry Sibelman

The author discusses bilingual education, its implications, and the two distinctly different approaches—mainstreaming vs. maintenance.

B. Legal Aspects

6. Trends in Bilingual Education and the Law, *43*
Herbert Teitelbaum and Richard J. Heller

This article focuses on the recent trend to utilize litigation to introduce bilingual education into the schools.

7. The Legal Vicissitudes of Bilingual Education, *48*
Perry A. Zirkel

The author outlines the historical development of laws, court decrees, and key issues affecting bilingual education.

8. Where is Bilingual Education Going? Historical and Legal Perspectives, *52*
Earl J. Ogletree

The historical, legislative and legal basis of bilingual education will be assessed in terms of the present and future state of the art.

9. Bilingual Education and Desegregation: A New Dimension In Legal and Educational Decision-Making, *58*
Ricardo R. Fernandez and Judith T. Guskin

This article discusses in general terms some of the critical issues which have arisen as a result of the contact between the thrusts for bilingual bicultural education and school desegregation in urban areas over the past several years.

10. Bilingual Education Legislation: The Boston Desegregation Case, *67*
Maria Estella Brisk

This article describes the intervention of the bilingual community in the Boston desegregation case. Through the description of this case the author points out the process, the issues that need research and preparation on the part of the community and the importance of monitoring the implementation.

Section II. Culture, 72

Introduction by Marco Hernandez

11. The Special Assimilation Problems of Americans of Spanish Speaking Origin, *74*
Eleanor Meyer Rogg

This article concentrates on the special adjustment problems of Hispanic Americans. The author discusses the Puerto Ricans, Cubans, Mexican-Americans, and Latin-Americans.

12. The Puerto Rican—An Organizational Alien, *80*
    John D. Vazquez

    The author discusses the alienation of the Puerto Rican and Hispanic in post-industrialized American Society, emphasizing socialization within two distinctive settings: the Anglo-Saxon and Latin-Mediterranean milieu.

13. Life In A Changing Multi-Ethnic School: Anglo Teachers and Their Views of Mexican Children, *84*
    Jean Meadowcroft and Douglas E. Foley

    This article is an interpretative description of how elementary school teachers in a small southern Texas school perceived and interacted with their Mexican students.

14. The Advantaged: The Bilingual Student, *89*
    Naomi Platt

    Emphasis is placed on employment opportunities available to the students whose ethnic heritage gives them characteristics different from the majority by virtue of their bilingualism.

15. Sensitizing the American Teacher to the Caribbean Student, *95*
    Clement London

    The author deals with some crucial cultural nuances which inevitably surface and affect the teacher-student interaction, during teaching-learning process.

16. Reflections on the Italian-American Community, *104*
    Stephen R. Aiello

    This article focused on the immigration patterns and problems of acculturation and assimilation of the Italian-Americans. Also, emphasis is given to the needs of Italian-Americans in the areas of education and social service.

17. American Jews: Their Culture and Language, *108*
    Perry Davis

    The author discusses the loss of Jewish culture and language during mass immigration to the United States, current status of Jewish culture and language, and Jewish contributions to American culture.

18. In Search of Identity: The Soviet Jewish Immigrant, *114*
    Stanley S. Seidner

    The author surveys historical, cultural and social antecedents of Soviet Jewry. He examines linguistic and cultural considerations relevant to new arrivals and current problems encountered in the new environment.

19. Bilingualism in Quebec: A Changing Perspective, *122*
    Alison d'Anglejan and Lise M. Simand

    The authors discuss the use of the public school system in Quebec as a primary agent for the implementation of language planning; i.e., the Official Language Act enacted in 1974 by the National Assembly of the Province of Quebec has designated French as the official language of the province.

20. Cross-Cultural Education in Alaska: Not How But Why?, *126*
    J. Steven Hikel

    An Alaskan elementary school principal questions the advisability of pursuing cross-cultural education for Eskimos.

21. Third-Culture Kids, *128*
    Ruth Hill Useem and Richard D. Downie

    The authors present the reactions of American third-culture kids (TCK's) who have come home after living abroad as dependents of parents who are employed overseas.

Section III. *Language Acquisition, 131*
    Introduction by Evelyn Colon LaFontaine

22. Language and Linguistics in Bilingual-Bicultural Education, *133*
    Rudolph C. Troike

    The author explores ways in which linguistics and language research is relevant to bilingual education.

23. A Few Thoughts About Language Assessment and A Sociolinguistic Alternative to the Lau Remedies, *137*
    Ed DeAvila and Sharon Duncan

    The authors examine the issue of language assessment in response to the Lau decision and subsequent Lau Remedies.

24. The ULPAN In Israel, *143*
    Ezri Atzmon

    This chapter describes the role, objective, and methodology of the Israeli Ulpan. The Ulpan is an institution which teaches Hebrew to new Israeli immigrants as well as aiding in their assimilation.

25. Native American Bilingualism, *150*
    Harvey Laudin

    The author discusses the process of acculturative influences upon native Americans and their language.

26. Teaching English to Speakers of Other Languages: The State of the Art, *156*
Christina Bratt Paulston

In this article the author examines the major achievements and recent trends of foreign and second language teaching in the United States, a summary of the "State of the Art." The theoretical issues of language acquisition are discussed.

27. ESL Is Alive and Well, *168*
David Krulik

The article attempts to point out the issues in an English As A Second Language program for students, teachers, and administrators.

28. Aspects of Language Transition—The School Bilingual Program, *174*
Arnold Raisner

The pace and patterns of new language acquisition varies from student to student. An effective design for a language transition program in the schools demands consideration for psychological and sociological influences as they vary in strength over *time* and through *developmental phases.* The development of new language domains, the significance of the ever-changing patterns of Language Dominance Configurations and the role of the native teacher are discussed and applied to the practical problem of planning teaching strategies in the bilingual classroom.

29. Chicano Children's Code-Switching: An Overview, *180*
Erica McClure and James Wentz

This article briefly characterizes the syntax of code-switching and more extensively discusses its situational and stylistic functions.

30. Language Use In A Kindergarten Program For Maintenance of Bilingualism, *185*
Celia Genishi

The author presents a summary of research on code-switching in kindergartens, followed by a discussion of the educational implications of the study for bilingual programs whose goal is to maintain the use of two languages.

Section IV. *Programs of Instruction, 191*
Introduction by Carmen Perez

31. A Typology of Bilingual Education, *192*
William F. Mackey

The author presents a way to classify bilingual education in the form of a typology which could be of help in designing experiments and in talking about bilingual education. A sociolinguistic approach is taken.

32. Bilingual Education for the Children of Migrant Workers: The Adaptation of General Models to a New Specific Challenge, *204*
Joshua A. Fishman

The author discusses the three major socio-curricular models of bilingual education which are utilized throughout the world (compensatory/transitional, language maintenance, and enrichment oriented with respect to their goals) and their applicability to "children of migrant workers" in Northern Europe.

33. French Immersion: An Attempt At Total Bilingualism, *209*
Jeffrey L. Derevensky and Tima L. Petrushka

The authors describe the immersion programs utilized in Quebec which represents an attempt to use the second language as a medium of instruction, thereby shifting the emphasis from a linguistic focus to one where language is seen as a vehicle for developing competence in academic subject matter.

34. Bilingual Ed: How Un-American Can You Get?, *217*
Karen Joseph Shender

The author explores our National Language Policy and believes that the days of the melting pot ideal—when conformity was forced upon children at the expense of their individual needs—are gone.

35. We Got A New Kid and He Don't Speak English, *224*
Nancy Naumann

A teacher describes how she met the challenge of teaching a student who did not speak English. The method and program is described.

36. Italian Bilingual Education In The United States: A Historical Perspective, *230*
Angelo Gimondo

The author analyzes the bilingual education needs of the Italian community. Although Italian bilingual/bicultural education in the United States is a recent phenomenon, the study of the Italian language goes back to the early days of our history.

37. Bilingual Education for Native Americans, *233*
Dale Little Soldier and Leona Foerster

The authors look at bilingual education for native Americans from a historical perspective; they discuss the issues and problems; and they provide some general guidelines for the planning and implementation of bilingual programs serving Indian students.

38. The Resurgence of Welsh, *238*
Frederick Shaw

The author focuses on the Welsh system of bilingual education.

39. Bilingual Education in Scotland, *241*
Richard E. Wood

Bilingual education for Gaelic speakers began in the 1950's and a funded three-year project is in progress. Teaching methods, materials and student attitudes are rapidly improving. The author discusses bilingual Gaelic programs in Scotland.

40. Focusing on the Strengths of Bilingual Children, *248*
Richard E. Baecher

Due to the ASPIRA consent decree and the need for a clear definition of bilingual education, a case is made by the author for focusing on the strengths of bilingual children through educational style analysis.

41. Bilingual Education for Mexican American Children, *256*
Alfredo R. Flores

Young Mexican American children learn best through a bilingual-bicultural teaching strategy. These children are linguistically and culturally different from majority culture children. The author describes a bilingual bicultural education approach for Mexican American children.

42. Bilingual Special Education: Ahora, *261*
Nancy Ayala-Vasquez

This article traces the history of Special Education and establishes a parallel with the development of bilingual education.

43. Bilingual Special Education: Meeting the Needs of the Non-English-Speaking Mentally Retarded Child, *268*
Edward Rich

This chapter presents some of the issues related to the development and implementation of effective bilingual instructional programs for the child identified as mentally retarded.

44. Innovative Approaches to Multi-Cultural Programming, *273*
K. Balasubramonian and C. Frederickson

In this article the authors contend that a well-planned multi-cultural program can benefit every child within the school setting.

45. Self-Determination Through Education: A Canadian Indian Example, *279*
June Deborah Wyatt

The author shows that through a patient approach to change of an all Indian community school board, which incorporates elements of both Indian and non-Indian society, contributes to the goal of cultural and educational autonomy.

Section V. Curriculum, 285
Introduction by Maria Medina Swanson

46. Will Foreign Languages Still Be Taught In The New Year 2000?, *286*
Joshua A. Fishman

The author discusses the probability of continued foreign language instruction.

47. Self-Identity and the Bicultural Classroom, *290*
H. Ned Seelye

This article focuses on both affective and cognitive stress centering on how bicultural youths perceive themselves.

48. Components of A Multicultural Curriculum, *299*
Leona M. Foerster

This chapter will provide arguments for implementing multicultural education in our schools for all pupils.

49. Educational Activities and Practical Implications for the Classroom, *303*
Christina Bratt Paulston

The author describes her own "experimental educational activities" and the practical applications in the classroom.

50. Using Literature With Bilingual Children, *313*
Jane M. Hornburger

The author outlines factors contributing to the plight of bilingual children and suggests ineffective school programs and negative teacher attitude as major causes of their low achievement and high dropout rates. She deplores the system which isolates them and restricts the use of their native language. Teaching strategies are offered and a list of bilingual resource materials is included.

51. Integrated Reading Approaches for Bilingual Learners, *320*
Angela Carrasquillo

This article intends to discuss the three stages of a developmental bilingual reading program. Bilingual educators must be aware of the students preferred mode of learning before selecting a method to use with them. Bilingual teacher's major concern should be to help children develop broader and more advanced reading tastes. This goal can be accomplished by providing children with a wide variety of integrated reading experiences.

52. Mathematics In Bicultural Education, *325*
William M. Perel

In bilingual and hence bicultural education, mathematics as a high prestige and accultural discipline can make an important contribution to bridging the gap between the two cultures and languages.

53. Art As A Communication System, *330*
George Szekely

The art class can become a special place where visual experiences are communicated between student and teacher. In this article the author cites the unique nature of art as a non-verbal communicator. It is especially useful in teaching the non-English speaking child.

54. Reinforcing Bilingual-Bicultural Early Childhood Instruction with Music and Movement Activities, *339*
Minerva Benitez Rosario

The author discusses how music and movement activities can be used as a means to convey and strengthen learning in a bilingual early childhood classroom.

Section VI. *Staff Development, 342*
Introduction by Lourdes Travieso

55. The Role of the Teacher in a Bilingual Bicultural Community, *343*
Theodore Andersson

The author discusses the role of the teacher of Spanish or Portuguese in a bilingual bicultural community as well as considering the roles of the school child, of his family, and of his community.

56. Multicultural Bilingual In-service Teacher Education, *348*
Richard E. Baecher

The author formulates assumptions of multicultural bilingual staff development and recommends the conceptual framework of teaching style to clarify the emerging role of teachers of multicultural education.

57. Training the Bilingual Teacher: The Case for Language Development, *353*
Guadalupe Valdes Fallis

The author discusses the problem of language development and language growth of the English dominant Spanish speaking student who hopes to increase his total command of the Spanish language in order to teach in bilingual programs.

58. Bilingual Teacher Training in Higher Education, *359*
Margarita Mir de Cid

This chapter explores a bilingual teacher training program. The author contends that the passage of the Bilingual Education Act and recent court decisions have brought the urgent need for competent bilingual/bicultural teachers trained in colleges and universities where attitudes, skills, knowledge, and experience are emphasized rather than courses and credit hours.

59. A Community Resource: The Bilingual Paraprofessional, *364*
Bernice Williams

This chapter explores the value of the bilingual paraprofessional in an educational setting.

60. Video Tape: A Means to Develop the Bilingual Professional In The Community College, *367*
Elliot S. Glass and Nancy Liberti

The authors describe an innovative video tape oriented method to improve the bilingual skills of Spanish-speaking students and provide a degree of professional proficiency in Spanish to English-speaking students.

Section VII. *Evaluation and Language Assessment, 370*
Introduction by Protrase Woodford

61. Evaluation and Testing in Bilingual Programs, *372*
Perry A. Zirkel

The author presents a review of the current state of the art with respect to the evaluation data and test instruments relating to bilingual education programs in the United States.

62. Problems in Assessing Language Ability in Bilingual Education Programs, *376*
Roger W. Shuy

The author discusses the recent efforts at determining which children in a school system need special English language services which have led to a clarification of the goals of language assessment in bilingual education programs.

63. The Testing of Minority Children—A Neo Piagetian Approach, *381*
Edward A. DeAvila and Barbara Havassy

The authors discuss the problems of translating existing intelligence or achievement tests for non-English speaking children.

64. On Language Testing: The Development of the Language Assessment Battery, *385*
Howard S. Tillis, William Weichun, and Richard F. Cumbo

The purpose of this article is to present to the reader some of the practical and technical problems inherent in the development of a test in two languages.

65. Summary of a Language Skills Assessment of Chinese Bilingual Students, *391*
Maria Estella Brisk, Mae Chu-Chang, and Donald L. Loritz

The authors report the results of a research study by comparing and contrasting Chinese and Spanish groups so as to highlight the similarity and diversity of ESL students of differing backgrounds.

Preface

Producing change in the educational practices we undertake in our public schools has always been a difficult and complex matter even when there is uniform support for the underlying concept. Consider then the challenge faced by educators attempting to promote the establishment and development of bilingual education in the United States. The potential for controversy and complexity is obviously great when we recognize that inherent in the philosophy of bilingual education is the call for an intensive reassessment and analysis of how we educate a significant segment of the student population in our schools whose language background differs from that of the national language. In addition to the normal inertia resisting any educational change, we have had to face political, social, and economic issues raised as barriers to the effective implementation of bilingual education programs. The often highly charged emotional climate in which these issues are raised serves only to further complicate attempts to address these problems in a rational and scholarly manner. Nevertheless, significant progress has been made since passage of federal legislation in 1968 for the financial support of bilingual education programs by the federal government. School systems throughout the country have embarked upon serious efforts to develop bilingual/bicultural programs for students whose participation in the traditional monolingual English instructional process has been limited or in some cases virtually non-existent. These efforts have resulted in programs which range from those focusing primarily on developing the student's skills in the English language to those in which a comprehensive program using two languages as media of instruction is offered. In many cases programs have been limited to a relatively small number of students in the school and in other cases the entire school population, regardless of language background, is participating in a bilingual program.

The wide variety of practices in bilingual education is sometimes criticized as evidence of lack of direction and lack of concern about basic philosophy and goals for the program. On the other hand, supporters point to the need for experimentation and exploration of many different approaches as a way to developing the most effective programs for specific groups of students in specific situations.

Diversity existing simultaneously with uniformity is not entirely as contradictory as it may sound and in fact the sections of this book demonstrate there is considerable agreement among many of the authors on some issues while there may be difference of opinion on others. As a guide to students of bilingual education, the book is not intended to promote any one point of view, but rather to encourage serious study of many issues in the field as a basis for the acquisition of facts and knowledge which will enable practitioners to make intelligent decisions about the programs in which they participate. Even though some articles are more general than others, each of the sections focuses on an area which reflects an important factor in the development of bilingual programs. Section I provides an overview of the policy and legal factors which had an impact on the efforts to establish bilingual education as an integral component of American education. The section on culture highlights the importance of recognizing students' cultural backgrounds as essential to the successful development of any educational program. The articles in Sections III, IV, and V focus more directly on pragmatic concerns related to language, program design, and curriculum considerations. Naturally, the success of any program depends in large part on the effectiveness of the personnel implementing the program and thus, Section VI includes articles which present key issues in the development of staff for bilingual programs. Finally, the concern with the process of evaluating bilingual programs, and especially the assessment of pupil performance in language, is the subject of the last section.

Clearly, any reader seeking to find in this book all

the answers to all the problems will be disappointed since the intent was not to produce a definitive textbook of practice in the field. Instead, this compilation of articles by such a diversified group of authors, can only serve to stimulate our thinking as it introduces us to the experiences and opinions of scholars, practitioners and others who have at one time or another considered the complexities of promoting educational change.

We trust that the discussion of these readings in classrooms, schools, and wherever people are concerned with bilingual education, will be the source for some of the answers necessary to guide us into a more scientific and less emotional period of development for bilingual-bicultural education.

Special thanks go to my co-editors, Dr. Leonard Golubchick and Dr. Barry Persky, and members of the Doctorate Association Editorial Review Board for their efforts in preparing this book. Special thanks go to Elaine Morenberg, Regina Persky and Judith Golubchick as well as Zenaida Tejada for their technical and editorial assistance. It is the belief of all of us that *Perspectives In Bilingual Education* will be a useful and valuable tool to students at the undergraduate and graduate levels as well as the professional in the field.

Hernan LaFontaine
Director, Center for Bilingual Education
New York City Board of Education

Section I

Overview: Legal Aspects and National Policy

Introduction by Joseph P. Fitzpatrick*

A profoundly human lesson is evident in the articles which follow, namely: how very valuable and humanly desirable is the experience of being able to learn in one's native language; yet, how difficult an achievement that is in a Nation like the United States. The keynote of these articles could be chosen from two brief statements in the remarkable article by A. Bruce Gaarder who has been involved as extensively as anyone in the effort to bring about genuine bilingualism. "It is safe to say that a great many—perhaps most—of the speakers of non-English languages wish that their languages and cultures could be maintained and strengthened . . . It is also safe to say that very few of them know what would be required in terms of political, economic and educational change in order to make that wish come true." The objective is clear, but the road to it is rocky, uphill and beset with endless hurdles. The article by Arnold Liebowitz provided excellent historical background. Bilingualism is nothing new in the American education experience, and much of its difficulty has stemmed from the fact that the dominant Anglo-Saxon, English-speaking citizens were never prepared to cope with the multilingual population which came to the new Nation from many parts of the world. A strange but persistent insecurity about foreign language has troubled the United States from the beginning. It is still the source of much opposition. Dr. Molina's article, "National Policy on Bilingual Education" is an accurate and detailed summary of the development of the present policy and strategies for implementing it. Dr. Gonzalez' article, "Bilingual Education: Ideologies of the Past Decade" presents the wide variety of attitudes, beliefs and theories around bilingual education. Bilingualism means many different things to many different people. And since the different meaning it has for different people will determine the programs they will promote and the strategies for implementing them, the many ideologies inevitably lead to conflicts of interest and conflicts of culture. This is where the Gaarder article becomes significant in its remarkable detail of the way conflicting interests and theories impact upon the quality of programs. The Sibelman article, "A Mosaic of Controversy" provides further elaboration of the nature of the controversy.

The controversies have found their way into the courts and a sizeable body of law is developing around the issue. Perry Zirkel's article "The Legal Vicissitudes of Bilingual Education" gives the background to earlier legal controversies about bilingual education; he also reviews the current scene. The Bilingual Education Act of 1968 proposed bilingual education as a "Voluntary" process; federal support would be available for proposed programs. The intervention of the courts has shifted the character to "compulsory" programs, mandated by court order after legal action. Zirkel's article suggests what other writers explicitly state: one consequence of Court interaction is the complicated situation of Courts mandating academic policy when they haven't the academic experience or sophistication to do so. The complication is well documented by Teitelbaum and Hiller, "Trends in Bilingual Education and the Courts." These two lawyers have been trailblazing in the consent decree whereby the New York City Board of Education has agreed to provide bilingual education to children of Spanish-speaking background who do not know English well enough to be instructed in it. After an excellent review of current cases, they discuss the problem involved in the Supreme Court's decision that a remedy must be found for the failure of States to instruct children in the language they understand, but left open the option of the particular remedy to persons with local responsibility. This can be manipulated in such a way that it may preclude the fulfillment of the objectives of bilingual education. The legal rights of children and families are still in the process of being clarified. Ogletree, "Where is Bilingual Education

*Dr. Joseph P. Fitzpatrick, S.J., Professor of Sociology, Fordham University, Bronx, N.Y.

1

Going?" is a review of the legal and theoretical issues involved. He finds difficulties in the fact that as an innovation in American education, "its expectations are unrealistically high, its implementation poorly planned and its evaluation has been an afterthought." Its failure, he is convinced, would condemn thousands of American children to academic failure as well. The two final articles about the relationship of bilingual education to problems of desegregation call attention to the problems which emerge from unrelated sociological and political developments. Fernandez and Guskin analyze the problem. The focal interests of the Hispanic community in bilingual education are very different from the interests of the Black community in desegregation. Efforts toward the second can easily conflict with the interests of the Hispanic communities, especially since they are not as aggresive in demanding programs as the Blacks. The final article

by Maria Estela Brisk describes the experience in Boston in detail and points out the need for the Hispanic community to be alert and aggressive in defining its own particular interests and in promoting them.

In summary, then, we are back at the remarks of Bruce Gaarder: the political, economic and educational changes required for effective bilingual programs which look to the perpetuation of language and culture are complicated and extremely difficult to effect. The lesson of these articles is clear: Language is not simply a matter of words; it penetrates the deepest aspects of a person's life, religious, social, cultural and political. Bilingual programs, therefore, will touch the population at the deepest levels of their experience. The reactions will inevitably be forceful and varied. The eventual accommodation of conflicts of interests and conflicts of culture will require enormous skill and more enormous patience.

Chapter 1
Language Policy in the United States
Arnold H. Leibowitz*

Introduction

"...language gives a people 'its sense of unity and brings in its train a whole complex of elements that go into the making of a peoplehood.' Furthermore, 'it brings into play the remembrance of past heroes and events of history, the customs, laws which regulate conflicts of interest and help to maintain the peace, and folkways which include characteristic forms of esthetic self-expression. Besides enabling a people to carry on social intercourse, a common language is thus a vehicle for factors which give context and meaning to that social intercourse.' "[1]

As the above quotation indicates, language is more than a means of communication. Some linguists have indicated that it determines our thought patterns. But we do not need to go as far as this to realize that to a people, language brings into play an entire range of experience and an attitude toward life which can be either immensely satisfying and comforting or, if imposed from without, threatening and forbidding. From a central government's standpoint, a common language forges a similarity of attitude and values which can have important unifying aspects, while different languages tend to divide and make direction from the center more difficult. Every Federal government—and the United States is no exception—has been concerned with balancing the role that a non-national mother tongue plays for its citizenry: on the other hand the annealing, productive, and harmonizing effect resulting from the comfort obtained in the course of its use by members somewhat alien to the culture of the dominant society, and on the other the divisive potential brought on by its retention and strengthening.

But if minority language usage can breed problems, its suppression by public authority leads to bitterness and estrangement to the very government which is trying to create loyalty and devotion in this alien section of the population. Superimposed upon this long-range policy question are a myriad of short-range economic and social interests which affect local attitudes toward the group and its most obvious symbol of its apartness: its language. Public officials in attempting to balance these varying interests and emotions have been caught in a series of painful decisions as they have directed and redirected policies with respect to the enforcement of English in various aspects of American life.

The difficulties have been most clearly seen in the school system, where the question of the use of English as the language of instruction to the exclusion of other languages has been a constant issue. Around this issue long-range and short-term visions and attitudes clashed most sharply and resulted in a lengthy travail for politicians, administrators, and educators—however well-meaning—as well as for the parents and children who spoke a different mother tongue than English.

By law, most states require that the language of instruction in the school system be English. These requirements developed over a period of years, most of them arising during the period of World War I and immediately after, when, in a combined fit of patriotism and xenophobia, some 19 states enacted this kind of legislation. Recently the policy has softened. A number of states pointedly disregard the enforcement of these statutes or have repealed them. Similarly, the Executive Branch, which for over a century in governing its territories and Indian reservations had insisted on exclusive use of English by the inhabitants, in the last 25 years has permitted, and even encouraged schools to teach in the native tongue. And, just a few years ago, in a complete reversal of policy, Congress passed the Bilingual Education Act of 1967, indicating the propriety of instruction in a language other than English and authorizing funds to encourage this.

The purpose of this essay is to analyze the reasons behind the governmental decision leading to the "English-only" instruction policy and now to its reversal. The thesis that will be presented here is that this issue had little to do with the ability of non-English-speaking children to learn more readily in their native tongue, although there was, and continues to be,

*Arnold Leibowitz, Attorney at Law, Washington, D. C.

considerable debate over the advantages, from the educational point of view, of teaching in either the native tongue or in English.

Nor does the decision have to do with the willingness of the non-English-speaking group to learn English. In many cases the group either knew English or participated fully in the public school (English-language) system but was merely seeking to preserve its own language and culture in addition to English. Further analysis of the record indicates that official acceptance or rejection of bilingualism in American schools is dependent upon whether the group involved is considered politically and socially acceptable. The decision to impose English as the exclusive language of instruction in the schools have reflected the popular attitudes toward the particular ethnic group and the degree of hostility evidenced toward that group's natural development. If the group is in some way (usually because of race, color or religion) viewed as irreconcilably alien to the prevailing concept of American culture, the United States has imposed harsh restrictions on its language practices; if not so viewed, study in the native language has gone largely unquestioned or even encouraged.

As might be expected, language restriction was only one limitation to be imposed. These language restrictions were always coupled with other discriminatory legislation and practices in other fields, including private indignities of various kinds, which made it clear that the issue was a broader one. To the minority group affected, this was very clear and, therefore, it was the act of imposition itself which created the reaction by the minority group rather than the substantive effects of the policy.

In presenting this thesis, we shall analyze in brief compass the experience of the German-American migrant group. We shall show the different behavior manifest by the government at various times toward that group and how the requirement that English be the exclusive language of instruction in the schools was imposed or withdrawn as government policy changed. We shall then examine the Bilingual Education Act as amended in 1974, the Supreme Court case of *Lau* v. *Nichols* and other lower federal court cases, and recently passed state laws. We shall suggest what these governmental acts portend for future government policy.

German-Americans

Prior to the last half of the nineteenth century, the German immigrants in the United States aroused little hostility. They had proved themselves to be aggressive patriots as early as the Revolutionary War, being well represented at the Philadelphia convention of 1774 and

1775[2] and in the Continental Army.[3] The Continental Congress even printed German versions of a number of documents, including the Articles of Confederation.[4]

All schools in the United States were financed by private funds at that time. The German schools of the 1700's were sectarian in character; ministers were commonly the teachers.[5] School instruction throughout Pennsylvania, Maryland, Virginia, and the Carolinas, was given in German, often to the exclusion of English.[6]

The number of German immigrants increased greatly during the 1817-1835 period. Unlike the 18th century group, these were refugees from political—not religious—oppression.

Among their activities, these "30ers" worked "to have granted to the German language a high degree of ...status in those states with strong German elements."[7]

Most of the newcomers concentrated in those districts where the land was most readily available and cheap: the Western frontier states of Indiana, Illinois, Ohio, Wisconsin, Minnesota, Michigan, Iowa, and Missouri. In these farming districts, the Germans initially had no teachers at their disposal who were familiar with English and, in any event, there was little need for a command of English during those early settlement years.[8] Thus, most of the earliest school laws made no mention of the language to be employed in the public schools.[9] If the language question was raised in these states, the "30ers" brought pressure to bear—successfully—at the polls. The Germans in Ohio, for example, gave much support to the Democrats in the 1836 election. Charging not only that they had paid taxes for public school support but also that the Democratic party owed them some recognition, the Germans fought to exercise influence on the course of study in the public schools of the state. They did not want English to be excluded but they asked that German be taught as well. In response to the German demand, the Ohio legislation passed a law by which the German language could be taught in the public schools in those districts where a large German population resided.[10] In the succeeding election of 1839, pledges were taken from the candidates that the wording of the law would be changed to prevent any loopholes.[11] Accordingly, the law was revised in 1840—the date of the introduction of German-English public schools in Ohio.

In this initial state of tolerance, Pennsylvania a few years earlier had gone even further than Ohio. In 1837 a Pennsylvania law was passed permitting German schools—in some all instruction was to be given in German—to be founded on an equal basis with English ones. This was the only state where such language equality in the public school system was asked for or obtained.[12]

At the local level, accommodations were also made

to the native German school populace. For example, in one district in Wisconsin one-third of the textbook funds were specified to be spent for German textbooks; in others school boards could hire only German-speaking teachers; and frequently local school-district records were kept in German.[13] In Wisconsin it became the norm that whenever a newly created school district contained a large German population, teachers were hired and the schools were conducted either exclusively in German or in both German and English.[14]

In addition to having German taught locally, the immigrants fought successfully to create a legal framework to prevent state authorities from interfering with such teaching. In most instances, the legal provisions were applicable to all languages; it was, however, the German community who initiated these statutes and who benefitted the most from them.[15]

It should be noted that the Germans were practically the sole immigrants of any significant number during the first half of the nineteenth century. Because they settled in the relatively unpopulated frontier areas of the country and were concentrated in these areas, their presence was relatively unnoticed. They were in the majority in the regions they inhabited; their English-speaking counterparts were the minority population, giving the German element a political and social advantage not available to other groups at that time.

Another explanation for the liberalism that prevailed involves again the intense patriotism demonstrated by the Germans during the several United States conflicts of the period. Beginning with the War of 1812 and ending with the Spanish War, the Germans were represented by large numbers in the American armies.[16]

The latter half of the 19th Century saw the rise of increasingly violent anti-Catholic feeling in the United States. The Know-Nothing Party captured the Massachusetts and Maryland state legislatures and was highly influential in Connecticut. English literacy tests, passed in Connecticut (1855) and Massachusetts (1857), were designed to disenfranchise the newly arrived Irish-Catholics.[17]

The Civil War broke up the politically powerful Know-Nothing movement before it had had any severe impact on the Germans, of whom a sizeable number were Catholic. However, after the War the forces of nativism banded together again and, led by the American Protective Association (APA), ended the period of leniency for the German community.

The teaching of German in the public schools came under severe attack in the 1880's, and the use of German was discontinued in St. Louis, Louisville, St. Paul, and San Francisco.[18]

Restriction of non-English language instruction was not rationalized on technical and educational grounds: rather, legislation was based on a number of political and economic considerations which, when combined, made the recent immigrants a formidable threat.

Immigration reached an all-time high in the 1880's and, since declarant aliens were permitted to vote, the new immigrants threatened to change the political balance in many states.[19] Most of the newcomers were Catholic. Thus, religious bigotry was added to xenophobia and to the economic threat caused by their cheap labor flooding the market.[20] The APA moved against aliens on two fronts: their language and their church.[21]

The remedy developed by the Germans was the use of the private and parochial schools for instruction in the mother-tongue,[22] since the restrictive school laws at that time made little, if any, mention of schools other than public schools. The practice became so widespread that, in largely German districts "the parochial schools in connection with the Roman Catholic and the Lutheran churches had, to a very considerable degree, displaced public schools."[23]

It was a remedy that was viewed by opponents as a direct insult, "contrary to the spirit, genius, and institutions of the United States"[24] and as a potential menace to American institutions. Thus, in 1889, legislation was proposed in a number of states attempting to prescribe the use of English in private and parochial schools.[25]

The Germans were strongly opposed to the laws not only on the school language grounds but also because these laws represented an attack on their religion, culture, and personal liberty:

> They (the Germans) were convinced that (the laws) arose from hatred to foreigners, that it was sinister in its purposes; in short, that is was intended as a blow against all they held most dear. They, on their part, protested that they had no hostility to the public schools nor to the English language...Germans understood that the law was aimed at the destruction of all religion. A panic fear seized upon the minds of the lovers of the German language and customs...[26]

Legislation against Catholics was being passed at this time and gave further justification to the fears expressed above by the German Catholics. New state constitutions included prohibition against sectarian instruction (e.g., Nebraska in 1875, Colorado in 1876, Idaho, Washington, and Wyoming in 1889); numerous states enacted legislation barring all sectarian books not only from the classroom but from school libraries (e.g., Kansas in 1876, Oklahoma in 1890, Idaho in 1893, South Dakota in 1901); prohibitions of state aid to church schools were strengthened by constitutional provisions (e.g., North Carolina and Texas in 1876, Delaware in

1897, Wisconsin in 1898, and in 39 states by 1903).[27]

Perhaps the most heated controversy about the use of English in the private and parochial schools took place in the German-populated states of Illinois and Wisconsin. The Edwards Law in Illinois and the Bennett Law in Wisconsin were passed in 1889. Both Laws required, for the first time, that parochial as well as public schools teach elementary subjects in the English language. The reasoning may be exemplified by an editorial in the *Chicago Tribune* on March 15, 1890:

> In Illinois and Wisconsin a contest between the supporters and enemies of the American free schools, between the right of Americans to make their own laws and the claim on an Italian priest living in Rome that he has the power to nullify them can have but one termination—the defeat of such arrogance and presumption.[28]

Roger Vail, Vice-President of the Catholic Truth Society, answered that Catholics "have nothing against the demand that reading, writing, arithmetic, and U. S. History be taught in the English language," but they objected to the sections that give local authorities power over the parochial school system.[29] The Catholic hierarchy in Wisconsin made a similar statement of protest to the Bennett Law.[30]

The German Lutherans of the states affected were caught in the middle of this anti-Catholic movement, for they had a sizable parochial school system as well. They saw these laws as a violation of the freedom of conscience by forcing children into the public schools or forcing upon them books "permeated by the toxins of atheism and irreligion."[31]

The Missouri Lutheran Synod appointed a General School Committee to direct the opposition to both the Bennett and Edwards Laws. In addition to other responsibilities, the Committee was empowered to solicit contributions and lend financial aid to district synods who could not meet the costs incurred in opposing these laws, publish articles in the secular press, and secure the nomination of candidates who supported their position on the school question.[32]

With the exception of the Lutherans, the majority of Protestant denominations favored the new school laws.[33]

In the 1890 elections the Democrats, supported by the German Lutherans, the Polish and German Catholics, the Scandinavian Lutherans, and the German Freethinkers, won in Wisconsin and Illinois on anti-Edwards and Bennett platforms.[34] Both acts were repealed in 1893 and the two states passed compulsory-attendance legislation without any reference to the English language. The attacks of 1889-1891 left their impact, however, on the German schools. For one, the Bennett and Edwards Laws were in operation for a number of years before their repeal, and the schools attempted to adjust to them: "The footing that English gained was not taken back even after the repeal of the...Acts."[35]

The question of German in the parochial schools was revived during the First World War. At the onset of the War, state officials maintained the right of private schools to give instruction in German. One such official declared:

> Private parochial schools have the legal right to conduct schools in the German language...so long as they do not violate the law or interfere with the carrying on of the War.[36]

But as anti-German feelings grew and Germans were considered a serious threat to U. S. security, a movement, led by the National Council of Defense, sought to stamp out the remnants of the German culture still in existence. A decree issued by the Victoria County Council of Defense in Texas read in 1918: "We call upon all Americans to abandon the use of the German language in public and private, as an utmost condemnation of the rule of the sword."[37] Although it was impossible to stop the use of German in the private sphere, council attempts to suppress its use in public were successful. In Findlay, Ohio, the town council levied a fine of $25 for the use of the German language on the streets.[38]

Given this political climate, restrictive legislation concerning the use of the German language in the schools was inevitable. In 1903, there were but fourteen states with some sort of provision requiring that instruction in the elementary schools should be in English, and seventeen such states in 1913. By 1923, however, thirty-four states required English.[39]

German was specifically mentioned in the laws of several states. But the German provisions in 1903 and 1913 were permissive while those in 1923 were prohibitive.[40] Ohio provides an excellent example in this regard. In 1903, the provision was as follows:

> The Board of any district shall cause the German language to be taught in any school under its control, during any school year, when a demand therefore is made, in writing, by 75 freeholders resident of the district, representing not less than forty pupils who are entitled to attend such school, and who, in good faith, desire and intend to study the German and English language together; but such demand shall be made at a regular meeting of the board, and prior to the beginning of the school year, and any board may cause German or other languages to be taught in any school under its control without such demand.

In 1913, it was changed to read:

> Boards of Education may provide for the teaching of the German language in the elemen-

tary and high schools of the District over which they have control but it shall only be taught in addition and as auxiliary to the English language. All the common branches in the public schools must be taught in the English language.[41]

By 1923 the statute, in appropriate part, read:

Sec. 7762-1. That all subjects and branches taught in the elementary schools of the State of Ohio below the eighth grade shall be taught in the English language only. The board of education... shall cause to be taught in the elementary schools all the branches named in the...General Code. *Provided that the German language shall not be taught below the eighth grade in any of elementary schools of this state.*[42]

The Ohio statute and similar laws against German language instruction were declared unconstitutional by the Supreme Court.[43]

The leading case in this area, *Meyer* v. *Nebraska*,[44] made clear that the prohibition or undue inhibition of the use or teaching of a foreign language is an unconstitutional violation of due process.[45] However, it also explicitly assumed, *in dicta*, that a state statutory requirement of English instruction in public and private schools was permitted by the Constitution.[46]

The case arose when, after World War I, Nebraska and a number of other states passed statutes inhibiting the teaching of foreign languages. The Nebraska statute was quite simple:

Section 1. No person, individually or as a teacher, shall, in any private, denominational, parochial or public school, teach any subject to any person in any language other than the English language.

Section 2. Languages, other than the English language, may be taught as languages only after a pupil shall have attained and successfully passed the eighth grade....[47]

The Court, Mr. Justice McReynolds writing the opinion (as he did for all the language cases arising in the twenties), held the statute unconstitutional:

It is said the purpose of the legislation was to promote civil development by inhibiting training and education of the immature in foreign tongues and ideals before they could learn English and acquire American ideals; and 'that the English language should be and become the mother tongue of all children reared in this State.' It is also affirmed that the foreign born population is very large, that certain communities commonly use foreign words, follow foreign leaders, move in a foreign atmosphere, and that the children are thereby hindered from becoming citizens of the most useful type and the public safety is imperiled.

...The protection of the Constitution extends to all, to those who speak other languages as well as to those born with English on the tongue. Perhaps it would be highly advantageous if all had ready understanding of our ordinary speech, but this cannot be coerced by methods which conflict with the Constitution—a desirable end cannot be prompted by prohibited means.

The desire of the legislature to foster a homogeneous people with American ideals prepared readily to understand current discussions of civil matters is easy to appreciate. Unfortunately experiences during the late war and aversion toward every characteristic of truculent adversaries were certainly enough to quicken that aspiration. But the means adopted, we think, exceed the limitations upon the power of the State and conflict with rights assured to plaintiff in error. The interference is plain enough and no adequate reason therefore in time of peace and domestic tranquility has been shown.

The power of the State to compel attendance at some schools and to make reasonable regulations for all schools, *including a requirement that they shall give instructions in English, is not questioned.* Nor has challenge been made of the State's power to prescribe a curriculum for institutions which it supports....Our concern is with the prohibition approved by the Supreme Court. ...No emergency has arisen which renders knowledge by a child of some language other than English so clearly harmful as to justify its inhibitions... We are constrained to conclude that the statute as applied is arbitrary and without reasonable relation to any end within the competency of the State.[48]

Justices Holmes and Sutherland would have upheld the state legislation, although they would have struck down a statute aimed specifically at one foreign language.

We all agree, I take it, that it is desirable that all the citizens of the United States should speak a common tongue, and therefore that the end aimed at by the statute is a lawful and proper one. ...I cannot bring my mind to believe that in some circumstances, and circumstances existing it is said in Nebraska, the statute might not be regarded as a reasonable or even necessary method of reaching the desired result....I agree with the Court as to the special proviso against the German language contained in the statute dealt with in Bohning v. Ohio.[49]

Despite the court rulings, the practical effect of World War I and the accompanying state legislation resulted in the German effectively being dropped from the high school curriculum. Thus, in 1915 approximately 324,000 students were studying German. By 1922, four years after the World War I ended, the high schools had less than 14,000 students of German.[50]

The road back was slow and World War II made matters doubly difficult. The result was than, although there was an increase in the total high school population from 1,300,000 in 1915 to 5,400,000 in 1948, German enrollment dropped in thos years from 324,000 (25 percent) to 43,000 (.8 percent).[51]

There was a growth in foreign language studies generally in the United States in the '50's and early '60's as a result of expanding post-war international activity and the National Defense Educational Act of 1958. German language study similarly expanded. However, general curricula instruction in German now seems to be a thing of the past.[52]

Bilingual Education Act

By 1967 when the Federal government for the first time, by its passage of the Bilingual Education Act, suggested the permissibility—even the desirability—of instruction in the native language, the political context had substantially changed. The Executive and Legislative Branches had both come out strongly for civil rights and focused on the deprivations suffered by various minority groups. The wave of ethnic nationalism which accompanied the civil rights movement and social changes in the '60's no longer required Spanish-speaking parents to remain mute or to soften their desire that the Spanish language be given a more meaningful role in their children's education.

The 1960 Census[53] counted the Spanish-surnamed population in the five Southwestern states of Arizona, California, Colorado, New Mexico and Texas, and the figures were indeed significant. The total Spanish-surnamed population had increased more than 50 percent over the 1950 totals: to 3,464,999 from 2,281,710. The 1960 figures from Texas showed that the Spanish surnamed population was 1,417,810 out of a total population of 9.5 million people, or almost 15 percent of that total. California had the largest Spanish-surnamed population, 1,426,538, a figure which showed an 87.6 percent increase over 1950.

In the other Southwestern states (Arizona, New Mexico, and Colorado) the Spanish-surnamed population was also identified and was in all cases approximately 10 percent or more.[54] On the East Coast, although not as numerically significant, there was a large number of Puerto Ricans—over 600,000 in New York City and, by 1966, almost 21 percent of the total public school population of that city[55]—for whom Spanish was the native tongue.

The Federal government and the individual states had begun to respond to this increased constituency. For example, in 1965 the Federal government established the Interagency Committee on Mexican-American Affairs[56] to concern itself with Mexican-American issues, and on July 1, 1967, a Mexican Affairs Unit began to function within the United States Office of Education. Within the next few years the Equal Employment Opportunity Commission published its first study of Mexican-Americans, *Spanish-Surnamed American Employment in the Southwest*, The U.S. Civil Rights Commission held its first hearings on Mexican-Americans and published its first report "Mexican-Americans and the Administration of Justice in the Southwest," and the Congress in the Voting Rights Act of 1965 permitted the suspension of literacy tests as a condition of voting where past performance indicated discriminatory administration of the test[57] or where the voter had completed the sixth grade in an American school where the language of instruction was other than English.[58] In extending the Act, in 1970 and then 1975, Congress suspended and then banned literacy tests altogether.[59]

At the local level the New York City Board of Education in 1958 published its comprehensive *Puerto Rican Study* dealing with the difficulties encountered by these native Spanish-speaking pupils in the New York school system.[60] The Texas Education Agency in 1965 investigated the problem of the pupils in the Texas schools having Spanish-surnames and Colorado published in 1967 a general study of the status of the Spanish-surnamed population in that state.[61]

As the state studies show, education was in the forefront of the concern of the Spanish-speaking. The 1960 Census statistics on the educational level of the Spanish-surnamed students in the five Southwestern states showed that Mexican-American children had completed an average of 8.12 years as compared to the White American average of more than 14 years of schooling. The high drop-out rate that these statistics evidenced caused great concern.

Moreover, educational theory had changed. Quite apart from the political developments mentioned above, there was an increasing interest in introducing foreign language programs in elementary schools. This activity was assisted by a series of government grants under the National Defense Education Act, passed in 1958 in response to the Russian launching of Sputnik. Title VI and—later—Title XI of that Act emphasized the retention and expansion of our foreign language resources. This renewed interest in foreign languages and foreign language teaching enabled new groups such as ACTFL (American Council for the Teaching of Foreign Languages) and TESOL (Teachers of English to Speakers of Other Languages) to assert themselves in educational circles.

The powerful National Education Association (NEA) in late 1966 sponsored a conference on the education of Spanish-speaking children in the schools of the southwest which led to the publication of NEA's report entitled "The Invisible Minority, Pero No Vencibles." This report strongly recommended instruction in Spanish for those children who speak Spanish as a native tongue. In April 1967, at the Texas conference for the Mexican-American at San Antonio, demonstrations were given of the work of bilingual and English as a second language program already established in a few elementary schools in Texas. One of the major conclusions of the conference was the need for bilingual education with a call to the Federal government to assume an important part of this responsibility.

These educational forces also conjoined to discredit the idea that instruction in English and American values and patriotism were inextricably linked although this view continued to be voiced at the hearings on the Bilingual Education Act, even by avowed advocates of the new law. The climax of these efforts was reached when, in 1967, Senator Ralph Yarborough of Texas introduced a bill[62] to amend existing elementary and secondary education act legislation to provide assistance to local educational agencies in support of bilingual education programs. Bilingual education was defined as the use of non-English mother tongue as a medium of instruction (together with English) in all or a significant portion of the regular school curriculum. Senator Yarborough's bill was limited to assisting the Spanish-surnamed populace only.

Although the Office of Education was at first reluctant to support new legislation for bilingual education, taking the position that this problem could be handled through existing statutes, especially Title I and Title II of the Elementary and Secondary Education Act, it finally advocated the bilingual bills. In the House of Representatives at about the same time a number of similar bills advocating bilingual education were introduced, most notably by Congressmen Augustus Hawkins and Edward Roybal of California and Congressman Jerome Scheuer of New York.[63] The Hawkins/Roybal bill expanded on the Yarborough bill to include assistance to the French-speaking as well, and the Scheuer bill authorized bilingual instruction to all children whose native tongue was not English.

The changed political and moral situation can be seen in the opening speeches of the sponsors of the legislation in the Senate, Senator Yarborough and Senator Paul Fannin. Much of the rhetoric— "disadvantaged" and "discrimination"—arose from the broader aspects of the civil rights movement and the number of people affected was immediately noted.

Mr. Yarborough. Mr.President, in the southwestern part of the United States—bordered by my State of Texas on the east, California on the west, and reaching to Colorado in the north— there exists, as in the rest of the country, a folklore that we have achieved equality of economic opportunity, that everyone has an equal chance to get ahead.

The reality lurking under this belief is that for a group of 3,465,000 persons, 12 percent of the population of the Southwestern States, equality of economic opportunity awaits the future. It is a myth, and not a reality, today for the Mexican-Americans of the Southwest....

I believe the time has come when we can no longer ignore the fact that 12 percent of the people of the Southwestern United States do not have equal access with the rest of the population to economic advancement. The time has come when we must do something about the poor schooling, low health standards, job discrimination, and the many other artificial barriers that stand in the way of the advancement of the Mexican-American people along the road to economic equality.[64]

Mr. Fannin. I need not remind any member of this special subcommittee that to overcome, educationally, the effects of a disadvantaged childhood is a formidable task. But to rise above the combined effects of a disadvantaged youth and a language barrier is for many children an educational impossibility.[65]

But the broader political context is most clearly seen in the way representatives of the Executive Branch stated the goal of education:

Brief references to two documents, 184 years apart in our history, should suffice on this point. The earlier document, the Bill of Rights of the Constitution, is unequivocally emphatic about the primacy and dignity of the individual as opposed to the power of the state. Justice Brandeis has epitomized this emphasis in the *Olmstead Case:* 'The makers of the Constitution...sought to protect Americans in their beliefs, their thoughts, their emotions and their sensations. They conferred, as against the Government, *the right to be let alone*, the most comprehensive of rights and the right most valued by civilized men.'

The second document, published in 1960 as *Goals for Americans*, contains the Report of President Eisenhower's Commission on National Goals together with certain essays on the same subject. Henry Wriston, chairman of the Commission, reminds us that human dignity is the basic value of freedom, that dignity does not consist in being well-housed, well-clothed and well-fed. And he goes on to say 'that it rests exclusively upon the lively faith that individuals are beings of infinite value.'

Some educational corollaries emerge from the above statement and restatements of principles:

1. If the first goal of education is individual self-fulfillment, all other goals, however important, such as preparation for citizenship, preparation for 'the world of work,' and assimilation to the 'mainstream of American life,' become secondary...

2. The child's parents and the child himself must have the major voice in determining what his education should be.

So we see that the 'right to be let alone' places self-fulfillment, self-determined, at the peak of all the desiderata of education.[66]

The passage of the 1968 Bilingual Education Act focused increased attention on the needs of the non-English speaking, and resulted in both State and Federal legal activity. A number of states passed legislation permitting the implementation of the new law.

Thus California, on May 24, 1967, passed a law authorizing bilingual instruction "when such instruction is educationally advantageous to the pupils—[if] it does not interfere with the systematic, sequential and regular instruction of all pupils in the English language."[67] The New Mexico Legislature adopted in 1969 a law permitting any school district to set up "a bilingual and bicultural program of study"[68] and Arizona in that same year passed legislation to permit school districts where pupils have English-language difficulties to provide special programs of bilingual instruction in the first three grades. In addition to Texas' provision for a special pre-school program for non-English-speaking children,[69] Texas revised its Educational Code in 1969[70] to permit school districts at their option to offer bilingual education.[71]

At the time the 1974 Bilingual Education Act was passed, eleven states had legislation of some kind concerning bilingual-bicultural education. Of those eleven, only six had funds set aside to carry out the legislation. The large majority of all bilingual programs were dependent on Title VII funding.[72]

Additional pressure was brought to bear for expansion of federal bilingual efforts, finally resulting in the 1974 Bilingual Education Act, by a combination of judicial and Executive Branch action. Thus, the National Advisory Council on the Education of Disadvantaged Children stated:

"The National Advisory Council on the Education of Disadvantaged Children (NACEDC) believes that a bilingual bicultural education is the right of every American child whose vernacular is not English, and that bilingual-bicultural education is needed by all of the children in a country where variety within unity has been, and continues to be, of the utmost importance. A child's bilingual-bicultural background is an untapped national resource, and the NACEDC recommends strongly that bilingual-bicultural education be an essential component of the educational program of a child with limited or no knowledge of the English language."[73]

More importantly, the Office of Civil Rights in the Department of Health, Education and Welfare, as part of its responsibilities to implement Title VI of the Civil Rights Act of 1964 which requires that there be no discrimination in any federally assisted program issued the following memorandum on May 25, 1970 "to school districts with more than five percent national origin minority group children." Referring to Title VI of the Civil Rights Act of 1964[74] and the [HEW] Departmental Regulation[75], promulgated thereunder, which required that there be no discrimination on the basis of race, color or national origin in the operation of any federally assisted programs, the memo stated that its purpose was to clarify HEW policy on issues concerning the responsibility of school districts to provide equal educational opportunity to national origin-minority group children deficient in English language skills. The key directive of the memo was as follows:

"Where inability to speak and understand the English language excludes national origin-minority group children from effective participation in the educational program offered by a school district, the district must take affirmative steps to rectify the language deficiency in order to open its instructional program to these students."[76]

So far under the May 25 Memorandum, there has been only one enforcement proceeding. HEW charged the Uvalde Texas Independent School District with unlawful segregation of Mexican-American students in elementary schools; discriminatory racial and ethnic teacher hiring and assignment; discriminatory ability grouping; and failure to provide bilingual-bicultural education.[77] The Reviewing Authority reversed the Administrative Law Judge and found a denial of equal educaional opportunity in all but the second charge of the HEW, thus requiring that the school district provide bilingual programs.[78] The major importance of the Memorandum stems from the affirmance of its policy view by the United States Supreme Court in *Lau* v. *Nichols*.[79]

Lau v. *Nichols* was a class action initiated in 1971 by 1800 non-English speaking Chinese students charging the San Francisco Unified School District with failing to provide all non-English speaking children with special language instruction. They alleged a violation of their Constitutional rights under the Equal Protection Clause of the Fourteenth Amendment and a violation of Title VI of the Civil Rights Act.

The Supreme Court supported the children but was careful to limit its holding to the statutory, not the Constitutional, ground:

> "...there is no equality of treatment merely by providing students with the same facilities, text-books, teachers and curriculum; for students who do not understand English are effectively fore-closed from any meaningful education...

> We know that those who do not understand English are certain to find their classroom experiences wholly incomprehensible and in no way meaningful...

> It seems obvious that the Chinese-speaking minority receives less benefits that the English-speaking majority from respondents' school system which denies them a meaningful opportunity to participate in the educational programs—all earmarks of the discrimination banned by the [HEW] Regulations..."[80]

The Court remanded the case for the district court to fashion appropriate relief, leaving it unclear how extensive a language program is required.

Other lower court cases were equally supportive in providing relief for students, requiring compensatory language instruction and went beyond the narrower language of the Supreme Court ruling and unclear remedy requirements. Thus in *United States* v. *Texas*,[81] the district court found de jure segregation of Mexican-American children and ordered the creation of a unitary school system in which "...neither English nor Spanish is presented as a more valued language."

"[There is] ...the need... for special educational consideration to be given to the Mexican-American students in assisting them in adjusting to those parts of their new school environment which presents a cultural and linguistic shock. Equally clear, however, is the need to avoid the creation of a stigma of inferiority akin to the 'badges and indicia of slavery' ...to avoid this result the Anglo-American students too must be called upon to adjust to their Mexican-American classmates, and to learn to understand and appreciate their different linguistic and cultural attributes."[82]

In *Serna* v. *Portales Municipal Schools*,[83] although the educational program at the predominantly Mexican-American school was "substantially equivalent" with other programs elsewhere, nevertheless, the court found that there was a denial of equal educational opportunity because the curriculum was tailored to the needs of English-speaking children without regard to the needs of Spanish native tongue children. The court rejected the school district's plan as a mere token to the needs of the Spanish-speaking children and ordered a bilingual-bicultural program to be put into effect.

In *ASPIRA* v. *Board of Education of the City of New York*,[84] the New York federal district court accepted a consent degree calling for bilingual education for all New York children who need it beginning with a pilot program including:

1) supplemental instruction in English with the objective of attaining early functioning competancy in English, and
2) instruction in substantive courses in Spanish, and
3) a planned and systematic program designed to reinforce and develop the child's use of Spanish.

Following *Keyes* v. *School District No. 1* (I), the Denver court in *Keyes* v. *School District No. 1* (II),[85] ordered implementation on a pilot basis of a bilingual-bicultural approach in several predominantly Chicano schools during the 1974-1975 school year with a long range goal of implementation throughout the district.

Internationally there was a similar interest in bilingual education. Much of this international work resulted from the growth of many new nations who were forced with polylingual, uneducated societies to make basic judgments on both political/legal and educational aspects of language. Careful examination of this experience had begun and there were produced a number of book length treatments in English setting this forth.[86]

This international experience, the HEW memorandum, the State laws, dependent upon federal funding, and the court cases, led to the Bilingual Education Act of 1974. The avowed purpose of the 1968 Bilingual Education Act was to provide funding to meet "the special education needs of large numbers of children of limited English-speaking ability in the United States."[87] The Act did not provide guidelines on the establishment or operation of such programs.[88] The limited requirement of the 1968 Act that the children served by the bilingual education programs, come from families with incomes below $3,000 per year[89] restricted considerably the effective scope of the Act. Further, of the $400,000,000 authorized to be spent under the Act for fiscal year (FY) 1969 through FY 1973[90] only $117,900,000 were actually appropriated by Congress.[91] Many needs brought forth by the Act went unserviced. Thus of the 3 million Mexican-American children who constitute 60 percent of all the non-English speaking school population and whose programs received $83.5 million of the $124 million spent under the Act between 1969 and 1973, less than 3 percent were being reached by bilingual programs.[92]

Besides complaints that the programs on the whole were too limited or biased toward certain bilingual groups, other shortcomings were noted. First, the Act was much less successful in reaching needy non-public students than public school children. Of the 1973 programs, 187 served 105,708 public school children while 35 served 3,755 non-public school children.[93]

Also, Title VII programs rarely reached students at the junior and senior high levels. In 1973, only 16 programs served secondary schools.[94] The Bilingual Education Act of 1974,[95] which superceded the 1968 Act attempts to remedy these defects by broadening considerably the scope of the federal government's involvement.

The 1974 Act eliminates the requirement that children served by its programs must come from low income families. It then defines what constitutes a bilingual education program in very broad terms.

"a program of instruction, designed for children of limited English-speaking ability in elementary or secondary schools, in which, with respect to the years of study to which such programs is applicable—there is instruction given in and study of, English and to the extent necessary to allow a child to progress effectively through the educational system, the native language of the children of limited English-speaking ability, and such instruction is given with appreciation for the cultural heritage of such children, and with respect to elementary school instruction, such instruction shall to the extent necessary, be in all courses or subjects of study which will allow a child to progress effectively through the educational system."[96]

This definition permits bilingual education not only in a remedial situation, as an aide to learning English, but also where cultural reinforcement is the goal.

The Bilingual Education program is upgraded to be headed by an office Director in HEW.[97] To improve the coordination and success of Title VII programs, the 1974 Act introduces a research aspect to bilingual education to be conducted by the National Institute of Education of HEW "in order to enhance the effectiveness of bilingual education programs."[98]

The needs of American Indians are given special attention under the 1974 Act with direct financing of bilingual programs permitted in Indian schools[99] or indirect through transfer to the Department of the Interior.[100]

Not surprisingly this liberal educational activity was parallelled in other areas. Thus the Equal Educational Opportunities Act of 1974,[101] declares that "No state shall deny equal educational opportunity to an individual on account of his or her race, color, sex, or national origin, by...the failure by an educational agency to take appropriate action to overcome language barriers that impede equal participation by its students in its instructional program."[102]

Conclusion

We have tried to show that the utilization of the English language as the language of instruction is the result of a decision reached on extra-educational grounds. Of course, the decision had an educational effect and was frequently designed to do so. But even when it did, it had an overriding political purpose and for that reason was coupled with discriminatory action of various kinds designed to suppress the minority group's normal development. What was important was the act of imposition itself which acted as a symbol to demonstrate official public hostility toward the particular group. Again, the educational policy was combined with other acts, both public and private: most notably, in the continental U. S., segregation, to achieve the desired political result.

The imposition of the English language and the discriminatory action accompanying it arose quite naturally out of the limited concept of pluralism present in the United States during its expansionist years. Until recently distinctive language and cultural development based upon religious and racial differences were viewed with great hostility, and public actions to inhibit cultural development in other than the preconceived mold were regarded as quite in order.[103]

The requirement of instruction in the English language, then, is a symbol of a broader societal discrimination which can usually be found in segregation and in limitations on employment opportunities. Confining ourselves to the English-language-instruction requirement, the issue is not whether the native tongue is used as the language of instruction or not, but only whether English is the *required* language of instruction. If English is not required or not imposed it becomes one more symbol of tolerance and openness, one more way in which society is stating that the natural development of the minority group involved is acceptable and appropriate and should be permitted. What language is to be chosen should be decided by the local community. The results will likely not make much difference as long as it accurately reflects the instincts and desires of the parents so that they feel that the opportunity for their child is maximized.

The United States, at both the Federal and state level, as we have seen, in balancing the unifying effect of English with the harmonizing benefits of native language retention has consistently favored English.

Even where the group was relatively small and the accommodation to be made was relatively short-term in character (one or two generations at most), the force of official sanction was used to impose English-language instruction and to limit native-language instruction. Whatever the benefits of such a policy were its necessarily concomitant discriminations have left a bitter legacy. At this time the government has realized and should continue to do so that the *option* of native language instruction should also be made available to be exercised as desired by local communities. The Federal system needs the sense of harmony, cultural equality, and devotion which such an option engenders.

Much of the material found here is also available in a longer monograph by the author entitled "Educational Policy and Political Acceptance: The Imposition of English as the Language of Instruction in American Schools" (Center for Applied Linguistics, Washington, D. C.). It has been specially updated for this essay. What has been totally omitted are the detailed chapters exploring the experience in the U. S. of the Japanese/Americans, Mexican/Americans, American Indians and Puerto Rican/Americans on the Island of Puerto Rico.

FOOTNOTES

[1] Excerpt from speech delivered by Antonia Pantoja. Puerto Rican Forum, Inc., *1964 Study of Poverty Conditions in the New York Puerto Rican Community* 78-79 (1965). Quoting from M. Kaplan, *The Future of the American Jew* 146 (1948).

[2] 1 A. Faust, *The German Element in the United States* 291 (1969). (Hereinafter cited as Faust.)

[3] *Id.* at 299.

[4] H. Kloss, *The Bilingual Tradition in the United States* 51 (1970). (Hereinafter cited as Kloss) The page numbering mentioned in this footnote and subsequent references to this work are to the manuscript version kindly made available by the publisher.

[5] 2 Faust 203.

[6] *Ibid.*

[7] Kloss 57.

[8] 2 Faust 204.

[9] For example, Missouri in 1817; Illinois in 1825; Michigan in 1835; and Iowa in 1841. Kloss 200.

[10] 2 Faust 151.

[11] *Ibid.*

[12] *Id.* at 152.

[13] L. Jorgenson, *The Founding of Public Education in Wisconsin* 146 (1956).;

[14] J. Fishman, *Language Loyalty in the United States* 234 (1966).

[15] *Id.* at 235. E.g., Missouri and the Territory of Dakota; and between 1854 and 1869 in Indiana, Wisconsin, Iowa, Illinois, Minnesota, and Kansas.

[16] 1 Faust 512, 524, 529.

[17] Leibowitz, "English Literacy: Legal Sanction for Discrimination," 45 *Notre Dame Lawyer* 35 (1969).

[18] Kloss 156.

[19] Leibowitz, supra note 17, at 35.

[20] N. McCluskey, *Catholic Education in America* 15 (1964).

[21] Kloss 157.

[22] J. Hawgood, *The Tragedy of German-America* 39 (1940).

[23] Bascom, "The Bennett Law," 1 *Educational Review* 48 (1891).

[24] D. Reilly, *The School Controversy (1891-1893)* 57 (1943).

[25] Kloss 153. E.g., New York, Ohio, Illinois, Winconsin, Nebraska, Kansas, and in 1890 the newly established states of North and South Dakota.

[26] Kellogg, "The Bennett Law in Wisconsin," 2 *The Wisconsin Magazine of History* 19 (1918).

[27] Beale, "A History of Freedom of Teaching in American Schools," in Amer. Hist. Ass'n. Com'n. on Social Studies, *Rep.* 208-209 (1941).

[28] D. Kucera, *Church-State Relationships in Education in Illinois* 114 (1955).

[29] Reilly, *op. cit. supra* note 24, at 56.

[30] Kucera, *op. cit. supra* note 28, at 114.

[31] *Id.* at 116.

[32] *Ibid.*

[33] *Id.* at 117.

[34] Kloss 154.

[35] *Id.* at 155.

[36] Kucera, *op. cit. supra* note 28, at 161.

[37] Kloss 111.

[38] *Id.* at 112.

[39] J. Flanders, *Legislative Control of the Elementary Curriculum* 18 (1925).

[40] Some twenty-two state legislatures specifically singled out German and prohibited its instruction. Zeydel, "The Teaching of German in the United States from Colonial Times to the Present," in Modern Language Association, *Reports of Surveys and Studies in the Teaching of Modern Languages* 361 (Nov. 1961). See also E. Hartmann, *The Movement to Americanize the Immigrant* 237-53 (1948).

[41] Flanders, *op. cit. supra* note 39, at 29.

[42] 108 Ohio Laws 614 (June 5, 1919).

[43] Bohning v. Ohio and Pohl v. Ohio, 262 U. S. 404 (1923).

[44] 262 U. S. 390 (1923).

[45] *Id.* at 403.

[46]*Id.* at 402.

[47]Ch. 249 Laws of Nebraska 1019 (1919).

[48]Meyer v. Nebraska, 262 U. S. 390, 401-3 (1923).

[49]Bartels v. Iowa, 262 U. S. 404, 412 (1923). (dissenting opinion.)

[50]Zeydel, *supra* note 40, at 361.

[51]*Id.* at 368.

[52]*Id.* 378-388.

[53]The 1930 Census identified "Mexicans" (persons of Spanish colonial descent) as a racial classification. In 1940, on the basis of a five percent sample, the Census counted persons speaking Spanish as the mother tongue. The 1950 and 1960 Censuses, on the basis of a 20 percent and 25 percent sample respectively, identified the Spanish-surnamed populace in the five Southwestern states. These states had accounted for more than 80 percent of all persons with Spanish as the mother tongue. The 1970 Census used four different means of identifying persons of Spanish ancestry: (1) birthplace, (2) Spanish surname, (3) mother tongue, and, (4) Spanish origin based on self-identification.

[54]The precise figures as of 1960 for these latter three states are: Arizona: 194,356 Spanish-surnamed out of a total population of 1,302,161; New Mexico: 269,122 out of a total population of 951,023; and Colorado: 157,173 out of a total population of 1,753,050.

[55]Hearings before the Sen. Special Subcommittee on Bilingual Education of the Committee on Labor and Public Welfare 90th Cong., 1st Sess., 75 (1967) (Hereinafter cited as *Sen. Hearings, Bilingual Education*).

[56]The Nixon Administration expanded its jurisdiction and renamed it the Cabinet Committee on Opportunity for the Spanish-Speaking.

[57]Upheld by the Supreme Court in *South Carolina* v. *Katzenbach* 383 U. S. 301 (1966).

[58]For practical purposes only those students who studied in Puerto Rico were affected. The provision was upheld by the Supreme Court in *Katzenbach* v. *Morgan* 384 U. S. 641 (1966) rev'g 247 F Supp. 196 (D.D.C. 1965). See Leibowitz, "English Literacy: Legal Sanction for Discrimination" 45 Notre Dame Lawyer 7 (1969).

[59]This action of the Congress was sustained by the Supreme Court. *Oregon* v. *Mitchell* 400 U. S. 112 (1972).

[60]New York City Board of Education, *Puerto Rican Study 1953-1957*, (1958).

[61]Colorado Commission on Spanish Citizens, *The Status of Spanish-Surnamed Citizens in Colorado* (1967).

[62]S. 428 in *Sen. Hearings, Bilingual Education.*

[63]*Bilingual Education Programs*, House of Rep., Hearings before the House General Subcommittee on Education of the Committee on Education and Labor on Bilingual Education Programs 90th Cong., 1st Sess. (1967). (Hereinafter cited as *House Hearings, Bilingual Programs.*)

[64]*Sen. Hearings, Bilingual Education* 16-17.

[65]*Id.* at 14.

[66]Statement of D. Bruce Gaarder, Chief, Modern Language Section, U. S. Office of Education in *House Hearings, Bilingual Programs* 351.

[67]Calif. Education Code, Sec. 71.

[68]N. Mex. Stats. Ann. 77-11-12 (1969).

[69]Tex. Rev. Circ. Stat. Ann., Art. 2654-lb (1965).

[70]Vernon's Anno. Tex. Stats. Education Code, Sec. 4.17 (1969).

[71]It was reported that in October 1970 a Mexican-American teacher in Crystal City, Texas, was indicated for teaching a high school class in Spanish contrary to the Texas Code. U. S. Commission on Civil Rights Draft Report II, *Cultural Exclusion of Mexican-Americans in the Schools of the Southwest*, Appoendix C, A Legal and Historical Backdrop, p. XV (1971).

[72]Education Legislation, 1973, Part 7, Hearings Before the Senate Subcommittee on Education of the Committee in Labor and Public Welfare (93rd Congress 1st Sess.) (Hereinafter, Senate Hearings, Educational Legislation) Testimony of Sen. Edward M. Kennedy at 2583. Although the trend is toward passage of support for bilingual programs, such legislative proposals are still susceptible to defeat. e.g. "French Set Back in New Hampshire" *Washington Post*, May 29, 1975, p. 20, which reports the defeat of a bill that would have directed schools to make French the state's "second language of international communication" by assuring that it would be offered as an optional language in all schools. Despite the fact that 40 percent of New Hampshire's population is of French extraction, opponents emphasized that "this is America and English is our language."

[73]National Advisory Council on the Education of Disadvantaged Children, *America's Educationally Neglected*, Annual Report to the President and the Congress, 1973 (Wash., D. C. 1973), p. 31.

[74]42 U.S.C. §2000 (d) (1964).

[75]45 CFR Part 80.

[76]May 25, 1970 Memorandum of the Department of Health, Education and Welfare 35 *Fed. Reg.* 11595, (July 18, 1970).

[77]Letter to Mr. R. E. Byron, Superintendent, Uvalde Independent School District, Uvalde, Texas, from Dorothy D. Stuck, Regional Director, Office for Civel Rights, Region VI (Dallas), June

15, 1971. U. S. Commission on Civil Rights, An Historical Overview of Language Minorities and Education, (Hereinafter *Historical Overview*) App. B. at 7 (1975).

[78]Administrative Proceedings in the Department of Health, Education, and Welfare and the National Science Foundation in the matter of Board of Education and Uvalde Independent School District, Uvalde, Texas and Texas Education Agency, Respondents. Final Decision of the Reviewing Authority (Civil Rights), July 24, 1974. *Historical Overview*, App. B at 8.

[79]*Lau* v. *Nichols*, 414 US 563. (1974).

[80]Ibid. at 564.

[81]342 F. Supp. 24 (E.E. Tex. 1971).

[82]Ibid. at 30.

[83]351 F. Supp. 1279 (D.N.M. 1973) aff'd. 499 F. 2d. 1147 (10th Cir. 1974).

[84]58 F.R.D. 62 (S.D.N.Y. 1973).

[85]380 F. Supp. 673 (D. Colo. 1974). The first *Keyes* case is reported at 413 U.S. 189 (1973).

[86]Fishman, Ferguson, & Das Gupta (ed.), *Language Problems of Developing Nations* (John Wiley & Sons 1968); Rubin & Jerrudd (ed.), *Can Language Be Planned: Sociolinguistic Theory and Practice for Developing Nations* (Univ. of Hawaii. 1971; B. R. Nayar, *National Communication and Language in India*, (Praeger 1968); Heath, *Telling Tongues, Language Policy in Mexico: Colony to Nation* (Columbia Univ., Teachers College, 1972); See also Report of The Royal Commission on Bilingualism and Biculturalism (Ottawa, Canada 1967).

[87]20 U.S.C. 880 b (1968), P.L. 90-247, Title VII, Sec. 702, 81 Stat. 816.

[88]20 U.S.C. 880 b-3 (1968) P.L. 90-247, Title VII, Sec. 705, 81 Stat. 817.

[89]20 U.S.C. 880 b-2 (1968) P.L. 90-247, Title VII, Sec. 704, 81 Stat. 817.

[90]The authorizations were:

FY 1968	$115,000,000
FY 1969	$130,000,000
FY 1970	$140,000,000
FY 1971	$180,000,000
FY 1972	$100,000,000
FY 1973	$135,000,000
FY 1973	$400,000,000

20 U.S.C. 880 b-1 (1968) P.L. 90-247, Title VII, Sec. 703, 81 Stat. 816.

[91]The appropriations were:

FY 1969	$116,700,000
FY 1970	$119,700,000
FY 1971	$125,500,000
FY 1972	$133,500,000
FY 1973	$133,200,000
FY 1973	$117,900,000

[92]*Senate Hearings, Education Legislation.* at 2575, 2598, 3064.

[93]*Senate Hearings, Education Legislation*, Testimony of Edward R. D'Alessio at 3183.

[94]*Historical Overview*, at 83.

[95]20 U.S.C. 880 b (1974), P.L. 93-380, 88 Stat. 502.

[96]20 U.S.C. 880 b-1 (1974), P.L. 93-380, Title VII, Sec. 703 (a) (4) (A), 88 Stat. 504.

[97]20 U.S.C. 880 b-10 (1974), P.L. 93-380, Title VII, Sec. 731, 88 Stat. 509-510.

[98]20 U.S.C. 880 b-12, (1974), P.L. 93-380, Title VII, Sec. 742, 88 Stat. 511.

[99]20 U.S.C. 880 b-8, (1974), P.L. 93-380, Title VII, Sec. 722 (a), 88 Stat. 507-508.

[100]The Interior Department's bilingual education activities vis-a-vis Indians had expanded as a result of the Indian Education Act of 1972 and changes in policy. See Bur. of Indian Affairs, *Bilingual Education for American Indians* (Wash. D. C. 1970); Turner, (ed.) *Bilingualism in The Southwest* (Univ. of Ariz. Press 1973).

[101]20 U.S.C. 1701, (1974), 88 Stat. 514.

[102]20 U.S.C. 1703, (1974), Sec. 204 (f), 88 Stat. 515.

[103]It is only fair to the reader to note at this point that Dr. Heinz Kloss, one of the leading scholars in the area of bilingualism, has concluded, quite contrary to the views expressed here, that the United States' legal norms have assisted in the preservation of ethnic identity in the schools and elsewhere:

> But as our study shows, the non-English ethnic groups in the U.S.A. were anglicized not *because* of nationality laws which were *unfavorable* towards their languages but *in spite* of nationality laws *favorable* to them. Not by legal provisions and measures of the authorities, not by the state did the nationalities become assimilated, but by the absorbing power of the unusually highly developed American Society. The nationalities could be given as many opportunities as possible to retain their identity, yet the achievements of the Anglo-American society and the possibilities for individual achievements and advancements which this society offered were so attractive that the descendants of the 'aliens' sooner or later voluntarily integrated themselves into this society.

H. Kloss, *Excerpts from the National Minority Laws of the U. S. of America* in East-West Center Institute of Advanced Projects, Occasional Papers of Research Translations 124 (1966). The complete original work is entitled *Das Nationalitatenracht der Vereinigten Staaten von Amerika* (1963).

Chapter 2
National Policy on Bilingual Education: An Historical View of the Federal Role
John C. Molina

Introduction

Few countries in the world have greater resources for providing at least an adequate education to children than does the United States. Many countries with far lesser means have recognized the ineffectiveness of attempting to educate children of diverse linguistic backgrounds in a language they cannot comprehend. Moreover, many countries rich in cultural resources have understood the mark of a truly educated individual to be one who can communicate beyond lingusitic and cultural barriers. Such countries have provided bilingual schooling for their educated elite as well as for their diverse linguistic populations for many years.

In the United States however, heightened civil rights awareness was required to arouse strong sentiment among groups concerning the educational needs of language minority children. Complaints to the Department of Health, Education, and Welfare (HEW) of violations of Title VI of the 1964 Civil Rights Act finally stimulated Congressional Hearings sponsored by Senator Yarborough. These hearings, held in different parts of the country, disclosed the language and cultural problems experienced by language minority children attempting to adjust to the English monolingual school. Testimony gave strong public advocacy urging that Federal funding be provided to school districts for the establishment of bilingual educational programs for language minority children. It was not until 1968 that the United States finally established a national policy for providing equal educational opportunity to language minority children through bilingual education.

The implementation of bilingual programs under the 1968 Bilingual Education Act, Title VII of the Elementary and Secondary Education Act, revealed the weaknesses of the Act as well as the complexity of establishing programs with conflicting goals, untrained personnel, and inadequate instructional materials and evaluation. The 1974 Bilingual Education Act has come closer to alleviating these difficulties by clarifying previous ambiguities. In addition, under this new Act, current bilingual education programs must focus on developing bilingual resources and building the capacity of institutions to provide such resources to state and local educational agencies. Such resources as teacher training, materials development, demonstration and dissemination of information on bilingual education approaches provide the base needed for extending to children of any language background the opportunity to receive bilingual schooling in the United States.

National Policy: The 1968 Bilingual Education Act

The 1968 Bilingual Education Act provided funds to agencies "to develop and carry out new and imaginative elementary and secondary school programs," to meet the special educational needs of children of limited English speaking ability.[1] The regulations defined bilingual education as "the use of two languages, one of which is English, as mediums of instruction."[2] Funds were authorized for the development and operation of such programs in school systems with high concentrations of children of limited English speaking ability from low income families and for the training of personnel to maintain such programs. Between 1969 and 1973 under the Act, $117.9 million was spent, 88 percent of which was allocated for classroom projects and 12 percent for various special projects. In 1969 the Office of Education established a Branch of Bilingual Education within the Division of Plans & Supplementary Centers, Title III to administer this Act.

During the first few years the new Federally funded bilingual education programs experienced many difficulties due to the inexperience of educators in this

*Dr. John Molina, Director, Office of Bilingual Education, Department of Health, Education, and Welfare, Washington, D. C. Dr. Molina acknowledges the contribution of Ms. Olga Harper for technical assistance in the research and writing of this article. This article was written by Dr. Molina in his private capacity. No official support or endorsement by the U. S. Office of Education is intended or should be inferred.

country as well as the vagueness inherent in the Act itself. Bilingual education was too new and philosophically threatening to be accepted by many school districts which often favored remedial and English language programs instead. The lack of appropriate materials in non-English languages, and the need for trained bilingual teachers made difficult the starting of new programs with appropriate emphasis on native languages.

In addition, minimal evaluation and research data contributed to the difficulty which plagued Title VII bilingual programs for many years. While the 1968 statute did not explicitly require evaluation, a succession of guidelines and regulations attempted to rectify this shortcoming. However evaluation reports from bilingual programs were developed so dissimilar that meaningful comparisons could not be made on a project basis. Programs often used locally made tests recognizing that many evaluation instruments on the market were either inadequate or inappropriate.[3] Regulations have since become more explicit and require pre and post-testing in both languages, achievement test results in all subject areas in both languages and comparison group testing.[4] But many programs are still unable to document achievement results due to inadequate evaluation techniques in the early years of their program.

While lack of bilingual resources hampered the initiation of effective bilingual programs, the lack of explicitness in the language of the 1968 Act and the regulations gave rise to practices which conflicted with the intent of the law for providing equal educational opportunity. For example, the provisions delineating the participants of bilingual education programs were not explicit. The broad definition of children of limited English speaking ability as "children who come from environments where the dominant language is other than English" made no distinction between language minority children who were English monolingual and those who had varying degrees of proficiency in English and the native language. Consequently, between 1968 and 1974, some school systems obtained Title VII funds and installed bilingual programs which concentrated on teaching English-dominant language minority children their minority language as a second language. Often they placed such students in remedial-type "bilingual programs" focusing on English skills development with minimal use of the non-English language. Moreover, the 1968 law made no provisions for the participation of English-speaking students in the bilingual program nor for the participation of the language minority children in integrated classrooms. Segregated "bilingual programs" were often the result.[5]

In 1971, the Division of Bilingual Education attempted to assist school districts more extensively by issuing guidelines which fully described the purpose of bilingual education and the use of two languages for instruction. In addition, the guidelines assisted school districts in the interpretation of program requirements and policies, outlining steps in program development, amplifying procedures for planning and submitting applications for implementation and continuation of bilingual education programs.

The 1971 guidelines stimulated controversy over the basic goals of bilingual education and the role of the Federal Government. Some felt the bilingual approach was necessary only until the student gained some proficiency in English at which time the transition would be made to an English monolingual classroom. Others thought this transitional approach was shortsighted. It overlooked the educational benefits a student receives in developing self-esteem and scholarliness in two languages when the native language is maintained throughout the student's school career.

The 1971 guidelines and the philosophical position of Title VII suggested a maintenance approach to bilingual education. The guidelines emphasized the intent that students in bilingual education programs would . . . "develop greater competence in English, and become more proficient in their dominant language . . . . . ."[6] In a position paper on Bilingual Education, developed in 1973 the newly formed Division of Bilingual Education defined bilingual education as "an approach which would effectively manifest itself in a well-planned, concrete educational program beginning at the pre-school level and continuing through a child's elementary school career, being maintained through language arts courses in the student's dominant language at the secondary level."[7]

However, legal interpretations of the 1970 General Education Provisions Act resulted in an Office of Education policy which nullified the use of the 1971 Guidelines. The interpretation of the General Education Provisions Act required that guidelines, like regulations, be based on particular sections of the law and published in the Federal Register. Because the guidelines were based on educational philosophy, they could have been interpreted as imposing a philosophical approach rather than simply as a guide to implement the law. The controversy centered around the issue of whether the Federal Government could financially support bilingual programs whose goals are to encourage the maintenance of non-English native languages or whether it should support bilingual programs whose primary objective is to use two languages to promote English language proficiency. This controversy continued until the enactment of the 1974 Bilingual Education Act.

National Policy: The 1974 Bilingual Education Act

Important educational legal development at the state and national levels paved the way for the stronger and expanded Bilingual Education Act in August, 1974. Passage of the 1968 Bilingual Education Act encouraged states to modify existing state legislation in order to support the implementation of state bilingual education programs. Several states established mandatory bilingual education laws and the number of those prohibiting the use of languages other than English in the classroom diminished.[8]

In January, 1974 the Supreme Court decision in the case of *Lau* vs. *Nichols* case directed national attention to the inadequacies of traditional education for providing equal educational opportunity to children of limited English-speaking ability. The *Lau* decision focused on placing the basic educational responsibility of providing effective educational programs to these children upon the state and local educational agencies.

The impact of this decision upon bilingual education was significant. While the court did not impose any specific educational approach, bilingual education was given prime consideration by a Task Force appointed by the Department of Health, Education, and Welfare to develop suggested remedies.[9]

The *Lau* decision and state bilingual education laws encouraged the use of bilingual education as a method for providing children of limited English-speaking proficiency with equal educational opportunity at the time the 1968 Bilingual Education Act was due to expire. The drafting of the new 1974 bilingual education legislation was impacted in two ways.

First, the scope of the Act was narrowed by more clearly defining the participants and goals of bilingual program. Thus, in 1974, the Bilingual Education Act defined, "children of limited English-speaking ability" to be individuals who "have difficulty in speaking and understanding instruction in the English language".[10] The goals of a bilingual program funded under this Act were very clearly to enable children of limited English-speaking ability to achieve competence in English[11] and to give instruction in the native language to the extent necessary to allow a child to progress effectively through the educational system.[12]

While narrowed in scope, the Act did not prohibit the funding of programs that had more extensive goals, i.e., development of the non-English language or its maintenance throughout the grades in the school curriculum. The 1974 law merely established the learning of English and effective progress as base line goals. School districts were free to establish broader objectives as long as their target population was of limited English-speaking ability.

Secondly, increased activity in bilingual education from state legislation and by school districts complying with *Lau* caused advocates to call for the expansion of bilingual education and the development of bilingual resources. The U.S. Civil Rights Commission called for specific provisions in the legislation in the areas of teacher training, curriculum development, research, and the funding of demonstration projects which would systematically provide information on alternative designs for bilingual education programs. Additionally, the Commission asked HEW to maintain the Title VII role in development of bilingual resources separate from Title VI Civil Rights enforcement.[13]

In December 1974, after the enactment of the 1974 Bilingual Education Act, the Undersecretary of HEW clarified the role of the federal government and declared it to be one of capacity building in bilingual education. This includes "research, testing, and dissemination of educational approaches, models, and techniques for teaching students with special educational needs, curriculum development, teacher training, and technical assistance to States and LEA's."[14]

Current Status of Bilingual Education Programs

The current status of bilingual education programs focuses on developing bilingual resources and building education for present and future needs. The 1974 Bilingual Education Act as reinforced and amplified by the regulations delineates a national policy with four major objectives. First, to continue funding programs on a limited scale those programs which serve as demonstration projects.[15] These projects should provide alternative program approaches while building the capacity of the local educational agency to implement bilingual programs on a broader scale. Title VII supported programs have increased in number from 76 in 1968 to 425 in 1976. These programs now serve a total of 65 different languages including 35 Native American, 18 Asian and Pacific Island American and 12 Indo-European languages. Appropriations have risen from $7,500,000 in 1968 to $69,594,764 for basic programs (including 15 percent for staff development within these basic programs).

The second major objective, according to the Title VII legislation directs the Commissioner of Education to "establish, publish, and distribute, with respect to programs of bilingual education, suggested models with respect to pupil-teacher ratios, teacher qualifications, and other factors affecting the quality of instruction offered in such programs."[16] Unfortunately, the Office of Bilingual Education has never been funded specifically to accomplish this task.

However, the Office of Education has considered at

least two ways of establishing bilingual educational models. One way is to design a theoretical model based upon preconceived philosophy and desired goals; such a model can be implemented and process and outcomes carefully documented for subsequent replication. An experimental design can be created in which variables in the model are changed and their relationships studied. The Office of Education, however, found it difficult to implement such an experimental control, and reluctance on the part of school systems to engage in experimental designs.[17]

An alternative approach taken by the Office of Education has been to identify exemplary programs in existence. In 1972, a survey was made of Title VII programs to select exemplary projects. Four projects were finally selected and descriptions of all aspects of the projects were assembled as Project Information Packages. After field testing and revision, these Packages may be used by school districts to facilitate the implementation of bilingual programs. The field testing phase will determine the clarity and usefulness of the Package descriptions in assisting school districts to implement bilingual programs. Although the exemplary programs are not considered to be models since their goals and objectives are not explicit, a study of their implementation may be the first step in finding ways to transport bilingual programs which have shown some evidence of success.[18] Moreover the careful implementation of these projects is one expedient way, given present limited resources, for Title VII to begin identifying effective bilingual educational approaches.

The third major objective is to provide financial assistance to prepare personnel to staff bilingual programs; to train teachers, administrators, paraprofessionals, aides and parents; and to train persons to teach and counsel such persons.[19]

While some classroom demonstration projects include some inservice training and curriculum development, they reach only a small number of students. The 1974 Bilingual Education Act addresses training needs by requiring that $16 million of the first $70 million appropriated be used for training, and that one-third of the amounts above $70 million be similarly earmarked. These funds enable institutions of higher education to provide teachers and administrators with some of the skills needed to work in bilingual education programs.

It is estimated that almost 129,000 bilingual teachers will be required to meet the needs of the non-English language target population. Data on the number of such teachers now available is being collected.[20] Present figures indicate that existing training programs in local school systems and in institutions of higher education do not meet the present or future needs.

Training programs include: inservice training for administrators, parents, counselors, teachers and aides participating in Title VII projects; scholarships to assist recipients achieve degrees or accreditation in the field of bilingual education; fellowships to provide additional graduate studies for teacher trainers in bilingual education in institutions of higher learning; and grants to institutions of higher education to support the development of their bilingual training capabilities.[21] Resource Training Centers discussed below provided another source of training.

The fourth major objective under the 1974 Act as expanded by the regulations is to provide technical assistance leading to the development of bilingual programs.[22] Such technical assistance through the establishment of resource training, materials development, and dissemination and assessment centers[23] addresses the urgent operational needs which have burdened bilingual programs for years.

Experience has shown the staff training provided by local programs has satisfied local immediate needs but could not be expected to build national resources in bilingual education. Local programs have attempted to develop their own materials and disseminate them through sporadic conferences. This has resulted in poorly designed materials lacking in sequence and limited to local use.

Three national materials development projects which were funded in 1970 and 1972, showed limited but encouraging progress. Based upon these experiences, a National Network of three types of centers was established in 1975.

The National Network consists of Resource Training Centers, Materials Development Centers and Dissemination/Assessment Centers. Each type of center functions both independently and interdependently to accomplish expected goals.

Resource Training Centers are primarily responsible for providing direct service to classroom teachers within funded local educational agencies and institutions of higher education as well as coordinating services with State education agencies. Their services are expanding to include technical assistance in program planning and operation, evaluation of programs, materials utilization, staff development, and dissemination of information on effective program practices and procedures. In addition, the Resource Training Centers are responsible for conducting needs assessments for the Materials Development Centers and for coordinating the field-testing of materials within a given region. In 1976, fifteen Resource Training Centers were awarded $5,000.000.

Materials Development Centers are responsible for developing bilingual-multicultural student materials for teaching specific skills and content in the languages of target groups to be served. Such materials are field-tested by local school districts with the assistance of the Resource Training Centers. The materials are then distributed by the Dissemination and Assessment Centers. In 1976 fourteen Materials Development Centers were awarded $5,425,000.

Dissemination and Assessment Centers' primary responsibility is to evaluate, publish, and distribute instructional materials and to disseminate information on curriculum, training, human resources, evaluation and assessment. These centers assess the appropriateness of materials designed for publication and their effectiveness when utilized in programs. Three Dissemination and Assessment Centers have been awarded $1,575,000 in 1976.

In addition to these major objectives, the Office of Bilingual Education has solicited the support of other offices and agencies within HEW to work cooperatively to assess and develop bilingual resources. The Office of Planning, Budget and Evaluation is currently conducting a study on the usage of bilingual instructional materials developed to date. The National Center for Educational Statistics is presently conducting studies on the number of limited English-speaking person in the United States and bilingual education teachers to update current information. The Office of Bilingual Education and the National Institute of Education are working jointly to establish a National Clearinghouse for Bilingual Education to assist educators, administrators and the general public in locating information regarding instructional materials, research, and other documents pertinent to bilingual education.

Future Perspectives

There is a continuing interest in extending to all children the opportunity to receive bilingual schooling. Witnesses at hearings of National Advisory Council on Bilingual Education in Portland, Albuquerque, and Philadelphia have stressed the importance of bilingual/multicultural education as a viable educational approach for children of every language background. They viewed bilingual education not as a remedial program for non-English dominant children, but as a positive approach to instill in every child knowledge and appreciation of the diversity of our national heritage. Generally, they endorsed a maintenance model of bilingual education and encouraged its expansion to English speaking students.[24]

Many efforts which would allow for the expansion of bilingual education are already in the planning stages. As the possibility of expanding bilingual education to include more children arises, increased emphasis will be placed on obtaining funds to provide

for immediate and long-range needs.

It is proposed that Title VII shift emphasis from demonstration programs to an "installation strategy." Such a strategy would provide funds for districts for a designated period of time to install a bilingual education program. The cost of such installation would be determined by the number of children to be served. This strategy will be examined with the field testing of exemplary projects. A study of the implementation of "Project Information Packages" will determine the feasibility and cost of installing effective bilingual education projects in school districts which chooses to adopt bilingual programs. Project Information Packages will give the districts enough information to eliminate most of the trial-and-error time limited resources and expenses usually present in the initiation of new bilingual programs. Start-up costs should be lowered and programs should be implemented more efficiently.

Increased activity in bilingual education research will continue to be a critical need. The National Institute of Education (NIE) is beginning to assume a stronger role in bilingual education research. Joint funding of research projects with the Office of Bilingual Education is now a reality. An example is the joint NIE/OBE efforts to initiate a National Bilingual Education Clearinghouse. A ten-year plan for immediate research is needed and is currently being discussed.

Moreover, present training programs funded will lead to the institutionalization of bilingual education degree programs in colleges and universities. This will most surely be followed by an increase in the number of states instituting specific bilingual teacher certification.

The human resources needed for expansion of bilingual education are now available. There are many more qualified bilingual education professionals. By 1977, about 1265 will have received training through the fellowship program. It is expected these and other graduates of bilingual education training programs in institutions of higher education will assume leadership roles in the creation of future policies in bilingual education.

Ultimately, the expansion of bilingual education in the U.S. will and should depend upon the desires of the national community. The school is an agent for promoting the values of society, and is thus, a reflection of the needs and desires of the people.

Emerging language minority groups who want bilingual education programs must begin to exert pressure upon their community representatives. They must accept nothing less than the kind of bilingual education programs they really desire. Presently, language minority groups desiring bilingual education tend to focus on the value of biculturalism because it supports ties with their ethnic communities. However, an increasing number are beginning to see the economic and inherent value of bilingualism. As successful members of the language minority groups emerge as models in the field of education, diplomacy, international business relations and other fields requiring bilingual skills, the economic value of having native-like speaking and writing skills in two languages will become a desirable goal. Presently small numbers of enlightened bilinguals are beginning to appreciate the cultural and esthetic value of becoming biliterate.

The responsibility for responding to the desires of the community rests clearly upon school board members of individual school districts. The federal role in education has been and will continue to be limited. As lay people in the community, school board members make decisions on educational programs based upon priorities within their community. When school districts cite monetary constraints as a reason for the lack of a bilingual education program it is clear that the education of language minority children and the value of bilingualism is not recognized as a priority need of the community.

School board members set language policy within their communities. If the primary concern of the community is to enable language minority children to learn English and use the native language only insofar as it enables them to reach that goal, then transitional bilingual programs will be instituted. If there is a belief in the value of bilingualism and a desire to develop the capability of students to become international citizens by becoming educated bilinguals, then maintenance bilingual education programs will emerge.

As our world grows progressively smaller and our nations become more and more interdependent, there is little doubt that educated bilinguals will be at a premium in this country. Just as we are beginning to understand that the diversity of species is critical for the survival of our "blue planet", so will we realize that the diversity of languages and cultures is necessary to the richness of life and the well being of the human spirit.

FOOTNOTES

[1]U.S.C. 880b. Enacted January 2, 1968, Public Law 90-247, Section 702.

[2]Grants for Bilingual Education Programs, Regulations of Title VII of the Elementary and Secondary Education Act of 1965 as amended. Title 45 - Chapter 1, Part 123 of the Code of Federal Regulations Reprinted from (January 7, 1969) 34 F.R. 201-205.

[3]For more information on weakness in evaluation in Title VII programs see U.S. Department of Health, Education, and Welfare, *A Process Evaluation of the Bilingual Education Program*, *Title VII*, *Elementary and Secondary Education Act*, Volume 1, prepared by Development Associates, Inc., under contract with the U.S. Office of Education, December, 1973.

[4]Criteria for Governing Grant Awards, Bilingual Education Programs—Title 45—Chapter 1, Part 123, Bilingual Education Programs, Part III of the *Federal Register*, June 11, 1976, Section 123.14(7).

[5]This situation did not begin to be rectified until the 1974 Bilingual Education Act and subsequent regulations clearly defined the term "children of limited English-speaking-ability" as applying to those persons who "have difficulty speaking and understanding instruction in the English language." The Act further prohibited a program from being designed explicitly to teach a foreign language to English-speaking children. Furthermore, the new law made provisions for the voluntary participation of native English-speaking children in the bilingual program and the regulations explicitly required provisions for children of limited English speaking ability in the bilingual program to participate in regular classes with native English-speaking children.

[6]1971 Guidelines, p. 1.

[7]Position Paper, December, 1973, p. 9.

[8]A survey of state legislation on bilingual education indicates that in 1971 no states had mandatory bilingual education laws whereas by 1975 ten states had such laws. The survey further indicates that whereas in 1971 twenty-two states mandated English as the only language of instruction permitted except in foreign language courses, by 1975 only eleven states had such English-only laws. For an overall discussion of State bilingual legislation, see Hanna N. Geffert, Robert J. Harper II, Salvador Sarmiento, and Daniel M. Schember, *Current Status of U.S. Bilingual Education Legislation*, Paper in Applied Linguistics, Bilingual Education Series: 4, (Center for Applied Linguistics: Arlington, Virginia, 1975).

[9]For more information see *Task Force Findings Specifying Remedies Available for Eliminating Past Educational Practices Ruled Unlawful Under Lau vs. Nichols;* Department of Health, Education, and Welfare, Office of Civil Rights, Summer, 1975.

[10]P.L. 93-380 Section 702(a).

[11]P.L. 93-380 Section 702(a)(B).

[12]P.L. 93-380 Section 703(a)(4)(A)(i).

[13]Statement of the U.S. Commission on Civil Rights on

Bilingual Bicultural Education before the General Education Subcommittee of the House Education and Labor Committee, April 12, 1974.

[14]Memorandum dated December 2, 1974 to the Assistant Secretary for Education from the Undersecretary, Frank Carlucci. Subject: Departmental Position on Bilingual Education.

[15]P.L. 93-380 Section 702(b).

[16]P.L. 93-380 Section 703(b).

[17]For more information on the difficulties of implementing an experimentally designed planned variation model bilingual program, see *A Proposed Approach to Implement Bilingual Education Programs: Research and Synthesis of Philosophical, Theoretical and Practical Implications*, research pursuant to a grant with the Office of Economic Opportunity, Executive Office of the President (National Puerto Rican Development and Training Institute, Inc., New York) pp. 1-5. Also see Joan Baratz and Janice C. Redish, *Development of Bilingual Bicultural Education Models*, a research pursuant to a grant with the Office of Economic Opportunity, Executive Office of the President, (Washington, D. D., Education Study Center, 1973).

[18]A survey of projects was made to determine which programs were effective and worthy of replication. Program effectiveness was demonstrated through significant gains in English for children with limited English language skills as well as achievement gains in content areas taught in the native language. Projects screened were required to include English language instruction for children with limited English skills, to provide academic instruction in the language of the target population, and to address the customs and cultural history of the target population. Other criteria considered important in the selection of the projects were defineable and describeable instructional and management components and reasonable startup and continuation costs. For more information on the study design see Evaluation of Bilingual Education Programs: The Exemplary Study, research pursuant to a contract with the Office of Planning, Budget and Evaluation, Office of Education, (American Institute for Research, Palo Alto, California, 1974).

[19]Public Law 93-380 Section 723(a).

[20]*The Condition of Bilingual Education in the Nation: First Annual Report to Congress*, Office of Education, November, 1976.

[21]In 1976, $10.2 million was spent on inservice training for 30,000 participants; $3.2 million provided scholarships to 856 trainees; approximately $4 million provided 708 fellowships; and about $6 million supported the institutional development of 100 institutes of higher education. See *First Annual Report to Congress*, Office of Education, Office of Bilingual Education, pp. 36-38.

[22]Criteria for Governing Grants Awards, Section 123.12(d).

[23]Ibid. Section 123.23.

[24]*Second Annual Report*. National Advisory Council on Bilingual Education, Office of Bilingual Education of the United States Office of Education, November, 1976, p. B-2.

BIBLIOGRAPHY

A Proposed Approach to Implement Bilingual Education Programs: Research and Synthesis of Philosophical, Theoretical and Practical Implications. Research pursuant to a grant with the Office of Economic Opportunity. Executive Office of the President. New York: Puerto Rican Development and Training Institute, Inc.

Baratz, J. and J. Redish, *Development of Bilingual Bicultural Education Models*. A research pursuant to a grant with the Office of Economic Opportunity. Executive Office of the President. Washington, D. C.: Education Study Center. 1973.

"Evaluation of Bilingual Education Programs: The Exemplary Study." Research pursuant to a contract with the Office of Planning Budget and Evaluation. Office of Education. Palo Alto, California: American Institute for Research. 1974.

Geffert, H., R. J. Harper II, S. Sarmiento, D. M. Schember, *Current Status of U.S. Bilingual Legislation*. Papers in Applied Linguistics Bilingual Education Series: IV, Arlington, VA. Center for Applied Linguistics, 1975.

U.S. Civil Rights Commission. Statement before the General Education Subcommittee of the House Education and Labor Committee. April 12, 1974.

U.S. Department of Health, Education, and Welfare. *A Process Evaluation of the Bilingual Education Program, Title VII, Elementary and Secondary Education Act*. Vol. 1 Prepared by Development Associates, Inc. for the U.S. Office of Education, December, 1973.

U.S. Department of Health, Education, and Welfare. Office of Civil Rights. *Task Force Findings Specifying Remedies Available for Eliminating Past Educational Practices Ruled Unlawful Under Lau vs. Nichols*. Summer, 1975.

U.S. Department of Health, Education, and Welfare.

Office of Education. *The Condition of Bilingual in the Nation: First Annual Report to Congress.* November, 1976.

U.S. Office of Education. Office of Bilingual Education. *Second Annual Report.* National Advisory Council on Bilingual Education. November, 1976.

Ken Robinson

Chapter 3
Bilingual Education: Ideologies of the Past Decade
Josué M. González*

While the use of two languages for instructional purposes is not a recent development in the U. S., the last ten years have brought a renewed interest in this aspect of multilingualism along with a flurry of theoretical recommendations and a variety of programmatic applications of those surmises (Gonzalez, 1975).

In 1968, the passage of the Title VII Amendment to the Elementary and Secondary Education Act of 1965 (Bilingual Education Act, 1968) brought to the fore policy issues and ideological differences which had been dormant for several decades. This law also led to far-reaching regulations and mandates by state legislatures, enforcement agencies and by the courts (Center for Law and Education, 1975).

Since that time bilingual education components have been added to other educational legislation. The Educational Amendments of 1974 included bilingual education components in seven of its eight titles. One analysis (U. S. Office...) notes that "the theme (of bilingual education) permeates amendments to more than twenty pieces of legislation enacted by Congress in the past quarter century" (p. 2).

With this prominent involvement by governmental entities came a concurrent revival of policy discussions on all of the facets of this instructional form: staffing, organization, scope, methods, governance, and its duration through the school years. One of the most intriguing aspects of bilingual education is the diversity of ideologies relating to its ultimate mission and goals. Equally noteworthy is the absence—whether benign or insidious—of an articulated policy which could unite the public interests, both of the majority group (of native English speakers), and diverse language minorities.

It might be argued no doubt, that the current absence of a clearly defined policy is salutory; that in its infancy, bilingual education is best served by not being overly constrained with policy restrictions which could give premature roots to one particular ideology. This view assumes that such inattention will eventually result in the spontaneous generation of a social policy which will be acceptable to all of the groups concerned. In truth however, much of the basis for social policy determination has already been established through legislative, regulatory, and judicial precedents and these bases could easily escalate into official policy. Succeeding developments of this type further cement underlying ideologies since it is customary for legislatures, courts and other agencies to determine future courses of action based on antecedent practices.

Goals and Approaches

The goal of this article is to document currently existing ideological differences. This will be accomplished through a double-faceted analysis. First, an attempt will be made to ascertain the nature of emerging public ideology and policy as they are reflected in recent legislation, court decisions, and the mandates of enforcement agencies. Secondly, other discernible ideologies in the lay and professional sectors will be summarized.

The underlying presumption is that these differences concerning rationale, clienteles, outcomes, and their corresponding views of home-language loyalty have been dynamic and consequential. It is further assumed that the interplay of these ideological camps is a continuing rather than an historical one and that their interactions and dialectics are likely to continue to influence future trends in the formulation of bilingual education policy.

No attempt will be made to suggest policy directions or to support or deny the need for a convergence of ideological currents. The study is further delimited in scope by the desire not to ascribe relative strength—political, persuasive, logical, pedagogical, sociological, etc.—to the various positions. What has been sought out is *the presence and range* of differences rather than a comparison of their relative virtue or merit.

*Dr. Josué González, Associate Professor of Education, Southern Methodist University

In tracing the evolution of recent *governmental policy* for bilingual education a documentary approach will be used. A number of education documents which were deemed significant because of their potential or demonstrated impact, will be analyzed. These representative statements will be examined with a view to glean from them insights into the ideological orientations which motivate their authors or constituencies. Additionally, their points of view regarding clienteles, home language, and linguistic diversity will be extracted whether the views be explicit or tacit.

The alternative ideologies which will be highlighted were collected in a series of educators' workshops held in several midwestern cities over a two-year period. Information was obtained through an open-ended interview technique in which the following cue questions were posed:

(1) Which *students* should participate in bilingual education? Who should have priority treatment?

(2) What should be the *goal(s)* of bilingual education? What can it accomplish that other types of schooling cannot?

(3) What is the significance of speaking a language other than English at home? ...at school? ...within one's own group? ...in the larger society?

(4) What, in your opinion, is the greatest *single reason* for having bilingual education in the public schools?

(5) For *how long* should students participate in bilingual education?

(6) Should bilingual schooling be *required*? If so, for whom? In which situations?

Follow-up questions were asked when it was felt necessary to elicit representative and comprehensive responses.

The interviewer defined bilingual education simply: "the use of two languages for instruction; one being English and the other the language of the child's national-origin group." Interviewees were encouraged to interpret the definition, to embellish it, modify it and finally to re-state it to serve them comfortably as a basis for their responses.

The answers to all questions and the definitions given were then analyzed to determine patterns and clusterings of similar responses. Finally, the data were organized into categories which seemed realistically representative of the discrete foci or orientations which the respondents felt bilingual education should have. The data presentation was organized into an outline format rather than a statistical analysis since this seemed to better serve the purposes of the study.

Approximately 60 percent of the persons interviewed were involved as support staff or teachers in bilingual or ESL programs. A few were parents and/or paraprofessionals. The rest were administrators; chiefly principals, assistant and associate superintendents, staff development personnel, and others involved with policy interpretation and clarification. All came from public school districts having national-origin populations in excess of five (5) percent.

In conducting this analysis it has been borne in mind that by their nature typologies such as the one presented here are deficient in at least three unavoidable respects. First, they cannot generate all possible views or categorizations since they are produced from a limited data corpus. Second, they are stated so as to represent salient, easily observable positions and therefore do not account for more eclectic or subtly variant stances. And third, the entire process could be tinted by the analyst's own perceptions or preconceptions. Nonetheless, while it is acknowledged that the analysis may suffer "from the problems of oversimplification and polarization inherent to all such schema," (Carter, 1971), it is hoped that the exercise documented here will be useful in understanding the multiple factors which are currently operating within this dynamic educational innovation.

Federal Policy: Haltingly Evolutionary

In 1967, the U. S. Senate held the first Congressional hearings ever on the subject of bilingual education. Within minutes of the beginning of the first hearing, (U. S. Congress, 1967), one of the Senators participating acknowledged the uncertainty that was being felt by some of the protagonists involved in these deliberations;

It would be a mistake ... for us to impose our notions of bilingual education on school officials, state or local. We are politicians, not educators....

My one reservation—and it is a serious one—is with the provisions that schools, in order to be eligible for aid, must teach Spanish as the native tongue and English as a second language. Educators with whom I have talked are unanimous in their belief that this would be a tragic mistake, every bit as tragic as has been the longstanding policy of requiring Spanish-speaking students to shun their Hispanic heritage (p. 15) ....

...we cannot accomplish that necessary (aim of local schools), by not teaching them the English language, or by not teaching it as well as we teach Spanish, or French, or Italian or German (p. 16).

Some of the witnesses also echoed the caution, restraint and ambivalence reflected in the Senator's statements. First, they were treading on new ground and they were uncertain about public reaction. And second, they were confused by the linguistic science notions of "first language" and "second language." These labels were being read by some as signals of a continuing divergence not only of a linguistic nature, but perhaps also, as a cultural and nationalistic departure from the perceived normativeness of the — "Melting Pot" ideology. The fear of ethnic divisiveness was clearly an issue even when the expressions of reserve were not openly xenophobic.

One Senator noted:

...we must remind ourselves that Spanish-speaking Americans, like the rest of us, can make their greatest contributions to themselves, their families and their country—our country—only when they acquire *the educational skills of most other Americans* (U.S. Congress, 1967, p. 16).

On reading the two volumes of testimony and supporting documentation collected by the Special Subcommittee on Bilingual Education (U.S. Congress, 1967), the true meaning of "the educational skills of most other Americans," becomes clear. What legislators and witnesses alike had in mind was the use of bilingual instruction to bring about a transition from the use of the vernacular in informal situations to the exclusive use of English in the formal setting of the schools. A concomitant assumption seemed to be that this linguistic assimilation was but one phase of a more comprehensive *cultural and nationalistic* assimilation which was perceived as being highly desirable.

Some witnesses in the Senate hearings stressed the then popular notions of "cultural disadvantagedness" in their explanations of the evils which bilingual education would help to exorcise. A Texas school superintendent noted that,

...a large group of students are handicapped by (1) inadequate attendance; (2) cultural background; (3) language deficiency; (4) migrancy; (5) low level of aspiration.

...through ... "compensatory education" we ... are trying to take steps ... which will compensate for these handicaps (U.S. Congress, 1967, p. 272).

When legislation was adopted in 1968, as Title VII of ESEA, it carried this same ideological tone in its preamble:

In recognition of the special educational needs of the large numbers of children of limited English-speaking ability ... (Bilingual Education Act, 1968).

In addition, the legislation required that "poverty criteria" be applied in determining the eligibility of children who were to participate in the programs to be funded by the Act. This was an additional affirmation that bilingual education was seen in the same way as Title I of ESEA: an educational strategy designed to remediate the effects of poverty and "cultural disadvantagedness." This position has not been unanimously accepted however, and differing interpretations as to the goals of Title VII have come up both within and outside HEW. As late as 1974, federal officials found it necessary to circulate an internal memorandum designed to clarify their understanding of the purposes of Title VII. This memorandum read in part;

The fundamental goal of a federally-supported bilingual education program is to enable children whose dominant language is other than English to develop competitive proficiency in English so that they can function successfully in the educational and occupational institutions of the larger society. ...this view of the federal goal regards the use of the home language and reinforcement of its culture and heritage as necessary and appropriate means of reaching the desired end of giving the children from the various language groups proficiency in the dominant language, and not as ends in themselves (Memorandum, 1974).

At about the same time, Molina (1975), then National Director of Title VII, reiterated this interpretation:

l... the legislation (Title VII), was specific in saying that this program must have as its fundamental goal the learning of English by the non-English-speaking child, and it stressed a quick transition to total instruction in the English language (p. 28).

The message is clear: the use of the vernacular for instruction was seen as an unfortunate requirement of the linguistic circumstances of language-minority children and as *nothing else*.

Title VII was not the sole determinant however, of a remedial/compensatory approach to the education of language-minority children. In 1970, the Office for Civil Rights (OCR) of DHEW circulated a memorandum to numerous school districts across the nation. The notice (Memorandum, 1970), advised the districts that they were mandated to "take affirmative steps to rectify the language deficiency" of students having an inadequate command of the English language. This was as interpretation of the Civil rights Act of 1964, which was subsequently reiterated by the U. S. Supreme Court in its historic *Lau v. Nichols* (414, U.S., 563) decision. This decision provided the strongest court ruling yet in support of the "language deficiency" perspective.

Writing in *Lau*, Justice Stewart said unequivocally: The Department (of HEW) has reasonably and consistently interpreted Section 601 (of the Civil Rights Act of 1964), to require affirmative remedial efforts to give special attention to *lin-*

guistically deprived children. ... For these reasons I concur with the judgment of the Court.

It was Justice Blackmun, however, who exemplified most clearly the popular bias towards linguistic assimilation in the English language. Writing in that same case he said:

> We may only guess as to why they (plaintiffs) have had no exposure to English in their pre-school years. Earlier generations of American ethnic groups have overcome *the language barrier* by earnest parental endeavor or by the hard fact of being pushed out of the family or community nest and into the realities of broader experience.

The same year of the *Lau* decision, Congress passed the Equal Educational Opportunity Act of 1974. Its name notwithstanding, this act was designed chiefly to restrain the use of large-scale busing of school children for desegregation purposes. The EEO Act included however, a reference to the linguistic deficiency model in enumerating practices which deny equal educational opportunity. The Act identifies as discriminatory

> the failure by an educational agency to take approaches necessary to overcome language barriers that impede equal participation by its students in its instructional program (Equal Educ. Op. Act, 1974).

None of this evidence distinguishes between "language barriers," and a barrier to a good education. In fact, the two concepts are used interchangeably in the hearings, opinions, suits, and other documentation which surround and support the pertinent decisions and legislation. The reasoning appears to be that, in the U. S., if an education is to be equitable, it must be accessible through the vehicle of the English language.

Until 1975, programs of English-as-a-Second Language (ESL) had been acceptable to most federal authorities as adequate means to overcome the "language barriers" of students. During the summer of 1975, however, a new position was taken by the Office for Civil Rights of HEW. It was contained in a document entitled "Task Force Findings Specifying Remedies Available for Eliminating Past Educational Practices Ruled Unlawful Under *Lau v. Nichols.*" This document was a follow-up to OCR's memorandum of May 25, 1970. It was also the awaited blueprint for enforcing *Lau*, since the decision had not dictated remedies of a specific type. In its document OCR did so in a fairly dramatic manner.

According to one interpretation (Center for Law and Education, 1975), of the new rulings,

> transitional bilingual education, bilingual-bicultural and multi-lingual-multi-cultural programs are approved (in the OCR document), without qualification and (ESL) programs are

not approved, or approved in only certain situations (p. 2).

In addition to limiting the use of ESL programs, the "Task Force..." document is significant in that it attemps to

(1) Re-define the Title VII concept of *bilingual education* by broadening its scope to include the further "developing (of) all the necessary skills in the student's native language and culture" (Center for Law..., p. 2).
(2) Distinguish between bilingual/bicultural education and *transitional* bilingual education, and
(3) Specify certain situations in which the more comprehensive (bilingual/bicultural) approach should be used.

It must be remembered however, that this issue has not yet been terminally resolved.

> An unanswered and critical question is the extend to which the courts will rely upon the HEW memorandum in formulating relief (Center for Law..., p. 2).

The Center for Law and Education (1975) has noted however that, "in the past, in some school desegregation cases, the courts did rely on analogous HEW standards" (p. 2).

A resolution of this matter would no doubt settle with some finality one aspect of the policy question; how much and what type of bilingual education will be required by the courts in their attempt to prescribe equal educational opportunity.

Other aspects of federal bilingual policy must also await further action by Congress and other agencies.

State Policy—All Deliberate Parallelism

Until relatively recent times, many states had statutory prohibitions against the use of languages other than English for instruction (CAL-ERIC/CLL, no. 23). Beginning in the early 1970's however, some states began *requiring* bilingual instruction in schools having substantial numbers of limited-English-speaking children.

A recent study (Cardenas, Bernal and Kean, 1976), notes that, by 1976,

> thirty of the fifty states and three territories, have some type of legislative prescription for bilingual education. Eight of the states plus Puerto Rico have mandatory provisions which make it legally binding (in certain situations) (p. 2).

The model legislation for this trend was enacted by Massachusetts in 1974. The Massachusetts Bilingual Act (Mass. Gen. Laws, Ch. 71) is noteworthy not only because it was the first state mandate, but also, because it has contributed much to institutionalize the concept of *transitional* bilingual education. The notion of transitional bilingual instruction represents a "hard line" of linguistic nativism in that it sets off bilingual education as an atypical departure from the normativeness of English-only instruction. Furthermore, it prescribes a fixed time after which children are expected to function solely in English. Home language preservation and the attendant linguistic pluralism in the society are thus excluded from the responsibility of the schools.

The Massachusetts influence can be seen readily upon a comparative reading of recent statutes from the different states whether the new enactments be permissive or mandatory in nature (CAL-ERIC/CLL, No. 23). Typical of the reluctance towards embracing the maintenance of linguistic pluralism are the policy-prologues to the bilingual education laws of Texas, California, and New York; all states having substantial non-English speaking populations:

California (1965):

It is the policy of the state to insure the mastery of English by all pupils in the schools; provided that bilingual instruction may be offered in those situations when such instruction is educationally advantageous to the pupils. Bilingual instruction is authorized to the extent that it does not interfere with the systematic, sequential, and regular instruction of all pupils in the English language.

New York:

In the teaching of the subjects of instruction prescribed by this section, English shall be the language of instruction, and textbooks used shall be written in English, except that for a period of three years, which period may be extended by the commissioner with respect to individual pupils, to a period not in excess of six years, from the date of enrollment in school. Pupils who, by reason of foreign birth, ancestry or otherwise, experience difficulty in reading and understanding English, may, ...be instructed in all subjects in their native language and in English.

Texas:

(a) English shall be the basic language of instruction in all schools.

(b) It is the policy of this state to insure the mastery of English by all pupils in the schools: provided that bilingual instruction may be offered or permitted in those situations when such instruction is necessary to insure their reasonable efficiency in the English language so as not to be educationally disadvantaged.

Summary of State and Federal Foci

(All citations are from the CAL-ERIC/Cll, No. 23 analysis.)

Our review of both federal and state enactments, agency regulations and the documentation which attends them, points towards a unified ideology which we can not categorize more succinctly. We can conclude that governmental policies are subsaturated with the following ideological elements:

Orientation: Assimilation/Compensation/Remediation.

Goal: To provide a greater equality of educational opportunity through an enhanced ability to use the English language.

View of non-English home language: Dysfunctional and limited as it pertains to school achievement and upward social mobility.

Participation: Children who come from "disadvantaged backgrounds"—economically, socially and culturally—and whose home language is other than English.

View of linguistic diversity: Neutral to negative.

Duration or scope of bilingual instruction: Short-term or intermittent; a "special" program for atypical populations who are expected to enter a more typical (English-language), instructional program as soon as this is feasible.

In juxtaposition to these ideological patterns emerging from actions of the state, a number of other perspectives co-exist within and outside the programs of bilingual education which are funded and regulated by state or federal agencies. Some of these, which embody discernible differences are summarized below.

Other Perspectives
Aesthetic/Enrichment Orientation

Programs of this type fall squarely within the traditional *humanities* or *liberal arts* approach to education. Its advocates believe that knowledge of more than one language is a sound educational goal for all students. Programs of this type are similar in structure to traditional foreign language classes. The parameters of this ideology can be summarized as follows:

1. *Goal.* Bilingual schooling of this type is designed to enrich the education and the intrinsic humanistic, and aesthetic qualities of an individual through the study of a language other than his/her own.

2. *View of non-English home language.* Home languages are seen as untapped natural resources. Not to maintain and improve the child's home language is considered an educational anachronism and a societal waste of valuable resources.

3. *Participation.* This view holds that bilingual education is good for *all* children, although in practice, it is usually the more affluent parents (whose children

attend private academies), who are the strongest proponents.

4. *View of Linguistic diversity.* Multilingualism is seen as positive although it is often based on a "conservative" (and secure), ethnocentrism which does not perceive political or economic threats in modest (and controlled), forms of cultural and linguistic pluralism.

5. *Duration or scope of bilingual instruction.* In this school of thought opinions vary from the more traditional one-hour-per-day study of a language to the immersion methods employed in expensive private schools. There is no conceptual limit of the number of years of bilingual schooling recommended, but extremes are generally avoided.

Civil Libertarian Orientation.

Some advocates of bilingual education view this form of schooling within the broader framework of a societal bilingualism which should be protected and even encouraged by law. This view is grounded on a broad conceptualization of freedom of speech, and the protection of inalienable human and civil rights. Its proponents seek the protection of minority-group interests from their potential exclusion within a society in which majority-rule is the prevailing, morally and socially sanctioned, norm for making decisions. Generally speaking, a civil libertarian approach to bilingualism is an attempt to counteract the cultural and linguistic imperialism which has developed around the hegemony of the U. S.; its institutions, language, values, and lifestyles being as pervasive as its military and economic might. In essence this ideology embraces the following:

1. *Goals.* The ultimate goal is to establish and maintain the right of linguistic minorities to study and use their home languages. Also sought is the establishment within particular jurisdictions, of the concept of "official" bilingualism in schools and society.

2. *View of non-English home language.* Mother tongues are cherished inheritances which are to be asserted and protected as a civil liberty and right.

3. *Participation.* Under this approach children who come from non-English speaking backgrounds should receive first priority in being afforded the option of bilingual schooling. Others could be required or encouraged to study a language or languages as a subject matter depending on the region or locality where they might live. Some proponents would require bilingual schooling of *all* children living in an area which has a majority of non-English-background residents.

4. *View of linguistic diversity.* Multiple languages are a societal reality which should be recognized and legally sanctioned.

5. *Duration or scope of bilingual schooling.* The *opportunity* to be educated bilingually throughout the public school and college years should be available to all. Some or all of this range may be required for certain students.

Pedagogical/Human Development Orientation

Some advocates of bilingual education base their rationale for this type of instruction on the developmental needs of children. In their opinion, bilingual education should be more than a mere linguistic adjustment. It should also embody the concept of culture-based curricula and cultural context teaching. In effect, these advocates suggest that in much the same way that children move from the known to the unknown in subject or content areas, they should do likewise in "culture and heritage" acquisition. Thus, considerable emphasis would be placed on learning the history of the child's own ethnolinguistic group and the many facets (Gonzalez, 1974) of his/her "culture."

Contemporary research (Ramirez and Castaneda, 1974) indicates that significant differences may exist among racial/ethnic groups in learning styles and incentive/motivation styles. Proponents of this emphasis in bilingual education claim that incompatibilities which are culture-based define a need for a bicultural and "bicognitive" approach to instruction. In addition, this humanistic approach also stresses the need to develop and maintain in children healthy concepts of self, of group membership, and of cultural diversity itself. It is suggested by some that the development of the affective domain is a prerequisite to continued effective functioning in the cognitive areas.

1. *Goals.* Primary goals are (1) to develop in the child healthy perceptions and feelings of him/herself through the positive reinforcement of home language and cultural heritage; and (2) to assist minority children to succeed in school through a healthy psychological-growth climate of home language and cultural heritage.

2. *View of non-English home language.* When properly utilized, the child's home language is seen as a useful tool for helping the child to adjust psychologically to his/her environment and succeed in school by virtue of an enhanced self-concept.

3. *Participation.* Emphasis for participation is on people "of color" who because of their existence in a racist society have been psychologically damaged to the extent that they do not participate effectively in school.

4. *View of linguistic diversity*. Multilingualism is seen as a reality to which schooling must adjust itself not only linguistically but also sociologically, psychologically, and methodologically. This adjustment must occur however, within a broader recognition of a dominant society which is ethnocentric and ethno-imperialistic.

5. *Scope and duration of bilingual instruction*. Bilingual schooling should continue throughout the public school years since the task of developing psychological feelings of secureness is a long-range one. Throughout these years the child is continuously exposed to negative experiences outside the classroom which can counteract the psychological gains made in the classroom.

Cultural Assertiveness Orientation.

To some minority-group activists, the maintenance of strong linguistic and cultural identification among racial/ethnic groups is a necessary strategy to prevent the groups from being "swallowed up" into an amorphous "American culture" or "way of life." And while such advocates may not be so extreme to be labelled as separatists, they perceive distinct social, economic and political advantages in maintaining pluralism and ethno-linguistic group identity. In their view, schools should reinforce this ethnic identification in their students because it is in the students' best interests as members of a competitive and alienating U. S. society.

1. *Goal*. The main thrust is to maintain, with the support of the schools, the ethno-linguistic differences which exist in the society for purposes of more vigorously and effectively seeking participation in social, economic and political processes in the greater society.

2. *View of non-English home language*. Home language is seen as an asset which language minorities should protect and maintain since it promotes group strength and solidarity within a society which holds many adversities for those who are members of those groups.

3. *Participation*. Stress is on the provision of opportunities for language maintenance to children from language groups who are also members of oppressed and excluded groups; groups characterized by a low socio-economic standing in U. S. society.

4. *View of linguistic diversity*. Linguistic identification is seen as an essential tool for the effective assertion and representation of excluded minorities in social, educational, political and economic institutions.

5. *Duration and scope of bilingual instruction*. Most advocates propose no specific limit. Some would

establish parallel programs and even alternative institutions at all levels. Such institutions would be devoted to the preservation of linguistic and cultural diversity.

Cultural Pluralism Orientation

This view of bilingual education is similar to the "cultural assertiveness" perspective. It differs from it however, in that the latter emphasizes the benefits which may accrue to the ethno-linguistic groups while the cultural pluralism view is based on *societal* advantages: the greatest good for the greatest number. The position rejects the need for a single official language and would maintain instead a *laissez-faire* linguistic policy which is culturally democratic and therefore potentially more harmonious than monolingualism. A carefully scored societal stringed ensemble would in effect be replaced by an equally melodious but less restricted jazz performance which accepts lead, background, or harmonizing roles according to the situation.

1. *Goal*. To create and maintain a linguistic democracy within the society, reduce the hegemony of English and thereby decrease the feelings of alienation and subservience of other language groups.

2. *View of non-English home language*. This is seen as a socio-linguistic reality which should be accepted because it can serve as a positive force for individual and group identity, security, and for an easier and more comfortable adaptation by language minorities into the society.

3. *Participation*. All children, but particularly those from non-English backgrounds should be encouraged to participate.

4. *View of linguistic diversity*. The numerous language groups are viewed as positive phenomena, a vital asset and an aesthetic improvement over a monoglot and ethnocentric society.

5. *Scope or duration of program*. The view is similar to that of the Civil Libertarian and Aesthetic/Enrichment schools of thought. Cultural pluralists may be assertive activists or may limit themselves to nominal conceptual support. In the latter case, they may be relatively passive in promoting a change which they see as attractive though not necessarily urgent.

Pragmatic/International/Work-related Orientation

This ideology is an extension of the cultural pluralism view. It stresses the need for U. S. citizens to be prepared to interact in work situations (both domestically and internationally), with other language groups *in the languages* of those groups. Although by no means widespread, several programs are currently in operation to prepare bilingual professionals in such fields as international commerce, agriculture, engineering, and others.

1. *Goal*. To prepare students to function professionally or vocationally in bilingual or non-English environments both domestically and internationally.

2. *View of non-English home language*. Bilingualism, whether inherited or acquired, is viewed as an asset which improves an individual's marketability in any vocation, art or profession in which contact with other language groups occurs.

3. *Participation*. Existing programs generally are not restricted to language-minority students. An almost equal emphasis is given to participation by native English speakers.

4. *View of linguistic diversity*. The existence of multiple national and world languages is recognized as an enduring and challenging reality to which workers must adjust by becoming bilingual. This is a departure from the mid-century view that English (or an artificial language), should and would become the universal language.

5. *Scope and duration of programs*. Participation continues until prescribed behavioral objectives are reached or a particular credential is earned.

Conclusion

It should be noted that in practice, few programs of bilingual education adhere *exclusively* to one or another of the orientations listed above. Most programs and practitioners utilize an eclectic approach which accommodates more than one view. What is not always apparent even to them, however, is the *underlying emphasis* which guides the elaboration of specific learning objectives, materials selection and staffing patterns. As Cardenas, Bernal and Kean (1976) have implied, it is not uncommon for schools to embark on a bilingual education venture without a clear ideological base. Schools sometimes use the nomenclature of bilingual schooling simply to avail themselves of additional "soft money" resources which are then applied as "general aid" funds.

Nor is it yet feasible to analyze bilingual education programs with a view to determine best practices using the taxonomy which has been presented here. We would expect to find solid justification for offering a variety of bilingual education programs to various student populations. Indeed it can be assumed that a universal ideology may not be realistic. The tailoring of programs to fit local climates and needs will probably continue. Hopefully, however, program architects, teachers, administrators and the public will seek a clarification of ultimate goals and underlying

ideologies and will attempt to participate fully in their definition. Similarly, teacher-training institutions should clarify and state clearly the orientations(s) on which the learning experiences of future bilingual teachers will be based. The anxiety, frustration and ambivalence which develops in the absence of a clear philosophy can have detrimental effects on the morale of teachers and students alike.

Finally, it should be emphasized that the ideological positions described above are acknowledged to be highly simplified manifestations of very complex issues which are highly interrelated and interdependent. The perspectives, both personal and collective which have been discerned, cannot be easily divorced from the exigencies of U. S. politics, personal and group values of a cultural nature, nationalistic ideosyncrasies, and other such phenomena.

Numerous and complex questions would no doubt arise were we to attempt a detailed analysis of these dynamics. Is the group psychology of contemporary U. S. society moving away from ethnocentrism or towards it? Is there a particular brand of xenophobia at work in the U. S. and if so, what are its policy manifestations? What changes in bilingual education may be expected to develop as the recognition of the myriad implications of this type of schooling dawns more fully?

Many more questions are indeed implicit in the schematic exposition presented here. Some of these are disturbing in that they appear to revive negative attitudes from past generations. Clearly, bilingual education has not demonstrated that it holds something for everybody. Consequently, there are many whose ideology about bilingualism is that *it should not exist*. We can only conjecture as King (1969) has done on a cognate topic as to the extent to which this opposition can

> ...be attributed to honest ignorance, how much deserves to be assigned to a decent sense of shame, or how much is accounted for by those ancient protective instincts which rouse themselves like barking dogs against the midnight footsteps of old dark fears installed by the myths, customs, and distortions of the past (p. vi).

Such intriguing conjectures are of course, topics for separate analyses. Suffice to say that all of the issues, questions and concerns raised by the recent resurgence of bilingual education serve the useful purpose of stimulating further study and analysis not only of educational structures but also of the society which has created them. This introspective process must be conducted if we are someday to arrive at a societal, parental, professional and political climate in which educational innovations can come forth and experience a fair trial of what they propose to contribute to their participants.

REFERENCES

Bilingual Education Act, 1968 (20 U.S.C. 800b) Enacted January 2, 1968, P.L. 90-247.

Brischetto, R. and Arciniega, T. "Examining the Examiners: A Look at Educators Perspectives on the Chicano Student." in Chicanos and Native Americans: The Territorial Minorities, edited by Rudolph O. de la Garza, et. al., Englewood Cliffs, New Jersey: Prentice-Hall, Inc., 1973.

Cal ERIC/CLL Series on Languages and Linguistics, Number 23. *The Current Status of U. S. Bilingual Education Legislation*, Arlington, Va.: Center for Applied Linguistics, 1975.

Cardenas, J. A., Bernal, J. J., and Kean, W. *Bilingual Education Cost Analysis*. San Antonio: Intercultural Development Research Association, 1976.

Carter, T. P. "The Persistence of a Perspective."*Mexican Americans and Educational Change*. Symposium at the University of California, Riverside, sponsored by Mexican American Studies Program (UC-Riverside), and Project Follow Through (USOE), Riverside, Cal., May 21-22, 1971.

Center for Law and Education. *Bilingual-Bicultural Education: A Handbook for Attorneys and Community Workers*. Cambrige, Mass.: Center for Law and Education, 1975.

Civil Rights Act, 1964, 42, U.S.C.S. Sec. 2000 eg. seq.

Equal Educational Opportunities Act, 1974, 20 U.S. C.S., 1701.

Gonzalez, J. M. "A Developmental and Sociological Rationale for Culture-Based Curricula and Cultural Context Teaching in the Early Instruction of Mexican American Children." Ed. D. Dissertation, Univ. of Mass., 1974.

Gonzalez, J. M. "Coming of Age in Bilingual/Bicultural Education: A Historical Perspective." *Inequality in Education*, Center for Law and Education (Harvard Univ.), No. 19, Feb., 1975.

King, L. L. *Confessions of a White Racist*. New York: The Viking Press, 1969.

Lau v. Nichols, 414, U. S., 563, (1974).

Massachusetts General Laws, Ch. 71A. (1972).

Memorandum, DHEW/OCR, May 25, 1970, to School Districts With More than Five Percent National Origin-Minority Group Children: From J. Stanley Pittinger, OCR; Subject: Identification of Discrimination and Denial of Services on the Basis of National Origin.

Memorandum, DHEW/USOE; August 6, 1974, to Jim Evans, BSS: From Pen Jackson, OPBE; Subject: Final Report, FY'74 Bilingual Education Objective.

Milina, J. C., "Bilingual Education in the U.S.A." in *Proceedings of the First Inter-American Conference on Bilingual Education*. Edited by Rudolph Troike and Nancy Modiano. Arlington, Va.: Center for Applied Linguistics, 1975.

Ramirez, M. and Castaneda, A. *Cultural Democracy, Bicognitive Development and Education*, New York: Academic Press, 1974.

U. S. Congress. Senate Committee on Labor and Public Welfare. *Bilingual Education Hearings* before a Special Subcommittee on Bilingual Education, U. S. Senate, on S428, 90th Cong., 1st sess., Parts 1 and 2, 1967.

U. S. Office of Education DHEW, Region VI, Office of the Regional Commissioner. "Bilingual Education in P. L. 93-380" Dallas, n. d. (Mimeographed)

Chapter 4
Bilingual Education: Central Questions and Concerns
A. Bruce Gaarder*

Program goals determine the meaning of bilingual education, but no less a determinant are the social and political dynamics of the bilingualism that exists in the learners and their parents.

An examination of bilingual education that does not first take into account different kinds of bilingualism itself would be futile. Without such an accounting, there would be no point of reference, for bilingual education necessarily flows out of and into some kind of bilingualism, and there are many different kinds.

For our purpose here, the most fundamental distinction is between voluntary bilingualism, developed in individuals, and obligatory bilingualism, which is a collective or group phenomenon. In the former case, the individual becomes bilingual of his own free will or that of his parents. The new skill is acquired from members of the family, tutors, or servants, from sojourns abroad, in special schools, or from simple foreign language study. Obligatory, collective bilingualism takes two main forms, but the principal one is the result of contact and conflict between two peoples in a single state or under a single government: a dominant people and a dominated people. The latter group becomes bilingual by necessity, from their need to eat, to survive.

Thus, the bilingualism of Americans or Frenchmen or Argentinians who learn Russian or German is voluntary, elitist, academic. The bilingualism of Puerto Ricans or Mexican-Americans (Chicanos) who have to learn English, of Catalans in Spain who must learn Spanish too, of Indians in South or North America who must learn Portuguese or Spanish or English—this is obligatory and collective. The dynamics—social, political, pedagogical—of the two kinds of dual-language acquisition are different and incompatible.

Factors Affecting Collective Bilingualism

In addition to the obligatory form of bilingualism that appears when one people is subordinated to another, it is not uncommon for a single people to use and prefer to use two languages. Examples of this are the Arabic nations, each of which has its own vernacular Arabic and also uses Koranic Arabic;

Greece, where Katharevusa and *Dimotiki* are common; the German cantons of Switzerland, where the population is generally bilingual in Schwyzertutsch and standard German. What differentiates this form of collective bilingualism from the other is the lack of inter-group conflict and the fact that there is no competition between the languages, since each is used by its speakers for a different set of purposes. Collective bilingualism in these cases—commonly known as diglossia—is a stable relationship.

The political stance toward linguistic and cultural diversity is another factor in the dynamics of bilingualism. Some countries notable for a strongly assimilative stance toward their minority peoples are the United States (despite the bilingual education movement and wishful wisps of cultural pluralism), France, Spain, and South American nations except Paraguay. The objective in states favoring assimilation is to promote national unity even if minority-group cultures and languages must thereby be eliminated.

Among the nations which—for whatever reason—practice true cultural pluralism are Switzerland, the Soviet Union, Czechoslavakia, Yugoslavia, Belgium, Finland, and in a very special way, Paraguay. This is usually done by means of laws which recognize the right of minority people to cultural autonomy or a status closely approaching that autonomy and which safeguard each people's language from aggression by others. (1) Cultural autonomy commonly means the right and the means to establish schools and colleges, to publish and use the air waves, to conduct business and legal matters, to practice religion and everything else in one's own language. It commonly supports the ideal of unilingualism, although not to the exclusion of learning one or more additional languages. There is recognition of the important difference between foreign language instruction and the much more powerful—and dangerous—use of the second tongue as a medium of school instruction.

*A. Bruce Gaarder, Special Assistant, Division of Educational Systems Development, Office of Education, Department of Health, Education, and Welfare. Reprinted with permission of the author and The N.Y.U. Education Quarterly.

Cultural autonomy is usually based on separate territories, but in some cases when two peoples live dispersed among each other there is recourse to the personal principle, which gives to each person language rights wherever he finds himself. Paraguay is unique because the merging there of two peoples, the indigenous and the European, has been marked by a oneness that includes retention and cultivation of the Guarani language by a majority of the people in a stable, diglossic, non-competitive relationship with Spanish.[2]

Two other important factors in the dynamics of bilingualism are power (political and economic) and prestige (the prestige of the languages concerned). Usually the power factor is overriding and is merely reinforced by the prestige of the more powerful people's language. In a few notable cases, however, the prestige of a language is great enough to override superior political and economic power. Examples of this latter anomaly are found in Belgium and the Republic of South Africa. In both these nations a Dutch-speaking people (Flemish and Afrikaaners) have achieved hegomony—over the French-speaking Walloons in Belgium and the English-speaking people in South Africa. The enormously greater prestige of French and English exercises such power of attraction over Flemish and Afrikaaner families, that they begin by becoming bilingual and end by becoming French- or English-speaking, and in both countries it has been found necessary to restrict severely the likelihood of bilingualism.

A final major factor (there are many more, but they cannot be identified here) is the extent, in demographic terms, of the bilingualism. Collective, compulsory bilingualism (two languages and peoples, one dominated by the other within a single nation) is essentially a transitional means of communication between two monolingual peoples. Here it should be borne in mind that it is invariably a one-sided phenomenon: the subordinated people alone becomes bilingual, the dominant one does not; the subordinated people's tongue alone (except in the anomalous cases noted above) suffers linguistic interference, with distortion of its syntax and swamping of its lexicon. As soon as most of the dominated people become speakers of both languages there is no further need for both of them, and the weaker tongue disappears. We then say that a language shift has occurred.

It follows that collective, compulsory bilingualism is an unstable, self-destructive linguistic phenomenon, for no people needs two languages for the same set of purposes. Therefore it matters a great deal, in terms of the imminence and danger of language shift, whether only a few people have become bilingual or whether almost all have so become.

The five major dynamic factors of collective bilingualism—its inevitability, the political stance, power, language prestige, and demography—plus its instability, plus the factors of religion and race and the wide variation of people's attitudes toward their language or languages—all these elements and more combine variedly to show fifty-four essentially different, contrasting kinds of bilingualism.[3]

Obligatory Bilingualism in the United States

After the above brief overview of bilingualism, some points become apparent about the language situation in the United States. First, it should be plain that there are fundamental, irreconcilable differences between, on the one hand, the millions of students in schools and colleges who are studying foreign languages and, on the other hand, the many more millions—perhaps one-tenth of our population—who have no choice about speaking two languages. For the first group learning the new language is an elitist gesture of cultural enrichment; for the others it is a form of assimilation which they would find almost impossible to avoid.

Why, it will be asked, cannot the second kind of bilingualism be as enriching as the first? The answer, not at all clear and unequivocal, is that it can be, indeed often is, but somehow in the great majority of cases it is not. Consider for a moment that at least half of all of our teachers of foreign language—predominantly those who teach the uncommon tongues—are native speakers drawn from the ranks of obligatory bilinguals. Consider too some possible reasons for the persistence of bilingualism in Mexican-Americans, in the Puerto Ricans in continental United States, and in native American Indians. What weight should be given to the fact of their being in large part "visible" minorities in a racist society and to the consequent negative factors of isolation, poverty, illiteracy, and discrimination? There are of course more positive factors which must be weighed too: the proximity of Mexico and Puerto Rico, the ease of travel, the historical primacy of these peoples (they are either aboriginal or identify ethnically with the aboriginals), and their professed unwillingness to be assimilated—to become like everyone else and lose their distinctive language and culture.

What then of bilingual education (the use of two languages, one of them English, as mediums of school instruction, plus emphasis on the history and culture of the children's forebears)? Can it be seen as other than encouragement to bilingualism? Yet, in view of the self-destructive nature of compulsory bilingualism, can bilingual education be other than a way of hastening the disappearance of all folk languages except English?

Pedagogical and Other Implications

There were only a few examples of bilingual education in the United States in recent times—including what may still have been the best attempt, Coral Way Elementary School in Dade County, Florida—before the Bilingual Education Act was passed in 1968. That act may fairly be called a national response to the Spanish-speakers' struggle for social justice. It was intelligently and ambiguously worded to give equal comfort to those who wanted bilingual education to be a mere one-way bridge to English and to those who hoped it might be extended into the secondary schools to maintain and develop full competence and literacy in Spanish and the other non-English tongues. Also out of political expediency, and most unfortunately in the view of those who saw each of the languages as the chief manifestation and instrument of a culture and a people, the act included a poverty criterion for use in identifying its beneficiaries. This has had the effect of stigmatizing bilingual education as an educational medicine specific to the poor and disadvantaged. It might instead have been seen as a superior kind of education for possible superior children.

There was nothing in the writings of those who provided the rationale for bilingual education to show that they were aware of the dilemma posed by the transitory, self-destructive nature of obligatory bisocietal bilingualism. "Research findings" were quickly produced to show that the child would less likely be retarded if allowed to learn in its mother tongue instead of being forced to delay a year or two or three until sufficient competence had been acquired in the use of English to permit its unrestricted use for instructional purposes. Other findings showed the greater ease with which a Spanish mother-tongue child becomes literate in comparison with one whose mother tongue is English, given the extraordinary incongruencies between the English pronunciation and writing systems. And so on. Not until 1973 did it occur to me that the only rationale either needed or worthy of being heeded for teaching a child through its mother tongue is the simple proposition that it is a fundamental human right for every people to rear—and educate—its children in its own image and language.[4]

Meanwhile, under the stress of creating proposals for the first Bilingual Education Act grants by 1969, patterns of federal and local administration of the program were quickly developed. It is my perception that the most significant of these was a tendency to minimize the importance of employing in bilingual education programs only well-prepared teachers and administrators, strongly literate in the non-English tongue and highly knowledgeable of the other culture.[5]

In retrospect it is not difficult to explain this attitude, even apart from the unavoidable haste in launching the national program. First, it would be unthinkable not to use—for example—the Spanish speakers themselves in the new effort to improve the education of their children. Yet, unavoidably, most of them are victims of educational policy which in the past denigrated their mother tongue, discouraged them from using it, and virtually assured their illiteracy in it. Second, due in part to the studied ambiguities of the Bilingual Education Act, there was from the beginning an inclination among school people to define bilingual education as any special educational treatment given to bilingual children, including the exclusive teaching of English "as a second language." Third, although it might have been possible to set standards of training and competence for the teachers, it would have been difficult (in personal and political terms) to rule out of a local program any teacher, already employed there, who was "bilingual" and then to bring in supposedly more competent outsiders, even members of the same ethnic group. Who would make the judgments? Fourth, there was no existing program of suitable training in the teacher training institutions, because no precedent existed for preparing teachers to work professionally through the medium of a non-English tongue. Fifth—and perhaps most weighty—it soon became politically inexpedient among important segments of the speakers themselves to suggest that teachers should use *el espanol comun* (world standard Spanish) for school work[6], rather than a vernacular somewhat analogous to "black English."

The result—one result—was that I had occasion in 1970 to identify one group of about thirty native Spanish speakers regularly employed and responsible for the Spanish side of bilingual education in Colorado and New Mexico, not one of whom had ever read a book in Spanish. Another such group in 1971 did not know the Spanish alphabet. Previous experience with similar groups of teachers in California attests to the same situation there. All of them were graduates of American schools and colleges, educated exclusively through English.

Another result of the negligible emphasis on strong literacy in the non-English tongue has been the preponderant use of English for professional purposes related to bilingual education: publications, meetings, record keeping, etc., and, most importantly, teacher training. With very few exceptions, I have found that the plans of studies in master's degree and doctoral programs offered in "bilingual education" consist essentially of a selection of standard education courses in English; a course or so in the history and culture of the minority people, also in English; something dealing with the "theory" or history of bilingual education, also in English, plus an invitation to enroll for courses in the institution's department of foreign languages.[7]

In contrast with this, it can be averred that in any other country where a minority people has won the right to educate its children through its own language, one of the first major concerns would be the establishment of a normal school to train the teachers. And the school would be staffed by educated, highly literate members of the minority language group and conducted exclusively in that language.

Incompatible Goals of Bilingual Education

Enough has been written here to lead us to the centermost of all concerns: the goal or goals of bilingual education. Clearly there are three major ones, each in basic opposition to the others: 1. development of a more effective, more "humane" one-way bridge to English; 2. more effective education for children whose mother tongue is not English, plus the long-term development and maintenance of that mother tongue; 3. provision of a source of jobs in education and of preferential treatment for members of the ethnic groups involved.

The U.S. Office of Education and Albert Shanker, president of the American Federation of Teachers, exemplify espousal of the first goal. Their view is very widely shared. In a letter to Senator Joseph Montoya of New Mexico dated November 15, 1974, the Commissioner of Education, Terrell H. Bell, discussing the question of ends and means, wrote:

I maintain that the proper goal of federally-supported Bilingual/Bicultural Education Programs is precisely that stated in the OE (Office of Education) staff paper cited in your letter—namely, "to enable children whose dominant language is other than English to develop competitive proficiency in English so that they can function successfully in the educational and occupational institutions of the larger society... What we know about the educational process tells us that the most effective and the most humane way to achieve this English language competency is through a Bilingual/Bicultural approach."

Mr. Shanker makes that position clear in an article related to the consent decree won by the plaintiffs in *ASPIRA vs. New York City Board of Education*, which mandates substantive instruction in Spanish for children whose English-language deficiencies prevent them from participating in the learning process in the New York City schools. Speaking in *New York Teacher* for January 26, 1975, Shanker said, "It should be made clear that this kind of instruction is transitional, and that children should be moved into regular instruction in English on an on-going basis as their English language skills are strengthened." Reiterating the transitional nature of bilingual education, he said that the bilingual programs should "self-destruct." "That is, the ultimate goal is to integrate non-English speaking children into the regular school program as quickly as possible."

The second goal was expressed typically by Spanish-speaking Senator Montoya in a letter to the U. S. Commissioner of Education on October 11, 1974.

It is my view...that bilingual education must have as its goal the fulfillment of what is inherent in its title: two languages. Children learn to speak a language at home or in their community. The school is, ideally, the place where children learn to read and write in that language, thus becoming literate.... If a bilingual program is available in his school, he can learn to speak two languages instead of one, and because he is instructed in two languages (as the law directs for bilingual programs) he can soon become literate in two languages instead of one.

It is safe to say that a great many—perhaps most—of the speakers of non-English languages wish that their languages and cultures could be maintained and strengthened. Perusal of the consent decree referred to above—from the point of view of the Puerto Rican—substantiates this statement. It is also safe to aver that very few of them know what would be required in terms of political, economic, and educational change in order to make that wish come true.

The third goal, jobs and preferment, is uncomfortably evident in what was said above about the lack of academic soundness in much that is called bilingual education at both the school level and the university level.

There is increasingly convincing evidence that educational policy which requires non-English mother-tongue children to be educated exclusively through English is severely detrimental to them. There is little evidence that bilingual education, as it is now practiced, is offsetting that detriment. A situation that used to be seen, ethnocentrically, as "the handicap of bilingualism"—and still is, very widely and for the same reason—is coming to be viewed as a denial of equal educational opportunity. The evidence of detriment comes chiefly from studies related to the measurement of intelligence and, to a lesser extent, of achievement. Stated summarily, the case rests on three points : use of non-Spanish-speaking testers, use of English as the testing medium, and use of tests which are culture-bound to the English language milieu. These factors, separately and combined, have been found to depress severely the performance of Spanish mother-tongue children.[8] However much the I.Q. testing program alone might be improved, the failure to provide equal educational opportunity (insofar as formal schooling is concerned) for Spanish-speaking children would be as great as ever in any classroom where the medium is English and the teacher other than a Spanish speaker well-trained to teach through Spanish.

Evaluation

All that has been said above suggests the difficulty of evaluating the effectiveness of a national program involving (in the 1972-73 school year) twenty-four languages and "dialects" in twenty-nine of the states, plus Guam, the Mariana Islands, Puerto Rico, and the Virgin Islands, and over 100,000 students in 652 schools.[9] Examination of the best attempt thus far to evaluate the bilingual education program suggests additional complications. In 1973, under contract with the U. S. Office of Education, an excellent "process evaluation" was made of a random sample of thirty-four projects supported under the Bilingual Education Act and serving Spanish speaking children.[10] Emphasis on the Spanish speakers—even as in this essay—was justified on grounds of consistency plus the fact that about 80 percent of the Bilingual Education Act projects deal with the Spanish language. The following observations on some of the findings of the evaluation are to be read in the light of what was said above about the dynamics of bilingualism.

The 14,043 children in the thirty-four projects were classified solely on the basis of "language dominance": 8,765 Spanish-dominant, 4,008 English-dominant, and 1,270 undetermined. This must be considered together with the Office of Education's official *Manual for Project Applicants and Grantees* (1971) which says that "children whose dominant language is English and who attend schools in the project area should be encouraged to participate, and provisions should be made for their participation in order to enhance the bilingual and bicultural aspects of the program." The same manual cites as a characteristic of approved bilingual education programs that "provision is made for increasing the instructional use of both languages for both groups in the same classroom."

What this means is that Anglo monolinguals and Spanish-speaking monolinguals (or bilinguals) are together in the same classroom, receiving instruction at the same time. Not only is there a basic incompatibility in such groupings in terms of the dynamics of bilingualism, as noted above, there is also a kind of pedagogical incompatibility. Teaching that uses Spanish as the medium of instruction for Spanish-speaking pupils permits vigorous, authentic, full use of that tongue. It is a much more powerful teaching mode than and basically incompatible with teaching Spanish

as a foreign language, which is inescapably required if there are English monolinguals in the class.

A disastrous compromise is possible: rapid switching by the teacher from one language to the other. I have seen this done continuously in projects in South Texas. The conclusion there was that the miraculous language learning of which young children are capable was not taking place, for the pupils had but to wait a few seconds to receive the same message in their own tongue. Language switching is a manifestation of acculturation and of the difficulty of keeping the two languages entirely separate.

The official evaluation had much to say about the extent of the teachers' preparation. Of the 510 teachers, only 22 had "lived for an extended period" in a Spanish-speaking country. There were no data on the extent to which any of these had actually studied through Spanish. Of the 510, 393 were "bilingual," but the evaluators noted that "the extent of functional bilingualism of teachers and aides was not determined."

Two of the 34 projects had no bilingual teachers and instead used bilingual aides. The project directors voiced a common concern for the inadequacy of their teachers' preparation. Most directors provided "orientation" and some in-service training for their staffs. One project sent the entire staff to Mexico two successive summers for five weeks of intensive training.

Regarding teaching materials in Spanish, the evaluation noted that most teachers found those published elsewhere to be somehow inadequate and that in many projects the bilingual staffs were preparing their own. It also referred extensively to the more than 20,000 items of published Spanish-language materials collected throughout the Spanish-speaking nations specifically for use in bilingual education projects. Of these it was observed that "teacher evaluation sheets show that foreign materials tend to be too difficult for American children." Even more revealingly, the evaluators remarked of those imported publications, "The language is evidently too difficult for those who are not fluent speakers and readers of Spanish."

About pupil achievement the evaluators had little to say. The pupils' "language competence in both English and Spanish was not measured" by the projects' staffs. "Spanish language skills of English-dominant students were imparted only minimally by current attempts at teaching subjects in Spanish." During about two-thirds of the school day "content" was taught in English; in one-third it was taught in Spanish. Some projects professed to be devoted to the transitional language-bridge philosophy; others professed to be aiming at long-term maintenance and development of the non-

English mother tongue. The evaluators found marked incongruity between those professions and what was actually happening in the projects.

The major concerns raised in this essay seem to be of little concern to those involved most closely in bilingual education. The questions raised and implied are not being answered. At the very least this suggests that before an evaluation of bilingual education in terms of pupil achievement is attempted, each project might well be scrutinized to see if what is happening there corresponds reasonably well to its stated aims. This would require careful consideration of the social, political and pedagogical dynamics of bilingualism. At the most it suggests that bilingual education could still be used to meet the noblest goals of the most generous of its supporters.

NOTES

[1] Jean Falch, *Contribution à l'étude du status des langues en Europe*, Québec: Presses de l'Universite Laval, 1973; and Bernard Touret, *L'amenagement constitutionelle des Etats de peuplement composite*, Québec: Presses de l'Universite Laval, 1973.

[2] Joan Rubin, *National Bilingualism in Paraguay*, unpublished doctoral dissertation, Yale University, 1963. Chapter VII appears in *Readings in the Sociology of Language*, Joshua A Fishman, ed., The Hague: Mouton, 1970.

[3] A. Bruce Gaarder, "Political Perspective on Bilingual Education," unpublished manuscript, 1974.

[4] Theodore Anderson and Mildred Boyer, "A Rationale for Bilingual Schooling," in *Bilingual Schooling in the United States*, Vol. I, Washington, D. C.: U. S. Government Printing Office, 1970.

[5] A. Bruce Gaarder, "The First Seventy-Six Bilingual Education Projects," in *Monograph Series on Languages and Linguistics*, No. 23, James A. Alatis, ed., Washington, D. C.: Georgetown University, 1970.

[6] On this subject see Estelle Chacón, "Pochismos," *El Grito*, 3, 1 (1969): 34-35; and Uvaldo Palomares, "Psychological Factors Teachers Must Recognize in the Bicultural Child," *Proceedings, National Converence on Bilingual Education*, Austin, Tex-

as: Dissemination Center for Bilingual Bicultural Education, 1972, pp. 210-220.

[7] The Education Amendments of 1974 Act, which amended and expanded significantly the original Bilingual Education Act of 1968, mandates that "for the fiscal year ending June 30, 1975, not less than 100 fellowships leading to a graduate degree shall be awarded...for preparing individuals to train teachers for programs of bilingual education." Additonal fellowships are to be awarded in subsequent years.

[8] Forty-seven randomly selected Spanish-speaking "retarded" children, half from urban, half from rural backgrounds in California were reexamined in the Spanish language by Spanish-speaking psychologists, and it was found that 42 of the 47 scored above the I.Q. ceiling of the mental retardate classification; 37 scored 75 or higher; over half scored 80 or above; 16 percent scored 90 or more. This was part of the evidence presented in *Diana, et al. vs. (California) Board of Education*, which led U. S. District Court Judge Robert E. Peckham to rule on February 5, 1970 that thenceforth school officials would be required a) to explain any disproportionate assignment of Spanish-speaking children to classes for mental retardates, and b) to have prepared an I.Q. test normed to the California Spanish-speaking child population; and that such children will be tested in both Spanish and English and be allowed to respond in either tongue. See also James Vásquez, "Measurement of Intelligence and Language Differences, *AZTLAN*, 3, 1 (1973): 155-163; and Jane R. Mercer, "Current Retardation Procedures and the Psychological and Social Implications on the Mexican-American," paper prepared for Southwestern Cooperative Education Laboratory, Albuquerque, April, 1970.

[9] *Guide to Title VII ESEA Bilingual Bicultural Projects in the United States*, Austin, Texas: Dissemination Center for Bilingual Bicultural Education (6504 Tracor Lane, 78721), 1973.

[10] *A Process Evaluation of the Bilingual Education Program, Title VII, Elementary and Secondary Education Act*, Vol. I. Washington, D. C.: Development Associates, 1973.

Chapter 5
Bilingual Education: A Mosaic of Controversy
Larry Sibelman*

The pattern of the past in most American public schools was to treat all children more or less the same regardless of their ethnic origins. Ethnicity was largely ignored in the construction of school programs and curricula. The melting pot concept was almost universally applied.

Children from families that came from all over the world were thrust into an English-speaking school environment with little or no consideration given to their ethnic origins. The general program was designed to move children into the mainstream of American life as soon as possible and the public schools were viewed as instruments in that process.

School authorities, teachers and parents were in general agreement that this was the proper approach. Immigrant parents were not only satisfied, they were happy over the notion that their children were going to a public school designed to make "Americans" out of them as soon as possible. Parents were proud and happy that their children read, wrote and spoke English. While there were stresses created by generational differences, it is fair to say that there was broad acceptance of this entire approach.

Literally millions of young people from immigrant homes representing every possible ethnic, national religious group from all over the world went to public schools to become Americans. In fact, one of the major philosophical arguments for the promotion of public schools was the need to create a greater uniformity out of immense diversity. A major aim of the public schools was to be a place where children of varying ethnic backgrounds would find common experiences, hopefully reducing ethnic divisions and strains. People came to the United States with many built-in prides and prejudices that were outgrowths of their ethnic history. Religious prejudice abounded. National prejudice was widespread.

The public schools were thought of as meeting places where the children could begin the process of mutual assimilation. Racial, national and religious tolerance was the watchword.

The extent to which this philosophy had positive and negative effects can be argued, but in general terms there is little question that ethnic differences among European immigrant groups have sharply diminished. Wave after wave of ethnic immigrants was absorbed, if not wholly, at least mainly, into the mainstream of American life.

Many of the children exposed to the American public schools in earlier times came from homes where English was either not spoken at all or was a second language often spoken with a heavy ethnic accent. Newspapers, magazines and books catering to the language of the parents were readily available and had wide readership. But the children went to schools that give little, if any, recognition of this fact and simply insisted that instruction be totally in English with the specific aim being language assimilation as quickly as possible.

Some ethnic and cultural groups set up extensive after school and weekend programs of private instruction in language, culture and religion in efforts to maintain vestiges of the culture of origin. But these evening, afternoon and weekend private efforts were not directed toward a negative view of the efforts of the public school in the direction of rapid assimilation. Rather, the prevalent view was positive. How else could an individual hope to read a paper, get a job, or function effectively in an English-speaking society?

In recent years, a different philosophy has been promulgated throughout the country. This new approach is called bilingual and sometimes bilingual/bicultural education. The thrust for bilingual education stems largely from frustration. Public schools today, it is claimed, fail to meet the needs of minority students. (Minority students are defined as coming from Black, Spanish-speaking, American-Indian and Asian-American families. All other ethnic groups are considered members of the majority population and are officially designated "other white" by federal dictum.)

*Larry Sibelman, Assistant to the President of American Federation of Teachers. Reprinted by permission of the American Federation of Teachers, AFL-CIO, American Teacher, December, 1976.

Students who are Black, Chicano, Puerto Rican, Asian, Indian and so on, are considered disadvantaged by either language or cultural deficiencies and are presumed to suffer from this disadvantage in the public schools. Bilingual education is viewed as necessary to accelerate the learning of minority children by utilizing their language of origin as an entree into language development in English. At the same time, a case is made that the language of origin should be promoted with the outcome a group of students who are proficient in both English and the native language of either the children or their parents.

The bicultural element is designed to maintain a relationship and familiarity with the culture from which the children or their parents originated. Black studies, Hispanic studies, Asian studies and Native American studies all stem from this philosophy. The idea is that children should come to a positive outlook on their own origins, enriching their own lives and the fabric of American society. Extreme proponents of bilingual/bicultural education view this approach as one that proceeds on into an indefinite future creating a multi-ethnic, multi-cultural societal mosaic with certain universals but with a positive view toward many societal differences, all promoted by the public schools.

The advent of bilingual education must then be viewed as a sharp departure from the practices of the past and careful analysis must be made of projected outcomes and immediate and long-range prospects. Since the education and nature of the teaching force in the public schools is also a factor, this must be considered and because there are large social and political implications, the entire question of bilingual education must be viewed seriously.

Is a child who comes from a Spanish-speaking home seriously disadvantaged in achieving in a standard English-speaking public school? The federal government says yes. Recent legislation and court decisions establish the legitimacy of the claim that severe disadvantage is felt by children introduced into the regular school program.

Was this always true? In the "melting pot" days of the past, children did feel that they were entering an alien environment. Children left the warmth of the family and found themselves confronting teachers who were Irish when they were Jewish; Jewish when they were Black; Anglo when they were Chicano and so on. There are initial insecurities. There are moments of dislocation. There are even bits of foolishness. It is ironic that tens of thousands of Jewish children in the New York city schools had music teachers who taught Christmas carols and never thought of introducing an Hannukah song. (There were no Israeli songs before Israel.) Yet, it is a radical extension of this fact to insist that only Puerto Rican teachers can be effective in educating youngsters from Puerto Rican families. Adequately prepared, warm decent human beings, thinking about the individual value and importance of each child, make good teachers, irrespective of race, religion or nationality.

There are two distinctly different approaches to the kind of program supporters of bilingual education push. The first is a program designed to bring children into the mainstream of the society. The bilingual component of the child's education is considered temporary until the child is "caught up" with children from English-speaking families. This approach assumes a public policy of assimilation over a given period of time and is called "mainstreaming." The second approach is called a "maintenance" or "maintenance of culture" approach, wherein a bilingual and/or bicultural program is established as a permanent part of the education of minority children and perceived as going on into future generations. The aim of such a program is not assimilation but rather assumes a public policy of perpetuating and promoting the separate or divergent social origins of the population into the indefinite future.

The differences between these two approaches are great. The implications for educators are also great. A permanent "maintenance of cultural differences" program would require a major change in the nature of the education of teachers. Tens of thousands of teachers would have to be trained in bilingual education on a continuous basis. If the extreme point of view that only persons of a given ethnicity can effectively teach children of that same ethnic group were to prevail, the ramifications for teachers would be considerable. Teachers would have to be selected, not on the basis of individual merit, but on the basis of their ethnic background.

The entire concept of treatment of individuals on the basis of individual worth would be seriously damaged. If the theory was applied to all ethnic groups, we would need set numbers of teachers from as many as 50 or 60 different ethnic groups. As the number of children from different ethnic backgrounds shifted and changed, the number of teachers needed to teach each group would also shift and change.

The "maintenance" concept clearly connotes a major revision in the contemporary value structure of our society and leads in directions which are probably unacceptable to the vast majority of people in the country. Certainly, teachers and their organizations would fight against this kind of construct.

If the "mainstream" idea becomes policy, the implications, though radically different, still present difficulties. Large numbers of teachers would need to be trained in bilingual education. This would require teachers conversant with the particular language and probably the culture of non-English-speaking groups. However, as children entered the mainstream, both in the educational system and in the society, the need for a continued program would diminish. Eventually, the outcome would be a sharply reduced need in some ethnic groups and perhaps different needs as immigration patterns change.

An additional dimension to the problems is the question of what linguists refer to as "Black English." This is the term used to describe the dialect widely used by Black Americans. Some linguists feel that learning impairment, especially in language skills, among Black students is due to their use of a distinct dialect outside of school, at home and in the community. "Standard English" and "Black English" are so different that bilingual approaches are suggested. This would require teachers and text material in still another language, "Black English." As in all other cases, the two basic approaches, mainstreaming and maintenance, apply to "Black English," and the same arguments pertain although there are probably fewer proponents of the maintenance position in regard to "Black English" than in the Spanish-speaking area.

Until quite recently, there were only a few laws or court decisions concerned with language usage or instruction. During World War I, in the midst of a period of xenophobic zeal, the State of Nebraska Supreme Court affirmed the conviction of a teacher for instructing students in the German language. The decision was based on the idea that English should be and become the "mother tongue of all children reared in this state." The United States Supreme Court overturned the conviction and declared any such statute unconstitutional. There are a few other cases of the same sort, but it is clear that the courts leaned in the direction of supporting English as the language of the American citizenry.

In 1974 the United States Supreme Court handed down a decision that altered the thrust of previous decisions and became the principal weapon in the fight to establish bilingual programs. This decision is called the *Lau* decision and results from the litigation in the *Lau* v. *Nichols* case. The case, brought by Chinese public school students against the San Francisco School District, squarely presented the issue of whether non-English-speaking, national origin minority-group students receive an equal educational opportunity when instructed in a language they could not understand. The absence of programs designed to meet the linguistic needs of these students violated, they claimed, the equal protection clause of the Fourteenth Amendment and Title VI of the Civil Rights Act of 1964.

The parties in *Lau* did not dispute that 1,790 Chinese students received no services designed to meet their linguistic needs. The lower courts ruled that the student's right to an equal education had been met by their receipt of the same education as tens of thousands of other students in the San Francisco schools. The Ninth Circuit affirmed and declared that English language instruction "was paramount in the schooling process." The Circuit Court said this is an English-speaking nation and the use of English in the schools was perfectly correct.

The case went on to the Supreme Court with the same basic premise presented by the *Lau* petitioners. By not understanding the language of the classroom, the students, it was argued, were deprived of even a minimally "adequate education."

The United States Supreme Court agreed with the plaintiffs, avoided the constitutional issue, and reversed the Ninth Circuit Court relying solely on Title VI of the Civil Rights Act. The Court reasoned as follows:

"Under these state-imposed standards there is no equality of treatment merely by providing students with the same facilities, textbooks, teachers and curriculum; for students who do not understand English are effectively foreclosed from any meaningful education."

The *Lau* decision does not, however, mandate bilingual programs. Mr. Justice Douglas noted at the outset of the Court's opinion:

"No specific remedy is urged upon us. Teaching English to the students of Chinese ancestry who do not speak the language is one choice. Giving instructions to this group in Chinese is another. There may be others. Petitioners ask only that the Board of Education is directed to apply its expertise to the problem and rectify the situation."

But the *Lau* decision in the background, HEW and the Office of Civil Rights enter the picture as prime movers. A long series of rulings and court decisions since the *Lau* decision has so confused the issue that very few people understand the legal status of bilingual education.

In an effort ot clarify the matter, HEW has issued a blueprint for compliance with *Lau* called the "*Lau Remedies.*" Among other things, the "*Lau Remedies*" outline the *educational* approaches found by HEW to be appropriate "affirmative steps" designed to "open the instructional programs" to non-English dominant students. If a school district found to be in non-compliance with Title VI has 20 or more students of the same language group other than English, the district is required to immediately develop specific voluntary compliance plans. If a district has even "one" such students, they must take some steps, although they need not submit a "voluntary compliance plan."

The *"Lau Remedies"* does not mandate bilingual education. At the high school and junior high level, ESL programs are specifically endorsed and even at the elementary level, bilingual education is not mandated. School authorities may propose and pursue other educational approaches, and deviate from the *"Lau Remedies";* but they must offer some demonstrable proof that the program they offer will be equally effective in ensuring equal educational opportunity.

Since HEW may refuse to fund federal grant programs to school districts which refuse to comply with compliance directives, there appears to be a strong potential that more and more school districts will perforce be offering bilingual programs, especially at the elementary school level. This is apparently the favored mechanism for remediating a failure on the part of school districts to offer equal educational opportunity to students who come to school from non-English language backgrounds.

So, a struggle is under way. With proponents of various points of view pressing through the political structure and the courts for programs that move public education in their direction. The implications for the teaching profession are profound. Likewise, teacher education will be greatly affected by the ultimate direction bilingual education takes.

It is true that in many places the issues and implications involved have little, if any, impact. On the other hand, throughout the Southwest, in all the major urban centers and in various other pockets around the country, the issue is very much alive and pressing.

The outcomes will not be known for some time, but the questions involved are of great concern to teachers and others interested in the nature of public education in America.

New York Teachers' Staff

Chapter 6
Trends in Bilingual Education and the Law
Herbert Teitelbaum and
Richard J. Hiller*

Bilingual education, which should be voluntarily introduced into schools but often is not, can be required of a school district through either state legislation, federal legislation and regulations, or judicial decree. This article focuses on the latter two devices, and in particular two recent events which have done much to help muddy already muddy waters surrounding the obligations of school districts towards language minority students: The 1975 "*Lau* Remedies" and the case of *Otero* v. *Mesa County School District No. 51*.[1]

An Overview of the Case Law

Although court ordered bilingual programs predate *Lau* v. *Nichols*,[2] that case represents the most important judicial bench mark for those who advocate bilingual education as a means toward achieving equality in education for language minority children. The United States Supreme Court unanimously determined in *Lau* that federally funded school districts must affirmatively provide to national origin minority students with English language disabilities, services which will secure for them equal access to the instructional program.[3] As is its practice, the High Court avoided prescribing a particular remedy and, as in all educational rights lawsuit, sent the case back to the lower court to forge appropriate relief. In *Brown* v. *Board of Education*[4] busing was not ordered, nor racial ratios fixed, nor compensatory programs devised, nor school discipline codes revised. At least in the first instance, these are chores for trial judges.

Accordingly, the Supreme Court in *Lau* did not mandate bilingual education. Nevertheless, there is a developing judicial trend, beginning several years prior to *Lau*, which points to bilingual education as the appropriate remedy. For example, in desegregation cases involving so-called tri-ethnic communities, bilingual programs of one sort or another were ordered to compensate for the effects of past discrimination. In 1971 in *United States* v. *Texas*,[5] a federal district court mandated a comprehensive bilingual program for the San Felipe Del Rio Consolidated Independent School District affecting curriculum, staffing, student assignment, classroom organization, community involvement, special education, funding, and evaluation. Implementation, however, was tied to the availability of adequate federal grants.

Other pre-*Lau* cases, most notably from Texas, (*e.g. Arvizu* v. *Waco Independent School District*;[6] *United States* v. *Texas*[7] [Austin]) contained remedial orders mandating bilingual education to secure an equal educational opportunity for language minority youngsters.

Since *Lau*, the introduction or strengthening of bilingual education programs in school districts under court jurisdiction has continued. *Serna* v. *Portales Municipal Schools*[8] required such programs as the fulfillment of the federal rights of Chicano children living in Portales, New Mexico, and *Aspira of New York* v. *Board of Education of the City of New York*,[9] ordered bilingual education, with the consent of the defendants, to meet the educational needs of Puerto Rican and other Hispanic school children in that metropolis. *Morgan* v. *Kerrigan*[10] and *Bradley* v. *Milliken*,[11] the latter a desegregation case in Detroit and the former in Boston, both required bilingual instruction as component parts of the overall desegregation plans ordered for schools in those cities. In *Morgan*, Judge Garrity's bilingual education mandate derived not only from the Massachusetts Transitional Bilingual Education Act, but from *Lau* as well, and extended bilingual programs to kindergarten and vocational education classes. Most recently, in *Evans* v. *Buchanan*[12], the Court in adopting a metropolitan desegregation plan affecting Wilmington, Delaware and the surrounding suburban school districts, prohibited the reduction of existing bilingual programs and cautioned responsible educational officials to comply with federal requirements relating to language minorities.

---

*Herbert Teitelbaum is the Legal Director and Richard J. Hiller a staff attorney with the Puerto Rican Legal Defense and Education Fund, Inc. in New York City. They are litigating lawsuits involving bilingual education in New York City, Philadelphia, Pennsylvania, Boston, Massachusetts, Suffolk County, New York, and Wilmington, Delaware.

Although in *Keyes* v. *Denver School District, No. 1*[13], the Tenth Circuit Court of Appeals reversed portions of the lower court's desegregation order dealing with Chicano children (the Cardenas plan), it sent the case back to the trial judge for a determination as to whether the *Lau* rights of the Denver students were being met. The plan rejected by the Tenth Circuit clearly was the most far-reaching and comprehensive ever proposed, going well beyond merely bilingual education even as defined by the Colorado legislature in its recent bilingual education Act. And, despite the Tenth Circuit's ruling that rectifying linguistic, cultural and other incompatabilities between students and schools is not required by the Fourteenth Amendment, and that bilingual education cannot be a substitute for desegregation, it did not overrule or limit its pronouncements in the *Serna* case, which it also decided, or limit the authority of the district court upon the remand of the case to mandate bilingual programs for students with English language problems.

Looking at the past five years of litigation, then, courts have more and more relied on bilingual education as a remedy. Indeed, even the words of limitation found in *San Antonio Independent School* v. *Rodriquez*[14], have not stopped courts in ordering bilingual programs once a violation of federal law is established.

The Otero Case

Much controversy is now stirring among educators and lawyers over a recent decision entitled *Otero* v. *Mesa County Valley School District*, handed down December 31, 1975 by a Colorado federal district court. For some, *Otero* represents a breach in a consistently well constructed judicial mandate for bilingual education. Admittedly, the decision should be viewed by proponents of bilingual education as a disruption of the momentum developed by other courts during the 1970's. In that sense, *Otero* is an aberration and should not be construed as a death knell to court ordered bilingual education.

Apart from the need to place *Otero* against the backdrop of the past five years of the successes achieved in bilingual education litigation, it is crucial to point out that the opinion, itself, does not modify the principles established in prior cases. *Lau* v. *Nichols*, *Serna* v. *Portales*, *United States* v. *Texas*, *Aspira*, and *Morgan* are alive and well and still governing school boards. Once passed the frequent, gratuitous, and injudicious comments regarding plaintiffs' counsel and expert witnesses, anyone reading the decision should realize that the *Otero* court neither made new law, nor narrowly interpreted prior law. Judge Winner only found that plaintiffs did not produce the necessary

facts to establish a violation of their educational rights as defined in *Lau* and *Serna*, two cases by which he was bound.

The *Otero* plaintiffs, ten Chicano children each suing through an adult parent or guardian, were either enrolled or had dropped out of school. They claimed that their rights under Title VI and the equal protection clause of the Fourteenth Amendment to the Constitution of the United States were being violated because the school district did not "take into account their linguistic and cultural differences," and as a result the students were "provide[d] an inadequate or unequal" education. Before *Otero* was decided, the Tenth Circuit in *Keyes* rejected the Cardenas Plan.

Relying heavily on the language in *Keyes* that the Constitution does not require a school district to "adapt to the cultural and economic needs of minority students," the *Otero* court predictably found that courts in the Tenth Circuit were not constitutionally mandated to resolve the cultural incompatabilities between the Chicano child and the school by the introduction of a comprehensive bilingual program.

The application of *Lau* and *Serna* was the only theory available to the Mesa County plaintiff school children, since these decisions were not based on the Constitution but solely on Title VI. However, Judge Winner gutted that aspect of plaintiffs' case by ruling that they did not prove there was sufficient students (even perhaps, any students), in the district with English language deficiency to trigger *Lau* rights. Choosing to find the defendant school district's experts more persuasive, the court placed virtually no value on a survey presented by plaintiffs through which they attempted to satisfy the *Serna* standard of demonstrating a sufficiently numerous class of students with English language difficulties.[15] Socioeconomic deprivation, and not language, the *Otero* court reasoned was the barrier to full enjoyment of the educational benefits offered by the school district. Simply put, the court determined there were no children in the school district who had English language deficiencies for purposes of setting in motion the mandate of *Lau*.

As with all litigation, the discretion of the *Otero* trial court in making factual findings was broad. Although idle speculation as to whether the *Otero* outcome would have been different before another judge adds nothing to one's understanding of the opinion, it does help put the case in perspective. Judges obviously differ from one another, and differ most in their interpretation of facts. What is unfortunate in *Otero* is not the court's view of the law, but its interpretation of the facts regarding language disabilities among the plaintiffs. For this reason, *Otero* is of little precedential value, since factual findings are binding on other courts in but a few instances.

The Lau Remedies: Background

In the summer of 1975 the U. S. Office of Education and the Office of Civil Rights jointly issued to the heads of state educational agencies the findings of its national task force, made up of educators predominantly.[16] The findings, among other things, outlined the educational approaches found to be appropriate "affirmative steps" designed to "open the instructional program" to non-English dominant students.

Where *Lau* violations have been determined to exist in school systems receiving federal financial assistance, the school districts are required to develop compliance plans consistent with the *"Lau* Remedies" or demonstrate affirmatively that alternative plans will be "equally effective in ensuring equal educational opportunity."[17]

Clearly, these *"Lau* Remedies," which have received the approval of the Secretary of HEW, are similar in purpose to the May 25, 1970 Memorandum upheld in *Lau* v. *Nichols,* and as such, minimally are entitled to great weight as an agency interpretation. An intransigent school board intent on resisting the *"Lau* Remedies" as beyond the scope of HEW's powers, ultimately should meet the same fate as the San Francisco School Board in *Lau.*

Preliminary Considerations

The *"Lau* Remedies" are applicable to school districts that are *found* to be in non-compliance with the provisions of Title VI of the Civil Rights Act of 1964, the HEW regulations promulgated pursuant thereto (45 C.F.R. Part 80), and the May 25, 1970 Memorandum interpreting these regulations.[18] But, on what basis is a school district determined to be in non-compliance? Must the strictures of the *"Lau* Remedies" be adhered to if a school district is to avoid committing *Lau* violations? Are the *"Lau* Remedies" to be given any weight at all in determining non-compliance? Expressed otherwise, if the *"Lau* Remedies" are the remedial standards against which to measure the appropriateness of an educational plan designed to eliminate past practices found unlawful, what is the standard of liability to be applied in determining whether past or existing educational practices are unlawful? These critical questions are as yet unanswered, but the *Lau* decision, itself, and OCR compliance reviews, past and ongoing, provide some guidance.

We know from *Lau* that school districts violate Title VI if they fail to take affirmative steps to rectify the English language deficiencies of their national origin minority group children so as to open the instructional program to them. *Lau* also teaches that districts which offer its non-English speaking students the same course of instruction provided to its English speaking students, violate Title VI. Likewise, it should be apparent, that merely offering the standard fare remedial programs, designed for and provided to under-achieving English speaking students, can scarcely consitute the "affirmative steps" comtemplated by the May 25, 1970 Memorandum.

But, what of ESL? Would providing ESL alone to *all* students with English language deficiencies enable a school district to escape a finding of non-compliance, and, thus, avoid the *"Lau* Remedies" altogether? The *"Lau* Remedies" find ESL, alone, an inappropriate program for elementary school students and monolingual, non-English speaking, intermediate level students. It would seem, then, that giving these same students only ESL would also constitute inadequate "affirmative steps," and thus, violate Title VI.

In determining whether Title VI violations exist where only ESL is offered, local school districts may be allowed the opportunity to affirmatively show that ESL has proven effective in opening the instructional system to students with linguistic deficiencies. This should present for them formidable problems[19] since the burden of proof should be theirs.

In assessing the merits and effectiveness of ESL, or other alternative approaches advanced by local school authorities, OCR in all probability will adopt the same standards as used in its past compliance reviews. That is, it will analyze relevant indicia such as student achievement data; retention, and drop out rates; promotion and graduation statistics; and ability grouping and tracking. Moreover, OCR can be expected to evaluate the language assessment procedures utilized; the curriculum; staff development; and evaluation systems used. Private individuals seeking to establish a claim under Title VI will be relying on the same indicia.

The Force and Effect of the "Lau Remedies"

Whether viewed and applied as a remedial standard or a standard of liability, or both, it is assumed, of course, that the *"Lau* Remedies" are valid and enforceable. Undoubtedly, some recalcitrant school officials will challenge such an assumption. The rationale given by at least one school district, the Seattle public schools, for defying the *"Lau* Remedies" is that failing to publish them in the Federal Register, renders the *"Lau* Remedies" without the "force of Law."[20]

While it is true that statements of general policy, or interpretations of general applicability, formulated or adopted by a federal agency must be published in the Federal Register,[21] local school districts which have actual notice of the "*Lau* Remedies", are not immunized from sanctions flowing from violations, even if the "*Lau* Remedies" remain unpublished.[22]

Considering that the "*Lau* Remedies" have been widely disseminated, it is difficult to imagine that an offending school official will be able to assert successfully lack of actual notice. The courts have consistently refused to follow blindly the requirement of publication in the Federal Register in circumstances when to do so would amount to a wooden application of the rule.[23]

One may be permitted to wonder why the "*Lau* Remedies" have yet to be published in the Federal Register. The May 25, 1970 Memorandum at issue in *Lau* was published with dispatch in July, 1970. Neither OCR nor the U. S. Office of Education have offered any reason why publication has not been effected, except to represent, when pressed, that publication is imminent. Recent pronouncements by OCR, (March 15, 1976), indicate that the "'*Lau* Remedies' will appear shortly in the Federal Register."[24]

OCR has stated that it is "not using the '*Lau* Remedies' as a regulation with the force of law," but that the "*Lau* Remedies" are "entitled to weight as an agency interpretation" and are to be considered "guidance having a uniform purpose as the May 25 Memorandum."[25] Whether labeled a guideline, or an agency interpretation entitled to great weight, or a regulation having the force of law, it is pristine clear that school districts are not free to disregard them.

There is ample reason to believe that the courts will rely heavily on the standards set forth in the "*Lau* Remedies." The *Lau* decision must be read not only as upholding the May 25, 1970 Memorandum, but as reaffirming the authority of HEW to issue and enforce reasonable interpretative guidelines consistent with the mandate of Title VI of the 1964 Civil Rights Act prohibiting national origin discrimination in federally assisted schools. The unanimous ruling in *Lau* firmly buttresses HEW's authority to "fix the terms on which [the Federal Government's] money allotments to the states shall be disbursed." And, Justice Stewart, in his concurring opinion remarked that, "the Department has reasonably and consistently interpreted paragraph 601 [Title VI] to require affirmative remedial efforts to give special attention to linguistically deprived children."

School districts will have difficulty convincing the courts that the "*Lau* Remedies" are unreasonable or inconsistent with Title VI. Programmatic options are presented, bilingual education is not, strictly speaking, *mandated* "as the only possible approach to compliance,"[26] and alternative educational programs

are to be considered and accepted if shown to be equally effective. If viewed as a federal agency interpretation, the "*Lau* Remedies" will not be upset unless they are found to be plainly erroneous.

In the past, in the context of school desegregation cases, courts relied heavily on analogous HEW standards in formulating relief. HEW's Office of Education first issued desegregation guidelines in April, 1965, which "fixed the minimum standards to be used in determining the qualifications for schools applying for federal financial aid."[27] School districts were given several choices for satisfying Title VI requirements. The courts consistently attached great weight to these guidelines.

In 1966, and again in 1968, HEW issued revised guidelines relating to school desegregation, and again courts accorded them "serious judicial deference, respectful consideration, and great weight,"[28] albeit refusing to abdicate their constitutional responsibilities to HEW entirely.

Conclusion

Bilingual-bicultural education is a relatively new phenomenon to both courts and legislatures. Creating new legal rights and duties predictably also will create uncertainties. Despite *Otero* and the April 8th Henderson memorandum, a clear trend has been established obligating school authorities to adopt bilingual programs as a means to secure for language minority school children an equal educational opportunity.

FOOTNOTES

[1]Civ. No. 74-W-279 (D. Colo. December 31, 1975).

[2]414 U. S. 563 (1974).

[3]The *Lau* decision was premised on Title VI of the Civil Rights Act of 1964, 42 U.S.C. §2000d, and its regulations and guidelines, one of which, commonly referred to as the May 25, 1970 Memorandum, requires that: "Where inability to speak and understand the English language excludes national origin-minority group children from effective participation in the educational program offered by a school district, the district must take affirmative steps to rectify the language dificiency in order to open its instructional program to these students." 35 Fed. Reg. 11595.

[4]347 U. S. 483 (1954).

[5]342 F. Supp. 24,27-38 (E.D. Tex. 1971), aff'd per curium, 466 F. 2d 518 (5th Cir. 1972).

[6]373 F. Supp. 1264 (W.D. Tex. 1973), aff'd in part, rev'd as to other issues, 495 F. 2d 499 (5th Cir. 1974).

[7]Civ. No. 73-3301 (W.D. Tex. 8/1/73).

[8]499 F. 2d 1147 (10th Cir. 1974).

[9]72 Civ. 4002 (S.D.N.Y. August 29, 1974); also 57 F.R.D. 62 (S.D.N.Y. 1973); 65 F.R.D. 541 (S.D.-N.Y. 1975); 394 F. Supp. 1161 (S.D.N.Y. 1975).

[10]401 F. Supp. 216, 242 (D. Mass. 1975), aff'd 523 F. 2d 917 (1st Cir. 1975).

[11]402 F. Supp. 1096, 1144 (E.D. Mich. 1975).

[12]Civ. Nos. 1816-1822 (D. Del. May 19, 1976).

[13]521 F. 2d 465 (10th Cir. 1975).

[14]411 U.S. 1 (1973). The Supreme Court in Rodriguez said, among other things, that developing educational policy does not fall within a court's expertise.

[15]Although the Supreme Court's opinion in *Lau* did not raise any requirement as to numbers of eligible children necessary to create rights to special programs, Mr. Justice Blackmun's concurring opinion did, and the Tenth Circuit in Serna chose to adopt Mr. Justice Blackmun's caveat.

[16]The *"Lau* Remedies" actually bear the following title: HEW Memorandum on "Evaluation of Voluntary Compliance Plans designed to eliminate educational practices which deny non-English dominant students equal educational opportunity," Summer, 1975.

[17]"Conceivably, other methods of achieving the goals set by the *"Lau* Remedies" may exist, but the Office for Civil Rights will accept an alternative approach only if there is a reasonable basis to believe that it is at least as effective as the guidance set in the *"Lau* Remedies." Letter from Lloyd R. Henderson, Director, Elementary and Secondary Education Division, Office for Civil Rights, to Rosa Castro Feinberg, *Lau* General Assistance Center (B), School of Education, University of Miami, dated March 15, 1976.

[18]Supra, n.3. Although OCR's initial enforcement efforts are focused on the 333 *Lau* districts, identified in January, 1975, the scope of the *"Lau* Remedies" extends beyond these districts. Designation as a *Lau* district did not signify, at least from OCR's perspective, a determination of non-compliance, but was based upon data indicating a probability of violations.

[19]For example, the New York City public schools (now operating under the mandate of a Consent Decree requiring bilingual education) would have been hard pressed to demonstrate that ESL, alone, given since 1954, is adequate in the face of data substantiating the disproportionately high dropout and retention rates, and disproportionately low achievement scores and graduation rates of its Hispanic students.

[20]Letter from Peter E. Holmes, Director of OCR to Dr. J. Loren Torxel, Superintendent, Seattle Public Schools, November 24, 1975. The "force of law" generally connotes that which has the force and effect of a statute, creating legally binding rights and obligations.

[21]5 U.S.C. §552 (a) (1) (D) (The Administrative Procedure Act"). See also 42 U.S.C. §1508 ("The Federal Register Act") which enumerates categories of documents required to be published in the Federal Register.

[22]5 U.S.C. §552 (a) (1) (E). See, Rodriguez v. Swank, 318 F. Supp. 289, 295 (N.D. I11. 1970) aff'd 403 U.S. 901 (1971) (welfare case); Kessler v. F.C.C., 326 F. 2d 673.690 (D.C. Cir. 1963); U.S. v. Aarons, 310 F. 2d 341,346 (2d Cir. 1962).

[23]Thorpe v. Housing Authority of Durham, 393 U.S. 268,276 (1969) (upholding a HUD Circular not published in the Federal Register requiring notice to tenants residing in federally assisted housing projects prior to their eviction); Like v. Carter, 448 F. 2d 798,803-804 (8th Cir. 1971) (rejecting arguments that the HEW Handbook of Public Assistance Administration did not have the force and effect of law because it was not published in the Federal Register); Andrews v. Knowlton, 509 F. 2d 898,905 (2d Cir. 1975) (suggesting that distribution of a federal agency policy under the auspices of that agency may be sufficient in lieu of publication in the Federal Register).

[24]Letter from Henderson to Feinberg, supra, n. 17.

[25]Id.

[26]Letter from Holmes to Troxel, supra, N. 20.

[27]Singleton v. Jackson Municipal Separate School District, 348 F. 2d 729,730, n. 6 (5th Cir. 1965).

[28]United States v. Jefferson County Board of Education, 380 F. 2d 385,390 (5th Cir.) (en banc), cert. denied sub. nom. Caddo Parish School Board v. United States, 380 U.S. 840 (1967). See also, Kemp v. Beasely, 389 F. 2d 178,185 (8th Cir. 1968); Whittenberg V. Greenville County School District, 298 F. Supp. 784 (S.C.D.C. 1969).

Chapter 7
The Legal Vicissitudes of Bilingual Education
Perry A. Zirkel*

Webster defines *vicissitudes* as "the rise and decline in phenomena: the successive alterations visible in...human affairs." Although bilingual education seems at first blush like a rather recent phenomenon, a closer and longer look reveals its historical vicissitudes.

Arnold Leibowitz attributes these legal ups and downs to political expediency rather than pedagogical effectiveness or lack thereof.[1] His logic is difficult to deny; certainly law and politics are not foreign to each other. Yet part of the problem lies in the pedagogue's failure to define and evaluate bilingual education adequately. And where educational practitioners and scholars fail to provide a solid basis for decision making legislators and courts are prone to vagaries and variations.

Bilingual education is admittedly less easily defined than vicissitudes. The typical definition, "instruction using two languages as media of instruction," obscures a wide range of philosophical and programmatic differences. One researcher identified more than 400 types of bilingual education, depending on such factors as goals of the program (e.g., assimilation or pluralism), extent of subject matter taught through each language (e.g., a "50-50" program, offering half of each day in each language), and the number of language groups being served (e.g., "two-way" or "one-way" programs.)[2]

Although there are appealing arguments from both compensatory and elitist points of view, the effectiveness of bilingual education is not readily clear. Despite increasing investments of federal and other funds for such programs, there remains an embarrassing scarcity of relevant research. Much of the data used to support arguments for bilingual programs is derived from limited experiments conducted abroad under linguistic, cultural, temporal, and socioeconomic conditions different from the modern milieu of national origin minority-group children in the U. S.[3] Studies conducted in the U. S. are largely limited in their results, design, and applicability. In the face of these incomplete and inconclusive findings, the Department of Health, Education, and Welfare belatedly funded a national study to evaluate bilingual education, and Congress recently enacted amendments to the Bilingual Education Act requiring extensive research in this area.

Reference to such legislative intervention moves us directly to an examination of the legal history of bilingual education in the U. S. Such a perspective not only furthers our understanding of bilingual education and its possible future, but also gives us insight into the relationship of the law and the public schools.

The history of bilingual education and of the laws affecting it begins in the early 1800s rather than, as many think, in the mid-1960s. An estimated one million children attended bilingual programs in public schools during the nineteenth century, not to mention the continuing tradition which started even earlier in sectarian schools. There were, for example, German-English public bilingual schools in several states, French-English programs in Louisiana, and Spanish-English programs in New Mexico prior to the Civil War. Most of the early school laws and administrative policies were silently permissive as to the languages of instruction. Some states specifically authorized using a language other than English as a medium of instruction. For example, a Pennsylvania statute passed in 1837 and an Ohio statute passed in 1839 specifically permitted German-English public schools. Similarly, the California and New Mexico constitutions were drafted in the context of linguistic equality between Spanish and English.

However, as a result of increasing immigration, anti-Catholicism, and nationalism, a wave of "English-only" legislation began to form toward the end of the century. During the years 1890-1923, which one commentator described as "the heyday of xenophobic legislation"[4] and which the U. S. Supreme Court later recognized as "the period of extreme nativism,"[5] the number of states requiring English to be the exclusive medium for instruction in public and private schools more than tripled, to approximately 34. In seven of

*Perry A. Zirkel is associate professor of education at the University of Hartford, where his duties include co-chairing the Division of Curriculum and Foundations and directing the Teacher Corps Cycle X Project. Reprinted with permission of Phi Delta Kappa, January, 1977.

these states the statutes provided for revoking certification if a teacher committed the "criminal act" of teaching in a language other than English.

World War I killed public bilingual schools in the U. S. and injured private ones, notwithstanding two restraining reactions by the U. S. Supreme Court. In *Meyer* v. *Nebraska*, the Court held unconstitutional a Nebraska statute prohibiting teaching in and of foreign languages in the public and private schools.[6] In *Farrington* v. *Tokushige*, it similarly struck down territorial legislation in Hawaii which regulated the islands' private foreign language schools.[7] Despite its invalidation of these apparently anti-German and anti-Japanese statutes, the Court left room for less sweeping statutory prohibitions focusing on bilingual rather than foreign language instruction. Thus in *Meyer* the Court reasoned that "no emergency has arisen which renders knowledge by a child of some language other than English so clearly harmful as to justify its inhibitions," but it in effect reserved the right of a state to require that all subject-matter instruction be given in English.

Despite the forgettably depressing early results of this pedagogical policy, the English-only era that began with World War I extended well beyond World War II. For it was not until the early 1960s that public bilingual schooling was reborn. Rebirth took place in 1963 at the Coral Way School in Dade County, Florida. The movement spread on a limited basis to locations in Texas and other parts of the Southwest, but was not until the passage of Title VII of the Elementary and Secondary Education Act in 1967 that it really took hold.

Known as the Bilingual Education Act (BEA), Title VII was permissive, not mandatory, legislation. It encouraged the development of bilingual programs by means of grants to local school districts upon competitive application. The appropriations for the BEA, which have increased steadily since 1967 despite decreases in many other areas of federal funding for education, alone accounted for well over 300 bilingual programs by 1974. Of equal importance, the BEA was the first piece of federal legislation which recognized the use of a language other than English in public school classrooms.

After an ambitious but abortive attempt to mandate bilingual education in the *Tijerina* v. *Henry* case in 1969,[8] pro-bilingual advocates did not experience success in the courts until the early 1970s. These advances came on two fronts: a series of desegregation decisions starting with *United States* v. *Texas* in 1971,[9] and other cases involving bilingual education in a context devoid of the segregation question beginning with *Serna* v. *Portales Municipal Schools* in 1972.[10] The desegregation decisions ordered bilingual education for Spanish-speaking students as part of a comprehensive plan of relief from illegal segregation in a school district. Thus such relief was mandated for Mexican-American pupils in the aforementioned *Texas* case and in *Arvizu* v. *Waco Independent School District*[11] and was similarly granted for Puerto Rican pupils in the Boston desegregation case.[12]

The plaintiffs in *Serna*, on the other front, sought bilingual education in a case where segregation was not at issue. The federal district court had held in favor of the Mexican-American plaintiffs, based on the equal protection clause of the Fourteenth Amendment, thus apparently creating a federal constitutional right to bilingual education. However, the sight of such a broadbased right was short-lived. For while the *Serna* decision was on appeal to the Tenth Circuit, the decision of the U. S. Supreme Court in *Lau* v. *Nichols* in 1974 was more limited in its basis and scope.[13] The Court ruled in favor of the plaintiff class of 1,800 pupils of Chinese ancestry, but based its decision on Title VI of the Civil Rights Act of 1964 and the subsequent regulations and guidelines[14] of the Office for Civil Rights rather than on the U. S. Constitution. Moreover, the Court did not mandate bilingual education as the remedy, leaving the determination to the district court level in stating, "Teaching English to the students of Chinese ancestry who do not speak the language is one choice. Giving instructions to the group in Chinese is another. There may be others." The Tenth Circuit Court of Appeals subsequently affirmed the bilingual relief in *Serna* but did so on the narrower statutory basis of *Lau*, leaving open the constitutional question.

At about the same time, the *Aspira* case was settled in New York City.[15] The results went further and faster than *Lau* or *Serna*, mandating an ambitious timetable for assessing bilingualism and establishing bilingual programs for Puerto Rican pupils in New York City's public schools. However, these results were in the form of a consent agreement, legally binding on the parties[16] but of negligible precedential effect on other school districts in the nation.

Similar signs of momentum were evident at the legislative and administrative levels. Several states reversed their earlier trend and enacted statutes specifically permitting bilingual education programs (although 12 states still have English-only statutes). Moreover, six states enacted mandatory legislation during the 1970s, the best known being a Massachusetts statute and the most recent a New York statute. Such laws typically require bilingual instruction in school districts having an enrollment of 20 or more children of limited English-speaking ability. Moreover, renewed federal legislative action was taken in the mid-1970s. The 1974 Educational Amendments to the ESEA expanded not only the amount but also the scope of funding available for bilingual education. Supporting activities such as research and teacher training were authorized under this legislation. The Equal Educational Opportunities Act legislatively confirmed *Lau* by strengthening the standard for and expanding the availability of judicial action in this area.

Encouraged by the Supreme Court's reliance in *Lau* on its administrative guidelines under Title VI, the Office for Civil Rights initiated steps to outline and enforce the "affirmative steps" required of school districts to rectify the English-language deficiencies of national origin minority-group children. In April, 1975, the OCR announced the start of a compliance review of 333 selected school districts. That summer the OCR issued a document titled "Task Force Findings Specifying Remedies Available for Eliminating Past Educational Practices Ruled Unlawful Under *Lau* v. *Nichols.*"[17] This document recommended some form of bilingual education as the appropriate remedy at almost every level of public schooling. Because of the subsequent furor regarding the legal force of the "Task Force Findings," the OCR issued a brief statement— taken by many as a careful retreat—that the findings were "guidelines" only, but that the burden of proving the acceptability of an alternate remedy rested upon the school districts involved.[18]

More recent court developments have concurred with the OCR's enforcement efforts. Based on strengthened state and federal statutory standards, the *Serna-Lau* line of cases moved toward a broader bilingual mandate in *Morales* v. *Shannon.*[19] In this case the federal district court judge had ruled against a claim of discrimination by Mexican-American students for failing to receive bilingual education. The Tenth Circuit Court of Appeals resurrected the possibility of such a claim, remanding the case for a fresh hearing in light of the new Texas and federal legislation.

At the same time, the desegregation line of bilingual decisions took significant steps back from mandating bilingual education in *Keyes* v. *School District No. 1, Denver.*[20] In the *Keyes* case (discussed in the April, 1976, *Kappan*), the Tenth Circuit reversed the district court's order which had originally instituted the Cardenas Plan, a comprehensive bilingual-bicultural program extending to matters of governance, philosophy, curriculum, testing, and noninstructional services. The Tenth Circuit found such pervasive and detailed relief to be an unwarranted incursion into the local school board's authority, concluding that "although enlightened education theory may well demand as much, the Constitution does not." Further, this court resolved possible tensions between bilingual education and desegregation in favor of the latter: "Bilingual education, moreover, is not a substitute for desegregation. Although bilingual instruction may be required to prevent the isolation of minority students in

a predominantly Anglo school system,...such instruction must be subordinate to a plan of school desegregation."

Relying upon *Keyes*, the federal district court in Colorado ruled in the case of *Otero* v. *Mesa Valley School District No. 51* that "under Tenth Circuit law there is no constitutional right to bilingual-bicultural education, and our appellate court has held that even where there is segregation [and there is none in District 51] a trial court cannot impose the Cardenas Plan on the school district."[21] The effect of *Otero* is uncertain, due to its factual limitations ("the case involves a very few, if any, students who have a real language deficiency"), and the judge's notable proclivity to defer to school district authorities.

The legal controversy surrounding bilingual education continues unabated, clouded by much uncertainty. Several federal suits are currently pending, including civil actions brought on behalf of Puerto Rican pupils in the cities of Hartford; New Haven; Patchogue, New York; and Philadelphia.[22] Bilingual suits in states which have strong constitutional provisions regarding education[23] are also likely. Persisting problems revolve around the need to more precisely define the class and prescribe the remedy.[24] Problems in the definition category include "alingual" pupils—children who are not proficient in either English or their native language. Similarly, what about the children of limited English-speaking ability and their parents who do not favor bilingual instruction? Problems in the remedy category include "singletons"—limited English-speaking children who are virtually alone because they are scattered across school sites or grades. Similarly, what part should culture play in fashioning appropriate relief, especially where there are limited English-speaking children of various cultural backgrounds? Further, if bilingual education is the answer, which type of bilingual program is best—e.g., a "two-way" program, which includes instruction through a second language for native English-speaking children, or a "one-way" program, which is limited to serving as a transition for non-English-speaking children?[25] A third category of questions concerns the nexus of bilingual education and other school programs which have special status in the eyes of the law. For example, what about the children who have special problems in terms of learning as well as language? Are they entitled to a "bilingual special education" program? Similarly, is desegregation more important for limited English-speaking children than bilingual education, even if it means sink or swim for them, with no transitional preparation for the "mainstream?"

The closer and longer you look at the situation, the larger the questions loom. Their equitable resolution depends at least as much upon educators' actively learning about and contributing to legal decisions as it does upon lawyers, judges, and legislators contributing to education. As Chester Nolte recently pointed out, the responsibility for court incursions into public education belongs as much to errant or passive school-people as it does to eager litigants or interfering judges.[26]

By taking a long, hard look at the legal history of bilingual education in the U. S., one can see that what at first appears to be a recent and rising monolith is actually a quite complex and persistent phenomenon characterized by distinct fits and starts and ups and downs. If future developments in this field are not to be vagaries dictated by personal predilections or political pressures, there must be close and active collaboration among educational and legal practitioners.

FOOTNOTES

[1] Arnold H. Leibowitz, "The Imposition of English as the Language of Instruction in American Schools," *Revista de Derecho Puertorriqueno*, October/December, 1970, pp. 175-244. See, for example, his reference to "language juggling" on p. 227.

[2] William F. Mackey, "A Typology of Bilingual Education," *Foreign Language Annals*, May, 1970, pp. 596-608.

[3] Richard Venezky, "Nonstandard Language and Reading," *Elementary English*, March, 1970, pp. 334-45; Patricia Lee Engle, "Language Medium in Early School Years for Minority Language Groups," *Review of Educational Research*, Spring, 1975, pp. 283-325.

[4] Arnold H. Leibowitz, "English Literacy; Legal Sanctions for Discrimination," *Notre Dame Lawyer*, Fall, 1969, pp. 35-42.

[5] *Loving* v. *Virginia*, 388 U. S. 1, 6 (1967).

[6] 262 U. S. 390 (1923).

[7] 273 U. S. 284 (1927).

[8] 48 F.R.D. 274 (D.N.M. 1969), *appeal dismissed*, 398 U. S. 922 (1970).

[9] 342 F. Supp. 24 (E.D. Tex. 1971), *aff'd*, 466 F.2d 518 (5th Cir. 1971).

[10] 351 F. Supp. 1279 (D.N.M. 1972), *aff'd*, 499 F.2d 1147 (10th Cir. 1974); cf. *Denetclarence* v. *Board of Educ.*, Civ. No. 8872 (D.N.M. stipulated agreement, December 14, 1973) (Navajo Indian Students).

[11] 373 F. Supp. 1264 (W.D. Tex. 1973).

[12] *Morgan* v. *Kerrigan*, 401 F. Supp. 216 (D. Mass. 1975), *aff'd*, 523 F.2d 917 (1st Cir. 1976).

[13] 414 U. S. 563 (1974).

[14] The May 25, 1970, memo required school districts to take "affirmative steps" to remedy the English language deficiencies of national origin minority-group children (35 *Fed. Reg.* 11595).

[15] *Aspira* v. *Board of Educ.*, Civ. No. 4002 (S.D.N.Y. consent agreement, August 29, 1974).

[16] The Board of Education and the School chancellor of New York City were recently ruled in contempt of court for failing to substantially comply with the *Aspira* consent decree. Civ. No. 4002 (S.D.-N.Y. October 29, 1976).

[17] Terrel H. Bell, commissioner of education, and Martin H. Gerry, acting director of the Office for Civil Rights, memorandum dated August 11, 1975, to chief state school officers.

[18] Lloyd Henderson, director of OCR Elementary and Secondary Division, memorandum dated April 8, 1976.

[19] 366 F. Supp. 813 (W.D. Tex. 1973), *rev'd in part*, 516 F.2d 411 (5th Cir. 1975).

[20] 521 F.2d 465 (10th Cir. 1975), *cert. denied*, 423 U. S. 1066 (1976).

[21] Civ. No. 74-W-279 (D. Colo. December 31, 1975).

[22] *Ramos* V. *Gaines*, Civ. No. H-76-38 (D. Conn. filed January 26, 1976); *Arroyo* v. *Barbarito*, Civ. No. 75-191 (D. Conn. filed August 6, 1974); *Rios* v. *Read*, Civ. No. 75. (E.D.N.Y. filed February 26, 1975); *Lopez* v. *Thomas*, Civ. No. 75-14 (E.D. Pa. filed January 6, 1975).

[23] E.g., *Robinson* v. *Cahill*, 62 N.J. 473, 303 A.2d 273 (1973), *cert. denied*, 414 U. S. 976 (1973); *Horton* v. *Meskill*, 31 Conn. Supp. 377, 332 A.2d 113 (Super. Ct. 1974).

[24] Perry A. Zirkel, "The Whys and Ways of Testing Bilinguality Before Teaching Bilingually," *Elementary School Journal*, March, 1976, pp. 323-30.

[25] Edwardo Seda Bonilla, "Ethnic and Bilingual Education for Cultural Pluralism," in Madelon D. Stent, William R. Hazard, Harry N. Rivlin, eds., *Cultural Pluralism in Education* (New York: Appleton-Century-Crofts, 1973).

[26] M. Chester Nolte, "Why Are We Begging the Courts To Run the Schools?" *American School Board Journal*, May, 1976, pp. 32, 33.

Chapter 8
Where is Bilingual Education Going? Historical and Legal Perspectives
Earl J. Ogletree*

The Bilingual Education Act of 1968 was enacted to meet the academic, social and economic needs of the increasing number of non-English and partial bilingual-speakers in the United States. It was recognized as far back as 1920, that the inability to understand the language of instruction was the chief cause of immigrant children's poor performance in school (Ide 1920). Current statistics are similar. The non-English-speaking child is one year behind by the third grade, two years by the seventh grade, and one of the fifty percent school dropout statistics by the twelfth grade (U. S. Office of Education 1975).

Today there are approximately five million children living in homes where a language other than English is spoken (U. S. Office of Education 1975). Of this group 1.8 to 2.5 million need special instruction in English.

Although the Bilingual Education Act (Title VII, ESEA) was initially promoted by Cuban immigrants relocating in Miami, Florida (U. S. has the fifth largest Spanish-speaking population in the world) it now includes speakers of German, French, Italian, Chinese, Japanese, Philippino (Tagalog) and several American Indian languages, to list a few. It was designed to help three to eighteen year old non-English-speakers to:

1. Achieve fluency and literacy in two languages (native and English).
2. Function effectively in the American and native cultures (bicultural component).
3. Progress in academic subjects at the same rate as non-immigrant, English speaking children.
4. Develop a positive self-concept and pride in the dual linguistic and cultural heritages (Condon 1974).

An important component of the Act is to involve the parents and community in the planning, implementation and evaluation of bilingual programs.

With the development of bilingual programs came a myriad of educational-linguistic concepts:

Bilingualism: The ability to function in two languages, but not necessarily with equal proficiency.

Biculturalism: The possibility to function in two cultures, as the occasion arises, but not necessarily with equal proficiency.

Bilingual Education: Instruction in two languages, enabling the person to function in another language in addition to his native language, with or without equal proficiency.

Bilingual/Bicultural Education: Instruction in and reinforcement of the native language and culture as well as the new or second language and culture.

Transitional Bilingual Program: The learning of English with no or little reinforcement of the native language, except as a starting point to help the student to make the transition from his native language to English as soon as possible. (This program is based on the "melting pot" concept of assimilation.)

Maintenance Bilingual Education: A self-sustaining, continuous program of developing the native language, while learning English with equal proficiency. (This program is based on the concept of cultural pluralism.)

According to Condon (1974), "in its ideal form, the overall purpose of bilingual-bicultural education is to produce bilingualism and biculturalism within the learners." However, idealistic programs are generally stifled by the time. Bilingual education is interpreted as a remedial compensatory model of education for minority groups not as a linguistic model in which all children would be bilingual. Instead, the Bilingual Act "functionally promotes the use of other languages only as means of learning English," while sacrificing the native idiom (Gonzales 1975). Federal and state statutes have favored transitional over maintenance bilingual programs. The confirmation of the melting pot rather than the pluralist philosophy of American society is reflected in the history of bilingual education.

This article will attempt to examine the historical evolution, legal basis and major issues of bilingual education.

*Dr. Earl Ogletree, Associate Professor of Education, Chicago State University.

Historical Perspectives of Bilingual Schooling

Bilingual schooling is not a new phenomena in the United States. Founded by immigrants, the U. S. has been populated by people from virtually every country. The earlier immigrants (1600-1880) faced cultural and linguistic problems in developing and adjusting to the American culture. However, it was the later immigrants that faced the greatest opposition to their native culture and language and overt pressure to change and to assimilate (Dimmerstein and Reimers 1975).

The first immigrant groups (mainly protestant, Scotch-Irish, French, English, Welsh, Germans and Dutch) lost their distinct national heritages/and languages to become part of the common American culture. Although English is the native language of the U. S., originally it was only one of the languages, together with French, Spanish, Dutch and German, brought to the colonies by the settlers. These early groups started their own bilingual and native language schools as a solution to meeting their children's educational needs.

Bilingual schooling dates back to the 1700's, when German, French, Scandinavian and Dutch established their own school, teaching English as a subject. From 1839-1880, German, French and Spanish groups established native language schools in the West, South and Southwest (Leibowitz 1971). "In New Mexico, the Spanish language had equal constitutional status with English and was in actual use as an official state language" (Chicago Board of Education 1974, p. 33). Even the Cherokees had a native and bilingual educational system that produced 90 percent literacy in its native language. It was reported "that Oklahoma Cherokees had a higher literacy level than the white populations of either Texas or Arkansas" (Leibowitz 1971, p. 78).

Between the mid 19th century and World War I, increasing numbers of Catholic, Jewish, Eastern Orthodox and Asian religious groups from Italy, Russia, Balkans and Asians immigrated (Kopan 1974). Unlike the earlier immigrants, they were largely illiterate.

Being ethnically and racially different and poor they posed a potential threat to the American nativists. They were the "socially or culturally disadvantaged" of their time. They were looked on as inferior and blamed for the crime and slums of the cities. Coming from undemocratic countries, they were also suspected of being political radicals, enemies of the American system. They were social outcasts, and subsequently experienced hostility and blatant discrimination. Anti-ethnic organized formed to pressure the government to restrict further immigration of these new ethnic groups. Immigration laws were passed restricting Asian and Southern European immigration, while giving preference to Northern and Western European immigrants (Hartman 1974).

Both the old and new immigrant groups together with the larger society attempted to "melt the overwhelming number of immigrants into American society by teaching them English" (Hartman 1974, p. 20). Although it was estimated, that over one million children attended some form of bilingual schooling, the great majority of children who were in school received no special consideration, despite their difficulty in learning English (Cubberley 1934).

During and after World War I, restrictive legislation and nationalistic and isolationist foreign policies lead to the "English only" policy in schools and institutions. Dimmerstein and Reimers (1975) outline reasons for and implications of the decline in foreign languages in the United States between the two wars:

1. The pressure to assimilate into American life and become "truly American."
2. The emphasis on knowing English for successful competition for jobs.
3. The decline of foreign language newspapers.
4. The declining use of foreign languages as the children learned English.
5. The nationalistic zeal that accompanied World War I and World War II.
6. The curtailment of immigration.
7. The enactment of state laws declaring that English was to be the only means of instruction in the schools.
8. The development of mass media in the English language.
9. The use of foreign languages was limited to the instruction of that language (p. 124).

Many states passed laws that restricted the use of other languages for school instruction except in a foreign language class.

During World War II, the U. S. armed forces saw a need to teach foreign cultures and languages to servicemen. Bilingual-bicultural courses were implemented. After the War, interest in foreign languages diminished. It was not revived until the passage of the National Defense Education Act of 1958. Gonzales (1975) believes this act not only legitimized the active study of foreign languages, but it was also responsible for "providing financial assistance to many minority group students to attend college and specialize in math, science and foreign language." It also gave impetus to the "development of language education as a specialized teaching field" (p. 8).

Until the 1960's, few public schools had bilingual programs. Twenty-five states, even those with large non-speaking populations, had "English only" laws regarding classroom instruction. In seven states it was a violation of the criminal code and could mean the loss of certification to teach in a foreign language (Chicago Board of Education 1974).

Contemporary Bilingual education in the public schools began with the Coral Way School (Miami, Florida) bilingual program, funded by private and public foundations. The Cuban refugees persuaded the Dade County, Florida schools to launch this model bilingual program, which soon became the unofficial demonstration model school for the nation (Cordasco 1969).

The Coral Way experiment made clear that bilingual education was possible. Soon leaders from Latin American communities across the country, especially in the Southwest, pressed for bilingual programs for their children.

In 1964, two programs were established in Texas, one in the Nye School of the United Consolidated Independent School District in Webb County, outside of Laredo, and the other in the San Antonio Independent School District. In 1965, bilingual programs were established in Pecos, New Mexico and Edinburg, Texas. In 1966, the Harlandale Independent School District of San Antonio, Del Rio, and Zapata, Texas, in Calexico and Marysville, California and Rough Rock, Arizona, bilingual programs were founded. By 1968 Las Cruces, New Mexico; Hoboken, New Jersey; Corpus Christi and Del Valle, Texas; and St. Croix in the Virgin Islands had programs. In 1967, the U. S. Senate Sub-Committee on Bilingual Education called for hearings and in 1969 the Elementary and Secondary Education Act of 1965 was amended and Title VII was added to the Act. During 1969-70, there were fifty-six bilingual programs plus seventy-six projects that were funded under Title VII. Today there are 383 classroom demonstration projects in 42 languages (23 in American Indian and Eskimo languages), plus five material centers (U. S. Office of Education 1975).

Besides Title VII (ESEA) funding, U. S. Office of Education and HEW supports a variety of bilingual programs under the Emergency School Aid, Title I ESEA, Teacher Corps, Follow Through, Adult Education, Indian Education, Right to Read and Education for the Handicapped among others. Sixty-eight million dollars were expended for bilingual programs under Title VII for the 1974-75 school year (U. S. Office of Education 1975).

Legal Basis of Bilingual Education

Judicial decisions have recognized the lack of language proficiency can be the basis of discrimination. Bilingual instruction was the remedy.

The following legislation and court decisions helped provide a foundation for bilingual education:

1. Meyer v. Nebraska (1923). The Supreme Court invalidated prohibitions against foreign language instruction in private schools.

2. Farrington v. Tokusnige (1927). The Hawaii territorial law regulated subjects taught, textbooks used, and the political beliefs of instructors and had a provision restricting foreign language instruction to one hour per day, six days per week, 38 weeks per year. The court invalidated the statute.

3. Title VII of the Elementary and Secondary Education Act of 1965 gave financial assistance to local educational agencies for the development of bilingual curricula to familiarize immigrant students with their history and culture. The program was voluntary.

4. Title VI of the Civil Rights Act of 1964 prohibited discrimination in federally funded programs and related activities. Under these regulations, no school system administering a federally-funded program may employ criteria or methods of administration which effectively frustrate the program's goals for persons of any particular national origin. In 1970, HEW issued a memorandum applying this standard to the problem of providing equal educational opportunity for national-origin minority group children deficient in English Language skills.

5. The Bilingual Education Act (1968). Congress authorized appropriations recognizing:
   a. That there are large numbers of children of limited English-speaking ability.
   b. That many of such children have a cultural heritage which differs from that of English-speaking persons.
   c. That a primary means by which a child learns is through the use of such child's language and cultural heritage.
   d. That, therefore, large numbers of children of limited English-speaking ability have educational needs which can be met by the use of bilingual education methods and techniques.
   e. That, in addition, children of limited English-speaking ability benefit through the fullest utilization of multiple language and cultural resources (Giffert, et. a. 1975).

6. Lau v. Nichols (1974). The U. S. Supreme Court determined that "there is no equality of treatment merely by providing students with the same facilities, textbooks, teachers, and curriculum, for students who do not understand

English are effectively foreclosed from any meaningful education." This case referred to Chinese-speaking children in the San Francisco school system who were not receiving equal education opportunities, under Title VI of the Civil Rights Act of 1964. The school system was ordered to remedy the situation.

7. Serna v. Portales (1964). The court relied on the Lau decision and affirmed a lower court decision to order bilingual programs as a remedy in a Title VI case. It was found that Spanish-speaking children in a New Mexico school district had not received equal educational opportunity and this had violated their constitutional right to equal protection.

The Lau decision facilitated the amendment of Title VII (Public Law 93-380). In addition to helping LEA's to serve non-English speaking children better, it also broadened the program to include more deliberate and systematic teacher training and curriculum development (U. S. Office of Education 1975). It is predicted that the supreme court ruling in the Lau v. Nichols decision that public schools must provide special language instruction for non-English speakers will lead to a proliferation of bilingual programs in the 1970's and 1980's.

Accompanying these changes at the federal level, was the amendment of state statutes which expressly or implicitly permit instruction in a language other than English. Fourteen states have no statutory provisions. Two states (Alaska and Penn.) describe only the circumstances under which non-English instruction in substantive courses is permitted. Five states have an "English-only" policy for the public schools, whereas seven states have an "English-only statute for both public and private schools (Giffert, et. al. 1975).

Grubb (1974) reasons there will be additional changes in local statutes in that failure to provide bilingual instruction where it is needed constitutes a violation of the constitutional provision for equal protection and due process. When considered in the context of compulsory education laws, this argument carries much weight. "If a state is interested in educating its population, it may justify compelling the children to attend schools. But when suitable educational instruction is not provided, compulsory schooling is reduced to confinement" (p. 241).

With the changes in federal laws and legislation and state statutes, a number of states have passed laws mandating the establishment of bilingual education. In 1972, Massachusetts was the first state to pass a mandatory bilingual education law, requiring bilingual programs in any school district with twenty or more students of the same language background. Illinois passed a similar law in 1973, followed in 1974 by

California, New Jersey, New Mexico, Texas and Alaska. Other states followed with administrative directives for the establishment of bilingual programs (Gonzales 1975).

However, all of the state legislation to date has been directed toward transitional rather and maintenance bilingual education. Bilingual education is the stepping-stone to learning English, rather than the foundation for the national program. Its educational and fiscal status confirms it standing in the American schools. In most states, bilingual programs are adjuncts to the regular curriculum, only limited English speaking children are eligible for bilingual instruction and their existence is based on the availability of federal and state "soft monies."

Issues in Bilingual Education

The proponents of bilingual education view it as a vehicle for cultural pluralism. They argue that bilingual education:

1. Gives the non-English-speaking child the opportunity to learn his own language and culture, and it influences self-concept and intellectual development during the formative years.
2. Approaches the child as advantaged rather than disadvantaged.
3. Helps to maintain the linguistic and cultural heritage of the ethnic group.
4. Is a legal right because it provides reasonable opportunity for academic success for non-English-speakers.
5. Should be a regular course of study, teaching two languages to all children.
6. Fosters educational change by challenging the assumption that an English based curriculum is suitable for all children.

Bilingual education supporters attempt to dispell some of the myths by claiming that: 1) It is not an expression of minority militancy, but a recognition of cultural pluralism; 2) It is not a compensatory or remedial English or reading program; 3) It is *not* based on the concept of ethnic segregation; 4) It is *not* specifically designed for the Spanish-speaking only; 5) It is not a watered-down or dumping ground program for the outcast non-English and partial bilingual speakers; and 6) It is not an unAmerican educational activity (Condon 1974).

Despite their altruistic motivations and forceful arguments, bilingual education has not, as yet, been accorded equal status with other programs. Opponents provide an equally compelling case against bilingual education. Their arguments are based on historical and social precedents and economic factors. They reason

that:
1. Every child must learn English to adequately function in American society.
2. The maintenance of an ethnic culture and language is the responsibility of the home, not school and tax payer.
3. Past generations of non-English children learned English without the benefit or special, public funded bilingual programs.
4. If an ethnic group or individual decides to reside in the U. S., they should take the responsibility upon themselves to learn English.
5. Special considerations are given to certain ethnic and racial groups over others in violation of the Civil Rights Act of 1964.
6. Bilingual education fosters a form of ethnic and racial segregation, counter to current trends of school and community integration (Condon 1974).
7. U. S. is a melting pot of citizens, not ethnic groups. No ethnic group is forced to give up its "character and distinctiveness as a price for participation in American society and polity" (Glazer 1975, p. 5).

Although the proponents of bilingual education may reject the latter statement by countering with the ethno-centricism or racism charge, others (Glazer 1975) would argue that the United States is a union of states, a "nation of free individuals, not a nation of politically defined ethnic groups" (p. 5). Glazer qualifies his position by making a differentiation between ethnicity and citizenry.

The ethnic group is one of the building blocks of American society, politics, and economy, none of which can be fully understood without reference to ethnic group formation and maintenance, but this type of group is not given any political recognition or formal status. No one is enrolled in an ethnic group, except American Indians, for whom we still maintain a formally distinct political status defined by birth. For public purposes, everyone else is only a citizen. No one may be denied the right to political participation, education, jobs because of ethnic status nor (given better access to socio-economic institutions) (p. 28).

It follows that no ethnic groups have been or should be allowed to establish an independent polity, since they possess no political status. Only the individual, the citizen has political status.

It is this question of ethnic group status that is the stumbling block for the acceptance and implementation of bilingual education and its goals.

Bilingual education seems to be moving against the currents of social trends. One of course, is the "melting pot" concept. The other is the incompatibilty between the principles of bilingual education and integration. For bilingual education to function effectively: 1) children of like language and cultural background must attend the same school, 2) the community and neighborhood school concept must be maintained, 3) teachers of similar cultural and language background must be assigned to schools with like pupil populations, and 4) parents are mandated to be involved in the development of bilingual programs.

Segregation rather than integration is by necessity an essential ingredient of bilingual education. An example of the desire for ethnic segregation was demonstrated by the refusal of a group of Chicago Latin parents to send their children out of the Latin community to a black high school. Another was illustrated in a recent survey of Chicago teachers' opinions of proposed teacher and pupil integration plans. It showed that 62 to 85 percent of Latin teachers rejected all four plans (Ogletree 1976).

Therefore, the issue of bilingual education centers on whether or not it is compatible with the political, social and educational philosophy of the American society. Many believe the transitional programs provide a compromise between the nativists and the immigrants. Maintenance programs are too divergent with current American thought and political action.

Current Trends

Bilingual education is being developed and funded on the basis of the transitional model. It is predicted that the Education Amendment of 1974 (Public Law 93-380), which amends Title VII of ESEA, will facilitate service to non-English speaking students. Under the Vocational Education Act training programs are being established to train or retrain limited English speaking persons, ages 16 and over.

As the number of bilingual programs swell to include over 200,000 children in 1976, it is estimated that between 48,000 and 77,000 teachers are needed. For the fiscal year 1976, the funding for bilingual education includes:
1. Inservice training of 9,000 teachers, paraprofessionals, parents, administrators and counselors.
2. Undergraduate and graduate training fellowship for over 1,300 bilingual teachers and professors.
3. Assistance for over 20 colleges and universities to expand and develop bilingual education programs.
4. Expansion of six resource centers to assist teachers, develop curriculum materials.
5. Surveys to assess the specific local and national needs of bilingual education programs (U. S.

Office of Education 1975).

Looking to the Future

Bilingual education is still in the developmental stage. It has not achieved its full potential. One reason is that like any new innovation, its expectations are unrealistically high, its implementation poorly planned and its evaluation insufficiently anticipated. Evaluation evidence has not kept pace with the growth of bilingual programs (Zirkel 1976); the state of the art of bilingual education and evaluation is still limited (Engle 1975).

Whether bilingual-bicultural education will become a change agent and secure equal status with other programs, as a desirable and essential aspect of the American educational process is still a question. Like all socio-political issues, its future depends upon the attitudes and beliefs of the populace. Failure to nurture it may doom thousands of non-English speaking children to academic failure.

REFERENCES

A Better Chance to Learn: Bilingual-Bicultural Education. Washington, D. C.: U. S. Commission on Civil Rights, Clearinghouse, 1975.

"Bilingual Education," *Education Briefing Paper*. Washington, D. C.: U. S. Department of Health, Education and Welfare/Education Division, 1975.

A Comprehensive Design for Bilingual-Bicultural Education. Chicago, Ill.: Chicago Board of Education, 1974.

Condon, E. C., "Bilingual, Bicultural Education" *NJ-EA Review*, 1974, *10*: 9-10.

Cordasco, F. "The Bilingual Education Act," *Phi Delta Kappan* 1969, *51*: 75-76.

Dimmerstein, L. and Reimers, D. M. *Ethnic Americans: A History of Immigration and Assimilation*. New York: Dodd and Mead, 1975.

Giffert, D., Harper, L., Sariento, C. and J. Schember, *The Current Status of U. S. Bilingual Education Legislation*, Arlington, Va.: Eric, Clearinghouse for Languages and Linguistics, 1975.

Glazer, N., *Affirmative Discrimination: Ethnic Inequality and Public Policy*. New York: Basic Books, Inc., 1975.

Gonzales, J. "Coming of Age in Bilingual/Bicultural Education: A Historical Perspective," *Inequality in Education*. 1975, *19*: 5-17.

Grubb, E. B., "The Right to Bilingual Education," *California Journal of Educational Research*. 1974, *25*: 240-4.

Hartman, E. G. *The Movement to Americanize the Immigrant Language in the United States*, New York: Columbia University Press, 1948, p. 7.

Ide, G. G. "*Spoken Language as Essential Tool*," *The Psychological Clinic*. 1920, *5*: 219.

Kopan, A. T. "Melting Pot: Myth or Reality?" *Cultural Pluralism*. ed. E. G. Epps. Berkeley, Calif.: McCutchan Publ. Co., 1974, p. 43.

Leibowitz, A. A. Educational Policy and Political Acceptance: *The Imposition of English as the Language of Instruction in American Schools*. Washington, D. C.: Eric Clearinghouse for Linguistics, 1971.

Ogletree, E. J. "Chicago Teachers Accept Integration, But Reject the Plans," *Illinois Schools Journal*. 1976, *56*: 56-60.

Zirkel, P. "Research on Bilingual Pupils and Programs," *News, Notes and Quotes*, 1976, XX: 4.

Chapter 9
Bilingual Education and Desegregation: A New Dimension In Legal and Educational Decision-Making
Ricardo R. Fernández and Judith T. Guskin*

The past decade has witnessed the rapid growth of bilingual bicultural programs throughout the United States. Beginning with the passage in 1968 of federal legislation and modest appropriations (Title VII of the Amendments to the 1965 ESEA), and with the support of enforced regulations and a number of significant court decisions which culminated in *Lau* v. *Nichols*, bilingual bicultural education has "come of age."[1] This process, which has been accompanied by the involvement of community groups from different language and cultural backgrounds, has resulted in the passage by several of various forms of state legislation pertaining to bilingual bicultural (B/B) Education.[2] Federal expenditures for bilingual education presently exceed $100 million, cover over 40 language groups, and additional expansion is anticipated since the majority of children in need of B/B Education are still not being served. Bilingual bicultural education represents one of the major thrusts in present U. S. public educational policy and its influence on the nation's educational system is evident, although it is as yet impossible to judge its eventual impact on society at large. Parallel to this phenomenon, over the same time period another thrust in public educational policy has become intensified—school desegregation in major urban areas outside of the south. Supported by a series of court decisions following the historic *Brown* case, the movement to end segregation of the nation's public schools, which had begun to gather momentum in the late fifties and early sixties in the South, began to expand to the North and to the West in the early 1970's. The issue of involuntary transfers and busing students to achieve "racial balance" in schools (a new definition of desegregation) emerged and controversy still abounds over this and related issues in major urban centers throughout the country. From San Francisco and Los Angeles to Denver, from Omaha and Chicago to Boston: from Minneapolis to Milwaukee to Houston and Austin, school districts are faced with litigation and court-ordered desegregation. While desegregation litigation was still concentrated in the South, there was no public consciousness regarding its effects on cultural and linguistic minorities who also face discrimination. Once suits were filed and remedies imposed in cities with significant minority populations in addition to Blacks, another element entered into the picture and it became necessary to consider these other racial and ethnic groups in planning and implementing desegregation.

This article will attempt to discuss in general terms some of the critical issues which have arisen as a result of the contact between the thrusts for bilingual bicultural education and school desegregation in urban areas over the past several years. Since these issues are quite recent and in many instances are still being debated in legal and educational circles, these comments, which are preliminary in nature, are advanced in the spirit of attempting to foster dialogue in the hope that this will lead to their eventual satisfactory resolution in terms not only of the political compromises underlying desegregation, but also the needs and desires of minority children, their families and communities.

Equal Educational Opportunity: Desegregation and/or Bilingual Bicultural Education

While Blacks and Hispanos and other minority groups as well espouse the same goal in terms of equality of educational opportunities, the means to achieve the same often appear to be in conflict. This apparent conflict is based on legal precedents, federal (and, at times, state) legislation and, very importantly, differing perceptions by specific communities on the goals (immediate and ultimate) of desegregation and its logical conclusion—integration.

The body of law and judicial precedents pertaining to desegregation of public educational systems is considerable. Inexorably, the courts have moved to dismantle "dual systems," which were found to be inherently unequal in *Brown*, and to strive toward the operation by school boards of "unitary systems,"

*Dr. Ricárdo Fernandez, Assistant Professor of Cultural Foundations, University of Wisconsin-Milwaukee. Dr. Judith Guskin, Bilingual Education Service Center, Arlington Hts., Illinois.

wherein equality of educational opportunity is more likely to exist. The literature on this subject is plentiful and, for the purposes of this article, we need not concern ourselves with this topic.[3]

Although in several decisions which preceded *Lau* federal courts sustained the soundness and appropriateness of bilingual bicultural education, and the right of children of limited English language skills to such programs (cf. *United States* v. *State of Texas* (San Felipe del Rio), *Serna* v. *Portales*), it was not until *Lau* that the issue received nationwide publicity when, in a unanimous decision delivered by Justice Douglas, the United States Supreme Court found that failure by the San Francisco Unified School District to address in a meaningful way the needs of a large group of children of limited English-speaking ability amounted to a violation of their civil rights under Title VI of the Civil Rights act of 1964. Although it was not clear, it appeared that the *Lau* decision recognized (or applied) only the rights of groups of students as opposed to rights of individuals. However, the Equal Educational Opportunity Act of 1974 went a step further in prohibiting the denial of equal educational opportunity to individuals in Section 1703, which states in part:

No state shall deny equal educational opportunity to an individual on account of his or her race, color, sex or national origin by—

(f) the failure by an educational agency to take appropriate action to overcome language barriers that impede equal participation in its instructional programs.[5]

The outcome of the possible conflict between group rights vs. individual rights is still undecided and judicial testing may be required to further define and delimit the scope of existing legal precedents and federal (and, where applicable, state) legislation.[6]

Spurred on by what are perceived to be significant victories, Hispanic and other language minorities throughout the United States have turned to federal courts or federal agencies (such as the Office for Civil Rights) to seek relief for unmet needs. Quite often, their demands are based on the group's preference for programs which go beyond the remedies prescribed by law or regulation, which are mainly compensatory and transitional in nature. In an age of ethnic consciousness for most ethnic/racial minority groups in the U. S., parents are increasingly demanding that the educational system change from its traditional assimilationist, stripping-away of ethnicity and language through a monocultural/monolingual mold to a new pluralistic, multilingual/multicultural model involving group pride, respect and adaptation in diverse ways to values and behaviors of the dominant society. This demand translates into an advocacy for bilingual bicultural programs which although aimed at

students with limited proficiency in English, can include those having some ability in English. New curriculum, materials and staff are necessary to implement these programs which place emphasis on developing communication skills (speaking, reading, writing and comprehension) in a language other than English and in the pupils home cultural and historical traditions.

The significant growth of the Hispanic community in the United States over the past decade and a half has resulted in most major urban areas developing concentrations of Hispanos (Mexican Americans, Puerto Ricans, Cubans, persons from the Caribbean, Central and South American, as applicable, depending on the region).[7] Immigration to the United States accounts in part for this growth but although a portion of Hispanos in urban areas are new arrivals, most are U. S. citizens who have migrated north and west from the Southwest, especially Texas, and from Puerto Rico. In some midwestern cities, Hispanic communities have existed for several decades. Within these urban centers, due to their low socio-economic level, Hispanos tend to be concentrated in central cities, where, together with Blacks (and, in some cities, other minorities—Asian Americans, Native Americans, etc.) they make up in some cases a majority of the population and in most cases a significant percentage of the minority school age population. The movement of Whites from central cities to the suburbs ("White flight") also accounts for the sudden increase of minority students in major urban school systems. Segregated housing patterns, together with past discriminatory policies by school boards with little or no minority representations, have resulted in segregated schools where minority students of various backgrounds are deprived of educational opportunities. It is in this context that litigation to desegregate schools enters the picture, and it is here that the dual thrusts (desegregation and bilingual bicultural education) come in contact and possible conflict. Parenthetically, it must be recognized that voluntary desegregation and voluntary bilingual education has taken place in several cities. The success of these ventures is dependent primarily on these factors: size of the city, percent of minority population and the quality of community leadership.

A cursory review of the recent litigation to desegregate schools reveals a consistent pattern: usually Black plaintiffs bring suit against school districts and, after many years of effort and expenditure of money, a judgment is entered in favor of the plaintiffs and, based on district-wide population data, desegregation is ordered along Black/White lines. Ratios of Black students and staff are established, and guidelines for phased implementation are developed as part of a comprehensive plan prepared by the plaintiffs or the district, subject to final approval by the court. Much of desegregation planning involves the movement of students for the purpose of achieving "racially balanced" schools which includes various amounts of busing and is usually done within the context of a court-ordered remedy addressed to the injuries sustained by the plaintiffs in the action.

In school districts with concentrations of Hispanos and other minorities, planning is usually done in the absence of any input from the Hispanic community, although it is clear that Hispanic pupils are affected by being transferred out of neighborhood schools and by other programmatic changes, especially with regard to staff. In order to protect the interests of Hispanic students, which are often tied to the viability of existing bilingual bicultural programs or programs to be created at schools where Hispanic children are transferred, Hispanic groups, often assisted by the Mexican American Legal Defense and Education Fund (MALDEF), the Puerto Rican Legal Defense and Education Fund (PRLDEF) and others, have intervened in a number of cases. The upshot of these interventions will be discussed at some length later on in this paper. Suffice it to say that these interventions have succeeded in obtaining recognition by courts, school districts and Black plaintiffs of the unique educational needs of Hispanos and other cultural and linguistic minorities and programs they advocate to meet their needs.

The fact that Blacks have led the legal struggle for desegregation and that only after a case is won do Hispanos take a manifest interest in it, has caused some advocates of desegregation, both Black and White, to conclude rather hastily that Hispanos are opposed to school desegregation and integration. Viewed against the background of the struggle of Blacks for equality in American society, it is understandable that Hispanos are looked at as relative newcomers to this struggle.

It should be noted, however, that although this may be the case in northern cities, Chicanos in the Southwest and California have long suffered the effects of segregation and discrimination. Today segregation appears to be increasing for Hispanos.[8] Placement of Hispanic children in disproportionate numbers in classes for retarded children is a painful example of another type of segregation.

To complicate matters further, language and culture are injected into the debate, which previously had focused on strict racial White vs. Black lines. Coupled with this are different perceptions of race and color, derived from varied cultural and historical experiences, which tend to give non-Black minorities a distinct perspective on the problem. It is not surprising, therefore, to have Hispanos, as well as American Indians, Asian Americans and others, view

desegregation of schools in terms of racial balance as primarily or even exclusively a Black/White issue. Although in theory desegregation may be beneficial in the long run to society as a whole, it is not seen by many Hispanos as an immediate priority for their children and their community.[9] It may well be that the vision of these Hispanos[10] as to what their place and role in American Society—a vision which is based on their values and their experiences in this society and on ideological reference points which shy away from assimilation and lead toward cultural socio-economic pluralism—differs fundamentally from that of a majority of the Black community.[11] The essential difference between these groups appears to be that while the Black struggle historically has centered around the *integration* of an involuntarily excluded and alienated segment of the population into the mainstream of social, cultural, economic and political life, the struggle of Hispanos and other culturally and linguistically (and racially different, whether in fact or merely perceived as such by the dominant society) groups has been one primarily of *adaptation* to social and cultural patterns, with some degree of participation in the economic and political spheres. This static description does not accurately portray the complexity of these processes which are directly influenced by societal discrimination and attitudes of the majority toward the various minority groups.

From the White perspective, one of the reasons why bilingual education and desegregation are seen as opposed is the tendency to describe all inter-group relations in Black/White terms. This perspective has led Whites to feel that if they could understand Blacks, they would understand other minority groups since Blacks were the most prominent minority group and the most clearly discriminated against. Progress towards the equal treatment of Blacks is seen as progress for all groups. The final resolution of these divergent perspectives still remains to be worked out in the dynamics of the various racial and ethnic groups competing in American society.

Latinos As An Identifiable Ethnic Minority Group

The earliest litigation by Mexican Americans against school authorities and their ethnic/cultural/linguistic background dates back to 1930.[12] A number of court cases in California and Texas followed during the forties and early fifties. Following *Brown* (1954), the question of how Mexican Americans would be classified in planning for school desegregation was still unresolved. Although in the Southwest and California there were no statutes requiring the segregation of Mexican American students, it is a fact that separation had existed for decades, at times justified on the grounds that students' limited English language skills necessitated separate schools or programs, ostensibly to provide special remedial help which usually never materialized.[13] It was not until 1970 that a federal district judge in Texas held that, for the purpose of school desegregation, Mexican Americans should be treated as an "identifiable ethnic minority group."[14] The body of precedents on this issue grew rapidly[15] and by the time that the case of *Keyes* v. School District No. 1, Denver[16] reached the *10th* Circuit on appeal, there existed clearer guidelines on how Mexican American students were to be dealt with in the planning of school desegregation. The situation prior to *Keyes* was at best ambiguous, with conflicting precedents such as the Houston desegregation case, where Mexican Americans were included in the White category.[17] *Keyes* ordered that Hispanos be included under a broader category of "minority" students (which included Blacks and Native Americans, and has subsequently been expanded to other Hispanos— Puerto Ricans, Cubans and others—as well as Asian Americans, based on the particular city's demographic profile). Hispanos were declared to be "an identifiable ethnic group" by the 5th Circuit and this finding was later accepted by the U. S. Supreme Court. Thus, the terminology of school desegregation planning was expanded by the use of the term "tri-ethnic" to refer to those districts where a third group was "numerically significant" to be considered separately in devising court-ordered remedies.[18]

Hispanos As Intervenors—Highlights Of Some Of The Major Cases

In spite of the *Keyes* precedent related to Hispanos as an identifiable ethnic group which deserves consideration in desegregation planning, in several major cities such planning proceeded along Black/White lines and Hispanos found it necessary to formally intervene at the remedy state to represent and safeguard the educational interests of Hispanic pupils in any comprehensive plan to be developed. Interventions of this nature have occurred in Boston, Wilmington (Delaware), Waterbury (Connecticut), and San Francisco,[19] to cite the most prominent, where Hispanic and other ethnic organizations, parents of school children and students themselves have successfully petitioned courts. As has been the pattern of involvement, when the original actions were begun by Black plaintiffs, the number of Hispanos in schools was small but by the time decisions were handed down years later, their numbers had grown significantly and they demanded and obtained recognition and inclusion in the planning.

It is important to note that interventions by Hispanos generally have been viewed as "friendly interventions" by Black plaintiffs because Hispanos have consistently argued in favor of desegregation, provided that bilingual bicultural education programs not be jeopardized in the process. Indeed, when B/B programs are recommended as a component of a plan, they are usually tailored to fit into the framework of the constitutional mandate to desegregate schools. *Keyes* posed the question of what takes precedence when both thrusts compete with one another. The legal precedent established in *Keyes* is clear, however: "Bilingual education, moreover, is not a *substitute* for desegregation. Although bilingual instruction may be required to prevent the isolation of minority students in a predominantly Anglo school system...such instruction must be subordinate to a plan of school desegregation." An obvious comment to be made here is that legally there is no difficulty with B/B education as *part* of the remedy but clearly it cannot be *the* remedy for segregated school systems or even portions thereof. The examples of desegregation efforts in Boston, Detroit and St. Paul, Minnesota present appropriate case studies on this matter.

Intervention efforts have been planned with *Keyes* in mind and are generally based on students' rights under *Lau* and federal legislation (and state legislation, where applicable), without recourse to a constitutional issue, which would involve relitigation and a separate finding of constitutional violation of the rights of Hispanic students. Thus, up to now, Hispanic intervenors have limited their petitions to statutory rights under the Civil Rights Act of 1964 (Title VI), and it is likely that this will be the pattern to be followed in the near future.

The shift in mood and attitude toward school desegregation throughout the United States, as manifested in recent U. S. Supreme Court decisions makes it impossible to predict the outcome of pending cases and future litigation on this issue. In general, it seems safe to assume that bilingual education litigation and interventions will not be curtailed by these trends, although there have been and may continue to be instances where bilingual bicultural education programs are adversely affected as a direct result of court-ordered desegregation. Perhaps only through the vigilance of community groups, parents/community organizations and interested persons will the integrity of present and future programs be protected and enhanced. It is reassuring to know, however, that a measure of protection for Hispanos and other ethnic/racial minorities does exist: "No remedy for the dual system can be acceptable if it operates to deprive members of a third ethnic group of the benefits of equal educational opportunity" (U. S. v. Texas Educational Agency (Austin), 467 F. 2d at 848).

Problems of Implementing Bilingual Bicultural Programs in Desegregating School Systems

One of the most important issues, the resolution of which will have great impact on the future of bilingual bicultural programming in a desegregated setting, is the issue of student and staff ratios. Student and staff desegretation is frequently measured by how well individual schools or in some instances zones reflect proportionately the average majority/minority group populations. In fashioning remedies, courts have at times assigned ratios which must be met by planners if they are to satisfy the court's mandate. In districts where Hispanos make up a small minority of pupils and which offer bilingual bicultural education for a portion of these students, a rigid application of court-assigned ratios can result in the destruction of these programs.[20] Pedagogical considerations require that there be a minimal, critical mass of students and staff present to insure the viability of a program and some courts have accepted this reasoning. In the Boston case, for example, bilingual education needs were recognized in the desegregation plan ordered by Judge Garrity, and some latitude was allowed on specific ratios of Hispanic students per school in order to satisfy a state law mandating bilingual education and because of the designation of some schools as citywide programs.[21]

Teacher ratios is also a concern, given the need for an adequate number of instructors, and exceptions have been made also in this regard, but conditions and results vary greatly from city to city. Most interventions include direct references to this important aspect of any plan, although the prospects are highly dependent on teacher unions and the strategies utilized by them to look after the interests of their membership. The desegregation of school staffs, including administration, was long overdue but the effects of staff desegregation are also complex. For example, Black teachers and administrators have lost their jobs over desegregation plans that involved changing community perceptions of previously all Black schools by placing White administrators and teachers in such schools. A similar situation could occur with regard to Hispanos.

The use of ratios has also stirred renewed controversy since in some cities it has become impossible to meet court-established ratios due to the increasing numbers of minority studtents. Indeed, in certain cities, such as Houston, courts consider schools legally integrated when its student body is less than 90 percent of one race or a combination of Black and Hispanic students.[22] A recent decision of the Supreme Court of California has raised doubts on the ratios to determine segregation in particular schools: "Moreover, in determining whether a particular school is "segregated" for constitutional purposes, we do not believe set racial or ethnic percentages can be established, either in absolute terms or in terms of the racial composition of a particular district's student population."[23] Although the issue pertains to the California state constitution, it may be an indication of possible future trends brought about by what might be termed a *reductio ad absurdum* of court-assigned ratios.

There are, to be sure, other specific issues which cannot be examined here for lack of space but which also impact significantly on the future development of bilingual education in the United States. These include classroom (vs. school) segregation,[24] ability groupings (bilingual education appears to fall under the category of *bona fide* groupings, as determined by federal regulations in force),[25] and costs.[26]

If entire schools devoted to bilingual bicultural education are not permitted by particular judges on the grounds that such schools will not fit the local definition of a desegregated school, this must not be allowed as an excuse by the local district to ignore the needs of linguistic minority children. It would be unfortunate to dismantle such programs since a concentration of resources, both in terms of staff and materials, is beneficial to the implementation of any new curricular change in education, and this is true for bilingual education as well. Dispersing students enrolled in such schools and not providing them with similar services in desegregated schools will place an undue burden on these children, is educationally unsound and indicates that the desegregation plan is not appropriate for the multi-ethnic/multilingual population in the district. Expansion of options for bilingual programming in other schools is often necessary. Some districts have experimented with pairing schools by grade levels, others by instituting half-day models which involve some transportation of students or teachers, still others by establishing pull-out type programs involving some tutoring and minimal language instructions. There are problems inherent in these alternative models, such as lack of sequencing instruction from grade level to grade level, the isolation of the few bilingual teachers in these programs and the increased demands on these teachers to individualize their teaching related to heterogeneous groups of students. Additional supportive services, such as in-service training for all staff, are needed.

Voluntary ability grouping is likely to be needed in implementing bilingual programming in these contexts. This should not be seen in the same light as imposed segregation, such as tracking, which implies a dead-end situation limiting students' aspirations. Such voluntary grouping should be seen instead as part of the current trend in education sometimes referred to as "continuous progress," which involves individualization of instruction.

In some cases, educational plans for bilingual education that call for some dispersal of staff and students under desegregation may be more expensive. If this is the case, such costs cannot be an excuse used to prevent implementation and additional monies will have to be made available for bilingual educational implementation within the context of desegregation. Local funding is not always a viable alternative, since these students often reside in the poorest districts. While it is understandable that these districts are feeling great pain in having to implement both desegregation and bilingual education, resources must be found. Federal funds are available through the Emergency School Assistant Act (ESAA) as well as on-going funding from Title I and Title VII of the ESEA. The greatest expense will involve start-up costs for bilingual programs (staff, materials, training) but this will not be a continuing burden on the district's finances.

The debate over these issues is likely to continue through the end of this decade in courts, political arenas and educational circles. A more encompassing debate on the merits of bilingual education as an enrichment program, free of the trappings of remediation, can also be anticipated as advocates of bilingual bicultural education seek to establish a more permanent support base for these programs in the 1980's.

The debate which has arisen over bilingual education in the context of desegregation will continue and, as with other issues, a definite outcome will not emerge quickly. Some Whites will reluctantly support desegregation of Blacks as an "American" remedy, since it focuses on individuals attempting to "melt" into the mainstream, but oppose bilingual education as a part of the remedy for equality since it stresses characteristics clearly associated with groups—language and culture. However, the fact remains that people of color have not been treated as individuals in our society, but as members of groups. Color has been a critical characteristic denying such groups the possibility of "melting" into American Society. Creating schools which instill respect for groups may aid individual mobility.

Americans opposed to bilingual education within the context of desegregation raise the fears of political instability. Separatism will be the result of bilingual education, they claim. This adds unnecessary confusion. Educational programs which are based on an understanding and respect for what the children bring to school are not separatist in a political nation-state sense. Groups which desire recognition and respect for this uniqueness can be contributing members of a political entity. There is no inherent conflict between love of family, and love of country. Love of family does not mean a desire to reject the economic and political life of a nation. Only in certain societies, where groups do not share respect for each other, and economic and political decision-making does not include them, have political movements for separatism arisen that use language differences as a symbol for mobilization for political purposes. Recognizing language issues and taking them into account in desegregation planning is not for the purpose of political separatism but rather to insure educational opportunity in a multi-lingual, multi-ethnic, multi-racial society.

It is clear that cultural and linguistic minority groups are not progressing adequately through urban school systems. Programs to address the needs of these students must be included as part of desegregation planning. Solutions will vary depending on judicial precedents, educational justification based on research and political compromises arrived at through pressure and bargaining. It may well be that as Hispanos and other groups continue to increase their numbers at present rates, their presence will become more visible and carry more weight in the next quarter century. But, apart from whatever implications this growth in numbers may hold, a concrete contribution which bilingual education has already made to the on-going debate on school desegregation is that curriculum innovation and change is essential, not only for bilingual programs but for school systems as a whole. In many cases, bilingual programming has opened the way for curriculum reform which addresses the needs of a multi-cultural student body. In the final analysis, this may well end up being the most important and lasting contribution of bilingual bicultural education to integrated education in the U. S.

FOOTNOTES

[1] For a concise yet comprehensive account of the growth of bilingual bicultural education in the United States, see the excellent article by Josué M. González, "Coming of Age in Bilingual/Bicultural Education: A Historical Perspective," *Inequality in Education*, Number 19 (Fedruary, 1975, pp. 5-17).

[2] See Hannah N. Geffert, Robert J. Harper, II, Salvador Sarmiento, Daniel M. Schember, *The Current Status of U. S. Bilingual Education Legislation*, Center for Applied Linguistics (Papers in Applied Linguistics, Bilingual Education Series: 4), Arlington, VA, May, 1975.

[3] Robert L. Crain *et. al.*, *The Politics of School Desegregation*, Chicago: Aldine Publishing Co., 1968.

Lino A Graglia, *Disaster by Decree: The Supreme Court Decisions on Race and the Schools*, Ithaca, N. Y.: Cornell University Press, 1976.

David J. Kirby, T. Robert Harris, Robert L. Crain, Christine H. Rossell, *Political Strategies in Northern School Desegregation*, Lexington, Mass.: Lexington Books (D. C. Heath and Co.), 1973.

Richard Kluger, *Simple Justice: The History of Brown v. Board of Education and Black America's Struggle for Equality*, New York: Knopp, 1976.

George R. La Noue, Bruce L. R. Smith, *The Politics of School Desegregation*, Lexington, Mass.: Lexington Books (D. C. Heath and Co.), 1973.

Nancy St. John, *School Desegregation: Outcomes for Children*, New York: John Wiley and Sons, 1975.

Meyer Weinberg, *School Integration: A Comprehensive Classified Bibliography of 3,100 References*, Chicago: Integrated Education Associates, 1967.

[4]*United States* v. *State of Texas*, 342 F. Supp. 24 (E. D. Texas 1971), *aff'd per curiam*, 446 F. 2d. 518 (5th circuit 1972) at 27-38.

[5]20 U.S.C. Section 1703.

[6]The Supreme Court did not find in *Lau* that the plaintiff's constitutional rights had been violated. Rather, it restricted its findings to the Civil Rights Act and decreed that measures must be undertaken to correct inequities attributable to language differences. *Lau* affirmed the soundness of previous Office for Civil Rights regulations, specifically the May 25, 1970 Memorandum and supported OCR's authority to issue and enforce such directives.

Since the *Lau* case was a class action suit, the rights of the approximately 1,800 children to special remedies appropriate to their condition of inequality were recognized. But the caveat contained in Judge Blackmun's concurring opinion cast a shadow of doubt on the applicability of *Lau* to individual rights:

> I merely wish to make plain that when, in another case, we are concerned with a few youngsters, or with just a single child who speaks only German or Polish or Spanish or any language other than English, I would not regard today's decision, or the separate concurrence, as conclusive upon the issue whether the statute and the guideline require the funded school district to provide special instruction. For me numbers are at the heart of this case and my concurrence is to be understood accordingly.

Following the *Lau* decision the San Francisco Unified School District was ordered to present a plan to the district court on how to provide services to children of limited English language skills. (LELS) The Center for Applied Linguistics was retained by the district to assist in the planning of the plan. In October, 1976 a consent decree was signed, wherein the district agrees to implement bilingual education programs for LELS children. (*The Linguistic Reporter*, Volume 19, December, 1976, p. 1).

[7]*Persons of Spanish Origin in the United States: March 1975* (Advance Report)—Population Characteristics, Current Population Reports, Series p-20, No. 283. Issued August, 1975 by the Bureau of the Census, U. S. Department of Commerce, Washington, D. C. This report states that in March, 1975 there were an estimated 11,202,000 persons of Spanish origin, which made up 5.3 percent of the total U. S. population. The median age for this segment of the population was 20.7 as compared to 28.6 for the entire U. S. population.

[8]During the 1974-75 school year, Hispanic children were more likely than Blacks to be attending predominantly minority schools. Such segregation is stable or growing in every region. "Twelve Years Later: Most Black and Chicano Children Still Attending Segregated Schools," in *Un Neuvo Dia*, Published by The Chicano Education Project—Lakewood, Colorado, Fall, 1976, Vo. 2, No. 3, pp. 7, 14.

[9]"L. A. Desegregation a Tall Order to Fill," *The Milwaukee Journal*, Sunday, January 16, 1977.

[10]Hispanos are indeed a heterogeneous group, and are not to be looked at as monolithic. To be sure, there is a wide spectrum of ideology and opinion within Hispanic communities throughout the U.S. The same is applicable to Black communities, of course. The intent is to underscore what appears to be the representative opinion on this subject by the majority of these groups, as articulated by leading spokespersons.

[11]The term "cultural-socio-economic pluralism" is taken from the essay by Antonia Pantoja and Barbara Blourock, "Cultural Pluralism Redefined," in *Badges and Indicia of Slavery: Cultural Pluralism Redefined*, Antonia Pantoja, Barbara Blourock and James Bowman, Editors, Study Commission on Undergraduate Education and the Education of Teachers, University of Nebraska, Lincoln, 1975, pp. 2-24.

[12]*Independent School District v. Salvatierra*, 33 S.W. 2d. 790 (Tex. Civ. App.—San Antonio 1930), *certiorari denied*, 284 U. S. 580 (1931). For an excellent overview of the struggle by Mexican Americans to gain their rights in the areas of education, employment, access to public accomodations and the administration of justice, see Guadalupe Salinas, "Mexican Americans and the Desegregation

of Schools in the Southwest," *El Grito*, Volume IV, No. 4 (Summer 1971), pp. 36-69. Another useful compendium of legal precedents on the subject of Mexican Americans as an ethnically identifiable group is Gerald M. Birnberg's article by that name in *Texas Law Review*, Volume 49 (1971), pp. 337-346.

[13]See *The Current Status of U. S. Bilingual Education Legislation*, cited above, for a list of states which statutes prohibiting the teaching in a language other than English in private and/or public schools (pp. 4-5; 122-123).

[14]*Cisneros v. Corpus Christi Independent School District* C.A. #68-C-k95 (S.D. Tex., June 4, 1970), 457 F. 2d 142 (5th Circuit 1972) (en banc) certiorari denied, 413 U. S. 920 (1973). Quoted by Salinas, op. cit., p. 36.

[15]*Alvarado* v. *El Paso Independent School District*, 445 F. 2d 1011 (5th Circuit 1971); *U. S.* v. *Texas Education Agency* (Austin), 467 F. 2d. 848, 862 (5th Circuit 1972), *Tasby* v. *Estes*, 517 F. 2d. 92, 107 (5th Circuit 1975).

[16]413 U. S. 189 (1973); 521 F. 2d 465 (1975) *certiorari denied*, 44 LW 3399 (January 12, 1976).

[17]*Ross* v. *Eckels*, 434 F. 2d. 1140 (5th Circuit 1970).See Salinas, op. cit., pp. 62-63, for an analysis of Judge Connally's curious reasoning in this case. A similar situation occurred in Miami, Florida.

[18]The issue is still being debated, however. In Milwaukee (*Amos et al.* v. *O'Connell, et al.*, C.A. No. 65-C-173), for example, court ordered desegregation was framed within Black/White ratios, although Hispanic pupils presently comprise 5 percent of the district enrollment and certain elementary schools have percentages of Hispanic pupils ranging up to 71 percent. Persistent requests by the City-Wide Bilingual Bicultural Advisory Committee (CWBBAC) caused the school board to formally petition the court to include Hispanos, Native Americans and Asian Americans as "minority students" along with Blacks, in formulation of the plan. The attorneys for the plaintiffs have opposed this request, arguing that "the issue of unconstitutional segregation of Hispanic pupils has not been litigated in this action" and that "the court did not find that Hispanic pupils were unconstitutionally segregated." (Letter from Lloyd A. Barbee and Irvin B. Charne to L. C. Hammond, Jr., attorney for the Milwaukee Board of School Directors, November 17, 1976). The CWBBAC is considering intervention given this state of affairs in January, 1977.

[19]See *Morgan* v. *Kerrigan*, 401 F. Supp. at 227; also of interest is the Student Desegregation Plan, C.A. No. 72-911-G, (May 19, 1975); *Evans* v. *Buchanan*,

C.A. Nos. 1816-1822, D-Del., (June 26, 1975; on October 21, 1975 the intervention was finally approved); *United States of America* v. *Board of Education of Waterbury*, C.A. No. 13, 465 (September 9, 1976); *Johnson* v. *San Francisco Unified School District*, 500 F. 2d. 349, 352-353 (9th Circuit 1974).

[20]Pomona, California is a good example of this (information obtained in a telephone conversation with Richard Hiller, staff attorney for the Puerto Rican Legal Defense and Educational Fund, New York, N. Y.).

[21]"Exceptions to these variation limits shall be permitted where necessary to allow appropriate bilingual assignments or to allow students in any racial or ethnic group to be assigned to a particular school in groups of at least twenty. As a result, some schools may have no other minority students in attendance." (p. 73). Later on in the plan, an exception is made regarding bilingual instruction: "(b) The (Rafael) Hernandez School, which contains a citywide Spanish-English bilingual program, may enroll a student body up to 65 percent Hispanic. Non-Hispanic other minority will be eligible along with White and Black students, within the remaining 35 percent of school capacity." (pp. 75-76) Cf. Student Desegregation Plan, *Morgan* v. *Kerrigan*, C.A. No. 72-911-6, May 10, 1975. Another issue, which was of crucial importance, was decided earlier when the Court accepted the plaintiffs-intervenors request that the City defendants' method of characterizing them as Black or White Spanish-surnamed be rejected and that Hispanos be treated instead as a distinct ethnic group for purposes of protecting their rights in any school desegregation plan. (Memorandum, Proposal, and Critique of Plaintiffs-Intervenors, *Morgan (and El Comite de Padres Pro Defensa de La Educacion Bilingue* v. *Kerrigan*, C.A. 72-911-G, February 3, 1975, p. 1).

[22]Article in the *New York Times*, July 24, 1976.

[23]*Crawford* v. *Board of Education of the City of Los Angeles*, C.A. 30485, 551 p. 2d. 28 at 43. Significant portions of this important decision are included for reference:

"...The Constitution does not require a school board to achieve a particular or identical "racial mix" or "racial balance" in each school; rather, the constitutional evil inheres in the existence of *segregated* schools...Experience has taught that the task of integration is an extremely complex one which entails much more than the percentages of pupils of different races or ethnic groups to the same school."

(Segregated schools are defined as) "schools in

which the minority students enrollment is so disproportionate or realistically to isolate minority students from other students and thus deprive minority students of an integrated educational experience."

"In addition to the racial and ethnic composition of a school's student body, other factors, such as the racial and ethnic composition of the staff, and the *community* and *administration attitudes* toward the school, must be taken into consideration."

[24]Jose A. Cardenas, "Bilingual Education, Segregation and A Third Alternative," *Inequality in Education*, Number 19 (February, 1975), pp. 19-22, provides valuable specific suggestions on how instruction can be individualized in a bilingual classroom.

[25]Cf. 45 C.F.R. Section 185.43 (c) for the specific requirements imposed by the rules.

[26]See Jose A. Cardenas, "Bilingual Education Cost Analysis," (a presentation to the CACTI (Lau Center) Multi-Cultural Education Materials Conference in Albuquerque, New Mexico on December 9, 10, 11, 1976).

Chapter 10
Bilingual Education Legislation: The Boston Desegregation Case
Maria Estella Brisk*

Language legislation in education is undergoing a drastic change. From policies that increasingly demanded the use of English as the only language of instruction in school to mandatory bilingual education in the native language of children and English. At least twenty-two states have enacted bilingual education legislation.[1] Following the *Lau* decision, all school districts in the United States are required to submit periodic reports to the Office of Civil Rights specifying the types of programs they offer to children of linguistic minorities. As a follow up, a number of school districts have been found not to comply fully with general guidelines; Hartford, Connecticut, for example, is not elaborating a program, as are many other school districts. There have been other cases in which parents of bilingual children have filed suit against their own school districts based on the inadequate education their children receive for lack of a coherent approach to bilingual education.

Bilingual communities have also entered as secondary parties in desegregation suits brought before federal courts by both the Department of Justice and private citizens, so that their children's educational interests are considered in the midst of integration. As this is written, language minorities are participating in the search for quality education in the cases of *Morgan* v. *Kerrigan* (Boston) and *Evans* v. *Buchanan* (Wilmington, Delaware). State legislation, private suits, and desegregation proceedings have combined in some cities to produce added pressure for bilingual programs.[2] The rise of public interest law firms throughout the United States will undoubtedly continue to spur such litigation in the future.[3]

Educational legislation and litigation are the result of political and economical pressures. Research as to what is the best education for the children is of lesser importance. Moreover this process does not guarantee implementation nor quality of the program. Bilingual communities at large—grassroots and professionals—must prepare and intervene to insure that the content of the legislation is sound and reflects the best possible education for their children. They also must follow the implementation to insure that the principles for which they fought so hard are indeed carried out.

This article will be limited to describing the intervention of the bilingual community in the Boston desegregation case. Through the description of this case I wish to point out the process, the issues that need research and preparation on the part of the community and the importance of monitoring the implementation.

This case reflects the concerns of a linguistic minority when their school district is ordered to desegregate due to the existence of a dual school system, black and white. Two things characterize the case of Boston. First the plaintiffs were representatives of the Black community concerned with the unfair treatment of Black children. This meant the Hispanic community had to defend the best interest of their children[4] within the context of integrating Black and White Americans. This was the case in Colorado (*Keyes* v. *Denver*)[5] but not in other court cases concerning bilingual education.[6] Second, bilingual education legislation was in existence. In 1971 Massachusetts passed the Transitional Bilingual Education Law[7] mandating bilingual education for children with limited English speaking ability. Presently in Boston there are approximately 6,000 children in bilingual education programs, distributed among seven language groups; Spanish, Chinese, Italian, Greek, Haitian, French, Portuguese, and Cape Verdean. The Spanish constitute about 75 percent of the children. A judge will more readily defend bilingual education in the context of existing legislation rather than have to force it as a new educational idea when the issue in question is desegregation and not bilingual education.

Since March 1972 Boston has been in the process of integrating the schools. The events that precipitated a complete and final plan for total desegregation issued by Judge Garrity on May 10, 1975 began only at the end of 1974. As a result of a Court order the School Committee of the City of Boston issued a plan on December 16, 1974 to complete desegregation in the Boston Public Schools. A second plan came out a month later with slight modifications.[8] The Plaintiffs

*Dr. Maria Brisk, Director, Bilingual Program, Boston University.

presented their own plan[9] and a number of groups filed critiques with alternative solutions. In the meantime the Spanish parents concerned by the fate of their children and the already existing bilingual education programs formed a committee, "El Comité de Padres Pro-Defensa de la Educación Bilingüe." Parents' groups were organized in each community with a leader in charge of gathering opinions and imparting information. They also secured the help of lawyers from the Puerto Rican Legal Defense and the Massachusetts Chapter of The National Lawyers Guild. A technical committee was formed to aid in the formalizing of the issues. "El Comité" presented the case to court and were allowed to enter the suit as plaintiffs-intervenors. A plan dealing particularly with bilingual education was written, expressing general agreement with the Plaintiffs' plan as a sensible vehicle for integrating Boston Public Schools, but since the bilingual issue was not properly nor fully considered, there was need for an additional plan dealing specifically with the bilingual issue. Only a few weeks elapsed since the formation of "El Comité" until the bilingual education plan was presented. The work was done under tremendous pressure and difficulty. Bilingual communities should prepare in advance if their city is going to undergo desegregation in order to insure that bilingual children and their needs are properly considered in the total plan for desegregation.

In order to arrive at a final solution, Judge Garity appointed four Masters and two experts to review the various plans, to hold hearings from the corresponding parties, and to eventually present him with a plan for his revision and final approval.

In general most groups were sympathetic to the bilingual education cause. In the other plans, however, bilingual education was not treated in any depth. Moreover, the Spanish children were classified as Spanish white and Spanish black; they were spread around the Boston schools, forming very small clusters in each school;[10] and the School Committee's Plan proposed the creation of a multicultural magnet school which was to be located in a school in terrible physical condition and which the Spanish parents were afraid would become the token bilingual program. In the light of these circumstances it was crucial for the Spanish parents to organize to defend bilingual education and in the final analysis obtain beneficial results not only for the Hispanic children but for all children of linguistic minorities.

The classification of black and white Spanish surnamed does not have any relevance in the context of the type of educational program that bilingual children should get. Their needs are based on difference in language and culture and not on race. Moreover, Spanish people are already integrated, there is racial mixture within families, so it is rather unrealistic to try to determine their race. This issue has legal precedent such as *U. S.* v. *Texas* and *Keyes* v. *Denver* where it was ruled that Mexican-Americans are a distinct ethnic minority. Another reason why this separation should not be allowed is because Spanish white children are used to fill the white percentage requirement, resulting again in a segregated school with all minority children, Spanish white and Black Americans.

In order to have a viable bilingual program, "El Comité" felt it was necessary to have at least four clusters of one language group in a given school at the elementary and middle school levels and seven to eight in high school. Having more clusters means more teachers and aides with a greater variety of expertise, more flexibility in the grouping and better possibility of having support personnel for the bilingual children. Any group of Spanish children in the Boston Area of the same age are at a variety of levels in their language, reading and other skills depending on the time they have lived in this country, previous schooling, place of origin and other factors.

At the high school level the need for specialized teachers increases. A high school curriculum can have up to four different kinds of mathematics, three kinds of sciences, various social studies and other subject matters. In order to have quality education and run a program parallel to the English program there is need for a number of specialized teachers. In addition, a school with a significant number of bilingual children will make a special effort to better serve these children by hiring a bilingual administrator, acquiring materials and books for their library and in general making a stronger commitment to bilingual education.

"El Comité" felt that clustering was sufficiently important to justify busing when needed to achieve the recommended number of clusters. To insure that the number of clusters and the location of the program would be suitable, "El Comité" had to determine the schools and distribution of the Spanish school age children in the city. The lack of data and the inaccuracy of that available made it a very difficult task. The State figures showed 2,709 bilingual children; the School Committee's figures added up to 1,811 while the Bilingual Department estimated 5,745 children in bilingual programs.

In order to plan adequately it is essential to have accurate information on the number of school age children in and out of school and the section of the city where they are living.

In the selection of the schools for bilingual programs the criteria was the size, location and existence of a suitable bilingual program. In order to insure four or more clusters per school without tipping the racial balance it was important to select schools with large capacity. One hundred to 120 students (5 to 6 clusters) in a school of 1,000 students constituted only 10 percent of the student body, an unquestionable percentage. Busing was the least worry for Spanish parents, but neighborhood schools were selected for the most part because in general all parties were trying to achieve integration with a minimum of busing. Besides, neighborhood schools lead to more parent participation and improvement of school-community relationships. It was also important to choose schools that their personnel had already demonstrated a sincere interest in bilingual education and an understanding of the bilingual children and their needs. Besides, these schools, by their good reputation, are likely to attract the children who are out of school.

In the "reuniones de barrio" (neighborhood meetings) held previously and during the preparation of El Comité's plan, a number of general concerns were expressed by the parents, such as the lack of programs with maintenance of language and culture after the child has tested out of the bilingual program, the lack of bilingual kindergartens, the placement of those Spanish children who do not need bilingual education according to the Transitional Bilingual Education Law. After numerous discussions it was decided that the two latter points could be argued within a general integration suit. The first issue, that of maintenance, had to do more with the existing law and this was not the place to bring it up.

Massachusetts Transitional Bilingual Education Law fails to mandate kindergarten. The community successfully argued this case in terms of language development, need to receive reading readiness in the child's own language since in first grade s/he is taught to read in it. Besides, by not using the native language the child cannot participate meaningfully in the kindergarten program which is a vital part of any child's education.

A great concern of the Spanish parents was what would happen to those Spanish children who are not considered eligible for bilingual education programs. The Teachers' Union critique expressed that "in assigning students to such [bilingual] clusters that they are advanced and integrated into a majority Anglo-speaking population as soon as possible and are not continuously assigned to a majority Hispanic program throughout the student's academic career."[11] This reflects the feeling of believers in "americanization" as fast as possible and at all cost, even if it means losing language, identity, and establishing deep gaps within families. There is value in being a balanced bilingual and that is not going to occur if the child is isolated from his language and culture. Besides the child who has learned English still thinks and acts the way other Spanish children do, if he is in a school where there is a

bilingual program there is a chance that there are going to be administrators, teachers and other personnel who are familiar with his culture and can communicate effectively with him; and since they know his language they can communicate effectively with his parents.

During the testimony of the bilingual expert, it became clear that the concern of the Masters and lawyers representing other parties was the value of bilingual education and whether there is incompatibility between bilingual education and desegregation. The following issues were questioned and discussed.:

(1) *Bilingual education tends to isolate the children and does not prepare them to face the mainstream of American life once they leave school.* This objection arises from the belief that bilingual education retards the process of learning English. A bilingual program emphasizes the teaching in and learning of two languages, one of them English. In addition, it avoids the retardation of the learning process in content areas and has a positive effect in the affective domain among linguistic minority children.

When bilingual education is only for the non-English speaker, it can be seen as a form of segregation. There are ways to avoid separation, either by teaching all children in a given school both languages; by emphasizing individualized instruction;[12] or by having the children together in non-verbal subject areas such as physical education, music, art and separating them for other subject matters where language comprehension is crucial.

It is also important to clarify that children of the linguistic minorities are quite mobile and enter school at all grade levels. Consequently, it is important to have programs at all levels. At the high school level, the existence of bilingual education becomes even more important because the individual at that age has even more difficulty than a young child in learning and adjusting to a new language and culture.

(2) *By preserving the mother tongue of non-English speaking children the parents lose the chance to learn English.* Frequently children are responsible for teaching this language to their parents. It is indeed necessary for parents to learn English, but this could be done through adult language programs and not at the cost of the children losing their mother tongue.

(3) *Bilingual education is remedial.* Teaching in another language is not remedial, since the curricula is similar to that of other countries where that particular language is the medium of instruction. There is, however, need for remedial education for non-native speakers of English, either because they have emotional problems, they are mentally retarded, or because some of these children are teenagers who never went to school. These students need programs

which are different from regular bilingual programs. The failure to differentiate regular from remedial bilingual education usually results in the lack of special programs for the bilingual children who need special education managed by specially trained personnel.

(4) *A large percentage of bilingual children in one school is against desegregation.* School desegregation usually implies schools with student bodies reflecting the racial distribution of the school district. Successful bilingual programs, however, have usually an equal proportion of children from each language group[13] or they have most children of one language group.[14] In the case of Boston, under school desegregation order, any of those two systems would be impossible. The population of Boston is constituted by 51 percent white, 37 percent black and only 12 percent other minority. In the case of Colorado, *Keyes* v. *Denver*, this issue was apparent also. At least in one school a great proportion of Mexican American children were allowed.

More research should be done on the importance of proportion of students in the success of a bilingual program. It should be studied and solved outside the context of desegregation to allow for objectivity.

Finally a certain degree of resentment was reflected in the questioning of the expert with respect to the fact that bilingual education was defended only for the interest of the Hispanic children. This was the case only because the Spanish parents were the ones who organized and entered their plan as plaintiff-intervenors. Of course the fact that they are the largest linguistic minority in Boston helped. All of the argumentation was done in defense of the principles of bilingual education which apply to any linguistic group who is interested in preserving their language and culture. In the final plan ordered by Judge Garrity all of the groups benefited since the provisions are for bilingual children in general.

For the most part the results of having participated in the decisions were positive. The Spanish community of Boston got organized and is highly conscious of the need to get interested in the education of their children. It was highly educational for most parents, who presently know a great deal more about bilingual education.

The need to address and serve the interests of the bilingual students in the process of segregating the schools was firmly established.

According to Judge Garrity's plan of May, 1975 bilingual programs at all levels, including kindergarten will be provided in desirable schools and in suitable clusters. The Boston School Department was ordered to translate the booklet explaining desegregation into various languages. Moreover, the Citywide Council of 40 members appointed to overview the proper

implementation of the plan had two Spanish and two Chinese members. Students were classified as white, black, Hispanic, Asian-American, American Indian or other. Bilingual students were supposed to be assigned before all others to the schools. No less than twenty students of one minority will be assigned to any given school, avoiding in this way the isolation of bilingual students who have tested out of a bilingual program. The well known examination schools for gifted children were ordered to recruit Black and Hispanic children to constitute up to 35 percent of the student body. Finally, universities were committed to help various districts in the education process including that of bilingual children.

In the implementation of this plan a number of things happened that did not allow the full implementation of what was ordered. The assignment of bilingual children was not accurate resulting in sending a number of bilingual children to schools without a bilingual program. Some clusters were not as large as desired. The fact that the Bilingual Department has no jurisdiction over kindergartens has slowed the much needed opening of bilingual kindergarten. The booklet explaining the desegregation process, although translated, was very long and written in rather complicated language. Moreover, many of the parents do not read.

In conclusion, it is highly beneficial for the bilingual community to organize and voice their demands when their school district is ordered to integrate or whenever legislation that will affect the education of bilingual children is being proposed. To maximize the effectiveness, however, two things must occur. The community should research and prepare so that the plans proposed are educationally sound. In second place a monitoring system should be built into the legislation with decision-making power to enable the implementation of what was established on paper.

FOOTNOTES

[1]See Hannah N. Geffert et al., "The Current Status of U. S. Bilingual Education Legislation, *Papers in Applied Linguistics* (Arlington, VA: Center for Applied Linguistics, 1975) and Center for Law and Education, *Bilingual-Bicultural Education: A Handbook for Attorneys and Community Workers* (Cambridge, MA: CLE, 1975).

[2]Such is the case of New York, Boston and Hartford.

[3]The two major firms are the Puerto Rican Legal Defense Fund and the Mexican American Legal Defense Fund. Local Legal Aid Offices also take up cases, sometimes with cooperation of one of the major ones.

[4]The Spanish parents were the only ones to organize

and enter the suit. What was learned from this experience could be applicable to any linguistic minority.

[5]Keyes v. Denver, 93 A Supreme Court Reporter, 2686 (1973).

[6]U. S. v. State of Texas, 342 Fed. Supp., 24 (1971); Morales v. Shannon, 366 Fed. Supp., 813 (1973); Serna v. Portales, 351 Fed. Supp. 1279 (1972); Aspira v. Board of Education of the City of New York, 58 F.R.D. 62 (S.D.N.Y. 1973); and Lau v. Nichols, 414 US 563 (1974).

[7]Massachusetts General Laws Chapter 71A.

[8]Boston School Committee, *Student Desegregation Plan* (December 16, 1974) and *idem* (January 27, 1975).

[9]Tallulah Morgan et al. v. John J. Kerrigan et al., Civil Action No. 72-911-G (January 20, 1975).

[10]A cluster is a group of 15 with a teacher or 20 students with a teacher and an aid.

[11]Boston Teachers Union, "Teachers Union's Evaluations as to Student Desegregation Plans and Proposals," (February 5, 1975), p. 22.

[12]See the plan for Del Rio School District in the case U. S. v. Texas and Jose A Cardenas "Bilingual Education, Segregation, and A Third Alternative" *Inequality in Educaion*, no. 19 (February, 1975), pp. 19-22.

[13]John F. Kennedy School in Berlin has 50 percent German students, 40 percent English speakers and 10 percent other; Coral Way School and other bilingual programs in Dade county keep their student body about half Spanish and half English.

[14]The St. Lambert project in Montreal is for English-speaking Canadians; a number of programs in Mexico, Peru, Guatemala and other Latin American countries are for Indian children only.

New York Teachers' Staff

Section II
Culture

Introduction by Marco A. Hernandez*

Very often in discussions regarding culture, the term culture is used in a variety of contexts. Our main interest in this section is to place culture within the educational setting and to develop its relative importance and meaning within this context. For although differences in definition might be difficult to eliminate, there is no doubt that scholars wrestling with this problem would have to agree that all societies known to man practice education vigorously and that it is the vehicle which transmits concepts such as language, customs, beliefs and values to members of a given society.

What difference does a concept such as culture make to our conception of the school curriculum? What difference does it make to the teaching-learning process? And finally, what difference does it make to the administration of the educational system? Whether the educator is aware of it or not, value judgments underlie each objective that is employed in directing the educational process. In dealing with the linguistically and culturally different child, a pervasive attitude that influences educational decisions has been one which equates differences with inferiority. The role of education has been traditionally viewed as one of reshaping the child which has been labeled as "disadvantaged" into an individual of the acceptable variety in ther dominant culture. If our goal or mission in education is to reverse the effects of deprivation in our schools, then we must change once and for all the attitudes inherent in our institutions which have characteristically equated being different with being inferior.

Many kinds of information are needed to better understand the problem of the culturally different and to assist in planning for the effective delivery of educational services. Among the many things that this information reveals is the large proportion of youngsters in the United States that have a native language other than English. In a survey of language usage conducted in 1975, the National Center for Education Statistics reported that of the total 83,150,000 school-age population in the United States, 10,639,000 were youngsters from households where a language other than English was spoken. The same year, in New York City, out of a total enrollment of 1,099,000, approximately 400,000 pupils were identified with a home language other than English.

Historically, in the United States, educational programs specifically designed for the non-English-speaking students have been limited in number, scope and financial and administrative support. Through the English only policy, which was traditional in our educational system, the emphasis had been on the suppression of the student's home language and culture. The introduction of English as a Second Language (ESL) approach may have improved the situation, but by itself failed to solve the problem. The child was still being placed in an environment that categorized his native language and culture as being inferior. Although we know that pupils from a non-English-speaking background bring to school well-established language skills and cultural values, the schools by and large did not capitalize upon the already developed concepts, skills and positive experiences of these children. Bilingual/bicultural programs came into existence when it was felt that the native language and culture of non-English-speaking pupils ought to be an integral part of the educational process, since the previous attempts and approaches had not been successful with this population. The program is a comprehensive educational approach which involves more than just imparting English skills. While it recognizes English as a vital component and an essential factor in the preparation of youngsters to scale the economic and social ladder, it also establishes a definite role for the native language and culture of each individual in the educational process.

The articles that appear in this section describe the experiences, thoughts and theories of ethnic groups residing in the United States and Canada.

*Marco A. Herandez, Deputy Executive Administrator, Center for Bilingual Education, New York City Board of Education.

They are intended to: (1) present the problems that minority groups have experienced and continue to encounter under our present educational system; (2) develop an understanding of the personal, historical and intellectual characteristics of these groups; (3) provide a picture of the diversity of cultures that characterizes America, and; (4) motivate educators to consider, evaluate and understand other cultures so that this information may be reflected in the curriculum and in the methodology in the teaching and learning process.

The most important objective of this section is to attempt to clear the air of any misconceptions so that we can move to develop an effective approach to educating students who happen to be different from the middle Americans for whom the educational system was designed.

There is no doubt that we Americans have always encountered ambivalent feelings regarding our multi-cultural origins. On one side we proudly acknowledge the fact that we are a unique hybrid of many ethnic and linguistic groups. On the other side we feel embarrassment about these mixed roots and have tried to suppress their traces. However, over the past ten years, the endorsement of the principle of cultural pluralism has been impressive. To support cultural pluralism is in effect to understand and appreciate the differences that exist among our nation's citizens. It adds a positive force to the continuing development of a society which professes a wholesome respect for the intrinsic worth of each individual.

Our educational institutions must be committed to the development of a social system whose fundamental tenets shall be based on the dignity of each individual. At this crucial period of history, our great nation must move forth and bring to full fruition the basic concepts of the American dream.

Chapter 11
The Special Assimilation Problems of Americans of Spanish Speaking Origin
Eleanor Meyer Rogg*

Americans of Spanish-speaking origin comprise the largest bilingual minority group in the United States. The United States Bureau of the Census estimates that as of 1976, Americans of Spanish-speaking origin make up 5.3% of the total population of the United States, some 11.1 million people.

If present birth rate and immigration trends continue, the population of Hispanic Americans should continue to increase substantially. For example, Mexico and Cuba have been leading countries of emigration to the United States even before immigration laws changed in 1968. Since the United States Bureau of the Census began using its current survey procedures for ethnic groups in 1973, the increase of Americans of Spanish-speaking origin has been estimated to be approximately one half million. (New York Times, Dec. 12, 1976, p.82.).

This article will concentrate on the special adjustment problems of Hispanic Americans. In the increasing body of literature dealing with the assimilation of Americans of Spanish-speaking origin, many articles have concentrated on individual ethnic groups classified according to country of origin. Substantial literature, however, is not yet available about the common problems confronting Hispanic Americans. Instead, we find substantial literature available about the problems of the 6.6 million Americans of Mexican origin and the 1.8 million mainland Americans of Puerto Rican origin. Some literature is available about the 687,000 Americans of Cuban origin as well as about other Spanish-speaking groups.

Perry and Perry (1976) question whether using common country of origin is a valid reason to group Americans together for study purposes. For example, they question whether Mexican-Americans' experiences have not differed considerably according to their state of residence, their time of arrival in the United States, their skin color as well as their social class origins. Mexican-Americans are a diverse group with members in many different stages of assimilation. Thus, if it is difficult to deal with the common experiences and problems of Mexican-Americans, it is even more difficult to deal with the common

experiences and problems of Hispanic Americans.

Hispanic Americans as a Group

We should proceed with caution to be sure that we are dealing with a group that really exists and with a useful model for study. Vander Zanden (1975) defines a group as "a collection of people with certain common attributes. (p.159)." By this very broad definition, Hispanic Americans are obviously a group, since they are a collection of people with the common attribute of coming from a Spanish-speaking background and/or having a Spanish surname.

Since 1973, the United States Bureau of the Census has collected data about Americans of Spanish-speaking origin and Spanish surname, lending further evidence to the existence of this group. Hispanic Americans then are at least a statistical aggregate created by demographers and sociologists, even though no monolithic group which is a unified community with a common culture and called Hispanic Americans exists.

Robert Bierstedt's classic typology for classifying groups (1948) provides us with three criteria to help us analyze Hispanic Americans. Groups can be differentiated according to (1) "a consciousness of kind" - the recognition that people have something in common, (2) "social relations between people" - whether people actually interact with each other because they have something in common, and (3) "formal organization" - a planned group designed to achieve specific goals and functions. (pp.700-710).

1. "Consciousness of kind" tends to develop among people when they face common problems and find they have a common interest. Indeed, Hispanic Americans may have found this common interest in maintaining and developing the use of Spanish, not only at home but in schools and other institutions. The successful

*Dr. Eleanor Rogg, Chairperson, Department of Sociology and Anthropology, Wagner College.

implementation of bilingual education programs may actually help create a sense of unity among Americans of Spanish-speaking origin. Shaw (1975) points out that the successful bilingual education program in Miami's Coral Way School, originally developed for Cuban emigrés sparked a group consciousness for bilingual programs among other native Spanish-speaking groups. A group consciousness of Hispanics may also develop from reading the same Spanish language newspapers and listening to Spanish Radio and T.V. programs.

2. Social Relations between Hispanic Americans are increasing. As bilingual education programs have developed in the United States, the need for Spanish-speaking personnel with special teaching credentials have combined to create shortages of qualified bilingual teachers. Cordasco and Castellanos (1973) found that Cuban educators through special certification programs have partially filled this need. "Caught in the dilemma of either having Spanish-speaking Cubans teach their children or having English-speaking Americans, the Puerto Rican leadership has accepted the former. While it is known that Cubans as a group tend to be prejudiced against Puerto Ricans, their prejudice takes the form of disdain rather than hostility. The strong militant elements in Puerto Rican communities have undertaken the task of sensitizing these teachers. p.237." Despite the tensions and competitiveness in this situation, interaction has inevitably begun.

Finally, some formal organizations are beginning to represent the common interests of all the Spanish-speaking. For example, Shaw (1975) notes that "Aspira, Inc., an association dedicated to helping mainland Puerto Ricans, initiated a class action to secure bilingual education for all Hispanic children in the city's schools whom it might benefit. p.106" Departments of Hispanic Studies have been established in some colleges and universities. As bilingual education programs have grown, formal organization has been developing as well.

In order to explore the common assimilation problems of Hispanic Americans, let us begin briefly by describing the three largest ethnic groups within this larger Spanish Language group classified as Hispanic Americans.

Mexican-Americans or Chicanos

Mexican-Americans are the second largest minority group in the United States. Mexican-Americans have been living in the Southwest part of the United States for more than 350 years, descendants of the original Spanish conquerors. Some early villages north of Sante Fe, New Mexico were settled as early as 1598. The descendants of these original Spanish settlers became residents of the United States in 1848 when they and their land were annexed to the United States. Many Mexican-Americans are native-born and are able to trace their native ancestry back for generations, while another large migration of Mexicans to the United States occurred in the early twentieth century. Five states (close to the Mexican border) including Arizona, California, Colorado, New Mexico and Texas, hold more than 85% of the Mexican-American population. (Alvirez and Bean, 1976)

The Mexican-American population has increased dramatically in the Southwest reflecting a high birth rate and continuing immigration to the United States. (Pettigrew, 1976) Mexican-Americans have been moving increasingly into urban areas and northward and westward to California.

Despite the fact that almost 50% of Mexican-Americans are third-generation American, Mexican-Americans have not experienced a great deal of upward mobility. They tend to be concentrated in low-skilled, poorly paid jobs. While research up to 1950 showed a similar pattern of prejudice and discrimination against Mexican-Americans as against Blacks in American society, D'Antonia and Samora (1962) contend that more recent findings show that Mexican-Americans are not in a caste-like relationship with Anglo-Americans. Pinkney (1970) believes that in the community he studied, "the possibility for improving the status of Mexican-Americans is greater than for Negro Americans. p.80. The Chicano movement began in the mid-1960's. This successful movement has been primarily political and cultural, helping cultivate a growing sense of pride and dignity among Mexican-Americans.

Puerto Ricans

In 1917, all Puerto Ricans were declared citizens of the United States. The almost three million Puerto Ricans living in the commonwealth of Puerto Rico and the 1.8 million Puerto Ricans living on the United States' mainland have developed into one social and cultural community. Most mainland Puerto Ricans live in cities along the Eastern seaboard, particularly New York City. Some live in large cities in the Mid-west. The Puerto Rican experience is unique in that large numbers of Puerto Ricans travel back and forth to Puerto Rico; many return to Puerto Rico permanently. Almost 1/3 of the Puerto Rican population have lived some part of their lives on the mainland, generally when they are young. This return migration has impeded the acculturation and political organization of Puerto Ricans.

Economically, Puerto Ricans are generally found on

the lowest socio-economic levels in the city of New York. Many live in Spanish Harlem. Puerto Ricans have encountered prejudice and discrimination based on their use of Spanish and their skin color which ranges from very light to dark. Puerto Ricans are usually labeled nonwhite.

A small but increasing proportion of Puerto Ricans who remain on the mainland are attaining some upward mobility, including movement to the suburbs.

Cubans

The majority of the 687,000 Cubans in the United States are recent arrivals; most have come as a result of the Cuban revolution of 1959. Many popularized articles have appeared in magazines indicating the spectacular success that Cubans have achieved in the United States in such a short time.

Cubans are a refugee group. They did not voluntarily leave their country for economic advancement, but they felt forced to leave Cuba because of a political situation they defined as intolerable. The hope of a quick return to Cuba helped them to accept their exile to the United States as temporary. As it has become apparent that there will not be a quick return home, Cubans have been forced to come to terms with a new life in the United States. Many Cubans live in Florida, but some large communities have developed in urban areas in the North and Midwest as well. Studies (Poertes, 1969 and Rogg, 1974) have shown that the middle class values and goals of the Cuban refugees have helped speed their rapid adjustment to life in the United States.

While emphasis has been placed on the middle class backgrounds and success of Cuban refugees, little attention has been paid to Cubans who are not middle class and who have not adjusted well. Much research is still needed to gain an adequate picture of all Cubans in the United States.

The Unique Problems of Hispanic Americans

By rapidly looking at the three largest ethnic groups of Americans of Spanish-speaking origin, we have seen how diverse their history and experiences have been in the United States. We could be justified in simply concentrating on these unique qualities of each group, but we are also justified in concentrating on the parts of their experiences which may lead to a natural growth of unity among them. If we consider the history of other immigrants to the United States, like the Italians, we find that when these immigrants first arrived in this country, they identified themselves by the province of Italy from which they came. Italy did not become unified until the middle of the nineteenth century. Before that time, these provinces were the only political, social and cultural reality for these people. They did not tend to think of

themselves primarily as Italians, but as immigrants from Sicily, Calabria, Lucania, Apulia or Compania. Once in the United States these immigrants found that Americans did not really recognize these provincial distinctions. Americans saw all of them as Italian. Slowly, these distinctions faded for a number of reasons, although they are still somewhat present even today. In the United States, these immigrants and their descendants began to identify themselves increasingly as Italian-Americans.

Perhaps, a similar sense of identity may emerge among Americans of Spanish-speaking origin, although in a modified form. If such an identity emerges, it may result from the unique but common problems confronting these Americans.

1. Lack of Immigration

The vast majority of Americans of Spanish-speaking origin are not immigrants to the United States. A number of studies (Moore, 1970, Gaviglio, 1976) point out that many Mexican-Americans did not ever move to become residents of the United States. They automatically found themselves "involuntary" residents, when the United States won the Southwest from Mexico. They were to some extent a conquered people whose culture has been valued in the Southwest for more than 200 years before they were overtaken. (Nava, 1970) Gaviglio (1976) believes that "no Chicano is really an immigrant in America. When they 'moved north', they felt that they were moving in an environment that was geographically, culturally and historically familiar. I would even say that in a political sense the border has been a nebulous entity. There was no border patrol until 1924 and there was not even a quota on Mexican immigration until 1965. (p.382)."

Like the Southwest, Puerto Rico was won in war by the United States. The Island became a U.S. possession at the end of the Spanish-American War on December 10, 1898. Thus, Puerto Ricans found themselves involuntary residents of the United States, as did Mexican-Americans. Their movement to the mainland required no passports or visas since Puerto Ricans were declared U.S. citizens in 1917. Thus any movement of Puerto Ricans to the mainland must be viewed as a migration and not an immigration.

Most Cubans are also not immigrants. Rogg (1974) notes that Cubans are refugess. Refugees are people who are pushed out of their homeland, unlike immigrants who are pulled or attracted to their new adoptive country. Immigrants tend to be young people from lower-class backgrounds, while refugees come from all age groups and social classes. Many come from middle-class and upper-class backgrounds, and have been forced to leave behind their homes and life-savings. Refugees often dream of returning to their homelands. Considering their stay in the receiving country as temporary, they spend far less energy adjusting to life in the host society than do immigrants who see their stay as permanent. While some Cuban refugees have realized that their chances of returning to Cuba are small, and consequently, are reorienting their lives to a permanent commitment to life in the United States, other Cubans are still dreaming of returning to Cuba.

Moore (1970) cautions that "the nature of the introduction into American society matters even more that race" in the adjustment and assimilation of Hispanic people (p.240). The way that many Americans of Spanish-speaking origin have been introduced to American society has been so different from the experiences of European immigrants that we cannot use the European immigration model to understand the Hispanic American role in American history. (Nava, 1970)

2. The Physical Closeness of Home

When the United States annexed the Southwest, Mexican-American culture was well-developed, autonomous and dominant in the region. This culture has been continually reinforced by the proximity of Mexico and, in part, has slowed the acculturation of Mexican-Americans. Gaviglio (1976) believes the border doesn't really exist. The differences between such border towns as Calexico and Mexicali, El Paso and Juarez and Brownsville and Matamoros are really political and economic, not geographical or cultural.

Fitzpatrick (1971) shows that "the proximity of the Island and the ease of return seem to prompt the Puerto Ricans to find in the Island the sense of strength, support and identify which former immigrants found in the clusters of their own kind in the immigrant communities of American cities. There is a great deal of truth in the comment that this is not a Puerto Rican migration, but a process of Puerto Rican commuting. (p.179)." Brahs (1973) stresses recognition of the fact that the Puerto Rican community on the Island and the mainland is one social and cultural community. Puerto Rican migrants maintain close family ties with the island and often return.

While Cubans in Miami are physically quite close to their former island homeland, unlike Mexican-Americans and Puerto Ricans, they are not able to return home. Instead they have created a very strong and concentrated ethnic community in the Miami-Dade County area. Some are trying hard to recreate a sense of being in Cuba and are trying to keep alive the dream of returning home. Some older Cubans are pressuring yourger Cubans to remain loyal to their Cuban heritage and the dream of returning to Cuba.

3. Identity Crisis - Who am I?

When people are uprooted and find themselves surrounded by a culture different from their own, they find they must adapt to a new way of perceiving themselves and others. They are confronted with redefining themselves. They must answer the question —who am I?

This quest for identity is common among immigrants, but it may really be part of a larger national questions of discovering who we Americans are. Are we evolving as a nation of homogenized "melted" Americans? Or are we evolving as groups of hyphenated Americans, culturally or structurally distinct from each other? Or is yet another pattern emerging?

In order for immigrants, refugees or native Americans in the United States in 1976 to answer the question of who they are individually, Americans may have to answer the question of who they are collectively as well.

It is not surprising then to find that many studies (Cabrera, 1971, Nava, 1979, Fitzpatrick, 1971, Brahs, 1973, Moore, 1976) indicate that a major problem confronting all Hispanic Americans is a lack of a sense of identity. Much energy in ethnic communities is used attempting to explore and discover an identity within the host society. Sometimes other groups in the receiving society help identify the group. Moore (1976) points out that only in interaction with "various elements in American society—Anglo, Chicano, Black and other Latin Americans" have official institutions "discovered" that Chicanos should be considered a disadvantaged *minority* group (p.10).

To identify oneself as Mexican-American, Puerto Rican or Cuban, almost inevitaby means to value Roman Catholicism, Spanish and familism as part of one's heritage. (Cabrera, 1971, Fitzpatrick, 1971, Rogg, 1974).

Spanish as One's Cultural Heritage and Identity.

Spanish has become a focal point for identification among Hispanic Americans. It serves not simply as a medium of communication, but as a bond, a living symbol of one's unique cultural heritage.

When a school system is intolerant of a child's use of Spanish, it reflects a philosophy intolerant of cultural pluralism. Nava (1970) believes that exclusive English language instruction is destructive to the Spanish-speaking child's self-image and ego. The most advanced educational programs build upon the Spanish language and Hispanic cultural backgrounds of their students as strengths, not weaknesses.

For many Spanish-speaking intellectuals, there is

concern that large numbers of children of Spanish-speaking origin are not able to speak either English or Spanish correctly. Instead they speak a mixture of the two langurages, and are losing the quality of both languages. Many hope that bilingual education programs will improve the children's ability in both languages.

Fitzpatrick (1971) expresses the concern that knowledge of English may be functional for a child's eventual assimilation but may cause a painful role reversal at home, when poorly educated parents must rely on their children to be interpretors for them. (p.144) This problem may be particularly acute in Hispanic homes where family roles are carefully defined.

5. Familism

Many studies (Rubel, 1966, Gil, 1968, Cabrera, 1971, Fitzpatrick, 1971, Rogg, 1974, Alvirez and Bean, 1976, Moore, 1976) attest to the great importance Hispanic Americans attach to family life. The family includes parents and children as well as extended relatives and godparents (compadrazgo). Respect, courtesy and affection are important family values. There is a strong sense of family obligation and hierarchy among Hispanics.

Fitzpatrick (1971) contends that in Latin culture generally, "personalism" is a basic value. Personalism stresses the inner value and qualities of the individual, the person's uniqueness and self-worth. Hispanic Americans tend to be less concerned with external symbols, less competitive and materialistic than other Americans stressing spiritual values instead.

"Machismo" or male dominance is the family characteristic most emphasized and perhaps overemphasized in the literature about Hispanic Americans. While emphasis is generally placed on the male's ability to conquer women, particularly sexually, Alvirez and Bean (1976) contend that the concept contains contradictory elements. What is less emphasized in the concept are "the elements of courage, honor and respect for others as well as the notion of providing fully for one's family and maintaining close ties with the extended family (p.278)." It is difficult to perform these latter obligations if one is supposed to be a great lover also. Cabrera (1971) adds that "machismo: is found in all world groups and may be as much a cultural stereotype of Hispanics as a reality. He argues that "machismo" is related more to low socio-economic status than it is to ethnicity. The double-standard, use of physical force and large families are really characteristics of low socio-economic status.

6. Confusion of Social Class and Ethnic Values.

Studies (Fitzpatrick, 1971, Rogg, 1974, Moor, 1976,

Gaviglio, 1976, Pettigrew, 1976) show that most Mexican-Americans, Puerto Ricans and Cubans are now urban residents, often found living in overcrowded, inadequate housing.

Cubans have been the most successful group in escaping from this situation. While often found in situations of underemployment in the United States, many Cubans still have the advantage of middle class values and optimism upon which to fall back.

Cabrera (1971), believes that "the losing of lower-class culture rather than ethnicity is most related to mobility upward (p.60)." If many Puerto Rican and Mexican-American families are characterized by many children, poverty, parents with poor educational backgrounds and unskilled occupationally, we are looking at lower class subcultural factors and not ethnic factors. Middle class Cuban families lack these lower class factors, but they are very much hispanic.

7. Racial Attitudes

Finally, Mexican-Americans, Puerto Ricans and Cubans have been strongly influenced by Spanish tradition in forming their attitudes about interracial mixing. Unlike American society, Hispanic culture has allowed much more intermingling racially. Mexican-Americans and Puerto Ricans have been even more tolerant of this pattern than Cubans. In Puerto Rican culture, the racial classification system allows more than the two possibilities of black or white. The term "trigueno," as well as other related terms, provides a third comfortable and positive alternative. Fitzpatrick (1971) indicated that in Puerto Rico one's social class determines in large measure how a person will be classified racially, whereas in the United States, the way a person is classified racially will strongly influence the social class to which the person will belong. When Hispanic Americans, particularly of medium color, find themselves in contact with Anglo culture, they become anxious over the two-fold classification system they find. They soon understand the advantages of being classified as white. Fitzpatrick (1971) notes that those who can't quite be classified as white may try to remain within the Puerto Rican community where they are not discriminated against. While Will Herberg expects Puerto Ricans to split into two groups based on race, Fitzpatrick does not see this happening at present. Fitzpatrick hopes that the Hispanic pattern will continue and spread among other American groups.

Summary

The presence of large numbers of Americans of Spanish-speaking origin interested in maintaining their Spanish language and heritage may serve as a focal point for a growing unity among Hispanic Americans. In order to understand the unique role of Hispanic Americans in American history, the problems common to Americans of Spanish-speaking origin should be considered. These special problems include (1) a lack of immigration to the United States (2) the physical closeness of home (3) an identity crisis (4) Spanish as one's cultural heritage and identity (5) familism (6) the confusion of social class and ethnic values and finally (7) racial attitudes.

BIBLIOGRAPHY

Alvirez, David; and Bean, Frank D. "The Mexican American Family." *In Ethnic Families in America: Patterns, and Variations*, edited by Charles H. Mindel and Robert W. Habenstein. New York: Elsevier, 1976.

Bierstedt, Robert. "The Sociology of Majorities." *American Sociological Review*, 1948, 13:700-710.

Brahs, Stuart J. *An Album of Puerto Ricans in the United States.* New York: Franklin Watts, Inc., 1973.

Burma, John H. "A Comparison of the Mexican-American Subculture with the Oscar Lewis Culture of Poverty Model." In *Mexican-Americans in the United States: A Reader*, edited by John H. Burma. Cambridge, Mass.: Schenkman Publishing Co., Inc., 1970.

Cabrera, Y. Arturo. *Emerging Faces: The Mexican-Americans.* New York: Wm.C. Brown Co., 1971.

Cordasco, Francesco; and Castellanos, Diego. "Teaching the Puerto Rican Experience." In *Teaching Ethnic Studies: Concepts and Strategies*, edited by James A. Banks. Washington, D.C.: National Council for the Social Studies, 43rd Yearbook, 1973.

D'Antonio, Wm. V; and Samora, Julian. "Occupational Stratification in Four Southwestern Communities: A Study of Ethnic Differential Employment in Hospitals." *Social Forces*, 1962, 41: 18-24.

Department of Health, Education and Welfare. "Cubans in our Midst." In *Social Science and Urban Crisis*, edited by Victor B. Ficker and Herbert S. Graves. New York: The Macmillan Co., 1971.

Fitzpatrick, Joseph P. *Puerto Rican Americans.* Englewood Cliffs, New Jersey; Prentice-Hall, Inc., 1971.

Gaviglio, Glen. "The Myths of the Mexican American." In *Society as It is: A Reader*, second edition, edited by Glen Gaviglio and David E. Raye. New York: Macmillan Publishing Co., Inc., 1976.

Herberg, Will. *Catholic, Protestant, Jew.* New York: Doubleday and Co., Inc., 1955.

Moore, Joan W. "Colonialism: The Case of the Mexican American." *Social Problems*, 1970, 17:463-472.

Moore, Joan W. *Mexican Americans*, second edition. Englewood Cliffs, New Jersey: Prentice-Hall, Inc., 1976.

Nava, Julian. "Cultural Backgrounds and Barriers that Affect Learning by Spanish-speaking Children." In *Mexican—Americans in the United States: A Reader*, edited by John H. Burma. Cambridge, Mass: Schenkman Publishing, Co., Inc., 1970.

Perry, John; and Perry, Erna. *The Social Web*, second edition. San Francisco: Canfield Press, 1976.

Pettigrew, Thomas Fraser. "Race and Intergroup Relations." In *Contemporary Social Problems*, fourth edition, edited by Robert K. Merton and Robert Nisbet. New York: Harcourt, Brace, Javanovich, Inc., 1976.

Pinkney, Alphonso. "Prejudice Toward Mexican and Negro Americans: A Comparison." In *Mexican-Americans in the United States: A Reader*, edited by John H. Burma. Cambridge, Mass: Schenkman Publishing Co., Inc., 1970.

Poertes, Alejandro. "Dilemmas of a Golden Exile: Integration of Cuban Refugee Families in Milwaukee." *American Sociological Review*, 1969, 34: 505-518.

Rogg, Eleanor Meyer. "Adjustment Problems of Bicultural School Children (A Comparison of Puerto Rican and Cuban School Children)." *Lutheran Education*, 1973, 109:103-115.

Rogg, Eleanor Meyer. *The Assimilation of Cuban Exiles: The Role of Community and Class.* New York: Aberdeen Press, 1974.

Rubel, Arthur J. *Across the Tracks.* Austin: University of Texas Press, 1966.

Santa Barbara County Board of Education. *The Emerging Minorities in America: A Resource Guide for Teachers.* Santa Barbara: American Bibliographical Center, Clio Press, 1972.

Shaw, Frederick. "Bilingual Education: An Idea Whose Times has come." *New York Affairs*, 1975, 3:94-111.

Vander Zanden, James W. *Sociology*, third edition. New York: Ronald Press, 1975.

Chapter 12
The Puerto Rican-An Organizational Alien
John D. Vazquez*

Introduction

In the United States there are over nine million children of school age that are non-Anglo Americans and as a result differ from the culturally dominant population. Approximately five million within this population come to school speaking a language other than English. Traditionally these children have been considered marginal and not worth educating. Most of these youngsters live in ghettos, reservations, or barrios. At least 50 to 60 percent of them leave school prematurely, (NEA Reporter, 1976). The other four to five million minority children speak English, but are also culturally and ethnically different from the dominant Anglo-American population. As a result they become alienated, excluded, and have poor grades which lead them to make up the bulk of early school leavers. Even though the United States has always been a land of ethnic diversity, our national institutions have perpetuated a white Anglo-Saxon, Protestant, monocultural standard. In addition the myth called the "melting pot" has made possible the continued paradox between ethnic diversity and a monocultural standard. (NEA Reporter, 1976).

According to the "melting pot" myth, education transforms people from diverse ethnic backgrounds into a homogeneous citizenry. In other words education is geared towards cultural assimilation and the inculcation of a national, American consciousness. It should be noted that the Americans who have obtained the greatest measure of opportunity, economic success and respect were those who most appropriately conformed to the melting "pot's" monocultural ideal.

However, cultural assimilation is often accompanied with painful conflict and a high emotional price. In order to enter the mainstream of American society many persons have attempted to strip themselves of their ethnic and cultural differences, they have changed their names, cut family ties, and have denied their heritage. Historically the public school along with other secondary institutions have perpetuated this situation.

To a great extent this is still true, in spite of bilingual, bicultural education.

According to the NEA task force established in January, 1974, "bilingual education is a process which uses a pupil's primary language as the principal medium of instruction while teaching the language of the predominant culture in a well organized program, encompassing a multicultural curriculum. (NEA, p.13). The emphasis supposedly addresses itself to the needs of the predominant society. In other words bilingual-bicultural education is to assist the child to comfortably, and with a minimum of conflict, relate to two cultures and the result should be a well-integrated entity. For example, a non-English speaking hispanic in a bilingual-bicultural program is to ascend as a well functioning, integrated citizen, who supposedly can function in his own culture and that of the dominant society.

My contention is that for a hispanic to ascend from a bilingual-bicultural program to a well-integrated personality, certain role models must be present. The classroom and the teacher must be consistent with his societal and cultural heritage. Especially since the class is an agent of socialization and allocation. It is within the classroom that a child is trained to be motivated and technically prepared for performing adult roles. It is here that the child learns commitment and responsibility. The classroom is to some extent an extension of the family, but rather than his ascribed status being important, it is his earned or achieved status that is rewarded. Ascribed status plays an important role in our lives, but in American society achieved status is cardinal. In order for the hispanic student to achieve he must be able to communicate in the classroom. This communication must be both verbal and nonverbal.

In observations made of the bilingual-bicultural program during the spring, 1975 term in Community School, District #23 (New York City), it was found that children in kindergarten through fifth grade, were normal, responsive, and motivated to learn. The bilingual-bicultural Puerto Rican teacher served as a catalyst for the children. The children's ability to identify with the teacher enhanced communications.

*Dr. John Vazquez, Professor of Sociology and Psychology, New York City Community College, City University of New York.

It must be noted at this point that verbal and nonverbal communications are culturally-rooted. In addition, the teacher's sensitivity and awareness permitted them to pickup culturally rooted signs and symbols which helped to breakdown the language barrier.

In the earlier grades the bilingual program appeared Spanish Dominant with the children being able to relate to the teacher in both Spanish and English. But as the child enters the sixth and seventh grades, the teacher, while being hispanic, primarily speaks and teaches in English. It is here that both teachers and children communicate more in English than in Spanish. It was found that communications between project directors and teachers was primarily in English. In essence, the bilingual education programs are concerned with using the native language as a tool to help children learn English.

The Puerto Ricans are not succeeding in adapting to their new surroundings. They are experiencing more liabilities than any other major immigrant group. Regardless of their natural citizenship, Puerto Ricans have been migrating to the United States since 1911 and this greatly increased after the Jones Act of 1917 (making Puerto Ricans American citizens). The influx of Puerto Ricans into the United States had reached its peak between 1951-1960 (U.S. Dept of Labor 1975). Approximately forty-seven percent (47%) of all Puerto Ricans coming to the United States settled in New York State between 1960-1970. In fact in New York City they constitute about eleven percent (11%) of the total population (U.S. Dept. of Labor, 1975). In addition, about forty-three percent (43%) are native born New Yorkers (Puerto Rican—American (U.S.Dept of Labor, 1975).) The fact that there is about 1.25 million Puerto Ricans in New York City is unimportant, they still have limited mobility in all the major areas of urban life, education, occupation, and economics.

Their educational attainment is the lowest of any other group in New York City. The median educational level for those 25 years or more is less than 9th grade, as compared with the 12th year median for all city residents. We find that among adult Puerto Ricans, only one in five has completed high school as compared to all other residents where the figure is one in two. In higher education, the gap widens. Only one in one hundred have a college degree as compared to one in nine for the rest of the city population. Among Puerto Ricans, age twenty-five and over, only twenty percent have a high school diploma. It should be noted that the majority of New Yorkers, age 20-24 who enter the labor market, have a high school diploma plus additional training. On the other hand, Puerto Ricans in the same group age are usually high school dropouts. Despite the increasing population of Puerto Ricans in Public schools, they are still less likely to take part in formal education than other groups in the city. In fact a smaller percentage of Puerto Rican children are in school before age seven and a higher percentage drop out by age sixteen (U.S. Dept. of Labor, 1975).

Within the age group, 16 to 21, one in four has completed high school. More than half the Puerto Rican male population is not in school. This gives a sixty-seven percent drop out rate for Puerto Ricans which is comparable to Black students (U.S. Dept. of Labor, 1975).

The educational attainment of the Puerto Rican is not totally disastrous. The 1970 census reported 12,030 of the city's Puerto Rican residents with one or more years of college education and that 8,117 are enrolled in college. By 1972, 13,563 Puerto Rican students were currently enrolled in City University, a number exceeding the total number of college graduates two years earlier (U.S. Dept. of Labor, 1975).

The limitations placed on the Puerto Rican educational attainment stems from the language barrier. It was found in 1970 census that 40 percent of adult Puerto Ricans living in the United States lacked basic literacy in English. In fact, among the 10-24 age groups, one out of five could not read or write English. "Public school records show that approximately one in three Puerto Rican students encountered problems in reading and understanding English." It is clear that language, job training and educational attainment are all interrelated. The language barrier is a major obstacle and to overcome this barrier will open many doors. Upward mobility is dependent on breaching this barrier. The responsibility falls both on the dominant society as well as the newcomer. The process of adaptability must be symbiotic.

New York City is dominated by white-collar workers. But Puerto Ricans are not part of this group, they are mainly blue-collar workers. Not only in New York City, but also, throughout the United States Puerto Ricans hold blue-collar jobs and have a higher than average unemployment rate.

Approximately fifty-eight percent of the residents of New York City have white-collar jobs while only thirty-three percent of the Puerto Rican's population are in this work force. In 1970, under five percent of the Puerto Ricans were in the professional and technical occupations. In addition, less than four percent were managers, officials, and proprietors. It was found that more than half the employed Puerto Ricans worked in semiskilled and unskilled operative and service jobs. The Puerto Rican's occupational distribution is heavily weighted on the low-skilled side as compared to the rest of the residents in the city's work force.

Within any of the major occupational classifications, Puerto Ricans are always at the bottom of the earning scale. In major areas like law, medicine, education, and engineering Puerto Ricans constitute about one percent.

Puerto Ricans are primarily involved in a declining sector of the city's economy, manufacturing. The jobs in the manufacturing sector have shrunk about one-third between 1950-1970. The city lost 285,000 jobs between 1970-74 and the majority were in the manufacturing sector. Thus affecting the Puerto Rican who is heavily employed in the manufacturing sector (Gray, 1975, pp.12-16).

In essence we can suggest that the concentration of Puerto Ricans in blue-collar, semiskilled, unskilled and low level white-collar occupations is due to his lack of job skills and educational attainment. Both of which are integral parts of the process of adaptability.

Becoming part of a declining sector of the economy reflects a lack of information and understanding of the American scene. This lack of being "tuned in" is clearly an illustration of limited acculturation. The problem of acculturation is reflected in the Puerto Ricans annual income. Money is a major instrument for acquisition and a commodity that permeates our high-income, modern society. However, the Puerto Rican's inability to successfully accumulate significant amounts demonstrates a lack of information.

In comparison to other New Yorkers, Puerto Ricans have the least desirable jobs and the lowest incomes. Their median family income is but little more than half the average for the city. One-third live at or below the poverty level. It was found that even when employment is steady and there is a regular income, Puerto Ricans earn substantially less than others with the same employment record (U.S. Dept. of Labor, 1975).

Puerto Ricans are at the bottom of the economic scale in New York City. In 1969, about one-half of New York City families had incomes over $10,000 annually. Less than one in six Puerto Ricans had the same or are above this income. Even though Puerto Ricans in the United States as a whole have a median income of $6,115 as compared to $5,575 for New York City Puerto Ricans, their annual median income as a group is comparatively less than for the rest of the population (U.S. Dept. of Labor, 1975). It should be noted that family income refers to the earnings, number, sex and age of family members who are employed. For the Puerto Rican household this creates a problem because women are less likely to be employed outside the home. This is unlike the national trend. Therefore it is clear that a family who depends on only one income will have less than a family with more than one wage earner. In addition, we know that Puerto Rican female headed households have the lowest incomes of all. A second wage earner in a Puerto Rican household often brings the family above the poverty line. For example, in 1969 Puerto Rican families with two earners had an average annual income of $9,064 as compared to a single wage earner with an annual income of $5,773. A working wife is a major factor in family income status (U.S. Dept. of Labor, 1975).

The Puerto Rican New Yorker's low income status reflects a combination of variables that handicaps his entrance into the mainstream of economic life: recency of arrival, lack of know-how in coping with urban customs and *patterns of behavior*, relative youth, below average education and skill training, and lack of fluency in English.

What is illustrated by the preceding information is that the Puerto Rican is undergoing a serious problem in acculturation to modern American society. The timetable of assimilation subprocesses is set back because of the incongruency between American and Latin-American culture. In addition, the problem reaches its zenith when you are dealing with an island, personal, simple, folk-type as opposed to an automated, advanced technological, complex type. It is well demonstrated by recent studies that the process of adaptability for the Puerto Rican in the United States will be slow.

The two most important socializing units are the family and the school. Both need to reinforce each other in orienting and preparing the child for participation in adult life. The family is primarily responsible for the initial socialization process and the school for reinforcing this initial socialization. The school and the family should be a continuum. However, neither one of these socializing units provide or give the Puerto Rican child support. His initial socialization process within the Puerto Rican household is often confusing and full of contradictions. Between 1911 and 1940, this was not true because of their small numbers and relegated state. But with the post World War II influx the setting changed. The large influx made him visible and subject to the liabilities of any newcomer, in addition to the fact that unlike other migrants before, his socio-cultural background was incompatible with that of the dominant culture. Therefore, his initial socialization process within the Puerto Rican family milieu was inconsistent with his socialization in the Anglo-Saxon American school system.

According to Schneider and Homans (1955) Americans are concerned with a single basic form, emphasing the nuclear family, and secondarily important kindred. But it is noted that within this particular framework, there is considerable room for variations. This variation is in terms of roles and relationships rather than in terms of basic kin-groups. The diversity focusing on a basic unit. This is in contrast to the Latin-American ethos where kinship, status, and the extended family play a major role. The individual is an extension of his family. It is the family's individual worth, dignity, and honor that is generated. In Puerto Rican society, the family is the center of life. The family *is* life. Puerto Rican culture emphasizes ascribed status, while American culture is oriented toward achieved status. In modern postindustrial America, the role of the family is different from that of the traditional Puerto Rican family. The direct influence of the dominant culture has caused and is causing a great deal of confusion and contradiction with the Puerto Rican family milieu. These contradictions are internalized by its individual members and personal disorganization becomes social disorganization as they are transferred to the secondary institution, e.g., the school.

Theoretically, the school is a formal organization that is geared toward serving a client group. In other words, it is a service organization whose prime beneficiaries are the students. This is not happening with the Puerto Rican student. This is substantiated by the fact that they have a sixty-seven percent drop-out rate. Educational attainment for the Puerto Rican in New York City and the United States in general is minimal. It should be noted that as a client group, he has no power. He is an alienated entity and has no decision making powers. In addition to his lack of orientation, there is the fact that organizations are especially careful to protect what Etzioni calls, "strategic positions" from the penetration of different or unknown types, e.g., Puerto Ricans. Particular positions like at national headquarters, communication centers, and socializing units. The Puerto Rican faces two different fields of battle: (a) his own role confusion derived from a contradictory family milieu, and (b) a system or structure that is unfamiliar and incompatible with his societal and cultural roots. Any pattern of realizations leading to enduring and meaningful social relations must be an integral part of the overall structural setting. It must be noted that there must be an "ordered relations of parts to a whole," that within this arrangement the elements of the social life are linked (Firth, 1951). In other words, for any group to

be an integral part of any society or structure of society, he must understand and relate to its order of patterned relations.

In the last analysis, the cultural dimension must be used as a vehicle for reaching and understanding the individual as an individual. He should not be buried behind generalizations about a group. Culture should then be referred "in part to the general style of interpersonal relations and related attitudes that are traditional in a given society (Leacock, 1968). Understanding cultural differences will enable secondary institutions like the school to see behind socially patterned behavior and allow for meaningful relationships. Thus, setting the scene for members of a particular group to contribute to the whole.

SELECTED BIBLIOGRAPHY

"America's Other Children" *NEA Reporter*, Vol. 15, No. 4, 1976

Firth, Raymond "Social Structure and Social Organization" *Elements of Social Organization* London: C. A. Watts, 1951.

Gallaher, Art, Jr., "Directed Change in Formal Organization: The School System" *Change Processes in the Public Schools*, (Center for the Advanced Study of Educational Administration, University Of Oregon), 1965.

Leacock, Eleanor, "The Concept of Culture and its Significance for School Counselors", Personnel and Guidance, Vol. 46, No. 9, May, 1968.

Schneider, David M. and Homan, George C., "Kinship Terminology and The American Kinship System", *American Anthropologist*, Vol. 57, 1955.

"The School Class as a Social System", *Harvard Educational Review*, Vol. 29, No. 4, 1959.

U.S. Department of Labor, "A Socio-Economic Profile of Puerto Rican New Yorkers", New York: Bureau of Labor Statistics, July, 1975.

Chapter 13

Life In A Changing Multi-Ethnic School: Anglo Teachers and Their Views of Mexican Children

Jean Meadowcroft and Douglas E. Foley*

This article is an interpretive description of how elementary school teachers in a small South Texas school perceived and interacted with their Mexicano students. Although this ethnographic analysis offers no suggestions for proper or "better" teacher attitudes and classroom behavior, the concerned teacher should be able to draw his/her own conclusions. Hopefully, the description provides a realistic and accurate portrait of Anglo teachers struggling to change in a changing community. If change is the only sure thing facing contemporary American teachers, perhaps there are some important lessons in this case for teachers in any multi-ethnic school.

The Setting and Procedures

This investigation is based on fifteen months of fieldwork by four anthropologists in a small (5,000) agricultural (vegetables, maize, peanuts and cotton) community located south of San Antonio, Texas, near the Mexican border.[1] The community, which will be referred to as North Town, was predominately Mexican American/Mexicano (75%), and since the early 1960's has had a history of sporadic political confrontations between organized Anglo and Mexicano groups. In the 1970's the development of a Chicano political party, *Raza Unida Party*, in various Texas towns and cities began to influence North Town ethnic relations and politics. Increasingly, a small group (30-40) of prominent local Mexican American businessmen, agricultural producers and professionals began organizing to compete in local elections for control of the school board and city council. The length of this article does not permit an extensive description of this ethnic conflict. It suffices to say that powerful, sometimes disruptive forces affected the daily life in schools. Actual field work in the elementary school lasted four months. Ms. Meadowcroft spent several hundred hours observing classes and interviewing teachers. There were approximately 450 students and 15 teachers in this grade 1-6 school program. The curriculum included the usual subjects of English, science, math, and social studies. The program also included music, physical education and two recess periods. Although 80% of the children were Mexicanos, the school had only one experimental bilingual education class in the first grade. There were no other experimental programs, and little indication that the district was particularly "progressive". Nor could the district have been labeled "backwards", by either the standards of the local people or the State Education Agency. The vast majority of the students came from low income families, however, and the mean scores on all subject areas in the national achievement tests were consistently below the national averages. The teachers came almost exclusively from the surrounding area and were educated in various regional teacher training colleges. The vast majority were Anglo (85%) and were from rural and small-town backgrounds of middle and lower-middle class standing.

Teacher Attitudes

At our first meeting with teachers, we were introduced to the kinds of attitudes that we would hear over and over again during our stay in North Town. One teacher, a longtime resident of the area, told us that "Latins" needed special grouping for their needs. Another teacher, new to the community, answered that ability grouping was better since it would prevent the slower children from feeling that they could not do better. We subsequently found many similar rationales for the low performance of Mexicanos. Many of these beliefs about Mexicano children stemmed from the teacher's presumed knowledge of homelife on the Mexicano side of town. It is important, therefore to briefly indicate the pattern of teacher-community relations observed before describing the general attitudes and beliefs of teachers.

Teachers' knowledge of Mexicano students' homes rarely was direct. Except for one or two cases, teachers did not visit their students' homes. There seemed to be no regular channel of contact between the home and

*Jean Meadowcroft is a Ph.D candidate in education and anthropology at Stanford University. Douglas E. Foley is an Assistant Professor of Education and of Anthropology at the University of Texas in Austin.

the school. There was no parent-teacher organization. Only if the principal or the teacher telephoned, or if the truant officer went to the home was there direct contact. Announcements and notices sent to the home were in English, although many parents did not read English well, if at all. A number of teachers complained that few parents came to the school, and that sometimes they failed to respond to failing notices or teachers' notes. Some Mexicano parents said that they did not go to the school often, only during visiting week or at the teacher's request. However, increasing numbers of parents, particularly those active in the Raza Unida, were visiting and challenging school policies and individual teachers. Yet overall, the great majority of Mexicano parents were inactive in school affairs, a fact which led to great consternation among Raza Unida activists. These activists were also critical of the teachers' isolation from the Mexicano community.

Anglo teachers frequently blamed the school difficulties of Mexicano students on their home life. They said that Mexicano children had a worse home life than Anglos. "Noisy", "overcrowded", "disorganized", "immoral" were some of the words used to describe Mexicano homes. One teacher suggested that his students were so noisy because "the Latins, the Mexicans, they're used to being shouted down in their homes, having to shout over the others to be heard". It was true that many Mexicano houses were smaller and more crowded than Anglo houses. Mexicano housing generally reflected the poverty of many barrio families. Generalities that Mexicano homes were disorganized and immoral were, of course, not accurate.

Interestingly, Anglo teachers pointed out that all ethnic groups were not unsuccessful. The German communities of South Texas were cited as a poor group that had worked hard and "made it". One teacher pointed out one of her students: "Talk about minorities! That little girl over there comes from a German family. She lives with her mother and her grandmother. There are nine children and they get welfare. Their father isn't home, but they work and they try." The implication here was that something in Mexican culture encouraged low achievement and a lack of industriousness.

Some teachers also said that Mexicano children were not as disciplined as Anglo children. They felt that they "talk back and misbehave because their parents let them do it at home".

Another attitude expressed by teachers was that Mexicano children did not know the value of money since many of them were thought to be on welfare. Teachers often criticized children who were on the free lunch program for buying candy and snacks. Furthermore, teachers said that the children expected everything to be free, from extra reading newspapers to materials for class projects. Some teachers claimed that

there were Anglo students who actually were poorer than the Mexicano students, but who did not get free lunch because they were not the "right" color.

Some teachers justified their views of Mexicanos by referring to various deprivation theories. One teacher thought that deprivation occurred through protein deficiency. She said that the common Mexicano diet of beans and tortillas is deficient in protein. However, other sources in the schools, including the school nurse, said that malnourishment was not a problem. Another deprivation view, shared by several teachers, was that Mexicano children no longer had traditional Mexican culture, nor had learned "American" culture, and culture-conflict existed.

The "good" Mexicano child was the one who was most like the Anglo child, who usually came from a more economically advantaged home. This was the child who came from a "better" home, who was quiet, who did not receive free lunch and who was nicely dressed. Teachers were quick to point out such "good" Mexicano children as proof that those who wanted to could do well in school.

To show that children who speak Spanish at home can succeed in English language schools, teachers also often compared local Mexicano youngsters with students who were recent immigrants from Mexico. These Mexican-born children often performed better in school than locally-born children. There are several probable reasons for this. First, these children had the opportunity to learn to read and write and do arithmetic in their own language. They did not have to master the fundamental concepts while at the same time learning a new language. Second, many of these children came from families where the parents were teachers or semi-professionals in Mexico. That is, they had a higher level of education than many local Mexicano parents. Once they had immigrated to the United States, the parents might work for a while at manual labor, but they soon sought better jobs, "learned English, and moved on up the ladder."

Third, it was apparent that many teachers had higher expectations for these children than for locally-born Mexicano children. This, in addition to the motivation and education of the parents, might contribute to these children's success in school. For example, one teacher defended an immigrant girl in her classroom. In English, the teacher told her to take her book to the blackboard. The girl went to the board, as the other students were doing, but she failed to take her book. The other students started laughing at her. The teacher looked at them firmly and said, "It's not her fault she doesn't know English".

Several teachers recognized that prejudices existed against the Mexicano students. Two were not outsiders, but locally born and raised Anglos. One considered her parents' generation to be bigots and thought that relations between Mexicanos and Anglos would improve in the future. In her view the point of school was to "allow him to cope with Anglo culture". The second expressed an awareness and concern over how the children were very conscious of their skin color, even at a very young age. Further, she noted that the present elementary school, located in the barrio, was built only for Mexicano children. But then the decision for integration was made, and the "people over there (Anglos) had to send their children over here". Another Anglo teacher cited the prejudice against Mexicanos, especially those "who made something of themselves, and still are not accepted by the Anglos", yet described herself as biased on a class basis. She felt that those who sacrifice and work hard can get ahead. She felt that differences between the Mexicano elite and the lower classes in San Antonio showed this. Another teacher, who usually seemed prejudiced against Mexicano students, could sympathize with the Mexicano principal of the school. She said that a number of teachers did not like him because he was "Latin", but that she felt he was well-qualified, and was doing a good job. Moreover, not just Anglos, but even middle-class Mexicano teachers were critical of lower class Mexicanos. One talked about the migrants, "A lot of them live at a place called Ranchero on the way to Model City. They say it's a pig farm and it sure looks like one. Those people live just like pigs."

Some Portraits of Teachers

Nearly all of the North Town elementary and intermediate school teachers were Texas born and raised. In spite of the fact that most of the teachers grew up in what might be characterized as traditional small town Anglo settings, there were significant differences in their attitudes and world view. It is exceedingly difficult to characterize local Anglo teachers into some "typical" types, but the following two portraits are an attempt to show the diversity and most common orientations that we encountered. The way Anglo teachers generally think about and teach Mexicano children tends to fall into one of these general orientations. Each case does not necessarily represent any one actual teacher, but is a composite developed through observation and conversations.

Nancy Donaldson has lived and taught in North Town for twenty years. She now is toward the end of a long career that included teaching at the old Mexicano school. She and her husband live on a ranch which they have worked hard to build up over the years. Mrs. Donaldson says the homes of a lot of Mexicano children are not very good. Families are very large, so the mothers do not have enough time to care for the

children. "With ten children how can they keep track of them, and teach them manners?" She says "families are illiterate, even in Spanish, so that children come to school with a five-hundred word vocabulary. Besides, they have forgotten Mexican culture and still haven't learned American culture. They don't know what a *serape* or a *siesta* is even though those are part of Mexican culture." Mexican people don't like each other to get ahead, according to Mrs. Donaldson. She doesn't like "this La Raza stuff", because it's an extremist movement that tells people they can get what they want by taking over, instead of working for it.

Mrs. Donaldson thinks it is hard for a child to go into a classroom where another language is spoken, but "English is the American language; they will need it. Mexican children should have intensive English, but the teachers should know some Spanish; but bilingual education would be difficult; we have to teach reading, math, and so many things in English, how would we have time to teach in Spanish, too? I like to teach the slower kids. I tell them, 'You can do it. Just try and you can do it.' I try and get them to be self-reliant and independent."

In the classroom several children run up to Mrs. Donaldson when she enters. They surround her desk and keep talking to her. She hugs a girl who has been out with a sore throat and tells her she is glad to see her. Later, Mrs. Donaldson is teaching one of the reading groups. The children are reading slowly and have trouble pronouncing words. She explains that "two is dos" and "too is tambien". A more advanced group finishes their reading and she gives them pictures to color. They start getting noisy. Mrs. Donaldson raps a paddle on her desk and threatens to put names on the board. Then she asks another boy if he has finished all of his work since he is reading a library book. Another boy is talking; Mrs. Donaldson walks over and paddles him, then asks the rest of the class if they want to get paddled too. Then she turns to work with a girl who wears thick glasses, and is nearly blind. Mrs. Donaldson had arranged to have special large print books for her, and today they start a math lesson. Some other children start talking again. One girl tatttles that another is not doing her work. Mrs. Donaldson takes the tape and scissors from her desk, and asks the class "Does anyone want a goat beard?" They fall silent.

Mrs. Donaldson, along with many other teachers, is sincere in her intention to help the Mexicano children she teaches. She is doing her best to teach them American ways, and to speak English.

Rose Carter's family has lived in the North Town area for generations. They are ranchers who have continued to work hard to develop their business and cope with the ups and downs of agriculture. They are progressives who try to keep up with the new technology to keep their ranch going. Since Rose Carter grew up on a ranch in the area she has known Mexicano families and spoken Spanish since childhood.

Mrs. Carter feels that Mexicano parents are taking more of an interest in their children's education now. She says children from large families, especially the youngest child, may have more problems in school; but she is not sure of this, since the children from some large families do very well. She feels she judges people not on race but on class. "People should work hard and try to make something of themselves. These days they (Mexicans) think agricultural labor is beneath them. They'd rather take welfare. They want the minimum wage and we can't afford it. Mexican Americans can make it the same way my family did, by hard work." She is apprehensive about La Raza,

"I don't know why but even the most educated people were influenced. We got along o.k. until the outside instigators came in. They don't say anything to me, but I don't know how I would feel if they took over. They want to take over the land, the offices, everything. It's not as if they wanted to buy it; they just want to take over. I guess when things get divided you go with your own." Still, she tries to understand the bitterness of educated Mexican Americans, who, she says, are discriminated against. "They have made something of themselves and still are not accepted by the Anglos."

If the schools required the teaching of Spanish, Mrs. Carter would teach in Spanish. She feels schools should help Mexicano children to adjust to Anglo culture. She noted that the reading books have little to do with Mexicanos, and said, "It would be nice if we had some readers with Mexican folk tales. Still all children need to master English that they will need for college and work." She tries to make school a positive learning experience. "I don't like to spank. Children should feel good about school. The only thing I wish is that they were more independent. They shouldn't have to ask the teacher everything, but should be able to learn on their own too."

At the beginning of the day, several children each ask to come to the front of the classroom. One tells a riddle; and another tells about a trip to San Antonio. Mrs. Carter thanks the children for sharing with the class. Later in the day she is teaching the children how to write a letter; they are writing letters to a classmate who is in the hospital. She has several children suggest things they might write, and she writes a sample letter on the blackboard. Some children do not follow the rules for paragraphs. She tells them in a loud voice to look at the letter on the board. The teacher asks one boy why he isn't doing anything. He says he doesn't know what to do and hasn't got a pencil. She tells him to listen and to follow directions.

Toward the end of the day, Mrs. Carter pairs off the children for a math review. Each child has a partner; the faster children help the ones who are having more difficulty with their homework. As children finish, they get out science and health packets Mrs. Carter has prepared. They go to the back of the room and cut out pictures to illustrate the lessons. Other children get library books. All children are working at something, and Mrs. Carter goes around the classroom to check with each child.

Mrs. Carter, like other Anglos, wants the children to learn American ways, and to use English. Her classroom has a positive, energetic enthusiasm that seems to challenge the students. She has all sorts of materials available and expects the children to be working. If children have finished their own work, then they are to work on extra materials or work with their partner. There is little conflict in her classroom, because she has made her standards clear, and because she herself constantly encourages the children. Also, through the partnerships she has provided a way that children can get the help they need without all of the children having to rely on one source of teaching. Mrs. Carter demands a great deal of the students but stresses cooperation so that everyone has a chance to accomplish the goals.

These are only two examples among the many teachers of North Town. These two happen to be teachers who are taking an interest in their Mexicano students.

Some teachers talked about Mexicanos in the teachers' lounge or with each other in classrooms before and after school. But they wouldn't say negative things in front of their Mexicano students. "We can't tell them not to speak Spanish any more. I try to encourage them to use English in the cafeteria, but the older students use Spanish and they just follow their example." Teachers often talked about La Raza party and political events in South Texas. They talked about "militants" who wanted to "take-over". Many felt that everyone was happy with things the way they were before (integration). "The teachers here try hard to teach the Mexicans. None of the teachers here are prejudiced. When we had the old school, we taught there because we wanted to. We did everything for the children. The teachers worked so hard to bring them up from where they were, to raise them up."

Most teachers felt that the educational system provided an equal opportunity for everyone who wanted to work and make something of himself. Others were bewildered by the idea that their own efforts to help Mexicanos were unappreciated. Of the two teachers portrayed here, both were sincere in their intention to help their students. The second was more successful than the first because she provided an environment that was more supportive of the students rather than forcefully imposing an Anglo environment on the students. But several other teachers observed seemed less aware of the effect of imposing Anglo culture and the English language on Mexicano children. Indeed, after months of extensive observation and discussion with local teachers, it was rare to find Anglo teachers who were actively concerned with promoting linguistic and cultural diversity. Some privately held the ideal of cultural diversity, but none were ever observed advocating or showing concern over the apparent lack of cultural materials on Mexicanos. More commonly teachers advocated the need for the schools to act as a "melting pot" or agency for Americanizing the culturally different Mexicans.

Summary and Conclusions

In short, teachers' attitudes toward their Mexicano students did differ, but very possibly none of them were as sympathetic to the culture and language of the Mexicano child as the new Chicano leaders desired. The most positive attitudes were still paternalistic and Anglo-oriented, even if sympathetic.   However, Anglo teachers, even those with the most negative attitudes, have had to change with the times. Teachers used to fail a high percentage of the first graders at the Spanish-only school, making them repeat the first grade until they learned enough English. The children became discouraged by such techniques and up to 75%

reportedly dropped out of school before finishing high school. Now because of parental pressure, teachers cannot fail so many students. Teachers no longer can prohibit the use of Spanish at school, or punish children for speaking Spanish. The most blatant forms of inequality and discrimination are gone, and the Anglo teachers of the '70's have apparently changed a great deal. Some of these changes have been forced upon them, some have sincerely tried to adapt to the new Chicano demands. From the local Chicano leaders' point of view, this "softening" of some Anglo teachers still does not represent sufficient change. They continue to seek a much more extensive bilingual-bicultural program, Chicano administrative control, a majority of Chicano teachers, and a school system that vigorously advocates their cultural traditions and that pushes Chicanos upward into higher education.

NOTES

[1]This research was sponsored under the National Institute of Education, Anthropology Panel Studies Grant. No. NE-G-00-30117. For a fuller treatment of the cultural and political change occurring in this community see: *North Town in Transition: Ethnic Relations in a South Texas Town from 1900-1975* by Douglas E. Foley and Ignacio Lozano, Clarice Mota, Donald Post, Mexican-American Studies Center, University of Texas Press, Austin (1977).

Chapter 14
The Advantaged: The Bilingual Student
Naomi Dornfeld Platt*

Introduction

Since the majority of us are either the children of or the grandchildren of immigrants, our interest in the migration of peoples to the United States should be aroused. The difficulties in coping with the educational problems raised by the newest arrivals to our metropolis are not new. Many of the immigrants remain in urban areas precisely because of the available educational opportunities. Today's minority students, as in previous times, look to educational institutions as the principal avenue of upward mobility. Cross (1971) stated that as a group, minority youth have high aspirations for a college education and that education is the pathway out of the cycle of poverty for many thousands of minority youths. Clarke (1972) agreed that because of the open admissions policy, the community college has become the most important avenue to higher education for minority group students. The urban colleges can bring to realization the educational aspirations of those students who have come to this country speaking a language other than English.

Immigration

When a person emigrates to another country, his feelings may be very strongly one directional, or they may be mixed. In the first case, he is not leaving a country as much as he is entering a new country and a new life. And in doing so, he ostensibly breaks all ties with the past. For the other person, immigration is not a permanent severing of ties. It is a temporary condition in which one enters a country, learns skills, accumulates wealth, and then either goes back to teach these skills to the people of his country of origin, or he moves on in search of new skills and new experiences. The first group seems to be more strongly committed to assimilation than the latter group. Straubenmueller (1906), Associate Superintendent of Schools, New York City, spoke of the heart of the immigrant of his day turning to the land of "limitless possibilities" in the same way as the heart of preceding generations of immigrants. Immigration then meant no turning back.

The immigrant of today who is an ethnic minority belongs more to the second category, and this is not to put a value judgment on his own attitude towards assimilation. The immigrant is neither days nor months away from his country of origin. He is only hours away by airplane and seconds away by telephone communication. There is neither the same need nor motivation nor realities for severing ties with the past. It is understandable that the immigrant today finds it much more difficult to establish an absolute commitment and allegiance to his adopted country in the same way that it would be hard to comprehend his giving up commitments and allegiance established during the early years of his childhood in his country of origin. A resultant of this situation is, however, that the modern immigrant sometimes experiences ambivalencies in attitude with either one or both comunties, and the degree of cultural disparity with the host country has an effect on psychological aspects of an immigrant's desire to assimilate (Wynar, 1975).

In the history of the immigration process, while the immigrating generation usually attempted to integrate, at least economically, into American society, it was usually the second or third generation American grouping who assimilated culturally into American society. Their first-generation elders did not (Cordasco & Bucchioni, 1972; Parenti, 1967).

Today, emphasis is being placed on understanding and helping present day immigrants to assimilate in those areas where they clearly wish to, and to help them clarify their motives in those areas where there is either ambivalency or traditional ethnic loyalties (Cordasco & Bucchioni, 1972). In discussing the process of assimilation into the American way of life, one has to question the socioeconomic striving of immigrant groups. Where an immigrant farming group from an agricultural or village environment may have spent literally a lifetime attempting to adjust to an urban lifestyle, where he finds himself at the bottom of the economic scale in the urban context (Meyers, 1974),

*Dr. Naomi Platt, Assistant Professor, Kingsborough Community College, City University of New York.

their American offspring, having it a little easier, were encouraged to think in terms of upward mobility. This meant thinking in terms of access to and success in higher education.

Clark (1970), pointed out that American colleges and universities, particularly the public and land-grant colleges, were some of the most effective instruments in facilitating the upward economic mobility of the children of immigrant groups. Concerning open admissions at the City University of New York, Clark maintains that the historic rationale established over one hundred years ago to facilitate the upward economic mobility of immigrant groups from southern and eastern Europe is being reinforced for the immigrant ethnic minority groups seeking upward mobiltiy today.

Perhaps the image of the modern immigrant is not one of "pitchfork in hand" or "bent back in a sweatshop." It nonetheless resembles these other generations in their willingness to look beyond the horizon and to pull up stakes in order to seek a new life (Jones, 1960).

The Immigrants

According to statistics published in March, 1975, the total population of the United States as of January, 1975, was close to reaching the 213 million mark, up 1.6 million from January, 1974 (U.S. Bureau of the Census, 1975). Population growth in the metropolitan areas, however, has slowed down since 1970, and while the South and the West have grown by seven percent over the five years between 1970 and 1974, the North has increased by less than two percent. This two percent increase is reflected by an increase in the number of black and other ethnic groups moving into central cities. As of 1970, within New York City, 42 percent of the population reflected people of foreign origin, 23 percent reflected blacks and other races, and 10 percent reflected the Puerto Rican population (U.S. Department of Labor, 1973b).

It is interesting to note that of the Spanish grouping, the Puerto Rican population in the United States is younger (the median age being 18) than the other groups, especially the Cuban grouping, where the median age is 34.1 years (U.S. Department of Labor, 1973a). Another interesting point is that with the influx of Puerto Rican and other Spanish speaking immigrants into urban areas and the surrounding suburbs, an increasing number of communities are, by necessity, becoming bilingual and bicultural, and in the older communities, where the old and the new have adjusted to each other, one might even see signs in store windows, "English Spoken Here" (Holsendolph, 1976).

What portion of the American population is vulnerable to the "immigrant condition?" According to Wheeler (1973), about one-third, if to the foreign born and second generation Americans are added the present non-white population. This means that about one-third of the American population is experiencing poverty, prejudice, uprooting and cultural conflict.

Of the immigrant groups from the Western Hemisphere who speak English as a second language, Puerto Ricans are by far the most numerous of the groups. As such, they have made the greatest impact of these groups on the mainland (LaGumin & Cavaioli, 1974). In fact, they are regarded by some as having emulated the roles of the Jewish and the Italian people who have come before them by retaining their rich heritage. Instead of giving up their cultural heritage in an attempt to blend in as rapidly as possible as some other immigrant groups have done, the Puerto Ricans have attempted to preserve their ethnicity by retaining their language and customs, and by creating numerous Puerto Rican clubs and associations (LaGumina & Cavaioli, 1974).

While maintaining their ethnicity has been a good thing, because it has guaranteed the transformation of a cultural heritage from one generation to another, it also has some negative ramifications. It makes moving up from a low economic strata much more difficult (Rogg, 1974). And in American society, one must acculturate in order to move up. It also affects them psychologically. Since Puerto Ricans are not so much regarded as immigrants, as they are migrants because they already are American citizens, many never feel quite at home in America (LaGumina & Cavaioli, 1974). For them, the migration process has never ended. Migration is not only an actuality; it is also a state of mind, and a state of mind does not always change, even when conditions do. To Agueros (1973), it will take leaders, like himself, trained in the university, tempered in the ghetto, to execute policies that will also change the "state of mind" condition of the Puerto Rican migrant.

The social and economic facts alone for Puerto Ricans are very discouraging and they add to the problem of assimilation. This group's annual median income in 1970 was lower than any other urban minority (U.S. Department of Labor, 1973b). This was also true in 1969 (Ryscavage & Mellor, 1973). And, according to Dinnerstein and Reimers (1975), the unemployment rate is twice as high as that of any other sector; a third of all Puerto Rican families living within the city live in poverty; and one out of every two families is receiving welfare. Concerning education, fewer Puerto Ricans complete high school or college than children of other ethnic backgrounds and more of their children in elementary school are reading below grade level than are children of other ethnic minorities. Dinnerstein and Reimers (1975) concluded that the Puerto Ricans are experiencing the same type of disabilities associated with lower class, as did poorly educated European immigrants.

The Haitians have been described as "New York's

most invisible minority" (Pousner, 1971). There has been a great influx of Haitians in the last ten years, most of them fleeing from the iron rule of their government. In terms of politics, to most of the Haitians, anything is better than Haiti (Pousner, 1971). Since about 200,000 Haitians live in the metropolitan area, it would seem that the new programs for French speaking children and the attempt of many city agencies to have French speaking personnel in areas with a heavy Haitian population are helping to ease the Haitians into the mainstream. They appear to have made a smooth transition. It also appears that the difference in immigration patterns between the Puerto Ricans and the Haitians is similar to previously stated trends. The Haitian grouping belongs to the traditional pattern of immigration where the immigrant is seen as one who is fleeing from his country for whatever reason: political, economical, or religious (Alvarez 1975). This type of immigrant seems to assimilate more quickly. The Puerto Rican, on the other hand, is usually motivated by economic factors rather than by persecutory factors, and he again, does not seem to have the same drive to assimilate rapidly.

Language

One of the first problems faced by the immigrant, aside from survival problems, deals with language. The traditional approach stressed learning English as quickly as possible in order that the rest of the process leading to Americanization could occur (Al-Khazraji & Al-Khazraji, 1969; Lambert & Tucker, 1972; Riis, 1890/1957). One would be accepted once one was Americanized. Essential in this approach is the overt discouragement of using one's native language. Children and future generations certainly were not encouraged to use this language (Ross, 1974). Since this approach is essentially a supremist one, it was soon regarded as undemocratic. The melting pot theory then emerged as better representing the American spirit (Rogg, 1974). In this theory, after a period of time for the immigrant, an American emerges combining the best ingredients of all the diverse immigrant cultures that had been "brewing" in the melting pot. This theory, however, does not really recognize "the reality and the legitimacy of the existence of ethnic groups" (Vecoli, 1970, p. 76).

A third theory, cultural pluralism, on the other hand, encourages the maintenance of ethnic differences within American society. This theory encourages ethnic clubs, public display of ethnic cultural heritage, and the retention of the native language in everyday activities. This theory reflects, to some extent, a resistance to complete assimilation. For adherents of this theory, if English is to be learned, it is for communication purposes with the majority culture and for functioning

in a monolingual school system in which instruction is presented in English; it is to be a supplement to the native language (Guerra, 1973). Some adherents of the pluralistic philosophy extend this theory to include the retention of the native language in the educational system as long as possible. This proposition has led to the creation of bilingual programs within the school system. The Federal government, acknowledging its responsibility to this philosophy, has begun to pursue a policy of bilingual language-maintenance, reinforcement, and development as a means of conserving the often neglected resources of American speakers of non-English languages (Fishman, 1967; Montoya, 1973). Ramirez (1970) stated that the resources of the bilingual students must be utilized. Up to the present, very few people have said, "You have strengths which are not being used" (p.51). In fact, the Department of Health, Education and Welfare estimates that between 1.8 and 2.5 million American children speak English so poorly that they must be taught in their native language in order for educational skills to be absorbed (Swift, 1976). State legislature, following federal directives, now require every school district to make bilingual education available upon parental request (Bilingual Schools Pass Albany Test," 1976).

Concerning the school, the community, and immigration, the school has always been viewed as a potential means of promoting the general welfare of the community. Purcell and Melican (1969) stated, "Essentially, if urban schools are to be a major vehicle of cultural assimilation for immigrant groups or for those socially bypassed, a kind of mutuality and reciprocity must be established that promotes community change and change in the school" (p. 442). Cordasco (1967) emphasized that the schools belong to the people and the schools should respond to what the people affirm and define to be their needs. As an interesting side issue now that bilingual programs are being implemented on a broad basis, some parents who have not been able to learn English are now pleading with individual school boards to teach their children in English so that the children will learn English faster (Bard, 1976)

Once bilingualism as a sound educational approach was established, it was possible again to emphasize the crucial need for becoming proficient in English. This is, retaining the native language is now an accepted given. However, alone, without a knowledge of English, cultural estrangement is an acknowledged penalty. Social intercourse between the two cultures, with a common linguistic code, in this case, English, is a must (Condon, 1969; Donahue, 1975). Once one becomes proficient in the language of the majority culture, then one can more comfortably think in terms of upward mobility. As Condon (1969) pointed out, language is a "visa on the passport of social and economic success" (p. 285). Without a proficiency in English, economic independence is very difficult to achieve in the United States.

According to the constitution of the National Association for Bilingual Education, bilingualism is committed to "the continuous use and preservation of two languages and their corresponding cultures" (Byrd, 1974, p. 40). This means that each child should become "functionally bilingual"; that is, to be able to "understand, speak, read, and write in both his first and second language effectively" (Cohen, 1975, p.263). The result emotionally for the child, as expressed at the International Bilingual-Bicultural Conference of May, 1974, will be a stronger sense of security and achievement in identifying openly and proudly with one's own cultural heritage, knowing that others of other cultural heritages are doing the same (Byrd, 1974). This had earlier been acknowledged by Gaarder (1965).

An attempt should clearly be made to keep these students in school, whether through a bilingual program or other programs for ethnic minorities who speak English as a second language, so that they can become productive and participating members of our society, instead of becoming the dropouts of the future. In addition to providing educational equality to these students, this would be an investment in the future well-being of this nation by opening new vistas and new doors for them. This approach includes, of course, retention of these students up to and including higher education. With higher education, they become a rich employment resource. Employment based on skills learned in college, to the ethnic minority, is employment which reflects upward mobility.

For the student who speaks English as a second language, one of the skills essential for upward occupational mobility based on college persistence and success, is proficiency in the English language. Al-Khazraji and Al-Khazraji (1969), pointed out that there is a relationship between the level of English mastery and occupational mobility. In general, proficiency in English has two benefits. One, a higher potential persistence rate in college; and two, more attractiveness as a job applicant. Where a native language is an ancillary to the employment criteria, retention of the native tongue is an additional asset (Fuller, 1974; Honig & Brod, 1974).

Since there is a definite connection between foreign languages and jobs, the student who speaks a language other than English as his native tongue should be made aware of the jobs that will be available to him utilizing his bilingual or multilingual skills. Because today's job market is difficult, possessing a marketable skill, plus a foreign language, may be the deciding factor in securing employment. Contrary to the assumption that jobs for language specialists are few in number and limited in scope, there are a number of jobs begging for people with language skills—but as a supplement to technical, business, or professional talents (Honig & Brod, 1974). The language should be the ancillary skill, not necessarily the primary job skill.

In a survey of American business, industry, and service organizations conducted by the Modern Language Association of America in 1972, nearly 70 percent of the respondents said they do use, could use, or expected to use people with foreign language skills. A substantial number of employers stated that given two job candidates with equal abilities in their area of specialization, they would hire the person who knows a foreign language. This need for bilingual employees applies all across the country and in American offices outside the country. Employers in areas as diverse as manufacturing, health care, government, banking, social service, technical and engineering positions, business and commerce, secretarial and clerical, financial personnel, social work, travel and tourism, hotels and motels, and transportation are begging for people with language skills as a supplement to skills and knowledge. The man or woman who is fluent in a second language has a very bright occupational future.

The student whose mother tongue is other than English whould be considered as "advantaged",whose ability should be developed to his full potential of being culturally and linguistically unique, and should be encouraged to develop and preserve intact the resource that is his background and cultural heritage.

The cities continue to be built by newcomers from other countries, speaking other languages and following different customs. The immigrant is faced with attractive alternatives of acculturation and ethnicity. "The school in America," Hillson (1969) stated, "is the major social institution that serves as the acculturation agency for the society" (p.46). Retention of a native language is a main issue related to ethnicity.

Summary

To summarize: (1) upward mobility is a common striving for ethnic minorities, including ethnic minorities who speak English as a second language; (2) education is the key to upward mobiltiy in our society; (3) education is the key to occupational mobility; (4) occupational mobility and ecomonic mobility are directly related; (5) ethnic minorities must strive for occupational mobility through educational opportunities in order to succeed; (6) the present policy of cultural pluralism towards immigrants, especially ethnic minorities, has led to an increase in ethnic pride and the establishment of bilingual and other programs which help to ease the ethnic minority into the mainstream; (7) a proficiency in English is essential for success in all levels of education and for success in employment situations; and (8) a proficiency in English leads to more comfortable socialization with Americans and a faster assimilation process.

BIBLIOGRAPHY

Agueros, J. Halfway to Dick and Jane: A Puerto Rican Pilgrimage. In T. Wheeler (Ed.), *The Immigrant Experience: The Anguish of Becoming American.* Maryland: Penguin Books, Inc., 1973.

Al-Khazraji, M., & Al-Khazraji, E. *Worcester's Spanish Speaking Residents: Dimensions in Social Adjustment.* Massachusetts: College of the Holy Cross, 1969.

Alvarez, A. N.Y.'s 'Other' Ethnics: The Haitians. *New York Post,* August 5, 1975, p. 23.

Bard, B. School in Spanish? A District Fumes. *New York Post,* February 6, 1976, p. 28A.

Bilingual Schools Pass Albany Test. *New York Post,* May 25, 1976, p. 23.

Byrd, S. Bilingual Education: Report on the International Bilingual-Bicultural Conference, May, 1974. *ADFS, Bulletin of the Association of Departments of Foreign Languages,* 1974, *6* (1), 39-41.

Clark, K.B. The Governance of Universities in the Cities of Man. *American Scholar,* 1970, *39* (4), 566-573.

Clarke, J. R. Student Personnel Work and Minority Groups. In T. O'Banion & A. Thurston (Eds.), *Student Development Programs in the Community Junior College.* New Jersey: Prentice-Hall, Inc., 1972.

Cohen, A. D. *A Sociolinguistic Approach to Bilingual Education.* Massachusetts: Newbury House Publishers, Inc., 1975.

Condon, E. C. English as a Second Language: A Bilingual Approach to a Practical Solution of the Inadequacies Found in Foreign Language Speakers and Educationally Disadvantaged Learners. In M. Hillson, F. Cordasco & F. P. Purcell (Eds.), *Education and the Urban Community.* New York: American Book Company, 1969.

Cordasco, F. The Non-English Speaking Child in the American School: Continuing Challenge to Education in a Democratic Society. *Hearings Before the General Subcommittee on Education of the Committee on Education and Labor,* House of Representatives, 90th Congress, First Session on H. R. 9840 and H. R. 10224. Washington, D. C.: U. S. Government Printing Office, 1967, pp. 262-275.

Cordasco, F. & Bucchioni, E. *The Puerto Rican Community and Its Children on the Mainland: A Source Book for Teachers, Social Workers and Other Professionals.* New Jersey: The Scarecrow Press, Inc., 1972.

Cross, K. P. *Beyond the Open Door.* California: Jossey-Bass, Inc., 1971.

Dinnerstein, L., & Reimers, D. M. *Ethnic Americans: A History of Immigration and Assimilation.* New York: Dodd, Mead & Company, 1975.

Donahue, K. "Buon Giorno" in the Bronx. *New York Teacher,* May 18, 1975, p. 17.

Fishman, J. *United States of America, Congressional Record.* Proceedings and Debates of the 90th Congress, First Session, Volume 113, Part 10, May 15, 1967 to May 24, 1967. Washington, D. C.: U. S. Government Printing Office, 1967, pp. 13747-13752.

Fuller, C. S. Language-oriented Careers in the Federal Government. *ADFL, Bulletin of the Association of Departments of Foreign Languages,* 1974, *6* (1), 45-51.

Gaarder, A. B. Teaching the Bilingual Child: Research, Development, and Policy. *The Modern Language Journal,* March, 1965, *49* (3), 165-175.

Guerra, M. H. Bilingual and Bicultural Education. In M. D. Stent, W. R. Hazard, & H. N. Rivlin (Eds.), *Cultural Pluralism in Education: A Mandate for Change.* New York: Appleton-Century-Crofts, 1973.

Hillson, M. The Reorganization of the School: Bringing About a Remission in the Problems Faced by Minority Children. In M. Hillson & F. Cordasco & F. P. Purcell (Eds.), *Education and the Urban Community.* New York: American Book Co., 1969.

Holsendolph, E. Official Urges National Assessment as Hispanic-American Population Rises Sharply. *The New York Times,* April 9, 1976, p. 13.

Honig, L. J., & Brod, R. I. Foreign Languages and Careers. *Occupational Outlook Quarterly,* 1974, *18* (4), 26-36.

Jones, M. A. *American Immigration.* Chicago: The University of Chicago Press, 1960.

LaGumina, S. J., & Cavaioli, F. J. *The Ethnic Dimension in American Society.* Boston: Holbrook Press, Inc., 1974.

Lambert, W. E., & Tucker, G. R. *Bilingual Education of Children.* Massachusetts: Newbury House, 1972.

Meyers, G. C. *Migration and the Labor Force* (U. S. Department of Labor). Washington, D. C.: Bureau of Labor Statistics, 1974.

Montoya, J. M. *United States of America, Congressional Record.* Proceedings and Debates of the 93rd Congress, First Session, Volume 119, Part 26, October 9, 1973. Washington, D. C.: U. S.

Government Printing Office, 1973, pp. 33236-33246.

Parenti, M. Ethnic Politics and the Persistence of Ethnic Identification. *The American Political Science Review*, September, 1967, *61* (3),717-726.

Pousner, M. Haitians: The Invisible Minority. *New York Daily News*, January 11, 1971, p. 32.

Purcell, F. P., & Melican, R. Politics, Social Legislation, and Education. In M. Hillson, F. Cordasco & F. P. Purcell (Eds.), *Education and Urban Community*. New York: American Book Company, 1969.

Ramirez, M. *Hearings Before the General Subcommittee on Education of the Committee on Education and Labor, House of Representatives, 91st Congress, Second Session on H. R. 14910*. A Bill to Provide a Program to Improve the Opportunity of Students in Elementary and Secondary Schools to Study Cultural Heritages of the Major Ethnic Groups in the Nation. Hearings Held in Washington, D. C., February 16, 17, 18, 24, 26; March 4, 5, 19; and May 6, 1970. Washington, D. C.: U. S. Government Printing Office, 1970.

Riis, J. A. *How the Other Half Lives*. New York: Hill and Wang, 1957. (Originally published, 1890.)

Rogg, E. M. Changing Immigration Patterns and the Schools of the Seventies. In L. H. Golubchick & B. Persky (Eds.), *Urban, Social, and Educational Issues*. Iowa: Kendall/Hunt Publishing Company, 1974.

Ryscavage, P. M., & Mellor, E. F. *The Economic Situation of Spanish Americans* (Monthly Labor Review, U. S. Department of Labor, Bureau of Labor Statistics, Volume 96, Number 4). Washington, D. C.: U. S. Government Printing Office,

April, 1973, pp. 3-9.

Senior, C. Puerto Ricans on the Mainland. *Americas, 13:* 36-43, August, 1961.

Straubenmueller, G. The Work of the New York Schools for the Immigrant Class. *Journal of Social Science*. Massachusetts: Damrell & Upham and the Boston Book Company, 1906, pp. 175-184.

Swift, P. Native Tongue. *Staten Island Advance*, April 25, 1976, p. 23.

U. S. Bureau of the Census, *Current Population Reports*, Series P-20, No. 279, "Population Profile of the United States: 1974," Washington, D. C.: U. S. Government Printing Office, 1975.

U. S. Department of Labor. *Census Data on Persons of Spanish Origin* (Monthly Labor Review, Volume 96, Number 3, Bureau of Labor Statistics). Washington, D. C.: U. S. Government Printing Office, March 1973. (a)

U.S. Department of Labor. *Diversity of New York City Described in Social and Economic Review; Puerto Rican Family Income Grows at Slower Rate Than Black or Total*. Washington, D. C.: Office of Information, May 31, 1973. (b)

Vecoli, R. J. *Ethnic Heritage Studies Centers* (U. S. Congress. House Committee on Education and Labor, H. 341-143, H. R. 14910, pp. 60-94). Washington, D. C.: U. S. Government Printing Office, 1970.

Wheeler, T. (Ed.). *The Immigrant Experience: The Anguish of Becoming American*. Maryland: Penguin Books, Inc., 1973.

Wynar, L. R. *The Encyclopedic Directory of Ethnic Organizations in the United States*. Colorado: Libraries Unlimited, Inc., 1975.

Chapter 15
Sensitizing the American Teacher to the Caribbean Student
Clement London*

In recent years, there has been a noticeable effort in operation throughout the country aimed at emphasizing cultural pluralism. Concomitantly, the development of teaching personnel as well as educational goods and resources to support this new emphasis, has also become increasingly visible.

Notwithstanding the severe criticism which proponents of this movement have had to face, the idea of a shift from the old 'melting pot theory' to a policy of an accommodation of cultural and ethnic identities, continues to find increasing support from persons, groups, and institutions alike.

Kallen (1956) is among those believers who have long felt that the dominant group in the United States culture stands to benefit from coexistence and interaction with cultures of other ethnic groups within the population. Wolfe (1967) suggests too, that the recognition of differences among peoples can serve to enrich all lives; and, he posits the view that the mission of the school should be partly one of helping prepare children for cultural diversity.

More recently, the impact of international economic and political repercussions has prompted writers such as Tildon (1972) to suggest that because of the overlapping composites of our diverse heritage, we share commonalities with the world community, and that the recognition and expression of this diversity must be seen in relation to the need for an outreach which undergirds global interdependence.

In attempting to assess the national indicators which relate to the shift towards cultural pluralism, Stent et al. (1973) observe that the United States is engaged in a social revolution which will thoroughly test her national policies and attitudes regarding human difference; and, that it signals the response to a concern which must transcend its physical boundaries and assume global proportions.

The actualization of the thrust for a culturally pluralistic society is best seen in terms of federal[1] appropriations which have been made for the promotion of bilingual-bicultural programs. Government support systems have generated a proliferation of educational goods and services in both the public and private sectors of education.

If the end product of the current trend towards cultural pluralism is assumed to be a more coping, caring, humane, literate, and dynamic society, then the facility of the school as a primary socializing institution is further legitimized. For, it is in this environment that the dynamics of the teacher-student interaction may best serve to effectuate the felt needs.

Since classroom teachers are expected to effectuate the blueprint for a literate society, then this mission should be buttressed by the provision of appropriate educational goods and services, as part of the preparation for dealing with the culturally different. Fortunately, work has already begun in this direction (Banks, 1973), but it is hoped that a corresponding momentum will be generated in the preparation of teachers, techniques, and materials for the culturally different, both within and without. For, as Brown (1963) observes, no society could hold together unless patterns of thinking, feelings, and acting are reasonably systematic and coherent, and at best, understood.

The Culturally Different Immigrant

Thousands of persons from other cultures come to the United States yearly; this is the continuation of a trend begun many decades ago. A goodly number of these immigrants belongs to the category of students who either stay on and become naturalized, or return to their homelands to become leaders. It is therefore, important that teachers and other 'significant others' who touch the lives of these students, help to prepare them for global, if not interplanetary living.

More and more, as the United States asserts her leadership in the world community, her function as a global facilitator becomes increasingly evident, as nations reach out for her technology. Part of this outreach will involve bridging gaps of social distance and discord, among social aggregations sometimes culturally different from her own.

*Dr. Clement London, Assistant Professor, School of Education, Fordham University, Lincoln Center Campus.

As one comes to understand people who live by institutions and values different from one's own, at the same time one comes to see that such people are, nevertheless, at bottom quite like one's own people. The alien culture at first appears to us as a mask, enigmatic or seemingly repugnant. On closer acquaintance we see it as a garment for the spirit; we understand its harmonies and appreciate them. Finally, as acquaintance goes deeper still, we do not see or for a time forget the culture, but look only to the common humanity of men and women beneath (Redfield, 1947).

Both teachers and students need to study the diverse and complex cultures which have developed in the Western Hemisphere, indeed the world. They need for instance, to view these cultures from a humane perspective, with respect to similarities and differences, and to regard all cultures as valid (Banks, 1975). According to Adler (1959), human beings would doubtless get along with each other better, and would approach each other more closely were they able to understnd one another better.

The Caribbean Universe:

a) *Migration*
With one of the world's highest birth rates and a declining death rate, the Caribbean region is expected to double its population by the end of the century.[2] Pressures of an expanding, increasingly urban population, have brought rising unemployment, food and fuel sacrifices, and mounting political and social anxiety among the twenty-five independent nations and territories in the Caribbean. More than three million people from the islands have migrated to the United States in the last quarter century. Still many will emigrate in the future.

The continuing influx of Caribbean immigrants within recent years is providing a concommitant inflow of students into American schools. Moreover, as the island-states gain their independence from European colonialism, the United States becomes the focal point for educational options, because there is no longer any compelling reason to patronize the educational institutions of the metropolitan 'Mother Countries.'

Also, in addition to the geographical proximity, there are other long-standing relationships of socio-economic and political proportions which tie the Caribbean to the United States. All of these factors have facilitated the flow of immigrants, and account for the large Caribbean presence here. However, despite these relationships, relatively little is known about the Caribbean and still less about the cultural background of the students who carry their own particular needs to the classroom, as they grapple with the problems of adjustment and acculturation.

b) *Geographical Considerations*
The Caribbean region is variously referred to as the 'West Indies,' 'The Islands,' or 'The Antilles.' The very name West Indies is a misnomer which arose out of confusion and ignorance. Columbus mistakenly named the region, believing it to have been the shores of the Orient which he had hoped to reach by sailing West. Today, the term Caribbean is used generally to refer to the politics now, as formerly, with the colonial system. Antilles and Caribbean are both used interchangeably.

Geographically speaking, the Caribbean archipelago forms a curved 1500-mile chain which extends from the Peninsula of Florida in North America to the Peninsula of Paria on the northeast coast of South America. (See Appendix A.) There are over twenty million people.

A West Indian then becomes an anomaly; he may be a Bahamian (the most northern dweller), or a Trinidadian (the most southern); he may be a Cuban, a Grenadian, a Chinese, an East Indian, A Puerto Rican, Frenchman, a Dutchman, an Irishman, a Jew, or an Arabian. He may be categorized from a time-place construct, or of racial, religious, or ethnic origin.

c) *Socio-cultural Considerations*
The history of the Caribbean has been marked by contact and clash, amalgamation and accommodation; even resistance to change. Within fifty years after Columbus' visit, the Spaniards had established their first bases in the Caribbean and had decimated both the native cultures and peoples of the islands—the Arawaks and Caribs (Augier, 1971).

Altogether, the region has experiences more than three hundred years of slavery,[3] colonialism, and exploitation; and it constitutes the oldest colonial sphere of Western European expansion. As slaves and immigrants arrived from Africa, Europe, India, and China, their old traditions were adapted to meet local conditions, and new ones developed, thereby creating an unusual and complex racial and ethnic combination of Amerindians, Europeans, Africans, and Asian (Horowitz, 1971). Thus, the Caribbean social history may be characterized as one of colonialism, massive migrations, plantations, and extensive use of slave and contact labor (Mintz, 1968).

One may argue that such conditions can be identified in the United States universe. However, in the case of the Caribbean, differences of habitat, economy, population, composition, political history and status are useful guides for a general understanding of the inhabitants who constitute more of a 'social area' than a 'cultural area' since its component societies probably share more social-structural features than they do cultural features. Hence, Pan-Caribbean uniformities wherever they exist, usually consist of parallels of economic and social structure and organization, the consequence of lengthy and rather rigid colonial rule (Horowitz, 1971).

The Caribbean in particular, with a few exceptions have several major characteristics of 'island ecosystems' (Fusberg, 1963). They are limited in size and stand in relative isolation. With the exception of Haiti which won its independence by revolution in 1803, all the islands have had a colonial status which reached well into the twentieth century, as well as a history of having changed hands several times. (See Appendix B.) In addition, there is the tendency towards a two-sector stratification consisting of a dominant plantocracy and subordinate agricultural proletariat (Horowitz, 1971).

Today, the rise of nationalism and cultural autonomy, the transition of many of the islands from dependent to independent status and, many unfulfilled expectations, have given the Caribbean increasing world attention.

The islands of the Caribbean contain some of the most complex societies in the world. According to Parry (1971), they are all mixed societies with unique individual distinctions of their own. Their complexities lie not in their size, degree of internal differentiation or technological development, but in the dependent and fragmented nature of their cultures, the ethnic diversity of the populations, the special nature of their dependent economies, the peculiarities of the political development, and the apparent incoherence of their social institutions (Smith, 1971).

Out of the merger of African and Asian antecedents coupled with western traditions of the colonial powers, in the very special environment, have come distinctive cultures which are neither African, Asian, or Western, but rather a synthesis of all. Within the framework of this synthesis lies the peculiarity of disparity. It is a disparity which arises among peoples strung out over more than a thousand miles of islands with such richly varied historical backgrounds and diverse cultural inheritance.

Considerations With Respect to Teaching

Considering the import of the preceding discussion, one may sense the difficulty inherent in the identification of Caribbean students, since they are likely to come in different dimensions as well as colorations and backgrounds.

A grasp of this complexity may be obtained by a careful study of a particular situation. It involves the interview (Dennis and Dennis, 1977) of a dark-skinned, green-eyed, auburn-haired Trinidadian housewife who told her American interviewers that her father is half black, half Chinese; her mother is three-quarters

English and one-quarter Spanish. Here it may be noticed that genealogy has been transferred to mathematical abstraction. But such is a 'West Indian' characteristic.

What therefore, is expected of teachers in New York City who are confronted with such a unique cultural millieu? Indeed, they have a challenge. To the degree that teachers are ignorant of patterns of cultural differences in their classrooms, they may be unable to effectively transmit instruction to learners whose cultural orientation is different from their own.

On the other hand, teachers must guard against faculty generalizations that ascribe certain cultural characteristics to all members of a given ethnic or cultural group. This would suggest that education programs designed to develop teachers who can work effectively with ethnically or culturally diverse students must grow out of theories of cultural differences as contrasted with theories of cultural difficiencies.

The need to develop intercultural sensitivity among teachers requires a focus on the differences among groups. It also requires a combined focus of patterns of cultural and individual differences. Such a combination is more effective than either component alone because it works to lessen invalid stereo-typing and develop a generic sensitivity to the cultural orientations of each child.

Button (1977) argues that teachers who possess a generic cultural sensitivity have the ability to detect potential cultural differences. Sensitivity of this nature helps alleviate the problem that teachers cannot become knowledgeable about all the potential points of cultural conflict among all the students they are likely to teach in the future. Teachers with this kind of sensitivity should be able to 'cue' into, get information about, and develop understandings of, familiar and unfamiliar sources of cultural conflict.

Thus, characteristics may or may not grow out of cultural differences and would include the learner's cognitive styles, learning skills, values, and preferred means of participation and communication.

Problems of culture shock which results from sudden removal from the Caribbean to an unknown and sometimes unfamiliar environment may often cause a student to respond in the classroom situation by being withdrawn and uncommunicative. Or, alternately, a student may act out aggressively. These are both well-known human reactions to being upset, to bewilderment or dislocation. And quite frequently, these kinds of behavior patterns are misunderstood as being permanent disturbance factors.

Ginott (1972) answers his own question: Where do we start if we are to improve life in the classroom? by suggesting that teachers should examine how they respond to students; because it is indeed, how a **teacher** communicates which is of decisive importance. This affects a student's life for good or bad. Ginott observes that usually while teachers are not overly concerned about whether their response conveys acceptance or rejection, yet to a student, this difference is fateful or fatal.

Part of a teacher's response to his/her students must focus on those unique non-verbal communicative vibrations which students radiate. A non-verbal symbol stands for a complex and diffuse type of experience which is emotional, cognitive, and conative. While words tend to represent consciously articulated mental states, the evocative power of non-verbal symbols stretches beyond consciousness into the unconsciousness. The specific function of non-verbal symbols is to articulate what cannot be normally articulated by words or by language in general.

In the teaching-learning relationship, the student's personality must become a serious consideration in his unique adjustment to his environment. Thus, what a teacher needs to know and do in the classroom, go far beyond responses and the teaching of his/her subject. A teacher needs to unlearn habitual language of rejection and acquire a new language of acceptance. Perhaps instead of blaming, shaming, preaching, moralizing, admonishing and accusing, ridiculing and belittling, threatening and bribing, diagnosing and promising which brutalize, vulgarize, and dehumanize, teachers should be about engendering trust through identification and application (Ginott, 1972).

A critic can always argue that a student, no matter what his cultural background, and given a certain amount of intelligence, will in time become oriented to American cultural nuances. The chances of this happening are usually enhanced by his youth. However, the process of acculturation must be gradual and structured. It should never be hastened and erratic, since this can have a deleterious, psychological impact on the individual.

The real value of a Caribbean student's orientation to the American mode lies in the success derived for the blending of all levels of communication, of the spoken word with whatever else is transmitted on the vocal wave length, with visual, language, (including body language) and self-imagery.

There is a sense in which the teacher-student relationship must generate sustenance from a spirit of reciprocity. From a teachers' point of view, there must be a willingness to deal realistically with students' cultural nuances, agreeing not to treat them as the butt of silly jest. It is not even necessary for a teacher to invest his political philosophy, nor abandon it in the process. He is asked only to become aware of others, if

they exist.

Beyond this factor lies the more profound issue of the teacher's own personality. His body language, tone of voice, allotment of speaking time to students who have the 'desired' speech pattern will indicate to all just where their teacher stands. What he says is as important as what he does not say, but does. The style of the teacher is an important factor.

But a teacher cannot be at peace or in harmony with his students until he is at peace with himself. Therefore, any method that is conceptualized for and used in, the domain of the classroom should have truth as its basis. The essence of truth is within ourselves; its use can only help to facilitate ourselves. It can better help to facilitate the process of education.

Becoming aware of the self and others in terms of human variations, needs, abilities, goals, and aspiration is of paramount importance for both teacher and student who, thrown together by educational circumstances, must establish rational relationships of understanding, as viable support systems of the teaching-learning act.

One may conclude that since studies of families in far away places have had their counterpart in the growing literature on the family among different ethnic, racial, and religious goups within American society (Jennings, 1974), then whatever set of sensitivities a teacher brings to bear on his/her interactions with students in general, will suffice for the Caribbean student. However, considering the peculiarities of the Caribbean student's unique background, the New York teacher will require other sensitizing support systems.

The New York teacher of the Caribbean student will require among other things, a sense of Caribbean history; a sensitivity towards the student's background, values, culture patterns, his environment, and specific influences which impinge upon him. He will require an understanding, that the Caribbean student's penchant for education has a basis respecting his unsung determination to satisfy personal and parental aspirations which emanate from a desire to both 'make it' and to please.

The New York teacher requires a sensitivity to non-American phenomena; that the Caribbean student's speech as well as his identity is not incorrect; it is only different. His spelling may be British oriented; in time he will adapt to the American mode. Be reminded that the Caribbean student has difficulty understanding his American teacher; do not therefore, add to his confusion and culture shock by hastening to Americanize him immediately, or to slip into the tendency to stereotype and denigrate the student's historic and cultural background (Wiggins, 1962).

A teacher needs to look beyond the immediacy of

the student. Get to know his student's parents by involving them in the endeavors of the school. Invite them as speakers, resource persons, or helpers in the school's educational operation. Demonstrate positive attitudes towards, and maintain high expectancies of the student.

A New York teacher will need to show a sensitivity towards the vicious impact of slavery, its attendant evils of discrimination, bigotry, and poverty, and the student's need to break out of the cycle of dependence and restrictions which have served to characterize life in his familiar parochial setting.

A teacher should avoid pre-conceived notions about a student's ability; he should not confuse learning styles with learning disability. Being different does not necessarily mean being difficult or disadvantaged. A teacher should be sensitive to the incidence of culture shock and culture conflict experienced by a student who attempts to maintain the old while embracing a new culture. Such a student should be helped to actualize the transition which is often fraught with inconsistencies and difficulties for him.

A New York teacher should show a sensitivity towards the reality of differences within and among groups of Caribbean students, in much the same way as one recognizes and deals with dominant American groups. Challenging stereotypes and respecting individuality among all students are moral stances.

It is acknowledged that all of these suggestions may be quite difficult, though not impossible to actualize. The difficulty may be compounded by such intangible factors as religious beliefs and practices, in addition to concerns of aesthetic styles, folklore, family structures, food, and clothing preferences. The New York teacher will therefore need, in addition to the above a demonstration of sensitivities which are indicative of good, positive, and warm human relationship techniques.

Without doubt, the New York City teacher is being asked to demonstrate an unusual kind of sensitivity towards the Caribbean student. The development of this kind of sensitivity depends very much upon the teacher's knowledge of the environment in which the student has lived or now lives, the social forces which impinge upon him with his life space: that is, the nature of his family life, and the important events in the history of his people; his racial, ethnic, economic, or socio-cultural group.

The demonstration of this sensitivity should constitute a part of the resourcefulness of the humanistic teacher, a resourcefulness which requires that the teacher respect each student as a unique human being, and with more potential than is evident (Patterson, 1973).

But there are needs that are common to all students

regardless of age, social class, race, religion, or national origin. The truth is that everyone wants to be accepted, to feel wanted, to develop a sense of belongingness; to achieve, to risk failure and experience success.

It is these commonalities which provide the underpinnings for some broad-based concerns about peoples and cultures. In this regard, they may serve as guidelines or reminders to teachers that they should be aware of stereotyped views of Caribbean students. The difficulty about stereotypes is that whether favorable or unfavorable, they are exaggerated beliefs associated with categories which may or may not apply to a particular individual.

Thus, a teacher should be able to see the common humanity of students amidst cultural diversities in the classroom, and to recognize that despite real cultural differences, students everywhere have a common humanity in their basic motivations and desires. This recognition should help a teacher to understand reversals of behavior. For instance, an American child sticks out his tongue to show defiance, while some Caribbean children do so to show simple disappointment.

A teacher should also recognize different scales of values in non-American social settings, for although many values are universals and cut across cultural lines, there are fundamental differences in value systems. It is important for one to distinguish, for example, between a statement of fact and a value judgment. A teacher must be careful not to be ethnocentric in judging a culture only according to an American scale of values or frame of reference. While an American family may consider a nursing home the ideal place for one of its senior members to spend his declining years, its Caribbean counterpart may, on the contrary, see the home base as the appropriate place instead.

Moreover, a teacher should develop empathy and concern for all students, and see education as part of a process of continuously extending both empathy and understanding in time and place. The discernment of unique relationships should serve to foster better acquaintances with students in all of their diversities, and thus help to reduce ethnocentricism and academic provincialism.

What is really needed is humanistic psychology expressly designed to deal with human aspects of personality and behavior, a psychology which does not ignore the student's belief systems, but makes them central to its concerns (Combs, 1972). Respect for the individual student should encompass all aspects of the democratic faith and process. Other critical concerns such as attitudinal, emotional, physical, and behavioral changes need to be maximized in teacher-training programs be they pre-service or in-service (Gazda, et al., 1977).

When a teacher has the ability to understand his students, has a sensitive awareness of the way the process of education and learning seems to him, then the likelihood of significant learning is increased (Rogers, 1969). A supportive understanding environment will serve to remove those causes of external threats, and thus permit a student to make due progress.

Learning to live together must depend to some degree, on the classroom climate which a teacher establishes for his students in their culturally pluralistic environment. In addition, a teacher must demonstrate that he is committed to the value, worth, respect, and dignity of every child in his classroom, regardless of his dedication or not, to issues of civil rights.

How a teacher acts out his feelings, beliefs, values and expectations, will set the pattern for his students. As he actualizes the tenets of intergroup relationships, he becomes a role model which his students pattern as they themselves learn to get along together. Of course,

these ideals do make many exacting demands on the teacher. They demand of him, for example, that he confront himself with respect to his own private attitudes and values. He may be forced to relinquish long-held myths and stereotypes, for truths about people. Students may even require of the teacher that he demystify himself and his mission in the classroom; to see himself in a reciprocal relationship with his students.

The multi-cultural classroom, such as that which the students of the Caribbean will constitute, confronts the New York City school teacher with the fact that people have certain similar needs, and that different societies develop culture differences as they try to satisfy these needs; that in his effort to develop healthy attitudes towards people, he should utilize a sensitivity which moves him from the level of 'tolerating differences' to one of seeing human differences as natural, desirable, and above all, providing no hindrances to educational growth and development.

Anthony Malave

POPULATION OF THE WEST INDIES*

COUNTRY	AREA (Sq. miles)	POPULATION
Jamaica	4,411	1,893,000 (1967 est.)
Trinidad and Tobago	1,978	1,010,100 (1967 est.)
Trinidad	1,864	
Tobago	116	
Barbados	166	248,161 (1966 est.)
Grenada	120	92,000 (1965)
St. Vincent	133	87,000 (1965)
St. Lucia	233	94,000 (1965)
Dominica	305	67,000 (1965)
Montserrat	39	13,000 (1965)
Antigua	108	60,000 (1965)
Barbuda	62	1,200 (approx.)
St. Kitts	68	38,300 (1960)
Nevis	36	12,700 (1960)
Anguilla	35	5,500 (1960)
Martinique	425	290,000 (1965)
Guadeloupe	583	316,000
Netherland Antilles	366 (Curacao, 173)	202,000 (1963)
Tortola, BVI	24	6,200
Bahamas	5,380	138,107 (1965)
Cuba	44,164	7,200,000 (1963)
Hispaniola (total)	29,525	7,780,000 (1963)
Haiti	10,714	4,450,000 (1963)
Dominican Republic	18,811	3,330,000 (1963)
Puerto Rico	3,435	2,520,000 (1963)
Belize (Br. Honduras)	8,867	106,000 (1965)
Guyana	83,000	638,000 (1964)

*Adapted from Michael Horowitz, ed. *Peoples and Cultures of the Caribbean*, Garden City, New York: The Natural Press, 1971, p. 4.

(Appendix B)

EUROPEAN COLONIAL OWNERSHIP OF THE WEST INDIES BETWEEN 1623-1814*

YEARS OF OWNERSHIP	CUBA	ST. KITTS	BARBADOS	NEVIS	ANTIGUA	MONTSERRAT	ST. LUCIA	JAMAICA	VIRGIN IS.	ST. DOMINIQUE	DOMINICA	GRENADA	ST VINCENT	TOBAGO	MARTINIQUE	GUADELOUPE	TRINIDAD	DEMERARA	ESSEQUIBO	BERBICE
1623	S	E						S		S							S	D	D	D
1624	S	E	E					S		S							S	D	D	D
1625	S	fe	E					S		S							S	D	D	D
1628	S	fe	E	E				S		S							S	D	D	D
1632	S	fe	E	E	E	E		S	Buccaneers	S							S	D	D	D
1639	S	fe	E	E	E	E	E	S	Buccaneers	S							S	D	D	D
1641	S	fe	E	E	E	E		S	Buccaneers	S							S	D	D	D
1650	S	ef	E	E	E	E	F	S	Dutch	S		F			F	F	S	D	D	D
1655	S	ef	E	E	E	E	F	E	Dutch	S		F			F	F	S	D	D	D
1664	S	ef	E	E	E	E	E	E	Dutch	S		F			F	F	S	D	D	D
1666	S	ef	E	E	E	E	F	E	E	S		F			F	F	S	D	D	D
1713	S	E	E	E	E	E	F	E	E	es		F			F	F	S	D	D	D
1759	S	E	E	E	E	E	F	E	E	es	E	F			F	F	S	D	D	D
1762	S	E	E	E	E	E	F	E	E	es	E	E			F	F	S	D	D	D
1763	S	E	E	E	E	E	F	E	E	es	E	E	E	E	F	F	S	D	D	D
1778	S	E	E	E	E	E	E	E	E	es	F	E	E	F	F	F	S	D	D	D
1779	S	E	E	E	E	E	E	E	E	es	F	F	F	F	F	F	S	D	D	D
1780	S	E	E	E	E	E	E	E	E	es	F	F	F	F	F	F	S	D	D	D
1782	S	F	E	E	E	E	E	E	E	es	F	F	F	F	F	F	S	D	D	D
1783	S	E	E	E	E	E	F	E	E	es	E	E	E	F	F	F	S	D	D	D
1793	S	E	E	E	E	E	F	E	E	es	E	E	E	E	F	F	S	D	D	D
1794	S	E	E	E	E	E	E	E	E	es	E	E	E	E	E	E	S	D	D	D
1794	S	E	E	E	E	E	E	E	E	es	E	E	E	E	E	F	S	D	D	D
1795	S	E	E	E	E	E	E	E	E	es	F	F	F	E	E	F	S	D	D	D
1796	S	E	E	E	E	E	E	E	E	F	E	E	E	E	E	F	S	D	D	D
1797	S	E	E	E	E	E	E	E	E	F	E	E	E	E	E	F	E	D	D	D
1801	S	E	E	E	E	E	E	E	E	F	E	E	E	E	E	F	E	D	D	D
1802	S	E	E	E	E	E	E	E	E	F	E	E	E	E	F	F	E	D	D	D
1803	S	E	E	E	E	E	E	E	E	F	E	E	E	E	F	F	E	E	E	E
1804	S	E	E	E	E	E	E	E	E		E	E	E	E	F	F	E	E	E	E
1807	S	E	E	E	E	E	E	E	E		E	E	E	E	F	F	E	E	E	E
1808	S	E	E	E	E	E	E	E	E	Haiti	E	E	E	E	F	F	E	E	E	E
1809	S	E	E	E	E	E	E	E	E	Haiti	E	E	E	E	E	F	E	E	E	E
1810	S	E	E	E	E	E	E	E	E	Haiti	E	E	E	E	E	E	E	E	E	E
1814	S	E	E	E	E	E	E	E	E	Haiti	E	E	E	E	E	E	E	E	E	E

Legend: S:SPANISH   E:ENGLISH   F:FRENCH   D:DUTCH

*Adapted from F.R. Augier and S.C. Gordon, *The Making of the West Indies.* London: Longmans, Green and Co., Ltd., 1964, p. 100.

FOOTNOTES

[1]See the Bilingual Education Act, Title VII of ESEA, 1968. Sponsored by Senator Yarborough of Texas in 1967.

[2]See Ford Foundation *Letter,* Volume 7, No. 6, December 1, 1976.

[3]In the Anglo-Caribbean colonies, slavery was abolished by Britain in 1834; France and Denmark in 1848; the Netherlands in 1863; Puerto Rico in 1873; and Cuba in 1880 (Mintz, 1968).

REFERENCES

Alder, A. Understanding *Human Nature*. New York: Premier Books, 1959.

Augier, F. R., & Gordon, S. C. *Sources of West Indian History*. Bristol, England: Western Printing Services Ltd., 1971.

Banks, J. D. (ed.) *Teaching Ethnic Studies*. Washington, D.C.: N.C.S.S., 43rd. Yearbook, 1973.
, *Teaching Strategies for Ethnic Studies*. Boston; Allyn and Bacon, Inc., 1975.

Brown, I. C. *Understanding Other Cultures*. Englewood Cliffs, New Jersey: Prentice-Hall, Inc., 1963.

Button, C. B. "Teaching for Individual and Cultural Differences." *Education Leadership*. 1977, *34*, 435-438.

Combs, A. W. *Educational Accountability*. Washington D.C.: ASCD, 1972.

Dennis, L., and Dennis L. "Trinidad and Tobago: A Nibbler's Paradise." *Essence Magazine*. 1977, *7*.

Fushberg, F. R. (ed.) *Man's Place in the Island Ecosystem*. Honolulu: Bishop Museum Press, 1963.

Gazda, G. M., etal al. *Human Relations Development*. 2nd ed., Boston, Mass.: Allyn and Bacon, 1977.

Ginott H. *Teacher and Child*. New York: The Macmillan Company, 1972.

Horowitz, M. (ed.) *Peoples and Cultures of the Caribbean*. Garden City, New York: The Natural History Press, 1971.

Jennings, F. G. *Teachers College Record*. 1974, *76*.

Kallen, M. H. *Cultural Pluralism and the American Idea*. Philadelphia: University of Pennsylvania Press, 1956.

Mintz, S. W. "Comments on the Socio-Historical Background of Pidginization and Creolization." Unpublished paper. Proceedings of a conference held at the University of the West Indies; April, 1968.

Parry, J. H., and Sherlock, P.M. *A Short History of the West Indies*. London: The Macmillan Press Ltd., 1971 (3rd edition).

Patterson, C. H. *Humanistic Education*. New Jersey: Prentice-Hall, Inc., 1973.

Redfield, R. "The Study of Culture in General Education." *Social Education*. 1947, *11*.

Rogers, C. R. *Freedom to Learn*. Columbus, Ohio: Charles E. Merrill Publishing Company, 1969.

Smith, M. G. *The West Indian Family Structure*. Seattle, Washington: University of Washington Press, 1962.

Smith M. G. *The Plural Society of the British West Indies*. Berkeley, California: University of California Press, 1965.

Stent, M. D., Hazard, W. R., and Rivlin, H. N., (eds.) *Cultural Pluralism in Education: A Mandate for Change*. New York: Appleton, Century - Crafts, 1973.

Tildon, T. J. *The Anglo Saxon Argony*. Philadelphia: Whitmore Publishing Company, 1972, *13*, 195-196.

Wiggins, G. A. *Education and Nationalism*. New York: McGraw-Hill, Book Company, 1962.

Wolfe, A. G. *Differences Can Enrich Our Lives: Helping Children to Prepare for Cultural Diversity*. New York: Public Affairs Committee, Inc., 1967.

Chapter 16
Reflections on the Italian-American Community
Stephen R. Aiello*

The Italian-American experience in the United States has been and continues to be diverse. The different kinds of people and the variety of materials which describe this experience, are themselves equally diverse and record the fortunes and vicissitudes of millions of Italians who were and are part of the great migrations to America. (Iorizzo and Mondello, 1971, p. 22).

The Italian emigration of modern times is one of the great mass migrations of a people; in size, in the multiplicity of its destinations, and in the complexity of the forces which brought it into being. It has been estimated that no fewer that 26 million Italians emigrated between *1861 and 1970*, and that since 1900, more that 10 million Italians have permanently left their country (Bucchioni and Cordasco, 1974, p. 3).

Italians migrating to the United States came mostly from southern Italy and Sicily. The official Italian statistics report that over five million Italians migrated to the United States between 1876-1930, and that 80 percent of the total were southerners (Tomasi, 1975, pp. 16 and 17).

The regional origin of southern immigrants indicates the predominance of Sicilians. In fact, over 27 percent came from Campavria, an area around Naples; 16 percent from Abruzzi and Molise; 7 percent from Apulia; 5 percent from Basilicata; 13 percent from Calabria; 29 percent from Sicily; and about 0.6 percent from Sardinia (Tomasi, pp. 17-18).

About 15 percent of all immigrants arriving from Italy between 1899 and 1910 had been in the United States previously. Because of this, the Italians became known as "birds of passage" in the New World. They were slow to sink their roots in any foreign soil. This indecision to settle permanently affected the development of organized life in the immigrant community. If America was only a temporary place or work and quick enrichment, it was perfectly normal for the immigrant to concentrate on economic profits rather than on his future place in American Society (Tomasi, pp. 20-21).

Although most Italian immigrants came from regions with agriculture as their main industry, they settled in urban centers concentrating in North Atlantic

States. Between 1900-1910, over 76 percent settled in the North Atlantic area; over 11 percent in the north central area; over 2 percent in the South Atlantic area; over 2 percent in the south central area; over 7 percent in the western area; and about .03 percent in Alaska, Hawaii, Puerto Rico and the Philippines (Tomasi, pp. 28-29).

It is these immigrants and their children, of whom I am one, that I present in this paper. To begin with, we are Italo-Americans and our history begins at Ellis Island - not in Ancient Rome, Renaissance Florence, or modern day Italy. Do not misunderstand me, Italo-Americans are proud to be the descendents of a rich Italian heritage and culture. However, our true, living history and experience is the one which has been forged by the American experience upon the Italian community.

In attempting to understand the concerns, fears, problems and hopes of the Italo-American community, one should keep in mind what Dr. Francis Arricale, Executive Director of Personnel, New York City Board of Education, calls the four A's - *Awareness, Ache, Anger* and *Affirmation*.

At present, the United States is experiencing a period of history, marked by a resurgence of ethnicity as a major component of its political, social and economic development (Novak, 1972). Until recently, this resurgence, especially as it characterizes the Italo-American community, was ignored by both historians and sociologists. In the last few years, however, the impact of ethnicity on everyday life has been so great that academicians, policy-makers, and agency personnel have been forced to recognize it, especially in terms of jobs, language and neighborhood stability.

Dr. Michael Novak has written in his book, *The Rise of the Unmeltable Ethnics*, (1972), "The new ethnicity is not a reduction of consciousness to an uncritical stage but the acquisition of a new competence in consciousness: A multicultural consciousness." It favors the development of a pluralistic personality. The

*Stephen Aiello, President, Board of Education, New York City.

pluralistic personality does not pretend to be universal; neither does it accept being stereotyped or limited to the resources of one cultural history only. Rather, the pluralistic personality recognizes its own roots, draws consciously from its own resources, and tries to become skilled both in self-knowledge and in the accurate perception of those with different roots (p. 48).

For members of the Italo-American community, this new awareness has and continues to have profound effects. For too many years, many newcomers to this land have become victims of *the Teutonic myth:* A belief in the racial superiority of Nordic peoples.

The United States, one would think, would be a most fertile culture favoring the development of cultural pluralism. However, many leaders of our country were so fearful and paranoic of division and so suspicious of "foreigners" that before granting American citizenship they expected the immigrant to be *molded* and *converted* totally to fit the White Anglo-Saxon Protestant model.

This philosophy and practice of discouraging immigrants and their children from retaining foreign languages and ties with foreign cultures was based upon a philosophy of racial *superiority.*

As Mondello and Iorizzo write in *"The Italian-Americans"*, "Physical hardships, nativist prejudice, and even an occasional lynching party in Louisiana, Mississippi, and Colorado greeted the southern Italian immigrant."

A New York City newspaper in the early 1900's expressed a not untypical view of the Italian immigrants:

"The flood gates are open. The bars are down. The sallyports are unguarded. The dam is washed away. The sewer is choked. Europe is vomiting: In other words, the scum of immigration is viscerating upon our shores. The horde of steerage slime is being siphoned upon us from continental mud tanks" (La Gumina, 1973, p. 221).

This racist philosophy was more clearly developed in 1916 in Madison Grant's book, *The Passing of the Great Race.* In this book, *Grant,* flaunting the imposing designations of chairman of the New York Zoological Society, Trustee of the American Museum of Natural History, and Councilor of the American Geographical Society, *didactically* asserted that the Nordics are supermen of the earth, and that races drawn from the lowest stratum of the Mediterranean basin and the Balkans were "human flotsam and the whole tone of American life, *social, moral* and *political* has been lowered and vulgarized by them" (Musmanno, 1965, p. 97).

This type of thinking and its resultant attitudes helped the Congress to pass the Johnson-Reed Immigration Law of 1924 supported by theories and implemented through restrictive quotas based on national origin.

The effects of this and other forms of institutional racism have been devastating for both the society at large and the individual. The hate, shame, and denial of one's heritage, parents and staff continue to have negative consequences for our society.

Thus, the ethnic *awareness* that is stirring in the United States has before it an important intellectual agenda. It gives promise of a new, true cultural pluralism.

As Professor Salvatore La Gumina (1973) states in his book, *"WOP; A History of Discrimination Against the Italian Americans"*, the *"awareness of recent years has more clearly focused on the ever present Ache of most thinking Italians".*

Italo-Americans feel that ache when they experience the continuing use of negative stereotypes and discrimination by the society at large. As the great Luigi Pirandello has written, "Look, I wouldn't like to commit an outrage, but I also wouldn't like others to commit an outrage and make use of me."

Writing in the 1969 issue of *"The American Scholar"*, Michael Lerner examined the bigotry towards Italian-Americans fashionable among upper class liberals. His points are telling:

"An extraordinary amount of bigotry on the part of elite liberal students goes unexamined. Directed at the lower middle class, it feeds on the biases of class perspective, the personality predilections of elite radicals and academic disciplines that support their views. Poles, Italians and others are safe objects for amusement, derision or hatred" (p. 223).

Italo-Americans are sick and tired of being seen as *bums, bigots,* or *buffoons.* Community leaders have instituted law suits and brought economic and moral pressures against those individuals and organizations which continue to discriminate against Italo-Americans.

Two areas where such discriminatory actions were commonplace are *social services* and *education.*

Recently, the Congress of Italian American Organizations released a study on the Italian-American community of New York City. One important aspect of this study related to the needs of the Italo-American poor and elderly. The study came as a shock to many people who *heretofore* believed that all Italians owned two-family homes, had good incomes, and needed little from the society at large. Let's consider some of CIAO's findings:

1. There are over 400,000 Italian poor in New York City alone.
2. Over 6 percent of Italian families survive on

$4,000 income per annum.

3. 3.9 percent have incomes between $4,000 - $7,000 per annum.

4. 24.9 percent have incomes of less than $10,000 per annum.

In other words, 53.4 percent of Italo-Americans in New York City are below the $10,000 income level. Until *very recently*, Italo-Americans were expected to survive on pride, endurance and just plain guts.

Let us now examine the area of education. The *New York Times*, April 12, 1970, issued a very disturbing report. Based upon research, a well-known non Italian educator stated that our school system was "failing not only for black and Puerto Rican children, but for white children as well". There were enough statistics to warrant serious investigation. However, nothing was done to follow up on the statistics as they pertained to the white students. Let us consider further the *educational system* and the Italo-American community.

As Richard Gambino (1975) points out in his book *"Blood of My Blood,"* The statistics of formal education of Italian Americans are both appalling and hopeful." They are appalling if one considers that except for Hispanic-Americans, Italo-Americans have scored the *lowest* in every category of educational accomplishment of all groups of European origin.

1. Of those over 35 years old, only 5.9 percent completed four years of college.

2. Of this age group, only 27.6 percent completed high school.

However, when one looks at the age group of those 25-34 years old, one sees the second highest 50.4 percent—amont those who have completed high school.

The statistics are hopeful in that during the last five years there has been an increase of those completing high school and going on to four year colleges (pp. 223-225).

However, many leading Italo-American educators think that the educational system must become more aware and sensitive to the needs of the Italo-American community; specifically in the area of bilingual-bicultural education.

Since 1965, with the repeal of the Johnson-Reed Law of 1924, over 20,000 Italian immigrants enter the United States annually (Tomasi, 35-37). In June 1973, the New York State Board of Regents described the plight of the non-English speaking student in this way, "Differences in language and culture effectively exclude about 300,000 students from meaningful participation in our educational system. Failure of schools to respond to the educational needs of these children results in academic failure, low reading scores, high drop-out rates and barriers to meaningful employment.

In July 1974, after almost 10 years of concerted organized and often frustrated efforts, the first Federal Title VII funds for Italian Bilingual Education were granted to New York City school districts.

This along with other educational programs, such as increased guidance services and Italian studies, which have only recently begun to surface for Italo-American school children, must become concrete realities.

Therefore, the *awareness*, *ache*, and *anger* can lead to one of two paths. We either deteriorate into a negative, devisive ethnocentrism or to a positive cultural pluralism based upon the dignity of each individual, pride and self-worth.

The aim, therefore, is unitive, not devisive; creative, not destruction; multicultural, not chauvinistic and a positive affirmation based upon a *real* cultural pluralism.

BIBLIOGRAPHY

Association of the Italian-American Faculty of the City University of New York. *Status of Italian-Americans in the City University of New York*. New York: Association of the Italian-American Faculty of the City University of New York, 1974.

Campisi, Paul, "Ethnic Family Patterns: The Italian Family in the United States," *American Journal of Sociology*, Vol. 53.

Casalena, Josephine, *A Portrait of the Italian-American Community in New York City*. New York: Congress of Italian-American Organizations, 1975.

Cordasco, Francesco and Eugene Bucchioni, Eds. *The Italians: Social Backgrounds of An American Group*, Clifton, New Jersey.

Covello, Leonard, *The Social Background of the Italo-American School Child*. Leiden: E. J. Brill, 1967.

DeConde, Alexander, *Half Bitter and Half Sweet*, New York: Scribners, 1971.

DiDonato, Pietro, *Christ in Concrete*. New York, 1939.

Gambino, Richard, *Blood of My Blood: The Dilemma of the Italian-Americans*. New York: Doubleday 1974.

Iorizzo, Louis and Salvatore Mondello, *The Italian-Americans*. New York: Twayne Publishers, 1971.
 .*WOP: A Documented History of Anti-Italian Discrimination in the United States*. San Francisco: Straight Arrow Books, 1973.

Musmanno, Michael, *The Story of Italians in America*. New York: Doubleday, 1965.

Novak, Michael, *The Rise of the Unmeltable Ethnics: The New Political Force of the Seventies*. New York Macmillan Company, 1972.

Patri, Angelo, *A School Master in the Great City*. New York: The Macmillan Company, 1917.

Pileggi, Nicholas, "Little Italy: Study of An Italian Ghetto," *New York Magazine*, Vol. I, August 12, 1968.

Rolle, Andrew, *The American-Italians: Their History and Culture*. Belmont, Calif.: Wadsworth Pub-lishing Company, 1972.

——.*Piety and Power: The Role of Italian Parishes in the New York Metropolitan Area (1880-1930)*. New York: Center for Migration Studies, 1975.

Tomasi, Silvano and M. Engels, Eds. *The Italian Experience in the United States*. New York: Center for Migration Studies, 1971.

Chapter 17
American Jews: Their Culture and Language
Perry Davis*

The Jews who fled their birthplace to settle in America did so for many reasons. For the most part, they sought a better life and an end to the oppression and hatred that had stifled their minds and souls. Once in America they found freedom and generously repaid the nation by molding its spirit and shaping its dreams. In all these aspects the Jews who came to America were quite similar to all other immigrant groups.

On the other hand, the Jews were unique because they came not from their homeland. Over a thousand years before they arrived in America the Jews had been forcibly scattered throughout the globe. And it was from the four corners of the world that they came to America. Their native languages differed as did their cultures and their Diaspora traditions. At the same time they were all Jews with a common ethno-religious heritage. They believed in the same God and the same scripture, they celebrated the same holy days. They shared a common heritage of pride but also of suffering and discrimination. In many cases they had one or even two common "Jewish" languages—Hebrew and Yiddish. And finally while some came to America to forget their Jewish roots, most shared an ardent desire—to survive not only as individuals but to survive additionally as a Jewish people. They succeeded, and Americans should be thankful for that success.

The Colonial Period of Jewish Immigration (1654-1815)

1492 was the year that Columbus discovered the "new world." It was also the year that the Jews of Spain were forcibly expelled from that country by the Monarchy. These Spanish, or Sephardic Jews, settled throughout the world and in 1631 a group of the descendants of these Jews settled in Recife Brazil—then a Dutch colony. When the Portuguese recaptured the colony in 1654 they expelled these Jews and 23 of them fled to New Amsterdam (New York).

These 23 Jews petitioned for the right to practice their religion and, at the same time, to act as full citizens of the Dutch colony in America—to own property, trade and set up a synagogue. Governor Peter Stuyvesant, under intense pressure, granted these

rights (except the synagogue) and thus set a precedent for religious freedom in America.

When the British replaced the Dutch in America, Jewish rights were continued. The early settlers flourished and new Jews arrived from western Europe. Now synagogues were built and fledgling Jewish communities sprang up in Newport, Rhode Island, Charleston, South Carolina and Lancaster, Pennsylvania. The synagogue became the center of life where Jews prayed, celebrated, mourned, cared for their needy and taught themselves the language of the country.

By the time the Liberty Bell was cast and inscribed with a verse from the Hebrew scriptures, there were 2,500 Jews in the 13 colonies. Their European experience helped them become successful merchants, shippers and manufacturers. During the Revolutionary War they were almost unanimous in their support of the patriot cause. They fought with Washington and Jews like Haym Salomon helped finance the war effort. Salomon later became an official of the Office of Finance of the United States.[1] Another Jew—Uriah Philips Levy was a naval officer and hero of the War of 1812.[2]

Most of the Jews in America at the start of the 19th century were *Ashkenazim* (from France, Germany and Eastern Europe). The Sephardim had come first and were the dominant group. This changed during the next wave of immigration.

The Period of German-Jewish Immigration (1848-1881)

In the first half of the 19th century, Jews in Germany and Austria-Hungary lived under the most intolerable conditions. They were herded together in cramped ghettos, land ownership was prohibited, and they were

*Dr. Perry Davis, Senior Special Assistant to the President, N.Y.C. Board of Education. Formerly Assistant to N.Y.C. Mayor John V. Lindsay.

barred from colleges and even restricted from marrying in order to keep their birthrate low. By the time of revolutions of 1848, Jews were being physically attacked. General economic conditions worsened and the retail businesses of the Jews failed.

The promise of land and jobs brought thousands of these Western European Jews to America. In 1830 there were 6,000 Jews in America. By 1840 the number jumped to 16,000. By 1860 the Jewish population had risen remarkably to 150,000 and then 250,000 by 1880. In 1860 there were 77 sizable synagogue congregations in this country.

The German-Jewish immigrants face acculturation and language problems when they arrived in America. Some sought to establish an agrarian community in Sholem, New York—but they failed. Financial crises in this country hurt the new laborers when they competed for low paying jobs with 2nd and 3rd generation Americans. Anti-foreign and anti-semetic feelings ran high and the new arrivals were forced to set up defense and self-help organizations like the B'nai B'rith.

Faced with conflicting needs to become accepted as Americans and at the same time maintain their cultural identity as Jews, these new immigrants set up fraternal organizations like the Young Men's Hebrew Association and the Free Sons of Israel. These provided alternatives to the synagogue that were less ghettoized and more Americanized.

But beyond this, it was felt that even the religion of the German-Jewish immigrants should be adopted and thus serve as an acculturation and linguistic aid. Rabbi Isaac Mayer Wise and Rabbi David Einhorn founded the reform movement which introduced English liturgy and simplified the services.

In coping with their economic woes, German-Jewish immigrants came to realize that their European skills in peddling and manufacturing were most useful. The growth of America and the Gold Rush of 1849 had created a massive need for manufactured goods. One peddler, Levi Strauss, came back to New York after the gold rush and began making special heavy pants needed by miners and laborers—these blue jeans are still known today as "Levis."

Peddling led to more established retail stores and the first department stores started by these Jews (the Strausses founded Macy's—other famous names were Lehman, Bloomingdale and Guggenheim). Other German-Jews became bankers, patrons of the arts and philanthropists.

The German-Jewish immigration period produced many giants of American industry and public life. It also created an elite, groups of millionaire families which minimized and sought to escape their Jewish cultural roots and establish their own social caste which they called "our crowd."[3]

The Period of Eastern European Jewish Migration (1881-1925)

The trickle of Jews coming to America before 1848 became a steady stream by the 1880's, but following that period, the floodgates opened and Eastern Europe unleashed a torrent of millions of Jews flocking to America. The rest of this chapter will describe this key period of immigration, the problems the Jews faced and the solutions they came up with. The contemporary situation will also be described because in a sense it continues to be a part of this same migratory episode.

The remarkable Jewish trait of adaptability was thoroughly tested in Eastern Europe during the last 3 centuries. In 1791 official anti-semitism on the part of the Monarchy and Church of Russia banished Jews to the western territories of Russia and parts of Poland called the *Pale of Settlement*. Later government initiated terror campaigns led to the forced conscription of Jewish youth into the Russian army and the kidnapping and massacre of thousands of Jews during pogroms that swept the area. The worst of these pogroms occurred in 1881 and was followed by laws barring Jews from owning land or even living in the very villages to which they were formerly banished. They were crowded into stifling urban ghettos and still forced to endure pogroms and other forms of official anti-semitism.

Reacting to the earlier expulsion to villages, Jews banded together in semi-agrarian settlements. The *shtetl*, as this kind of settlement was called, became a homogeneous and even supportive environment where Jews lived by age-old traditions, worked and studied and developed the common Jewish language of the Diaspora-Yiddish. Modernizing forces, however, threatened the serenity of *shtetl* life, but this inner threat was soon replaced by the ominous external threats of the pogroms of the 1880's. In the face of physical destruction, even Jewish adaptability found its limits and thousands of Jews fled to America.

Most of these Eastern European Jews settled in New York and the other major eastern cities. In 1880 there were 80,000 Jews in New York City alone. By 1910 there were a million and a quarter. Between 1881 and 1924, a total of two and one quarter million Eastern European Jews arrived in America seeking a good free life in a country whose streets they were told were "paved with gold."

These Jews brought with them the trades and skills developed in the *shtetl*. They brought also the schism of the *shtetl*—the love of Yiddish, the love of secular education and the often conflicting desire to preserve traditional Jewish culture. Emma Lazarus, a Jewish-

American, gave hope to her brethren by expressing in verse the symbolic promise of New York's Statue of Liberty—

"...Give me your tired your poor
your muddled masses yearning to breathe free,
the wretched refuse of your teeming shore.
Send these, the homeless, tempest—tost to me,
I lift my lamp beside the golden door."

Unfortunately, the hope that flourished with the decision to pack and leave for America quickly vanished. Because of restrictive legislation passed by the United States in 1891, 1897 and 1906, many would-be immigrants were kept from approaching the "golden door." Thousands of others perished in the horrible steerage voyage across the Atlantic. The millions who made it underwent a grueling inspection at New York's Ellis Island which becme known as the "island of tears." On it inevitable deportations followed discovery of disease or irrevocable poverty. Writing of her experience on Ellis Island Emma Goldman, destined to become a leading political activist wrote: "the atmosphere (was) charged with antagonism and harshness. Nowhere could one see a sympathetic face; there was no provision for comfort of the new arrivals...The first day on American soil proved a violent shock."[4]

Once in America the Jewish immigrants found a brand new set of enemies ready to take up where their old ones had left off. Organized labor hated them because they provided a cheap competitive source of workers and thus threatened existing wages. Groups like the Daughters of the American Revolution and the American Legion saw the Jews as radical subversives that threatened their sterile sense of patriotism. Big business leaders like Henry Ford spread anti-semitic myths. Ironically, even their brethren, the German Jews, saw these Eastern Europeans as inferior beings who threatened the high status they had built up since the mid 19th century. The German Jews devised the "Galveston Plan" to steer their fellow Eastern European Jews inland away from the big Eastern seacoast cities. The Hebrew Immigrant Aid Society (HIAS) was, however, set up by the German Jewish leadership to help the new arrivals, and as antagonisms softened, the Educational Alliance was started on New York's Lower East Side to help acculturate the newcomers.

Despite the "Galveston Plan" most Eastern European Jewish immigrants remained in the great port City of New York where they arrived. Thousands of them crowded into the wretched housing and unsanitary streets of the lower East Side. By 1904 there were 64,000 people in 5,897 tenements. In 1910 there were 542,000 people in this one neighborhood. In their new refuge the Jews often longed for the pastoral serenity of their old *shtetl*. Remembering her childhood misery in New York the Yiddish writer Anzia Yezierska wrote:

"Where was there a place for me to play? I looked out into the alley below and saw palefaced child ren scrambling in the gutter. 'Where is America?' cried my heart."[5]

The task of finding and keeping a job was a new misery. Some of the immigrants were skilled clothiers and the German-Jewish manufacturers hired them. Other Jews were unskilled and were forced to learn trades like hat making, carpentry, cigar and cigarette making. However, the sweatshop conditions endangered their health and the low wages they made forced women and children to work for long hours thus threatening the very bulwark of Jewish existence—the family. The American Labor Movement, the Unions and the improved working conditions they forced sprung up from this experience.

Once the shock of transition began to wear off, the Eastern European Jews set once again to their age old task—survival through adaptation. 'Here we are' they said—'free at last to live together as Jews—let us make the best of it!'

And so the lower East Side was transformed into a tool for collective survival. The great modern historian of the Jews—Irving Howe, called the lower East Side a "triumph of human resillience...for a few decades, as a subculture of migration, it bore a unique character, marvelously vital and expressive in its preoccupations. Unable to live wholly by the ways of the Old World but not yet ready to yield wholly to the ways of the New, the lower East Side chose to improvise a world of its own."[6]

This new world, this giant transplanted *shtetl* had as its native tongue the language of Yiddish. Yiddish had become a great friend to the East European Jews. It was a wonderful link that brought together thousands of different people from hundreds of towns and villages. It bridged geographical difference and when it was passed on to children it also spanned the generations. Somehow it held a mystical quality— perhaps if Yiddish were to survive, Jews were to survive. The Jews of the lower East Side therefore sought to preserve Yiddish. Religious Jews set up small part-time elementary school classes (*Hederim*) and larger full-time day schools (*Yeshivas*). These institutions taught scripture and Talmud in Yiddish. Aside from the Hebrew Prayers, the language of the Synagogues was Yiddish. In addition, secular Jewish schools set up by labor and Zionist organizations taught both Yiddish and Hebrew. Yiddish was the language of the street and of the home. Yiddish theatre and Yiddish literature and journalism flourished. Between 1880 and 1920 there were over 150 Yiddish newspapers and magazines giving advice to the lovelorn, teaching American culture and bringing messages of hope and success to the newly arrived Jews.

In addition to preserving their old language, the immigrants anxiously sought to learn the new. Children were sent to public school and adults taught themselves English or went to night school. The "people of the book" sought education for education's sake but also as a way to become successful Americans. By 1900 a great many students at New York's City College were Jewish. Public libraries were besieged by Jews of all ages. As a measure of this clamor for education, by 1910 the lower East Side boasted of a large number of "home-grown" doctors, lawyers and pharmacists. It had its own hospitals and even a separate medical society with its own journal.

If Jewish survival in America meant the preservation of a language and of educational excellence, it also meant survival of a culture. Perhaps the primary manifestation of Jewish culture throughout history has been the self-help nature of its communal social services. Precepts of non-demeaning charity, called *zedakah*, have their origins in the five books of Moses. The East European *shtetl* re-invigorated this tradition and it was carried over to America.

While the assistance of HIAS, the Educational Alliance and other settlement houses was useful, the immigrants could not help but feel the *noblesse oblige* attitude on the part of the German Jewish community that founded and often operated these organizations. In addition, government social services were either inferior or totally non-existent. As a result, the Eastern European Jews in America organized various kinds of self-help organizations. These included hospitals, orphanages, and nursing homes.

The most important of all self-help organizations developed out of a most ordinary social event. The thousands upon thousands of immigrants arrived in American searching for some renewed fraternity that could both duplicate the *shtetl* of old and still adapt to the needs of America. Social relationships were most easily formed with fellow immigrants from the same European towns and villages. These compatriots called *landsleit* created a new form of Jewish social society called a *landsmannschaft.* One of the earliest of these societies was the Bialystok Mutual Aid Society chartered in 1864. By 1877 there were 22 of these groups, and by 1910 over one half million Jews were members of this new social network.

Some of these *landsmannschaften* merged with other organizations like the "Workmen's Circle." Others chose to maintain their integrity and still exist today. These societies performed vital functions. They were social clubs that served to ease the pain of immigration and facilitate acculturation. They provided insurance and medical care. They celebrated births and birthdays, helped members find jobs and took care of burial needs. They often bought large cemetary plots so that members would be together in death as in life. During both world wars these societies helped in relief work overseas.

The world of the lower East Side had a profound affect on the future of both American Jewry and of America as well. For the Jews it was less of a melting pot and more of a cauldron. Its inhabitants were hardened, they survived, they changed, they grew. For America, the lower East Side was the place where its notion of humanity was tested—in terms of fair labor practices, political representation, religious freedom and care for the needy. The Eastern European Jews of the lower East Side truly shaped America—they smoothed its rough edges.[8]

The Culture and Language of American Jews—Today

Between 1926 and 1953, 400,000 Jews fled to America from Hitler's Holocaust. Six million of their brethren perished.

The holocaust and the birth of the State of Israel in 1948 were the most important events in Jewish history in 1900 years. These seminal events led to a rebirth of Jewish life in Americe. Bolstered by the newly arrived immigrants, young American Jews sought to find their roots. In some cases, descendants of lower East Side immigrants whose parents and grandparents had forsaken the practice of Judaism and forgotten Yiddish and Hebrew, began to seek Jewish education.

Today there are hundreds of Jewish day schools (Yeshivas) in America providing students with intensive religious as well as secular education. While most of these students come from orthodox environments, some come from non-traditional homes.

Thanks to the "release time" program, thousands of Jewish children attending public school leave their classes early during the week for Jewish instruction at Synagogue-run afternoon schools. In addition, college students often take advantage of newly formed Jewish studies programs in various major universities. More intensive Jewish higher education is available at the orthodox Yeshiva University, the conservative Jewish Theological Seminary (both in New York) and the reform Hebrew Union College (in Cincinnati).

While modern Jewish education stresses the knowledge of Hebrew, there is a growing concern for Yiddish. Yiddish newspapers are still in print and there is some Yiddish radio programming in New York City. Jewish student groups like *Yugntruph* gather for Yiddish poetry recitals. In the summer of 1976, thousands of people gathered in New York's Central Park to celebrate the 100th anniversary of the Yiddish theatre in America. While members of the crowd mourned the dying if not the death of Yiddish, some young people objected.

"Yiddish has been a part of me since I was small," said Sheva Zucker, 24. "By speaking Yiddish you place yourself in a context. There is a feeling of continuity."

According to Bernard Backer, President of the "Workman's Circle" which still seeks to strengthen Jewish identity,

"There is a need for identification on a cultural level today. There is more of a desire now to integrate with past. There is more interest in tradition."[9]

Despite this renaissance, the American Jewish Community continues to face major problems. Orthodox Jews have, until recently, suffered various forms of discrimination, most specifically in employment. New legislation and court decisions, often prompted by Jewish legal groups like the Jewish Commission on Law and Public Affairs (COLPA), have given orthodox Jews the right to observe their religious precepts and still benefit from non-discriminatory employment.

One out of nine Jews in America today is 65 years old or older. Many of these Jews are left poverty stricken in inner city slums and preyed upon by criminals.

In addition to these problems, new Jewish immigrants continue to arrive in America from Arab nations and from the Soviet Union where the coals of anti-semitism continue to smolder. The American Jewish community is again devising self-help programs to teach these new immigrants English and help them lead a new free life in America. HIAS and the New York Association of New Americans (NYANA) are two relief organizations that have refocused their activities to meet these new needs. Some public programs have also been set up to aid these newcomers. The New York Public School System is now developing curriculum aides in Russian to help the Soviet immigrants.

Perhaps the gravest threat facing American Jewry today is the threat of total assimilation. The number of Jews marrying non-Jews is an important measure of this loss of identity. In 1961 the intermarriage rate was 6.7 percent, by 1972 the rate was 31.7 percent and it continues to rise.[10] Increased emphasis on Jewish culture, language and education may reverse this trend, but assimilation is now a serious threat to Jewish survival that rivals the external enemies of old.

American Jewish Accomplishment and Contributions

According to Will Maslow of the American Jewish Congress "Jews are perhaps the best educated ethnic group in America. Fifty-four percent of all Jews 25 years or older have some college training; . . . As the age bracket lowers, the level of education rises; nearly half (48 percent) of the 25-29 group have taken post graduate training or earned professional degrees. By 1985, it is estimated, half of all Jews under 65, male and female, will be college graduates."

Jews have also been successful economically and 14 percent of American Jewish households earn $25,000 or more a year.[12] They are also geographically mobile and only 47.8 percent of American Jews live in the Northeast.[13]

Of course, American Jews have not just taken from our horn of plenty, they have also contributed to it. On an individual level they have given America its greatest gifts and have led its historical development. Benjamin Cardoza, Louis Brandeis and Arthur Goldberg influenced the very growth of the American Constitution and Judicial system by their actions as Supreme Court justices. Saul Bellow, who won the 1976 Nobel Prize for Literature, playwrite Moss Hart, humorist Jack Benny, Artist Ben Shahn, and scientist and philosopher Albert Einstein are among the hundreds of American Jews who drew upon their Jewish roots to express a marvelous vision of America.

Even more important, as a community, the Jews of America have contributed essential precepts of freedom and democracy — religious tolerance, concern for the downtrodden outside of our borders, social welfare with dignity for the needy of our own country, fair labor practices, civil rights for blacks and other minorities, and the very essence of pluralism that cherishes and nurtures diversity.

American Jews have held a mirror up to the face of America. They have shown this country its faults and its greatness. They have taught America to dream and then helped to fulfill that dream.

FOOTNOTES

[1]Jews played a very significant part in the Revolutionary War. For details see "Jews in the American Revolution" *Jewish Digest*. July-August 1976.

The Museum of American Jewish History opened 1976, one block away from the Liberty Bell in Philadelphia. Its first exhibit — "The Role of the Jew in the Forging of the Nation" was most illuminating and a catalogue of the exhibit is available.

[2]Other notable Jews included Aaron Lopez who built up the Newport Whaling industry and Bernard and Michael Gratz who were important fur traders. For more details see Feingold, Harry, *Zion in America*, N.Y., Hipporrene Books Inc., 1974.

[3]Birningham, Stephen, *Our Crowd*, N.Y., Dell, 1967. For a review of this general period see Raisin, Max, *A History of the Jews in Modern Times*, N.Y.C., Hebrew Publishing, 1918.

[4]Feingold, *Op. Cit.*,p.122.

[5]*Ibid.*, p.123.

[6]Howe, Irving. *The Lower East Side: Symbol and Fact.* Condensed by *Jewish Digest.* July-August 1976.

[7]An excellent anthology on the importance of Yiddish is by Howe, Irving and Greenberg. Eliezer, *Voices from the Yiddish.* Ann Arbor, University of Michigan Press, 1972.

[8]The best description of the Lower East Side Jewish Culture is by Howe, Irving, *World of Our Fathers*, N.Y., Harcourt, Brace, Jovanovich, 1976.

[9]*New York Times.* July 19, 1976.

[10]Maslow, Will, *The Structure and Functioning of the American Jewish Community.* N.Y., American Jewish Congress, 1974, p.9.

[11]*Ibid.*, p.7.

[12]*Ibid.*, p.9.

[13]*Ibid.*, p.10.

Bibliography

Angel, Marc D., "Sephardic Culture in America", *Jewish Life*, March-April, 1971.

Baum, Charlotte, Hyman, Paula and Michel, Sonya, *The Jewish Woman in America*, New York: Dial Press, 1976.

Becker, Evelyn, Goldenberg, Harvey and Sanders, Beverly, *Topics in Jewish American Heritage*, N.Y., U.F.T., 1975.

Blau, Joseph L. and Salo W. Baron, eds., *The Jews of the United States 1790-1840: A Documentary History*, New York, Columbia University Press, 1964. (3 Volumes).

Brotz, Howard, *The Black Jews of Harlem*, New York, Schocken, 1964.

Eisenberg, Azriel, *The Golden Land: A Literary Portrait of Jewish Life in America*, New York, Thomas Yoseloff, 1964.

Evans, Eli, *The Provincials: A Personal History of the Jews in the South*, New York, Atheneum, 1973.

Feingold, Henry, *Zion in America*, New York, Hippocrene Books, Inc., 1974.

Franck, Isaac, "The Jewish Community's Influence on American Culture," *Jewish Digest*, October,1976.

Glazer, Nathan, *American Judaism*, (2nd ed.) Chicago, University of Chicago Press, 1972.

Halperin, Samuel, *The Political World of American Zionism*, Detroit, Wayne State University Press, 1961.

Handlin, Oscar, *Adventure in Freedom: 300 Years of Jewish Life in America*, New York, McGraw-Hill, 1954.

Howe, Irving, *World of Our Fathers: The Journey of East European Jewry to America, and the Life They Found and Made*, New York, Harcourt, Brace, Jovanovich, 1976.

Isaacs, Stephen, *Jews and American Politics*, New York, Doubleday & Co., 1974.

Karp, Abraham J., *The Jewish Experience in America: Selected Studies from the publications of the American Jewish Historical Society.*

Karp, Abraham, "How Jewry has Served America", *Jewish Digest*, July-August, 1976.

Liebman, Charles, *The Ambivalent American Jew*, Philadelphia, Jew ish Publication Society, 1973.

Marcus, Jacob R., *American Jewry: Documents of the 18th Century*, Cincinnati, Hebrew Union College Press, 1959.

Maslow, Will, *The Structure and Functioning of the American Jewish Community*, New York, American Jewish Congress, 1974.

Rezneck, Samuel, *Unrecognized Patriots: Jews in the American Revolution*, Westport, CT., Greenwood Press, 1975.

Rosenberg, Stuart, *America is Different*, London, Thomas Nelson & Sons, 1964.

Rubin, Lawrence, "Analyzing Anti-Semitism", *Civil Rights Digest*, Winter, Spring, 1976.

Sklare, Marshall and Greenblum, Joseph, *Jewish Identity on the Suburban Frontier*, New York, Basic Books, 1967.

Sklare, Marshall, *America's Jews*, New York, Random House, 1971   ,*The Jew in American Society*, New York, Behrman House, 1974.

Sidorsky, David, ed., *The Future of the Jewish Community in America*, New York, Basic Books, 1973.

St. John, Robert, *Jews, Justice, and Judaism: The Role of the Jews in Shaping America*, New York Doubleday & Co., 1969.

Suhl, Yuri, *An Album of the Jews in America*, New York, Franklin Watts Co. and the Anti-Defamation League of B'nai B'rith, 1972.

Zeldner, Max, "Yiddish a Living Language", *Jewish Digest*, Winter, Spring, 1976.

Chapter 18
In Search of Identity: The Soviet Jewish Immigrant
Stanley S. Seidner*

I. The New Immigration

The recent arrival of thousands of Soviet Jewish immigrants in New York City opened new prospects for exploration and development in bilingual education. One encounters major concentrations of this target population in Brooklyn's Coney Island and Brighton section, commonly referred to as "Odessa by the sea", Queens' Jackson Heights region, with a similar sobriquet of "Little Leningrad", and the Queens area of Forest Hills. Although the majority of those who left for Israel chose to remain, a number faced economic, social or political disillusionment and treked onwards to the United States. Others found temporary havens-in-transit from Israel to American shores, or indicated the former as their intended destination with another objective in mind. While Soviet Jewish immigrants made their way to other major cities in the United States, New York City attracted the larger multitude. It is not known at present to what degree the combination of overt Jewish activism from within the Soviet Union, and pressure from foreign governments and private sectors had influenced the Kremlin to permit the exodus. Incidents such as the trial of the so-called "Leningrad Eleven" elicited waves of sympathy and storms of protest from the West which the Soviet government found difficult to ignore (*Present Tense*, no. 1 (III), 1975; Spenser, 1971; *New York Times*, Jan. 16, 1972; *Midstream*, Feb., 1971). The more immediate expediency of dealing with such issues as disarmament and the detente "umbrella", or of removing threats to crucial grain and general trade agreements appeared to motivate the Soviet leadership to loosen the constraints of emigration. At any rate, some 100,000 Jews were able to apply for exit visas between 1971-1974. In spite of this permission, Soviet authorities continued to place obstacles in the path of would-be immigrants. On frequent occasions, Jews were refused permission to leave the U.S.S.R. for reasons of occupation or security. A law passed in 1972 required departing Jews to recompense the State, by way of a progressive tax, based upon the educational level of the individual. The penalty which required Jews to pay as much as $25,000 was relaxed somewhat in 1973 (*Time*, March 26, 1973).

Undaunted, Soviet authorities continued in their attempts to suppress activists and diminish emigration by increasing trails (Dechter, 1973, Taylor, 1976). OVIR, the cryptonym for *Odel Viz i Registrat sii* (Visas and Registration Department) continued to interpret *ukases* and decrees to the detriment of increasing applicants.

The official Soviet census of 1970 showed a questionable statistic of 2,151,000 "ethnic" Jews in the U.S.S.R., a drop from 1959 by 117,000 (*Izvestia*, April 17, 1971). In contrast, the historian Roy Medvedev estimated the number to be anywhere from one to ten million (Feshbach, 1970, Smith, 1976). It would seem that the statistical decline served the interests of Brezhnev and others who faced predictions by *zapadniki* (militants) of acknowledged rises in population among the national minorities. More likely than not, the decline reflected the desire of anonymity by Jews of mixed parentage. It is a virtual impossibility to understand the plight of the estimated six to seven thousand Soviet Jews in New York City without exploring who they are, and the conditions that led to their emigration from the U.S.S.R. Consequently, the author will journey to the past before proceeding with the present.

II. Historic Antecedents to Identity Crises

During their long sojourn on lands that now comprise the Soviet Union, the Jews remained by and large a separate, identifiable community from the mainstream of the host populations. Jewish communities perpetuated their ethnic and religious distinctiveness as a matter of choice or from outside pressures and constraints. Jewish settlements were alleged by Brann and Chwolson (1894) to have developed in Armenia and the Caucasas shortly after the Babylonian Captivity in 586 B.C. The resistance to assimilation was accentuated during the Persian

*Dr. Seidner is a full-time Senior Research Associate at Teachers College, Columbia University—the Institute for Urban and Minority Education. He is also an Adjunct Professor at Glassboro State College.

invasion toward the latter part of the fourth century, when Sapor II conquered most of the Armenian cities and led thousands of Jews into captivity (*Regesti i Nadpisi* 1899, p.37). Aside from Armenia, Jewish settlements arose in Georgia, along the northern shore of the Black Sea, the Sea of Azor, and in the Crimea. In these last regions, a Turkic people called the Khazars established a kingdom and adopted Judaism as the official religion. Modern Soviet Jewry learned little or nothing about the important significance of the cultural development through the research of recognized scholars as Dubnow (1916). Koestler (1976) noted that Soviet pressure resulted in a distorted interpretation in M.I. Artamonov's study of the period. The actual Russian destruction of Khazaria left a surviving minority which "lost its nationality and turned into a parasitic class with a Jewish coloration" (p.94).

The citation in itself might appear insignificant to the reader, except for its accentuation of chronological scapegoatism from the fall of Khazaria through the current regime. Jews found themselves collectively identified within the framework of a viral theory of social contagion. They became an alien organism in a host environment whose successive suzerains pressed for either their expulsion, absorption, or annhiliation. The *Zhydovskiye vorota* (Jewish gates) separated Jews from other residents of ancient Kiev. Russian monarchs saw the Jews as an explicit threat to the state. Even the more liberal Tsar, Peter the Great, exclaimed (Poliakov, 1976):

"You know my friend, the character and customs of Jews; you also know the Russians; I, too, know them both, and believe me: the time has not yet come to unite these two peoples. Tell the Jews . . . I understand the advantages I might have derived from them, but I would have pitied them for having to live among Russians." (p.280)

Inevitably, with Russian expansion, more Jews were brought into the empire. In a consistent manner with prior policy, they were segregated in a pale, or settlement, within the western provinces as a kind of *cordon santaire*. Through the onset of the twentieth century, the *shtetl* or village community within the pale crystallized Jewish tradition into a distinctive culture. Refugees from earlier persecutions in Bohemia, Germany, and other regions carried varieties of the Yiddish language, which supplanted Hebrew as the spoken idiom. In a parallel vein, the label *Zhyd* (Jew) replaced *Yevrei* (Hebrew) as a pejorative characterization. (Under the Soviet regime, the stigmatization reversed to the former *Yevrei*). For over a century, the semblance of separation failed to protect the Jewish communities, which suffered excesses at the hand of surrounding populations. Russification policies, in anticipation of modern Soviet techniques,

attempted to forcefully assimilate them. Anti-Jewish feelings culminated in *pogroms* or severe riots against the Jews in many areas throughout the Russian empire. In 1881, 1903 and again in 1905, unofficial organizations such as the Black Hundreds and the *Soyusz ruskago naroda* (Union of Russian People) slaughtered Jews to cries of *Hep* (Hierosolyma est perdita). Consequently, the first of three immigrations (a second occurred in the political wake of 1917) materialized in the flight of Jews to the United States and to the shores of Palestine. With the tacit blessing of the Imperial regime, government officials condoned the bloodshed with earlier pronouncements, such as "The Western border is open to them (Jews). . . and nobody has put obstacles in the way of their immigration" (Wischnitzer, 1948, pp. 38-39). Accusations of ritual murder further served the authorities who sought rationale for extremist rule. On the eve of World War I, the Russian Empire with a population of over 126 million people, contained somewhere between five to six million Jews. The young revolutionary, Joseph Stalin, voiced a prevalent sentiment of foreboding prophecy before the Bolshevik takeover (Chesler, 1974):

". . . interspersed as national minorities in areas inhabited by other nationalities, the Jews as a rule serve 'foreign' nations as manufacturers and traders and as members of the liberal professions, naturally adapting themselves . . . in respect to language and so forth . . . The question of national autonomy for the Russian Jews consequently assumes a somewhat curious character: autonomy is being proposed for a nation whose future is denied and whose existence is yet to be proved!" (p.41).

III The Soviet Experience

The advent of the First World War brought little alleviation to suffering experienced by Jews in the pale, or in the frontline trenches as soldiers. Although the termination of Tsarist autocracy in 1917 resulted in repeal of anti-Jewish legislation, it failed to rectify deep-rooted hatreds and stereotyped characterizations. The October (November) revolution appeared to offer some promise of improvement in conditions since a number of Jews were observed to wield considerable influence in the ruling Communist Party. Lev Davidovitch Bronstein, popularly known as Leon Trotsky, served as Commander-in-Chief of the Red Armies and Minister of War. Jacob Sverdlov became the first president of the party's Central Committee. Grigorii Zinoviev was the President of the Third International launched in 1919 and a member of the

Politburo. The association of these and other Jews as prominent figures in the Communist hierarchy led to brutal retaliation against innocent Jewish communities in Civil War Russia and emerging east and central European states. The intentions of the Communists towards the Jews as a viable national group crystallized through the ensuing decades as phrases such as "class enemies","bourgeoisie", and "Zionist" replaced the old Tsarist anti-Semetic epithets. Although *Izvestia* (August 9, 1918) declared anti-Semitism as contrary to the interests of the revolution, Zionist adherents found themselves under attack from government circles. The concept of an alien organism reemerged as the Communists established the *Yevsektsiia*, or Jewish Section, in various bodies of government. Rothenberg concluded that the *Yevsektsiia* served the dual purpose of enforcing Soviet policies as well as dialectical materialism upon the Jewish populace (Kochan, 1970). Soviet policy took the form of cultural suppression whenever possible and the promulgation of assimilation. The government still found it difficult to ignore the existence of the Jews as a recognized minority within the framework of the U.S.S.R. The concept of nationality was strongly tied to that of territory. Trotsky had unsuccessfully championed the contention, in the mid-1920's, that Communists officially should promote and use regional as well as general idioms of communication. The proposal materialized to some degree as the Byelorussian leadership promolgated the use of Yiddish on all levels of government. The existence of Jewish *Soviets* (Councils) in the Ukraine and parts of greater Russia as well, suggested the logical establishment of a national territory in these regions. The leadership in Moscow had other intentions and purposes in mind. They looked to the south-eastern part of Siberia in the area of Biro-Bidzhan, where Chinese immigration caused uneasiness in the Kremlin and a Japanese threat loomed on the near horizon. In addition to these considerations, the potential displacement of population placed the Jews outside the confines of the Soviet Union for all practical purposes. The project failed in its expectations to attract large numbers of Jews, remaining a propaganda vehicle with the trapping of Yiddish culture without substance (Eliav, 1969, Kochan, 1971). Biro-Bidzhan in essence became a segregated area — a ghetto in the same manner as the *Zhydovskiye vorota*, Tsarist Pale.

It would suffice at this point to indicate that many scholars have concurred on the anti-Semetic policies practiced by Stalin in his projected cult of personality (among them, Medvedev, 1972, Deutscher, 1968). The more avid student can similarly turn to any number of sources treating Soviet policy and the Jews during the period of the Second World War (for instance,

Michaelis, 1970). It would appear that the exterminations at Babi Yar and other localities, or heroism by Soviet Jews meant little or nothing to Stalin, who, in 1948, dispersed the national Yiddish theater and eliminated publications and cultural-language schools. A short month before, Golda Meir arrived in Moscow as the first envoy from Israel to the probable chagrin of Soviet officials who witnessed her greeting by ecstatically jubilent Jews. Four years later, twenty-four leading Jewish poets and writers were executed (Saivetz and Woods, 1973). The notorious "Doctor's plot" failed to generate justification in 1953 for new anti-Semetic measures in view of Stalin's death which occurred soon after. Soviet Jewry found little relief from continued discrimination through the 1950's. Armstrong maintained that continued anti-Semetic policies resulted in Jewish alienation from the Soviet regime and the transfer of allegiance toward Israel. This alienation found reinforcement in the continuous pronouncements by Soviet journals. Despite a fledgling Jewish cultural revival, *Sovetskaya Moldavia* (July 23, 1959) declared in blatant tones that "Judaism destroyed love for the Soviet Motherland." The justification concerning the difficulty of eradicating "national predjudices, distrust and antagonism produced by the Tsarist autocracy" reappeared in publication (*Partiinaya Zhizn* (21), 1970, p.6). Indirect mention to possible emigration, by Kosygin in 1966 contained more form than substance, camouflaging Kremlin policies (Baron, 1976). Under Kruschev's premiership, the U.S.S.R. had refused to allow Jews to emigrate to Israel altogether, regardless of sex or age. The initial inquiry for exit originated from outside the Soviet Union. Focus upon the problem occurred within the U.S.S.R. through the artistic efforts of Yevtushenko and Shostakovich, among others (*Time*, July 26, 1976; Korey, 1969). The Israeli victory of 1967 awakened the "Jews of silence" within the Soviet Union to direct activism. Within two years, the judiciary at Kiev sentenced a Jewish engineer to a labor camp for seeking an exit visa to Israel. By this time, a loose coordination emerged between activists and petitioners in the U.S.S.R. and sympathizers in the West who began to apply various forms of pressure and persuasion upon the Kremlin leadership.

Between 1970 and 1972, some 30,000 Jews departed from Georgia, the Baltic Region, Russia and the Ukraine. 25,000 of this number from Georgia and the Baltic, according to Yakhot, comprised 20 percent of the Jewish population in these republics. The remainder represented about 0.5 percent of the Jews residing in Russia and Ukraine (Voronel, Yakhot, 1973). It should be noted that Jews from these regions displayed a deep sense of cultural and national identity. Considering the difficulties imposed upon the regime by the combination of internal and external pressures, one might expect Soviet cooperation in a policy of emigration or expulsion preferable to that of virtual captivity; however, the exodus of large numbers on one minority could possibly set a precedent for others. In order to gain additional insight regarding this concern and the Soviet Jewish dilemma, we will examine more closely the assimilatory pressure brought to bear in the guise of multinational-cultural and multilingual policies.

IV The Vehicles of Culture and Language

Some 250 million people live in 15 republic and other administrative divisions which comprise the U.S.S.R. Of this number, approximately 142 million people listed Russian as their native language in 1970, while another 42 million cited it as a second medium of communication (Katzner, 1975). The 1970 census indicated that 381,000 people claimed Yiddish as their native language. The figures showed a linguistic decline of 17.7 percent from the 1959 calculation (*Izvestia*, April 17, 1971). The decrease illustrated the degree of success of Soviet assimilation policies. It should be remembered that the possibility remained for Jews of dual minority parentage to switch their official ethnic status. This, in large part, could account as well for the linguistic decline. The only Jews to receive recognition as a national minority in the U.S.S.R. were Mountain Jews residing in Azerbaydzhan. This population speaks Jedeo-Tat as opposed to Yiddish. A smaller group, the Bucharis Jews of Central Asia use a modified form of Persian (Lewis, 1972). Sizable percentages of Jews are found in a number of republics. Intriguingly, several Yiddish languages are found to exist, including Judeo-Tadzhik, Judeo-Georgian, Judeo-Crimean Tatar, Yiddish, and the aforementioned Judeo-Tat. As a consequence, the Jew exists as several nationalities, suggested by Schapiro (Kochun, 1970), instead of a "Russian" or "Soviet" Jew. The same premise can be projected to Byelorussians, Ukranians, Poles and other minorities. Yiddish, *per se*, is excluded as a national medium of expression in Soviet bilingual education, consistent with the pronounced intention to assimilate this language group (*Izvestia* April 17, 1971). Bilingual instruction, writes Zhamin (1973) is conducted in over fifty languages, theoretically until after the student has the opportunity to choose the idiom of education. Hall's (1973) study of Soviet textbooks during the decade of the 1960's showed that the mother tongue was maintained for all grade levels in only 18 non-Russian languages. Although regional languages are encouraged on paper, Russian remains a *sine qua non*. The Russian language, according to *Pravda* (April 2,

1971) symbolizes "the banner of amity and brotherhood of peoples" (p.2). Ever-mindful of the ideological clash with definitions of *natzia* (nation), party spokemen allude to the Russian language as an international means of communication (*Kommunist*, no. 13, 1965, pp.55-56; Shevstov, 1974). Soviet Jews find themselves as other minorities, beginning Russian at different school levels depending upon the education policy prevalent in the Republics (see *Narodnoe Obrazovanie*, Nov., 1962, pp.14-16 and Dec. 162, pp. 8-10). The coexistent mediums of native and Russian languages has resulted in an extention in some geographic areas of the normal curriculum by another year (Fishman, 1976). Maxim Kim (1974) classified Russian as "the second native language for the vast majority of the reading public in all the Soviet Republics" (p.188). The regime confines much of this reading material to Communist theory and application. Soviet ideology rendered the existence of recognized national to one of status without sovereignty. As a group without stature within the framework of the U.S.S.R., Soviet Jewry continued to be the target of subjective treatment. Recognition of this sizeable minority suggests the repudiation of anti-Zionist attacks and concurrent definable national presence. The dis-allowance of language and culture as purveyors of ethnic identity relegated Soviet Jewry to a state of limbo. Fedoseyev (Grigulevich, 1974) condemned the "Zionist" contention of a special Jewish nation "a completely false and reactionary idea, as Lenin pointed out" (p.281). One finds additional comprehension of their situation in the following posture by a number of Soviet academicians (Chertikhin, Popov, Rudenko, et al, 1975):

Long before the Romans destroyed Jerusalem, Jews dispersed and settled in the prosperous provinces of the Roman empire. But assimilation did not suit the leaders of the Jewish communities. It would end their economic advantages. So they made the synagogue the main centre for the artificial preservation of closed Jewish communities. Judaism became an ideological tool. The specific nature of its aims turned Judaism into a religion of intolerance. Designed to prevent assimilation with the surrounding socio-ethnic environment, it worked to perpetuate the social pattern and way of life of Jewish communities... Modern Zionism is the product of its time — the epoch of imperialism. It is expressive of the crisis of the Jewish bourgeoisie, which is gradually assimilating, on the one hand, and dreads losing its position, resists this, on the other (pp.181-182).

The tortuous permutations and transitions from Tsars to Soviets emphasized a uniformity in attitude toward Jews and, in many instances, parallel *modi operandi*. Soviet Jewry emerged no less the alien thorn in the U.S.S.R. than in Tsarist Russia. The manifestation of a new temper among Soviet Jews is reminiscent of the conscious attempt by a past spectrum of generations to eliminate the invidious circumstances of their existence.

V Problems and Needs in a New Land

In comparison with other immigrations, Soviet Jews constitute a relatively small number. Some 20,000 have settled in the United States since the beginning of the exodus. The number may be much higher, considering their classification as other nationalities, dependent upon their lengths of stay in intermediary countries before arriving here. Parker (1976) found that approximately 35 percent of the emigres have a Bachelors degree or higher. Of this, 10 percent possess teaching credentials on the university level. Physicians and scientists comprise 40 percent of the number. This group of "academics and professionals" pose the most problems in resettlement and potential vocation (p.39). Standardization of credentials for this cross-section of immigrants varies greatly in criteria from the U.S.S.R. to the U.S. The current economic conditions apparently intensify the immediate problems of employment. A further complication arises with the lack of facility for the English language. Faubion Bowers (1976) relates the following:

> Efim had learned tailoring as a soldier in the Soviet Army; in civilian life he was a goldsmith. But everyone in America in these two trades that I spoke to stopped listening as soon as I said that Efim spoke not English. I found him a job as a back-elevator man in an apartment, which required no English. He quickly declined. 'I'm trained only in sewing and in jewelry,' he said, as if I were stupid. Another prospective employer who had had experience with this new breed of Soviet immigrants, said right off, 'They're too much trouble' — and he wasn't talking about the language barrier. (p.25)

Soviet Jewish immigrants have often been described in terms of arrogance, stubbornness and mistrustfulness of others. Russian-language publications in the U. S., namely *Novoye Russkoye Slovo* or the Soviet *Literaturnaya Gazeta*, reflect the frustrations and disillusionment of Jews who chose to remain or sought to return to the U.S.S.R. A few arrivals, like Mark Klionsky, achieve a degree of success and status through art forms (Sharp, 1977). This does not necessarily apply to the great majority who struggle with compound economic and social obstacles of daily life. Many sacrificed positions of status to fulfill a quest for cultural identity. To paraphrase "the streets

of gold" characteristic of past immigrations, not only did the new arrivals find them to be of cold cement, but a number of the highly talented found themselves figuratively paving them. Their experience of downward mobility in occupation and inverse correlation with education finds similar parallels with other Slavic groups in studies by Mostwin (1969), Sypek (1955) and Zurawicka (1965). One finds it difficult to ascertain how these conditions would benefit the Soviet Jews in formation of positive self-concepts. For over fifty years, the Soviet regime served as a somewhat omnicient and omnipotent incorporator and provider. In its *mission civilsatrice*, the Communists denied the Jewish populace points of cultural reference to the stage of relegating them as nationless. A system of censorship controlled activities and filtered the degree of information attainable regarding the Soviet Union and the world. Soviet Jews, claimed Parker (1976), anticipated reward for their sacrifice, an expectation strengthened by Communist positive reciprocation to defectors from the west.

> The Soviet emigre expects the same reasoning to apply here. He thinks a job will be waiting for him. In the Soviet Union, the employment expert would have a list of jobs, one of which would be his. Here he is told there are no lists; instead, he must go out and compete (p. 39).

The passage reflects the environment of regulation and control which typifies the Soviet regime. Thrust into new conditions, the Soviet Jews are expected to make decisions with an awareness of individuals used to exercising their prerogatives with democratic maturation. As a consequence of their inability to rapidly adjust, they act out many of their frustrations and hostilities. Acculturation usually takes the form of escape from the negative labeling and stereotyping prevalent in the U.S.S.R. In their desire to feel part of the host society, many Soviet Jews search out the most prevalent mode in areas such as music and clothing. Nor is this behavior limited to the adult population in their desire for acceptance. Upon visiting a school in the Brighton area of New York, a teacher working with Russian-speaking students related an incident concerning an elementary school-age immigrant child. The student refused to respond when his name was called. When asked why, he declared, "From now on, you do not call me Igor—that is name of monster on television." When asked which name he preferred, Igor answered, "James—that's for big American hero, James Bond." Any inference of comedy is dulled by the harsh reality of identity crisis. Many Soviet Jews attempt to remedy this situation by enrolling their children in Yeshivas. Unfortunately, many cannot afford the tuition fees and depend on public schools with programs in infant stages of development. The immediate outstanding educational need emerges, as with the adults, in the area of communication. In consideration of the multiplicity of idioms currently utilized in the U.S.S.R., a distinct need exists for the assessment of language dominence. This is suggested in the following testimony of a Soviet-Jewish emigre (Voronel and Yakhot, 1973):

> The language of my childhood was Ukranian: I was raised by a Ukranian nursemaid. I went to a Ukranian kindergarten...Until I was eight years old I had no idea that there was such a concept as 'nationality.' At home there was no talk about nationalities...I was sent to a Russian school without discussion (pp. 60-61).

Although the overwhelming majority of Soviet Jewish immigrants speak Russian, a teacher may encounter a youngster who speaks the language of a national geographic region. Some students on the primary grade level in Jackson Heights Yeshiva speak Georgian and know little or no Russian. Nor should the fluency or comprehension of Yiddish be taken for granted. With the exception of the older generation, many immigrants experienced their first contact with the Yiddish language upon coming to Israel or the United Stastes. The implications for bilingual education in New York are staggering if the city ever realized the large-scale influx of heterogenous language groupings from the U. S.S.R. Large economic resources are needed for the initial diagnostic-prescriptive testing. Additional funding would have to be found for staffing and program requirements. At present, a need exists for qualified Russian-speaking personnel in all subject areas and grade levels. Because of the diverse differences between the collective Soviet educational processes and those within our country, the local and central boards of education could be well advised to rely upon consultants with familiarization appropos to the problems of subject area scope and contents. Any investment does not necessarily mandate prolonged tenure or expansion of programs. Notwithstanding the possible increasing geometric rate of influx, the tendency for involved Russian-speaking parents is to favor the E. S. L. component as opposed to dual language mediums of instruction. In view of federal legislation governing the equity in education, however, bilingual instruction as such cannot be ignored. Part of this need is particularly accentuated on the secondary and post-secondary level. In addition to the traditional curriculum, the exigency is noted in the area of vocational training and retraining.

Once again, the potentiality of massive economic outlays portends a gloomy financial horizon for the New York City school system with its more than 37 language groups. Realistically, federal economic

intercession in collaboration with involved local agencies remains the most feasible alternative. Some headway has been made in this direction with the establishment of regional technical assistance and study centers. The Bilingual General Assistance Center (B.G.A.C., or "Lau" Center) in New York provides services in six pertinent areas of bilingual education to school districts free of charge. Personnel are currently working with Russian-speaking populations in various districts. Data from a home language assessment survey, recently conducted by the Northeast Center for Curriculum Development is expectantly awaited by involved educators. Still, restrictions upon these centers mandated by funding and operation guidelines prohibit the rendering of assistance in such crucial areas as staffing and curriculum materials. New York service centers such as NYANA (New York Association for New Americans) arrange some E.S.L. classes for the adult population and gear the English content to particular vocations. In conjunction with these efforts, Project ARI (Arriving Russian Immigrants) in Brighton Beach offers a limited number of E.S.L. classes for Soviet-Jewish youngsters, plans Yiddish cultural programs and provides information regarding social and medical services (Bilus, 1975). Several orientation manuals for the incoming arrivals have been produced by the American Immigration and Citizenship Conference (1974, 1975). However zealous and well-intentioned, the aforementioned and other concerned organizations are unable to adequately meet the full educational needs of students within the k-12 grade range. Numbers of school-aged children in need of the city's educational services are inexact and can range anywhere from 33% upwards of the total numbers of arrivals. Percentages of student attendance at private Yeshivas, as well as those in transition from private to public institutions have yet to be accurately compiled. Concerted efforts by private and public sectors should be directed toward the coordination of available resources, evaluation of existing strengths and deficiencies, and the pursuit of acquisition of requisite resources. The direction of cultural expression at present is still not certain and will require longitudinal observation for this assessment.

Questions of total social entry and the retention of ethnicity pose a paradox for the Soviet Jewish immigrants. The transition from a highly controlled society to one of more flexibility did not bring with it security in choice and decision. The state of these arrivals cannot be described in terms of ethnocentrism or xenophobism. On the contrary, the cycle which began with the destruction of the first temple is one of deprivation and quest. Certainly, this generation of immigrants in their search for identity and belonging are entitled to no less the resources and services of this host society already readily available to other groups. Responses from institutions which value individual development and contribution can only ease the arduous transition and diminish the almost instinctual pain of past centuries.

SELECTED BIBLIOGRAPHY AND SUGGESTED READINGS

Armstrong, John A. "The Jewish Predicament in the Soviet Union." *Midstream*, January, 1971, 21-31.

Barghoorn, Frederick C. *Detente and the Democratic Movement in the U.S.S.R.* New York: The Free Press, 1976.

Baron, Salo, *The Russian Jew Under Tsars and Soviets.* New York: Macmillan, 1976.

Ben Ami, *Between Hammer and Sickle.* Philadelphia: Jewish Publication Society, 1967.

Bernard, William S. *Guide to Practice Requirements for Foreign Trained Professionals in the United States of America.* New York: American Immiration and Citizenship Conference, 1975.

____. *Immigrating to the United States.* New York: American Immigration and Citizenship Conference, 1974.

Bowers, Faubion, "Only—and Lonely—in America." *The New York Times Magazine*, September 26, 1976, 25, 28, 32.

Brann, M. and Chwolson, D. "Yevrei." In *Entziklo pedia Slovar.* St Petersburg, 1894, vol. XI.

Chertikhin, V. Y., Popov, Y. N., and Rudenko, G. F., et. al. *The Revolutionary Movement of our Time and Nationalism.* Moscow: Progress Publishers, 1975.

Chesler, Evan, ed. *The Russian Jewry Reader.* New York: Behrman House, 1974.

Dechter, Moshe, ed. *Terror in Minsk.* New York: National Conference on Soviet Jewry, 1973.

____. *The Lonely Course of Lazar Liubarsky.* New York: National Council on Soviet Jewry, 1973.

Deutscher, Isaac, *Stalin.* New York: Oxford University Press, 1968.

Dubnow, Simon, *History of the Jews in Russia and Poland,* 3 vols. Philadelphia: Jewish Publication Society, 1916-1920.

Eliav, Arie, "Birobidjan is Dead: But it is Still a Threat to Soviet Jewry." *Hadassah Magazine*, no. 51, November 1969, 12-13, 31-32.

Feshbach, Murry, "Observations on the Soviet Census." *Problems of Communism*, no. 3, 1970, 58-64.

Fishman, Joshua, *Bilingual Education: An International Sociological Perspective.* Middle Road: Newbury House, 1976.

Gilboa, Yehoshua, *The Black Years of Soviet Jewry.* Boston: Little, Brown & Co., 1971.

Glassman, Leo, "Soviet Russia's Jews." *B'nai B'rith Magazine*, July-August, 1930, 386-389.

Goldberg, B. Z. *The Jewish Problem in the Soviet Union.* New York: Crown, 1961.

Grigulevich, I. R. *Races and Peoples: Contemporary Ethnic and Racial Problems.* Moscow: Progress Publishers, 1974.

Hall, Paul R. "Language Contact in the U.S.S.R.: Some Prospects for Language Maintenance among Soviet Minority Groups." Ph.D. Dissertation, Georgetown University, 1973.

Hertzberg, Arthur, ed. *The Zionist Idea.* Forge Village: Atheneum, 1975.

Katzner, Kenneth, *The Languages of the World.* New York: Funk & Wagnalls, 1975.

Kim, Maxim, *The Soviet People—A New Historic Community.* Moscow: Progress Publishers, 1974.

Kochan, Lionel, ed. *The Jews in Soviet Russia Since 1917.* London: Oxford University Press, 1970.

Koestler, Arthur, *The Thirteenth Tribe.* New York: Random House, 1976.

Korey, William, "Kuznetsov and the Unquiet Soviet Jews." *American Zionist*, October 1969, 21-24.

____. *The Soviet Cage: Anti-Semitism in Russia.* New York: Viking Press, 1973.

Lendvai, Paul, *Anti-Semitism in Eastern Europe.* London: Macdonald & Co., 1972.

Leon, Abram, *The Jewish Question: A Marxist Interpretation.* New York: Pathfinder, 1970.

Lewis, E. Glyn, *Multilingualism in the Soviet Union.* The Hague: Mouton, 1972.

Margolis, Max and Marx, Alexander, *A History of the Jewish People.* Forge Village: Atheneum, 1975.

Medvedev, Roy A. *Let History Judge: The Origins and Consequences of Stalinism.* New York: Alfred A. Knopf, 1972.

Mostwin, Danuta, "The Transplanted Family. A Study of the Social Adjustment of the Polish Immigrant Family to the United States after the Second World War." Ph.D. dissertation, Columbia University, 1969.

Parker, Lenore, "From Paternalism to Pluralism." *The Journal of Philanthropy*, 17 (5), 1976, 38-43.

Poliakov, Leon, *The History of Anti-Semitism.* New York: Schocken, 1976.

Raisin, Jacob, *The Haskalah Movement in Russia.* Philadelphia: Jewish Publication Society, 1913.

Redlich, Shimon, "The Jewish Anti-Fascist Committee in the Soviet Union." *Jewish Social Studies*, 1969, 25-36.

Roeh, Nirah, "Is Russian Jewry Doomed?" *Contemporary Russia*, 1938, 427-441.

Rubin, Ronald, ed. *The Unredeemed: Anti-Semitism in the Soviet Union.* Chicago: Quadrangle, 1968.

Saivetz, Carol R. and Woods, Sheila Levin, *The Night of the Murdered Poets*. New York: National Council on Soviet Jewry, 1973.

Sanford, Margey, ed. *Orphans of the Exodus*. Miami: National Conference on Soviet Jewry, 1976.

Schenker, Jonathan, ed. *Colonel Yefim Davidovich*. New York: National Conference on Soviet Jewry, 1976.

Sharp, Roger, "Canvas of Freedom." Transcript of T.V. production on *People, Places, Things*, January 1, 1977.

Shevstov, V. S. *National Sovereignty and the Soviet State*. Moscow: Progress Publishers, 1974.

Smolar, Joseph, *Soviet Jewry Today and Tomorrow*. New York: MacMillan, 1971.

Speiser, Lawrence, "Soviet Jews on Trial." *Civil Liberties*, no. 225, February 1971, 5-6.

Stalin, Joseph, *Marxism and the National Question*. Moscow: Foreign Language Publishing House, 1947.

Sypek, Stanislaw, "The Displaced Polish Immigrant Professional in the Greater Boston Area." Ph.D. dissertation, Fordham University, 1955.

St. Petersburg, *Regesty i Nadpisi*, 1899.

Szyszman, S. "Le Roi Balan et le probleme de la conversion des Khazars." *Actes du X. Congres international d'etudes byzantines*. Istanbul, 1957, 249-252.

Taylor, Telford, *Courts of Justice: Soviet Justice and Jewish Emigration*. New York: Vintage, 1976.

Voronel, Aleksander and Yakhot, Victor, eds. *Jewishness Rediscovered: Jewish Identity in the Soviet Union*. New York: B'nai B'rith, 1974.

——. *I am a Jew: Essays on Jewish Identity in the Soviet Union*. New York: B'nai B'rith, 1973.

Wischnitzer, Mark. *To Dwell in Safety*. Philadelphia: Jewish Publication Society, 1948.

Zhamin, V. *Education in the U.S.S.R.: Its Economy and Structure*. Moscow: Nostvoi, 1973.

Zurawicka, Janina. "Problematyka emigracyina w polonijnej prozie beletrystycznej po II wojnie swiatowej." *IV Rocznik Polonii Zagranicznej*, 1965, 83-117.

Additional Publications Consulted:

Izvestia

Literaturnaya Gazeta

Mainstream

Narodnoe Obrozovanie

New York Times

Novoye Russkoye Slovo

Partiinaya Zhizn

Pravda

Sovetskaya Moldavia

Time

Chapter 19
Bilingualism in Quebec: A Changing Perspective
Alison d'Anglejan and Lise M. Simand*

The Official Language Act (Bill No. 22) enacted in 1974 by the National Assembly of the Province of Quebec has designated French as the official language of the province. The act contains provisions to enhance the status and power of the French language by making it the sole official working language at all levels of government and industry. Thus, French has become the language of communication within the government; French is to be used by the public utilities and professional corporations (e.g. doctors, lawyers, psychologists) to communicate with the public and with the government; and French will be used at every level of business activity.One of the provisions of the act (Chapter 5) stipulates that the language of instruction in the schools of the province will be French. There will continue to be instruction in English for those children whose mother tongue is English or for pupils who have a sufficient knowledge of English. But all future immigrants to the province will be directed to French schools. English and French will continue to be taught as second languages. The use of the public school system as a primary agent for the implementation of language policy changes has characterized language planning activities in a variety of countries (e.g. Indonesia, India, the Philippines).

Prior to the passage of the Official Language Act, Quebec was *de facto* a bilingual province. Businesses were free to use English, French or both languages in their internal and external dealings and all parents were free to choose English or French schooling for their children. It is interesting to trace the evolution of the nationalistic movement in Quebec which has lead to this language policy decision—a deliberate attempt to shift the power structure of the province's two competing languages.

French is today the mother tongue of close to six million Canadians, 84 percent of whom live in the Province of Quebec (Statistics Canada, 1971). Although enclaves of French-speaking Canadians occur throughout Canada, English is rapidly replacing French as the language of the French-Canadian groups in all areas other than Quebec. Until recently, both the high birthrate in Quebec and the strong retention rate of French as a mother tongue in the Province served to maintain the position of French as one of Canada's two official languages and to provide an important shield against linguistic and cultural assimilation (Lieberson, 1970). However, more recent studies (Henripin, 1976) suggest that the survival of the French language and culture in Canada may be threatened by two critical factors: 1) a sudden decline of the birthrate in Quebec which is now the lowest of any province in Canada; and 2) the tendency of 95 percent of immigrants to Quebec to assimilate with the anglophone minority of the province.

The existence of a very close link between language and cultural survival or national identity has been discussed by Fishman (1972). He points out that nationalistic movements emphasize the critical role of language in safeguarding the sentimental and behavioral links between the speech community of today and its historical counterparts. Such considerations tend to take precedence over more practical concerns such as communication within the group or with other nations.

Lieberson (1970) hypothesized that governments in officially bilingual countries will provide support for one group or the other only when the group whose demands are not met is strong enough to undermine national stability and harmony by the threat of revolution or separatism. A retrospective look at language policy decisions in Quebec and Canada during the past 200 years lends support to this hypothesis. Although the British North American Act of 1967 recognized French and English as the two official languages of Canada, there is abundant evidence (Bouthillier & Meynaud, 1972); Gendron, 1972; Porter, 1958; Royal Commission on Bilingualism and Biculturalism, 1967) that the French language occupied a minor position in Canada and that even in Quebec, French Canadians were underrepresented in the higher echelons of business and industry where

*Dr. Alison d'Anglejan and Lise M. Simard, Université de Montreal, Quebec.

English became firmly entrenched as the working language. The eruption of terrorist activities in the early 1960's brought to the surface the feelings of resentment held by many French Canadians with respect to their inferior status. The following fifteen years have been marked by sporadic outbursts of violence and by the emergence of an official separatist party which was elected in a landslide victory in the provincial elections of November, 1976. During the same period we have seen a parallel acceleration in language policy developments at both the federal (The Official Languages Act, 1973) and provincial (The Official Language Act, 1974) levels. Indeed more has been done in the past decade to guarantee the maintenance and development of French as the *de jure* and *de facto* working language of Quebec than during the preceeding 200 years.

In view of the significant role which language plays in preserving a culture from extinction through assimilation, and the close relationship between language and nationalistic movements, it is not surprising to find that language matters occupy a position of priority on the Quebec political and educational scene.

By virtue of the changes resulting from the implementation of Quebec's Official Language Act, it should soon be possible for any Quebecer to be educated and to conduct his business and his social life entirely in French. Indeed, this situation now prevails in most rural areas of the province. Nonetheless, it is clear that no matter what the future political status of the province may be—that of a separate state or a member of the Canadian Confederation—its geographic location in the heart of a gigantic English speaking continent and its high level of industrialization will perpetuate and possibly even increase the need for a cadre of bilingual citizens.

At the present time many French Canadians are fluent in English as well as in French. This is particularly true in the Montréal area where the two linguistic groups come into contact in the sphere of business and commerce. Traditionally, it was the French Canadian who mastered English while the English Canadian remained monolingual. French parents often enrolled their children in the English school system for part of their schooling to assure that they would gain a good working knowledge of the language. Other French Canadians picked up the language when they went to work in businesses or industries where they mingled with anglophones.

The repercussions of official language policies, and explicit nationalistic sentiments are making it more possible and indeed more socially acceptable for the French Canadian to remain monolingual. It is no longer possible for the French-speaking child who does not already speak, understand, read and write English with ease, to enroll in the English public school system. Furthermore, since the language of work in all levels of business and industry is increasingly French, he is less likely to acquire English skills on the job. Thus the responsibility for assuring a working knowledge of English to those who so desire, has shifted to the French school system. Quebec's Official Language Act specifies that "the Minister of Education must also take the necessary measures to ensure instruction in English as a second language to pupils whose language of instruction is French" (p. 10). However, no more specific objectives are set out and it is clear that bilingualism for Quebecers is not an educational priority. In the past, French Canadians appear to have learned English despite, rather that because of the formal teaching of ESL in schools.

Today, according to the guidelines set out by the Ministry of Education of the province, English is introduced in French schools at grade 5, at the rate of one half hour period per day. In fact, however, both the level at which instruction is begun and the number of periods per week tend to vary. In the outlying areas of the province where there is little motivation to learn the language, and contacts with the English-speaking world are negligible, if non-existant, instruction in ESL may be delayed until the high school level.

In general both in the outlying areas and in metropolitan Montréal English is taught by francophones, who do not have specific ESL training and who may, or may not, be proficient in the language. In a recent survey of ESL teachers (Acheson, d'Anglejan, de Bagheera and Tucker, 1977) less than 10 percent of the respondents indicated that they had become English teachers on account of their English language skills or specialized training. A lack of alternative job opportunities was the most frequently cited reason. In addition, only 4 percent of respondents felt that the present ESL program was providing adequate training in English for Quebec children.

Attitudes toward the teaching of English in the province vary greatly. The educational establishment and teachers' unions tend to be nationalistic in orientation and to view the teaching of English as a threat as much to the child's cognitive and linguistic growth as to the survival of the French culture. Interestingly, no systematic studies appear to have been undertaken by Quebec educational authorities to determine the cognitive and linguistic consequences for Quebec children of instruction in English as a second language. However, an empirical study carried out by Anisfeld (1964) in the Montreal setting indicated that French-English bilingual children of French ethnic origin scored significantly above matched monolinguals on both verbal and non-verbal skills.

To date there appear to have been no official attempts to determine on any set of external criteria the level of proficiency in English achieved by the typical high school graduate. The potential importance of such information for young Quebecers headed for university studies is revealed in a report (Smith, 1972) on the use of English language texts at the Université Laval in Quebec City. The proportion of English language texts among the 30,948 volumes in the library was estimated at 68-80 percent. The official calendar for the faculty of science indicated that 426 of the 572 recommended or reference texts listed for undergraduate programs were in English.

A recent poll conducted on behalf of the Commission des Ecoles Catholiques de Montréal, the largest school board in the province, by the Université de Montreal sampled attitudes of different sets of parents with children enrolled in the English or in the French sectors toward the teaching of second languages. The results showed a wide discrepancy between responses of English and French parents with respect to their satisfaction with present second language teaching: 60 percent of parents whose children attend French schools expressed *dissatisfaction* with the teaching of ESL, whereas 66 percent of parents whose children attend English schools were *satisfied* with present ESL teaching practices. The majority of parents (69 percent) whose children attend French schools favor the introduction of ESL at the beginning of the elementary school cycle. Furthermore, more than 80 percent of these parents believe that the early introduction of ESL will not have any deletrious effects on a child's mastery of his mother tongue.

An additonal finding suggesting the extent to which current educational practices are at variance with the aspirations of these Quebec parents was their response when asked to indicate their order of preference for French, English or Bilingual schools. Surprisingly, bilingual schools were the first choice of 50 percent of parents whose children now attend French schools. At the present time it is difficult to interpret these findings, since the full impact of the Official Language Act has not yet been felt and parents may still consider English to be the key to occupational success.

Bilingual schooling does not now exist for French children. However, increasing numbers of Quebec's anglophone children attend bilingual programs in which both English and French are languages of instruction. These schools, the popularity of which has spread rapidly, appear to provide children with a working knowledge of French at no expense to the development of their native language skills (Lambert & Tucker, 1972). Bilingual programs involving French and English as teaching languages have also existed for many years on a limited scale for children in Montreal's Italian community (Toramanian, in preparation). However, the future of these schools is in jeopardy since they do not conform to the requirements of Quebec's Official Language Act which stipulates that children who do not speak English fluently must attend French schools.

One interesting observation that emerges from even a superficial survey of existing bilingual programs, is that none involve the intermingling of children from the province's two dominant language groups in the same classrooms. English and French children go their own ways as do English and French adults and there are few opportunities for cross-cultural communication. This has been demonstrated by Simard and Taylor (1973) who questioned French and English Quebecers about their social contacts and recorded detailed information concerning recent conversations. Of the total number of social encounters recorded, 99.9 percent were with members of the same language group. It has been suggested by these authors that in any attempt to promote interaction between members of different ethnolinguistic groups, the focus should be more on improving social or communicative competence than on the technical aspect of second-language learning (Taylor & Simard, 1975).

It appears that Quebec has reached a critical period in history. The accession to power of the Parti Quebecois, the official separatist party, assures the control of the province's educational and cultural institutions as agents for the promotion of a French ethno-cultural identity. Yet French Canadian nationalism is not necessarily isomorphic with separatism and the province's present leaders whose explicit goal is to gain political independance from Canada must, if they wish to retain widespread support for their policies, demonstrate Quebec's economic viability and stability as a modern technologically oriented society. There is reason to believe that the need for highly trained personnel to meet the province's needs may bring about changes, at the official level, in attitudes toward the teaching of English and in educational practices. For if French-speaking Quebecers are not equipped with the second language skills necessary to compete in the North American professional world, then the economic underpinnings so necessary to the promotion of cultural aspirations may be undermined. One serious threat could be the creation of a technocratic elite in which French-speaking Quebecers would be once again underrepresented.

While there is little reason to anticipate an increase in the amount of time allocated to the teaching of English as a second language, there is an obvious need to evaluate and to heighten the effectiveness of the allocation of resources for this purpose. The current emphasis on the development of oral skills may well be inappropriate for French Canadians in an essentially francophone society. On the other hand, students might derive considerable benefits from courses designed to develop literacy skills in English. Perhaps a series of options must be developed within the public school system to insure that those who require, or desire, varying levels of second language skills may freely pursue their objectives through effective programs.

In Quebec, as in many other countries, nationalistic aspirations must be weighed against economic realities. Here, the situation is particularly difficult to resolve since the province enjoys a high standard of living which its population might be reluctant to sacrifice as the price for cultural preservation. For researchers interested in language planning in education, Quebec provides an instructive setting in which to study the ongoing process of change and adaptation. The very rapid political and socio-cultural changes which we have described are causing pressures on the educational system and indeed on society in general. Only time will tell whether the recent language legislation will have the desired impact and how Quebec society will adjust to such rapidly evolving circumstances.

REFERENCES

Acheson, P., d'Anglejan, A., de Bagheera, I. and Tucker, G. R. English as the second language of Quebec: A teacher profile. Paper presented at TESOL, Miami, 1977.

Anisfeld, E. A comparison of the cognitive functioning of monolinguals and bilinguals. Unpublished Ph.D. dissertation, McGill University, 1964.

Bouthillier, G. et Meynaud, J. *Le choc des langues au Québec*. Montreal: Les presses de l'universite du Québec, 1972.

Fishman, J. A. *Language and Nationalism*. Rowley, Mass: Newbury House, 1972.

Gendron, J. D. *The position of the French language in Québec*. Quebéc: Editeur officiel du Quebec, 1972.

Henripin, Jacques, La population du Québec en l'an 2000. *Population et fait francais: Les dossiers du Devois*. Montréal: Imprimerie Populaire, 1976, 5-25.

Lambert, W. E. and Tucker, G. R. *Bilingual education of children: The St. Lambert experiment.* Rowley, Mass.: Newbury House Publishers, 1972.

Lieberson, S. *Language and ethnic relations in Canada*. New York: Wiley, 1970.

Official Language Act (Bill 22), Assembleé Nationale du Québec. Québec: Charles-Henri Dubé, Editeur officiel du Québec, 1974.

Official Languages Act. Ottawa: Queen's Printer, 1973.

Porter, J. Higher public servants in the bureaucratic elite in Canada. *Canadian Journal of Economics and Political Science*, 1958, 24, 483-501.

Royal Commission on Bilingualism and Biculturalism. Ottawa: Queen's Printer, 1967, Vol. 1.

Simard, L. M. and Taylor, D. M. The potential for cross-cultural communication in a dyadic situation. *Canadian Journal of Behavioral Science*, 1973, 5, 211-225.

Smith, Brian, Policy with respect to ESL at l'Université Laval. Unpublished research report. TESL Center, Concordia University, Montréal, 1972.

Statistics Canada. *Population by maternal tongue*, 1971.

Taylor, D. M. and Simard, L. M. Social interaction in a bilingual setting. *Canadian Psychological Review*, 1975, 16, 240-254.

Toramanian, Jacqueline, Le'école primaire bilingue pour les immigrants italiens: utopie ou réalité. M. A. Thesis in preparation. Université du Québec à Montréal.

Chapter 20
Cross-Cultural Education in Alaska: Not How But Why?
J. Steven Hikel*

Most articles on cross-cultural education deal with *how* to implement it. After two years-teaching experience in remote Alaskan Eskimo villages, I believe that another question should be asked first: not *how* but *why*?

Why should whites be there? Why should cross-cultural education be attempted at all? The basic issue is not how to do better what has been done, but rather: Should we be doing it? Should one culture try to graft its institutions and values upon another, especially when that graft does not seem to be taking?

Before moving to Alaska, I assumed that the curriculum of native schools would be adapted to the Eskimos' way of life. I was wrong. Education and advanced technology are disrupting the Eskimos' traditional life-style. The curriculum, mostly a carbon copy of that offered in any school in Illinois or Alabama, contributes very little to their well-being; at best, it teaches Eskimos how to fill out official forms necessary for welfare payments, medical care, and supplementary benefits. Native skills have been sacrificed to the almighty mail-order catalogue. A growing group of young people find it increasingly difficult to identify with either their own or the mainland culture. The lack of cultural identity seem to *increase* with educational attainment.

If the curriculum is a true indicator, the school administration has one motive: to assimilate the Eskimo into the mainstream of American culture. Attempts to retain native language, oral history, or native skills are not working. The formal structure of school and curriculum offerings are not wanted, are unnecessasry, and are not valued by the Eskimos. The goals of mainstream society do not apply. Its values are imposed but not assimilated.

Native schools, aimed at assimilation, give little sense of identity and do not allow the Eskimos to retain cultural autonomy. Why should school be meaningful to them when they have not been responsible for its development? In Uncle Sam's stifling paternalism, nearly everything is done for them, decided for them, built for them, purchased for them. Even meanings are determined for them.

Institutional behavior is an acquired habit that has little significance for these people. Interpersonal violence, suicide, alcoholism, and other forms of social disintegration have increased as the schools' influence has spread.

There are many reasons why the schools have not become part of Eskimo villages. One is that the natives can respond to concrete situations with positive, constructive, productive action; but they are less successful in dealing with abstract, intangible problems. In addition, the schools as constructed are an institution for change, but the natives are not educated to participate in, understand, or control change. A pervasive fatalism inherited from the past does not allow them to deal with change effectively. The schools are changing the Eskimo culture in many ways that the natives themselves asre unaware of and thus are unable to control. They have little knowledge of the choices available, little ability to communicate what they want, and little sense of a need to change their basic life-style. Their present welfare state is a poor substitute for the concentrated effort to sustain life that is their heritage.

Because Eskimo parents place little emphasis on formal education, their children are not inclined to value it. The children see their parents subsisting without education. In addition, they soon realize that the federal government makes few demands on them to produce or excel in order to qualify for benevolent aid. So they take advantage of this misplaced generosity and produce only the bare minimum.

Students have little interest in the curriculum—and a correspondingly poor retention of classroom lessons. Many teachers of native students are aware of this lack of retention, but are not aware of its causes. Students' lack of interest and retention makes it difficult for the teacher to feel gratification, or for the student to feel pride in schoolwork. Instead, schools should teach skills that are *valuable in the Eskimo community*.

*J. Steven Hikel is principal of the East Homer Elementary School, Homer, Alaska. Reprinted with permission, Phi Delta Kappan, January, 1977.

Present policy makers seem to desire a carbon copy of the standard white middle-class curriculum, rather than taking into account native heritage and culture. One potentially meaningful change was the introduction of native teacher aides through the Title I program, and the introduction of bicultural activities. The native aide bridges the gap between the local culture and the requirements of a white curriculum. In the bicultural portion of the program, skin sewing, ivory carving, and basket weaving are among the offerings. These programs receive some support from community members, but unfortunately the bicultural program was discontinued because there was no satisfactory way to measure results for the federal funding agency. In one instance the children lost interest in the program when free masterials were used up and the village was asked to contribute.

As Eskimo villages move from a subsistence to a money economy, many problems bearing on education are created. Any economic system makes certain demands on the life-style of those who are a part of it; as an economic system changes, so do its demands upon the people.

There are many governmental programs designed to encourage natives' economic independence. Each year, at great expense to the taxpayer, many youths are sent to receive training, mostly vocational in nature. The idea sounds good, but reality undermines its chances for success. In the initial stages many enrollees drop out before they arrive at the training locations or shortly thereafter. In the training sessions I was aware of personally, the majority of enrollees ended up in a bar, at a friend's house, or, in some cases, in jail for various offenses connected with drunkenness. Many of those who did make it to the training site quickly became disenchanted with the routine and dropped out. Not infrequently, the airline fare provided by the government is used to finance a short vacation away from the local village.

What of those who do complete the training? Unfortunately, their prospects are no brighter. Unless an individual trained in a marketable skill is willing to leave his native village, he has little chance of being employed. In a sense, the teacher who succeeds in educating a student to survive in white society fails the student's own society by forcing him to leave to find employment.

The prohibitive cost of transportation and the lack of local initiative are factors which help rule out the possibility of any financially profitable industry. The government would have to establish, supply, and market for an industry, wholly subsidizing the entire enterprise. Most of the available jobs are civil service, or they are connected with some other program supported at public expense. Furthermore, most natives who did have regular jobs in the villages received their training on the job or during the course of their employment.

Cottage crafts based on utilizing sea mammals are practicable, but increase dependence on the mainland economy. More modern housing, instead of the traditional partially underground dwelling which used skins and tundra sod, has created a demand for electricity and petroleum in place of seal oil lamps. This dependence is now nearly universal. Gasoline is needed for snowmobiles (many of which were purchased by the sale of ivory carvings), the modern-day equivalent of the dog sled. At native stores, more income from crafts has allowed the purchase of an increasing amount of carbohydrates in the form of cookies, crackers, sweetened cereals, sugar, and pasta products. Many dentists, doctors, and nutritionists maintain that, as a result of contact with white culture, the original native diet has worsened.

Because of these and other factors, a growing demand for more tax dollars is being created, without any appreciable increase in the natives' ability to establish a viable, productive economic base. Those few natives who do have regular jobs frequently have a large number of dependents and are able to contribute little toward the public welfare.

Hundreds of years of warfare, rampant famines and disease, and a harsh environment were unable to snuff out Eskimo life. What could not be done by nature or the most brutal instincts of man is being accomplished in the name of cross-cultural education, not because it is so effective but because of its by-products, which are largely ignored by those who are "saving" the native way of life. The Eskimos should be saved from their saviors.

Chapter 21
Third-Culture Kids
Ruth Hill Useem and Richard D. Downie*

The first day, the teacher stood me up in front of the class and said I was from Singapore. The kids at school were tough. They started calling me Chinaman and harassing me. I didn't like being called that. I thought it was something bad to be. I did well in school, though. The teachers liked me, and the school was easy. The schools I went to overseas were tougher."

"When I was 16, I came from Japan to a small town in Indiana. I remember the first time I was out on a date—all we did was drive around to McDonald's and different places. The whole night! I never really got involved much in the school life. A lot of the kids were not planning on going to college, and so we didn't have much in common to talk about. I think I was pretty strange for them, too."

"I think part of the problem when I came to the States was I looked American but I did things that were not quite American. I had fun trying to be an American. It was an act in a way."

No, these are not the observations of new immigrants or foreign visitors. These are the reactions of American third-culture kids (TCK's) who have come "home" after living abroad as dependents of parents who are employed overseas. Although they have grown up *in* foreign countries, they are not integral parts *of* those countries. When they come to their country of citizenship (some for the first time), they do not feel at home because they do not know the lingo or expectations of others—especially those of their own age.

Where they feel most like themselves is in that interstitial culture, the third culture, which is created, shared, and carried by persons who are relating societies, or sections thereof, to each other.

Although some Americans were living outside the United States before World War II, the great burgeoning in numbers of Americans moving overseas began after the War. Now, there are approximately 300,000 school-age American children overseas. Their fathers are missionaries; visiting professors and teachers; representatives of the U.S. government (e.g., employees of the Department of Defense, the Department of State, etc.); employees of international and multinational corporations and financial institutions (e.g., Exxon, First National City Bank, Bell Helicopter); and American employees of international organizations such as the World Health Organization and UNICEF. These fathers are usually highly educated or highly skilled people who are forging the networks that intertwine and interrelate the peoples of the world. (The mothers may be employed overseas, but in most cases, the families have moved because of the fathers' employment.)

To be sure, Americans are not the only ones involved in third cultures. For example, Japanese businessmen work and live in the United States and in Southeast Asia, and diplomats from all countries represent their governments in posts all over the world. Their dependent children can be found in university communities, in the United Nations International School in New York, in the capitals and large cities of the world, and in some of the same overseas schools as American children. In this article, we shall limit our discussion to American TCK's.

The parents' sponsor in the overseas area is crucial in determining the specific part of the third culture in which the TCK's live, the kind of school they attend, the host nationals and third country nationals they will know, and the languages they will learn. These children even have labels that reflect their parents' sponsors— "Army brats," "MK's" (missionary kids), "biz kids," and most recently "oil kids."

Overseas, one of the first questions a TCK asks a new arrival is "What does your father do?" or "Who is your father with?" The answer helps to place young people socially. If, after returning stateside, a TCK asks such a question of a young person who has been reared here, the latter's reaction may be one of puzzlement or resentment. Unlike that of TCK's, the social life of young people reared here is not directly influenced by the father's employer.

TCK's are attached to the third culture through their parents' employers, who hold parents responsible for

*Dr. Ruth Useem, Professor of Education and Sociology, Michigan State University and Dr. Richard Downe, Assistant Dean University of Florida. Reprinted with permission of *Today's Education*, September-October, 1976.

the behavior of their offspring. (If a dependent grossly misbehaves, he or she may be sent home, and the employer may reassign the father or terminate his employment.) Therefore, fathers take an active role in their children's lives and in making family decisions.

In one study of third-culture families, only 6 of 150 TCK's reported that their mothers always or usually made final decisions about family matters. (It should be remembered that almost all overseas American families have both parents present.) Fifty-three percent of Department of Defense dependents claimed that only their fathers made final decisions; 41 percent of children of missionaries said their fathers had the final say in family decisions; and the others involved in the study, including 75 percent of children of those representing the federal government, reported that both parents, and occasionally the children themselves, were involved in decision making.

Most children and youth overseas do not resent strict parental controls, because all of them attached to the same sponsor come under similar rules and, hence, there is community reinforcement. Besides, the overwhelming majority of TCK's (close to 90 percent) like, respect, and feel emotionally attached to their parents.

There are many reasons for this. The high mobility of third-culture families, who usually move every one, two, or four years, seems to have the effect of bringing individual family members closer together. They share the common experience of moving into unfamiliar territory and offer each other mutual support in the face of change and strangeness. Parents are often the only people with whom TCK's have a continuing relationship as they move from one location to another.

American families overseas spend more time together (unless the children are in boarding school) than do their stateside counterparts —and the time together is often not taken up with mundane aspects of living. Mothers are home managers rather than housewives, because they usually have servants to clean up the spilled milk, make the beds, cook the meals, and chauffeur the children. As one overseas mother said, "It's amazing how pleasant conversations with children can be when you are not frantically trying to get the supper on, answer the telephone, and nag the children to pick up their clothes."

The family provides one form of continuity for TCK's. The schools offer another.

There is a remarkable similarity among the approximately 600 schools attended by American children overseas. There are also great differences.

These include variations in the size of the student body (from 10 or 12 up to 6,000 or so); differences in sponsorship (e.g., Department of Defense schools, schools assisted by the Department of State, private and entrepreneurial schools, those sponsored by corporations, and those run by Catholic orders and Protestant churches); and widely different make-ups of student bodies (e.g., from Americans only to Americans in the minority).

All of these schools place a heavy emphasis upon academic performance, and the secondary schools are college-prep oriented. The curriculum resembles that of stateside schools with the same orientation, but the overseas schools usually offer enrichment courses in the local language and culture. Books and material (which often don't arrive or come late) are generally imported from the United States.

The avowed purpose of most American-sponsored overseas schools has been to prepare American pupils for entering the mainstream of American society; stateside schools and colleges, to the extent to which they notice TCK's at all, have been concerned with their "problems of adjustment" to their peers. Neither the overseas nor the stateside schools have seen the TCK's as people who, as adults, will be following in their parents' footsteps and fulfilling mediating roles in the increasingly conflictive but interdependent global system. Nor do the schools see that solving some "problems of adjustment" offers TCK's valuable experience that can help prepare them for their future roles—which will probably be international.

One reason the schools lack appreciation for the great potentialities of these young people is that few educators have studied TCK's. In a bibliography on third-culture education that we compiled at the Institute for International Studies in Education, only 10 of the 50 dissertations listed concern TCK's—how they feel and perform what they value, what they aspire to, and how they view the world and themselves in relation to it.

(Given the rather thin reeds on which to rest generalizations about these youth, and given the rapidity with which third cultures and national cultures change, we warn the readers that what we are reporting here is suggestive rather than definitive.)

One study of 150 college-enrolled TCK's of varying sponsorship and residence abroad (but all of whom had spent a minimum of one teen year overseas) produced a dramatic finding: Not one preferred to pursue a career exclusively in the United States. One-fourth named a specific place overseas where they would like to work (usually the location where they had lived during their teen years); 29 percent expressed interest in following an overseas-based occupation but wanted to move from country to country; 25 percent wanted to be headquartered in the United States with periodic one- or two-year assignments abroad; and 12 percent wanted to be employed in the United States but to have opportunity for overseas job-related travel.

In order to qualify for careers in the third culture, these young people recognize that they must be well-educated and/or highly skilled. (There are few unskilled or even semiskilled third-culture occupations.) Thus they aspire, even when in secondary school, to attain college degrees, and many anticipate getting professional and advanced degrees or mastering highly specialized skills.

One important reason that TCK's want to work in an international occupation, whether pursued entirely or partially abroad, is that they feel most "at home" in third-culture networks. Only 7 percent report feeling "at home" with their peers in the United States, while 74 percent say they feel most comfortable with people who are internationally oriented and who have lived abroad.

Yet such preferences do not imply that a person is rootless or has made a "poor adjustment." As one TCK with Asian experience says, "I guess I could live anywhere and be comfortable. I have always liked to think I get along with all different people. I don't feel bothered by a lack of roots, and I don't think I have a lot of problems because of that."

To be sure, some TCK's have severe emotional problems that cannot be resolved without outside help —and some problems not even then. But the rate is probably not greater among these foreign-experienced youth than it is among the general American population of the same age.

The reported experiences of these youth suggest that they cope rather than adjust, and, as one student of multicultural persons describes them, they become both "a part of" and "apart from" whatever situation they are in. A TCK with Asian and African experience explains, "I find myself sitting back and objectively observing Americans and American society, occasionally smiling and occasionally shaking my head. I get along comfortably with both, but then again, there is a bit of me that remains apart."

Most third-culture kids are more familiar with foreign languages than are their stateside counterparts. One researcher reports that 92 percent of the TCK's she studied learn one or more foreign languages, mostly languages used in many parts of the world, such as Spanish, German, and French. Twenty-six percent claim knowledge of languages other than, or in addition to these, such as Yoruba, Hausa, Urdu, Kijita, Swahili, Amharic, Kalagan, Marathi, Kisukuma, Chinese, and Quiche. (In U.S. public secondary schools, less than .5 percent learn languages other than French, Spanish, German, and Latin.)

TCK's learn some languages in schools abroad and some in their homes or in the marketplaces of a foreign land. One-third of these youngsters are children of cross-cultural marriages and/or foreign-born parents, and they use a language other than English at home or when visiting relatives. Some pick up languages from the servants in the home or from playmates in the neighborhood.

Although most third-culture kids lose their proficiency in the foreign language when they return to an all-English-speaking environment, many pursue languages they have already learned, and some become literate in the languages they can speak. Few have emotional blockages about learning a new language—particularly if they perceive it as useful for the career they want to pursue in the future.

What can stateside teachers do to assist these youth when they return to the United States? Perhaps the best answer is for teachers to challenge them academically, both because this gives them continuity with their past and because this helps prepare them for the futures they desire.

Teachers should also try not to make these students' uniqueness a problem for them in school. Each TCK wants to be treated as an individual, not stereotyped as the "new student from Kuwait."

One TCK who lived in the Far East sums up her feelings about her experiences upon returning to the United States in this way: "I was made to feel like an odd person, a creature from another place—and I wasn't. I speak English, and I understand everything Americans say. My teacher and the people in the town where I was living didn't really see *me*—they just saw the difference."

FOR FURTHER READING

Soddy, Kenneth, M.D., editor. *Identity: Mental Health and Value Systems.* Philadelphia: J.B. Lippincott Co., 1961.

U.S. Bureau of the Census, 1970 Census of Population. *Americans Living Abroad.* Subject Report PC (2)-10A. Washington, DC: U.S. Government Printing Office, 1973.

Useem, John; Donoghue, John D.; and Useem, Ruth HIll. "Men in the Middle of the Third Culture: The Roles of American and Non-Western Peoples in Cross-Cultural Administration." *Human Organization* 22: 169-79; Fall 1963.

Useem, Ruth Hill. "Third Culture Factors in Educational Change." *Cultural Challenges to Education* (Edited by Cole S. Brembeck and Walker H. Hill.) Lexington, Mass: D.C. Heath & Co., 1973.

Useem, Ruth Hill, editor. *Third Culture Children: An Annotated Bibliography.* East Lansing: Institute for International Studies in Education, Michigan State University, 1975.

Section III
Language Acquisition

Introduction by Evelyn Colon LaFontaine*

If there is any one aspect of bilingual education which surfaces as the most visible and most easily understood by the public at large, it is the concept of language development and language acquisition. The very term "bilingual" defines rath explicitly the fact that these programs center around the use of two languages. And yet, the development of bilingual programs throughout the country in the past ten years has sometimes been accompanied by confusing definitions and unclear goals. It would seem obvious that if nothing else, bilingual education programs must focus on efforts to maintain and develop the language skills of the participating students. Those of us who are practitioners in the field, know quite well that the philosophy and objectives of bilingual-bicultural programs, are far more comprehensive in scope. However, if we are to concentrate on one component at a time, it behooves us to consider the area of language acquisition as one of the most essatial aspect of bilingual programs. The articles in this section focus on this very subject.

Some of the articles, such as those by McClure and Wentz and Genishi, discuss specific aspects of language usage and the possible implications for bilingual programs. The two articles by these authors examine language use and code-switching among young children. The articles impress upon us the need for researchers to look more deeply into the question of how bilinguals or potential bilinguals, particularly young children, use two languages. Further inquiry by researchers into the process of language development and acquisition is needed in order to formulate a firmer theoretical base from which practitioners can improve, alter and/or strngthen methods for using as well as teaching languages in a bilingual program.

At present, there are divergent views with regard to the approaches and methods to be used for language development in bilingual programs. There are several articles in this section that consider the process by which students acquire language skills in the more structured setting of institutional schooling. The articles by Atzmon and Raisner describe students, including adults, as they progress from fundamental conversational language skills to more sophisticated skills of reading and writing. Krulik and Polston focus on many of the key issues faced in programs for teaching English as a second language, while Laudin discusses the influences that have affected the development of the languages of native Americans.

DeAvila and Duncan discuss more technical considerations related to the assessment of language performance. They present some of the major problems which face us and offer what they describe as a sociolinguistic alternative in this area. The need for more effective methods of assessing language is made clearly apparent in their article. Rudolph Troike underscores the need for more research with regard to language particularly in linguistics and wisely calls for practitioners of bilingual education to take greater advantage of the contributions of linguistics.

This collection of articles clearly does not cover all of the possible general areas that could be discussed regarding language acquisition. It serves well, however, to alert the novice and remind the advanced student that the development of language skills is a complex and uncertain process in any case, but that when one is concerned with the development of two languages the complexity increases dramatically. It is this complexity which must be addressed by practitioners in the field with scholarly perseverance if we are to develop programs which can effectively achieve the objective of producing students proficient in two languages.

During these first ten years of contemporary bilingual-bicultural education in this country, it has been necessary to spend the major part of our

*Mrs. Evelyn Colon LaFontaine, Assistant Principal, New York City Board of Education.

energy and time in fighting for the development and implementation of programs—convincing opponents, penetrating resistant and often hostile educational institutions, involving parents, recruiting and training teachers, searching for materials, etc. Little energy or time was left for pure research in critical areas such as language acquisition and language development. The future of "bilingual" education may well depend on how much time, energy and attention we donate to language research during the next ten years, and how well we use the information from this research to improve instructional approaches and strategies in the bilingual classroom.

Chapter 22
Language and Linguistics in Bilingual-Bicultural Education
Rudolph C. Troike*

Bilingual education, by whatever name—vernacular education, mother-tongue education, educación bilingüe—is undoubtedly the greatest single educational movement in the world today. Experience in many countries has shown—and it is my own profound conviction—that linguistics has an important, indeed crucial, contribution to make to the successful achievement of the goals of bilingual-bicultural education in this country. It is also my deep concern, and the motivation for my personal involvement in bilingual education during the past decade, that unless educators make use of the contributions which linguistics has to offer, this great movement may fail, and be rejected as another promising educational innovation that was regrettably unable to achieve its goals.

Since we pride ourselves in this country on how advanced we are, it is ironic that countries of the so-called "developing" or third world—Mexico, Peru, India, the Philippines, Nigeria—are far ahead of us in recognizing the need for input from linguistics, and in making use of linguists in all of their key policy-making, materials development, and teacher-training efforts. The United States is almost alone in not doing so, and it is urgent that educators in this country awake to the need and act on it before it is too late.

A conference to be held later this month in San Francisco under the sponsorship of the Center for Applied Linguistics, with support from the National Institute of Education, will explore in depth the ways in which linguistics and language research is relevant to bilingual education. In the present discussion I can only summarize some of the central aspects of the matter. First, it is essential to point out that linguistics, like all sciences, has many facets, and some of these are of more immediate relevance to educators than others. Secondly, there are *degrees* or *levels* of relevance, and while a knowledge of Einstein's theory of relativity was necessary for those who planned the voyages to the moon, for example, the men who built the rockets did not have to be theoretical physicists. However, *they did have to have knowledge pertinent to their particular tasks in the chain of responsibility,* or the space missions could never have succeeded. Thus teachers should not be expected to be linguistic theoreticians, but those who are responsible for curriculum planning, materials preparation, test development, or program supervision had better know the results of lingusitic research in detail if their programs are to succeed.

Why is linguistics, or the understanding that a knowledge of linguistics provides, basic to bilingual education? To begin with the obvious, bilingual education by its very definition involves the planned use of language—two or more languages, to be precise—to attain certain educational goals. Since linguistics is preeminently the science that deals with language, it is therefore evident on the face of it that linguistic knowledge must be of fundamental relevance to bilingual education.

Although social and cultural factors may be of overriding importance in many aspects of bilingual education, even these factors are significantly reflected in language, and language exerts a very powerful effect in both cognitive and affective aspects of learning. This fact is often overlooked by educators, however, because *language is so very much the hidden dimension of instruction, unrecognized because like the air we breathe, it appears to be simply a transparent medium through which we communicate.* Yet it is not, and it is in that fact that so much of the relevance of linguistics lies.

For one thing, people often have strong social attitudes toward language, both their own and that of others, which need to be recognized in the instructional process. These attitudes in turn have an important influence on behavior, including that of teachers, parents, and administrators, as well as students. Some of these attitudes, which may have a very negative effect on students' learning, arise from a lack of knowledge about language that linguistics can supply.

*Dr. Rudolph Troike, Director Center for Applied Linguistics, Washington, D. C.

To illustrate, let me present a few examples. We all know that languages vary in various ways, but because people do not understand how and why these variations occur, they often attribute unwarranted characteristics to them. They then guide their actions on the basis of these attributions, often with unfortunate results. One very common belief is that languages have, or should have, a pure or "correct" form, and that deviations from this supposed standard are inherently wrong or corrupt. So long as people believe this, they will act accordingly. But language is a human institution, and linguists have known for over a century that this variation is a natural and normal thing. It is not something to be either decried or rejected, but simply a fact to be understood and recognized. Once this is done, more intelligent and effective program decisions and instructional strategies can be adopted.

It is important, therefore, to understand how and why variation occurs in language, and what its significance is. We need to recognize, first of all, that every language is a historical product—the accumulated result of the experiences of its users over many centuries. Thus, in English, for example, words like *fish* and *father* go back thousands of years, as shown by their relationship to Spanish *pesca* and *padre*, while words like *chocolate* and *tomato* have been in the language only a few hundred years, having been borrowed from Spanish, which in turn borrowed them from Aztec. On the other hand, the word for "man," *wer* or *wir*, which both languages once shared, has been lost by both (except in such derived forms as *were-wolf* or *virilidad*).

Similarly, grammatical features come and go in the history of a language. The use of the *s* to mark the possessive in English is quite ancient, while the Veracruz and Sonora), are distinct regional varieties. Thus it is important to recognize that each of these varieties has a pedigree as ancient and honorable as any other, no matter who speaks its. Linguists express this by saying that no one variety of a language is inherently better or more logical or more beautiful or whatever than any other. (However, if a teacher *thinks* that it is, he or she may react to a student's use of a particular variety in a negative way, by criticizing the student or otherwise making him ashamed of his speech.)

Not all change proceeds just along regional lines. When a society becomes complex enough to have cities, with different social classes, change will occur differentially along social lines and between city and country. The usage of the upper classes, in the cities, becomes prestigious because of their social position and power. Social identity becomes bound up with linguistic form, which becomes a marker of status and a potential tool of social discrimination.

It is an interesting fact that change tends to go on most rapidly in cities and among the educated upper classes, while rural dwellers and lower class groups are often linguistically more conservative. Thus such forms as multiple negatives in English (e.g., *I don't have nothing*) were in regular use in upper-class speech until the seventeenth century, while a verb form such as *vide* in Spanish (instead of *vi* "I saw"), was used by none less than Julius Caesar in this famous line, *Vini, vidi, vici,* "I came, I saw, I conquered."

All of these facts become important to us in very vital ways in planning and conducting bilingual programs, for *language is not merely a social phenomena, but a psychological one as well, which is intimately bound up with self-concept, learning, and social interaction.* Indeed, language is at the very interface of social interaction, for it is the principal means for manipulating social relationships, and in one form or another, the principal medium for carrying out instruction.

The understanding of how languages change, and how varieties come to exist, then, is one area of linguistic knowledge of relevance to bilingual education. This gives us a scientific basis for, on the one hand, emphatically rejecting the notion that a child is linguistically handicapped or disadvantaged because he does not know English, and on the other, equally rejecting the notion that he is unintelligent or retarded because he does not speak an educated middle-class variety of Spanish or English. *While schools have the obligation to teach children an educated variety (there is no single such variety) of the national language, they also have an obligation to recognize and value the linguistic skills a child brings to school, and to use and build upon those skills to maximize the learning process, both cognitively and affectively. The teacher also needs to realize the extent to which the language a child uses is both a part of him and a badge of his group identity, and show respect and acceptance for his language while helping him develop his linguistic skills and acquire command of a more educated variety of the language. This is crucial to helping strengthen the child's self-concept and achieving one of the major goals of education.*

These facts are also relevant to such matters as test development, the teaching of reading, and special education, for it is important in all of these to recognize the significance of regional and social variety, and interpret it appropriately in the context of student performance. The evaluation of student achievement is heavily affected by reactions to language, and understanding of linguistic variety. We know, for example, that many tests are linguistically biased, whether they are in English or Spanish, and a better knowledge of language is needed both in the construction and interpretation of tests.

The area of sociolinguistic research in recent years has highlighted the need to recognize the significance of the *functional* dimension of language use in bilingualism and language development. *Linguists speak of language being learned and used for particular social purposes and in different domains. It is also used in different types of social settings. Learning a language, both one's native language or a second language, involves all of these.* In fact, linguists today strongly emphasizes that language is *not* something which is to be taught and studied in isolation, as an end in itself, but that language is deeply interwoven with culture, and that what one should aim to teach is not merely language, or linguistic competence, but *communicative competence*—the total ability to use a language in the widest range of communicative contexts, including all of the traditional skills of spoken as well as written language.

This is why in the master plan for the San Francisco schools, which the Center for Applied Linguistics developed in response to the Supreme Court decision in the *Lau* vs. *Nichols* case, we recommended that an ESL program alone was *not* adequate for teaching children from a different language background at the elementary level. This recommendation has been adopted in the recent Office of Civil Rights guidelines for compliance with the *Lau* decision. We further recommended that ESL instruction as traditionally conducted be rejected as inadequate, since it teaches the language as an *object* rather than as a *tool of learning and communication*. Traditional ESL was fundamentally assimilationist and ethnocentric, giving little or no recognition to other languages and cultures. In addition, it was primarily designed for use with adults and based on outmoded behaviorist models of learning. While inadequate for adults in the first place, it was highly inappropriate for children and frequently psychologically destructive. There is an urgent need for a complete overhaul of methods and approaches in teaching English to speakers from other language backgrounds, and linguistic theory provides an important basis for such an overhaul.

I can only mention in passing the other areas in which linguistics can make a significant contribution toward the achievement of quality in bilingual programs. Briefly, these are teacher training, curriculum development, evaluation, and language learning.

a. Teacher training: In addition to an understanding of the nature of language and a knowledge of the facts and causes of linguistic change and variation, teachers must have fluent competence in using the non-English language of instruction in ways appropriate to classroom settings. Linguists can help define the necessary content of such competence and aid in development training to achieve it.

b. Curriculum development: Most materials preparation and syllabus construction has gone on with no research input regarding the linguistic competencies of children of different age levels and language backgrounds. Millions of dollars have been spent on materials development compared with only a few thousand on research. Even on the basis of this limited research, however, and a knowledge of regional and social variation, linguists can make a significant contribution to the process of curriculum design and materials development. In fact, no materials development should be permitted without the participation of linguists in the process. I hope we may reach the time before long when this will be the case.

c. Evaluation: *One of the greatest needs right now in bilingual education is for better program evaluation and improved techniques and instruments for student assessment.* (The Center for Applied Linguistics currently has a project underway in Illinois to develop a model evaluation and produce guidelines for the evaluation of bilingual programs.) The tendency in most bilingual programs, as in other educational programs, to uncritically utilize educational psychologists or test and measurement specialists as evaluators and test developers, on the assumption that they are technically knowledgeable enough in all relevant areas of the program, has resulted in large numbers of often superficially sophisticated evaluation reports which are worthless either as contributions to the research data on bilingual education or as sources of guidance for the improvement of the programs concerned. So-called internal evaluations are of little more value, and not infrequently even less. More existing language tests are either biased or inappropriate, and very few have had any input from linguists. Unfortunately, in matters where their expertise could count the most, linguists are usually the last to be consulted, with often wasteful if not tragic consequences.

d. Language learning: A tremendous change is taking place today both in linguistics and in the language teaching field which is of great significance for bilingual education. We are coming to know a great deal more about the language learning process, both for first and second languages, and how to facilitate the acquisition of communication skills by the learner. It is interesting that, beginning from different bases, the two fields have been independently converging in their understandings. While there is still much more to be learned before a final synthesis can be reached, enough is known and agreed on now that it can and should form part of the training program for every teacher, supervisor, and curriculum developer. These changes have seriously obsoleted most existing materials, methods courses, and the training possessed by personnel now in service, and urgently require their revision if they are to be appropriate for bilingual programs. Here again, input from linguists is important. One thing these changes have done is to provide sound justification for bilingual-bicultural education as the right way to go in creating opportunities for individuals to fully realize their linguistic potential.

My point here has been that whatever role we assign language in bilingual-bicultural education, if we are at all interested in quality in our programs, it is essential that the input of linguistics and linguists be sought in all aspects of the effort, from teacher training to materials development and evaluation. Bilingual education is one of the greatest movements in the history of American education, and has an important contribution to make to the realization of a pluralistic society in the United States through the provision of equal education opportunity for all linguistic and cultural groups. If it is to fulfill its promise, however, the experience of other countries, which has demonstrated the central relevance of linguistics, should be taken into account, if we are not to waste millions of dollars and human lives attempting to reinvent the wheel.

Chapter 23

A Few Thoughts About Language Assessment and A Sociolinguistic Alternative to the Lau Remedies

Ed DeAvila and Sharon Duncan*

The opinion of the Supreme Court of the United States in the class suit Lau vs. Nichols was delivered January 21, 1974, but its mandate with respect to providing non-English-speaking children in this country a "meaningful opportunity to participate in the public educational program" is not yet close to being met.

The problem raised in the Lau action is a matter of language instruction—specifically, the failure of a school system "...to provide English language instruction to approximately 1,800 students...who do not speak English..." This failure violates section 601 of the Civil Rights Act of 1964, which bans discrimination based on race, color or national origin in programs receiving federal financial assistance.

Almost immediately after the Lau ruling, the Office of Civil Rights (OCR) required all districts receiving federal funds to conduct a "language survey" to identify those children whose home language was other than English. When OCR followed up the Lau decision with this survey and published a list of 333 school districts which were "out of compliance" with the *Lau* decision, and subsequently prepared a set of guidelines to be followed by these school districts, the issue of language became both a socio-political and legal issue for the entire country. At the very heart of this issue lay the strong implication that school districts found to be out of compliance with the *Lau* decision would run the risk of forfeiting federal assistance for special programs. Insofar as this meant a possible loss of revenues school districts can ill afford to lose, district officials sought guidance from OCR.

The upshot of all this was that OCR, in an effort to assist school districts, prepared a set of recommendations which have come to be known as the *Lau Remedies*. The recommendations in the Lau Remedies are meant to help school districts from running afoul with the law. As such, questions pertaining to assessment, linguistic development, classroom placement, program design, and so on, which were normally under the purview of the educators, psychologists, linguists and other social scientists became the default responsibility of OCR officials. And, in the absence of "good hard empirical evidence" OCR officials were called upon to set up recommendations to provide ready made and practical solutions to some of the knottiest intellectual problems which have for years beset practitioner and researcher alike.

As the basic issue in the Lau decision was the fact that the approximately 1,800 children involved in the case did not speak English, the question of language assessment became a focal point in the Lau Remedies. In fact, it would seem that the issue of language assessment formed the very basis of the Lau Remedies since all else seems to follow from a determination of the linguistic make-up of the schools. In the following, we would like to examine the issue of language assessment. As will be seen, an examination of this issue reveals a far more complicated picture than origianlly understood. Unfortunately, this is a picture which is characterized by paradoxes, dilemmas and any number of unresolved social and political issues which are not as amenable to change as we might think. In fact, it may turn out that language is not the problem. Rather it is a unique combination of attitudes toward language, ethnicity, self and society which contribute.

As a means for helping districts determine the extent of their problem, OCR, in the absence of a research base, developed a five-level system for categorizing school children's language patterns.

A. Monolingual speaker of the language other than English (speaks the language other than English exclusively).

B. Predominantly speaks the language other than English (speaks mostly the language other than English, but speaks some English).

C. Bilingual (speaks both the language other than English and English with equal ease).

D. Predominantly speaks English (speaks mostly English, but some of the language other than English).

E. Monolingual speaker of English (speaks English exclusively).

(Lau Remedies, 1975, p. 3)

With the possible exceptions of the two extreme levels (i.e. A and E) one is immediately struck by the loose manner in which these levels are defined. As such, they bear no resemblance to the "operational definitions" found in the sciences which require that definitions be given in terms of concrete operations, such as scores on tests, numbers of items passed and so on. What this means unfortunately, from the point of view of a researcher, is that there is no clear way of deciding which of these categories apply to actual behavior, whether it be in the school or in any other linguistic context. One is also left wondering if the partitions provided in this system bear any resemblance to the qualitative/quantitative stages found in second language acquisition. In which case, it may be that what we are referring to as a language deficit is simply the natural expression of the different levels or stages of second language acquisition.

From the measurement point of view, as it will be seen, the five level system set up by the Lau Task Force lacked either theoretical or empirical basis and, in that sense, was totally dictated by the practical need for having some system which could serve as a general guideline. The major difficulty lies not so much in the fact that the system was arbitrary but that its relation to either theory or explicit measurement procedures was unstated. In this very real way, school districts were left to their own devices. As will be seen from the following analysis, school districts have been hard put to find much in the way of meaningful solutions. Conversely, not wanting to place itself in the position of advocacy, OCR has found it equally difficult to offer very concrete recommendations beyond those dealing with the legal aspects of the court's ruling.

It is fortunate that the Federal Government has, within the past year, funded a series of *Lau* centers whose responsibility is to assist schools found to be "out of compliance." It will become the responsibility of the professionals working in these centers to provide the leadership in working through and clarifying some of the above mentioned issues. Insofar as these centers are only now getting settled, the present discussion will not include their various approaches to the different aspects of the problem.

The fundamental issue underlying the Lau decision lies in the fact that there are significant numbers of children who are being denied an equal educational opportunity by virtue of the fact that they may or may not have the English language skills necessary to full participation in the current educational system. It is therefore the responsibility of the educational leadership to find ways to assist these children so they can more readily participate. As matters currently stand in the United States they are not going to participate if they are not proficient in English.

On the surface, the problem would seem simple enough, and herein lies the first major obstacle in implementing the spirit of the Lau decision. If the problem is simply providing English language skills, as many seem to believe, then the solution is simply in deciding which children are in need and assigning them to special remedial classes. However, the problem is far more complex. Let us begin by considering the problem of testing.

Let us begin by asking a number of questions, independent of Lau, about why we are testing: are there available instruments; are these instruments compatible with the backgrounds of the children; do they provide the kind of information that will assist the learner or do they simply fulfill legal requirements? Do they provide results which are consistent across different linguistic contexts (does the child speak the same way in all situations)? Do they stand up psychometrically? Do they test all of the various aspects of language? Do they provide comparable results? Do they provide results which simultaneously meet legal and educational requirements? Lastly, are there specific programs for each level, and if so, do these programs carry equal status with other programs, or are they simply the old programs designed for the "culturally disadvantaged" in a new form? Let us consider some of these questions. As will be seen, we have no specific set of answers. We do, however, have a great many questions.

From the point of view of *Lau* the only defensible reason for testing is to determine which children do or do not have the requisite skills to allow them to participate in the current educational systems, i.e., the ones who are not sufficiently proficient enough in the English language to participate. The unfortunate part here is that while a test of language "dominance" may be a convenient way to satisfy the legal aspects of the Lau decision, it tells nothing about specific needs of an individual child. A student who scores in the 79 percentile in English and the 65 percentile in Spanish is easily classified as "English dominant." The real truth is that that child may have problems in both languages. Or what about a student who scores in the 65 percentile in both languages? According to the Lau categories, he or she would be classified as a perfect bilingual.

The real problem here is that the concept of "dominance" is as ill defined as the Lau categories. Moreover, how does the concept of dominance clarify the relation between the child's linguistic development and school achievement in such a way that we can do something about it? Another way of asking this question is by asking whether or not "dominance" in and of itself determines either what is learned or can be learned.

Immediately school administrators ask for help in deciding which test to use. The immediate answer is that they should use the valid one. But which one is valid? Inasmuch as the OCR Remedies specifically state that the intent behind the district's assessment of linguistic ability is "...to place the student(s) in one of the following categories by language," then it is the Lau decision that has served as criterion validation and the instruments a district uses are valid if they can place students into the five levels set out in the OCR Remedies.

What this has meant is that to a large extent, the normal process of research has been suspended as a result of the need for a practical action. Furthermore, this has placed OCR personnel in the precarious position of having to make judgment about an instrument's technical properties without the benefit of research or a background in the field. However, problems associated with issues of predictive concurrent, and other indicies of validity and reliability are technical in nature and not particularly within the scope of this discussion. The key point to the present discussion is that these are technical issues associated with attempts to deal with the question of whether or not a test really measures what it purports to in a reliable way. And, with few exceptions, these issues have been subordinated by practical necessity. Therefore, let us leave the more technical issues of psychometrics aside for the moment and briefly consider the question of what to measure.

Based on the Project Best (1974, 1975) descriptive bibliography of instruments available for use in the assessment of bilingual programs and from data compiled by the Texas Education Agency (1975) on oral language assessment instruments, as well as our own examination of available instruments, we have completed a preliminary analysis of 44 currently available language assessment instruments: twenty of these instruments are classified as "long dominance" tests; twenty-nine can be classified as "long proficiency" tests; and seven instruments measure both "dominance" and "proficiency." Further findings will be discussed below within the context of the nature and structure of language.

It is a generally accepted notion that language consists of four primary subsystems: The *phonemic system* (the basic sounds of the language), the *referential system* (the "words" of the language), the *syntactical system* (the rules for making meaningful sentences), and the *pragmatic system* (the use of language to obtain specific goals). It also assumes, following McElroy (1972), that a measure of language skill must be first concerned with what the person *can* do and not what he/she usually does.

The Phonemic System, the foundation of any language is its phonemic system. It is from this small set of basic sounds that all meaningful words of the language are constructed. For this reason if the student cannot hear the difference between these basic sounds

(*decode* them) then he/she will not be able to understand words constructed from them in daily and instructional conversations. On the other hand, if the student cannot pronounce the sounds (*encode* them) then others will have difficulties in understanding his/her communications. It is these phonemes and the variants or allophones, which present the most difficulties to the student moving from one language to another. In addition there is increasing evidence that familiarity with the phonemic system is a very important aspect of learning to read and write (C. Chomsky, 1970; N. Chomsky, 1970; Read, 1971).

Of the 44 language assessment instruments we examined, only three included a measure of phoneme production. Of these, three were tests of Spanish proficiency, one was a test of English proficiency. We found no instrument described as a test of language dominance which included a measure of phoneme production.

There were five tests which measured auditory discrimination. Three were tests of language proficiency, two assessed both proficiency and dominance.

It is our feeling that the purpose of including auditory discrimination and phoneme production items in an assessment of language is in order to determine if the subject has a problem with a *significant* aspect of language, i.e., does he or she have a communication problem and thus a need for help? Whether or not a child pronounces the initial "p" of the American English word party as an aspirated or as an unaspirated stop, there probably won't be any lack of communication. On the other hand, if the child cannot distinguish between "sheep" and "cheap" or "yellow" and "jello" in either coding or encoding, there will likely be a breakdown in communication and/or an occasion for ridicule, as in the case of a visiting foreign student who announced, "When I go out to dinner, I always wash the hostess." Thus it would seem that a measure of auditory discrimination or production should include the *significant* sounds in the target language.

The Referential System (Lexical), the next level of language, consists of the meaningful units constructed from the basic phonemes. It is this level of "words" (Lexical items or morphemes) which ultimately determines the meaning of any sentence (Langacker, 1967). In addition, it appears that a knowledge of at least some lexical items are extremely important if not absolutely necessary for acquiring syntax of the corresponding language (Moeser & Bregman, 1972; Moeser & Olson, 1974). Unfortunately, in assessing the repertoire of referential units, we encountered substantial extralinguistic factors, namely the student's level of education and environment. If the level of education is high and environment offers diverse experiences the student will learn a wide range of words. For the restricted student the opportunity for word acquisition is considerably less. It is for this reason that most vocabulary tests correlate very highly with I.Q. scores (Irwin, 1960) and socioeconomic class (e.g. Osser, Wang & Zaid, 1969).

Forty of the forty-four tests included in our analysis measured various levels of lexical ability: the ability to respond to isolated words. Twenty of these tests assessed aural lexical comprehension; fifteen measured oral lexical production; and six included a measure of written lexical comprehension (i.e. reading).

It is quite true, as Miller (1965) emphasizes, that a sentence is not "a linear sum of the significance of the words that comprise it." It is also true that words in isolation may have different meanings. However, the fact that a student has problems with American English lexical items is an indication of a weakness in overall language growth. Either the student has not abstracted commonly encountered words or the student has had little or no experience in the language. In either case, from the point of view of the educator, the student has a language need.

The third level of language is the syntactical system (the rules for combining words into a meaningful sentence). Syntax is essential for the understanding of the language because the relationship between words provides a major contribution to the meaning of communications in that language. For example, while the sentence "the cat chases the rat" has the same words as the sentence "the rat chases the cat", they have very different meanings. The meaning of a sentence also depends on how words are grouped. As in Miller's (1965) excellent example, the sentence, "They are hunting dogs", may have two distinct meanings depending on whether we group "are hunting" or "hunting dogs."

The usual method of assessing linguistic ability (and specifically, syntactical ability) is through the analysis of the subject's linguistic production. It should be noted that there are a number of problems inherent in using this method to assess syntax.

1. The meanings of the results are difficult to interpret because they do not distinguish between what the subject *can* do and what it *does* do (McNeill, 1970);

2. Substantial effects due to socioeconomic class have been observed (Moore, 1971);

3. Interactions between situation and sub-cultural groups are often found (Brukman, 1973);

4. It is very difficult to know the exact input the child is responding to;

5. The interpretation of the results must take into account the age of the subject; and

6. Variations in syntax do not mean communication is necessarily lost.

Thirty-three of the forty-one tests included items assessing oral syntax comprehension and thirty-one measured oral syntax production. Thirteen measured written syntax comprehension (i.e. reading), and nine included written syntax production.

In an effort to isolate those tests which most completely covered the four components of syntactical ability — listening, speaking, reading and writing — we found five instruments which measured both aural syntax comprehension, and oral production as well as written syntax comprehension and production. Of these five, two were proficiency tests for high school and adult students of languages other than English and three were Spanish and English "language dominance" tests covering grades K to 12, Pre K to 6 and K to 12 respectively.

The fourth subsystem of language is a person's ability to use the language for his/her own ends (pragmatics). Examples of pragmatic use of language include a student's ability to carry out relevant tasks requiring language; such as playing with peers, shopping at the store, reading a newspaper, asking directions from a policeman or writing a letter to a friend. This area has generally been overlooked in both research and application. Seven of the forty one tests we analyzed included items which could be classified as pragmatic. These usually took the form of an oral interview with the subject who was directly questioned regarding his/her language habits. All of these seven tests were classified as tests of "language dominance."

In summary, our review seems to show that different tests seem to measure different things. And no single test seems to measure all of the various aspects thought to be important. How well they do measure what they claim to is still another question. It would be foolhardy to attempt to review the multitudinous fashions in which authors have attempted to validate their works. There seems to be no consistent pattern. Moreover, since to our knowledge, none of these instruments was specifically designed to meet Lau requirements, it would be equally foolhardy to discuss whether or not they were validated against the five level category system. In closing then, let us consider a few issues in the more general sense.

If the question involved in the Lau decision is actually one of language, then there are three alternatives:

1. ESL

2. Immersion in English

3. Native Language Immersion with ESL

In most ESL programs, the child is pulled out of the regular classroom for a short period of time and given instruction in English language arts, then returned to the classroom where he does not comprehend and cannot respond for the rest of the day. This leaves the child outside of "participating" in a full educational experience. By the same token, it means that the child's linguistic experience (i.e. ESL class time) is outside of the normal educational context. That is, as the child learns English he/she is falling further and further behind in all other subject areas.

Complete immersion in English is certainly a viable alternative and one which should have the effect of preparing the child for participation in the educational process. Basically this is what we find in the schools today and there are any number of immigrants from Europe and other places throughout the world, who would speak for this sink-or-swim technique. With respect to the Chicano, Latin American, or any child living in a highly ethnically homogeneous neighborhood, the technique has little chance for success. The primary reason is that the children are simply not afforded language models outside of the school's which are really any different from themselves. In other words, there is little motivation for speaking standard English outside of the schools. Further, why even try when there is little in the way of positive reinforcement for trying. And anything less than perfect is labeled as "pocho", deficit or substandard.

Paradoxically, it is also of some value to note that this method has had the greatest success of any of the attempts to promote bilingualism (see Cohen, 1975: Lambert & Pearl, 1972). The bitter irony, however, is that it doesn't seem to work in the absence of equal status for both languages. In other words, Chicano children are simply not going to want to learn standard English as long as their own language (substandard though it may be) is held as an object of scorn and ridicule.

Potentially the third alternative is most unique and enriching. This approach offers full time instruction in the child's native language with simultaneous instruction in English as a second language in the same way that for quite a few years American students in some school districts have been receiving instruction in English with simultaneous instruction in French or in Spanish as a second language. Through this approach there is no longer any problem with getting the linguistically different child to a level at which he or she can participate; any child of school age is already there in his/her native language. The results of this kind of program are multiple.

The linguistically different child becomes a genuine bilingual. The native language is maintained and at the same time the school instruction and the dominant English language of his environment ensure that he/she becomes proficient in English. In addition, a total

second language eduction — whether it be Spanish or Chinese - is made available to the American English speaking child, with all the concurrent advantages in attitude and intelligence, and at no extra cost to the school district.

The assumption underlying the Lau decision and for that matter any programs aimed at the remediation of an English language deficit is that children from homes where English is not the first language will fail in the schools as long as they don't learn English. Given the present attitudinal and organizational structure of the schools, this is true. However, a deeper assumption implicit in these approaches is that *unless* the child learn English she/he *cannot* learn. This is simply not true. It has the net effect of shifting the burden from the adult educator to the child who can do little or nothing.

If we were to turn the question around and forget looking at language as an end in itself and look at what can be *learned* through promoting bilingualism an entirely different picture emerges. Recent work drawn from a variety of sources would suggest that the benefits of bilingualism would far exceed any short term educational (or linguistic) deficits.

In by far the most rigorously controlled series of experiments on the relationship between language, intellectual development and school related achievement, Peal and Lambert (1962) matched monolingual and bilingual groups to show that:

> The picture that emerges of the French/English bilingual in Montreal is that of a youngster whose wider experiences in two cultures have given him advantages which a monolingual does not enjoy. Intellectually his experience with two language systems seems to have left him with a mental flexibility, a superiority in concept formation, and a more diversified set of mental abilities, in the sense that the patterns of abilities developed by bilinguals were more heterogeneous . . . In contrast, the monolingual appears to have a more unitary structure of intelligence which he must use for all types of intellectual tasks (Peal and Lambert, 1963, p.6).

Further review of the literature on bilingualism would tend to support the above conclusions in research conducted throughout the world from Singapore (Torrance, et. al., 1970), Switzerland (Balkan, 1971), South Africa (Ianoco-Worrall, 1972), Israel and New York (Ben Zeev, 1972), Western Canada (Cummins and Gulustan, 1973), Montreal (Scott, 1973) and from the United States on Chicano populations (DeAvila and Havassy, 1975, 1976; Cohen, 1975; Feldman and Shen, 1972). According to Lambert (1976), there have not been any recent contradictions to these positive findings which show definite advantages on measures of cognitive flexibility, creativity and diversity. Finally, research implication drawn from the study of "metalinguistics" (Cazden, 1972) would seem to provide further, if not stronger support for the contention that bilingualism is an intellectual asset, and not a deficit as has been believed.

We thus come to what is perhaps the ultimate problem, which is that the issue addressed by the Lau decision is legal and its solution symptomatic of the very problem that produced the original litigation. This problem really cuts across every level of American society. The problem addressed by Lau is but one facet. As such, Lau is an indirect attempt to address the problem of language status through legal means which unfortunately are not based on what we know about education, or more importantly, about how and what children learn. That it produces as many questions as it attempts to answer is good in that it means that the educator, test developer and/or any other person working with children for whom English is not the primary language, will have to think a little bit more about what they are doing, lest we all become coconspirators.

Chapter 24
The ULPAN In Israel
Ezri Atzmon*

A. The Role of the Ulpan and its Objectives

With the establishment of the State in 1948, Israel was suddenly confronted with an intricate task of mammoth dimensions: to absorb economically, socially and culturally the new mass immigration hailing from over a hundred countries. To educate this conglomeration of people, this "ingathering of exiles"—and turn them into productive, well adjusted citizens of a modern democracy became one of the prime tasks of the newborn State.

The study of the modern Hebrew language, which was considered to be the primary cultural tool for welding the newcomers speaking seventy different languages into one nation, dates back to the pioneering days of the end of the nineteenth century. However, the method of study was extensive and not concerted. With the establishment of the State, it was decided to organize a statewide system of intensive study, with Hebrew, basic Jewish cultural values and good citizenship at its core. The overriding aim was to impart to the masses, and particularly to the members of the free professions, a familiarity with the Hebrew language as a means of communication in order to facilitate their integration with the labor market and their cultural absorption into the State of Israel. The institution designed specifically for this purpose was established in 1948 and it was called *ulpan* (pronounced ool-pun, plural *ulpanim*)—meaning workshop or school—a unique Israeli school for adults.

The Language Instruction and Adult Education Department of the Ministry of Education and Culture suggested in 1953 the following educational objectives for those institutions under its supervision which were teaching the Hebrew language to immigrants:[1]

"The immigrant who completes his course of study in the institutions sponsored by the Department shall attain a level of knowledge in the Hebrew language, culture and the Israeli way of life which will prepare him for his role as a citizen of the State.

"The acquisition of a basic knowledge of the language is the primary aim of the course, but simultaneously with it, the course must provide an insight into the national character and a knowledge of the country and its people.

"A Hebrew citizen of the State speaks its language, is involved in its affairs, problems and culture. This is the 'law' of the immigrant and it should be impressed upon him."

Originally, the ulpan was designed for immigrants with higher education and professionals only. However, as time went on, its doors were opened to the veterans of the country who for a variety of reasons had not managed to master the language and who now came to expiate "the primordial sin." Also, amongst those benefiting from instruction in the ulpan are a large number of non-Jews: members of the clergy, embassy officials of foreign countries, foreign students, converts and just plain admirers of the Hebrew language. The progress of gentiles in the study of Hebrew is generally comparable to that of their Jewish counterparts who did not have a Hebrew background. Frequently, visitors from abroad spend some time in the ulpanim and learn Hebrew before returning to their countries of origin.

B. The Sponsoring Agencies

Adult Education in Israel, and particularly the Hebrew language instruction enterprise, while predominantly directed and supervised by the Department of Language Instruction and Adult Education of the Ministry of Education and Culture, is a joint venture of a variety of partners. They are: 1) The Jewish Agency; 2) The Defense Army of Israel; 3) The Hebrew University and other institutions of higher learning; 4) The Police Force of Israel; 5) The General Federation of Labor (*Histadrut*) which operates its Cultural Center and Cultural Committees of the Workers' Councils; The Mizrahi Labor Organization (the religious trend); 7) Local Civic Authorities; and 8) various other Zionist organizations like "Malben", The Organization of Zionist Women, The Women of

*Dr. Ezri Atzmon is Professor of Education at Jersey City State College, Jersey City, New Jersey.

Agudat Israel (the Orthodox trend), various hospitals, etc.

These agencies and institutions sponsor a large network of daytime and evening classes founded and maintained by them, but they all acknowledge the authority of the Ministry's Department of Language Instruction and Adult Education (the Department) in all educational matters i.e. curriculum, supervision and the resolution of educational problems. In most cities and larger population centers there is a Department of Culture attached to the municipality or local council which provides facilities for the ulpanim. On the average, the Department covers 50 percent of the operation expenses.

C. The Types of Ulpanim[2]

With the passage of time, the ulpan concept has crystallized, and as a result of various conditions and specific needs, has assumed a variety of forms. The major types that have evolved are as follows:

a) *The Residential Ulpan.* As its name implies, this is an ulpan with rooming and boarding facilities for adult immigrants who spend in it five months attending classes for five hours a day. The afternoons and evenings are devoted to doing homework and to social and cultural activities. The age of the students ranges from 18 to 70, the average age being 40. Usually there are ten such ulpanim located in urban centers in various parts of the country, however their number oscillates, depending on the momentum of immigration and the demand for classes in a given area.

There are residential ulpanim designed for particular categories of students (e.g. schools for members of the Police Force) or a single interest group of students (e.g. foreign students). In such cases, the curriculum is designed to suit the needs of the particular type of students. An educational director appointed by the Department is in charge of educational matters, while the Jewish Agency administers the living quarters.

b) *The Day Ulpan* is non-residential and is found in large urban centers. It is designed for immigrants who have succeeded in finding their own permanent accommodation. The studies are intensive and take up 30 hours a week. This type of ulpan is sponsored by the Jewish Agency, by municipalities, workers' councils, etc. It is usually maintained or subsidized by the Department which supervises the educational work. Though the educational atmosphere in this type of ulpan is not as dynamic as in the Residential Ulpan, the participants can absorb Hebrew from the natural environment around them.

c) *The Popular Ulpan* has morning and evening classes 12-16 hours a week. This type of ulpan is designed for immigrants or veteran citizens interested in learning Hebrew as fast as possible but who for occupational reasons cannot devote much time to study. This type of ulpan is operated throughout the school year and is scattered over the entire country in towns and immigrant centers. The number depends on the rate of immigration. The partners in this enterprise are the Jewish Agency, local authorities, workers' councils, etc.

d) *The Kibbutz Ulpan* is found in 60 kibbutzim throughout the country and is designed for young immigrants up to the age of 35 who work in the country or are continuing their general education. Here the studies are very intensive. The day is evenly divided into four hours of study and four hours of work, the latter being designed to cover tuition and upkeep. The term is six months long. The daily contact of the students with the kibbutz members and the small size of the classes are a contributing factor in the social integration of the participants and their speedy mastery of the language. The Agency organizes the ulpanim and refers the immigrant students, while the kibbutz, which houses the ulpan, receives from the Agency a financial subsidy to cover current expenses.

e) *The Youth Ulpan*, which caters to teenagers, is divided into two categories: 1) *The Residential Youth Ulpan* for young immigrants of secondary school background who intend to continue their studies in Israel. The term of study is eight months, and in addition to Hebrew, includes an introduction to Jewish history, the geography of Israel, citizenship, selections from the Bible and Hebrew literature. 2) *Youth Centers* for immigrant teenagers who have had minimal or no elementary education. These are day centers with four hours of study per day for a period of six months. A major part of the curriculum is devoted to the Three R's and to familiarizing the youngsters with the elements of Hebrew culture.

f) *The Summer Ulpan.* During summer vacations, two types of brief, intensive courses are offered to persons who are interested in improving their knowledge of Hebrew: 1) *A Month of Study* in which one-month intensive refresher courses are offered to graduates of regular ulpanim who, after an interval of a year or more, wish to continue their Hebrew studies. Admission is also open to those who, for one reason or another, could not take a regular course upon their arrival in the country and now, having settled down, want to catch up with their Hebrew studies either residentially or externally; 2) *A Course for Immigrant Teachers* which is a seven hours a day six-week course designed for immigrants who are qualified teachers. The purpose is to equip them with a general Hebrew vocabulary and professional terminology in the field of their specialization in order to enable them to function effectively in the Israeli classroom.

The Summer Ulpan has proven to be extremely successful due to the fact that the participants are highly motivated and determined individuals who know exactly what they want and who do their utmost to get it.

g) *The Ulpanit.* Despite the existence of all the types of courses described above, there are still a large number of persons who, for a variety of reasons, cannot attend any of them on account of the intensive nature of the curriculum. It has therefore become necessary to establish a nationwide network of classes with an extensive method of study. Such a class, called *ulpanit* (diminutive for ulpan, plural: ulpaniyot) is held two or three times a week predominantly in the evening and in a number of places, largely at the insistence of female participants, during morning hours. The co-sponsors are: local authorities, workers' councils, and various organizations and institutions. Also the government, interested in improving the knowledge of the Hebrew language among its officials and employees, co-operates in the establishment of ulpaniyot. In isolated places, there are also maintained ulpaniyot.

The ulpanit is the most popular of all language instruction institutions for adults in the country and enjoys the highest enrollment. It is set up in all parts of the country—in towns, villages, transit camps and any place where new settlers are concentrated. The majority of the participants are immigrants who find the normal ulpan impractical, often because they start working immediately upon their arrival in the country.

The ulpanit is open throughout the school year and oftentimes also during the entire calendar year. The attendance fluctuates with the intensity of immigration. The number of classes in an ulpanit is usually small and the composition of the students heterogeneous in terms of age-group, educational standards and background. As a result, progress in an ulpanit is slower than in a regular ulpan.

Ulpanit participants are usually not satisfied with one year of study and they periodically return for additional instruction.

h) *Home Groups.* This form of study is designed for complete illiterates, particularly for women who for various reasons cannot leave their homes to attend an ulpanit. The home groups consist of 3-6 participants, and the teacher comes to the house once or twice a week. These visits are of an informal character and greatly contribute to the social integration of the newcomers who in most cases hail from socio-economically and culturally disadvantaged countries.

D. Some Principles of Adult Education[3]

The teaching of an adult is contingent upon his readiness to learn, but his perseverance depends on the teacher's ability to motivate him since his mind is usually on his work and on other personal problems rather than on his studies. It would seem that the student's presence at the ulpan is sufficient evidence of his willingness to learn, however in reality it is not exactly so. One thing is to make the adult embark on his studies and another to make him stick to them. It is therefore incumbent upon the teacher to plan his teaching against the adult's specific psychological background. In particular, the teacher has to be aware of the learner's purposefulness, impatience, sensitivity and shyness, and finally, of his physiological condition. Moreover, the general classroom atmosphere is a most decisive factor in the endeavor.

1) *Purposefulness.* The adult comes to the ulpan on his own accord in the hope that his efforts will be crowned with palpable results and that the acquired knowledge will be useful to him in his daily life. If he does not see that his studies are getting him closer to his goal, he will stop learning. Conversely, if the positive results of his efforts are noticeable to him, he will make a genuine and major effort to persevere and to succeed. Therefore, the teacher has to clarify the ends and means of the course at the outset and to show the learner how to get results.

2) *Impatience.* Adult learners are by nature impatient about achievements. They want immediate returns on the sacrifice they are making. Experts maintain that adults want to achieve in six months what a child can accomplish in twelve years. Since this is hardly feasible, the adult attributes his failure to his advanced age which he believes has deprived him of his ability to learn. The fact, however, is that the adult does not lose his ability to learn, only that the speed with which he can assimilate knowledge diminishes with his age. This the teacher has to explain to his adult student right at the beginning and save him the disappointment and frustration. He should then outline attainable goals for each student and daily point out to him the degree of his success. Adults need praise more than children and are more sensitive to castigation and failure.

3) *Sensitivity and Shyness.* The adult enjoys a certain status outside the classroom. It is oftentimes difficult for him to sit in a class due to possible negative associations with his schooldays in childhood or due to the fact that being a student testifies to his ignorance.

4) *The Physiological Condition.* Age impairs the sharpness of the senses—sight, hearing and reaction speed. The fear of this physiological handicap may negatively affect the learning effort of the adult, a fact with which the teacher has to reckon.

5) *The General Classroom Atmosphere.* One ought to consider the general atmosphere in which adult

students function. They are saddled with worries, various ailments, and physical and moral fatigue. Therefore, the teaching process has to be made attractive to them and they have to be activated both physically and mentally. The teacher's interest in the student's occupation and personal problems as well as various social activities will engender a good rapport between him and his students.

The teacher should look upon himself as a guide in his area of specialization rather than a know-all. He ought to show his students a degree of respect, point out their maturity and even consult them in matters concerning the field of their individual expertise.

Finally, it out to be pointed out that while, according to Thorndike, after the age of twenty-four, the human ability to learn diminishes gradually, as does the memory, there are mental qualities the power of which increases with age, e.g.: the power of concentration, the ability to organize the learning material and the ability to make an effort. Unlike a child, whose memory is mechanical, the adult's memory is associative. Consequently, in the teaching of adults, associations have to be engendered. Moreover, the memory of adults is selective. Adults are also less flexible, they bring to class their life's experience, willpower, motivation, judgmental ability and individual language habits. All this has to be kept in mind in the teaching of adult students.

E. The Syllabus[4]

With the establishment of the State of Israel, an initial effort was made to formulate a detailed syllabus for all institutions teaching Hebrew in the country. This syllabus has been undergoing a series of modifications in the light of the acquired experience and in keeping with educational innovations introduced over the years.

The syllabus has been drawn up in accordance with the proclaimed fundamental objectives of adult education elicited earlier. Thus, the syllabus for the ulpanim and ulpaniyot, which is nationally binding in order to facilitate student transfer from one place to another, is composed of the following elements:

1) Speech (basic Hebrew vocabulary and idioms) enabling the student to carry on a simple conversation and to understand a popular lecture.

2) Fluent reading (with and without vowel points).

3) Legible writing, reasonable spelling a simple and clear style.

4) Grammar—the rules of conjugation and other basic elements of Hebrew usage.

5) Literature—selected passages from classical and modern Hebrew works.

6) Bible—a general knowledge of the Pentateuch and the First Book of the Prophets as well as passages from other Prophetic Books and the Chronicles.

7) The geography of Israel—a general familiarity with the country's geography, its areas and settlements.

8) Hebrew Legends (*Agadah*)—selected passages.

9) The History of Israel and Zionism—a general knowledge.

10) Citizenship and national institutions.

11) Singing—folk songs, songs about festivals, the homeland and work.

The studies are divided into the following three stages:

1) The first stage (135 hours) is devoted to the teaching of basic vocabulary related to everyday life (365 words and phrases).

2) The second stage (125 hours) is devoted to the expansion of the vocabulary (540 words and phrases).

In the first two stages the basic concepts and values of Hebrew culture are taught, and an introduction is offered to the variegated nature of the population of Israel and Israel's geography. The participants listen to the news and other suitable radio broadcasts and talks and read a simple newspaper called *For the Beginner (Lamathil)* especially published for this purpose by the Ministry of Education and Culture. They also learn popular phrases and songs.

3) The third stage (250 hours) concentrated on written Hebrew. Instruction is also given in the geography and history of the country as well as in Bible and Hebrew literature. In this stage, the "latent vocabulary" (words picked up from hearing and reading) is greatly enriched.

At the conclusion of each stage, a nationwide examination takes place. This serves as a instrument for measuring the achievements and consequently is of great importance to the students, the teachers and the Department of Language Instruction.

During the final month of studies, special instruction is given to people of different occupations to familiarize them with working conditions in their respective fields of endeavor and the necessary technical terminology.

There are also diverse social and informal educational activities conducted in the ulpan of which the following deserve particular mention.

1) *Excursions*: Trips to places of interest and projects in the vicinity of the ulpan and tours further afield designed to acquaint the students with sites of historical and contemporary significance.

2) *Special Days*: Every fortnight students stay at the ulpan over the Sabbath to join in some special cultural program. This may take the form of festive meals, convivial gatherings, hikes, guest lectures, debates and so forth. Appropriate programs are also arranged to mark religious and national festivals.

3) *Gatherings:* Throughout the term, the students organize at the ulpan numerous get-togethers. The most important educational aspect of these is their preparation which involves large numbers of students working together in planning and implementing a program conducted exclusively in Hebrew. The participants gain invaluable practice in expressing themselves articulately orally and in written form. The climax of these get-togethers is always the end of the term party during which the students humorously review their studies, their life in the ulpan, their achievements and the highlights of their ulpan experience.

4) *Newspapers:* In most classes wall-newspapers and newssheets are prepared by the students. As the end of the term approaches, all students participate in the preparation of a comprehensive scrapbook. These publications are an important educational stimulus for most students to improve their capacity for self-expression in written form.

F. The Methodology[5]

Since the establishment of the ulpan enterprise, careful thought has been given to the elaboration of a suitable methodology for this type of school. The one that has crystallized is a composite of the modern methods of teaching adults and can be generally identified as the direct or natural method, which uses Hebrew as the sole language of instruction and avoids translation as a matter of principle. Conversation and dramatization are the central features of the lesson, and functional grammar is studied inductively. Other than that, each teacher is free to improvise and employ whatever methods and techniques he considers suitable for his students—all within the framework of the following major principles which were formulated in 1964:

1) Learning a language is essentially the acquisition of a skill involving a new pattern of habits. Thus, exercises, properly graded, have to be planned for each aspect of the language (hearing-understanding, speaking, reading, writing). The bulk (80 percent) of the language lesson has to be devoted to the practice of the particular aspect taught.

2) Language is a vehicle of communication, and the main aim of its study is acquiring skill in its use (as opposed to "knowing" the language). Speech is more useful than writing, and it is the former that constitutes the basis for learning the written word. In the ulpan method one begins by hearing and speaking (no textbook is used during the initial fortnight), the students being free to record in their notebooks whatever they deem useful. For hearing, like speaking, requires guidance and practice.

3) The material is based on a basic vocabulary (some 2,000 "active" words). During stages one and two, grammar is not taught systematically; it is learned through use on the basis of a sentence pattern of graded exercises. Similarly, vocabulary is not taught independently but as an integral part of a sentence.

4) Starting with the first lesson, the teacher uses Hebrew only and avoids translation. The students may jot down their own translations or equivalents of words and idioms in their native language.

5) Teachers are trained to identify distinctive study handicaps hampering the students, particularly the problem of muddled speech stemming from the confusion of Hebrew words with those in their native tongue. For the purpose of combating this problem, lists of characteristic word confusions have been drawn up covering almost all languages spoken in the country.

6) The primary aim in the first two stages is the development of oral communication skills. In the third stage, reading and writing competence is emphasized.

The main teaching aids and techniques employed in the teaching process are:

Dramatization—this constitutes a major feature of every lesson and is adapted to the requirements of each stage of instruction. During the first lessons, prepared dialogues are learned and enacted. Later on, variations are introduced leading to independent preparations of dialogues and talks at various levels.

The Tape Recorder—this is the most common audio-visual instrument used for a variety of purposes: practice in listening and articulation, training in speech, the teaching of songs, etc.

Pictures of various types are also widely used. Association and multi-detail pictures, placards and picture books relating to diverse topics studied are also frequently resorted to.

7) Many of the procedures, whether inside the classroom or out, are conducted in small groups of three to five students. Group work is considered expremely suitable for the inculcation of values, for the modification of attitudes, and in general socialization of the adult immigrant.

G. Teaching Aids and Materials

1) *Textbooks.* A good textbook is still considered a basic teaching tool in adult classes. At the suggestion of the Department, a suitable textbook, specially conceived for the purpose, has been written. Its title is *A Thousand Words.* However, there are also other textbooks in use.

2) *Additional Reading Material.* In order to encourage the learner to read by himself, books and pamphlets in easy Hebrew are regularly published. The idea is to make available to the beginning reader

good literature in *correct* Hebrew edited for an adult whose vocabulary is limited and whose patience shall not be overtaxed.

3) *Lamathil* (For the Beginner) is a weekly newspaper in simple Hebrew which enjoys a wide circulation among Jews and gentiles alike.

4) *Omer* (The Word) is the only daily newspaper with vowel points. It is extremely helpful to readers on an intermediate level who cannot as yet read the regular daily press which is printed without vowel points.

5) *Shaar* (A Gate) and other publications are pamphlets containing adaptations of classical Hebrew works in easy Hebrew and printed with vowel points.

6) *Audio-Visual Equipment and Learning with Pictures.* The common audio-visual tools that are used in the teaching process are: the picture, the filmstrip, the record, the motion picture and the tape recorder. In addition, colored wall posters on selected topics with a list of appropriate terms on the margin are used. The topics are: traffic, with the family at home, the artisans' street, in the market, in the park, in the fields of Israel, good citizenship, and the like, Also, special sheets are in use containing basic vocabulary on the following subjects: in the cafe and in the restaurant, in the country, in the field and in the garden, women's clothes, Hebrew on the road, in the clinic, in the store and in the grocery, at the greengrocer's, in the post office, etc.

7) *A Hebrew Column in Foreign Language Newspapers* is another technique resorted to by the Department and designed to stimulate independent reading.

8) *Broadcasts in Easy Hebrew on "The Voice of Israel."* Hebrew courses are offered on the radio and T.V. to students whose native tongue is English, French, Yiddish, Ladino, Mograbi, etc. Successful experiments have been made to supply listeners and T.V. viewers with the broadcast lessons in writing for a minimal fee.

9) *News in East Hebrew* is also broadcast with increasing popularity by "The Voice of Israel" broadcasting station.

H. Teacher Training[6]

There is no need nowadays to prove that specialized training is required for the teaching of adults. When the ulpanim were first set up, ulpan teachers were trained in a special one-year seminar established by the Hebrew University in Jerusalem. However, since the number of full-time positions was not large, this seminar was eventually closed down. Ever since, adult teacher training has been carried out along two lines: 1) Teacher training colleges conduct a number of study groups, one of them being devoted to adult education. This is a popular course since many student teachers have an intrinsic interest in the subject and, as regards women, the great attraction is the fact that they are able to work in adult education during their period of compulsory military service. Later, there are ample opportunities open to them to obtain supplementary or part-time employment once they establish families of their own. 2) During the long summer vacation, the Ministry of Education and Cuture conducts a course in adult education for qualified primary school teachers. Similar courses are also held throughout the school year. Of a short, intensive nature, and lasting two to three weeks, the courses cover the principles of adult instruction, and the participants are trained in conducting classes in any of the three stages of the ulpan. Educational advisors are appointed to assist teachers who complete their basic training in one of the two frameworks mentioned above. During the initial year of work, and sometimes even later, these instructors are on hand to offer to the novices advice and guidance on any educational problem that might arise. Guidance is offered both orally and in writing.

The Department has four central offices in various parts of the country. Each office is staffed by an inspector, a number of administrative assistants and educational advisors who attend to the daily educational needs of all the teachers.

The personal guidance of newly appointed teachers is ensured by regular supervisory visits of the inspectors who may be directly consulted on any educational problem. Regular seminars are conducted for teachers in every distict as are short courses in various subjects as the need arises. Such courses are conducted both intensively (on a short-term basis) and extensively (in weekly meetings over a period of several months).

Teacher guidance is also offered by correspondence by the Department in consultation with inspectors and advisors. Moreover, two regular publications are issued for teacher guidance purposes—a bi-monthly *Letter to the Teacher*, which deals with practical problems, and a yearbook *Pathways*, which serves as a clearing house for fundamental issues of a theoretical nature and is accompanied by practical suggestions. Senior staff members of the Department have also made available a number of workbooks and guidance instructions for teachers and students.

Finally, the Department's Executive Branch carries out surveys and educational experiments in the various aspects of educational work. The findings are subsequently brought to the attention of ulpan directors and teachers.

I. Conclusions[7]

The ulpan enterprise, in its various forms, has proven to be an important tool for meeting the challenges of adult education and immigrant absorption in Israel. Added to this is the ulpan's contribution to the process of national consolidation and the moulding of newcomers from a vast variety of lands into a united homogeneous society.

As for methodology, the intensive method of study has proven to be most effective. Moreover, it confirms the conslusions of educational research concerning the capacity of adults and older persons to study in general and to learn a new language in particular. Indeed, it has been demonstrated that with regard to Hebrew, the average progress made by adults in the ulpan is even greater than that of children learning a new language (except for the accent factor of course). The progress of the ulpan student, however, depends on a number of conditions: the student's motivation, the availability of suitable and appropriately graded instructional material, and the adaptation of teaching methods and techniques to the psycho-physiological background of the student.

Much is to be said for the concept of combining the study of language with the social and general education program, this being the advantage of the Residential Ulpan over other teaching institutions. In Israel, this concept has been proven to be valid also with regard to the extensive method of study.

Moreover, attendance at an ulpan has a positive influence upon the student by strengthening his self-confidence, making him realize that he has a capacity for learning and that he is capable of achieving satisfactory results. Meeting the challenge of mastering the language, which at first appears to most immigrants to be an impossible, or at best, an extremely difficult task, is of utmost importance since not only does it satisfy the inherent desire of the adult to succeed in his undertakings but it gives him a greater awareness of his talents. This sense of accomplishment can add much to the psychological adjustment of the newcomer to the conditions of life in his new country.

The ulpan enterprise has attracted the attention of many educators abroad. Quite a few of them who have visited Israel in order to study what is going on in the field of education have published their impressions of the ulpan system in professional publications in their own countries.

NOTES

[1] Shaked, Joseph, "The Education of New Immigrant Workers in Israel", *UNESCO Educational Studies and Documents*, 1955, No. XVI. *Some Studies in Education of Immigrants for Citizenship.* Paris: UNESCO, 1955, p. 32.

[2] Kodesh, Shlomo, *From a Babel of Tongues to One Language: Aims and Activities.* State of Israel, Ministry of Education and Culture. The Division for Popular Instruction in Hebrew and Adult Education. Jerusalem, 1960. Pp. 4-7. Dulzin, Leon. "New Epoch of Immigration and Absorption" in *The Israel Yearbook*, Jerusalem, 1966. Pp. 7-9. Haramati, Shlomo. *What is an Ulpan?* Department of Education and Culture of the Jewish Agency. New York, N.Y. 1022. (n.d.) Pp. 8-12. Katzir, Issakhar. *The Teaching of Hebrew to Adults in the Diaspora* (n.d.) (In Hebrew) (Mimeographed). P. 4.

[3] Katzir, *Op. Cit.* Pp. 2-3.

[4] Kodesh, *Op. Cit.* Pp. 24-26. Dulzin. *Op. Cit.* Pp. 11-13. Haramati. *Op. Cit.* Pp. 12-14. Katzir. *Op. Cit.* P. 5.

[5] Dulzin, *Op. Cit.* P. 13. Katzir. *Op. Cit.* Pp. 6, 17-18. Haramati, Shlomo. *The Ulpan Method: Its Origin, Nature and Development.* Jerusalem: The Council for Language Instruction. The Department of Education and Culture in the Diaspora of The World Zionist Organization and The Department of Language Instruction and Education. The Department of Education and Culture, 1972. (In Hebrew).

[6] Dulzin, *Op. Cit.* Pp. 14-15. Haramati. *What is an Ulpan? Op. Cit.* Pp. 17-19.

[7] Dulzin, *Op. Cit.* P. 15-16.

Chapter 25
Native American Bilingualism
Harvey Laudin*

The languages of native Americans came under acculturative influences wherever there were continuing contacts with Europeans and later with Americans. The process has continued over the centuries with varying consequences among Indian societies, depending on a number of factors. In some instances, there was a willingness to go white, while in other cases, there was fierce resistance to change. Assimilation in some situations was a strong variable, while in others, it made little difference. While it is always hazardous to generalize, it may be a safe assumption to note that more Indians today are learning both native and English in their schools. The media also play an important role, as will be seen. In an age of electronic communication, it is no longer possible to see any native groups in total cultural isolation. The television sets among the Hopi bring English into their homes as they do for the Taos Pueblo in New Mexico. Native American bilingualism no longer is a matter of chance but is more a matter of choice. The reestablishment of native language instruction in schools attended by Indian children appears at this writing to be well along the pathway toward revivalism. How long this trend will continue only time will tell. Where languages have suffered severe attrition or have disappeared altogether, there is little likelihood there will be successful revitalization.

Eastern Long Island clan groups speaking Algonkian dialects had suffered devastating language loss after about 150 years of contact with whites. Thomas Jefferson, on January 31, 1791, at "Pusspatuck" in the Long Island Town of Brookhaven, held in his hand a list that, according to Tooker (1962) "consisted of 161 words, including the first four numerals," representing "all that remain of the language once spoken from Staten Island to Montauk Point." This incident took place only 151 years after the first Pilgrims came down from Lynn, Massachusetts, and landed at Conscience Point in 1640 where they were greeted by the friendly Sachem Nowedonah of the Shinnecock Tribe. Twenty years later, a few miles distant, the village of Southampton was established, the first incorporated village in the State of New York.

In 1972, I did field work among this group and found no one who could speak the language. Only a few words remained which were understandable to the late Princess Nowedonah whose Christian name was Lois Marie Hunter. She had written a book about her people (1950) and had attended college which subsequently led to a teaching career on the Shinnecock Reservation. In my field trials of a questionnaire which was used in the fall of 1972 at the Shinnecock Annual Powwow, I asked many of the elders if they could speak or understand any native words and none could do so. Princess Nowedonah was interested to learn that her grandfather's name, Wyckham Cuffee, meant *House* Cuffee, suggesting that the house in which she lived and in which her grandfather had been born in 1826 may have been the first house on the Shinnecock Reservation, marking a major material cultural shift from the wigwam to the type of housing used off the reservation.

Red Thunder Cloud, a Catawba friend who lives in Easthampton, Long Island, was recorded at the Massachusetts Institute of Technology. He is the last person who speaks this Algonkian dialect.

David Owl, an Eastern Cherokee, came as a young man to serve as pastor among the Seneca living at Cattaraugus in upstate New York. Most of the parishioners spoke Seneca, a language he had to master quickly. However, in a matter of only two decades, from the 1920's to the 1940's, English came into general usage everywhere on the reservation. Interestingly, David Owl could still recite the "Lord's Prayer" in Cherokee at age eighty-one, after years of removal from persons using this language. On this occasion I recorded a moving recital of "The Trail of Tears" story, an event in which one of his own grandfathers perished.

Martin E. Johnson, rector of the Tuscarora Baptist Church, in 1973 said that the Tuscarora language had recently been revived in the elementary school on the

*Dr. Harvey Laudin has taught the "North American Indian" course since 1969 at C. W. Post College of Long Island University. He has traveled over 30,000 miles visiting Indian reservations in the U. S. and in Canada.

reservation and that it would be introduced the following year at the junior high school level. The Tuscarora must speak English since most of them work in occupations off their reservation. Johnson spoke fluent English and was a professional singer who was a skilled guitarist.

Native languages are being taught today in schools on reservations. One finds the most unlikely mixtures and even anachronisms. At Hopi, Acoma, Santo Domingo, at Santa Fe along the sidewalks in the Plaza, the natives could speak English at a level of comprehension superior to the mumblings of children and youths living in Long Island all their lives. It *is* startling to see television antennas sprouting above the looming cliffs at Polacca clearly visible from the front doorway of the Pahona home where the chief means of making a livelihood for the young man of the house is creating highly artistic kachina dolls. Inside, one can see an American flag hanging upside down in a frame on a bedroom wall, symbolizing some degree of disdain or rejection. The radio and television set, however, bring the American values, beliefs, and attitudes into the Pahona and other nearby homes. While the old man may be the chief religious leader of the Snake clan among his people, his son sits transfixed before the screen absorbing images and sounds alien to the ideologies of his father's father.

The radio station in Gallup, New Mexico, broadcasts commercials and songs in Navajo. On the White Mountain Apache Reservation in Arizona, a mother said with feeling, "we want our children to speak English so they can function in the outside world." In the general store on her reservation one could hear a mix of English and Apache.

There are strong ethnic stirrings occurring on American reservations and on Canadian reserves as well. The location is not particularly important. One can talk with an elderly white woman, married for many years to a Fort Thompson, South Dakota, native American and feel comfortable. The husband can lead his visitor around an old frame building and explain in detail the various interesting points. Everything said is understood and he understands the words of the visitor from academe.

At Taos Pueblo, one can purchase fresh-baked bread from a young mother whose baby sleeps on the front seat of the pickup truck. The dollar will help her college expenses in the fall. Inside the ancient building, her mother speaks a halting English. She willingly takes down two ears of purple Indian corn from the wall and asks for two dollars. Her son does a little dancing while she drums and he gets a small tip for his efforts. Both speak English, she very poorly; he very adequately. The older sister who goes to college, very fluently. Across the broad, dusty field that separates this scene

from the building where an old woman bakes pots, one listens to the voices of American tourists mingling with those of the Taos men busily repainting their mission church.

South of Taos, at the Ranches of Taos, cute little native children stand obligingly in front of an adobe wall. Their grins are the universal faces of youngsters suddenly asked to pose for a picture taken by a stranger. They are terribly shy. The photograph scene is finished and they are asked some simple questions. They can speak in English, Spanish, and their native tongue. Across the street, the postmistress speaks in Taos to the patrons. Above her head on the wall is an oil painting that combines the spirit of native and Anglo elements.

Along the highway leading toward Taos, Larry Martinez operates his "Spanish Dandy" shop. He makes his own designs in silver and repairs items at very reasonable cost. His wife holds a small girl who looks oriental, with shiny black hair and a suggestion of epicanthic fold in the corners of the eyes. Larry and his wife speak softly with a trace of an accent. Is it Spanish or native? The surname is confusing. One makes assumptions that may not be valid. After four hundred years, what is "native?"

Kenneth White sits all day at his work bench in the Cortez Silver and Turquoise Co. It is a combination factory-retail store in Cortez, Colorado. He is a master silversmith. He is Navajo as are all the other employees in the place, all of whom are women. He is very affable and speaks rapidly and with a sense of excitement as he talks about his work. He explains that the "H" stamped inside an object means handmade. He, too, speaks with an accent. It is all right to take his picture. He is cooperative; however, the women on a brief rest break are not so cooperative. They glance down to avoid looking into the camera. They remain silent and their faces are impassive.

Not far away, at the Canyon Pottery along Highway 14, five miles into Cedar Canyon, a young man makes pots. He is not Indian but Anglo. He features stoneware, handicrafts, and art works. He is disappointed when the selection is something his associate has made—an egg separator—and not one of his own creations. The visitors return after a brief consultation and make another purchase of one of his own objects. He speaks perfect English and claims to enjoy living along a dirt roadway that is used almost exclusively by Navajo sheep herders. Along this fifty-two mile dusty stretch is nothing but emptiness and a few children watching their sheep. One of the sheep moves up to inspect the car and then bleats in his own language as the car moves again slowly. Despairing of finding civilization again along this forsaken roadway, the distant cloud of dust seems to be growing nearer. In a few minutes a pickup truck stops to offer assistance. The lined face points ahead and in understandable English brings tidings of imminent relief in the form of a paved road with food and water oases ahead. He is off in a flash of dust and this offense is overlooked, under the circumstances.

In Santo Domingo Pueblo in New Mexico, Lorenzo B. Coriz offers "Indian Handmade Jewelry—Special Orders." His name also reflects the common heritage flowing from two different genealogical lines.

In Albuquerque, in the window of the Wagon Wheels store, two expert silversmiths sit making jewelry. One of them poses for the camera that will record him fitting two silver watch tips set with turquoise and coral to an expanding strap. The flash is bright but he remains calm. He speaks with slow deliberate tones with a slight accent. He is very proud because his work is signed and is known throughout the nation. His partner also speaks fluent English, although both speak a few words in Navajo to each other and laugh.

It is the same story throughout the West among the Sioux, Crow, and the Montana Blackfeet. In Wisconsin, the Winnebago offer programs in English in a large amphitheater at the Dells. The crowds listen to explanations in English and songs that are more American than Indian, such as "In the Land of the Sky-Blue Water." The old man who is Sac and Fox attending this show explains that his people in Iowa hold powwows yearly and it would be very nice if his show could be visited later that summer. He talks slowly and his manner is somehow reminiscent of the old chiefs who-did-business with the American Army generals between the time of Sand Creek and Wounded Knee. He does not know whether the statement made at the Winnebago show by the master of ceremonies was really ture, that this tribe gave the sign language to the Plains culture tribes.

Up in Alberta, there is an installation ceremony and two white men are being made honorary Indian chiefs. The program is taped but the voice is indistinct as the high wind slams against the microphone. Even when the wind subsides, his voice and those of others coming to the microphone are hard to follow. They speak English but their accents are very heavy. The clear, crisp, thank yous of the honored men—one was the premier of Alberta—is a pleasant relief.

Mrs. Baker runs an Indian arts and crafts shop in Vancouver, B. C. She is the wife of the tribal headman. Her people are Coast Salish and once were deep water fishermen. They made totems and in the rear yard behind her store a fifty foot totem was being built in someone's spare time. The local men bring their work to the store and she tries to sell them to tourists. She speaks impeccable English and her home adjacent to the shop is well kept and a typical middle-class residence. Mrs. Baker's features do not suggest her native genealogy. Her flesh is a little darker than that of a white Canadian. There is a talking stick that is attractive. It is bought as a souvenir of the local culture area. She explains the various cuttings and her words are recorded for my students.

Albert is eighteen years old and stutters a little, especially when he tries to remember how many siblings he has and how many died from childhood and infant diseases. He takes a long time to answer simple questions. During the interview that occurred just outside his aunt's handicrafts shop on the Stoney Mountain Indian Reserve, a white man and his son passed behind me. The man gave the Hollywood Indian warhoop, laughed, and continued on his merry way. Albert said, "I don't feel very good whenever I hear that. It makes me feel very bad inside." I tried to explain that in time perhaps people would not do such things any longer.

We shifted the subject. What was his big dream? He had none. The idea was pursued a little longer. Finally, after much deliberation, Albert said, "I'd like to own a rock station." What kind of programs would he have on his rock station? "I'd play rock music," he replied.

Again, his voice was the slow, halting, delivery one gets to expect whenever talking with a reservation native. Although all of the people living on his reserve speak English, most of them also can speak in their native language. In fact, more natives live on reserves that live in cities in Canada. This is true of Indians living in the States, although the proportion among our own natives is not the same. In 1960, 400 thousand of our own Indians lived on reservations and 200 thousand lived in cities. In 1970, there were 500 thousand living on reservations and 300 thousand living in cities. In Canada, the proportion living on reservations would be considerably higher. This proportion of reserve to city dweller will probably change as more Canadian Indians, following the Indians in the States, enter college and settle in urban residences. The number of languages are fewer in Canada, with Algonkian and Athapascan dialects predominating.

Down in Rosebud, South Dakota, an old woman walks slowly toward Martin in 110 degree heat. She accepts a ride in the air conditioned car. Her name is Elsie Flood and she is known locally as the Turtle Woman. She has beadwork in her large bag. She takes out a unique headband made with small seed and the larger pony beads. The ends are tied with smudgy white shoelaces. This is the Indian way. One uses available materials. She had no leather strings and so she simply improvised. She asks six dollars for work that took many hours of painstaking effort. The money is passed. Her work is one-of-a-kind. The beauty is shown throughout the West. None of the natives have seen anything of its kind.

Alice speaks from the top of her lungs. She sounds as though she has asthma or tuberculosis. She is not so old after all. She is fifty. Where is she going? "To Martin. It's only forty miles down the road. I do it all the time." At a small general store we stop for cold drinks. She counts to ten in Lakota, the language of her people. She giggles frequently, like a school girl. A young mother seated nearby with four youngsters all under five years of age talks with them in the native language. One hears an occasional word in English.

As we say goodbye, the Turtle Woman, loaded down with her personal trinkets most of which bore turtle likenesses in a variety of styles and made from different materials, trudges slowly down the road toward Martin. One cannot help wondering how a human being can manage all that distance in such heat and do it "all the time."

In recent times, Pan-Indianism has effected much rapid change in language and in customs. Ernest Okaloran, a Seminole, told me in 1972 at the Annual Shinnecock Powwow:

"We all know the same songs. We all sing our own songs, though. We have our own dances and steps that we still do here, but we—through the years—have gotten to know each other's songs and dances. So it has become Pan-Indian. We call it Pan-Indianism, and some tribes are wearing things from other tribes."

Language, dance, and costumes have all changed through acculturative influences. The Shinnecock Indians "lost their dances and songs with their adoption in 1641 of the principles of Presbyterianism by their treaty with the Presbytery of Scotland" (Laudin, 1973). Similarly, government Americanization policies and Christian missionary policies that peaked in the 1870's and '80's, helped to transform American Indians into Indian Americans (Laudin, 1976). The functionalism thesis comes into play here:

The functional view of culture insists upon the principle that every type of civilisation, every custom, material object, idea, and belief fulfills some vital function, has some task to accomplish, represents an indispensable part within a working whole (Malinowski, 1936).

Language, seen in this context as "custom," is no exception to the general principle. Sapir (1946) has noted that social realities are shaped by language. Where social realities change through culture change, languages also must be viewed as part of this process. Whorf (1956) saw language as a means whereby human perception is shaped and the mechanism for the classification of experiences. As cultural situations change, the other factors in a society also will have to change. Thus, one sees how cultural situations are

functions of ideological, attitudinal, and behavioral situations. This view of culture change is treated more fully elsewhere (Laudin, 1973), but in this present context it need only be said that the approximately three hundred separate languages spoken by native Americans living north of Mexico, according to Yost (1976), all without exception have experienced profound changes. The erosion of customs, including languages, will undoubtedly continue unabated, regardless of any attempts to arrest this rate of change by adopting language instruction in native schools.

In 1970, I had a class of students in a North American Indian course write to all the native American groups in the nation. While the return rate was predictably low, the two dozen responses helped to satisfy the goals sought. We wanted to know which language was used and which was preferred. There is a strain toward consistency in these documents. The elderly tend to be more fluent than the young. The greater the contact with the general society, the higher the probability English will be used. The principle of functionalism is self-evident from random selections offered here.

On a letterhead from the Tribal Executive Board, Assiniboine and Sioux Tribes, Fort Peck Indian Reservation in Poplar, Montana, William Youpee, chairman of the Fort Peck Tribes replies:

"In my opinion, the language most in use by the Indians on the reservation is English. The elderly or grandparents speak mostly Assiniboine or Sioux in their homes. Most of the middle-aged Indians understand their tongue, but do not speak Assiniboine or Sioux. The younger children and students neither understand nor speak their language. Just recently, some of the students belonging to Indian clubs, etc. and some of the older people have indicated an interest in learning and speaking their native tongue by attending classes taught by older Indians, who speak Assiniboine and Sioux fluently, and *write it also*."

Other responses from the Papago Tribe, for example, indicate a desire to use their native language. This group is located in Sells, Arizona, just across the Mexican border and generally removed from high density traffic patterns. Their language retention, therefore, should be seen in the light of this variable. To their north, on the Pima-Maricopa Reservation in Scottsdale, Arizona, Filmore Carlos, past chairman, replied:

"This reservation has two member tribes, Pima and Maricopa. They both speak their own distinctively different languages. However, the Pima is the predominate tribe, thus the Pima language is more spoken. So far as a choice of language for daily conversation, English for the most part is used. And oft times a mixture of the two. However, this is not to say that the Pima and Maricopa people do not wish to use their language as the occasion arises."

At the San Carlos Apache Reservation, established in 1872, the Indians cling to their native language, as Sandra E. Belvado, secretary, Indian Development District of Arizona, stated in her reply: "Our people use most of the time is Apache language." In 1976, when I visited this group, Mrs. Belvado had been promoted to the position of assistant to the judge of the court on the reservation.

An unusually complicated situation exists in Louisiana. Due to intermarriage among the Choctaw-Biloxi, Biloxi-Ofo-Avoyelles, and Tunica-Ofo-Biloxi, a process that has been "going on for about 200 Years," according to Claude Medford, Jr., writing for Chief Joseph A Pierite, Sr., who states rather poignantly:

"The situation here at the present time is one of hostility against the almost 5,000 Indian people now living in Louisiana. The Indian way of life, the ceremonials, the languages in those tribes that now speak their own languages, are considered pagan, silly, and a waste of time by the local French and other white people."

He adds:

"Miss Hohmann, I hoped I have given you some idea of the picture here in Marksville. I am almost 29 years old and I have known all of the tribes here in Louisiana, in East-Texas, and Mississippi all of my life as my grandfather was Choctaw and I used to visit "around" with him in the various Indian communities. I am mostly Scotch-Irish."

The Hualapais in Arizona "use and speak both languages," according to Rupert Parker, responding to student Adrianne Petz in the course.

Tony Machukay, administrative assistant to the tribal chairman of the White Mountain Apache Tribe in Whiteriver, Arizona, a place I visited in 1976, replied:

"Our total membership is up to 6,010. The majority of these people certainly do prefer their own Apache tribal language now that the people are beginning to take pride in themselves in relation to a dominant society and its ways which has only resulted in needless anomie."

Mrs. Christine Yazzie, secretary of the Ahtna Tanah Ninnah Association (Copper River Indian Association) in Copper Center, Alaska, responded:

". . . The Ahtna Tanah Ninnah Association uses both English and the Athabascan language; the thirty members prefer English.

Mrs. Clara Carroll, writing for the Fairbanks Native Community Center in Fairbanks, Alaska, responded:

"The older native people still speak our language and use it frequently. But they have

to rely on English to get along. The younger people tend to not speak their language even when they know how. All of the young people prefer English, the older people are forced to speak English, while they do prefer their own language."

F.J. Houle, Jr., Tribal Secretary of The Confederated Salish and Kootenai Tribes of the Flathead Reservation in Dixon, Montana, stated that the 5,520 members do speak English which "is the predominant language of the members of these tribes." He adds some points that warrant repeating:

"If you are referring to Indian languages, Salish and Kootenai are spoken by a minority of the people. This reservation was opened for homesteading in 1910. Inter-marriage with the whites has left only a few people recognizable as Indians with the non-Indians outnumbering tribal members about 8 to 1."

Landless Indians of the Montana Landless Indians, Inc., according to Ed Belgard, president in 1970, number "an estimated 1200 to 1500 Landless Indians in Montana . . . Cree is used when Indian language is spoken, but for the most part English is primary since these people are living among the non-Indian race."

The Northern Piaute of Fort Bidwell in California, in Madoc County, also known as the "Splinter Group, because the greater portion of this large tribe is located in Nevada," according to Beatrice Pollard, tribal member, speaks only the Piaute language. She estimated that the tribal membership was about 250. She asked for help from some foundation so that "if we could open up a center we could put our work on display and sell right there." Her tribe does buckskin work that is well known for its high quality workmanship. She concluded her letter by saying that financial help from the outside "would be one way that you could help us to help ourselves towards a more meaningful *Indian America*."

Indian college students have problems with language. Ned Anderson (1970), in an article entitled, "I Broke The Barrier," appearing in a publication of The University of Arizona, stated:

Because the native student's native language differs with English tremendously, ways of thinking and reasoning in one language must be reformulated in the other language."

Anderson points out the main consequence of this language barrier:

American Indians as individuals range from being thoroughly acculturated to Anglo-American society to having little or no contact with Anglos. Most Indians fall between these two extremes. But to many Indian students, attending college is their first intensive contact with Anglo culture. Naturally, as a consequence, they would feel ill at ease with the majority of the students in the classroom.

This would appear to substantiate the Sapir and Whorf citations above. The movement toward adoption of native languages in Indian curricula has moved in a logical progression through kindergarten up to the high school level and beyond. In the fall of 1976, Indian and non-Indian college students could learn the Dakota and Ojibway languages at the University of Minnesota. According to an article published in *Wassaja* in September, 1976,

> Classes in Ojibway (Chippewa) were started in 1969, when the American Indian studies department was established. The Dakota (Sioux) language program was initiated in 1973. Dakota and Ojibway are now being taught in some Minnesota public schools that have high Indian enrollments.

Federal programs have been launched to help improve the educational opportunities for Saginaw Chippewa children, as reported in the same issue of *Wassaja*. To help arrest school dropout cases that generally occur at about the fifth or sixth grade levels, the native language is being used at every opportunity, such as a local ethnic festival, sponsored at an elementary school. One of those who did drop out complained:

> "I mean, we're just starting to get back our own tribe's language and traditions here. What do I know about southwestern Indians?"

Attempts to establish bilingual programs have been reviewed recently in San Francisco by the National Advisory Council on Bilingual Education. Testimony was heard by native Americans, Chicanos, Chinese, Vietnamese and other language and ethnic groups. Jeanette Henry, editor of *Wassaja*, in an article entitled, "Natives in Bilingual Programs: A Disgrace," (1977) quoted expressions such as "disappointing", "inefficient" and "ineffective", that described how the participants felt about such programs insofar as they concerned Indians. The most glaring faults cited were "understaffing of the resource centers, lack of training for teachers, lack of funds for development of alphabets and instructional materials, and confusion over goals." One such confusion raises the issue whether "to provide a transitional bilingual program model or a maintenance bilingual program", according to one of those who took part in these deliberations, Estella Morris.

The bilingual programs are spotty when viewed globally. The Rosebud, South Dakota Community College program appears to be successful, with an impressive curriculum going forward. This impression was the result of an interview in the summer of 1974 with the college's secretary. I asked if they could use any education majors from C.W. Post College during the summer sessions and this suggestion was politely declined. The principal reason was that faculty used the Lakota language, while a secondary reason was that Wounded Knee II had stirred up tensions involving the American Indian Movement and local tribal leadership supporters. The factions were creating deep tensions. The last thing they needed were some do-gooders from the East who "loved little Indian children."

The Indian is today a frustrated human being. More appropriately, there is no one "Indian" mind, as one observer has managed to express very well in this observation (Svensson, 1973), "How are these proud, touchy, independent, and often alien people to be treated? Carefully—that is, thoughtfully."

Attempts to keep alive customs including bilingualism may continue for a long time. In a statement released by the Eskimo Brotherhood of Canada in May 1977, and reported by Trumbull (1977)

> Canadian Eskimos will meet with ethnic kin from Alaska, Greenland, and possibly Siberia next month in Barrow, Alaska, to form the first international organization of the indigenous inhabitants of the Arctic.

One of the long-term objectives, according to Jens Lyberth, a Greenland Eskimo living in Canada, "will be the development of a standard system of writing for the variations of the Eskimo language, in place of the eight methods now used." This eventually will lead to a "a common script that will enable Eskimos with different languages to communicate on paper."

Finally, and perhaps even symbolically, according to Cody (1970), "Sign language is slowly passing on and Iron Eyes hopes that the youth of today will find it interesting enough to keep it alive for future generations to come." The means by which native Americans once communicated among themselves before the arrival of Europeans now appears to be fading into oblivion.

Strong present ethnic interest in the nation may also be helping to sustain bilingualism among Indian Americans. I suspect ultimate decline and obsolescence of bilingualism in the general society will coincide with similar phenomena among The First Americans. This will occur when the last among them who speaks a native language or dialect dies and goes to meet Wakan Tanka.

Chapter 26
Teaching English To Speakers of Other Languages: The State of the Art
Christina Bratt Paulston*

The Domains of TESOL

In her opening address at the 1972 TESOL convention, Betty Wallace Robinett defined the teaching of English as a continuum, with the areas between the two extremes as the proper domains of TESOL:

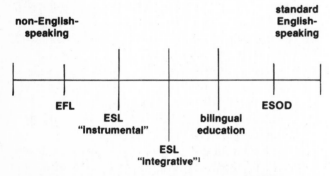

EFL represents English as a foreign language "where English is looked upon as cultural acquisition." ESL "instrumental" (the terms are Lambert's)[2] refers to the learning of English for "specific functional purposes," i.e., for economic advantage, while "integrative" deals with interpersonal, assimilative purposes. Bilingual education refers to programs where equal emphasis is placed onlearning the native language and learning English. ESOD represents English to speakers of other dialects.

The revisions of the TESOL[3] constitution, ratified in 1974, subdivide these domains into the following interest groups:[4] 91 0 EFL in foreign countries, (2) EFL for foreign students in the United States,[5] (3) ESL for United States residents in general, (4) ESL in bilingual education, (5) ESL in adult education, (6) standard English as a second dialect, and (7) applied linguistics.

In discussing TESOL trends, methods, and techniques, it is very important to keep in mind which of these particular groups one is dealing with. The theoretical approach is the same, but the objectives and techniques often differ according to the special needs of each group. Although most methods texts still address themselves primarily to foreign language teaching,[6], the revision of the TESOL constitution and the implementation of these revisions in the program of the TESOL conferences show our increasing sensitivity to the necessity to recognize the diverse needs of the various learners.

The first six TESOL special interest groups focus on the requirements of the learners, while the last category relates primarily to the concerns of the teacher trainers. The major part of this paper deals with trends and developments in EFL from the viewpoint of applied linguistics. The groups that are involved in these two areas are no different today than they were ten years ago. I would also like to discuss, however, three groups of learners whose particular needs and concerns have become increasingly recognized, namely ESL in bilingual education, ESL in adult education, and standard English as a second dialect. As early as 1970, David Garris commented in his presidential report to TESOL membership on TESOL's growing involvement in domestic programs, and these three interest groups are all representative of that growth. *Bilingual Education.* The major developments in the field of TESOL have been within bilingual education. With the passing in 1968 of the so-called "Bilingual Education Act" and the decision of the Supreme Court to uphold that legislation in the 1974 Lau vs. Nichols case,[7] educational authorities have had to revise their priorities in those parts of the country which have a sizable population whose mother tongue is not English. (Spanish, Chinese, French, and Amerindian languages are the major languages involved.) As the National Institute of Education's admirable report on *Spanish-English Bilingual Education in the United States* points out, the situation is far from clear because:

> . . . the principal piece of legislation, the Title VII amendment to the 1965 ESE (Elementary and

*Dr. Christina Bratt Paulston, Professor, Dept. of General Linguistics, University of Pittsburg.

Secondary Education) Act, is designed to meet the needs of children of limited English-speaking ability from low income families, so that these children will gain sufficient proficiency in English to keep up with their monolingual English-speaking peers in the educational system. Although the Title VII amendment is often referred to as "The Bilingual Education Act," this is rather misleading, since the long-range goal is not bilingualism but proficiency in English.[8]

In short, the programs are compensatory from the legislators' viewpoint. However, the major proponents for bilingual education, especially those members of the ethnic groups involved in implementing the new directives, invariably refer to the programs as bilingual/bicultural. The objectives of the bilingual/bicultural programs are a stable bilingualism with maintenance of the home culture as well as the home language, the "pluralistic model" in Kjolseth's terms.[9]

The compensatory programs, whose objective is a more rapid and efficient acquisition of English, he calls the "assimilation model." The NIE report points out that in practice the guidelines for Title VII programs have been interpreted loosely enough to allow for the existence of both models. With considerable funding available (total Department of Health, Education and Welfare expenditures on bilingual education and/or ESL projects for fiscal year 1973 amounted to nearly $67 million)[10] and the occasional tendency to hold up bilingual education as a panacea, *it is crucial,*" the NIE report states, *That the aims and objectives of bilingual education should be clarified and made explicit so that progress toward the goal can be evaluated.*" This has not yet taken place, but it is conceivable that when the Center for Applied Linguistics makes available its guidelines for the implementation of the Lau decision in San Francisco, its pluralistic model may become a standard for the rest of the country. At present, the interpretation of the objectives of bilingual education in the United States is based on politicoideological rather than linguistic criteria.

ESL in Adult Education is the interest group for those who teach English to adult immigrants in the United States. Academics rarely come in contact with these programs (many of them are in the nonformal education sector), and they are probably the least studied and researched courses in the field of language teaching and learning. The interest group itself has shown remarkable vigor during the last five years and has given research a high priority. We are likely to see a considerable increase of research in this area which is particularly theoretically interesting since learning strategies of students in adult education seem to differ from those who are academically oriented. In any case, it is an urgent practical problem that is arousing a

growing interest. The recent CAL - ERIC/CLL publication *A Selected Bibliography on Teaching English as a Second Language to the Illiterate*[11] bears witness to this concern.

Standard English as a Second Dialect is the interest group for those who teach English to American blacks whose home language is a distinct English dialect, variously called Nonstandard Negro English, Afro-American English, Black English vernacular, or, most commonly, Black English. Black English has been the focus of intense scholarly activity during the last ten years, and the teaching of standard English reflects this interest.[12] At the beginning of this period, there were attempts to use or adapt foreign language teaching techniques, but they were not very successful—especially when the techniques were of the mechanical, audiolingual variety—and most people today would agree with Virginia Allen that "A Second Dialect is Not a Foreign Language."[13] Some of the major academic contributions have been (1) Labov's sociolinguistic study of nonstandard English;[14] (2) applications of the linguistic descriptions of black English to studies of interference in reading and writing and their pedagogical implications;[15] (3) studies of the history of black English, to be used for teaching cultural pride and identity through understanding the legitimacy of black English as a dialect in its own right;[16] (4) the establishment of the legitimacy of black culture and the identification of speech acts, such as rapping, sounding, and jiving;[17] and (5) studies on language attitudes.[18]

In concluding this section on the domains of TESOL, I should point out that as a result of the fact that most scholars study as subjects those persons to whom they have easiest access, the bulk of the experimentation with language teaching techniques—and most of the empirical verification of hypotheses as to their various efficacy—is done with college or high school students who are either American students studying a foreign language or foreign students studying English in the United States. Both groups are involved in foreign language learning, a situation where social, political, economical, and cultural factors represent a minimum of interference compared with other language teaching situations. We are likely to continue to expect most new developments in methods and techniques of language teaching to come from a background of foreign language teaching at least until the bilingual education situation becomes stable. But it must be stressed that due caution is needed in generalizing from findings in foreign language teaching to other groups as the social, political, economical and cultural factors tend to be of far more significance in influencing eductional results than any language teaching methods *per se.*

TESOL: Developments Since 1969

In 1969 the ERIC Clearinghouse for Linguistics published Ronald Wardhaugh's state-of-the-art paper on TESOL. I would like to take my point of departure from this report. Wardhaugh characterized the state of the art of TESOL by the word *uncertainty*, the uncertainty arising "from the current ferment in those disciplines which underlie second language teaching: linguistics, psychology, and pedagogy."[19] I see much less of this uncertainty today, partially because we have come to a viewpoint which Christophersen sums up in his State of the Art chapter in *Second Language Learning*, 1973:

> We still know all too little in some of these areas (referring to disciplines relevant to language teaching); but there is probably a greater realization now than a couple of decades ago of the limits of our knowledge, and the earlier unshakeable faith in 'all-inclusive magico-scientific solutions (Ferguson, 1971) to the problem of language learning has partly—but only partly—given way to a more realistic appraisal.[20]

The three major areas I have discussed above—bilingual education, adult education, and SESD—are all concerned with social problems; I think today only the naive language teaching specialist talks about linguistic solution to social ills. Rather, as Spolsky puts it:

> Establishing a language policy like this (bilingual education) will not solve society's ills: it won't overcome racial prejudice, or do away with economic and social injustice. But it will be a valuable step in this direction and a contribution of linguistics to society.[21]

I sense today in the field of TESOL a great urgency to find viable alternatives in dealing with language as it intersects with racial prejudice and social and economic injustice. We simply cannot afford Wardhaugh's uncertainty.

Wardhaugh's 1969 paper is divided into six topics: (1) linguistics and language teaching, (2) psychology and language teaching, (3) language teaching and pedagogy, (4) linguistics, psychology and pedagogy, (5) teacher training, and (6) second dialect teaching. I will discuss each of these issues from my current viewpoint.

Linguistics and Language Teaching

Wardhaugh's original section on this topic contains a succinct summary of the tenets of transformational-generative grammar. He concludes:

> Generative-transformational grammar provides language teachers with new insights into

language. For example, no one can read *English Transformational Grammar* by P.A. Jacobs and P.S. Rosenbaum (Waltham, Mass.: Blaisdell, 1968) without being impressed by the insights into English structure that it contains. However, neither the grammar nor existing descriptions give teachers any way of teaching these insights nor do they provide any way of assigning a truth value to the insights on an absolute scale, apparent claims to the contrary notwithstanding.[22]

Nothing has happened since 1969 to change the "truth value" of that remark. The most intelligent statement of the value of TGG for language teaching was Robin Lakoff's "Transformational Grammar and Language Teaching," and she has since retracted her remarks, saying that she was mistaken.[23] A carefully reasoned criticism is found in Bruce Derwing's *Transformational Grammar as a Theory of Language Acquisition:*

> I have been suggesting that linguists in recent years have been concerned primarily to develop conceptual schemes designed to account for the form of utterances. Since these linguists have characteristically refrained from any sort of experimental investigations, these schemes remain untested (and in many cases untestable) and can be dismissed at present as brilliant but unsupported exercises in creative imagination.[24]

Stong words, but it is entirely possible that Derwing's book will greatly influence applied linguists for the next decade.

There can be no doubt that Chomsky changed the climate of linguistic thought in the United States and that this change became reflected in applied as well as in theoretical linguistics. In applied linguistics, it was the new attitudes and beliefs about the nature of language that effected new directions in language teaching. Of Moulton's (1961) five "slogans of the day" (a list of the major guidelines for applying the results of linguistic research to language teaching), only one is still viable. We no longer believe that language is only speech, nor a set of habits, nor that all languages are basically different. I doubt that Chomsky can take credit for the opposition to "teach the language, not about the language," but in the new climate it became possible to question that dictum. Of course, such a change of beliefs has resulted in different ways of getting people to learn languages.

But these beliefs do not really constitute what we mean by linguistics proper in its narrow sense. I see no evidence to support the claim that transformational descriptions of English have influenced language teaching methodology. I do see some confusion which results when a teacher writes *en* + on the board and insists—in spite of the students' objections—that it is the regular past particple. In short, I can be no more hopeful than Wardhaugh about the influence of TGG on language teaching. Naturally this is a controversial view. Betty Robinett writes:

> I disagree with your statement about the influence of TG on language teaching because I think more teacher trainers are emphasizing meaning than ever before, and the best way to get to meaning is through some of the newer grammatical and semantic insights. This may not have shown up in books yet, and I agree with you there, but more teachers can use TG (even to the extent that Quirk *et al* uses it) in contrasting items—factive, non-factive verbs and their relationship to progressives and imperatives, etc.; universals in relationship to such things as placement of relative clauses and adjective pre- or post- modification patterns. I would be the last to say that there is any close relationship between TG and ESL teaching, but I think it is an influence on teaching in the largest sense.[25]

There have been some recent influences on language teaching, however, from the field of generative sematics. Perkins and Yorio turned up some interesting findings about reading errors caused by misinterpretation of presuppositions and entailment, a new way of looking at an old problem.[26] Lakoff's (1974) paper on linguistic theory and the real world also contains some interesting ideas, even if the practical classroom implications are far from clear at present.[27] Allen's sector analysis is certainly eminently useful for teaching purposes but, except for its influence on his own students, it has not caught on as a major linguistic influence on his own students, it has not caught on as a major linguistic influence on language teaching.[28] There are various claims for other linguistic theories as well, such as case grammar and tagmemics[29]—in fact, I think stratificational grammar is the only current school of linguistic thought that no one has claimed to be pedagogically useful. But in general, the eclectic approach exemplified by Quirk and Greenbaum[30] (and Quirk, Greenbaum, Svartvik, and Leech)[31] prevails at present in language teaching. Furthermore, Furey finds in an analysis of grammatical rules and explanations very few differences among textbooks having audiolingual, direct method, TGG, or eclectic orientations. Presumably this is the result, she says, of the pedagogical necessity for simplification of the rules.[32]

The major recent influence on language teaching has come from sociolinguistics. One factor has been Labov's and others'work with Black English, another has been Hymes' criticism of the notion of the ideal hearer-speaker with no regard for the function of speech.[33] Hymes stresses the need for *communicative competence* rather than linguistic competence. Communicative competence entails not only being familiar with the linguistic forms of the language, but also being aware of when, how, and to whom it is appropriate to use these forms—in Grimshaw's terms "the systemic sets of social interactional rules."[34] I have discussed the implications for language teaching of Hymes' theoretical notions in my article "Linguistic and Communicative Competence."[35]

Another reason for the recent input from sociolinguistics is the reaction against the cultural deprivation theories[36] and the contention—especially in teacher training—that the members of various subordinate ethnic groups are culturally different, but certainly not culturally deprived. This emphasis has necessitated a more accurate description and understanding of other cultures and how they function, and has in turn influenced language teaching, especially in bilingual education, where one of the major aims in the "pluralistic" model is to teach children an acceptance of their home culture, frequently stigmatized by the larger society.[37]

There is also an attempt to understand on a theoretical level the social factors which contribute to bilingual education, and although language policy ultimately is set by political decisions, certainly a body of work is being developed which holds implications for future decisions about language teaching.[38] The Canadian data[39] is exceedingly interesting in this regard with the carefully researched immersion programs.[40]

Psychology and Language Teaching

Wardhaugh predicted that cognitive psychology would influence language teaching for many years to come, and so far his prediction has held true: Ausubel[41] is still frequently cited in footnotes; everyone agrees that language learning must be meaningful; no one claims that language learning is a straightforward matter of habit formation; and there seems to be a consensus that grammatical rules and explanations are beneficial to adults. Carroll, in his excellent article "Learning Theory for the Classroom Teacher," sums up the implications of the present tenets of psychology for language teaching. For classroom teachers he recommends a "commonsense" approach involving

> ...setting up pleasant and interesting learning conditions in which students feel they are making progress towards their goals and having their efforts rewarded, making the instruction as meaningful as possible by making the foreign language come alive in meaningful communication situations, making sure students understand what they are to learn, trying to predict the effect

of instructional presentations on students' minds, intellectualizing foreign language learning tasks in early stages by providing explanations of material to be learned (to the extent that the intellectual maturity of a student permits this), and providing ample and varied opportunities to practice and perfect what has been learned.

Carrol suggests that instructional materials should (1) explain to the student what he is to learn and how it fits in with or relates to what he already knows; (2) describe *how* the foreign language is put together, at the same time avoiding explanations of why; (3) prescribe learning sequences in which there is a maximal amount of reference to meaning and situation; (4) emphasize similarities and contrasts of forms and meanings when presenting new materials; (5) make provision for frequent review; and (6) provide a rich and varied selection of materials on which the student will be encouraged to try his skill.[42]

Krashen and Hartnett found in a study of direction of eye movement "that college students successful at an analytic, deductive system of learning Spanish, showed more right eye movement than students successful at a system requiring more inductive learning. This finding implies that the right hemisphere may play a role in certain kinds of foreign language learning."[43] And this is where the real action is to be found today in language learning and teaching on a theoretical level—in psycholinguistics and neurolinguistics. Douglas Brown's editorial in the December 1974 issue of *Language Learning* documents this well:

> There is an excited mood of anticipation among second language (L2) researchers today as a "new wave" of research in L2 acquisition gathers momentum. To be sure, the field is many centuries old; however, for perhaps the first time in history, L2 research is characterized by a rigorous empirical approach coupled with cautious rationalism. That is, the rationalistic but empirically substantiated approach to first language acquisition typical of the last decade is now being applied to L2 research.
>
> ...Such a wave comes at an important moment in history. The United States has begun to face seriously the problem of bilingualism, and the more we can discover about the process of L2 acquisition the better we may know how to deal with the educational and social complexities of bilingualism. We are also at a crucial moment in the history of language teaching: a new methodology—based on "communicative competence" and on cognitive and affective factory—is being developed in reaction to rote, oral-aural methods which began in the 1950's. The results of current L2 research will indeed have a great impact on

shaping a new method.[44]

It is too early yet to see what the implications will be—as people like Tarone and Swain[45] are careful to point out—and any premature recommendations for specific techniques are to be taken with a grain of salt. It is difficult to single out any specific studies. The issues of the last three years of *Language Learning* and the proceedings of the 1975 Georgetown Round Table are a good introduction, but the best place to begin is probably Roger Brown's *A First Language*. His basic finding is that "there is an approximately invariant order to acquisition for the 14 morphemes we have studied and behind this invariance lies not modeling frequency but semantic and grammatical complexity."[46] He also posits the concept of semantic saliency, a notion which may hold direct implications for language teaching.

Even though the implications of this "new wave" of L2 acquisition research for language teaching are not yet clear, Douglas Brown is right in pointing out a factor of major significance: the turning to empirical evidence rather than relying on unsubstantiated claims and counterclaims. This is the direction Derwing would like to see theoretical linguistics take as well.

Language Teaching Pedagogy

The audiolingual method has been totally discredited, perhaps at times unfairly so, as it has been interpreted in ways that Fries certainly never intended. A careful reading of his *Teaching and Learning English as a Second Language* will reveal it as being as sensible a book today as the day it was written.[47] Cognitive code (Carroll's term), with its emphasis on meaningful learning and careful analysis of linguistic structures, is generally recognized to be the new trend. An excellent account of this approach can be found in Chastain, *The Development of Modern Language Skills: Theory to Practice*.[48]

The difficulty with cognitive code is that I do not know of a single textbook for beginning students that can be classified as utilizing a strict cognitive code approach. In practice, most language teaching specialists are eclectic and so are the textbooks they write. In 1973 I wrote:

> John Carroll, the psychologist, holds that there is nothing mutually exclusive in the theories of Skinner and of Lenneberg-Chomsky about language learning, but rather that these theories are complementary. This opinion is reflected in the eclectic approach to methodology in language teaching, representative of the best work being done today in this field in the United States, by people like Douglas Brown, Frank Johnson, John Oller, Wilga Rivers, Ronald Wardhaugh, to men-

tion just a few. But then it is a biased statement as it is my own position.[49]

I see no reason to change that statement today except for the addition of some names to the list. Diller, however, disagrees. He claims that "a temporary phase of eclecticism is giving way to a reasoned choice of methods and techniques."[50] Although I don't understand his distinction between "eclecticism" and a "reasoned choice," it should be recognized that there are dissenting views on the value of eclecticism.

In addition to the prevailing eclecticism, two new methods have gained visibility in the United States, the Silent Way[51] and Community Language Learning.[52] In the Silent Way, the teacher uses Cuisiniere rods, a color-coded wallchart and speaks each new word only *once*; the responsibility for learning and talking is shifted to the students. Even correction is handled through gestures and mime by the teacher with no further modeling.

In Community Language Learning, the students sit in a circle and talk about whatever interests them. They speak first in their native language, and the teacher (who is not a teacher but a friendly counselor) translates for them into the target language, which they then repeat. The non-teacher analyzes the sentences on the blackboard, and the students write their own textbooks by copying these sentences.

Both of these methods have generated considerable interest and excitement, and Stevick gives a very favorable account of both.[53] Rather than to dismiss them as fads, which incidentally I think they are, both methods need to be studied objectively in order to identify just which elements, if any, within them contribute to efficient learning.

Wardhaugh concludes his section on pedagogy with some remarks on testing. The sources he cites all favor discrete item testing. One new trend has been toward abandoning discrete item testing in favor of global testing, expecially Cloze and dictation. Oller is probably the best source of information on global testing.[54]

Much of the interest in testing has been related to the invalidity of cross-cultural testing, i.e., evaluating minority group children with instruments whose norms have been established for white middle-class children.[55]

Linguistics, Psychology and Pedagogy

In his very brief section on this topic, Wardhaugh points out that "there is much uncertainty about how a second language should be taught...at the moment there is no consensus as to what it would be like, nor do any recent writings indicate that someone is shortly going to articulate a new set of principles to guide

language teachers."[56]

As I mentioned before, there is now less uncertainty and, I think, some consensus. We agree that all four skills—listening, speaking, reading, and writing—should be introduced simultaneously without undue postponement of any one. The importance of writing as a service activity for the other skills is generally recognized, and there is considerable interest in controlled composition. No one talks any longer about memorizing dialogs. Listening comprehension is still poorly understood on a theoretical level, but Morley's fine text has effected greater emphasis on the teaching of that skill.[57] The crucial importance of vocabulary, which was ignored in the audiolingual approach, is becoming increasingly accepted. The appearance of Barnard's text makes it possible to focus on this specific teaching point.[58]

There has been a major trend toward the use of error analysis, rather than contrastive analysis, as a teaching aid. Error analysis has, of course, also played an integral part in language acquisition research studies; the 888-item *Selected Bibliography on Language Learners' Systems and Error Analysis*[59] bears witness to this fact. One study in particular is worth mentioning, as it may indicate a new trend. Jacquelyn Schachter points out in her "An Error in Error Analysis" that "if a student finds a particular construction in the target language difficult to comprehend, it is very likely that he will try to avoid producing it."[60] There will then be no error to analyze, and only contrastive analysis could have predicted such avoidance. She concludes sensibly that CA and error analysis complement each other.

I think we agree with Chastain that "perhaps too much attention has been given to proper pronunciation,"[61] and we now tend to think that it is more important for the learner to communicate his ideas than to practice utterances with perfect pronunciation. The one thing that everyone is absolutely certain about is the necessity to use language for communicative purposes in the classroom. As early as 1968, Oller and Obrecht pointed out that communicative activity should be a central point of pattern drills from the very first stages of language learning.[62] Savignon's extensively cited dissertation (1971) confirmed this beyond a doubt.[63]

Mary Bruder's widely used textbook, MMC: *Developing Communicative Competence in English as a Second Language*,[64] exemplifies this approach. It is also used at Michigan whose English Language Institute staff are the first to point out that the Michigan method (as the aural-oral approach is frequently referred to overseas) is no longer used at Michigan.

No, I think there is more agreement than disagreement today on what language teaching should be about. And if a few bridle at pattern drills, it is not very important because we agree on the basic principle of meaningful learning for the purpose of communication. And that basic principle is indicative of what may be the most significant trend: our increasing concentration on our students' learning rather than on our teaching.[65]

Teacher Training

There is relatively little to add to Wardhaugh's section on this subject, which is to say that there have been no significant new developments in this area during the last seven years. Wardhaugh is correct in his assertion that in the United States most ESL teacher training is at the M.A. level and offers a good background in linguistics. In the past, ESL training has very frequently been tied to a department of linguistics, as in the case of my own students, who graduate with an M.A. in linguistics and a Certificate in TESOL. But with the urgent need to train teachers for bilingual education programs, which are usually on the elementary level and require teacher certification for the public schools, there are an increasing number of training programs for bilingual education/ESL in departments or schools of education.

Teachers in the public schools are certified by the state in which they teach, and there is now a rush of activity throughout the country to prepare teacher certification guidelines for the mandatory bilingual education. My own state, Pennsylvania, to date has no teacher certification program in ESL, and that is the rule rather than the exception. ESL certification will have to come soon, and this development can be directly traced to the Bilingual Education Act.

The professional organization TESOL (Teachers of English to Speakers of Other Languages) celebrates its ten year anniversary next year. It serves as a clearinghouse for the activities, interests, and problems associated with EFL, ESL, BE and SESD. TESOL'S publications include Charles Blatchford's *TESOL Training Program Directory 1974-76,*[66] which lists all of the programs in ESL teacher training, with a complete description of courses, requirements, staff, etc. The national organization has, during the last few years, encouraged regional affiliates, so that most states now have a local TESOL association. In addition, there are affiliates in Canada, Ireland, Mexico, Venezuela, and the Dominican Republic.

The last few years have also seen the founding of NABE, the National Associated for Bilingual Education, which serves the specific interests and problems of those involved with bilingual education in the United States.

An important source of information for teachers and teacher trainers is the ERIC Clearinghouse on Languages and Linguistics, which publishes the CAL•ERIC/CLL Series on Languages and Linguistics. Many of the titles in this series are very useful bibliographies. The Center for Applied Linguistics also offers extensive services to the profession. Some of CAL's recent publications include its Bilingual Education Series and its Vietnamese Refugee Education Series.

Wardhaugh closes his section on teacher training with a list of ten "basic methodology texts and books of readings which have been found to be useful in work with teachers." Today our students read only two of these entries, namely, Charles Fries, *Teaching and Learning English as a Foreign Language* and Wilga Rivers, *Teaching Foreign-Language Skills.*[67] Here is my list of publications since 1969 which have been found useful in teaching training:

Allen, H. and R. Campbell, *Teaching English as a Second Language.* New York: McGraw-Hill, 1972.

Chastain, K. *The Development of Modern Language Skills: Theory to Practice.* Philadelphia: Center for Curriculum Development, 1971.

Croft, K. *Readings on English as a Second Language.* Cambridge, Mass.: Winthrop, 1972.

George, H. V. *Common Errors in Language Learning.* Rowley, Mass.: Newbury House, 1972.

Harris, D. P. *Testing English as a Second Language.* New York: McGraw-Hill, 1969.

Lester, M. *Readings in Applied Transformational Grammar.* New York: Holt, Rinehart and Winston, 1973.

Lugton, R. *Toward a Cognitive Approach to Second Language Acquisition.* Philadelphia: Center for Curriculum Development, 1971.

Oller, J. and J. C. Richards, *Focus on the Learner.* Rowley, Mass.: Newbury House, 1973.

Paulston, C. B. and M. N. Bruder, *Teaching English as a Second Language: Techniques and Procedures.* Cambridge, Mass.: Winthrop, 1975.

Paulston, C. B. and M. N. Bruder. *From Substitution to Substances: A Handbook of Structural Pattern Drills.* Rowley, Mass.: Newbury House, 1975.

Rivers, W. *Speaking Many Tongues: Essays in Foreign Language Teaching.* Rowley, Mass.: Newbury House, 1972.

Saville-Troike, M. *Foundations for Teaching English as a Second Language.* New York: Prentice-Hall, 1976.

Schumann, J. and N. Stenson, *New Frontiers in Second Language Learning.* Rowley, Mass.: Newbury House, 1975.

Stevick, E. *Adapting and Writing Language Lessons*. Washington, D.C.: Foreign Service Institute, 1971.

Teaching a Second Dialect

I have already discussed this topic from the viewpoint of a special interest group Wardhaugh included it as a special topic, presumably because it was so recent a development in 1969. Today we recognize SESD as a regular domain of TESOL. Certainly considerably more research is needed on the disparate processes of second language and second dialect learning, but at least it is now routine to recognize and discuss the problems of this particular group of language learners.

Conclusion

There have been a number of recent developments in language teaching in the United States, and I have discussed those that I see as most significant in TESOL. Much of what I have said is true for foreign language teaching as well, even if many teachers in the public schools continue to follow the audiolingual approach. It takes considerable time until recent academic findings and opinions permeate into the regular classrooms, and it should be stressed that the view expressed here represents the view from a major university, not the assessment of actual teaching in the country.

NOTES

[1]Betty W. Robinett, "The Domains of TESOL," *TESOL Quarterly* 6 (September 1971): 197-207.

[2]Wallace E. Lambert, "Psychological Approaches to the Study of Language," in *Teaching English as a Second Language*, ed. Harold Allen (New York: McGraw-Hill, 1965), pp. 25-50. See also R. C. Gardner and W. E. Lambert, *Attitudes and Motivation in Second Language Learning* (Rowley, Mass.: Newbury House, 1972).

[3]TESOL (Teachers of English to Speakers of Other Languages)—a professional organization for those concerned with the teaching of English as a second dialect. James E. Alatis, Executive Secretary, School of Languages and Linguistics, Georgetown University, Washington, D. C. 20007.

[4]Current (1976) chairmen of special interest groups: (1) EFL in Foreign Countries—Frank Otto, Brigham Young University, Provo, UT 84602; (2) EFL for Foreign Students in the U.S.—Mary

Bruder, Dept. of General Linguistics, University of Pittsburgh, Pittsburgh, PA 15260; (3) ESL for U.S. Residents in General—Dennis Muchisky, 401 Sycamore Street, S.E., Albuquerque,NM 87106; (4) ESL in Bilingual Education—Sonia Rivera, 70 West 95th St., No. 9A, New York, NY 10025; (5) ESL in Adult Education—Donna Ilyin, 76 Sixth Avenue, San Francisco, CA 94118; (6) Standard English as a Second Dialect—Marcyliena Morgan, Dept. of Black Studies, University of Illinois at Chicago Circle, Chicago, IL 60680; (7) Applied Linguistics—Thomas Buckingham, 601 West Green Street, Urbana, IL 61801.

[5]In Robinett's terms, this would be ESL instrumental. There is some disagreement over this category; I myself use the TESOL definition. In my view a second language is the non-home but official language of a nation which *must* be learned by its citizens for full social, economic and political participation in the life of that nation. It is the relationship between the super and subordinate groups which gives the significant characteristics to second language learning, rather that the particular usage to which the language is put.

[6]Foreign language teaching here refers either to the teaching in the U.S. of languages such as French Spanish, or German, or to the teaching of English to foreign students. Textbook titles typically use English as a Second Language because publishers tend to find the word *foreign* pejorative in conjunction with English. A number of publications on bilingual education exist, mostly anthologies, but none can be said to be language teaching methodology texts. Possible exceptions are Muriel R. Saville and Rudolph C. Troike, *A Handbook of Bilingual Education* (Washington, D.C.: TESOL, 1971) and Henry Burger, *Ethno-Pedagogy: Cross-Cultural Teaching Techniques* (Albuquerque: Southwestern Cooperative Educational Laboratory, 1971).

[7]H. Geffert, R. J. Harper II, S. Sarmiento, and D. Schember, *The Current Status of U.S. Bilingual Education Legislation*, CAL•ERIC/CLL Series on Languages and Linguistics No. 23 (Arlington, Va.: Center for Applied Linguistics, 1975), ED 107 135.

[8]M. Ramirez III, R. K. S. Macaulay, A. Gonzalez, B. Cox, and M. Perez, "Spanish-English Bilingual Education in the United States: Current Issues, Resources and Recommended Funding Priorities for Research," National Institute of Education, ms., n.d., p. 6.

[9]Rolf Kjolseth, "Bilingual Education Programs in the United States: For Assimilation or Pluralism?" in *Bilingualism in the Southwest* ed. P. R. Turner

(Tucson: University of Arizona Press, 1973), pp. 3-27. See also Theodore Andersson and Mildred Boyer, *Bilingual Schooling in the United States* (Washington, D.C.: U.S. Government Printing Office, 1970); and Rodolfo G. Serrano, "Public Relations to CAE Bilingual/Bicultural Resolutions," *Council on Anthropology and Education Quarterly* 6 (May 1975): 36-38.

[10]DHEW, Office of Education, *American Education* (July 1974): 40.

[11]G. Joseph, K. McLane, and L. Taylor, *A Selected Bibliography on Teaching English as a Second Language to the Illiterate*, CAL•ERIC/CLL Series on Languages and Linguistics No. 25 (Arlington, Va.: ERIC Clearinghouse on Languages and Linguistics, 1975), ED 104 168.

[12]A Good bibliography is to be found in J. L. Dillard, *Black English: Its History and Usage in the United States* (New York: Random House, 1972). See also the review of Dillard by W. Wolfram in *Language* 49 (September 1973): 670-79.

[13]Virginia French Allen, "A Second Dialect is Not a Foreign Language," in *Georgetown University Round Table on Languages and Linguistics 1969*, ed. J. Alatis (Washington, D.C.: Georgetown University Press, 1969), pp. 189-95.

[14]William Labov, *A Study of Non-Standard English* (Washington, D.C.: ERIC Clearinghouse for Linguistics, 1969), ED 024 053.

[15]See the following publications of the Center for Applied Linguistics: J. Baratz and R. Shuy, *Teaching Black Children to Read* (1969), ED 025 761; W. Wolfram, *A Sociolinguistics Description of Detroit Negro Speech* (1969), Ed 028 431; R. Fasold and R. Shuy, *Teaching Standard English in the Inner City* (1970), Ed 037 720; D. Gunderson, *Language and Reading*, (1970), Ed. 037 722; W. Wolfram and N. Clarke, *Black-White Speech Relationships* (1971), ED 079 735; R. Fasold, *Tense Marking in Black English* (1972); W. Wolfram, *Sociolinguistic Aspects of Assimilation* (1974), ED 091 933.

[16]See Dillard. See also the many articles by William Stewart in the *Florida FL Reporter* and in D. L. Shores, *Contemporary English* (Philadelphia: Lippincott, 1972).

[17]See Thomas Kochman, ed., *Rappin' and Stylin' out: Communication in Urban Black America* (Chicago: University of Illinois Press, 1972); Claudia Mitchell-Kernan, *Language Behavior in a Black Urban Community*, Monographs of the Language-Behavior Research Laboratory No. 2, University of California at Berkeley, 1971; and W. E. Whitten and John F. Szwed, eds., *Afro-American Anthropology: Contemporary Per-*

spectives (New York: Free Press, 1970).

[18]See Frederick Williams, "Language, Attitude, and Social Change," in *Language and Poverty*, ed. F. Williams (Chicago: Markham Publishing Co., 1970), pp. 380-99 and its bibliography; and R. Shuy and R. Fasold, *Language Attitudes: Current Trends and Perspectives* (Washington, D.C.: Georgetown University Press, 1973).

[19]Ronald Wardhaugh, *Teaching English to Speakers of Other Languages: The State of the Art* (Washington, D.C.: ERIC Clearinghouse for Linquistics, 1969) p. 6, ED 030 119. See also W. Norris, *TESOL at the Beginning of the 70's: Trends, Topics, and Research Needs* (Pittsburgh: University Center for International Studies, 1972), and B. Spolsky, "TESOL," in *The Britannica Review of Foreign Language Education*, vol. 2, ed. D. Lange (Chicago: Encyclopaedia Britannica, 1970), pp. 323-40.

[20]Paul Christophersen, *Second-Language Learning* (Harmondsworth, England: Penquin Books, 1973), p. 13.

[21]Bernard Spolsky, "The Limits of Language Education," *The Linguistic Reporter* 13 (Summer 1971): 5.

[22]Wardhaugh, p. 11. To update Jacobs and Rosenbaum, see R. P. Stockwell, P. Schachter, and B. H. Partee, *The Major Syntactic Structures of English* (New York: Holt, Rinehart and Winston, 1973).

[23]Robin Lakoff, "Transformational Grammar and Language Teaching," *Language Learning* 19 (June 1969): 117-40; retracted in address, "Linguistic Theory and the Real World," at the 1974 TESOL Convention, Denver, Colorado.

[24]Bruce Derwing, *Transformational Grammar as a Theory of Language Acquisition* (Cambridge, England: University Press, 1973), p. 307.

[25]Betty W. Robinett, personal communication, October 9, 1975.

[26]Kyle Perkins and Carlos A. Yorio, "Grammatical Complexity and the Teaching of Reading in an ESL Program," University of Michigan, ms.

[27]Robin Lakoff, "Linguistic Theory and the Real World," paper presented at the 1974 TESOL Convention, Denver, Colorado.

[28]Robert Allen, *English Grammars and English Grammar* (New York: Scribner's, 1972). For a text based partially on this approach, See Marcella Frank, *Modern English: Exercises for Non-Native Speakers* (Englewood Cliffs, N. J.: Prentice-Hall, 1972).

[29]See Don L. F. Nilsen, "The Use of Case Grammar in Teaching English as a Foreign Language," *TESOL Quarterly* 5 (December 1971): 293-300.

[30]R. Quirk and S. Greenbaum, *A Concise Grammar of Contemporary English* (New York: Harcourt, Brace, Jovanovich, 1973).

[31]R. Quirk et al., *A Grammar of Contemporary English* (New York: Seminar Press, 1972).

[32]Patricia Furey, "Grammar Explanations in Foreign Language Teaching" (M.A. thesis, University of Pittsburgh, 1972).

[33]Dell Hymes, "The Anthropology of Communications," in *Human Communication Theory*, ed. F. Dance (New York: Holt, Rinehart and Winston, 1967); "Models of the Interaction of Language and Social Life," in *Directions in Sociolinguistics*, eds. John Gumperz and Dell Hymes (New York: Holt, Rinehart and Winston, 1972); Editorial introduction, *Language in Society* 1 (April 1972): 1-14; Introduction, *The Functions of Language in the Classroom*, eds. Courtney Cazden, Vera John and Dell Hymes (New York: Teachers College Press, 1972); "On Communicative Competence," in *Sociolinguistics, eds. J. B. Pride and J. Holmes (Harmondsworth, England: Penguin Books, 1972); Foundations in Sociolinguistics* (Philadelphia: University of Pennsylvania Press, 1974).

[34]Allen D. Grimshaw, "Rules, Social Interaction and Language Behavior," *TESOL Quarterly* 7 (June 1973k): 109.

[35]C. B. Paulston, "Linguistic and Communicative Competence," *TESOL Quarterly* 8 (December 1974): 347-62.

[36]Unfortunately these have had widespread influence in the U.S. educational setting. See Carl Bereiter and Siegfried Engelmann, *Teaching Disadvantaged Children in the Preschool* (Englewood Cliffs, N.J.: Prentice-Hall, 1966), and Martin Deutsch, Irwin Katz, and Arthur Jensen, eds., *Social Class, Race, and Psychological Development* (New York: Holt, Rinehart and Winston, 1968).

There has also been a strong reaction among linguists against Arthur Jensen's "How Much Can We Boost I.Q. and Scholastic Achievement?" *Harvard Educational Review* 39 (Winter 1969). The Linguistic Society of America voted in 1972 to publicly oppose his work.

[37]A. Aarons et al., eds., *Linguistic-Cultural Differences and American Education, Florida FL Reporter* 7 (Special Spring/Summer 1969 issue); R. Abrahams and R. Troike, *Language and Culture Diversity in American Education* (Englewood Cliffs, N.J.: Prentice-Hall, 1972); J. Alatis, ed., *Bilingualism and Language Contact: Anthropological, Linguistic, Psychological and Sociological Aspects* (Washington, D.C.: Georgetown University Press, 1970); Cazden et. al. (See note 33); Burger (see note 6); U. Hannerz, *Soulside* (New York; Columbia University Press, 1969); T. D. Horn, ed., *Reading for the Disadvantaged* (New York: Harcourt, Brace and World, 1970); R. Jacobson, "Studies in English to Speakers of Other Languages and Standard English to Speakers of a Non-Standard Dialect," *The English Record* 21 (April 1971); D. Shores, *Contemporary English* (New York: Lippincott, 1972); B. Spolsky, ed., *The Language Education of Minority Children* (Rowley, Mass.: Newbury House, 1972); Williams (see note 18).

[38]J. Fishman and J. Lovas, "Bilingual Education in Sociolinguistic Perspective," and W. Mackey, "A Typology of Bilingual Education," in *Teaching English as a Second Language*, eds. H. Allen and R. Campbell (New York: McGraw-Hill, 1972), ED 040 404; N. Modiano, W. Leap and R. Troike, *Recommendations for Language Policy in Indian Education* (Arlington, Va.: Center for Applied Linguistics, 1973); C. B. Paulston, *Implications of Language Learning Theory for Language Planning: Concerns in Bilingual Education* (Arlington, VA.: Center for Applied Linguistics, 1974), ED 102 866; "Ethnic Relations and Bilingual Education: Accounting for Contradictory Date" in *The Proceedings of the First Inter-American Conference on Bilingual Education*, eds. N. Modiano and R. Troike (Arlington, Va.: Center for Applied Linguistics, 1975); B. Spolsky et al., *A Model for the Description, Analysis and Perhaps Evaluation of Bilingual Education*, Navajo Reading Study Progress Report No. 23 (University of New Mexico, 1974).

[39]For the literature on the Canadian immersion programs, see J. D. Bowen, "Linguistic Perspectives in Bilingual Education," and M. Swain and H. C. Barik, "Bilingual Education in Canada: French and English," in *Current Trends in Bilingual Education*, eds. B. Spolsky and R. Cooper, forthcoming; S. T. Carey, *Bilingualism, Biculturalism and Education* (University of Alberta, 1974); H. P. Edwards and M. C. Casserly, annual research and evaluation of second language programs, 1971, 1972, 1973 (Ottawa: The Ottawa Roman Catholic Separate School Board); F. Genesee et al., series of evaluations of the 1973-74 French immersion classes submitted to the Protestant School Board of Greater Montreal; W. E. Lambert and G. R. Tucker, *Bilingual Education of Children* (Rowley, Mass.: Newbury House, 1972); W. F. Mackey, *Bilingual Education in a Binational School* (Rowley, Mass.: Newbury House, 1972); J. McNamara, "Perspectives on

Bilingual Education in Canada," *Canadian Psychologist* 13 (October 1972): 341-49; H. H. Stern, *The Position of the French Language in Quebec* [Gendron Report] (Quebec: The Quebec Official Publisher); M. Swain, ed., *Bilingual Schooling: Some Experiences in Canada and the United States* (1972), ED 061 849; M. Swain, "Some Issues in Bilingual Education in Canada," paper presented at Indiana University, March 1974; M. Swain, "French Immersion Programs across Canada: Research Findings," *Canadian Modern Language Review*, in press; and G. R. Tucker et al., "French Immersion Programs; A Pilot Investigation," *Language Sciences* 25 (April 1973): 19-26.

[40]I regret that an inclusion of Canadian work is outside the scope of this paper. In fact, Canadian and American scholars in language teaching work in close cooperation, attend the same conferences,; and read each other's publications. A statement on the state of the art of TESOL in North America would have closer reflected the reality of the situation.

[41]David P. Ausubel, *Educational Psychology: A Cognitive View* (New York: Holt, Rinehart and Winston, 1968).

[42]John Carroll, "Learning Theory for the Classroom Teacher," in *The Challenge of Communication*, ed. G. A. Jarvis (Skokie, Ill.: National Textbook Company, 1974).

[43]Steven Krashen and D. Hartnett, "Lateral Eye Movement and Acquisition of a Second Language," Queens College, ms.

[44]Douglas Brown, Editorial, *Language Learning* 24 (December 1974): v-vi.

[45]E. Tarone, M. Swain and A. Sathman, "Some Limitations to the Classroom Applications of Current Second Language Acquisition Research," *TESOL Quarterly* 10 (March 1976): 19-32.

[46]Roger Brown, *A First Language: The Early Stages* Harvard University Press, 1973), p. 379.

[47]Charles Fries, *Teaching and Learning English as a Foreign Language* (Ann Arbor: University of Michigan Press, 1945).

[48]Kenneth Chastain, *The Development of Modern Language Skills: Theory to Practice* Philadelphia: Center for Curriculum Development, 1971).

[49]C. B. Paulston, *Implications, p. 14. The reference to Carroll is John Carroll, "Current Issues in Psycholinguistics and Second Language Teaching," TESOL Quarterly* 5 (June 1971): 101-14.

[50]Karl C. Diller, "Some New Trends for Applied Linguistics and Foreign Language Teaching in the United States," *TESOL Quarterly* 9 (March 1975): 65.

[51]Caleb Gattegno, *Teaching Foreign Languages in Schools: The Silent Way* (New York: Educational Solutions, 1972).

[52]Charles A. Curran, *Counseling: A Whole Person Model for Education* (New York: Grune and Stratton, 1972).

[53]Earl Stevick, review of *Teaching Foreign Languages in Schools: The Silent Way*, in *TESOL Quarterly* 8 (September 1974): 305-13, and review of *Counseling-Learning: A Whole Person Model for Education*, in *Language Learning* 23 (December 1973): 259-71.

[54]John W. Oller, *Research with Cloze Procedure in Measuring the Proficiency of Non-Native Speakers of English*, CAL•ERIC/CLL Series on Languages and Linguistics No. 13 (Arlington, Va.: ERIC Clearinghouse on Languages and Linguistics, 1975), ED 104 154. See also B. Spolsky and L. Palmer, *Papers on Language Testing 1967-74* (Wahington, D.C.: TESOL, 1975).

[55]See Jennifer Sullivan, "A Sociolinguistic Review of the Iowa Tests of Basic Skills," in *Languages and Linguistics: Working Papers No. 5: Sociolinguistics*, eds. W. K. Riley and D. M. Smith (Washington, D.C.: George University Press, 1972).

[56]Wardhaugh, pp. 19-20.

[57]Joan Morley, *Improving Aural Comprehension* (Ann Arbor: University of Michigan Press, 1972).

[58]Helen Barnard, *Advanced English Vocabulary I,II* (Rowley, Mass.: Newbury House, 1971).

[59]A. Valdman and J. Walz, *A Selected Bibliography on Language Learners' Systems and Error Analysis*, CAL•ERIC/Cll Series on Languages and Linguistics No. 21 (Arlington, Va.: ERIC Clearinghouse on Languages and Linguistics, 1975), ED 105 772.

[60]Jacquelyn Schachter, "An Error in Error Analysis," *Language Learning* 24 (December 1974): 213.

[61]Chastain, p. 203.

[62]John Oller and D. H. Obrecht, "Pattern Drill and Communicative Activity: A Psycholinguistic Experiment," *IRAL* 6 (May 1968): 165-74.

[63]Sandra Savignon, *Communicative Competence: An Experiment in Foreign Language Teaching* (Philadelphia: Center for Curriculum Development, 1972).

[64]Mary N. Bruder, *MMC: Developing Communicative Competence in English as a Second Language* (Pittsburgh: University Center for International Studies, 1974), ED 105 711.

[65]See J. Oller and J. C. Richards, *Focus on the Learner* (Rowley, Mass.: Newbury House, 1973).

[66]Charles Blatchford, *TESOL Training Program*

Directory 1974-1976 (Washington, D.D.: TESOL, 1974).
[67]Charles Fries, *Teaching and Learning English,* and Wilga Rivers, *Teaching Foreign-Language Skills* (Chicago: University of Chicago Press, 1968).

Chapter 27
ESL Is Alive and Well
David Krulik*

English as a Second Language is "alive and well and living in New York City." In this huge urban metropolis, much is being done in the everyday work of the administration of the program. This article is presented from the administrative point of view.

The primary long-range goal is to reach all youngsters for whom English is a second language. An immediate goal is to enable pupils to accelerate in the acquisition of oral language skills and the companion skills of listening, reading, and writing.

Youth today must develop adequate communication skills in English. Opportunities which will present themselves will demand mobility and ability to adapt to new challenges in an environment where English is the primary language.

In New York City, the English as a Second Language unit is part of the Office of Bilingual Education. A myriad of services emanate from this unit.

The need and the demand for the English as a Second Language program are evident. Consider the statistics compiled from the 1973 data by the Bureau of Educational Program Research and Statistics.

In our schools are 256,492 Puerto Rican pupils and 40,516 other Spanish-speaking students. Of these, 79,116 Puerto Rican and 19,797 other Spanish-speaking pupils were classified as having English language difficulty. These two groups constitute the largest part of the non-English speaking population for which our schools provide special services. The other major groups with English language difficulty are Chinese, 6,183, Italian, 4,147, Greek, 1,770, and French, 3,747.[1] As is evident, the major portion of language-handicapped youngsters is Spanish. These staggering statistics underline the fact that we have a tremendous task on our hands.

Even at this writing, new statistics are being gathered as a result of the testing being done under the "Aspira Consent Decree" which states, in essence, that all non-English speaking youngsters are to be provided a program having the following elements:

A. Intensive instruction in English
B. Instruction in substantive subject areas in their native language
C. Reinforcement and development of the pup-il's native language
D. Provisions for pupils to spend maximum time with other children so as to avoid isoltion and segregation from their peers.

The need for the ESL program keeps growing with the passing of each day. The influx of students is a steady stream. In the past, the major group of newcomers was from Puerto Rico. The new arrivals come from South America (Chile, Colombia), Central America, Honduras, Costa Rica, Haiti, Japan, China, Yugoslovia, Greece, Italy, and from practically every other country in the world. In the representation in the English as a Second Language Program, the major native language is Spanish followed by Chinese, Italian, Greek, and French.

It should be emphasized that children, speaking 43 different native languages, are included in the English as a Second Language Program. It is obvious from the breakdown of languages involved that a multitude of youngsters would be isolated were it not for the English-as-a-Second-Language instruction.

With the advent of decentralization, the operations of the high schools are under central control. The expenditure of funds for English-as-a-Second-Language instruction for primary and junior high schools in the districts is controlled at that level. It is clear, of course, that each one of the school boards is limited by the budgetary stringency affecting the entire educational program of the city.

The basic philosophy in the teaching of English as a second language may vary from school to school, from city to city and from state to state. Basically, ESL is taught through the Audio-Lingual approach which was developed during World War II. However, it must be realized that a strong ESL program must develop four basic skills; listening, speaking, reading and writing.

"During the initial stages every grammatical structure, sound pattern and vocabulary item should have been presented orally before they are met in print, and

*Mr. David Krulik, Assistant Director, Center for Bilingual Education, English as a Second Language.

pupils should be asked to write only what they have read and spoken."[2]

The above approach is the one most widely used in teaching English as a second language. However, there are those who think that the written word should be introduced with the spoken word so that the sequence of hear, say, do may be taught with the "see" component preceeding the first two. In many instances the sequence is determined by the philosophy of the teacher and the maturity level of the student.

There is a great need for an objective screening device. It is most important to know at what level of competency a non-English speaking student is performing. Many schools and districts have developed their own scale for measuring a student's ability in English.

In New York City, we use a scale that was developed by the Puerto Rican Study in 1954. This scale rates a pupil in listening and speaking ability. It is administered by a knowledgeable teacher or ESL coordinator and to a certain degree is subjective. The student who is screened by the coordinator using this scale is placed in one of these levels; beginning, intermediate, or advanced. The placement of these students by use of this scale has been quite successful. This has been proved by the results achieved on a standardized reading and auditory comprehension test. Teacher judgement based on the above mentioned scale is a valid criterion.

With the growth of bilingual education throughout the country, ESL has shown greater strength. All advocates of bilingual education maintain that ESL must be an important component of any successful bilingual program. However, there are those who attempt to put down ESL. Rudolph Troike wrote an article with the title, "The View From The Center: Warning — ESL (Traditional) May Be Hazardous to Children."[3] In this article Mr. Troike makes broad generalizations that ESL instruction has done little good for students, and on balance may have been more harmful than beneficial.

Instead of clarifying the role of ESL in a bilingual program, Mr. Troike implies that pupils would be better off without it. In place of ESL he advocates that teachers of ESL use bilingual education.

No attempt is made to define bilingual education as an approach, a method, a philosophical viewpoint, or anything other than the antidote to the perniciousness of ESL. Interestingly, the distinction between ESL and English instruction in bilingual settings is never made clear.

Those who are currently teaching ESL in bilingual education programs know that a bilingual program without ESL is hardly viable. A bilingual program without intensive English instruction is, in fact, unthinkable. Moreover, such a state of circumstances is illegal, according to the mandate of the Aspira Consent Decree. What else but some sort of ESL approach is intensive English instuction for students learning English for the first time? Call it what you will, English is the other language—that is, the second language of students in bilingual education programs.

The English as a Second Language Unit of the Office of Bilingual Education is now a recognized resource center for New York City and visitors from other states and from abroad.

From the initial steps of coordinating a structured program, the unit has helped innovate, organize, and assist in the development of educational programs and projects which facilitate the rapid and effective adjustment of students learning English as a second language on all levels. These programs include devising and planning of strategies which develop clearer insights into the problems of the (a) initial placement of newly arrived students learning English as a second language, (b) class organization, (c) time allotment for language instruction, (d) use of various media of instruction in teaching English as a second language, (e) development of instruments of assessment for diagnostic and achievement purposes, and (f) evaluative strategies.

In the high school program, it has been necessary to test the pupils as required by Title I guidelines. After a great deal of discussion and deliberation, it was decided to use the Stanford Primary Test, level II for beginners and level III fro the advanced students. The students were tested in reading and auditory comprehension.

The number of students tested was 5,400. The mean reading score for beginning students was 2.2. The mean score for advanced students was 3.6. The auditory comprehension score for beginners was 1.5 and for advanced students 2.5. It should be evident from these pre-test results that the ESL youngsters on the high school level can succeed only if there is a special program for them.

Content areas, using an ESL approach have been set up. Such ESL programs give beginning youngsters 80 minutes for ESL instruction from a Title I funded teacher and 40 minutes from a tax-levy teacher. The post-test scores show an average growth of 6 to 8 months in the course of a 10-month school year.

The ESL youngsters come higly motivated, and it is incumbent upon the programs to sustain that motivation. For these youngsters, an environment must be created that is conducive to success. The articulation among the high schools has produced a coordinated and structured program which has rapidly moved in this direction. Therefore, all teachers must be included and trained in ESL techniques.

It has been the finding that the majority of students needs at least two years in a special ESL program before going into the mainstream. It had also been found necessary to create a transitional ESL class for the students to help them go from ESL to regular English.

The second focal point was to develop an ongoing teacher-training program that would aid not only the teacher of English as a second language, but also those teachers involved in the general instruction of the ESL pupil so that the students meet with success in the curricula areas as well. Therefore, after conferring with the principals, intensive, daily, on-the-job training in the classroom was arranged, as well as workshops. To provide for additional training, in-service courses for all teachers in the areas of methods and materials in ESL and techniques in teaching reading to ESL students are offered.

To further teacher training, a series of institutes was planned. Chairmen, paraprofessionals, and teachers involved in the program attended them. The agendas for these institutes were carefully drawn and thought out. Guest speakers, our own staff, and staff from the field made presentations. Different types of programs and materials were discussed, tried, and evaluated. After a consensus was taken, materials could be ordered, and curriculum materials produced.

For example, two interesting institutes were conducted. At the first, teacher representatives of the Italian, Chinese, Puerto Rican, Haitian, and Greek ethnic groups gave a short presentation on the educational experiences of students in their native lands, their cultural background and their particular needs in the United States. After the presentation, there was a question-and-answer period.

At the second institute, student representatives from these groups who were in the high school program talked to the high school personnel about the program and about their expectations from the high school programs. Articulation among the high schools and feeding schools was an important outcome.

These two institutes were video-taped and have been on loan to colleges. They are very useful for teacher-training and understanding of human relations. At these institutes, there has always been representation from the local colleges and from the district offices and schools. Every attempt is made to create a sound articulation program on all levels. Workshops have been given at the local colleges for ESL teachers in training.

For these pupils, it is most important that the class size be no more than 15 to 20 pupils, thereby allowing for greater individualization of instruction and for a closer relationship between teacher and pupil. It is only through federal and state funds has it been made possible to set up programs that restrict class size to 15 or 20. In other classes, there may be over thirty pupils.

The teachers program a double period of ESL. The first period is audio-lingual, the second period deals with the development of reading and writing skills. The teachers find that the double period makes it possible to develop these lessons more fully and to teach in a less hurried atmosphere. The ESL teacher develops lessons based on the vocabulary that the pupils will need to better understand the science and social studies lessons. The importance of ongoing, on-the-job teacher-training cannot be overemphasized. It is nuclear to the success of the program.

In continuing to assess the needs of the ESL students in the city, it has been found that one of the most consistent complaints of teachers of English as a second language was "What do I do with an illiterate youngster or one who can barely read his own language?"

A survey showed that there were over 2,000 high school students who are so severely retarded in reading and writing that they cannot function in either language. To meet the needs of these youngsters, a Native Language Arts Program (NLA) was designed. The NLA Program is designed to:

1. Make it possible for these pupils to learn to read and write in their native language.
2. Help them adjust to a completely alien situation by having foreign language speaking personnel. Give them a feeling of security by making it possible for them to learn basic language arts skills in their native language.
3. Make it possible for these pupils to learn to speak and understand English.
4. Deter the high dropout rate among foreign language speaking pupils by giving them a feeling of belonging, accomplishment, responsiblity, and success through the intensive use of their native language.
5. Provide smaller classes for instruction in Spanish and English so that there will be greater individual attention to needs.

The evaluation of this program has been most positive with a recommendation that it be continued. It is in 23 high schools at the present time. This year, the program focuses on Spanish and French. It is planned to include other ethnic groups as the need rises.

The program has been successful for a number of reasons:

1. The class size is 15 to 20.
2. The teachers are bilingual.
3. There is 80 minutes of native language instruction.
4. There is 80 minutes of English as a second language instruction.
5. There is integration with other pupils in the

mainstream.

6. There are materials especially selected in Spanish, French and English to meet the needs of these youngsters.

"Reading in English for the pupil who can already read his own language is a very different kind of learning task. This pupil has his spoken language. He can understand and speak, he has meaning stored. He can reach back into his memory both for receiving and for expressing himself in the vernacular. He possesses a fully developed oral language band of his mother tongue. To this well-developed verbal system, he has added the graphic band. He knows the written system of his language; he has the necessary associations between the print and speech of his language and he can make graphic representations of his speech. He is literature—thus he is able to express and to receive written language."[4]

Another innovative program has been the introduction of Music Language Arts (MLA). Music is a natural audio-lingual motivation for students. High schools have facilities for music programs. Teaching a language through music is a logical outgrowth. A complete curriculum was prepared and is being reproduced. This program is funded under Title I and has met with enthusiasm and success. The language emphasis and the participation by the students accelerate learning English language arts through music. Again, with funding, this program can be expanded.

English as A Second Language and Bilingual Education are cooperative, coexisting programs to help youngsters find success and happiness in the pluralistic American society. Bilingual, as the word indicates, is a combination of two languages.

"Some pupils who are speakers of other languages bring very few images, little information, and poor understanding of themselves and of their surroundings in the classroom. They have enjoyed few experiences from which concepts, and therefore, language may have grown. Their lives may not have been filled with an abundance of objects for which they have learned names. They may have enjoyed very limited encounters with their surroundings. They may have had little exposure to language. These boys and girls bring neither previously acquired concepts nor native language to the learning of English. An oral language development program in English which will provide the background needed for learning to read English is very different from the one which merely adds new language learnings to good native language and rich experiences. They will need to have many sensory opportunities. They need to

see, to smell, to feel, to touch, to hear, to move, to manipulate the countless ways in which humans know about things and people. As these sensory explorations are made, the language which describes, explains, and mediates meaning must accompany them."[5]

In the United States, English must be one of them. In the bilingual program, the child receives academic instruction for a certain portion of the school day in his native language and the remaining portion in English. These proportions vary as the student becomes more adept in his second language. Therefore, while the youngster studies his academic work in a bilingual program, it is equally important to re-enforce his acquisitions of communication skills in a small-group setting, in English so that he may function in the society in which he lives. Bilingual programs are now in existence in Spanish, Chinese, French, Italian, and Greek. English-as-a-Second Language programs encompass a wide range of languages as stated above. Therefore, there is sound reason for a strong English-as-a-Second -Language program as an important component of bilingual education and as a strong independent program.

Since thousands of youngsters in non-Title I schools are not receiving assistance for these special programs because they are not considered disadvantaged students, there is a definite need to change this ruling so that all language-handicapped youngsters might benefit from such programs.

Parents and community interests and support are crucial to the English-as-a-Second Language programs.

"Utilize the community resources and bring the people in the community into your program. This is important not only because it provides additional stimulation for the students but also because it will foster interest in English language learning in the community."[6]

Dialogues between communities and school boards lead to the expansion of programs and the strengthening of existing programs.

Within the framework of decentralization, the ESL Unit functions in a resource and consultative capacity for setting up and implementing elementary and junior high school programs. Upon request, the Unit offers all its services to the decentralized districts.

The central program services 37 high schools where there are large numbers of non-English speaking pupils. It should be noted that in the Title I funded programs for English as a Second Language, children speaking Spanish are the dominant group. However, students speaking such varied languages as Papiamento, Greek, Turkish, Chinese, and the Slavic language and many others are represented in the program.

The Unit does not work alone in the implementation of its programs. It is in constant communication with the Bureau of Educational Research, Bureau of Curriculum Development, Bureau of Bilingual Education, the directors of the various curriculum areas, the Bureau of Recruitment, The New York State Department of Education in Albany, and the Department of Education and Welfare in Washington.

There is some confusion about the role of ESL in a bilingual program. "ESL is an important component of bilingual education; but unless the home language is used as a medium for teaching a part or the whole of the curriculum, we believe education cannot be called bilingual."[7]

With the growth of bilingual education in the United States, it should be obvious that ESL will have to grow with it. However, we must make sure that ESL is taught by teachers who have native fluency in the language, that they are well trained in the methodology of ESL, and that the proper materials are available for the teacher and the pupil. It behooves the administrator to see to it that a positive philosophy is established for all teachers concerned with the teaching of ESL pupils. It is most important that the administration and staff have some knowledge of the culture and language of the ESL pupil and it is most important that the youngster be given the opportunity to learn about his culture and his language.

Side by side, ESL and bilingual instruction can create an atmosphere in the schools where our pupils will meet with success and a feeling of belonging.

From an administrator's point of view, several factors must be considered. On the high school level it is important that a strong articulation program be set up with the feeding schools. It is most important that the administrator and guidance personnel visit the feeding schools and outline the types of programs available to students and how the guidance staff and teachers of the feeding schools submit this information.

The administrator should, wherever possible have a flexible program. This is importnat for the mobility of the students in the program. If the administrator can set up parallel classes, it will be possible for the students to be moved from level to level. As the student advances in his studies so he can advance from a beginning level to intermediate or advanced without disrupting his program.

It is also important for the administrator to set up the teachers' programs so that they have a common free period. This gives the administrator and the teachers an opportunity to exchange ideas and to recommend the movement of pupils from level to level. Finally, on the high school level as well as all levels of instruction, the administrator, through workshops, in-service training and intervisitations should make the entire faculty aware of the culture and language of the pupils in the program.

On the intermediate or junior high school levels, the administrator would carry out the same type of program. Since this is a difficult age for all students, the administrator should make a concerted effort to obtain bilingual guidance services for all pupils.

On the elementary level, the situation is quite different. Since there is no departmentalization on this level, there will be an ESL pull-out program or special classes for the non-English speaking pupil. The administrator must be certain that there is a screening committee for incoming students. There must also be some sort of screening device to determine the level of ability of the student in English as well as his native language.

Usually some prepared quaestions based on a series of pictures will be a quick way to determine fluency and content of language. A paragraph from a basal reader would help determine the level of achievement. A word of caution, in a special high school ESL program students were tested with the Stanford Achievement Test Primary Level II Form B. The mean reading score was 2.2 and the mean auditory comprehension was 1.5. This should make it evident that for a beginning ESL student, knowledge of the second language will be at best minimal.

It is important that the administrator involve parents in the program. This can be done in a number of ways. One very desirable way is to set up ESL classes for parents. This will help the school help the parent work with the children. Another way is to involve parents with plays commemorating historical holidays. For example, parents can assist the teachers involved in making costumes or scenery. Parents could be invited to talk about life in the country from which they came. At all times, the school should try to provide bilingual personnel for the parents so that they are secure in the knowledge that there is someone in school with whom they can communicate.

In conclusion, it is important for the administration, working with a myriad of educational, economical, political, and social factors, to remember that its client is the student. In that way, the administration will steer a true course.

The administrator must plan, innovate, and constantly re-evaluate the programs. He must have first-hand personal knowledge of what is going on in the field.

Not only the administrator, but also his choice of staff must represent a broad spectrum of expertise in the field of ESL, including speech and reading, innovative programming, audio-visual instruction, testing, and writing proposals. Good interpersonal relationships are also a factor in the optimum workings of the programs, as well as an accomplished secretarial staff. Dialogue with those in the field and with students is crucial.

Using the ESL mnemonic, "STAMPS," the administrator and his staff must be able to offer—Special Services, Teacher—Training, Assistance in the Field, Material and Curriculum, Planning, and Selective Programming.

State and Federal funding are essential to the success of these programs, especially in the wake of the fiscal crisis in the city.

The program has made great strides in New York City. There is much more that can and should be done. A great deal of excellent teaching goes on in the high schools. ESL children do learn and advance into the mainstream and go on to college. It is with the cooperation of all concerned that the program will continue in its efforts to make it possible for its students to meet with success in the schools.

In an evaluation done in the school year 1975-76, Dr. Eleanor Kelly, (1975) an objective evaluator maintained that "Teaching English as a second language to high school pupils in small groups and with appropriate materials appears to significantly improve their auditory ability and reading comprehension. This improvement was measured by the Stanford Achievement Test by pre and post test scores (p.9)."

Mrs. Rhoda Stern (1975) an objective evaluator for another phase of an ESL program stated, "Statistically significant gains in reading and auditory comprehension in English were recorded for the majority of participating pupils (p.18)."

The evaluation of the past five years all done by outside, objective evaluators tell the same story. ESL is a viable, practical approach to the teaching of English to non-English speaking pupils.

NOTES

[1]N.Y.C. Board of Education Office of Business and Administration "Annual Census of School Population." June 1973.

[2]Dacanay Fe and Bowen, Donald *Techniques and Procedures in Second Language Teaching.* Dobbs Ferry, New York: Oceana Publications, 1967.

[3]Troike, Rudolph "The View From The Center: Warning—ESL (Traditional) May Be Hazardous to Children" *The Linguistic Reporter,* September-October 1976.

[4]Thonis, Eleanor Wall "Teaching Reading to Non-English Speakers," Collier-McMillan, 1970, p. 107.

[5]Ibid. p. 106.

[6]Finocchiaro, Mary *English as a Second Language From Theory to Practice*, New Edition, Regents Publishing Company, Inc. 1974, p. 121.

[7]Cordasco, Francisco "Bilingual Schoolboy in the United States," A Sourcebook for Educational Personnel, McGraw Hill Book Company, 1976.

BIBLIOGRAPHY

Bureau of Curriculum Development: *Handbook for Language Arts Pre-K, Kindergarten, Grades One and Two*, Board of Education of the City of New York, 1968.

Bureau of Curriculum Development: *Teaching English as a Second Language*, Board of Education of the City of New York, 1971.

Cordasco, Francisco: *Bilingual Schoolboy in the United States*, A Sourcebook for Educational Personnel, McGraw Hill Book Company, 1976.

Dacanay Fe and Bowen, Donald: *Techniques and Procedures in Second Language Teaching*, Oceana Publications, Dobbs Ferry, New York, 1967.

Educational Program Research and Statistics: "Annual Census of School Population, Board of Education of the City of New York, June, 1972.

Finocchiaro, Mary: *English As A Second Language From Theory to Practice*, Regents Publishing Company, 1974.

Thonis, Eleanor Wall: *Teaching Reading to Non-English Speakers*, Collier-Macmillan, 1970.

Chapter 28
Aspects of Language Transition – The School Bilingual Program
Arnold Raisner*

In 1970 the Census Bureau told us that over 4.5 million Spanish-speaking students under 20 years of age spoke Spanish at home. These students were not being brought into the mainstream of academic life. Their large numbers were disproportionately represented in the high school drop-out statistics. Their school achievement was generally characterized as a disaster and their prospects for upward socio-economic mobility were comparably dismal. It seemed obvious to everyone that these minority children would continue to have a most difficult time keeping up with their monolingual schoolmates as long as English remained the exclusive language of instruction. What exactly was to be done?

In 1974 the United States Supreme Court held in the case of *Lau* v. *Nicholas* that: "school districts receiving federal funds cannot discriminate against children of limited or non-English speaking ability by denying them the language training they need for meaningful participation in the educational process." It was further stated, that: "There is no equality of treatment merely by providing students with the same facilities, textbooks, teachers and curriculum; for students who do not understand English are effectively foreclosed from any meaningful education."

Surely it must have been understood at the writing of the decision that just as the sole use of English postponed the students' ability to grasp subject-content material in the classroom, so too, the exclusive use of the native tongue would postpone and possibly interfere with that critical language contact so essential for the proper acquisition of English.

The best of both worlds would require a balanced and possibly extended school day. It would provide for the learning of subject matter at a pace that would maintain the student's grade-level achievement while maximizing his opportunity to learn the English language. At the same time, the perfect program would maintain and improve the students' native language skills while imparting a sense of personal pride and appreciation for both his new and native culture. The multiplicity of programs that have been organized range across the full spectrum. Their configurations depend upon such diverse influencing factors as: the presence of political pressure, the district financial capability, the number of "foreign" students, and the initial extent of their English language deficit.

Let us look at programs at the ends of the spectrum.

One "traditional" approach placed the newly arrived student in a class with his English-speaking peers; seats him when possible, next to a pupil prompter who is one or two steps ahead on the language ability scale; has him periodically separated from the class, for time periods ranging from 20 minutes to one hour, in order to receive intensive English-language instruction, and then hopes that very soon, a combination of inborn talent and social exposure will catapult him up to the same level of language proficiency enjoyed by the home town boy across the aisle. It may have happened, sometimes,— but it was a rarity! More frequently the endless hours spent in the half light of dimly understood instructions were converted into periods of withdrawal, quiet desperation, and finally personal resentment and a search for other activity to salve the ego and gain peer recognition. Yes, some areas of English language participation are ultimately achieved, but the price is high in terms of the drop in grade-level achievement and the decline of self-image. The classic "melting pot"—total immersion, sink or swim approach—has produced some powerful swimmers in the past. The others sank into a societal matrix that provided jobs for the unskilled, and social ghettos that were to last for at least a generation. The cheap language-deficient labor force was actually an asset for the economy at that time. However, what was a plus in that past era can constitute "social dynamite" in our present time. The phenomena of increasing industrial automation coupled with a new employment emphasis on proficient language skills places the school deficient

*Dr. Arnold Raisner is School Community Superindent of District 28 in New York City. The District has 25,000 students with a large proportion of pupils of Spanish-speaking background.

candidate on an endless cycle of economic desperation.

Now consider the other end of the language-program spectrum. It is popularly called Bilingual-Bicultural education. In its most crystalized form the English-language deficient child is placed in a class of all similarly language profiled students and a "bilingual" teacher proceeds to give instruction in most vital content areas using the student's own language. In this way, it is hoped that he will keep on grade level with his English-speaking peers in the adjoining classroom. His books may be all in Spanish and his teacher and classmates all speak his native tongue. He will be taught English as a foreign language, as he probably was in his homeland, except, it is assumed, that he will incidentally receive massive reinforcement by the surrounding community influences (T.V., supermarket, playmates, newsprint) outside of school hours. Opportunities to study in English are expanded on a readiness basis until he gains a balanced proficiency and can even begin to take all his classes in English while still being enrolled in a native language maintenance program. Thus, he theoretically avoids, in the course of his school career, the psychological trauma of language isolation and does not stand still academically while waiting to gain proficiency in English. The question remains: Can he master English in this way, and gain subject matter proficiency within the time allotted to his pre-high school or even college preparatory schooling?

Some opponents of this latter design wonder if the bilingual class is not a theoretical "wonderkind" but a practical "flop." They feel that practically speaking it is little more than a direct transplant of a foreign classroom, in its entirety, into an American schoolhouse. Similar, for example, to the structure of the American School in Turkey for children of American army officers. Those children eventually return home without much of a capacity to understand the Turkish language. There is a deep concern that delay and postponement of the task of learning English will harden into an inability to ever master the language skills well enough to enable the students to compete on an equal footing with native born young adults. While the native child progressed through the grades working at capacity to master the intricate, graduated, cyclical skills of reading, writing, spelling and composition, his opposite number, of equal intelligence and academic capacity, spent his time going through a slow language transition. Can the language minority student hope to complete his time table for the development of second language proficiency in time to compete for a place in law or medical school?

Do physical and language barriers that are too long retained lead to ethnic isolation and political balkanization for the adult population? These quiet fears have indeed caused many minority language parents to request that their children not be placed in a "bilingual" track. Educators ask whether bilingual education, as described here briefly, is an effective means of providing "meaningful participation in the educational process" or whether total and immediate immersion in the linguistic "melting pot" more definitively fulfills our long range educational goals.

Any educational program that is planned and any instructional strategies that are devised must take into account both our immediate and long range purposes. The concerned educator would seek to avoid the expedience of simplistic shibboleths which may offer quick and direct answers but serve ultimately as a lock-step restriction against the implementation of the process and producing the product which reflects our ultimate hopes. For example, by accommodating the immediate concern of maintaining grade level achievement at the cost of postponing English-language acquisition we may be inadvertently frustrating our long range goal of providing maximum opportunity for the success of our students. The reverse may be true as well: by deferring subject matter instruction for too long a period in favor of an exclusive stress on the English language we may be too late to recoup our loss in academic progress. Now that we have a focus on the problem let us examine some of the influencing variables that would determine our final instructional strategy.

Let us assume that we have an ultimate 12 year success image in mind for the first grade child of Spanish-speaking background who is now entering school with a clear English-language disability. That projected image no doubt pictures a young adult who can, as a result of his or her K-12 experience qualify for advanced study and meet the keen competition of those of his peers who did not have the initial language difficulty and have with equal diligence, intelligence and academic capacity completed the course of study in English alone for 12 years. Our success image has acquired the full range of English language skills while retaining a sense of personal pride and confidence in his ability to learn. He has avoided cognitive retardation in all areas while in the process of learning English and has succeeded in maintaining competence in the skills of his native language, at least to the extent that it can be applied in the practice of the student's future profession or in his social life.

By whichever organizational method we ultimately select to reach our hypothetical success model there are some fundamental psycholinguistic considerations that should be taken into account. These concerns would apply universally in the area of second language acquisition through the in-school experience.

Diachronic Tracing of Language Shift Phenomena

Studies in descriptive linguistics often center about the relationship between two languages as they are used by an individual, side by side at a particular time (synchronic). But, languages in contact present an ever changing dynamic interaction with advance and retreat of one language or the other in the face of time, usage and attitude. The diachonic (change over a time period) significance of language acquisition hold the key to the insight needed to plan school based instructional programs.

If one were to follow the progress of any individual as he moves from monolingual to bilingual competence and eventual dominance in the new language one would begin to understand the interacting roles of *experience* and *time*. The quality, quantity and sequence of experience as developed over time are critical in the language shift mechanism. Setting aside for the moment significant individual influencing variables such as age, intelligence and inherent language learning competence we are confronted with the universal needs for exposure, motivation and use.

Exposure to a second language in a particular setting or area of use (consider perhaps the cafeteria for a hungry immigrant) establishes a beachhead in the struggle to acquire the new skill. This effort represents the start of the development of a language domain. Avoidance of hunger as a motivation will cause him to *switch* from his native language into the new expressive domain where cafeteria terms in English are dominant. Note the first tiny movement in the establishment of a new, individual language dominance configuration.

The diachonic analysis of language shift would reveal fertile areas for emphasis through planned experiences for students at different stages of bilingual development. Perhaps instructional methodolgy should not focus on an "all or none" language experience but should designate graded experience domains of involvement for developing bilingualism. For example, dramatic songs and poems or daily recorded experience charts may develop quickly toward the establishment of the exclusive domain of English for first and second graders. How much of each language is being used at any one time? In which direction and with what force should the vector of single language use operate?

Uriel Weinreich (1953) has pointed out the significance of determining the extent of use and the context of use for each language in a so-called bilingual system. The extent of the use of either language can be marked theoretically on a scale which extends from little use to total use. To superimpose the "area of use" scale of one language on a similar scale constructed for a second language, is to determine a "use configuration" which could help to profile the progress and the readiness of pupils to work and study in new areas.

More specifically Weinreich proposed that a *dominance configuration* be established for the two languages for each individual. This configuration would be determined by the bilingual's relative proficience, his mode of use, frequency of use, emotional involvement, function in social advance, and literary-cultural value. At the hurried pace of public education the development and use of such profiles would be impossible. But, our awareness of the dynamic process is invaluable as it affects our program planning.

Joshua Fishman (1965) tells us, "Dominance configurations may be used to summarize data on the bilingual behavior of many individuals who constitute a defined sub-population. Repeated dominance configuration for the same population, studied over time, may be used to represent the direction (or flow) of language maintenance and language shift in a particular multi-lingual setting." It is precisely the pace and completeness of this shift which gives us the clue to the contrastive effects of different methods or strategies for instruction which are most effective during the processes of both acculturation and cognition.

The way in which one functions as a bilingual can be related to the way in which one became a bilingual. It has been theorized that there are two types of bilingualism; one in which each language is learned in its own environment or context, and the other in which the second language is learned by translation through the first. The former method results in a *coordinate* bilingual system, while the latter leads to a *compound* bilingual system. Coordinate bilingualism—to the extent that it is desired for its quality of inducing fewer language interference—can best be achieved by having the learner abandon his native language while he undertakes the learning of his second tongue. Research indicates that separated language learning enhances the effectively separated use of the bilingual's two languages, where content area, science, for example is learned first in one language the student is likely to reserve that domain of thinking for the language in which it was originally studied. In comparable social situations a child who learned and spoke only a particular language with his grandmother is likely to switch to that language in thoughts relating to her. Obviously, this is not a hard and fast rule but rather an indication of tendencies that are subject to change by other influencing factors.

Immigrants working in a factory are likely to establish an entire domain of competence in discussing production operations but founder frequently on the linguistic switching and interference mechanism when talking about politics or personal problems. The context of exposure is important in establishing the moving line of language dominance configuration.

Central to the new language acquisition process is the operation of a suitable teaching linguistic model. Language learning is largely imitative and there is no substitute for a native speaker. I recall arrriving in Puerto Rico during the Korean conflict to assume responsibility for a portion of the English Language Instruction Program which was designed to prepare insular soldiers for their combat responsibilities at the side of their continental comrades. Upon making my early orientation observances I was dismayed at not being able to understand the lecturing "bilingual" drill sergeant who was shouting phrases to be repeated and learned by the troops. I thought that he was using a singularly esoteric form of colloquial Spanish that had completely escaped my castillian competence. My dismay turned to alarm when I realized that he thought he was pronouncing English words and the troops were repeating his utterances in the hope that they would soon be speaking the new language. Subsequent staff reassignment replaced the "bilingual" sergeants with non-Spanish speaking drill models—and to a somewhat greater extent, the program was on its way to success. Apart from the mimicry aspect of language learning there appeared to be a compelling psycho-social need to try the new speech since the instructors could not understand Spanish (poor fellows). The teacher interaction model is a vital element in establishing base competence in the new language domain. This should be seriously considered in staff planning for bilingual transition programs. Native speakers in both English and Spanish are essential to the bilingual program.

Having briefly touched upon the importance of models, the process of expansion of language domains and the importance of attitude and motivation let us return to the two instructional strategies discussed earlier in this paper.

The first model which required virtual elimination of the native language from the learning process was found to be faulty because of the stress on compulsion and the threat of failure whith all their attendant psychological and attitudinal scarring. In additon, the extended deferral of the learning of content areas (science, math, etc.) until English language operational competence is achieved has a built-in assurance that the student will incur an insurmountable academic retardation. Assuming that the curriculum for the monolingual child is normally full and demanding, the dual obligation to learn a new language and the normal course of study, in the same time period, is oppressive and unreasonable. The exceptionally bright and language capable child is too frequently called upon to exemplify the workability of a process that is unreasonable for the normal child.

The second model involving the extensive (and sometimes exclusive) use of native language in order to avoid the loss of grade level attainment in "subject" areas now faces the problem that the learning of English will be postponed to a period when the timely impetus for the development of new domain has passed. The child is "set in his way" of approaching new content. He has already "fixed" the area of use as a native language domain. He must now undertake the mastery of the new language through the use of his first language in a "compound" bilingual system. The language dominance configuration must be changed rather than be initially created. The full panoply of phonic, grammatical and lexical interference comes into play. English can be mastered but it takes a little longer and time is an irreplaceable ingredient in the success mix.

Ingredients of the Success Mix

The recently arrived student with a total English language deficit has a hard enough psycho-social adjustment problem without having to be subjected to the blank world of an alien language. A "vestibule" class in which his native language is spoken has a vital place in his emotional, social and intellectual orientation. Where a class cannot be organized because of the relatively small number of children in the non-English speaking category there should be a "buddy team" or a least a bilingual person to whom the newcomer may refer. This idea is not new—but it should not be overlooked in the haste of new program construction.

The transition from monolingualism to bilingualism should be marked off in progress *phases*.

We may think in terms of five "phases of progress" with phase 3 as the approximate "switching point" from a native language dominance to an English dominant use configuration. We can identify the pupil's operational phase in any grade and provide an "extent of usage" based program at the point of need. In phase one the instructional program would seek to establish a "domain of exclusive use" within the sea of native language use. In phase two the number and size of the domains are extended and subsequently connected through "bridge" or direct language instruction. Each grade would have materials and resources for presenting an instructional program picking up at the appropriate phase of transition and nurturing the growing edge of the thrust toward new language acquisition. In grade four, for example, the teacher would be aware of the phase of transition for each student. Those in phase *one* and *two* would actually take instruction in a bilingual class where instruction is presented in the native language.

"Use presentation" of structured linguistic patterns should constitute an intrinsic part of the transition phase instruction. Too frequently a cascade of random words (without domain pertinence) presented in a haphazard grammatical sequence results in a "fixing" of inappropriate tense and structure. This becomes truly difficult to undo through subsequent modified usage.

In a dual language use environment the myriad significant influencing factors must be taken into account if the student is to be challenged at the point of his maximum achievement level. The program must recognize the differences in the extent of home use of the language; the out-of-school peer and play use of the dominant and second language; the attitude of parents and siblings toward the use of the two languages; the foreign language acquisition talent of the student and the age and previous formal "language mix" exposure of the pupil. The picture is further complicated by a distinct difference between ability to understand and ability to speak the new language. The naturally shy or purposefully shy child can give the appearance of total inability in the second language.

It is for these reasons that the need to individualize and personalize the transition phases of instruction becomes critical. The researchers, program designers, authors and teachers need a closer look at the level mix, sequencing and pacing their transition material. For example, the presentation of domain oriented poems and rote or story songs should be connected to daily usage domains by a common vocabulary and a syntactic bridge.

The move through transition phases implies a need for individualization of instruction and the extension of available time.

It is here proposed that an extended school day for transition pupils is the only way to provide for the double burden of new language and new subject mastery. The Jewish "Yeshivas" for example, teach all subjects relating to the Hebrew language and religion and then extend the school day to teach content areas in English on a par with the public schools. Similarly, other parochial schools which seek to teach more than is mandated by state law simply provide more time without assuming that a "magical method" can be found to teach two things in the time it normally takes to teach one.

The earlier stress upon the importance of using native language teachers implies the need to have two teachers with the class (or a teacher and an appropriately trained paraprofessionsl). This need can, in part, be met by scheduling transition classes for part of the day with the English teacher and part of the day with the native language teacher. The proportions of the day and the content being taught at any one time would vary with the phase work undertaken at the planning stage. Two classes of approximately thirty students each might be taught by a team-teaching combination of two teachers and a paraprofessional. An expansion of the scheduling and program design would depend upon the character of the student population and the resources of the community.

The formulation of further design alternatives and the compilation of additional material suitable for use in the bilingual class depends largely upon the findings of new research. Action research is necessary for the development of testing instruments capable of measuring student language performance. The construction of such instruments should take into account not only the student's response to written form (as most current tests do) but also the power of self-expression and comprehension of the spoken word. The testing program should be designed to provide a continuing record of progress in order to supply data relating to shift of language use and dominance.

Languages in social contact present both problems of interference and loyalty, and opportunities for practice and reinforcement. How influential are the factors of societal pressure? How does the media affect language use and competence at different age levels? How can the positive effects of the dual language society be incorporated into the formalized instructional program?

Do children who are in the process of second language acquisition have to be subjected to the same teaching methodolgy developed originally for adults or are there cognitive implications which would be revealed through a deeper understanding of language readiness and maturation process.

The five million Spanigh-speaking students now in the United States will have a significant impact upon the national development and economic welfare of our nation. Time, energy and cooperative effort can turn the prospective problem into a promising potential.

BIBLIOGRAPHY

Ervin, S.; Osgood, D. E. "Second Language Learning and Bilingualism." In C. E. Osgood and T. A. Sebcok (Eds.) *Psycholinguistics*: A Survey of Theory and Research Problems, New York: Holt, Rinehart, Winston, 1961.

Fishman, J. A. "Bilingualism, Intelligence and Language Learning." *Modern Language Journal*, April, 1965. Vol. XLIX. No. 4, p. 233.

Lambert, W. E.; Havelka, F.; Crosby, C. "The Influence of Language Acquisition Contexts on Bilingualism." *Journal of Abnormal and Social Psychology*, 56, 1958. p. 239-244.

Raisner, A. *Oral English Program for Spanish-Speaking Personnel;* Manual for Instructors, Troop Information and Education Division, United States Armed Forces Antilles, Fort Brooke, Puerto Rico, November, 1953.

Raisner, A. "New Horizons for the Student of Spanish-Speaking Background," *Problems and Practices in New York City Schools*, New York Society for the Experimental Study of Education, Yearbook 1965, pp. 103-106.

Weinreich, V. *Languages in Contact*, New York: Linguistic Circle of New York, 1953, pp. 74-80.

Chapter 29
Chicano Children's Code-Switching: An Overview
Erica McClure and James Wentz *

1. Introduction

Code-switching is the alternation of codes in communication in accordance with a set of learned rules. A code is a system defined by a consistent set of co-occurring rules, and it may be either a specific language or a variety of a particular language. In order to describe code-switching accurately, both the grammatical and the socio-linguistic aspects (the form and function) must be considered. From a grammatical standpoint, it is useful to view code-switching as comprising two separate devices which are a part of an individual's linguistic competence: code-changing and code-mixing. Code-changing is the alternation of linguistic codes at the level of the constituent (e.g., NP, VP, sentence). The code-change is a complete shift to another language system. All function words such as articles, pronouns, prepositions and all morphology and syntax are abruptly changed as in:

(1) I put the forks *en la mesa*.

Code-mixing, on the other hand, does not involve a complete shift of the discourse to the opposite code, but rather incorporates elements of one code into discourse being conducted·in the other.

Code-mixing is done within constituents, and there is always at some level an indication that the code-mixed item is marked for use in a sentence of another code. For example, in the sentence:

(2) I put the *tenedores* (forks) on the table.

the noun phrase "the tenedores" is marked for use in an English sentence by the article "the". The morphology and phonology of "tenedores" (/tenedor+es/) is entirely Spanish nonetheless. Consequently, it is unlikely that, among bilinguals, such an occurrence would represent a lexical borrowing. In the sentence

(3) I want a motorcycle *verde*.

we can say that the Spanish adjective "verde" is code-mixed into an English sentence. Spanish placement of "verde" indicates it is not a borrowing. The noun phrase "a motorcycle verde" is marked by "a" as being an English noun phrase. It could not be used in a Spanish sentence, but "un motorcycle verde" could, in which case "motorcycle" might be either a borrowed or code-mixed noun. Its status is ambiguous because

there are no clear morphological or syntactic indicators. Phonology is only one clue in disambiguating the status of opposite language elements, because they often contain a mixture of Spanish and English sounds or phonemes. The sentence above and others containing code-mixes are generally perceived by bilinguals to be sentences of one language containing elements of the other. Sentences in which internal code-changes occur are felt to begin in one code and change to the other.

The dichotomy between code-changing and code-mixing which was occasioned by syntactic considerations is also useful in describing the functional aspects of code-switching. Code-mixing occurs when a person is momentarily unable to access a term for a concept in the language which he is using but can access it in another code, or when he doesn't have a term in the code he is using which exactly expresses the concept he wishes to convey, as for example in joking and punning. The need to code mix for these reasons may often trigger a total change. These two cases may reflect different relationships among signs and their referents for the bilingual. When code-mixing occurs because of inability to access a term in the language being spoken, it is probable that the signs are compounded; where code-mixing occurs because of the lack of a precise term in the discourse code, coordinate signs may exist. A sign combines a unit of expression and a unit of content. A compound sign is one in which a unit of expression in each of two languages references the same unit of content. Coordinate signs are separate units in each language which involve similar but not identical units of content. The distinction between compound and coordinate signs may be expressed schematically as in (4).

* Erica McClure, Assistant Professor of Educational Psychology, University of Illinois, at Urbana-Champaign.
* James Wentz, doctoral candidate in the Linguistics Department, University of Illinois, at Urbana-Champaign.

(4)

'book'   'libro'   'book' ≡ 'libro'
 | | /   \
/buk/   /libro/   /buk/   /libro/
coordinate signs   a compound sign

Code-mixing of color terms by the Mexican-American children we have studied provides a good example of the former since detailed analysis shows that for these children color terms in Spanish and English have identical referential and affective meanings.

(5) No van a hablar con una mujer que *can't calk business.*

is an example of the latter type of code-mixing. "Can't talk business" is derived from an idiomatic unit in English which has for the speaker no precise culturally appropriate Spanish equivalent. The use of "que" instead of "who" to introduce this relative clause suggests that the phrase is a code-mix and not a code-change.

Code-changing is influenced by two basic types of considerations—situational and stylistic. The degree to which situation constrains code choices varies widely. In some situations the use of a particular code may be nearly obligatory, while in others it is only probable. In the former instances a speaker's failure to use the expected code is interpreted by the bilingual listener as either being aberrant or conveying additional information. However, strict constraints upon code choice are comparatively rare among Mexican-American children we have studied. Moreover, in some cases what is important is the fact that a code-change has taken place rather than a particular code has been selected.

2. Code-Changing and Situation

Changes in situation tend to be reflected in changes in code. A situation is defined both physically and psychologically in terms of features such as participants, topic, physical setting, and psychological setting or cultural definition of a situation. The children we studied tend to be most sensitive to changes involving participants. Their earliest systematic code-switching is associated with changes in the category "participants." The inappropriate choice of code when addressing a monolingual is relatively rare. Thus, although children with little prior experience with the Anglo community were observed to use Spanish with Anglophone school teachers and pupils upon entering school, such behavior was no longer observed after the first month of classes. Those children lacking even a minimal facility in English soon resorted to one of two strategies: silence and passivity or the use of nonverbal communication through gesture. That children quickly develop a facility in code-switching according to

addressee is further demonstrated by the fact that such code-switching takes place even within turns of speaking. An example is:

(6) B(girl/16): "Ask daddy [for the matches]." (to sister/5)
 S(girl/5): "Oh, daddy have it. (to sister/16) Papi, 'on 'tan las matches? Dame."
 (to father)

Code-switching according to persons among young children appears to depend on binary judgments of linguistic competence. A person is considered either to know or not know a language. The youngest children studied did not seem to be able to gauge degrees of ability or else seemed to ignore such assessments in choosing a suitable code. Thus, for example, those children five or younger who were Spanish dominant spoke to the first author in Spanish, the language in which they were most comfortable, despite the fact that their English was more fluent than her Spanish. Older children make finer discriminations in selecting a code for use with a given individual. They consider both language facility and preference. The older children used Spanish in addressing four others whose knowledge of English was rudimentary. Assessments of language facility also appear to account at least partially for the fact that although as children grow older they increasingly use English with those who understand it, with pre-schoolers they continue to use Spanish predominantly. A random selection of fifteen one hour recordings contained 188 utterances directed to pre-schoolers, 67 percent of which were in Spanish. The use of English with pre-schoolers is generally restricted to short, routinized expressions—Spanish being used for most utterances with a high informational load. Siblings of pre-schoolers tend to use more English with them than do others. In our corpus 43 percent of the 118 utterances addressed by siblings to pre-schoolers were in English. Only 22 percent of the 70 utterances addressed by non-siblings to pre-schoolers were in English.

Not only are features of the addressee important, but also the role relationships which exist between them are significant in describing code-choice. There appears to be a characteristic pattern of language use associated with every role relationship. Given a situation that dictates the portrayal of only one role, the pattern of language use will remain invariant. For example, only one role relationship is available in an interaction between child and parent, and the pattern of language use is very consistent. In most families such interactions take place in Spanish. Teacher-pupil interactions also involve a fixed role relationship. English has been established as the appropriate language for these interactions, since the bilingual program was introduced only two years before the beginning of our study. Consequently, the bilingual teacher had difficulty in getting children who know English to respond to her in Spanish. A final example of a situation in which a child's role selection was rigidly constrained involved a nine-year-old girl and a male, Mexican-American researcher. The researcher defined the situation as a formal interview, his role being interviewer, the child's interviewee. He used Spanish, and the child followed suit, although she showed a marked preference for using English with the other researchers, male and female, who defined their roles vis-á-vis the children more informally.

Situations also exist in which a child has freedom of choice with respect to the selection of a role. Shifting role relationships among children are often marked by code alternation just as Blom and Gumperz (1972) have demonstrated among adults. Interactions between children which involve sibling relationships and peer relationships tend to be in English. Interactions between children which involve caretaker-child relationships are almost always in Spanish. We observed that when a younger child was hurt, it was comforted by an older child in Spanish even though an immediately preceding interaction between the children may have taken place in English. The following sequence is typical:

(7) P (girl/9): "Stop it Roli. You're stupid!"

    R (brother/3): "You stupid Pat."

    P: "Don't hit me!" (laughing and holding R off)

    R: (trips and begins to cry)

    P: "Ay, Roli! Mi hijito qué pasó?"

Likewise, we found that when children assumed a position of authority they issued commands in Spanish. Thus, when one of our research assistants went by herself to collect data from a group of children in the project mobile home, rather than as usual in the company of several other researchers, one of the older boys spontaneously assumed the role of the one responsible for keeping order among the rest. His orders in this role were issued in Spanish. It would appear that behavior in the caretaker-child role is patterned after that in the home where such interactions take place in Spanish.

The children at play have also been observed to switch from Spanish to English when switching from a peer role relationship with another child to a teacher-pupil relationship. Code alternation to mark role shifting is, of course, more common among older children than among younger children, since the former have access to more roles.

Topic does not appear to have as large an effect upon code switching in the children we studied as do participants. The children are able to and in fact do converse about anything in their experience in both languages. However the discussion of a few topics is more likely to occur in one language than in the other. Topics related to the family—child care, kinship and food preparation—are most often discussed in Spanish, whereas romance, sports and holidays such as Halloween and Thanksgiving are more often discussed in English. When a topic which is habitually discussed in one language happens to come up in a conversation in the other language, a high incidence of lexical borrowing and intrasentential code switching may be observed.

Setting also has an effect upon the choice of code. However, it like topics does not produce absolute effects—only relative ones. Thus, while Spanish used with greater frequency in the home than in any other setting, English is also heard there—more in the case of some families, less in the case of others. Similarly, while English is the only language of instruction and response in the school outside of the bilingual classrooms, interactions among the Mexican-Americans in the classroom and on the playground are often in Spanish. The community park and project car and mobile home, the other settings in which observations were made, appeared to be neutral with respect to language choice.

The categories topic, participants and setting are useful analytic constructs which have enabled the authors to account for a large proportion of code selection behavior. It is probable that at least the categories topic and participants also have some psychological validity for the subjects studied, since metalinguistic comments concerning these categories have been recorded. Examples are provided below:

(8) F (boy/4) : "Cómo es que hablas como nosotros," (to Anglo bilingual elementary school teacher)

(9) E (boy/10) : "In English or Spanish?"

    J (Anglo researcher): "En espanol si puedes."

    E: "Aw, I can't tell that in Spanish."

    J: "Just try, OK?"

3. Code-Changing and Style

Gumperz and Hernandez (1972) have shown that code-switching has a stylistic function for adult bilinguals. Our data suggest that style is also a very relevant parameter for analyzing the code switching of children. We have found that children's code switching may serve the following stylistic functions:

3.1 *Emphasis.* Code-switching for emphasis may occur from Spanish to English or from English to Spanish. The majority of such code-switches involve direct translation.

(10) P (girl/9): "Stay here Roli. Te quedas aqui."

3.2 *Focus.* Focus is here used to refer to the bringing

into prominence of a part of a sentence, in contrast to emphasis here used to apply to the entire sentence. One method of focusing upon a portion of the meaning of a sentence is topicalization. Code-switched topicalized subjects of the type illustrated in (11) below are perhaps used to indicate the ethnicity of the individual who is being discussed. In our data all examples of code-switched topicalizations were Spanish phrases in otherwise English sentences.

(11) E (Boy/8) : "Este Ernest, he's cheating."

Another example of focus is

(12) j (Boy/7) : "Pegó right there."

3.3 *Elaboration.*

(13) P (Girl/9) : "Roli, put that, ahi ponla en el sacate, [hi]jito."

This pattern of speech in which utterances are expanded is very similar to that observed in young children during the process of first language acquisition (*vide e.g.,* Clark, 1974).

3.4 *Clarification.* Immediate repetition in translation of an utterance appears to function as a means of resolving ambiguity or clarifying a potential or apparent misunderstanding.

(14) P (Girl/9) : "Qué tiene? . . . Will you watch your cards! Fijate en las cartas!"
(to brother/3)

3.5 *Attention Attraction or Retention.* Within a conversation a child may use a code-switch as a device to attract or retain the attention of his audience. It seems to us that some of such code-switching serves the same function as a raised voice, vocatives, gestures, physical contact or eye contact.

(15) M (Girl/9) : "Now let me do it. Put your feets down. Mira! It's Leti's turn again. Hi Leti!"

Still other cases appear to be a means of avoiding the tedium or insistence caused by multiple repetition. This type of repetition in translation has the impact of a paraphrase, not a repetition.

(16) P (Girl/9) : "A ver, a ver . . . let me see, let me see."

3.6 *Mode Shift.* Children's utterances involve a number of modes of discourse: conversational, rhetorical, soliloquy and commentary. It is clear that code-switching sometimes marks a point of transition between modes. For example, code-switching frequently occurs when a child interrupts a story he is telling to make a comment external to the narrative.

(17) T (Boy/8) : [final sentence of story told in Spanish] . . . respiran las llantas del tren, y that's all I could think."

Formulaic introductions and closings as well as descriptions may be in one language while the dialogue of characters in the narrative alternates between codes in the same principled way code alternation occurs in natural conversation.

Similarly, children often code-switch when interrupting a conversation with a self-directed or rhetorical statement.

(18) L (Girl/5) : "mira mi [hi] jito. La leche de tu mamá. Oh, darn, now what!"

Children also code-switch when moving from the factual to the imaginary.

(19) L (Girl/5) : "Echenle maś ahí, mucho! Pretend that was water, OK?"

3.7 *Shifts from Neutral to Affect Loaded Content.* Labov found that narratives involving a speaker's near encounter with death "almost always show a shift of style away from careful speech towards the vernacular," (Labov, 1971, p. 171). Similarly, Gumperz and Hernandez (1972) document a shift between Spanish and English in a social worker's account of her attempt to give up smoking. English was used in giving a clinical report, Spanish in giving a personal account. The alternation between Spanish and English also marks changing affect in the speech of the children studied.

(20) R (Girl/9) : "No son cuates . . . quedar a ver todas las listas. Yesterday, I almost fell down in the car. Yesterday, veniámos de Watseka, I almost fell down, cause Ramon veniá atrás, y entonces me senté . . ."

4. Conclusion

It is clear that the studied children's alternation between languages is not the result of a linguistic deficit. Their code-switching proceeds in accordance with grammatical and functional principles. Socially based principles operating within their speech community permit these children not only to integrate one code into discourse being carried out in another (code-mixing) but also to alternate the actual code of the discourse (code-changing). One purpose served by this sophisticated use of linguistic signs is to identify individual bilinguals as members of a particular community. Code-switching for the bilingual also functions to mark situational changes and stylistic expression more clearly than does register alternation for the monolingual. The adept use of code-switching by the bilingual can be viewed as analogous to the creative use of language by a skilled monolingual author or orator.

FOOTNOTES

1. Much of the material presented here appeared in E. McClure and J. Wentz "Functions of Code-Switching among Mexican-American Children."

SELECTED BIBLIOGRAPHY

Beltramo, A. & DePorcel, A. Some lexical characteristics of San Jose Spanish. In E. Hernandez-Chavex, A.D. Cohen, and A.F. Beltramo (eds.), *El Lenguaje de los Chicanos.* Arlington, Virginia Center for Applied Linguistics, 1975.

Blom, J. P. and Gumperz, J. Some social determinants of verbal behavior. In J. Gumperz and D. Hymes (eds.), *Directions in Sociolinguistics.* New York: Holt, Rinehart and Winston, 1972.

Clark, R. Performing without competence. *Journal of Child Language.* 1974, 1, 1-10.

Ervin-Tripp, S. On sociolinguistic rules: alternation and co-occurrence. In J. Gumperz and D. Hymes (eds.), *Directions in Sociolinguistics.* New York: Holt, Rinehart and Winston, 1972.

Gingras, R. C. Problems in the description of Spanish-English intrasentential code-switching. In Garland D.Bills(eds.), *Southwest Area Linguistics.* San Diego, California: Institute for Cultural Pluralism, School of Education, San Diego State University, 1974.

Gumperz, J.J. and Hernandez-Chavez, E. Bilingualism, bidialectalism, and classroom interaction. In C.B. Cazden, V.P. John and D. Hymes (eds.). *Functions of Language in the Classroom.* New York: Teachers College Press, 1972.

Lance, D.M., Spanish-English code-switching. In E. Hernandez-Chavez, A.D. Cohen, and A.F. Beltramo (eds.), *El lenguaje de los Chicanos.* Arlington, Virginia: Center for Applied Linguistics, 1975.

Labov, W. The study of language in its social context. In J.A. Fishman (ed.), *Advances in the Sociology of Language.* The Hague: Monton, 1971.

McClure, E. and McClure, M. Code-switching among Mexican-American children. In H. Sharifi (ed.), *From Meaning to Sound.* University of Nebraska, College of Arts and Sciences, 1975.

McClure, E. and Wentz, J. Functions of code-switching among Mexican-American children. In R.E. Grossman, L.J. San, and T.J. Vance (eds.), *Proceeding of the Paresession on Functionalism of the Chicago Linguistic Society.* Chicago: Chicago Linguistic Society, 1975.

Pfaff, C.W. Functional and structural constraints on syntactic variation in code-switching. In S.B. Steruer, C.A.Walker and S.S. Mufwene (eds.), *Papers from the Paresession on Diachronic Syntax.* Chicago: Chicago Linguistics Society, 1976.

Wentz, J. McClure, E. Aspects of the syntax of the code-switched discourse of bilingual children. In F. Ingemann (ed.), *Mid-America Linguistics Conference Papers.* Lawrence, Kansas: The Linguistics Department, University of Kansas, 1976.

New York Teacher's Staff

and linguistic competencies.

In the last 20 years there has been a great deal of interest in language development in young children. Until recently, however, there was a greater focus on the child's acquisition of forms or grammar than on how children use those forms in daily conversations or interactions in school settings.

When sociolinguists like Labov (1966) began to look at the use of language, they found that people use the forms of their language or dialects in different ways, depending on the social situations in which they find themselves. Other researchers (Blom and Gumperz, 1972; Fishman, 1968) studied bilingual speakers and found that they too use their languages differently, according to setting, and that to some extent you can predict what language a bilingual will speak to whom and in what social context.

A basic question sociolinguists ask is, how do we convey information about our ethnic ties, our education, or our regional background through language? Or how do we do this without stating directly, "I am highly educated," "I'm from the Midwest," or "I'm Chicano?" What is it about the way we pronounce the words that we choose and about our style of speaking that shows what we are?

A major reason why sociolinguists believe this is an important question is that different uses of language serve to maintain a social group's ethnic identity or sense of unity. For example, among some Blacks, the use of Black English dialect forms emphasizes a contrast between "us," the social ingroup, and "them,"

for example, Chicano speakers may signal the end of a gossip session by switching from colloquial Spanish to English when a stranger joins their group. This kind of switching, which follows a change in speakers, topic, or activity, is called *situational* switching (Blom and Gumperz, 1972).

Speakers also code-switch in more subtle ways. They may switch in the middle of a conversation or a sentence to make a point or specify which one of several people they are addressing. This is called *conversational* or *metaphorical* switching. For example, I heard a supervising teacher say to her student teacher in a conference with me, "You need to relax a little when you're teaching. *Me Entiendes?*" (translation: do you understand?) The teacher could have switched from English to Spanish for at least two reasons. She might have wanted to mark an ethnic bond between Chicana and Chicana and possibly exclude me from the conversation; and second, since Spanish was their "home" language, or the language of

*Dr. Celia Genishi, Assistant Professor, Department of Curriculum and Instruction, University of Texas at Austin.

This chapter is a revised version of a talk presented at the annual conference of the National Association for the Education of Young Children (NAEYC), Anaheim, California, 1976, and is based on the author's dissertation, Genishi, C. S. *Rules of code-switching in young Spanish-English speakers: An exploratory study of language socialization.* Unpublished doctoral dissertation, University of California, Berkeley, ©1976.

the ingroup, "Me entiendes" softened the teacher's criticism.

Most research on code-switching has been done with adult speakers. The main purpose of this study was to see how four six-year-olds code-switched in a school setting. The research questions were:

1. Which of the following situational variables seemed to affect the children's choice of language?
   (a) Physical setting (classroom vs. playground)
   (b) Activity (free play vs. teacher-structured task)
   (c) Features of the addressee or listener (age, ethnicity, linguistic ability)
   (d) Topic of conversation (television show, family dog, etc.)
   (e) Linguistic intention (requesting help, arguing, etc.)
2. Were the children's rules situational or conversational?
3. How did these six-year-olds' rules of code-switching differ from adult's rules?

Method

To see how four children actually chose between their languages, I carried out an observational study to collect samples of speech in naturalistic settings, not under experimental conditions. The categories used for analysis were developed by studying the daily activities and conversations of the children in three settings, the kindergarten classroom, the playground, and the day care center.

The site of the study was a combined day care center-kindergarten for children from three to seven years of age. Twenty of the 50 children in day care also attended the affiliated kindergarten in the mornings. The center was an alternative school, which was established by a group of Chicano parents in the San Francisco Bay Area. The parents and staff valued highly the maintenance of the Spanish language and their Mexical or Latin American heritage. The educational approach was what may be called a "whole child" approach. Teachers were concerned with the cognitive, emotional, and even political aspects of education. The kindergartners, for example, heard several lectures on Mexican history and politics during the period of data collection.

All teachers and aides at the site were either bilingual in Spanish and English or monolingual in Spanish. There were two women kindergarten teachers, who spoke both Spanish and English with the children, and one male teacher, who was born in Mexico and spoke only Spanish to the children although he too was bilingual. The woman aide in the kindergarten was a Spanish monolingual from Mexico.

The four children studied were chosen on the basis of (1) my observations in the kindergarten and day care center over a two-month preliminary period and (2) the three kindergarten teachers' rank-ordering of the "most bilingual" kindergartners. Three of the children were boys; one was a girl. They ranged in age from 6;0 to 6;2. The parents of two boys and one girl were not college-educated while the parents of one boy were both graduate students. In interviews with the parents, I found that they all favored the goals of the center to maintain their children's ability to speak Spanish and actively teach about Mexican/Chicano culture.

Data were collected in two phases. During the first, or preliminary, phase I familiarized myself with the routines of the children and staff while they became accustomed to me and the use of a tape recorder.

During the second, or recording, phase, either the second observer or I* observed, one at a time, for a one- to two-hour period and essentially followed the four children around to audiotape their speech and write a brief record of concurrent behaviors. Data were collected most often in the morning, between 9:00 a.m. and 12:00 n. Although the method of recording was obtrusive, the children became accustomed to it quickly.

Results

At the end of seven weeks, an assistant and I had recorded 17.5 hours of spontaneous talk during 45 hours of observation, chiefly in the kindergarten building, which was separate from the day care center. The children's speech in the playground, in a nearby park, and in the day care center was also recorded.

Seven types of activity settings or group types were identified in which the children used language in different ways:

(1) *Whole class*: teachers usually talked most of the time and children talked very little

(2) *Small group-task*: children were engaged in task-oriented activity, e.g., art work or language arts, initiated by the teacher

(3) *Small group-game*: children themselves chose to play a game with rules

(4) *Small group-dramatic play*: children assigned roles for fantasy play

(5) *Small group-free play*: children engaged in unstructured, self-chosen activity, e.g., playing on swings or at a water table

---

*I am Japanese-American, bilingual in English and Spanish, more proficient or dominant in English. The second observer was a male Anglo, also English dominant. Anglo is used here to mean someone who is not a member of an ethnic minority. It is used descriptively, not pejoratively.

(6) *Small group-eating*: snack or lunchtime with teachers and other children from kindergarten and the day care center

(7) *Dyad*: an adult with one of the four children, often either myself or my assistant asking for information about the children's activities.

All four children were most talkative in the activities they chose themselves, that is, the game and play categories.

Within the seven activities, I found four common speech patterns:

(1) *lecture*: one person, usually a teacher, talked most of the time and other participants talked rarely

(2) *conversation*: participants took turns so that all speakers ideally contributed equally to the interaction

(3) *commentary*: primarily children's talk which did not involve turn-taking. This included comments about what other children were doing, addressed to a general audience, which rarely brought verbal responses from others. During a game, for example, children might say things like, "He's winning," "You're cheating," "Come on, it's your turn." The focus is on the game, not on the content of talk

(4) *interview*: question-answer sequences, usually between adult and child, is sustained by the adult.

In order to analyze the kinds of code-switching that occurred within these activity settings, I transcribed the recorded segments that contained code-switches for later analysis. All recorded segments were categorized according to linguistic units of three kinds, the *episode*, the *utterance*, and the *subepisode*.

There was a total of 370 episodes for all four children and 187 subepisodes. Episodes lasted from a few seconds to more than half an hour, for example, when the interactive focus was a game. Using the episode as a framework, we coded 306 examples of situational switches and only 64 conversational switches.

The only variable that had a clear effect on the children's choice of language was one feature of the addressee: the listener's linguistic ability. By the end of the data collection period, we had assigned all staff and children to five categories, according to their ability to produce Spanish and English:

(1) Spanish monolingual (SM)
(2) Spanish dominant bilingual (SD)
(3) Balanced bilingual (BB)
(4) English dominant bilingual (ED)
(5) English monolingual (EM).

Tabulation of episodes in which the identity of the child's listener(s) was known showed that the children generally chose the listener's dominant language. The major finding of the study was that these four children were able to choose and maintain the language that their listeners spoke best in both instructional and noninstructional settings. Although there were wide individual variations when they spoke to bilinguals, all four spoke Spanish to SMs and English to EMs between 84 and 100 percent of the time. (Since the monolinguals with one exception *comprehended* the language they did not speak, the use of that language probably did not lead to gaps in communication.)

The four children had relatively few episodes containing mid-episode, or conversational, switches. Of these 64 conversational switches, only a dozen contained midutterance switches. The answer to the second research question, are the children's rules conversational or situational, then, was that they were situational. One specific aspect of the situation, listener's linguistic ability, seemed to determine their language choice. Code-switches within conversations occurred primarily to accommodate the differing abilities of listeners, so that they conveyed a straightforward message, "I am speaking to X in the language he/she speaks best."

This does not mean that there was no evidence of conversational rules. The children did seem to switch within episodes to (1) specify one addressee when speaking to more than one bilingual (e.g., a SD and an ED), and (2) to quote another person's speech in the language of the quotation. These are both functions of code-switching in adult speech (Gumperz, 1974).

The major difference between adults' speech and the four children's samples was the lack of conversational code-switching. Frequent switching among adults is a way of marking the differences between one group of speakers and another. The ability to do this would depend on the speakers' awareness that they can highlight ethnic differences through choice of the appropriate language. Although one of the four children stated that he was ethnically different (Mexican, not American) during an interview, none of the four seemed to mark this kind of awareness by code-switching.

There were examples in the data of the four children excluding other children from play areas, or "territories." Their way of excluding outgroup members was direct and did not involve code-switching. For example, one subject told a younger child from the day care center, "You can't come in!" to inform her that only kindergartners were allowed in the classroom. In addition, we did not observe bilingual children excluding monolingual speakers from conversations by switching to the language the monolingual did not speak.

Educational Implications

The second purpose for this chapter was to deal with implications for educational practice. While working for a bilingual program in public schools, I heard administrators', teachers', and others' opinions about bilingual children. Some of these adults thought that poor minority children did not achieve in school because they knew neither their home language nor English well. Phrases like "limited language," "bilingual deficits," or even "alingual" were used to describe Spanish, Chinese, or other non-English speaking students.

I questioned whether being bilingual was necessarily associated with a lack of linguistic or communicative ability. This study shows that when observed in school settings with teachers and peers of their own ethnic group, specific bilingual kindergartners demonstrated that they were competent speakers.

During the last decade there has been a major concern in American education with the development of bilingual programs for children of ethnic minorities. Although there is a broad range of bilingual curricula available (Andersson and Boyer, 1970, John and Horner, 1971) an objective common to many of them is to teach English as soon as possible to the children who do not speak it.

While children are learning English, teachers often assess pupils' linguistic ability with tests of language proficiency or dominance. Test results that ideally show which language a child knows better may be used to place him in either a bilingual or English-only program. The reliability and validity of these new measures are still undetermined so that, unavoidably, some children are wrongly assessed. Children who might benefit from bilingual programs, in which their home language is used in instruction, may be in classes taught by monolingual English speakers.

One result of errors in placement is that teachers who are not bilingual may describe non-English speakers as limited in both their home language and English. For these adults, the child who is linguistically competent is the one who speaks English well so that maintenance of the home language has been a secondary goal in bilingual programs.

The four children of this study were not linguistically limited. They spoke both Spanish and English fluently although none had had formal instruction in either language. They had developed their competencies informally through interactions with parents, teachers, and peers. The positive result of this development and informal learning, their bilingualism, challenges the impression that Spanish-speaking can use only "Spanglish," a mixture of Spanish and English.

A practical implication for bilingual programs for young children is that a child's use of a language other than English should not automatically lead to his placement in a special program. An assessment of each child's ability to speak both languages in naturalistic situations seems to be an essential step in determining what kind of language training, if any, is needed.

Maintaining Spanish with English

In bilingual communities, the decision to teach in the home language (Spanish, in this case) and/or English is a matter for parents and school personnel. The decision is best based on those groups' values.

At the site of this study, parents and staff stressed the use of Spanish. The parents of the four children were more concerned with maintaining their children's Spanish than with their acquisition of English. When parents and staff agree that linguistic and cultural maintenance is their goal, a suitable curriculum includes the consistent use of both languages.

In terms of models of bilingual education, this site was an example of a *pluralistic* one. It was initiated by members of the community and was "a social issue around which the ethnic community becomes politically mobilized. The program's administration provides reciprocal control between the school and the community" (Kjolseth, 1972, p. 99). At this school and center there was an unusual integration of educational, cultural, and political components. The use of Spanish was an important aspect of all three. And the frequent *use* of any language is the only way to maintain it as an integral, important part of the culture.

Yet the results of this study show that even in this optimal situation for maintaining Spanish, English was often the "language of choice." There were more ED children than SD, which often led to the use of English in play settings; the bilingual kindergarten teachers used English in conversations with each other (not with the bilingual children); at the end of the recording phase, our impression was that two of the subjects used English more than at the beginning; and, also at the end of the data collection, two of the SM boys were starting to say full sentences in English.

After a teacher encouraged him to start speaking more English, one of these boys made a poignant remark during a lesson about the Mexican hero, Benito Juárez, "*Pero él no sabiá inglés*" (translation: But *he* didn't know English). The boy's point was that if Spanish was the hero's language, couldn't it also be his? Educators in the United States would have to respond that Juárez did not need to know English because he didn't live in this country where most people expect one to speak it.

Parents' and staff preference for Spanish *with* English at this site probably will not guarantee maintenance of both languages in the future. My observations in many public schools indicate that the trend is toward the increased use of English. Shultz (1975) made a similar observation in his study in Boston. Fishman (1968), too, found that younger children in Jersey City, New Jersey, used English significantly more than older ones and that for all children English was associated with education.

Parents and staff who administer or are planning a maintenance program might consider three factors: (1) the interest and cooperation of the children's families, (2) the role of the monolingual speaker of either language to maintain both languages, and (3) the role of code-switching in a bilingual program.

Cooperation From Families

The first consideration, the families' interest and cooperation, seems a necessary support for any educational program. All four of the children's parents in the study shared a strong commitment of bilingual-bicultural education, and this probably was not coincidental. Their interest contributed much to the development of their children's bilingualism.

Importance of Monolinguals

Second, the data show that monolingual speakers at the school performed a major function in ensuring that the bilingual children did speak both languages. The four children used Spanish and English almost exclusively with SMs and EMs, respectively, because it was the most effective way to communicate. During structured lessons, the kindergarten teachers often acted as if they were monolingual. Their use of Spanish elicited responses primarily in Spanish from the four children. The teachers, however, used Spanish and English in informal situations or when they translated for EMs. They also encouraged SMs to begin to speak English to "get ready" for the first grade.

Since students in most schools in this country are expected to learn English at some time, perhaps teachers in programs whose goal is to maintain two languages might plan their curriculum to benefit monolinguals and bilinguals. In day care centers, preschools or kindergartens, administrators could have a combination of bilingual and monolingual adults and children to maintain and encourage bilingualism informally.

In the primary and middle grades, where formal lessons are the rule, teachers might reserve two periods each day for speaking each language. At those times they could organize several small groups so that most students in each group are monolingual. The others would be in the process of learning the language of the monolinguals, or the target language. *All* students would then have to use the target language in order to communicate.

Monolingual adult visitors from the children's families, aides, teachers who speak only one language in the classroom, and children who are monolingual in the target language would be the "group monolinguals." The subject matter during these periods would vary and should not be just the vocabulary or syntax of the target language.

A constant influx of at least some monolingual non-English speakers is necessary for such a program to continue. This would be a problem in some speech communites. In Spanish-speaking communities, however, there is usually a continuous immigration of SMs to the United States. In almost all of this country's communities there are numerous EMs who could serve as the group monolinguals when English is the target language.

Monolingual students who are beginning to learn their second language might need additional language instruction. A satisfactory approach might combine the use of highly structured techniques, including memorization and repetition of patterned responses for short periods daily, with opportunities for less structured interactions with peers and adults who speak the target language.

Role of Code-switching

The third consideration was the role of code-switching in a maintenance program. Code-switching was defined as the bilinguals' alternation of languages to convey social meaning. It is part of a speaker's communicative competence and is learned informally. Frequent alternation between languages seems to be at odds with a curriculum that maintains two languages by using each separately for specified periods of time.

The natural phenomenon of code-switching should not be forbidden in a maintenance program. (I doubt that any program, even one that is nominally "English only," could prevent bilinguals' spontaneous code-switches.) In class periods other than those designated for speaking only one language, on the playground or in the cafeteria, students would make language choices according to their own and their listeners' language dominance or perhaps according to the degree of familiarity with the listener.

For educators to work toward language maintenance while they leave time for unstructured verbal interactions, they need to understand the social meaning of switching from one language to another. Conversational switches may be signals that the students feel a common bond among themselves, or between themselves and a teacher. Permitting the expression of this feeling may increase students' motivation and promote learning. Acceptance of the functions that different languages serve might produce better academic results than a constant preoccupation with maintaining a single language.

Summary

This observational study focused on four six-year-old bilingual children's use of Spanish and English in instructional and noninstructional settings in the kindergarten, day care center, and playground. The main source of data was spontaneous talk. Analysis showed that the four children consistently applied one rule in choosing between languages, "Speak the language your listener knows or speaks best." Effective communication, or "getting the message across," seemed to be the children's main goal. With other bilinguals, the children often chose to speak English, but they spoke Spanish or English almost exclusively with Spanish or English monolinguals, respectively. These findings raised the question of how we can maintain Spanish with English.

No claim is made that the findings apply generally to six-year-old Spanish-English bilinguals because of the small number of children in the study. However, in naturalistic settings these four children were able to speak two languages fluently and use a variety of styles within each language to demonstrate their sociolinguistic competencies.

In terms of educational practice, maintaining these bilingual competencies requires a strong commitment from parents and staff to *use* both Spanish and English frequently. In any bilingual program, monolingual speakers of each language might play a major role in promoting maintenance.

BIBLIOGRAPHY

Andersson, T.; and Boyer, M. *Bilingual Schooling in the United States*. Austin: Southwest Educational Development Laboratory, 1970.

Blom, J. P.; and Gumperz, J. J. "Social Meaning in Linguistic Structures: Code-switching in Norway." In *Directions in Sociolinguistics*, edited by J. J. Gumperz and D. Hymes. New York: Holt, Rinehart and Winston, 1972.

Ervin-Tripp, S. M. "An Analysis of the Interaction of Language, Topic, and Listener." *American Anthropologist*, 1964, 66:86-102.

Fishman, J. A. *Bilingualism in the Barrio*. Final Report O.E.C.-1-7-062817-0297. New York: Yeshiva University, 1968.

Gumperz, J. J. "The Semantics of Code-switching in Conversation." Manuscript, University of California, Berkeley, 1974.

Gumperz, J. J.; and Hernandez-Chavez, E. "Bilingualism, Bidialectalism and Classroom Interaction." In *Functions of Language in the Classroom*, edited by C. B. Cazden; V. P. John; and D. Hymes. New York: Teachers College Press, 1972.

Hymes, D. *Language in Culture and Society*. New York: Harper and Row, 1976.

John, V. P.; and Horner, V. M. *Early Childhood Bilingual Education*. New York: Modern Language Association, 1971.

Kjolseth, R. "Bilingual Education Programs in the United States: For Assimilation or Pluralism?" In *The Language Education of Minority Children*, edited by B. Spolsky. Rowley, Mass.: Newbury House, 1972.

Labov, W. *The Social Stratification of English in New York City*. Washington, D.C.: Center for Applied Linguistics, 1966.

Shultz, J. "Language Use in Bilingual Classrooms." Paper presented at the Annual Convention of Teachers of English to Speakers of Other Languages (TESOL), Los Angeles, California, 1975.

Wright, H. F. *Recording and Analyzing Child Behavior*. New York: Harper and Row, 1967.

Section IV
Programs of Instruction

Introduction by Carmen A. Perez[*]

The success of bilingual education requires the development of carefully designed instructional programs which consider the specific conditions affecting the target populations. Recognizing that no single program model or design will satisfy the needs of all linguistic/cultural communities, this chapter examines unique situations, individual experiences, and diverse philosophies, and proposes practical suggestions for the establishment of bilingual programs. Consequently, the articles reflect a comprehensive summary of current thoughts on bilingual program models.

Mackey views bilingual education as a four dimensional phenomena composed of (1) the home, (2) the curriculum, (3) the community, and (4) the language. After defining the nature and role of each variable, the author presents a system for the classification of all possible types of bilingual programs.

Fishman's selection describes the three major socio-curricular bilingual education models currently operating throughout the world. The article focuses on bilingual education for the children of migrant workers in a variety of communities.

Four separate authors present a combination of theoretical and practical views on bilingual programs outside the United States. For example, selections by Shaw, Wood, and Derevensky are summary descriptions of bilingual education in Wales, Scotland, and Canada respectively.

The ulpan, an Israeli school for adults, was designed for the purpose of imparting the Hebrew language and Jewish culture to immigrants from over a hundred countries. The article by Atzmon is a description of the objectives of the ulpanim, including the syllabus for instruction, methodological condsiderations, and comments on teacher training.

The articles addressing bilingual education in the United States and Canada reflect the existing diversity of languages and cultures in North America.

Factors affecting the implementation of programs for Native Americans in the United States and Canada are the subject of the articles by Foerster and Wyatt. Foerster addresses the variables which should be considered in developing bilingual programs for Native Americans in the United States and Wyatt describes how an Indian community in Canada succeeded in establishing an educational program appropriate to their unique situation.

Balasubramonian and Frederickson promote the concept that retention of cultural and linguistic identity by ethnic communities in the U.S.A. is beneficial for the whole society. The selection includes descriptions of various types of bilingual programs implemented in Illinois.

Gimondo traces the history of Italian studies in the United States and concludes with a discussion of the current status of bilingual education for 2,000 Italian students in New York City. In another selection, Newman narrates her personal experiences as a non-Italian speaking teacher suddenly faced with an Italian monolingual student in her class.

In a general discussion of the rationale for bilingual education Flores focuses on the educational needs of the Mexican American population in the United States.

Baecher elaborates upon the implications of cognitive style analysis for the successful implementation of bilingual education. Clarification of the use of cognitive style mapping and a sample cognitive style map are included in the article.

The last two selections in this chapter address bilingual special education. Ayala-Vazquex presents evidence supporting bilingual special education for non-English speakers while Rich addresses factors affecting the implementation of bilingual programs for mentally retarded limited English speakers.

*Dr. Carmen A. Perez, Director, Bilingual Education, State University at Albany, New York.

Chapter 31
A Typology of Bilingual Education
William F. Mackey*

Introduction

There are few countries where one cannot find some instances of bilingual education. In the past decade the demand for bilingual education has been increasing in most parts of the world. In the developing or emerging nations the demand is caused by the rise in the status of one or more of the vernacular languages combined with the need to maintain an international language for purposes of secondary and higher education. In other nations, where the official language has already attained international status, a changing climate of tolerance toward minorities has often made it possible for ethnic groups speaking a language other than that of the national majority to organize with official approval their own schools in their own language.

Some of these changes have been the results of regional necessity; others are the fruits of local accommodations, based on purely political motives. It is important that the pressures of politics be distinguished from local linguistic needs. And linguistic needs must not be confused with linguistic desires. Language minorities have often been the victims of emotional exploitation from within by the few who can use it as a level to personal political power.

One of the pawns in the politics of local minorities has been the question of bilingual schooling. This is a question which often arouses bitter conflicts which are rarely resolved by the sort of objective analysis and impartial study needed. The situation is aggravated by the lack of knowledge on the advantages and disadvantages of bilingual education and on the conditions under which it is useful or harmful.

What has made it difficult to obtain such knowledge is the lack of some stable references to the many sorts of bilingual education and also because of the lack of standard measures for the numerous variables.

Schools in the United Kingdom where half the subjects are taught in English are called bilingual schools. Schools in Canada in which all subjects are taught in English to French Canadian children are called bilingual schools. Schools in the Soviet Union in which all subjects except Russian are taught in English are bilingual schools, as are schools in which some of the subjects are taught in Georgian and the rest in Russian. Schools in the United States where English is taught as a second language are called bilingual schools, as are parochial schools and even weekend ethnic schools.

Bilingual situations of entirely different patterns have unwittingly been grouped together under bilingual schools and used as a basis for research on bilingual education. This is partly because the concept of "bilingual school" has been used without qualification to cover such a wide range of uses of two languages in education. The term "bilingual school" means many things, even within the same country, and in any discussion is likely to mean different things to different persons. It cannot therefore, in its present denotation, be taken as an object for research.

Since we are faced with various combinations of various factors, any single definition of bilingual schooling would be either too wide or too narrow to be of any use in planning and research, for what is true for one combination of factors may be untrue for another. And since the causes and effects of bilingual schooling are to be found outside the school, it is important to take these into consideration. What is needed, therefore, is not another definition of bilingual schooling or bilingual education but a classification of the field to account for all possible types—in other words, typology.

Since bilingual education contains so many variables, a systematic classification of them in the form of a typology could be of help in designing experiments and in talking about bilingual education; it could contribute to the systematization of bilingual

*William F. Mackey, Director, International Center for Research on Bilingualism, Quebec.

**Prepared for a Research Conference on Bilingual Education Under the Auspices of the Bureau of Research of the United States Office of Education, June, 1969.

school programs and suggest ways of coordinating research and development in this expanding era of enquiry. As a preliminary to any typology, it is necessary to determine how much it will take into account.

Since the terms "bilingual education" and "bilingual school" are used to cover a wide range of different cases, it will be advantageous to have the widest possible inclusion. Otherwise we would have more use for definitions than for a typology. Instead of trying to change any current usage, we shall simply adopt the most inclusive . This will enable us to classify cases ranging from the unilingual education of bilingual children in unilingual communities to the bilingual education of unilingual children in bilingual communities. It will make it possible to include schools where some or all subjects are in the other language. It is necessary to isolate and classify all types of bilingual education before measuring their components. This is preliminary to any research.

In order to be of use to researchers, such a typology has to be entirely objective and based on criteria that are observable and quantifiable. Such criteria may be found in the pattern of distribution of languages in (1) the behavior of the bilingual at home, (2) the curriculum in the school, (3) the community of the immediate area within the nation, and (4) the status of the languages themselves. In other words, bilingual education is a phenomenon in four dimensions. Let us take a look at the first.

1. The Learner in the Home

If we study the language behavior of the learner at home in relation to the language requirements of his schools, we find that, classified according to language usage, there are five types of bilingual learners.

A learner who speaks only one language at home and the same language in the school, even though it may not be the language of the community, is in quite a different position from that of the learner who uses two languages at home and the same two at school.

Without going into the degree of language proficiency, which will be accounted for below, we may divide our five types into two categories: those covering learners from unilingual homes (U) and those from bilingual homes (B). In each category, there are the cases where one home language is used as a school language (+S) and those where no home language is used as a school language (-S); in the bilingual category there are the cases where both home languages are used as school languages (+SS). This gives us our five types of learner:

1. Unilingual home: language is school language (U+S).
2. Unilingual home: language is not school language (U-S).
3. Bilingual home: languages include one school language (B+S).
4. Bilingual home: languages exclude school languages (B-S).
5. Bilingual home: languages include both school languages (B+SS).

Trilingual, quadringual, and other multilingual cases are simply numerical extensions of the above.

If we use a small square for the home, a larger one for school, and shading for the languages, we may visualize the types thus:

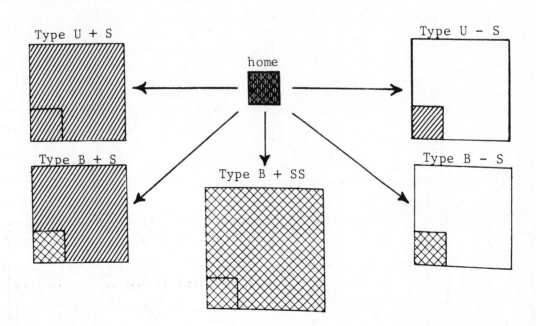

Type U + S

Type U − S

home

Type B + S

Type B + SS

Type B − S

2. The Curriculum in the School

Belonging to any one of these five types, each learner, with his acquired language habits ranging anywhere from complete unilingualism in one language to complete unilingualism in the other, enters a school where the importance and uses of the languages may not correspond to what they are at home. His place on the scale of bilingual usage—the ratio of his use of his two languages—is likely to be different from that of the school. Only at the extreme ends of the scale, the unilingual school for the corresponding unilingual learner (U+S), are the two points likely to correspond exactly. In all other cases, there is no guarantee that the ratio of bilingualism in the entering language behavior of the learner will correspond to the linguistic assumptions of a bilingual curriculum. For the curriculum patterns of bilingual schools vary as to (1) medium of instruction, (2) development, (3) distribution, (4) direction, and (5) change.

(1) The medium of instruction may be one language, two languages, or more; in other words the school may have a single medium (S) or a dual medium (D) curriculum. (2) The development pattern may be one of maintenance (M) of two or more languages, or of transfer (T) from one medium of instruction to another. (3) The distribution of the languages may be different (D) or equal and the same (E). (4) The direction may be toward assimilation into a dominant culture, toward acculturation (A), or toward integration into a resurgent one, that is, toward irredentism (I). Or it may be neither one nor the other, but simply the maintenance of the languages at an equal level. In this case, the languages may be equal but different (D), or equal and equivalent (E). (5) Finally, the change from one medium to another may be complete (C) or gradual (G).

2.1 Medium: Single or Dual

Schools may be classified according to their languages used to convey knowledge, in contradistinction to the languages taught as subjects. Knowledge may be conveyed in one language, in two, or more.

2.1.1 Single-Medium Schools (S)

Single-medium schools are bilingual insofar as they serve children whose home language is different from the school language, the area language, or the national language. This may be the only language used for all subjects at all times.

2.1.2 Dual-Medium Schools (D)

In contradistinction to the type of school using a single medium of instruction are those which use two media—both the home and the second language, as the case may be, to convey knowledge. These are the dual-medium schools. Some subjects are taught in one language, some in the other language. In parts of Wales, history, geography, literature, and the fine arts are taught in Welsh; mathematics, social studies, biology, and other sciences are taught in English. Dual-medium schools vary not only in what is taught but also in how much. It is thus that they may be distinguished and classified. They can be compared quantitatively by measuring the amount of time devoted to the use of each language.

So far, we have made only a static or synchronic distinction between bilingual schools—single-medium and dual-medium schools. But since education is progressive by its nature, these distinctions must also be viewed developmentally, that is, on a time scale.

2.2 Development: Transfer or Maintenance

If we examine bilingual schools on the time scale, that is, from the point of view of the distribution of the languages from the first to the last year of the school's program—or a section of it—we find two patterns: The transfer pattern and the maintenance pattern, both applying to single- and dual-medium schools.

2.2.1 Transfer (T)

The transfer pattern has been used to convert from one medium of instruction to another. For example, in some nationality schools in the Soviet Union a child may start all his instruction in his home language, perhaps that of an autonomous Soviet republic, and gradually end up taking all his instruction in the language of the Soviet Union. In schools of this type, the transfer may be gradual or abrupt, regular or irregular, the degree of regularity and gradualness being the variables available to distinguish one school

M E D I U M	Development	Transfer	Maintenance
	Single		
	Dual		

from another.

2.2.2 Maintenance (M)

Contrariwise, the object of the bilingual school may be to maintain both languages at an equal level. This is often the pattern when both are languages of wider communication or are subject to legal provisions in the constitution which oblige schools to put both languages on an equal footing. The maintenance may be done by differentiation or by equalization.

2.3 Direction: Acculturation or Irredentism (A-I)

The direction taken by the curriculum may be toward the language of wider culture, toward acculturation; or toward that of the regional, national, or neo-national culture—the direction or irredentism.

2.4 Distribution: Different or Equal (D—E)

The subjects in the curriculum may be distributed differently, using different subjects for each; or equally, alternating or repeating the instruction from one language to the other.

2.5 Change: Complete or Gradual (C-G)

The change in direction or distribution may be complete and abrupt—using, for instance, one language one year and the other language the next—or gradual—adding more and more instruction in the other language.

2.6 Curriculum Patterns

The interplay of these basic distinctions generates a limited number of possible patterns, as illustrated in the following figure:

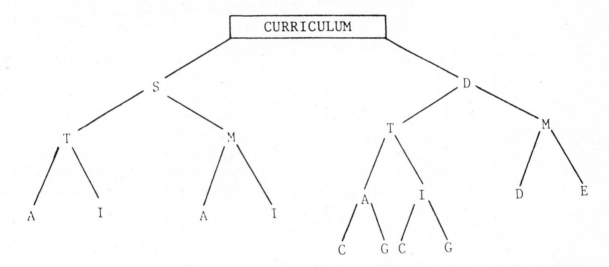

The distinctions between single (S) and dual (D) medium schools, accultural (A) and irredental (I), transfer (T) and maintenance (M), and complete (C) and gradual (G) change generate ten possible types of curriculum patterns. These are: SAT, SAM, SIT, SIM, DAT(C), DAT(G), DIT(C), DIT(G), and DEM. Let us see what each of these involves.

What is patterned in bilingual schooling is the use of two or more languages, one, all, or neither of which may be native to the learner and have a certain degree of dominance in his home environment. Any of the five types of home-school language relationship described above may enter the curriculum patterns described below. To represent these we shall take the unilingual home, where the language used may or may not be the school language or one of the school languages.

The curriculum, made up of subjects (vertical columns) and time units in which they are taught (horizontal columns) will be symbolized in a grid:

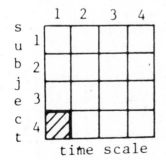

The home is placed beside the school, covering the lower left corner of the grid. It makes use of a language which may be different from that of the school, of the community, or of the nation. The extent to which the language is used is not a question of type but a matter of measurement—not of "what" is used, but of "how much." (See 4.1).

2.6.1   Type SAT (Single-Medium Accultural Transfer)

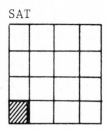

This type may transfer the language of learning from that of the home to that of the school. It may be completely accultural in that it takes no account of the language of the home. This type of single-medium acculturation is common among schools attended by the children of immigrants; for example, the English medium schools of Italian or French immigrants in the United States.

2.6.2   Type SAM (Single-Medium Accultural Maintenance)

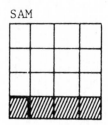

In some cases, as in the bilingual schools of certain parts of Canada, the home language or dominant home language is taught as a subject, without however being used as a medium of instruction. The maintenance of the home language as a subject may be the avowed purpose, as in the English-medium schools for French Canadians in Western Canada.

2.6.3   Type SIT (Single-Medium Irredental Transfer)

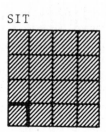

The converse also goes by the name of bilingual schooling. Here the home or dominant home language is used as a medium. Examples of this may be found in the multiple cases of language transfer, along the borderlands of Europe, resulting from the reconquest of territory. Witness, for example, the history of transfer of languages of instruction along the frontiers of the former Austro-Hungarian Empire.

2.6.4   Type SIM (Single-Medium Irredental Maintenance)

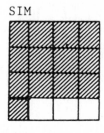

In some schools the dominant or formerly dominant national language is maintained as a school subject, as in the case of English in certain Gaelic schools of the West of Ireland.

2.6.5 Type DAT (Dual-Medium Accultural Transfer)

DAT–C

DAT–G

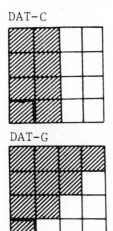

This type which, for obvious reasons of power and prestige is a common type, prepares children to take the rest of their education in a language or a dialect which is not dominant in the home—often a language of wider communication. Many of the schools in the emerging nations were, before they emerged, of this type. English in Africa was sometimes used after the third year. In other parts of Africa it was gradually introduced from the first year.

2.6.6 Type DIT (Dual-Medium Irredental Transfer)

DIT–C

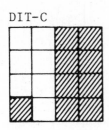

Conversely, in areas long dominated by a foreign language, the medium of instruction may revert to the language of the home, the foreign language being kept as a subject. Early Arabization of schooling in the Sudan illustrates this type.

DIT–G

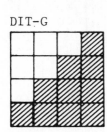

2.6.7 Type DDM (Dual-Medium Differential Maintenance)

DDM

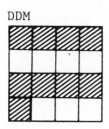

In maintaining two languages for different purposes, the difference may be established by subject matter, according to the likely contribution of each culture. Often the culture-based subjects like art, history, literature, and geography are in the dominant home language. Bilingual schools in certain parts of Wales are of this type.

2.6.8   Type DEM (Dual-Medium Equal Maintenance)

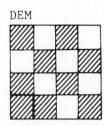

DEM

In some schools, as those found in certain parts of Belgium, South Africa, and Canada, it has been necessary—often for political reasons—not to distinguish between languages and to give an equal chance to both languages in all domains. This is done by alternating on the time scale—day, week, month, or year—from one language to the other.

We have seen that, from the point of view of patterning, the curriculum of bilingual schools can be distinguished between single- and dual-medium schools, each following transfer or maintenance patterns—transfer being accultural or irredental, maintenance based on differentiation or equalization.

These patterns may remain stable or evolve, slowly or rapidly, along with changes in pressures and policies. If, for example, one studies the changes in the laws of Louisiana during the past century, one notices several changes in approved patterns of bilingual schooling. The law of 1839 assumes the existence of both French and English single-medium schools. The constitution of 1879 authorizes that all subjects be given in both languages (Article 226). Whereas the 1898 constitution authorizes the teaching of French only as a subject (Article 251). In the constitution of 1921 all allusion to French disappears. Recent cultural accords between Louisiana and Quebec again encourage the use of French in instruction.

It is necessary, however, to distinguish between the patterns of language education used in a community and their avowed purposes. For example, a community may have language maintenance as its purpose, but be saddled with a transfer-type curriculum.

3. The Community in the Nation

Any one of these ten types of curriculum patterns (SAT, SAM, SIT, SIM, DAT-C, DAT-G, DIT-C, DIT-G, DDM, DEM) may function in a number of different types of language areas and national states.

It makes a great difference whether one of the languages used in school is that of the surrounding community, or that of the wider community. The home and community contexts in which the language is used must be taken into consideration if the language is to be used in school, since it is on the assumption of usage and consequent knowledge that the teaching is based. There is a difference, for example, in using English as a medium of instruction in one of the special language schools of Kiev and using it as a medium of instruction in the Ukrainian bilingual schools outside Edmonton.

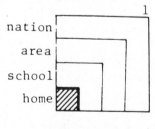

1. The school may be located in a place where the language of both the area and the national language is not that of the home.

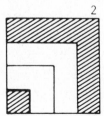

2. It may be in a country where the language of the home but not that of the area is the national tongue.

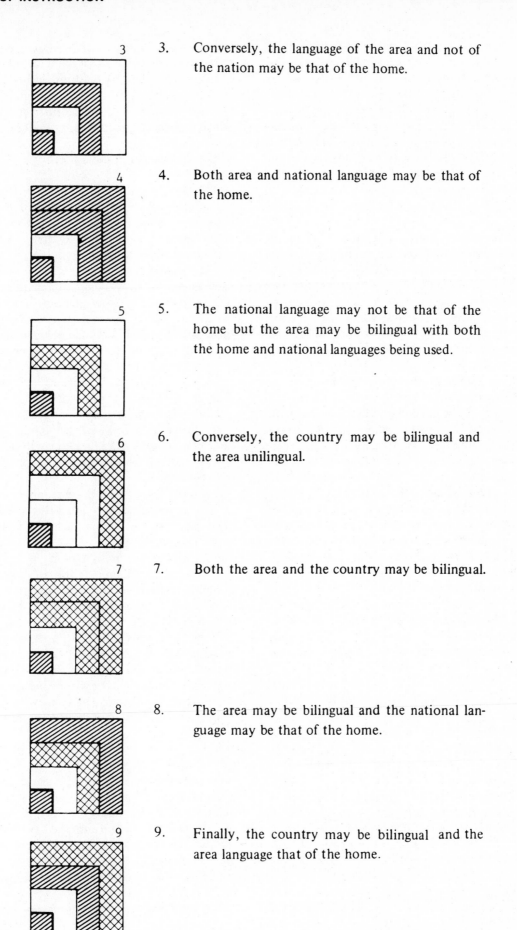

3. Conversely, the language of the area and not of the nation may be that of the home.

4. Both area and national language may be that of the home.

5. The national language may not be that of the home but the area may be bilingual with both the home and national languages being used.

6. Conversely, the country may be bilingual and the area unilingual.

7. Both the area and the country may be bilingual.

8. The area may be bilingual and the national language may be that of the home.

9. Finally, the country may be bilingual and the area language that of the home.

The typology so far elaborated has been based on variations in language patterning in the usage of the nation, the area, and the school; but much depends on which laguages are used and what sort.

Certain languages may be worth maintaining regardless of the community. If Spanish and French, for example, are regarded as legitimate specialties for the unilingual, why should they not also be for the bilingual whose other language is one of these? On the other hand, the language may not lead far, even though the probability of community maintenance may be high.

If each of these nine contexts can absorb each of the ten types of curriculum patterns, then there are ninety basically different patterns of bilingual schooling, giving us the typology which appears in the appended figure. Each of these ninety patterns may absorb one or more of the five home-school categories. If we eliminate mutually exclusive combinations, this leaves some 250 integrated types, ranging from (U-S)SAT 1 to (B+SS) DEM 9.

This should permit us to plan for the elaboration of objective distinctions between bilingual education and bilingual schooling. For example, a bilingual classroom with a DAT curriculum pattern may contain learners with different patterns of bilingual education, depending on the category of relationship with the home language. All five types may find themselves in the same classroom, all doing the same thing. Whether it is wise to put them in the same class is another question; but it cannot be answered until something is known about the different home language behavior patterns of the learners. What type of curriculum pattern is suitable for which type of bilingual is a question yet to be resolved.

A number of these curriculum patterns may be in operation within the same school system, in the same area, or in the same country. Which type of curriculum is most appropriate for which type of area is another question.

Before any of these questions can be answered with any degree of certainty some means must be found of quantifying the variable within each type. All that the typology can do at present is to enable us to distinguish one bilingual education situation from another in order to observe both of them systematically. But within each type there may be quantitative variations. The DAT type, for example, indicates that some school subjects are taught in one language and some in another; it does not tell us which ones or how many. It is only by using the typology to obtain a more detailed profile of each program of bilingual schooling that it will be possible to find out exactly what is going on in any area in the field of bilingual education, as compared with what may be going on some place else. This is what has been

attempted in the appended questionnaire, designed as it is to pattern descriptions of bilingual schooling into the typology for purposes of study and comparison.

The greatest problem of pattern quantification, however, remains in the fourth area—that of the contact between the languages themselves.

4. The Languages in the Pattern

The component common to all types at all levels is language. In fact, the entire typology may be viewed as a series of patterns of distribution of two or more languages in the area of the learner, within the home, the school, the area, and the nation.

This common component is itself a variable. So that each language appears in each pattern at a certain degree of intensity. Any planning or research design has to take this into account in trying to fit persons into the right patterns. For it makes a difference whether or not a child's proficiency in one or more languages is on a par with that of the rest of the class, and whether the level of proficiency is sufficient for the language to be used as a medium of instruction.

In order to understand the nature of the language variable in bilingual education it is important to make a distinction between the function of the languages, their status and the linguistic and cultural differences between them.

4.1 The Functions of the Languages

The languages involved in bilingual education may have different functions in the home, in the school, and in the country.

4.1.1 Languages in the Home

The learner brings to the school a pattern of language behavior and configuration of language dominance. It is not only a question of which language is involved, but to what extent.

There is a wide range of possible variation in the competence of the learner in each of his languages. Each language may be of a standard acceptable for unilingual education, or only one may be acceptable to a unilingual teacher, or neither may be comparable in degree to the language proficiency of unilingual speakers.

To study what happens to this entering behavior under the influence of bilingual schooling, standardized screening instruments are needed—both wide-mesh and fine-mesh. We need easily used and validated wide-mesh screens for quantitative analysis of bilingual population samples. We need fine-mesh screens for small laboratory-type studies and depth analysis of individual cases. There is need for the application of language proficiency measures suitable for bilingual children.

But the child's proficiency may be limited in some

domains and extensive in others, depending on his pattern of language behavior outside the school; he may, for instance, speak about certain things in one language to his father and about others in another language to his mother and her relatives. There is need therefore for simple scales to measure the degree of dominance in each of the child's domains.

If the child comes from a home where two or more languages are used, he may find it difficult to separate them. The extent and degree of language mixture may vary considerably from one bilingual child to the next, and from one domain to another. Tests will be needed to show how well a bilingual child keeps his languages apart.

4.1.2 Languages in the School

The language component also varies within the school—in the curriculum and in inter-pupil communication.

It is first important to determine the sort and amount of both languages used in the classroom. Two identical curriculum patterns may vary in the proportion of time devoted to each language. This is measurable by simple computation. But they may also vary in the domains in which each language is used. In one curriculum the second language may be used for history and geography; in the other it may be used for science and mathematics. In practice, each curriculum pattern would have to be quantified for each language in terms of proportion and domain of use. (See appended questionnaire.)

What is the language of the playground and of the street? In inter-pupil communication, it makes a difference how many of the other learners speak the language or languages of the child, and to what extent. It also makes a difference whether or not the child uses the same language at play as he does in school or at home. Some simple measure of the use of language or languages in the immediate context of the learner's activity would be a help in planning for bilingual education.

4.1.3 Languages in the Community

The extent to which the language or languages of the school may be used in the area in whch it is located is an important variable in the language education of the child. Some measurement of this is prerequisite to any planning or research into bilingual education.

The role that each language plays in the nation is also of importance. It makes a difference whether both or only one of the languages is rated as official or national. The legal status of a language may be limited to a juridical subdivision of the nation. Both the proportion of the population using each language and its distribution throughout the nation may have some influence on the curriculum pattern selected. So will the international status of the languages and the distance between them.

4.2 The Status of the Languages

If the languages involved are languages of wider communication, like Spanish and French, the bilingual situation is bound to be different from those involving local languages like Navajo. It is also important to find out the extent to which each language is dynamic or recessive, concentrated or diffuse, both at the international and at the national or regional level.

International Status

In order to determine the international status of a modern language as one factor in planning the curriculum, languages in a bilingual school may be rated according to five indices:

1. Degree of standardization.
2. Demographic Index: Population figures.
3. Economic Index: Population/Gross national product.
4. Distributional Index: Number and spread of areas in which the language is spoken.
5. Cultural Index: Annual production of printed matter/Cumulative production.

4.2.2 National or Regional Status

The dialects of the languages used may differ in the extent to which each deviates from the norm or norms that may have been established for them. If two international languages are used as instructional media, the dialect version of one may differ little from the standard speech comprehensible anywhere the language is used. The other language, however, may be available in the area only in a local sub-standard variety. And this variety may not be the same, either as the one used in the home, the school, or the nation. The Alemanic home dialects of German Switzerland, for example, are far removed from the sort of Standard German taught in Swiss schools.

4.3 The Differences Between the Languages

The rapidity with which a learner is likely to understand another language, used to teach him school subjects, depends on the degree of difference or distance between both languages. Because of the close relationship between Portuguese and Spanish a learner whose mother tongue is Portuguese may take less time to learn to understand instruction given in Spanish than instruction given in more distant languages like English or Chinese.

This same similarity, which facilitates understanding (listening and reading) may be the cause of multiple mistakes in speaking and writing—due to the interference caused by the closeness of both languages. We need measures of the closeness and mutual intelligibility of the languages involved in bilingual instruction and means of predicting the effects of the languages on the comprehension nd expression of the bilingual learner.

Regardless of similarities and differences in structure and vocabulary, the two languages may differ considerably in available cultural concepts. For example, Hungarian is genetically as distant from English as is Eskimo; but it is culturally closer, since both English and Hungarian embody many common European cultural concepts, which can be assumed as a basis for bilingual education. Before making use of this variable in research into bilingual education, however, it would be most useful to determine some way of quantifying it.

Conclusion

Once we have reduced our language variables to appropriate measures within the various types of bilingual education, it will be easier to analyze and classify specific cases.

It is only after we have taken all the variables into account and applied appropriate measures of them that we can achieve any degree of certainty in our planning in this important and complex field. Toward this end it is hoped that this preliminary typology may be of some help.

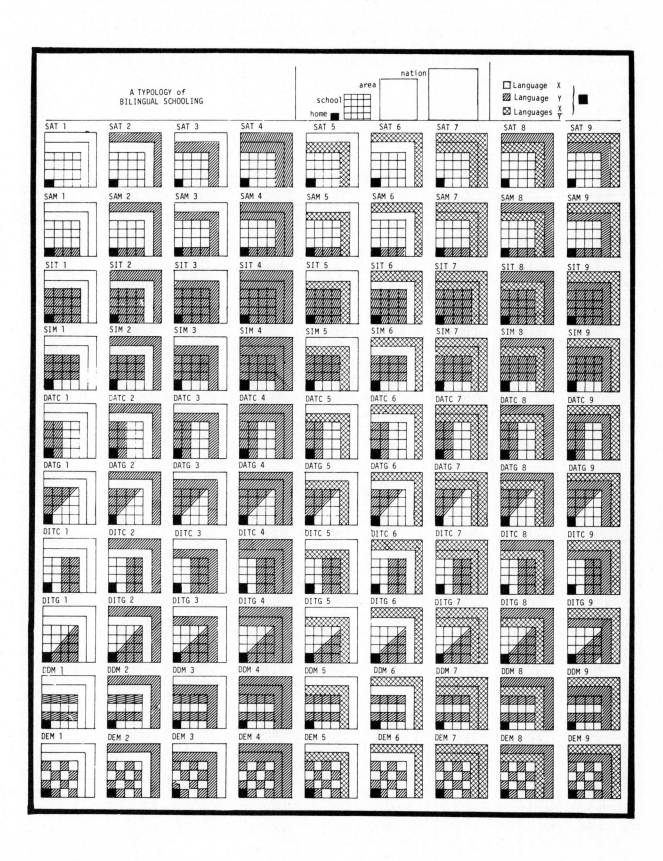

A TYPOLOGY of BILINGUAL SCHOOLING

Chapter 32

Bilingual Education for the Children of Migrant Workers: the Adaptation of General Models to a New Specific Challenge

Joshua A. Fishman*

Most of the nearly 100,000 bilingual elementary schools and 5,000 bilingual secondary schools throughout the world, located in over 100 countries, serve indigenous and sedentary populations (Fishman 1976a), rather than migrant populations from within or without their national boundaries. Nevertheless, the various sociocurricular constellations represented by these schools provide models which may well have both interest and validity for the education of "children of migrant workers" in present day Europe. Indeed, as more and more of the "migrants" become long term and finally permanent immigrants, their children acquire more and more similarity to other "marked language" children throughout the world. It, therefore, becomes even more appropriate to compare their education to the various educational approaches that have been developed within the framework of bilingual education, particularly as pursued in settings where it has had more time to become stabilized than is yet generally the case in connection with the education offered to children of migrant, Southern European workers recently arrived in Northern Europe. In this connection it should be realized, first of all, that bilingual education is a geographically omnipresent, quantitatively significant and historically continuous endeavor. Second of all, it should be realized that it is currently being fostered by two worldwide tendencies that are far stronger than the "migrant worker" phenomenon in Northern Europe, namely, the continuing *vernacularization* of at least part of the education of pupils hitherto educated via languages of wider communication *not* their mother tongues, on the one hand, and the *addition* of a (or of another) language of wider communication as a co-medium of education for pupils already being educated via their vernacular, on the other hand (Fishman, 1976b). These two complementary processes have contributed mightily to the increase of bilingual education in the past decade and can be expected to continue to do so for the forseeable future.

The three major socia-curricular models of bilingual education throughout the world are: compensatory/transitional, language maintenance and enrichment oriented with respect to their goals, listed in inverse order with respect to their incidence. The appearance on the Northern European scene of thousands upon thousands of "children of migrant workers" raises the question as to whether additional societal models of bilingual education will be forthcoming as a result or whether the prior three will continue to serve. Thus, not only can the education of the "children of migrant workers" benefit from an examination of bilingual education as a whole but bilingual education per se can doubtlessly benefit from a closer look at the education of "children of migrant workers."

Bilingual Education for the Down and Out

Compensatory/transitional bilingual education seeks to provide *marked-language children* with an opportunity to master the unmarked language of school and society as quickly as possible. During the relatively brief period in which they remain deficient with respect to mastery of the unmarked language (and this should be no longer than 2-6 years, depending on their age at arrival and upon the educational resources of hours of instruction, materials, and manpower devoted to their "unmarking") their own mother tongues are used as co-media of education. This approach to bilingual education is employed not only with most of the "children of migrant workers" in Northern Europe but with other socially, economically and politically disadvantaged marked-language children the world over. If, strictly speaking, it nevertheless deserves to be called bilingual education, it is however bilingual education of a most reluctant sort, a self-liquidating kind of bilingual education. No matter how successful it may be linguistically it generates several problems of a rather recurring and typical sort. First of all, it tends to weaken the marked language child's home and native community ties.

*Dr. Joshua Fishman, Professor of Sociology, Yeshiva University. Member, 1975-76, Institute for Advanced Study, Princeton, New Jersey. Prepared for AIMAV's International Conference on Educational Problems of Migrant Children, Ghent, Belgium, May 26-30, 1976.

Thereby not only adding to the child's own difficulties qua "migrant" but also weakening the two sources from which he might have drawn consolation and guidance. Secondly, compensatory/transitional bilingual education typically is "granted" or "imposed" by the unmarked language community and, as such, it does not seek nor attain the marked language community's involvement in, nor control over, the education of its own children. Thus an opportunity is lost for providing the marked language community with a type of adult responsibility and participation which it frequently feels it deserves and which could, at any rate, help "normalize" its existence in its new settings. Thirdly, the implied opportunity for social mobility into the unmarked community which compensatory/transitional bilingual education dangles before the hearts and minds of the marked language pupils may actually turn out not to be feasible, or not to be feasible to the extent or at the rate implied. This may be a devastating disappointment indeed for pupils who have, in the meantime, been weaned away from their original home and community bonds and who are left "neither here nor there." Finally compensatory/transitional bilingual education is often mistakenly "sold" to adults in the marked language community under the false flag of language maintenance bilingual education (or the adults delude themselves that such will be its impact on their children) and, once again, their disappointment is great. Can compensastory/transitional bilingual education for the "children of migrant workers" learn to avoid the difficulties and devastations that this kind of bilingual education has run into in other contexts? Perhaps so, but it will take both joint social planning and genuine social mobility for the marked populations if that is, indeed, to be the case, even in part.

Language Maintenance Bilingual Education

Somewhat more prevalent throughout the world, and often a sequentially later development growing out of the disappointments of the compensatory/transitional models is *language maintenance* bilingual education. In this approach the marked language is the preferred, emphasized and more stably implemented medium of instruction, whereas the unmarked language is introduced in small, slow and variable degrees (with parity between the two often being reached only in the upper grades if at all). This model is favored by marked language populations that have gained access to at least a modicum of political, economic and social power (e.g., in Quebec, Wales, parts of the Soviet Union, and "expatriate colony" settings). Although it is a more genuine manifestation of bilingual education, in view of its more thorough-

going medium-sharing and power-sharing character, it too inevitably is accompanied by typically recurring problems. The first of these problems has already been alluded to, namely that the unmarked language which can provide the marked language pupils with a viable link to the unmarked community and to the economic, social and political processes under its greater control, is sometimes only indifferently implemented. As a result, the marked language pupils often find themselves segregated from the broader national community, not only culturally and residentially but also communicationally and economically as well. No wonder then that language maintenance bilingual education is sometimes politically exploited for the redress of real, fancied or created grievances.

The segregation of the marked language pupils and of their corresponding adult communities from the unmarked "mainstream" is particularly severe when the languages and cultures that they carry are rather minor and non-prestigeful on the larger world scene. As a result, few unmarked students or adults can be expected to seek to learn these languages or to learn about these cultures (as many would if it were only English or French that were marked) via the educational resources and processes under their own control. Finally, yet another segregating factor that at times effects language maintenance bilingual education, is one which stems entirely from the unmarked community and its power structure, namely: a desire to discourage the marked community from remaining *in situ* and, instead, a desire to encourage its emmigration (or re-migration) elsewhere. Under these circumstances it is the unmarked community that imposes language maintenance bilingual education upon the marked community, seriously restricting the amount of unmarked language instruction made available to it. In this fashion the graduates of the language maintenance bilingual education programs are rendered unemployable or only minimally employable in the unmarked market place and their "return home" is fostered thereby. The Bavarian approach to *gastarbeiterkinder* has been accused of just such a tactic. Nevertheless, language maintenance bilingual education is growing throughout the world, in rich lands and in poor ones, on the part of indigenous as well as immigrant minorities, and on behalf of comfortably middle class (or above) as well as uncomfortably lower class schools and communities. It basically corresponds to a deeply engrained desire of adults throughout modern history to see their offspring educated in their own mother tongue at least to the extent of being a co-medium in instruction. This principle has been widely adopted by the poor and by the dispossessed of our day and age who differ from their predecessors of the past century only in their more vociferous demands that the schools serve them accordingly. These demands also face bilingual education with a more serious tactical challenge. Maintenance requires a far greater commitment of resources (teachers, curricula, texts, materials, time) than does compensatory/transitional bilingual education. Unlike the latter it is by no means self-liquidating within a few years, but, rather, self-developing and self-intensifying.

Enrichment Bilingual Education

By far the most prevalent type of bilingual education as well as historically the type of longest vintage and socially the type of greatest prestige, is that engaged in by unmarked populations for themselves and for their own children. It recognizes (as elites have recognized throughout recorded educational history) that bilingual education provides an invaluable expansion of intellectual, emotional, aesthetic and economic horizons. The enrichment potential of bilingual education has now been recognized far beyond the elitist, private school sector. Indeed, it is now not only firmly entrenched in the public school sector in certain countries but appeals equally to unmarked children whose vernaculars are small languages on the world scene (e.g., Philipino) as well as to unmarked children whose vernaculars are among the languages of wider communication of this day and age (e.g., Russian, Swahili, Chinese). Nevertheless, although enrichment bilingual education serves relatively advantaged and generally unmarked student populations, it is no more problem-free than any other type of bilingual education, nor for that matter than is monolingual education per se. However, the problems of enrichment bilingual education *are* different than the problems of either compensatory/transitional or language maintenance bilingual education. The former suffered from the disadvantaged position of their protagonists in the entire social order whereas the latter suffers from the fact that its favors are frequently still limited as to their availability. Whose children will be admitted into the bilingual stream, so that they can get at least part of their education in a language of wider communication not their own, is often a matter of great competition in the schools of the USSR, Canada, or Saudi Arabia. As the recognition of enrichment bilingual education increases, its mainstream availability in Western society is also destined to grow, particularly in the USA and Western Europe, where it is still largely an elitist preserve. It is only when the masses demand some of the good things in life (that only the rich have hitherto been able to enjoy) that enrichment bilingual education begins to appear problematic. Actually it is the epitome of bilingual education at its best and the only problem connected with it is how to make it available to as many as possible.

Contextual Factory

As our comments above imply, the reception afforded bilingual education is a byproduct of the relations obtaining between marked and unmarked populations and the particular social, economic, cultural and, therefore, political and philosophical factors that are brought into play between them. Numbers make a difference, as does the age of students, as does their expected/desired length of stay. Large numbers of young, marked-origin students that are expected to stay indefinitely are likely to be given compensatory/transitional bilingual education unless they can muster strong political leverage on behalf of enrichment or maintenance oriented approaches to their needs. Smaller numbers, older pupils and temporary newcomers predispose the powers that be to language maintenance bilingual education. Finally only when a substantial power base indeed is at the command of marked pupils is their language likely to stimulate the enrichment phantasies and passions of the unmarked.

Concrete factors such as those mentioned above finally prompt philosophical-ideological responses. This is not to say that ideology is secondary but merely to acknowledge the human capacity to justify and to moralize all actions that for one reason or another seem desireable, profitable, status generating or power protective. Compensatory/transititional bilingual education is absorptive in its avowed goals. When it holds sway the unmarked group's language of education swamps the marked group's home language. Nevertheless, this type of bilingual education is usually ideologized not as dislocative but as relocative. Marked languages and cultures are dubbed vestigal and facilitating the marked child's escape from his family and community is viewed as a noble and fraternal act on the part of the unmarked. "Thou shalt not kill, but needst not strive officiously to keep alive" becomes a self-satisfying response of the unmarked power structure. Frequently, however the full depth and breadth of genuine absorption is not really deliverable and anomie rather than fraternity results as social class divisions remain without the vibrant cultural props that previously existed.

If compensatory/transitional bilingual education is *absorptive* then language maintenance bilingual education is *separative* with linkage potential "in the wings." If this potential is realized then a diglossia situation can be forthcoming such that the marked population preserves its home and community language for internal purposes while utilizing the unmarked language for external relations with government, the broader economy and the educational experiences related to both. However, note that this diglossia arrangement pertains only to the marked populations. The unmarked population continues on its merry way as before, oblivious of bilingual education and it is in this sense that maintenance oriented bilingual education is *separative* not only because of the goals of the marked population but because of those of the unmarked population as well.

It is only when a double diglossia situation appears, such that both marked and unmarked populations engage in bilingual education, that enrichment may be said to obtain. What is primarily a school-related language for one population is primarily a home-and-neighborhood language for the other and vice versa. Thus, enrichment bilingual education is neither absorptive nor separative but additive and it is so whether one population (unmarked along) or two populations (both marked and unmarked) are involved.

The Problem Gradient

The problematic embeddedness of bilingual education is itself a variable, a differential that can be low, medium or high, depending on the extent to which negative features co-occur. This can be illustrated if we deal even with a small number of dimensions, e.g., (a) migrant status, (b) class status, and (c) vernacular status. Each of these dimensions is conceivable in terms of dichotomous features: (a) (im)migrant vs. indigenous status, (b) middle/upper vs. lower class status, and (c) language of wider communication vs. language of small scope. There are eight permutations of three dichotomous variables ($2^3 = 8$) and these can be arranged as follows in terms of the number of co-occurring negative features that can be revealed by the *marked pupils*:

I *No Negative Features*
1. Indigenous, middle/upper class, language of wider communication.

II *One Negative Feature*
2. Indigenous, middle/upper class, *language of narrower scope*
3. Indigenous, *lower class*, language of wider communication
4. *(Im)migrant*, middle/upper class, language of wider communication.

III *Two Negative Features*
5. Indigenous, *lower class, language of narrower scope*.
6. *(Im)migrant, lower class*, language of wider communication.

7. *(Im)migrant*, middle/upper class, *language of narrower scope*.

IV *Three Negative Features*
8. *(Im)migrant, lower class, language of narrower scope*.

It is clear from the above enumerations that most of the children of migrant workers in Northern Europe today are characterized by all three of the negative features (type 8 above) that we have chosen for illustrative purposes here (as well as by several others, e.g., many are non-Christian or not of the same Christian grouping as their "host" unmarked population). As a result, their bilingual education can be expected to be exceedingly complicated by accompanying social problems that are really *unrelated to bilingual education per se*. Indeed, were only unmarked monolingual education to be offered to such children the problematic nexus of their education would change little if at all.

If we compare the bilingual education context for most "children of migrant workers" in Northern Europe today with that now offered to most Hispanic children in the USA we move from context 8 above to either context 6 or 3. In the former case (context 6) we are dealing either with Puerto Rican children who have come to the mainland or with Chicano children who have moved out of the Southwest, and, therefore, with migrant and lower class children. In the latter case (context 3) we are dealing with Chicano children who have remained in their home region. In both cases we are dealing with a marked student population whose vernacular is recognized as related to a language of wider communication. Although the problem load is still substantial in both instances, it is at least somewhat less than that faced by Turkish, Greek, Yugoslav, Italian or Portuguese children in Northern Europe today. With improvement in class position (from context 6 to context 4) the American experience is already a far happier one, e.g., in connection with middle class Cuban children in Florida whose bilingual education has moved from a language maintenance to an enrichment rationale in the period of the past decade. The J. F. Kennedy School in Berlin is in this category, as are the expatriate elitist schools for Anglophone and Francophone children abroad.

Finally, we come to bilingual education which is entirely outside of the typical problem contexts that we have recognized above. In such circumstances (context 1) we find bilingual education proceeding most favorably as in the case of bilingual schools for elitist children in their homelands, e.g., the immersion programs in Montreal and Toronto, as well as the best bilingual programs in Wales, Singapore and elsewhere, all of which cater to far more than marked children alone.

Concluding Sentiments

Bilingual education for the children of migrant workers often seems to be hopelessly encumbered by problems. This may be less so if the problems are understood as societal aberrations really unrelated to bilingual education per se (aberrations that would and do plague monolingual education as well, even for indigenous lower class children). It is even less so if bilingual education for the children of migrant workers is viewed in the light of the few socio-curricular models that are found on a recurring basis throughout the world. There is no unproblematic education and if there is anything unique about bilingual education it is really not its greater problem-load but its greater potential pay-off.

REFERENCES

Fishman, Joshua A. *Bilingual Education: An International Sociological Perspective*, Rowley (Mass.), Newbury House, 1976a.

Fishman, Joshua A. *Bilingual Education as a Field of Social Science Inquiry*, Arlington, Center for Applied Linguistics, 1976b. Mimeographed.

Chapter 33
French Immersion: An Attempt At Total Bilingualism
Jeffrey L. Derevensky and Tima L. Petrushka*

The past decade has seen world developments necessitate a radical change in educational policies and practices toward the teaching of foreign languages. The inherent importance of incorporating the cultural diversity and background of a multitude of thnic groups within North America has stimulated a renewed and increased interest in the acquisition of a second language. As a result, educators have moved from the teaching of *foreign languages* to the teaching of *second languages*. Concomitant with this change in terminology has been a change in attitude by anglophones toward other non-English languages and a movement toward the value of acquiring these "second" languages (Genesee, 1976a). The growing recognition, awareness and appreciation of the ethno-linguistic mosaic, which can be found in numerous communities, has served to provide the necessary stimulus for researching new and more effective methods for the teaching of a second language.

During the past fifteen years the federal and provincial levels of government in Canada have initiated rapid changes in the language policy. While the British North America Act of 1867 designated English and French as the two official languages of Canada, the French language has in the past been relegated to a subservient positon in Canada. Since the time of Confederation, English has become the working language of business and industry (Lieberson, 1970). Politically, Canada has tried to resolve in a constructive manner the problems which have arisen between the English and French national groups. *The Report of the Royal Commission on Bilingualism and Biculturalism* (1967-1971), a six volume study incorporating the present thoughts and policies on bilingual and bicultural issues involved in industry, education, government and culture, sought to recognize the legitimacy of national development through both English and French. Furthermore, it sought, through the Official Languages Act of 1969, to resolve areas of potential conflict, frustration and disparate ideologies by reaffirming its intent toward a bilingual nation (Stern, 1973). In the past, English speaking Canadians had made relatively little effort or sacrifice to learn French beyond what was offered in traditional French-as-a-second language programs, whereas French speaking Canadians were compelled to make a concerted effort to learn English if they were to be successful in social, political and economic circles.

In the Province of Quebec where French Canadians comprise a sizeable majority of the population it is now imperative for all English speaking children to acquire a demonstrable working knowledge of French within their school curriculum:

> The curricula must ensure that pupils receiving their instruction in English acquire a knowledge of spoken and written French, and the Ministry of Education shall adopt the necessary measures to that effect (Province of Quebec, Bill No. 22, Title III, Chapter V, Article 44, 1972.)

Furthermore, a working knowledge of French is a mandatory requirement for most professional licenses; and the provincial government has exerted direct pressure on large companies and industries to collaborate with them in ensuring that French become the working language of employees at all levels. At the federal level, bilingualism has become a prerequisite for advancement, and immediate financial incentives are now being offered to individuals who are bilingual (Lambert, 1974).

It is not surprising that much of the research concerning second language teaching has originated in Canada, for bilingualism in Canada, and in Quebec in particular, is no longer a privilege but an economic necessity (Genesee, 1976b). The primary purpose of this paper is to critically review the existing programs which seek to ensure that all children will become functionally bilingual.

Anyone attempting to evaluate whether or not an individual is bilingual is immediately confronted with the problem of determining who is bilingual and to what extent. Wtihout elaborating upon the definition, a person can be regarded as bilingual when he is

*Dr. Jeffrey Derevensky, Assistant Professor of Educational Psychology, McGill University. Tima Petrushka, graduate student, Dept. of Educational Psychology, McGill University.

capable of using either of two languages without apparent difficulty whenever a particular situation necessitates one medium of expression or another (Stern, 1967). While various definitions have been proposed, it is generally accepted that bilingualism can be considered along a continuum, or a series of continua, which vary amongst individuals along a variety of dimensions (Macnamara, 1967). Thus, intra-individual differences exist in the ability to speak, listen, read and write in a second language.

Stern (1976)[1] has clearly delineated three levels of competence in the acquisition of a second language. The "first" level is concerned with a *basic competence*. Here it is argued that every educated Canadian should achieve a basic literacy in French as well as a knowledge of the French-Canadian culture and heritage. Acquiring this basic competence in French would provide a foundation from which the individual could build should he need or desire to attain additional communication skills. The next "middle" level provides for a *working knowledge* of French. While incorporating basic literacy, a meaningful command of the language for reading, listening and communicating with French-Canadians is inherent in this level of competence. The third or "top" level of competence would enable the individual to become a "quasi-natural" speaker, that is, the individual is *bilingual* and capable of effectively functioning in the second language. The individual attaining this level could be termed "balanced" (Macnamara, 1967), or synonymously, equilingual, ambilingual, or possessing a dual language command (Stern, 1967). The problem of defining a bilingual is further complicated by the fact that an individual's proficiency in a second language can vary along four skill areas (speaking, listening, reading, writing), all important concepts when initiating programs designed to enhance bilingualism (Macnamara, 1967).

Bilingual Education in Canada

The French language programs in Canada, and in Quebec in particular, can be grouped into three major categories based on the grade level at which the child enters the program, the amount of time devoted to teaching French and the method of language instruction. These three alternatives are commonly referred to as:

1) Traditional Second Language Programs
2) Immersion Programs
3) Submersion Programs

The traditional second language program involves the study of a second (target) language *per se*, for a prescribed number of minutes per day, on a specified number of days per week, all beginning at a given grade level. This traditional orientation enjoyed widespread popularity during the 1960's. An extensive range of instructional paradigms (e.g. direct method, reading method, intensive method, audio-lingual method, audio-visual method) have been developed within the traditional second language program reflecting underlying differences in psycholinguistic theory (Mackey, 1965). Despite the proliferation of language teaching strategies, only a very small percentage of those individuals taught a second language in the classroom have attained a relatively high level of linguistic competence (Kennedy, 1973). Concurrent with these disappointing results came the theoretical notion that native-language acquisition and second language learning are not disparate operations but rather involve analagous processes (Brown, 1973; Kennedy, 1973; Dulay & Burt, 1974). The concomitant pedagogical implications suggests that the primary objective of a second language program should be the creation of a native-like language environment where the focus of activity is on communication and where the quality of discourse will be judged on the basis of content rather than on the appropriateness of grammatical form (Lambert, 1974; Lambert & Tucker, 1972; Tucker, 1974).

Immersion Programs

The immersion programs represent an attempt to use the second language as a medium of instruction, thereby shifting the emphasis from a linguistic focus to one where language is seen as a vehicle for developing competence in academic subject matter. Two major types of immersion programs (early, late), varying in terms of the grade level at which the second language is introduced, have gained widespread popularity in Canadian schools (Tucker & d'Anglejan, 1975).

The *early immersion* program involves the use of the second language as the sole medium of instruction at the early grade levels with the introduction of the first language in a language arts class in Grades 2 or 3. Gradually certain content areas are taught in the child's first language so that by the late elementary years instruction is almost equally divided between the first and second language.

The St. Lambert project, a pioneering attempt at early French immersion, was designed to promote functional bilingualism among English-speaking elementary school students through a policy of home (English)—school (French) language switch (Lambert & Tucker, 1972).

A considerable amount of research has been carried out to evaluate the effectiveness of the St. Lambert approach. The progress of the pupils in the immersion classes are compared each year with carefully selected control classes (equated for socio-economic class and intelligence) of French children instructed in French, and English pupils taught in English. Results have consistently shown that early immersion pupils develop academically, cognitively and linguistically at par with their anglophone peers educated in traditional programs. In addition, the early immersion participants have attained a level of communicative proficiency in French which is far superior to that of their non-immersion English counterparts, at no cost to the development of their native language skills. They also demonstrate a greater awareness of and empathy towards French Canadian culture with no concomitant weakening of their own ethnic identity (for a complete review of the longitudinal evaluation procedures and results, see Bruck, Lambert & Tucker, 1974, 1975, 1976, in press; Genesee, 1974; Lambert & Tucker, 1972; Tucker, 1975).

The success of the St. Lambert experiment has generated a massive attempt to create similar French immersion programs across the country. These programs have generally met with favorable results. (See Cohen & Swain, 1976; Swain, 1972, 1974, 1976, in press; Swain & Barik, 1973).

The *late immersion* approach, the second major type of immersion program, involves several years of traditional second language study followed by a year of total immersion (e.g. grade 7 or 8). This immersion period is then followed by a return to regular instruction in which the student continues to study a majority of content subjects in English and selected subjects in French.

A number of empirical studies have revealed that students in the program show considerable improvement (as compared with students in the traditional French-as-a-second-language program) in the ability to speak, read, write and understand French, and at the same time are able to master content subjects at the appropriate grade level (e.g. Barik & Swain, in press; Bruck, Lambert & Tucker, 1976).

Are there differences in second language proficiency between early and late immersion students? More generally, does the age of entry into a bilingual program affect eventual mastery of the second language? In a comparison of the relative efficacy of the two programs Bruck, Lambert & Tucker (1976) found that early immersion students attain a level of French proficiency which exceeds that reached by students involved in the later (one year) immersion program. However, they are careful to note the preliminary nature of these findings:

On the basis of the present analysis we cannot state explicitly the ways in which the linguistic abilities of the two groups differ nor can we speculate in an informed way about the ways in which

these students will generalize their immersion experiences during the remainder of secondary school as the amount of French language input is reduced (Bruck et al, 1976, p. 35).

One of the most exhaustive studies dealing with the question of optimal age for second language learning was implemented in England and Wales by Burstall and her colleagues (Burstall, Hamieson, Cohen & Hargreaves, 1974) in order to determine whether it would be both administratively feasible and educationally desirable to extend the teaching of French as a second language into the early grades. This longitudinal (10 year) investigation failed to support the efficacy of an early language program. The results suggest that pupils taught French as a second langague from the age of eight did not subsequently reveal any significant gains in achievement as compared with a control group of pupils who started three years later. It was concluded that the more mature language learner (i.e. the child who begins second language instruction at 11 years as opposed to 8 years) is better able to make effective use of language learning strategies (Burstall et al, 1974).

There is no doubt that the results of this rigorous investigation deserve careful consideration. However, the suggestions in favor of a delayed introduction to the second language cannot be directly applied to the Canadian situation. The language policies and instructional programs of the two countries are not analagous and it is unwise to extrapolate from one setting to another. Until the results of longitudinal investigations and comparative evaluations of the differential success of early and late programs within a *Canadian milieu* are made available, no definitive answer to the question of optimal age of entry into a bilingual program can be provided.

Submersion Programs

Submersion programs, a third approach to second language teaching, involve the instruction of children within a school system that does not operate in their native tongue. Submersion programs are not implemented on an official basis; rather parents elect to enroll their children in these programs, in lieu of other bilingually-oriented approaches. For example, English Canadian children may attend full-fledged all French schools within a predominantly French-based school system. Whereas in the immersion programs all of the children are anglophone the submersion situation 'deposits' the child among native French speaking peers (Genesee, 1976a).

Multiple-language models, lack of formal French instruction, necessity to communicate with French classmates and day-to-day exposure to French-

Canadian culture are characteristic of the submersion program. The focus of the language acquisition process is thereby shifted from teacher to language learner. If first and second language learning are indeed analagous processes (Dulay & Burt, 1974), the submersion approach may prove very effective as a medium of instruction, for it simulates most closely the native language acquisition conditions which allow the learner to use his inherent learning strategies.

An empirical finding in support of the efficacy of such programs is reported by Macnamara (1975). He found that by grade four, anglophone students in a submersion program were linguistically indistinguishable from their francophone peers. While these results are encouraging, more long-range evaluations of the development of both French and English skills (which are not introduced until Grade 5) must be undertaken in order to determine the overall value of the submersion approach.

The success of the immersion programs has led to their widespread implementation (Swain, 1974). It should be noted however, that the majority of the research reports and programs are based upon a restricted and select population; namely, predominantly middle class, majority-group children of average or above average intelligence. Many of these children tend to receive support and encouragement from their parents and consequently have a high degree of motivation to succeed (Genesee, 1976b).

Although the economic and political fervour in Quebec necessitates the learning of French by *all* children, there is a scarcity of research involving the suitability of French immersion programs for the following groups of children[2]:

a) children of low intellectual and academic ability
b) children from low socio-economic status environments
c) children from minority groups (native language being neither English nor French)

These three groups of children represent a sizeable minority in the educational process. Educators, having in the past adopted an egalitarian ethic toward providing equal educational opportunities, are now confronted with the challange of creating bilingual education programs for all children. An examination of the existing research reports concerning the above mentioned groups should provide considerable insight into the question of the suitability and/or consequences of French immersion for all children.

Intellectual and Academic Factors

While relatively few bilingual investigations have been concerned with children with low intellectual ability (as measured by traditional standardized tests of intelligence), Gardner and Lambert (1972), Genesee and his colleagues (Genesee, 1975, 1976b; Genesee, Morin & Allister, 1974a, 1974b, 1974c) have reported evidence which suggests that, in terms of communicative skills, an individual's intellectual level does not appear to be a major factor in predicting successful acquisition of a second language. Rather, the research suggests that children of low intellectual ability comprehend an equal amount of French as compared with those children of high intellectual ability. Furthermore, low ability students were rated highly on measures of oral production, interpersonal communication, vocabulary, grammatical structure, and pronunciation. However, while the results suggest that children of different intellectual and academic abilities are equally able, or nearly equally able, to acquire particular interpersonal communication skills, their ability to acquire other functional skills (reading and writing) appears to be highly correlated with intellectual level. Since I.Q. scores are highly correlated with academic achievement this finding should not be surprising.

There is some evidence to suggest that when children with diagnosed language difficulties (the child's native language being poorly developed) are placed in an immersion program, they will acquire more communicative French than they would in a traditional program (Bruck, Rabinovitch and Oates, 1975). This evidence is speculative at best. The limited number of subjects and the lack of follow-up clearly indicates that more research is necessary before any definitive conclusions can be drawn concerning the effect of immersion on children with perceived perceptual and learning disabilities.

The empirical evidence to date suggests that all children, independent of intellectual level, possess the ability to acquire those interpersonal communicative skills of the second language. Thus, it would appear that the level of success of a second language program for low achieving students is highly dependent upon whether the program goals pertain to proficiency in non-academic communication skills (speaking, listening) or whether the goals emphasize proficiency in academic skills (reading, writing), all of which are important in producing a balanced bilingual (Macnamara, 1967). It is noteworthy that since many children with low intellectual ability experience difficulty in the academic areas and as there presently exists no remedial services in French within the immersion schools, many parents quickly decide to withdraw their children from these programs. The withdrawal of these children has fostered the existence of immersion programs which have a relatively homogeneous population consisting of children with average and/or above average intellectual ability.

Socio-economic Status and Second Language Learning

To what extent does a child's socio-economic background have an affect upon the acquisition of a second language? Recent studies (Bruck, Tucker & Jakimik, in press; Cziko, 1975; Tucker, Lambert & d'Anglejan, 1973) suggest that working class students enrolled in French immersion schools perform as well as their working class peers in traditional French-as-a-second language programs in terms of English skills. Furthermore, they perform as well as middle class immersion children on tests of French communicative ability (Cziko, 1975). Genesee (1976b) therefore suggests that working class French immersion students may profit from their bilingual training without endangering the development of native language competence.

Here again, however, the lack of longitudinal evaluations and follow-up of students withdrawing from these programs, and the lack of investigation into the attitudes of the parents of these children, makes it difficult to form any substantive conclusions. Indeed, research has clearly indicated that although most parents agree on the benefits of bilingualism, particular subsets of parents dependent in large part upon their ethnicity and the community in which they live, have distinct attitudes and motives toward the acquisition of a second language (Frasure-Smith, Lambert & Taylor, 1975). It may well be that the critical factor is not socio-economic status *per se*, but rather the attitudes and motives associated with a particular socio-economic group.

The Ethnic-Minority Group and Second Language Acquisition

An important consideration in the examination of the suitability of bilingual programs for all children is the question of their applicability to the non-English-speaking minority child. Lambert (1976) view this problem in terms of an 'additive' vs. 'subtractive' form of bilingualism. He suggests that the majority child who acquires another language is adding a second socially relevant language to his repertoire. This addition is achieved with no detriment to his native language or culture. For the minority child, on the other hand, an attempt at bilinguality often represents a threat to—or substraction from—his ethno-linguistic and cultural identity. In order to transform this negative-subtractive form of bilingualism into the more positive-additive form, precautions must be

taken to preserve the linguistic and cultural heritage of the non-dominant group (Genesee, 1976a; Lambert, 1976; Tucker, 1976). Tucker (1974) suggests the sequencing of the first and second languages such that priority for early schooling be given to the language or languages most likely to be neglected (i.e. the first language in the case of the minority child).

The use of the mother tongue will enhance the development of pride, self-esteem, and cultural awareness (in the minority child) and its use may well facilitate cognitive development or other readiness skills that will result in increased content subject mastery (Tucker, 1976, p. 83). Empirical assessments of bilingual education programs for the minority child (see Genesee, 1976b for a review) similarly suggest that in order for successful mastery of a second language to occur, the bilingual program must be adapted to the ethnocultural idiosyncratic needs of the minority group.

Motivational Variables

As has been suggested, much research energy has been channelled into the organization and evaluation of educational programs whose purpose is to develop and foster native-like proficiency in a second language. There is, however, a growing body of research that is concerned not with the methodological characteristics of effective bilingual programs but rather with those characteristics of the language learner *himself* that are predictors of success in mastering a second language (Gardner & Lambert, 1972). Many of these investigations have focused on the motivational variables associated with second language acquisition. These motivational factors reflect not merely a desire to learn the language but an "attitudinal syndrome"—a complex constellation of factors involving the learner's ethnocentric values and his attitudes toward members of other cultural-linguistic groups.

Gardner and Lambert (1972) have distinguished two types of motivational orientation which contribute to differential achievement in the second language:

The orientation is *instrumental* in form if, for example, the purpose of language study reflect the more utilitarian value of linguistic achievement, such as getting ahead in one's occupation and is *integrative* if the student is oriented to learn more about the other cultural community, as if he desired to become a potential member of the other group (Lambert, 1967, p. 102).

The integratively oriented second language learner seeks maximum proximity in order to identify with the new linguistic-cultural group. Contrastly, the instrumentally oriented learner would attain a degree of solidarity that would only be commensurate with his goals (Schumann, 1975). Success in second language acquisition is generally considered to be more likely in the integrative case.

Gardner and Smythe (1975, p. 222) explored the nature of motivational properties associated with learning French as a second language. They presented a 'taxonomy of motivational characteristics' under the following headings:

1. Group specific attitudes
    Attitudes toward French Canadians
    Attitudes toward European French
2. Course related characteristics
    Attitudes toward learning French
    Attitudes toward French course
    Attitudes toward French teacher
    Parental encouragement to learn French
3. Motivational Indices
    Integrative orientation
    Motivational intensity
    Desire to learn French
4. Generalized attitudes
    Interest in foreign languages
    Ethnocentrism
    Authoritarianism
    Anomie
    Machiavellianism
    Need achievement

These authors maintain that measures of language aptitude have consistently been found to be independent of attitudinal-motivational indices, though both are correlated with measures of French achievement. Thus, there may be two separate roads to success in second language acquisition—aptitude and motivation. Language aptitude is believed to be a relatively static characteristic (Smythe, Stennett & Feenstra, 1972), whereas a motivational profile is considered to be slightly more amenable to change. How can attitudinal variables be modified once the student has acquired the existing stereotypes or expectations of his parents and his community? Educational intervention strategies, involving cross-cultural exchanges (e.g. field trips, movies), have been introduced in an attempt to decrease the student's native ethnocentrism and increase his empathy toward other linguistic cultures. In order to be successful such incentive programs must be carefully designed to provide for the multidimensional nature of the motivational process. It is the out-of-classroom variables that must be considered when attempting to influence attitudes toward another cultural group. Such a perspective takes second language learning out of a soley educational mold and views it as a social-psychological process (Tucker & Lambert, 1973).

The economic, political and social necessity of acquiring French in Canada has created a proliferation of bilingual immersion programs throughout the country. A better understanding of the multiplicity of cognitive, psychological and sociological factors inherent in second language learning has provided further impetus for the widespread implementation of these programs. Yet, the question still remains—Are the immersion programs equally successful in producing functional bilingualism for *all* children? The preceding review suggests two conclusions. In order to determine whether these immersion programs are successful, one must examine what is meant by "functional bilingualism." If the underlying assumption is that these children successfully employ interpersonal communication skills (e.g. verbal and auditory fluency), the research suggests that immersion programs are highly successful with most children. If the intent is to produce balanced bilinguals the research is less supportive for children who are members of a minority group, who come from low socio-economic environments and/or who have below average intellectual and academic ability. Furthermore, it becomes essential to not only document and follow the progress of individuals who have become functional and balanced bilinguals, but to also examine those individuals who failed to profit from the instructional program.

The "group" research in the past has been useful in providing sufficient indices that immersion programs are successful in allowing the individual to acquire competence in a second language without any detriment to his native linguistic and academic skills. However, the group research, by focusing on unidimensional factors, has often tended to mask the large number of interacting factors which are essential in second language learning. It is encouraging that recently many researchers (e.g. Genesee, 1976b; Stern, 1976 Tucker, 1976, Tucker & d'Anglejan, 1975; Tucker, Hamayan & Genesee, 1976) have indicated the need for applying an individual difference approach to second language acquisition.

The question should not merely be—can all children function well in an immersion program? Rather, an Aptitude-Treatment Interaction (ATI) (Cronbach & Snow, 1969) or Trait-Treatment Interaction (TTI) (Berlinger & Cahen, 1973) approach suggests the more fruitful question—What are the differential learning rates in the acquisition of a second language for children with certain characteristics in a variety of immersion programs? Elucidation of the interactive effects of learner characteristics and instructional variables may provide bilingual programs that are tailored to the individual needs (both linguistic and extralinguistic) of the language learner.

FOOTNOTES

[1]These levels of competence are based upon a report of the Ontario Ministerial Committee on the Teaching of French, the Gillin Report (1974).

[2]A more comprehensive review can be found in Genesee (1976b).

REFERENCES

Barik, H. C. and Swain, M. A Canadian experiment in bilingual education at the grade eight and nine levels: The Peel Study. *Foreign Language Annals*. In press.

Berliner, D. C. and Cahen, L. S. Trait-treatment interaction and learning. In F. N. Kerlinger (Ed.), *Review of research in education*. Illinois: F. E. Peacock Publishers, 1973, 58-94.

Brown, R. *A first language: The early stages*. Cambridge: Harvard University Press, 1973.

Bruck, M., Lambert, W. E. and Tucker, G. R. Bilingual schooling through the elementary grades: The St. Lambert project at grade seven. *Language Learning*, 1974, *24*, 183-204.

Bruck, M., Lambert, W. E. and Tucker, G. R. Assessing functional bilingualism within a bilingual program: The St. Lambert experiment at grade eight. McGill University, 1975. (Mimeo).

Bruck, M., Lambert, W. E. and Tucker, G. R. Alternative forms of immerstion for second language teaching. McGill University, 1976. (Mimeo).

Bruck, M., Lambert, W. E. and Tucker, G. R. Cognitive and attitudinal consequences of bilingual schooling: The St. Lambert project through grade six. *International Journal of Psycholinguistics*. In press.

Bruck, M., Rabinovitch, S. and Oates, M. The effects of French immersion programs on children with language disabilities. *Working Papers on Bilingualism*, 1975, *5*, 47-86.

Bruck, M., Tucker, G. R. and Jakimik, J. Are French programs suitable for working class children? In W. Engel (Ed.), *Prospects in child language*. Amsterdam: Royal Vangorcum. In press.

Burstall, D., Jamieson, M., Cohen, S. and Hargreaves, M. *Primary French in the balance*. Windsor, England: NFER Publishing Company, Ltd., 1974.

Cohen, A. D. and Swain, M. Bilingual education: The immersion model in the North American context. *TESOL Quarterly*, 1976, *10*, 45-54.

Cronbach, L. J. and Snow, R. E. Individual differences in learning ability as a function of instructional variables. Final Report, Contract No. OEC-r-6-061269-1217, U.S. Office of Education, 1969.

Cziko, G. The effects of different French immersion programs on the language and academic skills of children from various socio-economic backgrounds. Unpublished M.A. Thesis, Department of Psychology, McGill University, 1975.

Dulay, H. and Burt, M. A new perspective on the creative construction process in child language acquisition. *Working Papers on Bilingualism*, 1974, *4*, 71-98.

Frasure-Smith, N., Lambert, W. E. and Taylor, D. M. Choosing the language of instruction for one's children: A Quebec study. *Journal of Cross-Cultural Psychology*, 1975, *6*, 131-155.

Gardner, R. C. and Lambert, W. E. *Attitudes and motivation in second language learning*. Rowley, Mass: Newbury House, 1972.

Gardner, R. C. and Smythe, P. C. Motivation and second language acquisition. *The Canadian Modern Language Review*, 1975, *31*, 218-230.

Genesee, F. An experimental French immersion program at the secondary school level—1969-1974. Protestant School Board of Greater Montreal, 1974. (Mimeo).

Genesee, F. The role of intelligence and second language learning. Curriculum Department, The Protestant School Board of Greater Montreal, 1975.

Genesee, F. Some Canadian experiments in developing intercultural communication. Paper presented at the Central States Conference on the Teaching of Foreign Language, Detroit, 1976. (a)

Genesee, F. The suitability of immersion programs for all children. *The Canadian Modern Language Review*, 1976, *32*, 494-515. (b)

Genesee, F., Morin, S., and Allister, T. Evaluation of the 1973-74 Grade seven French immersion class, June. Curriculum Department, The Protestant School Board of Greater Montreal, September, 1974. (a)

Genesee, F., Morin, S., and Allister, T. Evaluation of the 1973-74 pilot grade eleven French immersion class. Curriculum Department, The Protestant School Board of Greater Montreal, 1974. (b)

Genesee, F., Morin, S., and Allister, T. Evaluation of the 1973-74 grade four French immersion class. Curriculum Department, The Protestant School Board of Greater Montreal, 1974 (c)

Kennedy, G. K. Conditions for language learning. In J. W. Oller and J. C. Richards (Eds.), *Focus on the learner: Pragmatic perspectives for the language teacher*. Rowley, Mass: Newbury House, 1973, 66-80.

Lambert, W. E. A Canadian experiment in the development of bilingual competence. *The Canadian Modern Language Review*, 1974, *31*, 108-116.

Lambert, W. E. The effects of bilingualism on the individual: Cognitive and socio-cultural consequences. Paper presented at the Multidisciplinary Conference on Bilingualism, State University at Plattsburgh, 1976.

Lambert, W. E. and Tucker, G. R. *Bilingual education of children. The St. Lambert experiment.* Rowley, Mass: Newbury House, 1972.

Lieberson, S. *Language and ethnic relations in Canada.* New York: Wiley, 1970.

Mackey, W. F. *Language teaching analysis.* London: Longmans, 1965.

Macnamara, J. The bilingual's linguistic performance— A psychological overview. *Journal of Social Issues,* 1967, *23,* 58-77.

Macnamara, J. What happens to children whose home language is not that of the school? McGill University, 1975. (Mimeo).

Report of the Ministerial Committee on the Teaching of French (The Gillin Report) Toronto: The Ontario Ministery of Education, 1974.

Report of the Royal Commission on Bilingualism and Biculturalism, Books I-VI. Ottawa: Queen's Printer, 1967-1971.

Schumann, J. H. Second language acquisition: the pidginization hypothesis. Unpublished doctoral Thesis, Harvard University, 1975.

Smythe, P. C., Stennett, R. C. and Feenstra, H. J. Attitude, aptitude and type of instructional program in second language acquisition. Canadian Journal of Behavioral Science, 1972, *4,* 307-321.

Stern, H. H. *Foreign languages in primary education.* London: Oxford University Press, 1967.

Stern, H. H. Bilingual schooling and second language teaching: A review of the recent North American experience. In J. W. Oller and J. R. Richards (Eds.), *Focus on the learner: Pragmatic perspectives for the language teacher.* Rowley, Mass: Newbury House, 1973, 274-282.

Stern, H. H. Optimal age: Myth or reality? *The Canadian Modern Language Review,* 1976, *32,* 283-294.

Swain, M. *Bilingual schooling: Some experiences in Canada and the United States.* Toronto: The Ontario Institute for Studies in Education, 1972.

Swain, M. French immersion programs across Canada: Research findings. *The Canadian Modern Language Review,* 1974, *31,* 117-129.

Swain, M. Bibliography: Research on immersion education for the majority child. *The Canadian Modern Language Review,* 1976, *32,* 592-596.

Swain, M. Second language and content learning: A Canadian bilingual education program at the secondary grade levels. In E. Briere (Ed.), *Language Development in a Bilingual Setting.* In press.

Swain, M. and Barik, H. C. French immersion classes: A promising route to bilingualism. *Orbit,* 1973, *4,* 1-8.

Tucker, G. R. Methods of second language teaching. The Canadian Modern Language Review, 1974, *31,* 102-107.

Tucker, G. R. The development of reading skills within a bilingual education program. In S. S. Smiley and J. C. Towner (Eds.), *Language and reading.* Bellingham, Washington: Western Washington State College, 1975, 49-60.

Tucker, G. R. Cross disciplinary perspectives in bilingual education. Linguistics review paper. Paper prepared for the Center for Applied Linguistics Project on Cross Disciplinary Perspectives on Bilingual Education, 1976.

Tucker, G. R. and d'Anglejan, A. New directions in second language teaching. In R. C. Troike and N. Modiano (Eds.), *Proceedings of the First Inter-American Conference on Bilingual Education.* Arlington, Va.: Center for Applied Linguistics, 1975.

Tucker, G. R., Hamayan, E. and Genesee, F. Affective, cognitive and social factors in second language acquisition. *The Canadian Modern Language Review,* 1976, *32,* 215-226.

Tucker, G. R. and Lambert, W. E. Sociocultural aspects of language study. In J. W. Oller and J. C. Richards (Eds.), *Focus on the learner: Pragmatic perspectives for the language teacher.* Rowley, Mass: Newbury House, 1973, 246-250.

Tucker, G. R., Lambert, W. E. and d'Anglejan, A. French immersion programs: A pilot investigation, *Language Sciences,* 1973, *25,* 19-26.

Chapter 34
Bilingual Ed:
How Un-American Can You Get?
Karen Joseph Shender*

At first glance, Sherwood School doesn't look much different from the other flat, grim, utilitarian buildings that sit alongside Highway 101 as it cuts through the Salinas Valley. It could as well house the production of canned artichokes as the teaching of children. Nowhere are there the amenities—the shade trees, the playground equipment, the bright murals—that might comfort the eye or spirit of the poor children who go to school here. Inside, it seems even more drab and impersonal, an unreconstructed 1930s school.

During its first three decades, Sherwood had an even more direct way of telling its Spanish-speaking youngsters that they were not welcome, that their homes and origins were suspect. Like most schools, it adhered to the "English only" code which was law only in California and several other Southwestern states but which was de facto policy in most schools with language minority students. Its enforcement effectively curtailed the educational advancement of millions of non-English-speaking schoolchildren and in many cases contributed to hostile feelings toward self, home and school. A student testifying fefore the U.S. Commission on Civil Rights noted: "If they caught you talking Spanish, they would send you to the office and give you a warning. They would give you a long lecture about if you wanted to be an American, you have got to speak English....They are telling you that your language is bad, [that] your mother and father speak a bad language."

There has been considerable ongoing disagreement over which qualities go toward making a "good American." Language is so closely identified with nationality that, in the past, it was inconceivable for a person to speak a language other than English and also pledge allegiance to the United States. And although the melting-pot myth is no longer held up as a model, the old assimilationist ideas of a Teddy Roosevelt still fuel prejudice against those who speak a different language.

But things are changing at Sherwood School. In the teachers' lounge, colleagues converse in both Spanish and English. In the office, a bus driver speaks in Spanish with several Chicano children, then turns and converses in Spanish with another Anglo. Bulletin boards carry messages like *"Apre demos a leer y escribir en ingles y espanol."* (We are learning to read and write in English and Spanish.) Since 80 to 90 percent—depending upon the movement of the migrant workers—of the 850 students at Sherwood have Spanish surnames, both Spanish and English are used in teaching.

The Salinas Union High School District receives $234,000 in federal funds for its bilingual education program annually, thanks to monies from Title VII of the Elementary and Secondary Education Act—often called the Bilingual Education Act. The Salinas City School District (grades K-6) received $215,000 annually from Title VII and $58,000 from the state bilingual program. Sherwood uses its share—some $152,000—for hiring bilingual teacher aides, providing in-service training for its staff, and acquiring bilingual materials. The program, now in its fifth year, serves approximately 24 non-English- or limited-English-speaking and 130 English-speaking students, all volunteers, between preschool and fifth grade. It employs a Spanish reading specialist and 14 bilingual teachers, each with an aide (Aides hired under separate migrant education funding give Spanish-speaking children not in the program a more limited exposure to bilingual approach.)

First, the Mother Tongue

Sonia Lee, who is Chilean, is one of the kindergarden teachers in the Title VII program. "The good bilingual teacher puts out tremendous effort and energy," she says, "because of having to hunt for good materials and sometimes develop her own" Lee leads her students in discussing *En el Hogar y en la Escuela*, a text developed in Puerto Rico. The children sharpen their prereading skills by talking about the pictures. The lesson is conducted totally in Spanish, while an aide works with English-speaking children on a similar lesson.

*Karen Shender, Freelance writer. Reprinted with permission from Learning Magazine, October, 1976.

Later the class sings a Mexican nursery rhyme, with the six English-speaking students joining in. An aide comments that through their everyday exposure to the language, they are picking up Spanish rapidly.

The Spanish-speaking children in Sherwood's Project Esperanza begin school in their native language for several reasons. Many experts agree that the minority child's self-concept is enhanced if he is taught first in his mother tongue. (Children who speak the language of the dominant culture are not threatened by learning a new language, as their entire culture reinforces their positive self-concept, and language learning carries no hint of rejecting old ways.) In addition, it is difficult, if not impossible, to assess a student's true learning potential when he is working in a second language.

The air of eagerness in Maria Avila's bilingual first grade is a striking contrast to the atmosphere of boredom and defeat which can be seen in a non-bilingual class down the hall. While Avila works with a small group of children on consonant-vowel combination, the rest of her 33 students play word games—in Spanish. "We start some of the children reading English in the first grade," says Avila, "but only if we are sure they are ready for it. Most of the children have one hour a day of oral English skills, and they learn to read in Spanish." All of Avila's students are native Spanish speakers.

Both Avila and Lee agree that parent involvement is vital. "we have workshops, and our parents not only come, they bring neighbors!" beams Lee.

"Through conferences and home visits, I have helped parents see the importance of maintaining the Spanish language while learning English," says Avila. "I have met some confused people—like the man who thought we were going to teach his child 'pocho'—street Spanish. Others have worried that we will teach Castilian Spanish. But when they see that we are using standard Mexican Spanish, the kind that would be in print, they are pleased."

Lee notes that efforts to make the school a hub of after-hours school activity have boosted parental support for the program. "In Chile," she says, "the principal lives in the school and is as important a peacemaker as the judge or chief of police. People sometimes come to him in the middle of the night to solve problems or break up fights. We need to make the school here that central, that important to the community. But the community has to shape the program along with the school authorities."

Bilingual is the Mainstream

Respecting cultural needs is vital to Project Esperanza. Teachers are paired to provide both Spanish and English cultural and language models in each grade. Students in this voluntary program study most subjects in their native language, but for two hours each day they receive instruction in a second language. In second grade Juanita Miranda and Linda Mitchell are paired. For the first 15 minutes of the day, each teacher conducts her own bilingual class. Then the English speakers go to Mitchell and the Spanish speakers go to Miranda. There the students study reading, math and other subjects in the language they most often speak. Then another switch occurs for the afternoon. The Spanish speakers go to Mitchell for English as a Second Language instruction and the English speakers go to Miranda for similar instruction in Spanish.

Although all the children in these two classes have Spanish surnames, 20 of the 60 students are English dominant. Their families are far removed from their Latin heritage and do not speak Spanish, although they are eager for their children to learn it. Thirty-one percent of Sherwood's students speak limited or no English. Their Spanish-speaking parents are acutely aware of the economic value of good English, and may have expressed fear that their children will not learn English well enough to break free from the cycle of poor education and poor jobs.

In one district, doubts about bilingual education were dispelled when parents were told that Spanish would be used as a bridge to learning English well. Parents were told that their children would learn English more slowly but also more thoroughly, and would also continue to study their native language and to appreciate their home culture. Babysitting and transportation were provided so parents could observe in classrooms and spread the word that bilingual education was a positive tool, not another means of exclusion.

One parent who suffered through U.S. schooling when bilingual education was unheard of described his experience: "I went through eighth grade, and I still am embarrassed to speak in English. They didn't let me speak Spanish, and every time I spoke a few words of English they corrected and corrected. Most of the time I didn't talk at all. But I want something different for my children I want them to know both languages, to read well in both, and to choose their jobs not by what they can do in Spanish, but by what their minds see as good for their lives."

Some teachers have a difficult time understanding the desire to maintain one's own language while learning a second, dominant one. In a Sherwood staff meeting to explain the program, Juanita Miranda admits there were some arguments. "Some teachers were thinking in terms of English and Spanish, and we were thinking bilingually. We were asked when the children would be moved out of the bilingual program and into the mainstream, and we replied that we *are* the mainstream!"

The Way To Go Is Still Debated

Not everyone agrees with this cultural pluralism objective. Richard Shipp is head of Sherwood's language lab and coordinator of the school's "transitional bilingual program." He speaks with nostalgia of the days when more of the non-English-speaking students' time was spent learning English. After a court ruling on "pull-out" programs such as Shipp's, the time was cut to one hour a day. Says Shipp, "We use Spanish for explanation, giving instructions, not for teaching. English is the goal here, since the children already know Spanish."

Shipp and his two aides use a variety of multisensory games, language games with a focus on the audio-lingual method, and other teacher-prepared and commercial materials to teach their students, who come from classes not funded by the Title VII program. Students who read Spanish are given an alphabet keyed to Spanish pronunciation which begins "A—ai, B—bi, C—si." Shipp comments that once they have bridged the gap between Spanish and English pronunciation, they have few problems reading English. Yet reading scores at the school undercut his contention.

One of the language lab aides, a Filipino, voices the philosophy of the program. "My kids don't speak Tagalog, though I speak it fluently. If they want to learn it, that's O.K. But we are in America now, and English is what is important."

No one argues the necessity for a thorough knowledge of English; to attain a sound education—the key to most other achievements— one must be fluent in it. It seems logical, then, to increase efforts in English as a Second Language (ESL) instruction. But most ESL programs bypass the sequence of language learning—listening comprehension, speaking, reading and writing. (Although ESL methodology dictates this sequence, children who learn ESL in brief pull-out classes must follow the regular English curriculum along with their native English-speaking peers. Thus first graders must learn to read and write English as they are learning to understand and speak English.) And Bureau of the Census and U.S. Office of Education data reveal some startling facts about U.S. language minority populations which indicate that ESL's single goal of achieving fluency in English has not been achieved.

According to the 1970 census, 33.2 million Americans, or roughly 16 percent of the population, speak a first language other than English. Although precise data is not yet available on the numbers of limited- or non-English-speaking schoolchildren, the U.S. Office of Education estimates that at least five million need special language programs. And compared to the median number of 12 school years completed for whites, the median is 8.1 for Mexican Americans, 8.6 for Puerto Ricans, and 9.8 for Native Americans. This higher dropout rate is often attributed to frustration and lack of confidence, which in turn is due to language problems.

As one teacher put it, "If you have ever faced a child who can't understand a word you say, you know the need for Title VII type programs." The basic goals for such programs are generally agreed upon: improved self-concept, socioeconomic development, academic achievement, and an appreciation of the many linguistic and cultural heritages in the United States.

The debate is over which of the goals is paramount and should serve as the *modus operandi* of a given bilingual program. Some say that since academic achievement requires English skills, intensive ESL instruction—perhaps through an immersion process—is most important. Others reason that the child whose identity has been damaged through a loss of language will not succeed academically, regardless of English language skills. Still others contend that there must be a melding of language learning and increased appreciation for dominant and minority cultures—a truly bicultural or multicultural approach.

Setting Up a Program

Helpful materials and technical expertise for schools setting up bilingual programs have often come from the Center for Applied Linguistics, an association of linguists committed to putting linguistic research into practice in schools and businesses. A recipient of many public and private grants to work on linguistic problems relating to desegregation and urban and rural population shifts, the Center has worked on various aspects of bilingual education, and was recently contracted by the San Francisco Unified School District to help design a multilingual education plan.

According to Center linguists, there are two basic types of bilingual education programs in the United States, with several variations. In transitional bilingualism, the mother tongue is phased out as fluency in English increases. In maintenance (or full) bilingualism, fluency and literacy in both the mother tongue and the second language are developed.

The decision as to which of the two types of programs to implement is often made on the basis of available bilingual staff, adequate facilities, and other factors unrelated to educational philosophy. But the community which must accept the program, its willingness to try new methods and the extent of its commitment to bilingual education are also determining factors. In some areas school districts have rejected federal and state grants in the mistaken belief that, if they have no "outside" funding, they are not bound by state and federal laws requiring special educational programs for non-English-speaking students.

Obviously not every teacher who knows two languages will make an effective bilingual educator. According to the Center for Applied Linguistics, the bilingual teacher must not only know the two languages to be used in the program, but must have equal respect for the regional and social variations in both. He or she must understand second language teaching techniques, and must be able to use the child's language as a positive tool in teaching. He must also be able to develop curriculum activities to deal with the contrast in language structures. And he must be aware of the contributions the child's culture has made in U. S. history. An understanding of the cultural differences in behavior is also essential (a Mexican child is not being evasive by avoiding the eyes of his teacher; he is showing respect).

Although universities are now training teachers in bilingual education, the supply is not yet adequate, and some educators wonder if bilingual education has a chance to succeed nationally. At the state level, however, the forecast is different. Emelina D. Pacheco, director of bilingual education for New Mexico's sprawling Albuquerque school district, has no doubt that bilingual education is succeeding there. "Forty percent of our 81,000 students have Spanish surnames," she says, "but of our 3,000 teachers, only 10 percent are bilingual. So we meet the needs of our students in other ways. We provide lots of inservice training to help our teachers better understand their students' culture. We assure our often-threatened monolingual teachers that we are not trying to replace them; we are merely helping them gain new skills. We use team teaching in some classrooms, aides in others, and a variety of materials, some of which we have developed ourselves." In 1969, Albuquerque began with one bilingual pilot school which included four kindergarten classes through seventh grade, serving 6,500 children in 20 schools and 227 classrooms.

Successful programs like Albuquerque's have found that community education and involvement goes hand in hand with teacher education. In a given district, a committee of community members and school personnel should study the language makeup of the community, its economic base, and its attitudes toward bilingual education. This committee should help in setting goals and in hiring aides, teachers and the program director.

Rough Rock Demonstration School in Chinle, Arizona, embodies the elements which are essential to successful bilingual education. For ten years the Navaho community has been refining a program which director Ethelou Yazzie describes as "bilingual, bicultural and bicognitive." Defining the last term, she says, "If people are to operate in two cultures, they have to think in two ways, and we teach our children that skill."

The program is conducted in Navaho and English, with literacy skills first achieved in the native language, and English reading introduced after three to four years of oral English instruction. Studies include rug work, sand painting, and Navaho history and tradition, along with the more typically taught courses. Emphasis is on instilling in the children a sense of pride in their Indian identity, while preparing them to cope with the world beyond the Navaho Nation. Says Yazzie: "We see the destruction of Black Mesa by Peabody Coal; our water rights are ignored. These problems require sophisticated legal and financial analysis. We must prepare our children well."

Rough Rock has the reputation of doing precisely that, and Navaho parents outside Arizona send their children to board and study there. State evaluators have noted that Rough Rock students exhibit none of the confusion and unhappiness observed in so many Indian students—disrespect for parents, heavy drinking, misconduct in class or general apathy. The average number of school years completed for Navahos is five, but many Rough Rock students complete high school, and some, like Yazzie, complete professional studies.

Although Rough Rock's school board is entirely Navaho, there are some Anglo teachers in the school system. These teachers and their children, who attend the demonstration school, provide a different cultural model for the students. Of Rough Rock's 450 students, only 8 are Anglo, and they too are required to complete Navaho studies. "They are given no special treatment," says Yazzie, "and they like that."

The Courts Deliver a Mandate

Despite funding from Title VII and other sources, most U.S. schools had been moving cautiously with bilingual education until the *Lau* v. *Nichols* decision in 1974. This case had begun back in March 1970, when 13 non-English-speaking Chinese students filed suit in the Federal District Court in San Francisco against the Board of Education, whose president was Alan Nichols. The class action suit, on behalf of nearly 1,800 Chinese students, claimed that by denying them special English instruction, the school was "dooming these children to become dropouts and to join the rolls of the unemployed." The Chinese students declared that they should be taught by bilingual teachers, instead of merely learning to parrot what a monolingual teacher said. The court ruled against the students, saying that they receive "the same education made available on the same terms and conditions to the other tens of thousands of students in the San Francisco Unified School District."

In January 1973, the U.S. Court of Appeals for the Ninth Circuit upheld this decision, adding that the problems suffered by the children were "not the result of law enacted by the state...but the result of deficiencies created by the [students] themselves in failing to learn the English language."

When the U.S. Supreme Cort heard the case, however, it drew on the Civil Rights Act of 1964, and said that any school district which did not provide special English instruction for its non-English-speaking students was missing "a meaningful opportunity to participate in the equal treatment of unequals" and making "a mockery of public education." And on January 21, 1974, it ruled that the San Francisco Unified School District was discriminating against its non-English-speaking Chinese students, stating: "There is no equality of treatment merely by providing students with the same facilities, textbooks, teachers and curriculum; for students who do not understand any English are effectively foreclosed from any meaningful education."

The San Francisco Unified School District is now developing a bilingual education program which will serve not only its Chinese-speaking students, but also its Spanish-, Filipino- and Japanese-speaking students. It is being helped by the Center for Applied Linguistics and by a dynamic Citizens' Task Force.

Later in 1974, courts in New York, Colorado and New Mexico heard cases similar to San Francisco's. In every instance the *Lau* case was cited as precedent and interpreted as a mandate for bilingual education. (*Sema* v. *Portales Municipal Schools*, New Mexico, July 19, 1974; *Aspira* v. *Board of Education of the City of New York*, New York, August 29, 1974; *Keyes* v. *School District No. 1*, Denver Colorado, April 9, 1974.)

In addition to state court rulings on bilingual education, *Lau* v. *Nichols* has spawned a network of "Lau Centers" across the country. Nine education centers noted for their expertise in bilingual education have received contracts from HEW's Office for Civil Rights. These centers are equipped to provide technical assistance to school districts which do not comply with Title VI of the Civil Rights Act of 1964 which requires schools to meet the language needs of students when the difference in the home language and the language used in school excludes children from "effective participation" in the educational program.

A minor development in the *Lau*-sparked interest in bilingual education occurred in April 1976, when the U.S. Office of Education issued a memorandum to clarify the *Lau Remedies*. The *Remedies*, which had been developed by a task force within HEW's Office for Civil Rights, were very strongly worded, and many school districts feared that they would have to design bilingual programs for every language minority within their bounds. (The Arlington, Virginia, school district, for example, has many children from embassy families, and asked whether it would be required to provide a special program for two Hindi-speaking children, another for a Punjab-speaking child, and yet another for a handful of children from Japan.) The April 8 memorandum stated that the *Lau Remedies* were intended as guidelines, not as a mandate, and were only for the use of the 334 districts which had been declared out of compliance with the 1964 Civil Rights Act. This memorandum, given wide coverage in school districts where bilingual education is unpopular but sorely needed, in no way weakened the *Lau* decision itself.

According to Patricia Nakano, manager of the Lau Center in Berkeley, California, the centers will provide school districts with guidance in setting up a bilingual education program. "We come upon a school district's request," says Nakano, "and we stress from the beginning that we are neither punitive nor enforcement-oriented. We are here to provide the district with the help it needs in determining its goals and how to achieve them. We can provide workshops on bilingual education, a review of available materials, and assistance with designing programs. And we like to continue our relationship with the district after the program is in operation." Nakano added that thus far districts have been very receptive, and that even once-skeptical teachers and community members have become optimistic about bilingual education. "We show them that educational achievement for the entire population rises with the implementation of a workable bilingual program," says Nakano, "and that is what counts."

Quebec's Language Immersion Model

The aim of another interesting program in bilingual education—the Culver City Spanish Immersion Program—is to weed out social, political and racial overtones leaving only the issue of language acquisition. The project was born in March 1971, when some professors from UCLA approached schools in the Los Angeles area about replicating a language-immersion project that was working successfully in Quebec, Canada. Known as the "St. Lambert's Project," this program immersed English-speaking Canadians in the French language, beginning with kindergarten. The children were taught with the standard French texts, and not as though they were learning a second language.

English language arts was introduced to the St. Lambert's children in second grade. Gradually the amount of instruction in English language arts increased, and at the end of grade four the children could read, write and speak English as well as their English-monolingual peers. They could also read and write French better than students who had studied it in a typical second language program. St. Lambert's first immersion class is now in the seventh grade, and extensive testing shows that it is bilingual—almost equally fluent—in French and English, and that it is not retarded in any other subject area.

When professors Russell Campbell and Donald Bowen of UCLA presented these research findings to school administrators, Vera Jashni was enthusiastic. Then principal at Linwood E. Howe Elementary School in Culver City, Jashni recalls: "There was quite a high percentage of Spanish-speaking children in our school and I thought it would be nice if the English-speaking children could interact with them before they learned English."

Jashni and the UCLA people presented the language immersion scheme to parents of kindergartners at Linwood E. Howe. When not enough parents were interested, they opened the program to other kindergartners in the Culver City Unified School District. Says Jashni: "We ran into the fear of the unknown—'What will happen to my child's English?' 'Will he learn math?' These concerns were legitimate, and I could give no answers other than what the St. Lambert's study indicated."

After orientation for both teachers and consenting parents, the Culver City Spanish Immersion Program (SIP) began in Septmber 1971. The kindergartners were encouraged to speak as much Spanish as possible, and their teacher, Irma Wright, spoke to them only in Spanish. Initially one of the ground rules was that Wright would purposefully not understand English, so that students would have to tug her or pantomime if they could not express their needs in Spanish. But, says Wright, "we discovered that this was just too frustrating, so even during the first year of the program, we decided we would have to understand English. Now if a child asks to go to the bathroom in English, I respond, *Quieres ir al bano?*"

Most children leave the SIP kindergarten speaking words and phrases in Spanish, and understanding a great deal. In first grade, the teacher "understands" less and less English, and the children are expected to speak more and more Spanish. The teacher always speaks in regularly paced conversational Spanish, and by the time the children are in the second grade, they are

speaking, reading and writing Spanish and use no English except during English language arts classes. One teacher comments: "I won't speak in English, even to visitors. I use the children to translate for me. Once when I asked a child to translate for me, he hesitated a moment. Then he turned and paraphrased everything I had said into simpler terms in Spanish, thinking that maybe this way our English-speaking visitor would understand."

In second grade the children are well founded in encoding and decoding skills, and they begin one hour a day of English reading. Teachers find that their students need drilling on the eifferences between English and Spanish pronunciation, but the literacy skill is there, and they transfer easily to English reading.

Tests show that at the kindergarten level there is no difference between the English verbal skills of SIP and non-SIP children. In first grade, those in SIP score lower on standardized reading tests than non-SIP children; they have had no formal introduction to it. But in second grade, after introduction to reading in English, there is no difference between their reading skills and those of non-SIP children. Except, that is, that they can also read and comprehend Spanish.

The Spanish Immersion Program, now in its sixth year, has had some native Spanish speakers in it from the start. Says Jashni: "We found a tremendous difference between the attitudes of the SIP Chicano children and those of non-SIP Chicano students. The children in the immersion program have marvelous enthusiasm and want to attend even when they are sick, unlike those in regular classes."

Since the Chicano children in regular English-speaking classes are working in a second language—which, on the surface, would appear to be a mirror image of what the Anglo children in SIP are doing—one might wonder why their interest in school lags behind that of the English-speaking children. The answer lies in the SIP orientation UCLA provides parents, teachers and school personnel. Those connected with SIP are schooled in the assumption that normal children can learn a second language and concepts in that language concurrently. Teachers and parents are conditioned to *expect* that the children would learn, never to doubt it. At the same time they are led to a genuine respect for what the children would be accomplishing—mastery of a second language. The formula is simple: high expectations and high praise for achieving what is expected.

This is often quite different from what the child speaking a minority language experiences. His teacher's attitude is often one of concern over his socioeconomic background and confusion about how to teach him, particularly if the teacher does not speak his language. Often, too, the child who does venture into English receives an endless list of grammar corrections from his zealous teacher.

Jashni offered a concrete example of this double standard: "A publishing company developed a bilingual test and needed some children to provide spontaneous demonstrations for its salesmen. We sent two of our first graders, Daniel and Mike. When Mike responded to test questions in Spanish, there was a show of pleasure, with murmurs and some applause. But when Daniel, whose first language was Spanish, gave correct responses in English, there was no applause, no excitement, no positive feedback. He was in the U.S., so he was expected to speak English."

A loss of this kind of ethnocentrism is one of the valuable by-products of the Spanish Immersion Program. Says Mrs. Paul Bardin, mother of two SIP children: "Many SIP parents are interested in going to Mexico for the first time. They bring back books and games. Some go to school at night to learn Spanish. We have a new appreciation for the Mexican culture, and our children have helped us to meet one another in ways we wouldn't have before. Now we speak our little bit of Spanish and the Mexican parents speak their little bit of English, and we laugh together."

Enthusiasm runs high among students as well. When asked which language he spoke best, one first grader announced, "I talk both really good!" "I was borned English," said another child, "so it is good to know Spanish." And a little girl marveled, "When we go to a Mexican restaurant where the people know I speak Spanish, everybody adores me. I don't know why."

The Spanish Immersion Program in Culver City now has a waiting list and has moved to El Marino School where there is more space. The program receives no outside funding and spends no more than the district average per pupil expenditure. SIP suggests that it is relatively unimportant whether the first or second language is used as the medium of instruction. The key factor is whether the teacher expects the child to succeed in that language, and respects the child's home language.

As federal and state laws and increased research efforts move our nation's schools more quickly into bilingual education, one thing is evident. The days of the melting-pot ideal—when conformity was forced on children at the expense of their individual needs—are gone. Perhaps now, be it through dual language instruction or single language immersion, we can get about the business of developing the full potential of every student who comes into the classroom.

Chapter 35
We Got A New Kid and He Don't Speak English
Nancy Naumann*

How well I remember that day. It was Friday, exactly one month after the beginning of school. I sat at my desk trying to absorb the few remaining moments of quiet before the troops marched in. I had no thoughts more noble than just trying to endure until 3:00 when I could leave behind the third grade world of kids for two whole days. Still, there was that nagging sensation that things really weren't falling into place this year. I can live with the pitter-patter of little feet across the floor and the quiet hum of activity in the interest of individualized programs and do-your-own-thing education. But this year motion had degenerated into commotion, and the "quiet hum" was getting decidedly too loud.

Friday isn't the best day for revising life in the classroom. But since I wasn't surviving too well in the prevailing confused atmosphere, I decided it was time to confront the situation head-on.

"What could we do?" The question, and first order of business for the day, at least excited some interest and responsiveness on the part of the children. They all admitted there was a problem that needed to be solved. There was basically no spirit of give and take in the room, we agreed—a hard-to-define pulling apart where there should have been pulling together.

The answers we arrived at were good, sensible ones, and I wondered why I hadn't had this discussion earlier rather than mumbling in the teachers room about this "difficult class." The kids' suggestions involved mostly procedural changes in reading and math periods designed to streamline activity and cut down on "traffic congestion" at learning centers.

So we embarked on our new, more efficient management system and what we hoped would be the reign of peace and quiet. Everyone was trying to live up to his or her part of the bargain—in an eight-year-old sort of way. I was doing whatever a teacher does and was apparently fairly involved in doing it, because I didn't hear the knock at the door.

Philip poked me with his pencil. "There's Miss Reardon and a bunch of people." I looked up and, sure enough, there was Miss Reardon, the principal, and "a bunch of people" standing in the doorway. The principal was wearing one of those smiles that says,

"We're supposed to be *happy* about this," although the look in her eye told me I might not be that easily convinced. "We have a little surprise for you—a new third grader," she said. "His name is Luciano and he only speaks Italian." After a few more words (I have no memory of them in panic-stricken state), Luciano's escorts left, and there he and I stood, hand in hand, alone in the doorway.

A hundred uninvited thoughts passed through my mind. "I can't handle this...They didn't prepare me for this kind of thing in college...I can't speak Italian...Where do I begin...and how...and help!"

No sooner had Luciano sat down at the one avilable desk than the whole class simultaneously descended upon him; they knew this was no ordinary new kid. Admittedly, I had not as yet invented any plan for introducing our new friend, but it was clear there had to be a better way than this. With the help of an evil stare, order was restored and I briefly told everyone about Luciano. Except it was actually they who did the telling. From the sidelines, they had taken in every last detail of the conversation at the door and were more than happy to provide an instant replay—who was there, what each said, who could speak English and who couldn't.

It was hard to tell what Luciano thought of his center-ring position. He seemed so small sitting there, hardly big enough to be a third grader. His eyes showed no particular fright but I imagined how confused he must be by all the words exchanged between the rest of us which made him the focal point of our attention yet also excluded him.

From those first few moments we established the tone that was to carry us through the year. "We're very lucky to have Luciano in our room," I said. "It's a big responsibility teaching someone the things they need to know to live in a new country. Miss Reardon must think we're grown up enough in here to handle the job." That

*Nancy Naumann, Third grade teacher, North Haven, Conn. Reprinted with permission from Learning Magazine, October, 1976.

the real reason for Luciano's placement was actually that our class was the smallest of the three third grades was immaterial. Children are in constant search of signs of their own maturity. To be recognized for this—and bestowed an honor in addition—is a matter of great significance. We were off to a good start.

The kids made an attempt to return to their reading chores as I unearthed a new box of crayons for Luciano and got him a piece of drawing paper. These implements speak for themselves with no invitation or explanation needed. He picked up a crayon and began designing what quickly became a very intricate airplane. He obviously had some talent in this area, for which I was glad. But at the same time, I hoped the year would develop more than his artistic inclinations.

I couldn't help smiling to myself as I pretended not to notice the many pairs of eyes stealing secret glances in the direction of Luciano, intent upon his sketching. I felt my own eyes traveling that same route as I gave myself a brief scolding for my initial defeatist reaction to this situation.

"How will we teach him?" I asked the class. "He doesn't speak English and we don't speak Italian."

"Lucy does," a voice echoed from the back of the room. "Lucy speaks Italian."

I looked back and there was Lucy—ironically, at the desk right beside Luciano—looking very embarrassed. I had quite forgotten that Lucy's family spoke Italian at home and was more than pleased to be reminded of it now. She was immediately elected official translator, and began demonstrating her skill by giving a few welcoming remarks.

I attempted to refocus our discussion. "Let's teach him French!" That idea came from a number of children who thought their suggestion brilliant. We had barely begun a study of the language ourselves; perhaps they thought Luciano would feel less awkward if we were all equally confused. Meanwhile, Walter was whooping around the room like an Indian, trying to interest us in a little instruction in the fine art of sign language.

Since our thoughts were on language, it seemed logical to contemplate the hierarchy of language development. We reviewed how we had gone about learning French and arrived at the first two steps of language learning: listening and speaking. We could see how this would eventually expand to include reading and writing.

"What vocabulary would be most essential for Luciano?" We made lists of different categories—numbers, colors, "classroom words," parts of the body, and so on. Then, because helpfulness was literally oozing out of everybody, we set about to do some teaching. With the help of a box of crayons, "red" and "blue" were mastered by lunchtime.

It had been an eventful morning. Luciano had 18 willing bodyguards to escort him to the cafeteria, and as many volunteers anxious to sit next to him, help him with his tray, open his carton of milk, and otherwise take care of him. He was being treated with a combination of reverence and doting affection. I made a mental note to remind the kids that we needed to make a distinction between just helping Luciano and helping him to help himself.

Teachers-room chatter is always slightly incoherent of Fridays, but on this day, the conversation seemed even more boisterous than usual. By the time I arrived, the news of the morning was known to all and the source of much amusement. Only two of the other teachers and I weren't laughing; there were three children in Luciano's family.

Two other teachers volunteered to help with our problem—the reading specialist and a fifth grade teacher who spoke Italian. Nothing too definite could ever be assumed from a Friday lunch period, but for now, moral support was sufficient.

Back in the classroom, it was obvious that the kids were taking their new teacher roles very seriously. They must have drilled Luciano on numbers from his first bite of fish fillet through his final mouthful of yesterday's chocolate cake, for now they could hardly wait to show off his expertise. Tentatively he counted from one to ten, and it was impossible to determine who was more pleased with his accomplishment—he or the rest of the class.

Music, next on our daily agenda, is one of the cheeriest parts of our day. We gather around the piano and belt out a few songs together. For those of us inclined to be actors, it's a real opportunity to perform, and for the more timid souls among us, a chance for some nonthreatening participation. Luciano created a new category all for himself: for those who can't communicate any other way, music truly is a universal language. Even a hum or some indistinct sounds blended with the other voices inspires a sense of belonging. "He's singing!" was the astounded declaration made by Lisa, whose face always radiates particular pleasure during the music period. And so he was. From that very first day he sang "like one of the gang."

I hoped the language of mathematics would be universal as well, but was not looking forward to explaining the system under which our individualized program operated. For now I would be satisfied doling out separate worksheets on different levels from which I would try to glean the extent of Luciano's skills. "When in Rome, do as the Romans"—but was there a reciprocal agreement? We would soon find out how our own new math corresponded to foreign standards.

That was painless enough. Eight-year-old concepts

are more or less eight-year-old concepts, regardless of nationality. No, math would not be too traumatic. Except for group work, life would be much simpler as he learned to think in English—as opposed to merely translating 7 to *sette* to *seven*.

The clock ticked on toward 3:00. Everybody would have willingly stayed through the weekend if only I had let them; suddenly school had much more appeal than it had previously. Personally, I wasn't the least bit disappointed when the dismissal bell sounded. The morning's idle thoughts of leaving school behind for two days were pipe dreams now. Would two days be long enough for a crash course in bilingual education?

I grabbed a couple of fourth grade alumni of the previous year as they headed for their bus and asked if they'd like to help me shop the next day for some language-oriented materials. Maybe walking up and down the aisles of a toy department would trigger some ideas that could eventually find expression in some cut-and-paste creations of my own or in old and forgotten toys the children might bring in from home.

Early Saturday morning the three of us embarked on a shopping spree. We scrutinized the shelves of our local discount store, contemplating the potential usefulness of this game and that book. We bought a readiness type workbook that dealt with letter-sound association and developed some high-frequency vocabulary as it progressed from A to Z. For the teacher, we invested in an English-Italian dictionary.

On Monday I headed straight for the school library's picture book department. *Yertle the Turtle* and *Curious George* are delightful when you can understand their humerous escapades. But where were the books with those big uncomplicated pictures of fire engines and farm animals? From the age of the dusty relics I finally uncovered, it would seem that the suburban elementary school seldom needs to concern itself with developing really basic vocabulary.

I did blow the cobwebs off a few books that met our qualifications, including a story about a grocer peddling some artistically distorted versions of fruits and vegetables, and a 1950s edition of Junior's trip to the zoo—in which Junior had such a short haircut that I expected he would be as much of an oddity as some of the animals.

The Media Center had more to offer. Early primary education must be building its concepts these days through those bigger-than-life graphic portrayals of "Community Helpers," "The World of Work," and the like, because the study-print department was overflowing with packets to meet every need. I borrowed as many as I could carry.

When a group of little girls met me in the hall to tell me Lucy was absent, I assumed this was their idea of a joke. Unfortunately, it was true. Luciano was sitting next to a vacant seat—no Lucy, no interpreter. We would have to bridge the language gap without her assistance today as we began seriously the journey from one world to another.

One quick trip through the alphabet confirmed the fact that sound-symbol relationships in the two languages are different, and I had a further hunch (later proven true) from the problems Luciano was having that some of our letters had no counterparts for him. We struggled together with this for a while, but I'm sure I was learning more about him and the task ahead of us than he was about our phonetic system.

Next we tried a large picture book (circa 1940) on modes of transportation. We skipped a few obsolete vehicles, such as horse-drawn milk wagons, and concentrated on more familiar ones—trains, boats, cars. I would point to the names of the things before saying them, and Luciano would sound them out with little difficulty. Several pronunciations were incorrect according to our phonic rules, but the speed and ease with which he did this led me to believe that in his own tongue he had probably been a fairly good reader. I resolved, therefore, not to exclude written English from his beginning language instruction. The printed word was not a threat to him and could aid him in unlocking this strange new code.

Even in her absence Lucy had not forgotten us, and during the afternoon she called to find out how things were going and to apologize for having a sore throat. That was the first time I'd had a sick child inquire as to *my* welfare. Her concern was well founded and much appreciated. I encouraged her to get well soon and hurry back to school. Happily, she returned the following day.

Monday afternoon, all involved parties met with the principal to outline the needs of Luciano and his brothers and to assess the personnel available for helping to meet these needs. It was decided that he and his fourth grade sibling would share the services each day of the reading specialist for one half hour and attend the Title 1 instructional clinic for a similar length of time. The rest would be up to the classroom teacher.

I must admit that I never had any carefully calculated plans to carry out my part of the bargain— no knowledge of which methods might be most appropriate. I used an eclectic approach. We worked first from the books and prints from the store and library, then with a dollhouse and some puzzles brought in by the children.

Initially we dealt with words in isolation—"mother," "father," "train," "truck." Colors and numbers were learned simultaneously, and before long we were able to string together three concepts in written form, such as "one blue ball," "two yellow birds." Luciano demonstrated his comprehension of these by drawing them on a paper divided into boxes—about eight such phrases per morning was our usual number. I tried to keep the work varied and at a lively pace to avoid its becoming boring, which could easily happen with an eight-year-old boy forced to relearn preschool concepts.

Gradually more abstract ideas were added: *big, little, in, out, happy, sad, stop, go*. These were easy to depict and their meanings got through quickly. Phrases soon became sentences. Sentences turned to short paragraphs.

Around this time I raided the reading specialist's supply closet and inventoried the selection of preprimers and related workbooks. I chose Houghton Mifflin's *Tigers, Lions* and *Dinosaurs* because they supplemented the word-picture comprehension unit we were working on and because mastery of their vocabulary might make it possible for Luciano to be placed in a basal more on grade level.

For the sake of diversity we digressed occasionally to enjoy a Scholastic paperback and to attempt the accompanying questions. Luciano regarded this as a major step forward because "paperbacks" was an activity pursued by the rest of the class; his work wasn't all that different any more. Writing and spelling came naturally to him. As soon as he gained the confidence to trust his knowledge of our linguistic patterns, he wrote and spelled as well as the average third grader.

For a month or so I stationed myself beside Luciano for morning work sessions; the other children came to his desk for help on their assignments. His wasn't the kind of work that could be done independently, and each task was too short to allow me to venture too far away from him.

Parents helped to alleviate this situation. At the beginning of the year I had implemented a volunteer program whereby a few parents donated their services to aid our reading program. They quickly became central figures in Luciano's education, combining their own resourcefulness with guidelines established by me. They took my place beside him and supervised word-picture associations, the completion of workbook pages, and written answers to book questions. They also established an index card file of vocabulary by category, and later acted as scribes as he dictated sentences or short stories which he then read back and copied in order to make the language truly his.

The kids themselves also assumed some of my work overload. Helping Luciano became one of the options available when other work was completed, and they seemed to thrive on the involvement: "May I help Luciano with his letters?" "Has anyone gone over his flash cards with him today?" "Can I teach him the Pledge of Allegiance?" Everyone got into the act.

Peer teaching had real benefits for one little boy in particular. Joey was still basically a nonreader and had too few occasions within the classroom to feel pride in his academic achievements. He developed a technique with the flash cards that was very efficient—first reviewing old and familiar vocabulary and then concentrating on the new, more difficult words, building separate piles for "mastery" and "nonmastery."

Joey's patience and ability to relate to those who learn more slowly also won him the position of "math tutor." While Luciano had a reasonable grasp of addition and subtraction, using them to deal with "carrying" and "borrowing" was another story. He could handle the mechanics of the process in group work by watching what the others did, but confronted with a page of examples of different types, he was lost. I concluded from this that the verbal input in math teaching is more important than I had thought. Numbers have no magic without the reasoning behind them.

Joey would fill the board with examples, then step back to watch his protege work them out. "No, no, Luciano, not that way. You can't take away a bigger number from a littler number." Joey never tired of repetition. He was quite content with the slow but very real progress of his student and approached his teacher role with dignity. Luciano, always very willing to cooperate with both his peer and parent tutors, thrived on the attention and praise.

A final member of our "teaching team" was a Language Master. One of our resource teachers provided Luciano with cards to feed this tape-recorder-based teaching device, and he plugged himself into it every day for a few minutes of practice exercises. The cards he inserted were mostly sentences emphasizing correct pronunciation—"*H* is for *house* and *horse*." "*C* is for *car* and *cow*." The earphone arrangement kept the lessons from disturbing the rest of the class and allowed Luciano to check his pronunciation against the model by playing the recorder back as many times as he wished before moving on to the new example.

Our eclectic approach rewarded us nicely. Being immersed in an environment with as much animated discussion as our room had couldn't help but promote listening skills. Speaking, reading and writing evolved in due time from the methods outlined here, as well as through the efforts of the reading specialist and the instructional clinician.

Both of these teachers used a more systematic approach than my own. The reading specialist confronted the business of syntax, singular and plural, negatives, subject-verb agreements, and tenses—on paper as well as in speech. She also dealt with other vocabulary by category. She preferred a linguistic approach.

Our Title 1 clinician was fairly fluent in Italian and was therefore able to communicate with Luciano more fully than the rest of us. Using an aural-oral approach, this teacher worked to strengthen vocabulary in English, but also dealt with the concepts which the words represented—orientation in time, opposites, money, and so on.

At the beginning, new vocabulary had a way of slipping away over a weekend or after an extended absence from school, because Luciano reverted to his native Italian at home. In general, though, progress was consistent right from the start. Someone in the school asked him, when he had been with us just about a week, if he had learned any English words yet. With perfect clarity and not a moment's hesitation he answered, "sit down." (Incidental learnings are often the ones that count.) I also remember his first pictorial representation of some words he was learning. The directions stated, "Make a teacher." Luciano made a tiger, complete with big mouth and fiery eyes. I convinced myself it was a honest mistake.

Luciano never lost the shyness with which he came to us; nor did he develop the independence I would have liked him to have—but that was due partly to his nature. He needed constant reassurance that he was doing his work correctly and was at my side continually for this purpose. "What's the matter?" I questioned one day after his third appearance to verify progress on one workbook page that I knew he could do without assistance. "Nothing's the matter," volunteered Maria, who was seeking help on her own assignment and really needed it; "he just wants to *see* you." I suspect she was right.

He caught on easily to the lyrics of the songs we sang, if not the corrrect season to which some belonged. Thus we honored requests for "Jingle Bells" in January, and didn't mind a chorus or two of "Peter Cottontail" after Easter was long gone.

Stories read aloud were hard for him to grasp and held his interest least well of all classroom activities. Social studies gave him similar problems. Third graders can get fairly involved discussing issues, and it bothered me that Luciano could never really communicate his ideas at these times. I wondered what thoughts lurked behind the language barrier and how lonely it must be to be unable to speak spontaneously as other children do.

He could—and did—become involved in hands-on kinds of social studies and science projects, and there was plenty of opportunity for that. The children worked in pairs on a SCIS "Populations" unit, and he was as intrigued as his partner as he gazed through the magnifier to find out about those funny-looking brown things in the salt-water solution. "They move!" he informed me as I stopped by his desk. And so they did. Luciano had discovered one of the attributes of animal life.

If the message was not a critical one, Luciano often chose to remain silent; he was a person of few words. In an emergency, however, the right words could be found. One afternoon, a colonial-cooking session, directed by one of our parent volunteers, yielded a pot of New England corn chowder. After their first spoonful, most of the children concurred that this dish ranked somewhere between brussels sprouts and pea soup on their list of food choices—and Luciano agreed. He wasted no time raising his hand and announcing, "I don't like this," and donating his cupful to the birds.

Each step forward was a victory not only for Luciano but for those who contributed to his success. Teachers know well the joy derived from seeing new knowledge awakened in a child. But children are seldom able to share this same wonderful experience.

As a group this class would perhaps never seek glory in academic achievements. Their favorite subject was social studies, with the accent on the "social," although initially they hardly excelled in person-to-person relationships. Their common interest in Luciano united them and taught them the meaning of compassion better than any lecture I might have given.

Together we introduced him to such American traditions as Halloween parties and valentines. The day of the Halloween parade, Luciano arrived at the school with no costume and no mask. A group of his classmates alerted me to the situation with much concern. "He *has* to have *something* to wear," they insisted. Improvising a costume preempted our penmanship exercises. We found a large shopping bag and quickly transformed it into a robot-type head. Then we put a blanket around him and added some jewels donated by a Halloween gypsy. The end result was something of a wealthy Indian from outer space— a respectable enough disguise.

Valentine's Day caught Luciano unprepared too. He didn't have any cards to pass out, but he opened each one he received with pure delight. "This one's from Mrs. Esposito...."I got two just the same!" He may not have known exactly what Valentine's Day was, but the spirit of love was certainly present.

Was the obvious boost to Luciano's self-concept an intended result or a by-product of the exuberance that came from our own sense of self-fulfillment? In this game, everyone would win. I often thought how wonderful it would be if each child who entered school could feel this same sense of concern for his well-being, this same realization that he had the unfailing support of every other person in the class.

I remember the cheers and applause Luciano

received the first time he wrote a story and read it to the class. Three short lines—certainly nothing outstanding—but it was a milestone for him, and his efforts were respected. We were all beginning to feel that sense of community which had seemed so far away in September.

Is there a moral to this story? Can we gain new insights into bilingual education from it? From our point of view, the important thing was that a new dimension of humanism was added to our classroom. We hoped we had given Luciano the basic tools he would need to communicate in this country, but he taught us a lot about communication too. Language suddenly gained new significance for us as words, our words, helped Luciano to relate to a world previously inaccessible to him. Words alone, though, don't constitute language. The happy feelings that this experience created among us found expression through more than verbal means—a touch of tenderness, a twinkle in the eye, a warm smile. They were the source of a new sense of comradeship, manifested more in spirit than in actual doings. Teacher and children alike learned a valuable lesson in the sensitivity and sharing that must be a part of any growing relationship.

Chapter 36
Italian Bilingual Education In The United States: A Historical Perspective
Angelo Gimondo*

Italian Bilingual Bicultural Education in the United States is a recent phenomenon. However, the study of the Italian language goes back to the early days of our history. Italian in this country was quite fashionable from early colonial days to the Civil War period. This interest in Italian was a direct consequence of the strong pro-Italian tradition which the Anglo-American colonies had inherited from England where Italian culture had been popular since the times of Chaucer. Thomas Jefferson, for instance was a notable inheritor and propagator of that tradition. In 1785, while pointing out to a young American friend the merits of an American college education in contrast with the defects of a European one, he indicated clearly his feeling that European languages were a vital part of a college curriculum and that American students ought to include Italian in their study of modern tongues: "But why send an American youth to Europe for education? What are the objects of a useful American education? Classical knowledge, modern languages, chiefly French, Spanish, and Italian; Mathematics, Natural philosophy, Natural history, Civil history, and Ethics."[1]

Prior to the Civil War, some northern universities, as well as Jefferson's University of Virginia, included Italian studies in their curricula. Emigrant Italian intellectuals became the driving force behind the establishment of courses in Italian culture and language in New York City. A restless revolutionary spirit sent Orazio de Attelis here in the 1820's; he later opened his own school for teaching Italian in Manhattan, and he lectured in Italian history at Columbia University. Perhaps the most famous teacher of all was Lorenzo da Ponte, the noted Mozart librettist, who taught Italian at Columbia from 1825 until his death in 1838. And his son, Lorenzo L. da Ponte, became the first teacher of Italian at New York University where he served until 1840.[2]

Generally, the intellectual climate in the early history of the new nation was more favorable to Italian-language study than it is today.[3] Knowledge of Italian influenced the thinking of some eminent American intellectuals, scholars, and artists. Among the numerous native italiantes were the already-mentioned Jefferson, the two Adamses, Edward Everett, J. S. Chamberlain, Edward Rutledge, Longfellow, Bryant, Irving, Poe, Emerson, and Hawthorne. Some of these were the first to produce translations and studies of Italian literature in this country; some even championed the cause of Italian democracy.

Strange as it may seem, the influx of Italian immigrants in the second half of the century negatively affected the study of Italian in this country. There seems to be very little doubt about the attitude of Americans toward the new type of immigrants and its relationship to the decline of Italian studies in the United States. The new immigrants were not generally people of the educated middle and upper classes but workers and peasants, most of whom were illiterate. In *Beyond the Melting Pot*, Glazer and Moynihan provide striking evidence of the size of this influx and point out that even the Italian-language press had difficulty reaching this new undereducated population:

[Mass]migration from Italy did not begin until the 1870's. Then it became modern history's greatest and most sustained movement of population from a single country. This migration was a proletarian one, made up of peasants and landless laborers, large numbers of craftsmen and building workers, and much smaller numbers of professional people......Illiteracy seriously hampered the development of settlements into a single ethnic group, for differences in dialect, which in turn engendered mutual suspicion, tended to endure in the absence of widespread written communication. The Italian press was hampered not only by the illiteracy of its clientele but also by the existence of a great gap between the ordinary spoken language and the official language of the press.

In the last quarter of the century the study of Italian was also negatively affected by arbitrary college requirements which excluded all language except

*Angelo Gimondo, Assistant Administrator, Center for Bilingual Education, Program Planning and Implementation Unit, New York City Board of Education.

French and German. This situation did not improve until the 1920's when, largely through the encouragement of Mario Cosenza and Leonard Dovello, the enrollment in Italian-language courses in New York City high schools rose from a mere 898 in 1921 to 16,000 in 1937.[4] Many of these gains were attributed to Dean Cosenza's questionnaire which ascertained that 364 institutions of higher learning were willing to accept Italian as an entrance requirement.

Events of the 1930's and World War II, of course, dealt a crippling blow to the study of Italian, and by the end of the war Italian had disappeared from two-thirds of the schools.

The pattern of declining enrollment in Italian language classes during the post-war years has begun to change significantly. In New York City high schools, for example, the enrollment figure for the academic year 1974-75 was 6,658, an increase of almost 575 students over the previous year. If we include data from the elementary and junior high schools, the figure increases to a respectable 18,667. Such progress is expected to continue, especially in this age when the melting-pot concept is being replaced by the idea of cultural pluralism, and bilingual education is becoming increasingly more accepted by educators and ethnic communities throughout the United States.

Italian bilingual bicultural education which was introduced in 1972 in the Boston public schools as a result of legislation passed by the State of Massachusetts, contributed significantly to the growing enrollment of students of Italian.

Italian bilingual programs in the United States were initiated as a result of the growth of bilingual education in general and in response to the large numbers of immigrants arriving from Italy since the liberalization of immigration laws.

The Center for Migration Studies reports that the largest percentage of recent Italian immigrants settle in New York and New Jersey. The other states with concentrations of Italian immigrants are Connecticut, Illinois, Massachusetts, Pennsylvania and California.

Since the liberalization of United States Immigration Laws in 1965, the number of Italian immigrants has grown a great deal. The volume of immigration has remained consistently above 20,000 per year. To this number, one must add approximately five to six thousand illegal aliens who enter the country every year. Furthermore, large numbers of non-immigrant Italians are constantly entering the United States. For example, in 1972, over 150,000 Italians were admitted into the country as students, trade commissioners, tourists, etc. Most of them settle in New York City.

The majority of Italians who settle in the United States come from the rural south where economical conditions are least favorable. They often settle in the same area as people from the same region or town. Therefore, it is not unusual to find in one neighborhood, large numbers of people from the same town.

Since most Italians tend to settle in the New York Metropolitan area, New York City has, by far, the largest Italian bilingual program of any city in the nation.

The population of Italian children of limited English speaking ability in the New York City public schools is approximately five to six thousand.

Presently, there are eight districts and three high schools in New York City that have Italian bilingual programs servicing a total of approximately 1,800 students. Other Italian bilingual programs have been established in Boston, Chicago, Connecticut, Denver, Hoboken, Louisiana and various parts of New York State such as Syracuse and Long Island.

While mass media and compulsory education have increased exposure to standard Italian and have resulted in a leveling off of regional dialectal variations, most of the Italian immigrant children entering American schools continue to speak the regional dialect in the home.

Divorced from the continous re-enforcement of standard Italian which they would have received had they remained in Italy, their main exposure to Italian in America must come from the school system. For those children entering school for the first time in kindergarten or first grade, Italian-speaking skills are generally the most deficient. As a result, the bilingual program is left with the dual task of developing proficiency in both English and standard Italian.

While Anderson and Boyer (1970) question the desirability of bilingual education for Italian dominant students, in view of dialect diversities, the experience in New York City dispels concern over communication problems and comprehension of materials written in standard Italian. The general practice followed is for the teacher to speak only standard Italian, while the children communicate in dialect as proficiency in the standard variety is developed.

Students are encouraged to learn Italian as the language of education and wider communication. Dialect, it is explained, is the language of more informal social situations.

While most Italian bilingual programs are of a transitional nature reflecting strong assimilation patterns of the Italian-American community, every effort should be made to develop literacy skills in Italian. Such instruction should continue when the child has been removed from the bilingual program and placed in the mainstream. Literacy skills must be based upon well-developed speaking and listening skills. The question is, therefore, faced with the task of developing these skills in two relatively unfamiliar languages, English and standard Italian, how may this be accomplished most effectively and efficiently? This problem is solved very satisfactorily in District #32, New York City where perhaps the best Italian bilingual program in the country is functioning.

Dr. Rosemary Salomone-Levy, the Project Director of that program recommends a team teaching approach, especially in the early grades utilizing an Italian-dominant and English-dominant teacher. While both teachers should be bilingual, each will communicate with the students in the dominant language, while students may respond in either language and be understood by the teacher. She further recommends that the use of two languages be separate, not only as to person, but also as to time and place. This may be accomplished through the use of two separate but adjacent classrooms, one creating a totally American "language acquisition context" and the other, a totally Italian one through the use of instructional materials, textbooks, and audio-visual aides appropriate to the respective languages and culture.

The time element may be handled through an alternate days or a morning/afternoon approach with each teacher responsible for reading and language arts, as well as for certain content areas. The language of instruction in the content area may change over time. For example, while initial instruction in mathematics may be in Italian, the transitional program should switch to mathematics in English as early as possible, as this is the one area least depended upon verbal ability.

One of the problems faced by administrators of Italian bilingual programs is of an organizational type, since often there aren't sufficient children to form a complete bilingual track. In order to deal with this problem it is recommended that open classroom and Montessori approaches be utilized. Materials have been another area of concern. To date, most materials used in Italian bilingual programs have been imported from Italy. However, with the establishment of the Northeast Regional Curriculum Development Center which has an Italian component, it is hoped that more relevant materials of instruction will be developed in the near future.

Recently, the Italian Bilingual Educators Association (IBEA) was formed in New York City in order to deal with the problems faced by Italian Bilingual Educators in the areas of curriculum, teacher training, instructional materials, methodology and community attitudes. The organization, though New York based, is encouraging the establishment of chapters in States where there are large numbers of Italian dominant.

In conclusion, I should like to say that, while a great deal of progress has been made in the area of Italian bilingual education, much remains to be done. It is hoped that legislation mandating bilingual education and organizational activities, will help in reaching the desired goal.

FOOTNOTES

[1] Enzo Ficile, *Storia degli Italiani di New York* (New York: Italian-American Center for Urban Affairs, Inc., 1975), pp. 23-25.

[2] Fuciala, *op. cit.*, pp. 60-73.

[3] Nathan Glazer and Daniel Patrick Moynihan, *Beyond the Melting Pot* (Cambridge: The M. I. T. Press, 1963), pp. 182-186.

[4] Fucilla, *op. cit.*, p. 261.

Chapter 37
Bilingual Education for Native Americans
Dale Little Soldier and Leona Foerster*

Introduction

One of the most promising trends in Indian education is the development of bilingual programs for Native American pupils (Foerster and Little Soldier, 1975). On the other hand, bilingual education has become one of the salient issues in Indian education with both protagonists and antagonists offering sound rationales for their respective positions. Perhaps the issue is not so much the viability of bilingual education for Native Americans in general. Instead, the more specific questions of: for whom? when and for how long? and what kind of bilingual program will best fit the needs of the children to be served? appear to provide the fuel for the fire which has clouded the whole issue of bilingual programs and polarized educators who are concerned with providing optimum educational experiences for Indian pupils.

It is impossible to do justice to the entire topic of Native American bilingual education in an article of this length. However, first, the present authors will attempt to provide the reader with an historical perspective of Native American bilingual programs including the present status. The matter of bilingual programs for Indian pupils is a complex one. Thus next the authors hope to point out to the reader something of the complexity of this issue and the problems involved. Finally, it is the intent of this article to provide some general guidelines for the planning and implementation of bilingual programs in schools which serve Indian students.

Historical Perspective and Present Status

It is important for the reader to understand that bilingual education for Native Americans is quite recent in origin. Historically, the thrust of Indian education as provided by the federal government through the Bureau of Indian Affairs (BIA) was one of cultural annihilation and total assimilation of the Indian into the mainstream of American society. Not only were the vast linguistic and cultural differences among Indian tribes ignored, but rather the attempt was to provide schooling which would "civilize" the population and make Indians over into "good Americans." Boarding schools were provided which removed the children from the supposedly "negative" influences of home and tribe and to make cultural destruction more efficient and effective. Children were punished for speaking tribal languages in school and practicing the customs of their tribe. Schools for Indians were controlled largely by white educators who had little understanding of or appreciation for the wealth of culture and language brought to school by the Indian pupils with whom they worked. Education for citizenship and vocations was basic government policy up until the sixties. (For an excellent historical description of Indian education in the United States the reader is referred to a 1972 volume entitled, *To Live on This Earth* by Fuchs and Havighurst.)

Not all Indian students attend BIA schools. The BIA schools presently supplement but do not replace public school systems which also serve many Indian youngsters. Approximately a fourth of the more than 200,000 Indian students attend Federal schools; about two-thirds or 134,000 attend local public schools; around 18,000 are enrolled in mission or other private schools (Bureau of Indian Affairs, 1973, p. 6). The BIA maintains a position of encouraging pupils to enroll in public schools when possible.

Regardless of the type of school in which the Indian child was enrolled, however, until the sixties, the major goal of Indian education remained to help the Indian assimilate. The shift in philosophy which gradually occurred in the sixties resulted first in an awareness of and respect for Indian cultures and languages. The dreadful failure of American education to meet the needs of Indian pupils could no longer be ignored. Something indeed was very wrong and the prognosis was not good. Attempts to pinpoint possible causes for the educational ills of Indian pupils determined that the informal education brought to school by Indian

*Dale Little Soldier, Mandan/Hidatsa Indian and a graduate student at Texas Tech. University.
*Dr. Leona Foerster, Professor of Education, Texas Tech. University, Lubbock, Texas.

children not only simply did not mesh with school experiences but at times clashed violently. As a result, major efforts were launched to provide English as a Second Language (ESL) training for Indian pupils who came to school with little or no facility in the English language. It appears that Indian pupils and their parents by and large do accept the need to learn and study English if they are to function adequately in American society today (Fuchs and Havighurst, 1972, pp. 206-207). However, gradually parents and Indian educators came to perceive that in addition to competency in English, there was a need for preserving tribal languages and cultures as well. Thus Indian education has undergone a drastic metamorphosis. Shifting from an era in which the use of Indian languages was forbidden, the BIA, along with state departments of education and local school districts, is attempting to provide bilingual/bicultural programs in many schools where the need and interest in such programs exist.

It is difficult to estimate the number of children who enter school with little or no facility in English. In BIA schools, the estimate is about two-thirds of the children attending these schools (Fuchs and Havighurst, 1972, p. 207). The greatest need for bilingual programs seems to be among Navajo children who reside on the vast Navajo reservation which is comprised of 16 million acres which sprawl across the northern portions of Arizona and New Mexico and a section of southern Utah. Some of the cultural and linguistic implications of teaching these children have been outlined by one of the present authors (Foerster, 1974). Another crucial need has been among Alaskan native children. Efforts toward meeting the needs for bilingual programs for these two populations follow.

The Rough Rock Demonstration School on the Navajo reservation in Arizona has attracted national attention for its innovative efforts in the area of bilingual/bicultural education. Rough Rock is a BIA contract school which means that it is operated by the Navajos themselves with BIA funding. Its purpose was to create a school more responsive to the needs of the Indial community it serves. Bilingual/bicultural education is provided in all grades for Navajo pupils who attend this school. A wealth of culturally relevant curriculum materials has been produced at this school and disseminated for use in other schools serving Navajo children. Rough Rock is not unique, however, Noteworthy bilingual programs at other BIA schools on the Navajo reservation in Arizona include the Toyei Boarding School and Rock Point Boarding School. Bilingual education has spread to other schools serving Navajos including public and private schools. However, many of these programs are for younger children only and the use of Navajo language may be minimal in the upper grades. Head Start programs frequently are bilingual/bicultural in nature, responding to the crucial need for making early experiences for children in schools comfortable and for developing positive concepts of self and feelings of adequacy.

Bilingual education in Alaska is noteworthy too. The Southwestern Alaska Bilingual Program was developed as a means of preserving the Eskimo language and identity in the Yupik-speaking area of the state (Bureau of Indian Affairs, 1973, pp. 8-9). This program was begun as a pilot study in 1970 in Southwestern Alaska where Yupik is the dominant language among the 18,000 Eskimos who reside there. Students in the program are taught mainly in Yupik dialect of Eskimo with short periods each day devoted to the study of English as a foreign language. The major thrust of the program is to help students become literate in both Eskimo and English. Eskimo is stressed in the early grades and as children proceed through school, more and more emphasis is placed upon learning in English. The original program which involved four schools has been extended to include at least nine others. The University of Alaska has begun training bilingual Eskimos from Southwestern Alaska as teachers and teaching materials continue to be developed. Research data gathered from this project support its continuation. In addition, parents and students are enthusiastic about the program.

Many other bilingual programs for Native Americans have surfaced recently, too. Just a few will be mentioned here. For example, an excellent bilingual program has been developed at the elementary school on the Rocky Boy Reservation, Montana. At this school, the writers observed an impressive emphasis on Cree language and culture, the development of an array of curriculum materials and provision of a culturally relevant atmosphere within the school. The school is part of an independent public school district and it is controlled by an all-Indian, five-member school board. Federal funds have helped Rocky Boy in the development and implementation of their program.

The Wisconsin Native American Language and Culture Project (Roth, 1976) began in 1972 and had three primary goals. The first was to locate Wisconsin Indians who spoke their tribal language and to train them as teachers and resource persons. The second thrust was to develop instructional and reference materials in the five tribal languages—Chippewa, Oneida, Menominee, Potawatomi, and Winnebago—and to keep them from disappearing forever. The last goal was to provide linguistic and educational advisory services to language programs and other cultural and education projects for Native Americans in Wisconsin. Because of the number of languages involved and the research and development efforts which were needed, this program is still in its infancy. Early reports appear quite favorable, however, and educators involved in the program are looking forward to continued growth and expansion.

Space prohibits a complete listing of bilingual/ bicultural programs for Native Americans currently underway. In addition to the programs cited above, it should be noted that almost every state with a sizeable population of Indians has made serious efforts toward providing bilingual instruction in schools serving these pupils. In Oklahoma, the state containing the largest proportion of Indians, efforts to teach Cherokee children initially in their native language have been initiated in the eastern portion of the state. California, New Mexico, the Dakotas, Montana, etc. all provide some degree of bilingual education for their Native American population. It goes without saying that bilingual education has been established as a viable alternative for many Indian pupils, particularly in the early years. It has been successful in meeting its goals, has been well-received and should be expected to continue to increase in the future. Why, then, is bilingual education such a controversial topic? Delving into some of the problems involved should help shed some light on this matter.

Related Problems and Issues

Perhaps one of the most basic issues in bilingual education is that not all Native American parents favor it. Among Pauites and Shoshones in northern Nevada, for example, an informal survey of parents residing on the reservation outside of the community of Fallon revealed that most were opposed to the teaching of the tribal language in the schools, Objections given were that these languages were dying out and thus no longer useful for communication; since proficiency in English is necessasry to succeed in present-day America, that is what should be taught; the schools should not be involved in teaching the culture and language. Because many parents came through the educational system at a time when the speaking of their tribal language was prohibited, it is understandable that they may be confused by this change in philosophy and lack understanding of the rationale behind bilingual programs. Some parents may be aware of their own English deficiencies and how these deficiencies may have prevented them from going further in school or obtaining jobs they wanted. Thus, parents may be understandably concerned with the acquisition of English by their offspring in school so that their children may have social, economic and educational opportunities which they themselves feel were denied because of lack of English proficiency.

The All Pueblo Tribal Council has gone on record for opposing the teaching of language and culture in the schools (Fuchs and Havighurst, 1972, p. 212). The Council reasoned that the learning of language and culture among Pueblo Indians is the responsibility of the families. School is viewed primarily as the means of helping students acquire the skills, including language, necessary to survive in the non-Indian world. Certainly this is a point of view that needs to be respected.

In addition to the fact that many Indian parents oppose bilingual education for a variety of reasons, other problems abound. Among the most serious is the lack of an adequate supply of qualified teachers for such programs. Sometimes this problem is dealt with by employing bilingual community persons as aides in the schools and utilizing such persons to help in the implementation of bilingual materials. At other times, the thrust is toward recruiting native speakers into teacher training programs utilizing such lures as stipends and scholarships, and offering college courses on the reservation. On some reservations, Rocky Boy for example, aides work toward certification while on the job. Because the learning of Indian languages is difficult, it appears a more rational course to train persons who are native speakers to become teachers rather than to teach the monolingual speaker the tribal tongue. Progress is being made to remediate this problem but a great need for bilingual teachers in many programs continues to exist.

The matter of bilingual education becomes even more complex when one considers the linguistic variation displayed by the Native American population. It is simply not the same situation one finds among Mexican Americans in the Southwest who speak Spanish as a first language, Chinese in San Francisco, or Puerto Ricans in New York. Something of the linguistic diversity involved may be grasped by making even a cursory study of Indian languages. At least fifty-eight distinct linguistic families of languages of North American Indian tribes have been identified. It has been estimated that there may have been more than three hundred very different Indian languages spoken in North America, many of which were mutually unintelligible, at the time Columbus blundered to our shores as a result of gigantic navigational error. Many of these languages are still in existence today. Within one state, for example New Mexico, the researcher will find an array of languages spoken ranging from the related languages of Navajo and Apache to Hopi, Zuni and a vast variety of languages and dialects spoken in the various Pueblos north of Albuquerque. The five major languages of Wisconsin were mentioned earlier. Each state in which a sizeable proportion of Indians is to be found will contain Native Americans of diverse cultural and linguistic backgrounds.

Large urban areas, too, may attract Indians from all over the country. Dallas, for example, is purported to have up to 10,000 Indians residing within its limits. At a recent pow-wow held in the Dallas area and attended by one of the writers, the diversity of the Indian population in the Dallas area was quite obvious in the array of colorful and diverse costumes worn by participants in the Indian dancing. Obviously, a single bilingual program would be inappropriate for a large urban area. Also, the Indian population is so scattered among the schools as to restrict the feasibility of implementing any bilingual educational program within the area's schools.

The fact that the Indian languages were unwritten further hinders the development of many bilingual programs. As in the Wisconsin Native American Language and Culture Project cited earlier, the first hurdle to be surmounted was that of developing a written system for the five languages involved in the project. Until such a system becomes a reality, the production of curriculum materials in the languages involved is an impossibility. Such a system requires the intense study of linguists and demands a block of time in which to accomplish this goal. Thus some may feel that the time, money, and effort which is involved in producing written materials in the native language may simply not be worth it. And perhaps it isn't if interest is lacking and the demand for a bilingual program is minimal.

Conflicts over the scope of bilingual programs exist, too. Some educators feel that bilingual programs are a viable alternative in kindergarten and early grades only—to ease the child into school. Others feel that language and culture are inextricably bound and should be reinforced throughout the student's school experience; that literacy both in the tribal language and English is extremely important; that instruction in both languages should continue into the secondary school and beyond.

Tribal politics may get in the way of some bilingual programs. Funding problems are a reality, also. Federal and state monies are available for bilingual programs. But proposals have to be written and program design must be accomplished. Some public school districts simply don't want Federal or state monies because of the administrative red tape involved and the "strings" which may be attached. It is unfortunate when bilingual education is denied pupils on the basis of such reasons. However, these are real stumbling blocks that have hampered the development or expansion of bilingual programs in some locales where the need exists.

Guidelines for Program Planning and Implementation

The continuation of bilingual programs for Native American pupils is likely to occur in the future. However, careful assessment of needs and adequate planning procedures should precede any efforts to expand bilingual education for Native Americans. The writers would like to suggest a list of questions which might be used to guide the planning implementation of bilingual programs for Indian children. The list follows:

(1) Has a community assessment been made? Are parents in favor of the program?

(2) What is the dominant language of the pupils to be served by the program?

(3) Is the language (or languages) spoken in the homes? To what extent?

(4) Has a written system of the language been developed? What written materials are available?

(5) What community resources exist?

(6) Who will be involved in the planning and administration of the program?

(7) How will parent/community involvement be assured?

(8) What will be the major goals of the program?

(9) How will the program be monitored?

(10) Has the scope of the program been determined?

(11) What monies are available and how may they be obtained?

(12) What testing procedures will be employed? Who will test and for what purposes?

(13) What in-service training will be needed?

(14) What curriculum materials will be needed? How will they be created or obtained?

(15) What outside expertise will be necessary?

(16) What are the benefits which will be derived by children participating in the program.

(17) Are the personnel who will be involved in the program *convinced* that the program is worthwhile and *determined* that it will succeed?

(18) Is it worth the time and money which will be required for program implementation?

The responses to questions like these suggested here should provide program planners with the data needed to make rational decisions about the kind of program which should be developed if indeed signals indicate that the program should receive a green light. There is no single answer to the question of bilingual programs for Native Americans. The local community served by the school must be involved in the decision-making of all such programs. No single model could possibly meet the needs of the various local situations. The wisest course of action in some cases may be to provide no bilingual education at all. Perhaps ESL is the answer instead. In other cases, a limited bilingual program may offer the wisest alternative. The local situation must dictate the choice of language programs to be employed in the schools.

Although the controversies which surround the topic of bilingual education for Native American pupils are not likely to subside in the near future, it is reasonable to state that such programs will continue to be developed and expanded and that good results will be produced. What is most important to note, then, is that bilingual education is a reality for many Native American pupils who are being offered an educational opportunity which simply did not exist for their parents. Through these programs, they are being helped to develop positive concepts of self and a sense of prideful identity which should enable them to function more effectively both in the Indian and non-Indian world and to lead fuller and richer lives.

SUMMARY

Bilingual Education for Native Americans

Bilingual education is a promising trend and

controversial issue in Indian education. Problems surround the planning and implementation of bilingual programs. Local situations must determine the kinds of programs to be offered.

BIBLIOGRAPHY

Bureau of Indian Affairs, *Indian Education: Steps to Progress in the 70's.* Washington, D. C.: U.S. Department of the Interior, 1973.

Foerster, Leona M. and Little Soldier, Dale, "What's New and Good in Indian Education Today?" *Educational Leadership*, Vol. 33, No. 3. Washington, D. C.: Association for Supervision and Curriculum Development, 1975.

Foerster, Leona M. "Teaching the Navajo Child: Cultural and Linguistic Implications." Texas Tech. Journal of Education, Vol. 1, Nos. 2 and 3. Lubbock, Texas: Texas Tech. Press, 1974.

Fuchs, Estelle and Havighurst, Robert, *To Live On This Earth.* New York: Doubleday and Company, 1972.

Roth, Edith Brill, "Lato: Lats—Hunting in the Indian Languages." *American Education*, Vol. 12, No. 7. Washington, D. C.: U.S. Department of Health Education, and Welfare, 1976.

Chapter 38
The Resurgence of Welsh
Frederick Shaw*

Recent explosions of violence have reminded us of the role that language often plays in political strife. In South Africa, for example, an attempt to teach the Afrikaans language in black schools led to bloody riots, evoking shuttle diplomacy by Dr. Henry Kissinger. The death of a New York police officer who handled a bomb manufactured by Croatian nationalists and hijackers is another case in point. Finally, the execution of Basque terrorists by the Spanish government not long before elicited protests in many European capitals. Their respective languages, of course, play salient roles in the Basque and Croatian autonomy movements.

By way of contrast, Welsh dissidents have been relatively moderate in their political demands. Only a small minority adheres to the Plaid Cymru, the Welsh nationalist party, and its strategy stresses peaceful rather than violent methods. In the absence of sensational (read "newsworthy") incidents generated by this source, few Americans have become aware of the resurgence of Welsh culture. The pages that follow, based on visits in 1976 with Dr. E. Glynn Lewis, a Welsh scholar living near Cardiff, and the Education Office for Wales in that city, as well as a perusal of relevant literature on the subject in London's British Museum, will focus largely on one phase of that renaissance, the Welsh system of education.

The Welsh demonstrate their pride on their language's antiquity when they inform the visitor that theirs is the oldest living language in Europe. Two waves of invaders brought Celtic languages to the British Isles in the 6th and 4th centuries B.C. A definitive separation took place between two distinct dialects in the 5th century A.D. The Brythonic, now spoken in Wales, Cornwall, and Brittany, had partially merged with Latin, the language of the Roman conquerors, while the Goedelic, the native language of Ireland, Scotland, and the Isle of Man, was spoken by groups outside Roman dominion. Welsh is also distinguished by a rich literature that began in the 14th century. These facts provide a rationale for Welsh biculturalism.

For centuries the Welsh were a partially submerged people (despite the fact that the Tudor dynasty on the

English throne—1483-1603—was Welsh). Their language was not considered fashionable nor was it used by intellectuals. It was, in fact, considered a laboring classes *patois*. What is more, as a group the Welsh did not adhere to the Church of England. This was underscored by the fact that beginning with the late 17th century, nonconformist schools in Wales started offering instruction in the Welsh vernacular. Missions of the Church of England followed suit, for they discovered that instruction in English was ineffective: it was a foreign langage to most of the indigenous population. Denominational colleges also deliberately prepared theologican students for preaching in the Welsh language.

Following the establishment of universal free public education in Wales (1842), many voices were raised in favor of teaching Welsh in state-supported schools. At the turn of the century, Welsh gradually began to appear in these institutions, first as an optional subject for the children of the "upper classes," then as a foreign language. As early as 1912, about half the pupils in Cardiff studied Welsh. By 1926 a pattern was emerging in the Rhondda Valleys: Welsh became the medium of instruction in infants' schools (ages 5 to 7). Eleven secondary schools (ages 11-18) taught Welsh as a language, and they were encouraged to employ it as well for curricular offering as far as possible.

From the 1930's to 1950 the use of Welsh as the medium of instruction in primary schools in geographic areas in which Welsh was the indigenous language gradually took hold. They were located largely in the northern and eastern sections. The more populated (industrialized) sections of the south and east had been Anglicized, and their primary schools were conducted almost exclusively in English. In the latter regions, however, a quiet but distinct shift in thinking was taking place, particularly among parents whose ethnic origins were Welsh. They began to realize that they had been partly uprooted from their origins (largely as a result of their English education), and they

*Dr. Frederick Shaw, Director, Research and Statistics, Office of Bilingual Education, New York City Board of Education.

were anxious to have their children's ethnic identities restored. In Northern and Eastern Wales, which was less Anglicized, a Director of Education initiated comparable education. Accordingly, in 1939, the first school in an Anglicized area specifically designated as bilingual, a private school on Cardogan Bay, was established. Since then, Welsh education authorities have made strenuous efforts to promote education of this kind, for the decennial census returns have revealed considerable losses in speakers of the language.

As we have seen, the events outlined above took place between the 1930's and the 1950's, chiefly in Northern and Western Wales, the principal regions in which Welsh is spoken indigenously. In those regions, the schools are predominantly Welsh-speaking. (During the last few years they have partly restored English in order to prepare their pupils for grammar schools in which education is conducted almost exclusively in that language. As a matter of fact, until 1956 there were no secondary schools which were Welsh-speaking or bilingual.) In 1962 Mr. Gwilyam Humphreys became principal of the first bilingual Welsh school of this kind in an Anglicized area. It was a comprehensive school. That is, it accepted pupils with varying degrees of scholastic ability. Recent years have witnessed a steady expansion of Welsh bilingual schools in the Anglicized areas. Among them 52 are primary schools (ages 5 to 11) and eight secondary schools (ages 11 to 16). Two more bilingual secondary schools are now in the offing.

Paradoxically, bilingual education has made remarkable progress in recent years because the use of the Welsh language has been declining, a trend documented by successive decennial censuses. In 1840, for example, more than two-thirds of the population of Wales spoke Welsh, and about half of these were monolingual. Today, according to Dr. E. Glynn Lewis, only 26 percent of the population speaks Welsh at all. About 8 percent speak it as their native language, many being uncomfortable in English; about 6 percent, fluently; about 8 percent were brought up in Welsh, but speak English as well as Welsh (largely as a result of schooling and the need for the use of English at work); about 4 percent obviously learned it as a second language. The highest proportion of speakers of Welsh lies in Northern and Western Wales (areas to which Welsh militants have asked the Welsh population to withdraw). These are regions that are relatively sparsely populated. Paradoxically, the largest group of speakers of Welsh, in the aggregate, lie in the Anglicized areas of Wales, in the South and East.

These regions are predominantly English in speech, but they contain the greatest numbers of Wales' residents.

How may we account for the constant encroachment of English on native Welsh? A publication of the former Ministry of Education offers the following reasons:

1. The greatest reservoir of Welsh speakers has been in agricultural areas. These areas have witnessed a constant exodus of laborers.

2. Many Welsh, in fact, have emigrated to England, where a high degree of intermarriage has taken place. The children born of these marriages speak English.

3. In Welsh towns, the progress in means of travel and communication have led to increased degrees of Welsh tourism and more time spent on radio, television, and the cinema. All have proven Anglicizing influences.

4. The central government has pursued a policy of "afforestation" in Wales, bringing in forestry workers from English-speaking parts of the United Kingdom.

5. Industrialization in Wales has attracted many English-speaking families. In addition, the superintendents and foremen were frequently English.

6. World War II drew many young men and women out of areas where they would have been exposed to Welsh during their most impressionable and formative years.

7. The evacuation of children during that war brought many English-speaking children from large cities into the remotest regions of Wales. Demographic movements of this kind tended to dilute the strength of Welsh in its native land.

8. The Welsh have failed to adapt their language to science and mathematics. In an age of technology, that means instruction in these subjects must necessarily be in English.

In recent years, a remarkable change has taken place in the popular attitude towards learning Welsh in "state-aided schools." (The term, "public schools," of course, does not mean the same thing in the United Kingdom as in the United States.) Formerly the study of Welsh was not considered appropriate for the intelligentsia. Welsh, in fact was considered a proletarian or non-intellectual language, used by a submerged subnationality.

Today the climate of opinion has changed. Many professional parents want their children to learn Welsh, and some have become quite militant on the subject. Welsh is considered a proper subject for intelligent pupils with good future prospects, partly because their parents do not want these children to lose their identities in an English world (as these parents began to lose their own), partly because those same parents believe a study of another language, particularly one that is indigenous to the area, will help their children develop more well-rounded personalities. Certain forward-looking educators have been eager to promote the progress of Welsh, to forestall the disappearance of the language. The result has been a steady, impressive growth of bilingual education with both English and Welsh as mediums of instruction.

This trend was accelerated when educators found that children of above average intelligence who pursued courses in bilingual education tended to attain higher levels of achievement than their peers who did not. Analysis of the differences, however, indicated that they were not statistically significant.

Several final observations follow.

1. As they gained experience in this area, Welsh educators found that they could establish bilingual programs for younger children than previously believed possible.

2. Public education does *not* fall into two distinct areas—bilingual education and all the rest. Bilingual education has a great deal in common with other types of education. However, it has its own distinct requirements and needs.

3. In the course of my interviews, I found school administrators and scholars agreed on one principle: educational decisions and educational administration are best conducted by competent and experienced professionals.

By and large, efforts to promote Welsh bilingual education in the twentieth century have produced gratifying results. The following influences help account for this relative success:

●Enlightened public opinion in Wales and the Welsh educators appear to agree that the Welsh language should be maintained, perhaps even restored, among members of the rising generation.

●Educators' views about this controversial area do not appear to be marked by deep cleavages (although Welsh militants tend to espouse more drastic measures than the rank and file of their colleagues). All groups apparently concur on the desirability of bilingual education.

●Professional educators are convinced that this area of education requires trained and experienced teachers and administrators. What is more, they recommend that the best available staff be employed for this purpose.

●They have also thrown the full weight of the profession behing this endeavor, including not only school personnel, but also top management, curriculum experts, researchers, university scholars, and the like.

●A remarkable shift in thinking has taken place, both within the profession and among the more enlightened sectors of the public. The study of the Welsh language and curricular instruction in Welsh was once regarded as a proletarian enterprise. Today middle class and professional parents—both in the indigenous Welsh-speaking and Anglicized areas of Wales—appear anxious to provide bilingual education for their children. A vernacular once regarded as lowbrow is now deemed appropriate for the most intelligent and promising youngsters, partly to maintain their identity, partly to assure them a more well-rounded background than would be possible under a system of monoglot instruction.

The Welsh experience with bilingual education suggests the conditions which may promote the establishment and maintenance of successful programs in bilingual settings. They are the following:

1. The community should regard bilingual education in a favorable light, for this form of education rises or falls in the context of its political and cultural environment. The good will of the professional and managerial classes is particularly important.

2. The general public may favor bilingual instruction, and laymen may spearhead a movement to establish it. Only professionals, however, are competent to put it into effect.

3. At least a substantial majority, and preferably the entire educational organization should be thoroughly committed to it. Shared conviction will enable top educational leaders to utilize the talents of their entire staff in planning and implementing a bilingual program.

4. The key to success in the classroom is the presence of thoroughly competent administrators to supervise the program and highly qualified teachers as classroom instructors.

The lessons derived from the Welsh experience, as outlined above, may prove useful in helping ensure success in launching and administering bilingual programs wherever they are contemplated or already under way.

Chapter 39
Bilingual Education in Scotland
Richard E. Wood*

An ancient country with a distinctive history and culture, Scotland was also the first country in Europe to introduce mass compulsory education, some two centuries before its neighbor to the south, England. The two countries have been politically united for centuries; but they remain strikingly different in lifestyle and in that intangible which may be labeled national character. A powerful Scottish nationalist movement, long dormant, has revived, and the government of Great Britain is taking hasty steps to grant devolution (national autonomy in limited sectors, including the opening of a Scottish Assembly or parliament) in the hope of forestalling continuing demands for total independence.

While the Scottish national movement is today—as it was not even ten years ago—above all a political one, much more than a cultural one, there has been an upsurge of cultural pride in Scotland. The Scots have perceived that their national traditions, emphasizing thrift, democratic education, hard work, enterprise, close links with overseas countries, and certain specific fields such as medicine and engineering, equip them better than most peoples to survive and prosper in an economically troubled world.

The linguistic situation in Scotland is more complex than it seems. *Prima facie*, it seems to be an overwhelmingly English-speaking country. The mass media are, with few exceptions, in English. English is the language of the universities and of the huge majority of the schools. Yet Scotland is far from homogeneous linguistically and culturally, and with the resurgence of the national movement, the English face of Scottish public is being questioned.

When Scotland was an independent kingdom, until 1603, the language of the Edinburgh court was Scots, and offshoot of the northern Anglian dialects of Anglo-Saxon. It was a rather standardized language; Aitken (1976) suggests that it was more standardized than the English of the period. However, it was never fully separate from English, being descended from the same source, and even in the heyday of the Kingdom of Scotland, in the 15th and 16th centuries, Scots poets switched between a Scots standard and an English standard for poetic effect (Aitken 1976). Today, the identity of Scots as a separate language is not universally recognized, whether by dispassionate linguists or by its own speakers. Rather, there is what Aitken describes as a bipolar situation, with Broad Scots at one end and (Standard) English at the other end of a continuum of linguistic variation, with speakers ranging over different segments of the continuum and moving from point to point on the spectrum as circumstances dictate. Attention to Scots as the daily native language of pupils who confront English in the classroom has begun only recently, particularly with the holding of a conference and in-service course for educators, on "The Scots Language in Education," in Aberdeen in 1974. The results are presented in McClure (1974). Bilingual or bidialectal education in Scots and English has hardly begun, indeed, the need for it is hardly recognized, particularly by parents. A study of the problem could most fruitfully be conducted in contrast and comparison with other instances of bilingual or bidialectal education in which one language variety is standard English while the other is U.S. Black English, Jamaican English, Guyanese English, Appalachian English, etc., i.e., any moderately to highly divergent, generally non-standard, often socially stigmatized social dialect spoken by disadvantaged populations living in societies dominated by Standard English speakers. Though the linguistic details are different, the attitudinal and other social circumstances surrounding U.S. urban Black English and the Scots, or Scottish English, of the industrial cities of Lowland Scotland, are notably similar. Parallels can also be observed in the consciousness-raising activities of educators working with the U.S. Black community in tracing features of U.S. Black English to non-European historic roots, showing origins in Africa and related phenomena in the Caribbean and other areas of the Black diaspora, and Scots educators working with speakers of stigmatized, considerably anglicized urban varieties of Scots, pointing to the glorious

*Dr. Richard E. Wood, Associate Professor, Dept. of Languages and International Studies, Adelphi University, Garden City, N. Y.

historical roots of the language and combatting negative self-images on the part of speakers (cf. especially Macaulay and Trevelyan 1973).

Scots (or Lallans, "Lowlands") is, in the terminology of Kloss, an *Ausbausprache*, genetically related to English but developed as a partially independent standard language in the days of the Kingdom of Scotland; and still the language of Scots Law, which remains separate from the Common Law of England. Since then it has been overshadowed by English and re-dialectalized, but a national literary movement has in this century again raised it to the level of a vehicle for literature. However, the reaction of the largely anglicized upper-and middle-class urban Scots has been lukewarm and even hostile. The present writer has elsewhere (Wood forthcoming) explored the question of the standard (English) and the proposed counter-standard (Scots, Lallans) in contemporary Scotland.

We will devote the rest of the article to bilingual education conducted in English and the third language of Scotland, Gaelic, which is in Kloss's terms an *Abstandsprache*. Gaelic is naturally distinct from English/Scots by virtue of its identity as a Celtic language with an overwhelmingly different lexicon, syntax, phonology and morphology from those of the Germanic language(s), Scots/English.

According to the census of 1971, there are 88,892 speakers of Gaelic in Scotland, all but 477 bilingual in English. The latter, however, are essentially infants who will undoubtedly learn English upon exposure to the school system, the communications media and other influences outside the home. It is still disputed as to whether or not Gaelic was ever the language of all Scotland. Gaelic, a Q-Celtic language, was introduced from Ireland, whose closest point is only fourteen miles from the Scottish coast, in the 4th century A.D. At that time, P-Celtic, whose present descendant is Welsh, was spoken throughout most of the island of Britain, including what was to become Scotland. Germanic established itself in the Lothians, where Lowland Scots was to develop, and in northern coastal regions, where North Germanic was brought in by Norsemen, to survive as Norn in Shetland, until the beginning of the 19th century, leaving a strong substratum in the contemporary Scots dialects now spoken there. Gaelic, on the other hand, was strong enough to replace P-Celtic, and later, to supplant Norse in areas such as the Hebrides where it remains in place names and family names, as well as loan words in Gaelic.

The conversion of Gaelic into a minority language and of the Gaels into a minority people began around 1070 with the replacement of Gaelic as the language of the royal court by Scots. The path toward the gradual assimilation of Scots by English opened up even as Scots itself developed. Events moved quickly in the 16th century. Lowland Scotland was converted to Calvinism and a Presbyterian Church was established. It accepted an English bible and introduced mass education, aimed principally at basic literacy and ability to read the Gospels, in English. The Highlands, home of a traditional feudal culture dominated by warring clan chiefs with their extended families, remained outside domination of court and Kirk and adhered to feudal values and the old Celtic/bardic culture, while Lowland Scotland became in many ways the first modern, distinctly post-medieval, nation, with close links with two other countries also adhering to Calvinistic doctrines of personal responsibility, enterprise, thrift and innovation: The Netherlands and Switzerland. Soon after, James VI of Scotland moved to London and became James I of England. The Gaelic Highlands were then more distant, more different and more insignificant than before.

Campbell (1950) divided the official attitude of mainstream Scotland to Gaelic into a sectarian phase from 1609 to 1767, a utilitarian phase from 1767 to 1872 and a bureaucratic phase from 1872 until the time of writing. Space does not permit a full discussion of the tragic historical decline of Gaelic. At present, however, the Gaels can be described as a declining minority people living in remote, rugged, climatically rigorous mountain and island areas. They have been brought by a state educational system and other social forces to a state of self-abasement and widespread illiteracy in their native language, to the extent that some Gaels are unwilling to admit their knowledge of the language. The descendants of the clan chieftains have been anglicized (two hundred years ago the perspicacious and very English Dr. Samuel Johnson saw this coming and regretted it, saying that a Highland chief should never be permitted south of Aberdeen), even the middle class alienated and lost to the culture. What was once a high culture with intimate interchange with the fellow-Gaelic-speakers of Ireland and thence with the whole of Catholic Europe, has become a folk-culture, its village bards and scholars trying to impart to the younger generation values which are ignored or stifled by the anglicizing, alienating official education system.

A Gaelic revival movement began in the 1930's when Sorley MacLean and other poets forged Gaelic into a literary vehicle able to treat contemporary topics as well as traditional ones. While decay at the folk-life level in the Gaidhealtachd (Gaelic-speaking areas) continued, intellectuals and the grandchildren of Gaelic immigrants in the non-Gaelic-speaking cities began to shape new attitudes of self-respect. Flowing back from the cities with their universities, teachers' colleges, magazines and radio programs distributed in Gaidhealtachd areas, these cultural streams began to revive the dispirited Gaels. They are still the main cources of support for Gaelic culture. Finally, however, political and educational bases of support within the Gaidhealtachd itself have been established, chiefly within the last four years.

In a progressive reorganization of local government which was completed only in 1975, the whole of Great Britain was reshaped into regions, which especially in Scotland replaced the traditional counties as administrative units. Three of the new large regions which were set up in Scotland had significant Gaelic-speaking population: the Central, the Highland, and the Western Isles regions. It is the last-named, the Western Isles, which is our main concern, since through its creation a rather homogeneous, overwhelmingly Gaelic-speaking population was at least concentrated in a single political unit, rather than being balkanized as a series of western appendages to predominantly English-speaking traditional counties.

The Western Isles Council, in Gaelic Comhairle nan Eilean, declared itself legally bilingual and promulgated a policy for the official use of Gaelic at various levels throughout its region. Most importantly, it initiated a well-funded, well-planned Bilingual Education Project which since 1975 has already made considerable progress in redressing the harmful effects of centuries of neglect and discrimination. Before examining the Project, let us look at the history of Gaelic in education in Scotland.

Around the beginning of the 18th century, the Church of Scotland stepped up its efforts to convert the Highlands. It founded the Scottish Society for the Promotion of Christian Knowledge, whose main purpose was to convert the Gaels and change them into Presbyterian English-speakers. With the Highland clearances after the crushing defeat of the Rebellion of 1745, Gaels emigrated in large numbers, not only overseas (especially to Canada, where Gaelic is still spoken on Cape Breton Island, N.S.; on Prince Edward Island; and in Glengarry, Ont.) but also to the cities of the central industrial belt of Scotland, where, again for evangelical purposes, Gaelic schools were set up. They were known as Sgoilean Chriosd (Schools of Christ) (Stephens 1976, p. 62). Meanwhile, in the Highlands, dissatisfaction with the Established Church caused the formation of the Free Church of Scotland and the Free Presbyterian Church, which adopted Gaelic in Gaelic-speaking areas and opened schools in which it was the main language. State schools, on the other hand, ignored Gaelic and strove to eradicate it. The Education Act of 1872 made no mention of Gaelic. It nationalized the schools formerly run by the churches, thereby excluding Gaelic from them. Societies, mostly based in English-speaking areas including London, fought for Gaelic and recommendations were made for its

introduction into the schools, e.g., in 1885, but further Acts, those of 1892, 1901 and 1908, continued to neglect Gaelic (Stephens 1976, p.64). In the first half of the present century, Gaelic was used in schools only as a transitional language. Once a pupil knew resonable English, no more Gaelic was used with him. Later, Gaelic was studied to a small extent as a subject in upper primary classes, but as an academic subject, poorly taught in English, rather than as the natural linguistic expression of the life experience of the Highland Gael.

The Highland Society, An Comunn Gaidhealach, undertook a survey on the linguistic situation in 1936. It noted in part that "The majority of Gaelic-speaking parents are averse to the speaking of Gaelic to their children; they discourage the use of it so that their children have very imperfect English and no Gaelic." (quoted in Stephen 1976, p. 65). The report recommended the use of Gaelic, and improved teaching methods. But it went largely unheeded.

Another survey, conducted by Christine A. Smith in 1943-4, is of interest in that it attempted to measure the intelligence of bilingual children. It is interesting to compare the findings with those reported from Ireland in the early 1960's which, in suggesting and apparent retardatory effect of bilingual education upon the general intellectual and cognitive development of Irish children as compared with their monolingual English counterparts, had a negative effect on the growth of bilingual education worldwide until contradictory results much more favorable to bilingual education as an aid to educational development of the child were reported in the well-known St. Lambert experiment in Canada.

Gaelic-English bilingual education in Ireland and in Scotland is both similar and different. The languages involved are very similar. On the other hand, we must note that in the Republic of Ireland, Gaelic (Irish) is the first official language of the country and the government encourages its use to such an extent that natively English-speaking pupils are taught in (often inadequate) Gaelic by natively English-speaking teachers. Thus, the blind lead the blind and Gaelic, far from being a natural linguistic medium, is perceived as the language of government and bureaucracy, the language of form-filling and educational compulsion, a necessary evil imposed as a kind of reverse discrimination, a turning of the tables after years of oppression of Irish and Irish-speakers by English and English-speakers. It becomes a matter of game-playing and pretence, Irish serving more as a symbol of national identity than as an actually functional vehicle of information and enlightenment. This paradoxical situation, coupled with inadequate, archaic textbooks and teaching methods, lies at the root of the reportedly retardatory effect of Irish-English bilingual education.

This cannot be the case in Scotland. There, Gaelic had very little official status until regional officialization in the Western Isles, and even there numerous legal battles on such issues as Gaelic roadsigns remain to be fought (Rae 1976). Gaelic was not and is not likely to become the language of officialdom and bureaucracy; quite the reverse.

Smith, in her survey in 1943-4 sponsored by the Scottish Council for Research in Education and its Committee on Bilingualism, pointed out that the cultural content of education in the Highlands was alien to pupils. In these circumstances, IQ scores were naturally poor and students seemed to be distracted, absent-minded, shy and tardy. Their textbooks spoke of railway stations in lonely glens and sea-loch valleys where there was no railroads. They spoke of fathers returning from the office, when in fact the pupils' fathers were deep-sea fishermen, away for months at a time off the Grand Banks of Newfoundland. They described lamp-posts to the tenants of remote farms and crofts and cricket bats to natives of the rugged Highlands where there is none of the flat land with smooth, cropped grass needed for a cricket pitch, even if the Highlanders had the time or inclination for the slow-moving, leisurely, gentlemanly English game in the first place.

By the 1950's, action on bilingual education finally began. Gaelic distinctiveness was no longer perceived as a threat. Rather, it was a resource, if only as an attraction for the growing tourist trade in the scenic Highlands (Gaelic culture is likewise made much of on Canada's Cape Breton Island, where prominent bilingual Gaelic-English street signs are posted more with an eye to tourist snapshots than to the practical needs of the remaining ageing Gaelic population). An increase in Soviet submarine and reconnaissance-ship activity around the lonely Scottish coasts pointed to the strategic dangers of continued depopulation, neglect and alienation. An American nuclear-submarine base at Holy Loch, in a Gaidhealtachd, became the focus of nuclear-disarmament demonstrations some of which were associated with now-reviving Scottish nationalism which saw Gaels not as members of an alien culture but perhaps as the true Scots, one undeniable symbol of Scottish cultural identity.

Thus, bilingual education was introduced in Inverness-shire, Ross-shire and to some extent in Argyll, where Gaelic became a medium of instruction in county rpimary schools from 1958 on. The same bodies which sponsored the Smith report commissioned another in 1957 and 1959.

Gaelic is now usually the first language of instruction in infant classes and the medium for most subjects throughout the primary stage (Stephens 1976, p. 68-9).

At the secondary level English is used for almost all purposes, even, as Stephens points out, for the teaching of Gaelic to Gaelic-speaking pupils. Radio broadcasting for schools over BBC Scotland began in 1970. Stephens notes that it "has had an excellent influence on the teaching of the language" (1976, p. 69).

In a further step, Gaelic was introduced as a second language into about two-thirds of the primary schools of the mainland of Inverness-shire. This is a positive step in the reintroduction of Gaelic into a county which includes Inverness, the capital of the Highlands, but where the 1971 census shows percentages of Gaelic speakers ranging, in mainland civil parishes, only between 0 and 19.

Finlay MacLeod, Primary Schools Gaelic Advisor to the Western Isles Regional Council, conducted a survey in 1973-74. Of the sixty primary schools in the Region at that time, 56 were bilingual, and they had a total of some 2,700 bilingual pupils, of whom 88% had some knowledge of Gaelic, 68% were fluent Gaelic-speakers and 12% had no Gaelic at all, (MacLeod, quoted in Stephens 1976, p. 69). There were four all-English schools, but even there 68% of the pupils had a knowledge of Gaelic, though only 7% were fluent speakers. MacLeod's survey also noted that of the 200 primary-school teachers in the Western Isles in the 1973-74 school year, 158 were fluent Gaelic speakers, 14 knew the Celtic tongue moderately and 28 not at all. American readers surprised at the high number of schools and low number of pupils should recall that we are speaking of a remote, underpopulated region with climatic and cultural conditions comparable, in North American terms, to those of parts of Alaska, Labrador or Newfoundland, rather than the continental U.S.

MacLeod, a trained bilingual educator with a sound knowledge of bilingual education programs and trends in Canada, the U.S., The Netherlands and other countries, comments perceptively on the approach adopted once the initial decision was made to include Gaelic in the curriculum:

> The model selected was that used for teaching the classics. The basis of the work was conscious study of the grammatical structure of the language — through English. There was an exclusive concern with the language itself and how it was put together. One's ability to translate to and from English was given high priority. This approach permeated the whole of Gaelic schooling from the primary stage to university. Which uses of Gaelic as a language were brought to the fore for study within the school system? It has been used with a heavy reliance on the written word, and on literary sources (MacLeod 1976, p. 1).

MacLeod notes that the kind of Gaelic used was the standard developed for the bible translation and poetry of the 18th century, a formal literary register inappropriate to less formal settings and quite foreign to the everyday spoken Gaelic of the pupils. They are therefore induced to feel that their own Gaelic is inadequate, or perhaps not real Gaelic at all, since they can barely understand the archaic, convoluted language of the poems and literary texts. It was in the light of this that Finlay MacLeod entitled his 1974 paper "Gaelic: Out-Of-Date Model Slows Drive to Bilingualism."

Much progress has been made since then, and the change can be seen by comparing MacLeod 1974 and MacLeod 1976. The improvements are found in all fields: in teacher training, curriculum development, preparation of instructional materials, etc., but also in the crucially important field of student attitudes. Parents who have been conditioned to despise their own heritage may try to hide it from their children. In a provocative article on "Gaelic and Island Youth," Roderick Morrison (1976), headmaster of the Laxdale School in the Isle of Lewis, says:

> There are parents even today who honestly take the view that Gaelic, while it may not necessarily be a hindrance to the educational progress of their children, is only of minor significance. Dr. Finlay MacLeod . . . says that this attitude is seldom shared by the youngsters themselves. When asked what their attitude to the language is their answer is almost always positive. Yes, they are glad that they can speak Gaelic. Indeed many of those who speak the language seem surprised that any should ask them questions of this nature (p. 13).

Morrison reports on a survey conducted among almost a hundred senior pupils in Gaelic classes in the Nicolson Institute in Stornoway, capital of the Isle of Lewis and administrative center of the 90-percent Gaelic-speaking Western Isles Region. Ninety percent of the respondents expressed annoyance with those who pretended not to speak Gaelic, and a similar percentage expressed a desire that the Gaelic language should survive. Since parents may have negative attitudes to their native language, Morrison emphasizes that teachers in the bilingual program cannot rely on parents to build up Gaelic vocabulary at home. The attitude of the teacher is crucially important. Commenting on the Western Isles Bilingual Education Project, Morrison observes that

> The purpose of the scheme is not primarily to help Gaelic to flourish (though this could very well be a by-product of it), but simply to provide a better education for the children involved (p. 15).

Let us examine some of the details of the current Project, which is sponsored jointly by the Scottish Education Department and Comhairle nan Eilean (the Western Isles Council). An initial grant £34,000 was made by the Department and will be followed by a second in the same amount, to a total of £68,000 (somewhat over $100,000 since the most recent devaluation of the pound). It is administered by the Jordanhill College of Education in Glasgow, the largest city in Scotland and one outside though close to the indigenous Gaelic-speaking region. Its Vice-Principal, Mr. J. A. Smith, himself a Gael from the Isle of Lewis, is the Chairman of the Consultative Committee. The Director is Mr. John Murray, former Director of the Gaelic Books Council. Two primary teachers have been seconded to work full-time on the project; there is a full-time secretary. The Project operates from two centers—Stornoway, Lewis, where it is headquartered close to the Council offices, and Cladach Kirkibost on North Uist. They work at "devising situations and activities which will stimulate children to use Gaelic as a natural language for exploration and description of experiences" (quoted in Morrison 1976, p. 15). Twenty primary schools in the islands have been selected to act as pilot schools for the materials and resources devised. In-service courses provide training for the teaching staff. The project began in 1975 for a three-year period. The first year concentrated on infant classes but by 1978 all primary classes will be involved. MacLeod (1976) observes:

> Changes are taking place in today's primary classrooms in the Gaelic-speaking areas, and much of that is resulting from a change of attitude by teachers towards language itself and the different ways it can be used by children as well as adults. The language is being streamlined so as to be capable of coping with the children's everyday experiences, just as any living language has to do. Different registers are being evolved. Different levels of competence are being tolerated (p. 2).

MacLeod emphasizes the advantages of radio broadcasting for schools:

> There are now two primary series in Gaelic. The ways in which the language is being used to tackle different topics and the linguistic codes through which this is achieved provide most important guides to new ways of approaching Gaelic as a learning medium. Since broadcasts are more flexible, more direct than books and since they strengthen the current emphasis on oral work, their contribution towards a livelier and more imaginative use of Gaelic in schools cannot be overemphasized (p. 2).

Books, too, are not neglected:

> Recent children's books in Gaelic have been written with an eye on the kind of Gaelic used by

the children themselves. These books tend to extend from the children's present language situation rather than come at them with forms of language which are alien to them (MacLeod, 1976, p. 2).

As the primary school pupils involved in the Bilingual Project move ahead with their education, secondary schools must be ready to receive them and to build on the bilingual foundation. Beyond that, colleges and universities must be prepared. This has been a severe deficiency in the past. Bright Gaels were shipped out of the Gaidhealtachd to senior boarding schools in Inverness, Glasgow and other anglophone cities; and all the universities are in the Lowlands and teach Gaelic or Celtic Studies, where they do so at all, through the medium of English. A recent incident which exacerbated Highland-Lowland differences just at a time when they had shown signs of remarkable improvement, in part through the awakening of a new common sense of nationhood, involved the establishment of a new university. Highlanders, nationalists and others supported the candidacy of Inverness, the Highland capital. But Stirling, a Lowland city, was selected. Worse, the new University of Stirling steadfastly refused to establish courses in Gaelic; it turned into a *cause célèbre*, with sit-ins and demonstrations. The issue is still not resolved to the satisfaction of supporters and would-be Stirling students of Gaelic.

Secondary schools and colleges are now improving, and moving toward bilingual education. Morrison (1976) reports:

> The Nicolson Institute in Stornoway, the only Senior Secondary School in the Western Isles—it is planned to build another in the Southern Isles—has for years now made Gaelic an essential subject in the Common Course which pupils follow when they enter the first year. Pupils are divided into classes for Native Speakers and for Learners, and they can continue studying the language until the fourth and fifth years when they can set their Leaving Certificate at 0 Grade and Higher levels. They may, of course, drop the subject if they so choose, like other subjects in the curriculum. It is perhaps not without significance that two schools in the Highlands—The Nicolson and Oban High School—that have non-Native-Gaelic-speaking Rectors have adopted this practice (p. 16).

The Scottish Certificate of Education now offers papers in Gaelic at 0 (ordinary) and A (advanced) levels.

In 1973 the Gaelic College, Sabhal Mór Ostaig, opened at Teanga on the beautiful Isle of Skye. Its establishment there was an act of faith and daring, as Skye, while shown by the 1971 census as ranging between the 40 percent and 100 percent parameters of Gaelic-speaking population, is subject to the strong and growing anglicizing pressures of the tourist and winter-sports industries. Stephens (1976, p. 73) reports that the College, while administered as a charitable trust, belongs to Iain Noble, an enterprising businessman who has established on Skye a number of small-scale economic enterprises which use Gaelic for business purposes—a truly innovative step in a region whose population has been trained for centuries to consider English the natural language of business. Sabhal Mor Ostaig functions as a Community Center, promotes education and the study of Gaelic-speaking communities in Scotland and throughout the world. It has attracted the attention of the Gaels of Canada. It holds courses in Gaelic for those who wish to learn it as a second language. In this way Teanga has begun to function similarly to the Gaeltachts of Ireland, where the Republic's government supports local Irish-speaking communities which take in boarders and visitors from the English-speaking towns, to learn and use Irish in a natural setting. Tourism and Gaelic culture need not, the College believes, be mutually antagonistic, provided the visitor treats his residence in the Gaidhealtachd as a learning experience.

Sabhal Mór Ostaig is installed in a former partially derelict farmstead. The Director, Mr. Farquhar MacLennan, invites people everywhere to join the Friends of the Gaelic College (as this writer, himself not a native Gael but a Lowlander, a native of Dundee, has done). Its address is Teanga, Isle of Skye, IV44 BRQ, Scotland, and the minimum annual membership fee is a modest £2 ($3.50). Its aims are primarily to:

(1) Provide education in Gaelic in every subject and especially in the literature, history, philosophy and culture of the Gaels:
(2) Offer an opportunity to people world-wide to learn about the culture of the Gaels and to learn the Gaelic language;
(3) Be a social center for people living in Skye or visiting it;
(4) Supplement schools and Education Authorities in their Gaelic policies:
(5) Strive for the restoration of Gaelic as the main language of the Highlands and Islands and as the second language of Scotland as a whole.

What are the cognitive and developmental benefits of bilingualism in Gaelic and English? The cultural benefits to Gaels in overcoming centuries of humiliation and neglect are obvious, but what insights and perceptions does Gaelic offer which cannot be obtained through that segmentation of extralinguistic reality which English provides? Expressed in sweepingly broad terms, English is a language of actions, of yes/no questions, of past-, present- and future-tense verbs. Gaelic is a very different kind of language. The sentence tends to begin with the verb, a stative verb, frequently the verb *to be* or the equivalent of *there is/there are*; then, nouns or pronouns are added filling in the details and building a gradually-emerging picture of the situation in question. Modifiers such as adjectives tend to follow the noun. There are no equivalents for *yes* and *no*. Direct informational questions on the English model, particularly of the *yes/no*, *true/false* kind, are unacceptably brusque and alien to the Gael. With languages so different, the applicability of the Whorfian hypothesis seems evident, and the failings of the old education system based upon English-Gaelic, Gaelic-English translation are obvious.

It is in part a recognition of the cognitive and intellectual experiences and fresh insights to be obtained from a study of Gaelic which has encouraged non-Gaelic-speaking Scotsmen to take up Gaelic as a second language, as they have now begun to do as never before. In the metropolis of Glasgow, for example, a Gaelic Intensive Course of 100 hours is in operation; its sole aim is to produce Gaelic speakers. While French and German were generally selected as second languages in the past, perceptive anglophone Scots now realize that, by selecting Gaelic, they can come to understand the life and thought of their own countrymen and, in many cases, their own ancestors. MacLeod (1976) notes:

> The concept "modern languages" is itself an interesting one. In the past, little of the connotation of "modern" rubbed off on Gaelic at a national level. And yet the connotation of Gaelic is changing. No longer is it seen as the language used only for sad songs, emigrant longing and lengthy sermons. Its image is changing rapidly ...It might even be selected...if its relevance in present day Scotland is recognized more widely (p. 3).

As bilingual education in Scotland develops at the secondary and post-secondary levels, there will be more reports, more curricular innovations and test designs. In view of the traditionally high standards of education in Scotland—the first country in the world to introduce a modern education system—and of the excellent training and awareness of international developments in bilingual education on the part of Scottish bilingual educators, findings of road theoretical significance and general applicability to other instances of bilingual education where one of the two languages is English can be expected. We look forward to them.

BIBLIOGRAPHY

Aitken, A. J. "The Scots Language and the Teacher of English in Scotland." In *Scottish Literature in the Secondary School*. Edinburgh: Scottish Education Department, Her Majesty's Stationery Office, 1976.

Census 1971. (Scotland). Edinburgh: Her Majesty's Stationery Office, 1975.

Davies, A., ed. *Problems of Language and Learning*. London: Heinemann, 1975.

Hechter, Michael, *Internal Colonialism. The Celtic Fringe in British National Development, 1536-1966*. Berkeley and Los Angeles: University of California Press, 1975.

Macaulay, Ronald K. S., and Trevelyan, Gavin D. *Language, Education and Employment in Glasgow*. 2 vols., mimeo. Edinburgh: Social Science Research Council, 1973.

MacDonald, J. A. "Gaelic in Secondary Education—In Areas Outwith the Gaelic Speaking Area," Unpublished paper read at Conference on Scottish Studies and Gaelic in Scottish Schools, Aberdeen, 1976.

MacLennan, Farquhar, "The Raison d'Etre of Sabhal Mor Ostaig." *New Edinburgh Review*, 1976, 33: 11-12, 23.

MacLeod, Finlay, "Gaelic: Out-of-Date Model Slows Drive to Bilingualism." *Education in the North*, 1974, 2: 16-22.

_____,"Gaelic in Education in the Western Isles," Stornoway: Comhairle nan Eilean, mimeo., 1975.

_____, "Gaelic in Primary Schools." Unpublished paper read at Conference on Scottish Studies and Gaelic in Scottish Schools, Aberdeen, 1976.

McClure, J. Derrick, ed. *The Scots Language in Education*. Aberdeen: Aberdeen College of Education and Association for Scottish Literary Studies, 1974.

Morrison, Roderick, "Gaelic and Island Youth." *New Edinburgh Review*, 1976, 33: 13-16.

Nisbet, J. "Bilingualism and the School." *Scottish Gaelic Studies*, 1963, 10: 44-52.

Rae, Steven, "Gaelic and Comhairle nan Eilean [sic]." *New Edinburgh Review*, 1976, 33: 4-10.

Stephens, Meic, *Linguistic Minorities in Western Europe*. Llandysul: Gomer Press, 1976.

Thomson, Derick, ed. *Gaidhlig an Albainn. Gaelic in Scotland*. Glaschu, Gairm Publications, 1976.

Van Eerde, John, "Gaelic in Scotland." *Language Problems and Language Planning*, 1977, 19.

Wood, Richard E. "Linguistic Organizations in Scotland." *Language Problems and Language Planning*, 1977, 19.

_____, "Potential Issues for Language Planning in Scotland." *Language Planning Newsletter*, 1977, 3: 1-4, 7.

_____, "Sociolinguistics in Scotland." *Sociolinguistics Newsletter*, forthcoming.

_____, "Standard and Counter-Standard: The Case of Scotland." Paper presented to International Linguistic Association, Worcester, Mass., March, 1977.

Chapter 40
Focusing on the Strengths of Bilingual Children
Richard E. Baecher*

I Need for a New Focus

The educational reform movement described as "bilingual education" has made great strides since the passage of the Bilingual Education Act in 1968. Through the injection of federal funds into the schools—mainly Title VII monies—many children from backgrounds where English is not the native language, such as Hispanic American, Chinese, and Italian, have been the recipients of a more meaningful educational experience.

Despite the positive advances in teaching children in two languages—the child's native language and English—signs of dissatisfaction are becoming increasingly evident. These concerns pertain to the conceptual outlook of bilingual education, the implementation of a definite set of criteria, and the identification of the particular strengths of bilingual children.

For instance, a study of the National Puerto Rican Development and Training Institute, Inc., (Rivera, 1973), has referred to the "quick-fix solutions" and "crisis-crash syndrome" that has distorted the serious problems confronting bilingual education. Among the Institute's proposals is the articulation of a conceptual outlook, or a new focus, for the instruction of bilingual pupils.

In her exhaustive report on bilingual schooling and English as a Second Language (ESL) practices in New York City, Steinberg (1974) enumerates the following findings:

1. No systematic method to assess the educational needs of pupils with limited English-speaking ability has been devised by the N.Y.C. Board of Education;
2. Neither the Central Board nor community school boards have established guidelines for bilingual programs.

These conclusions, indeed, reveal the erratic nature of many current bilingual programs and ESL approaches. These results served as a prelude to a far more important decree, the ASPIRA decision.

II The ASPIRA Decree

The most dramatic decision to highlight the need for a new focus in bilingual education and perhaps the entire spectrum of education was handed down on August 29, 1974, in *ASPIRA et al. vs. Board of Education Consent Decree.* Faced with high dropout rates among Puerto Rican students, increased enrollments of pupils with limited English-speaking ability, and an insufficient number of bilingual teachers (Fitzpatrick 1971; Steinberg 1973; La Fontaine 1974, 1975), the New York City Board of Education has now implemented a viable and more effective educational program for its Spanish-speaking pupils.

ASPIRA, a national organization representing the educational advancement of Puerto Ricans, brought a class action against the New York City Board of Education. This action called for an improved method of identifying and classifying children who are Spanish-speaking or Spanish surnamed. Since many of these students have limited English-speaking ability, thereby hindering them from effective participation in the learning process, ASPIRA demanded that special educational programs be developed for these students in their own native language.

The basic elements of the program are given as follows: (1) intensive instruction in English; (2) instruction in subject areas in Spanish, e.g., mathematics, science, and social studies; and (3) the reinforcement and development of the pupil's use of Spanish, and reading comprehension skills in Spanish where a need is evident. Additionally, the Central Board established minimum educational standards for this special program. "Special Circular No. 32 (1974)" states:

*Dr. Richard Baecher is Assistant Professor of Education, Fordham University, Lincoln Center Campus.

This circular is addressed to the training needs of both regular and bilingual personnel, to fill the numerous positions in carrying out the program. This staff training program will include: (1) the refinement of Spanish and English language skills; (2) development of pedagogical skills and techniques where necessary; (3) development of content in subject areas such as mathematics, science, and social studies; (4) cultural elements to the degree that they are directly related to other segments in the program.

To accomplish the mission of this program, a teacher-training component will be initiated to assist teachers currently serving in the New York City system to become prepared for participation in the implementation of the ASPIRA decree. Examples of courses for the program are: (1) intensive English and Spanish programs for Common Branches teachers whose primary languages are English or Spanish language skills; (2) intensive English and Spanish programs for intermediate, junior, and senior high school teachers whose primary languages are English or Spanish and who are in need of improvement in English and Spanish language skills; (3) intensive Spanish language arts program for teachers of all levels so that they will be able to reinforce the pupils' use of Spanish in basic communication skills, especially reading; and (4) an intensive Spanish program for teachers of all levels to improve their communication skills in the conduct of their professional duties with the students, parents, and community. By means of this program, the decision to instruct students bilingually will challenge New York City teachers to engage in the process of functional bilingualism, i.e., the conscious use of the child's native language in relevant, meaningful contexts.

A second implication of the ASPIRA decree is the creation of enormous manpower needs to staff these special programs. Individuals with bilingual skills and knowledgeable in the content areas will be necessary to make the program successful. It has been estimated that 40,000 to 60,000 pupils will be identified to participate in the ASPIRA programs. This estimate, in itself, reflects the great staff needs in the future.

A third implication is the lack of sensitive and relevant instrumentalities. If these pupils are to be accurately identified and screened, then new instruments and techniques—global and diagnostic in nature—will be essential. Both the language and cultural backgrounds of the student population will have to be seriously considered in any effort to probe the communication and mathematical abilities of these children.

From the Steinberg report and the *ASPIRA Consent Decree*, therefore, a growing concern has surfaced among educators, administrators, and teachers on how best to educate its second largest minority group. The emergence of a new focus on bilingual education, children with limited English-speaking ability, and the training of teachers "for speakers of other languages" has become a priority.

Vasquez (1974) summarizes the bilingual scene in New York State in these terms:

1. Bilingual education has not been defined as a collective effort for the communication of sound teaching strategies and techniques for the bilingual and potentially bilingual student; and

2. its current, sole concern is with the linguistic performance of the pupil, thereby neglecting the implementation of a coherent conceptual system which considers the ways in which the student comes to relate to the world around him.

According to Vasquez, these inadequacies result in bilingual education being viewed as solely a vehicle of compensatory education instead of as an enrichment for all. All indications, then, point to the need for a new focus in bilingual education.

To partially meet the serious implications of the ASPIRA decree, and the need for a new focus within bilingual education, this paper seeks to: (1) briefly identify a conceptual framework for education that bilingual educators and ESL specialists may find helpful in their professional efforts; (2) illustrate the technique of "cognitive style mapping" by focusing on the strengths of bilingual children; (3) suggest assessment approaches through an outline description of the author's own research; and (4) list implications of cognitive style analysis for bilingual education.

III The Educational Sciences as a Framework

If bilingual programs and ESL techniques are to realize their great responsibilities, it is necessary to investigate various conceptual frameworks.

One perspective that seeks to foster the educational success of bilingual individuals and their total education is found in "The Educational Sciences." Hill (1973) states that "The Educational Sciences" provide a "conceptual and scientific language for the applied fields of education," thereby making possible the articulation of phenomena and problems related to education. This conceptual framework attempts to reduce misconceptions among educators due to a lack of communication. It seeks to bring precision to the resolution of educational problems including those of special relevance to bilingual education (Baecher 1973).

Essential to these "sciences" are the following assumptions:

1. Education is the process of searching for meaning.
2. Thought is different from language.
3. Man is a social creature with a unique capacity for deriving meaning from his environment and personal experiences through the creation and use of symbols.
4. Not content with biological satisfactions alone, man continually seeks meaning (Hill 1973).

These four assumptions are primary considerations in focusing upon the strengths of the bilingual child, or, in understanding the "cognitive style" of bilingual pupils.

Briefly, the "cognitive style" of a bilingual student refers to the way he comes to know the world he lives in, and how he relates to it. In determining the cognitive style of the student with limited English-speaking ability, these questions become paramount:

1. How does he take note of his surroundings?
2. What symbols (Spanish-English for example) does he prefer to use in solving problems?
3. Is the bilingual student a listener or a reader?
4. Is he more capable and comfortable in his own mother tongue for understanding concepts?
5. Does he make up his own mind or seek consensus with his peers?
6. Does he follow the directions of an authority figure?
7. Does he reason in categories like a mathematician, or in relationships as a social scientist might?

These are only a few of the important questions that are asked in observing how the bilingual pupil comes to know, or his "cognitive style." Answers to these questions are used to produce a cognitive style "map" for each student.

IV Cognitive Style Mapping

Using cognitive style "mapping," teachers can determine which pupils can and do learn well from TV or programmed instruction or group work, for example. A student's cognitive style map identifies the unique ways, or strengths, in which that bilingual pupil can master an educational task most readily.

Through observations and questioning, i.e., cognitive mapping, teachers seek answers to how the student used symbols to solve problems, how he is affected by these symbols in cultural contexts, and how he categorizes, contrasts, and/or relates information.

Three principal areas comprise the individual's map and are explored by the teacher through continuous questioning and observations:

The first area of exploration is *Symbols And Their Meanings*. The teacher, trained in observation and formulating behavioral descriptions, looks for indications of the bilingual pupil's use of symbols. The teacher may discover that the child is more successful in listening tasks in the child's own native language; or, that reading activities in English provide greater success. The teacher's attention may be drawn to the fact that the student excels in the use of mathematical symbols and numerical relationships. Moreover, the observant teacher may note how much the pupil depends on his sense of hearing and touch in coming to know, how readily he empathizes with others in the same group or class, the degree to which he accurately knows himself in various educational tasks, and even his ability to "read" gestures in speaking. These elements, or symbols, provide clues to the strength to be found in bilingual pupils. They are indicators of the ways in which meaning is sought and of the feelings, commitments, and values of the bilingual child. The reader is encouraged to investigate the bibliography for more information about *Symbols And Their Meanings*, and the section entitled "A Brief Guide to Cognitive Style Mapping."

Cultural Determinants, the second area of exploration, guides the teacher in ascertaining the influence of social groups on how the bilingual child perceives his role in life situations. His peers, or associates, may contribute significantly to how he views the world. The members of his family provide standards and guidelines for behavior from the earliest years, lasting well into school age. The teacher may note that the student's own individuality has a strong influence in his actions. His awareness of the factors that make him different from other pupils, and how he looks upon these differences, both positively and negatively, determines his behavior and how he assigns meanings to symbols. *Cultural Determinants*, then, can offer the teacher of bilingual children a profound insight into their world of human relationships.

The third area, *Modalities of Inference*, refers to the processes by which the student reaches decisions, i.e., his method of thinking. The teacher may observe that some bilingual children are quick to place items into classes or categories, and to use rules and norms in determining courses of action. Other students may be observed to use differences in their reasoning patterns; they are prone to compare things on the basis of a single characteristic. Still others may look for multiple relationships in what they perceive. Some children combine all of these methods of thinking in arriving at conclusions. A few pupils use the deductive reasoning method of the mathematician in making decisions.

Cognitive mapping, therefore, entails the use of a common language, and a variety of questioning and observational techniques. The common language that describes these three areas in mapping takes the form of an algebraic-visual shorthand.

For example, bilingual student number one, a fourth grader reading below grade level in English and Spanish, is a proficient listener. He is successful with materials requiring listening in English and Spanish. The numbers above each set of notations, T(AL)—T(VL), indicate his present "developmental" level of education at the time he was mapped. The subscripts e and s refer to the English and Spanish forms of tests used to determine the symbolic orientation of the bilingual pupil. Moreover, this bilingual student empathizes with others, appreciates the "beauty" discovered in scenes and music, and is dedicated to a set of principles. He's an individualist, and reaches decisions through a form of categorical reasoning.

Bilingual student number two, a fourth grader reading above grade level in English and Spanish, is a reader. He is influenced by his peers, derives meaning from visual materials, and perceives multiple relationships among things and events. Their maps are shown on both these pages.

A cognitive style map, then, in addition to identifying the ways in which a student can be most successful in mastering an educational task, can provide him the self-knowledge essential to direct him to realistic educational goals. Cognitive style is not fixed and static; it represents a dynamic and growing search for meaning on the part of the bilingual student.

Each map, like each student, is different, and thereby requires a personalized educational program. It can be augmented. Missing strengths required can be built on a student's existing strengths. The map is a starting point for the teacher. From it the teacher initiates a "prescription," i.e., develops a personalized educational program geared to the bilingual student's strengths and weaknesses.

V Educational Prescriptions

To promote the educational success of bilingual student number one, the teacher might prescribe the use of audio tapes to take advantage of this student's listening strength. These tapes and records could be in Spanish or English. He could receive his directions verbally and could work individually in a carrel with programmed materials. Instructions should be given to him in short, easy steps. Activities that incorporate music, and other related features can be planned. The teacher might augment his reading skills by means of these general prescriptions, or working through these strengths and other cognitive style elements that the teacher judges to be relevant (Radike 1973; Bowman et al., 1974). Other activities might include: (1) modality selection, whereby this bilingual pupil selects his own way of learning, in this case listening, and (2) choosing from alternatives such as contract teaching.

For bilingual student number two, the teacher would prescribe written materials and give directions in writing. These materials can be expressed in English or Spanish, and emphasis should be placed upon the use of visuals in helping this pupil. Since he works well with his peers, the teacher might provide for youth-tutor-youth learning situations. Activities calling upon his motoric abilities might be planned in an integrated manner with reading materials. Educational tasks that have him sorting and classifying things might increase his method of categorical thinking. Examples of other activities are open grouping for reading, peer instruction, and modality selection emphasizing the use of visuals.

These are only a few of the numerous educational prescriptions that the teacher can derive from these maps. Each teacher can begin to "match" the cognitive style of the bilingual student with available classroom resources, thereby personalizing education for successful completion of educational tasks. This focus on the strengths of bilingual children are the outcomes of the application of instruments and techniques that teachers can use in assessing the cognitive styles of their bilingual students.

VI Educational Assessment of Bilingual Children

By "educational assessment," I mean that process which systematically seeks to determine the presence or absence of cognitive style elements within the bilingual student. This process involves the human judgments and decision making of teachers, based upon a variety of observations and other forms of information. Various instruments and techniques can be utilized in accomplishing the aims of assessing bilingual children. Only a brief outline description of the author's own research, and those of "The Educational Series" (Berry and Sutton 1973) can be given in an article of this nature.

With respect to *Symbols And Their Meanings*, especially theoretical symbols, or that knowledge acquired through oral and written symbols, these instruments can be used:

1. Tests of basic skills in English and Spanish.
2. Reading tests—Spanish and English versions.
3. Math tests—Spanish and English forms.
4. Judgment of competent teachers.

Nonlinguistic or "qualitative" symbols, e.g., picture clues and kinesics, can be determined through direct measures and/or observations of sensory, programmatic, and "cultural codes." (The reader can refer to the section on "A Brief Guide to Cognitive Style Mapping" for more information.)

The author's own research has employed, adapted, and modified standardized tests, in English and

Fourth Grade Student   2.7   READING GRADE LEVEL (English)
                                        2.7   READING GRADE LEVEL (Spanish)

$$\left\{\begin{array}{ll} T(\overset{5}{AL})_e & T'(\overset{3}{VL})_e \\ T(\overset{4}{AL})_s & T(\overset{2}{VL})_s \\ Q(CEM)_e & \\ Q(CES)_e & \\ Q(CET)_e & \end{array}\right\} X \left\{\begin{array}{c} I \\ \\ F' \end{array}\right\} \left\{ X \left\{\begin{array}{c} M \\ \\ D' \end{array}\right\}\right.$$

IN WRITING IT WOULD LOOK LIKE THIS:

Processes more informa-
tion from listening than
from printed mated ma-
terials, in both English
and Spanish. . .

Is able to identify with
another person's role. . .

Can appreciate "beauty"
of ideas and things. . .

Dedicated to a set of rules
and principles. Works
hard at assignments. . .

Is an indi-
vidualist. Makes
up his own mind.

Will take direc-
tions from an
authority figure.

Categorizes and
classifies things
and events. . . .

Compares and con-
trasts on a one-
to-one basis.
Perceives many
differences. . . .

BILINGUAL STUDENT NUMBER ONE

Fourth Grade Student   5.8 READING GRADE LEVEL (English)
                                        5.3 READING GRADE LEVEL (Spanish)

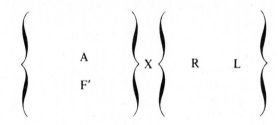

$$\left\{\begin{array}{ll} T(\overset{3}{AL})_e & T'(\overset{4}{VL})_e \\ T(\overset{4}{AL})_s & T(\overset{5}{VL})_s \\ Q(CKH)_s & \\ Q(V)_s & \end{array}\right\} X \left\{\begin{array}{c} A \\ \\ F' \end{array}\right\} \left\{ X \left\{\begin{array}{cc} R & L \end{array}\right\}\right.$$

IN WRITING IT WOULD LOOK LIKE THIS:

Gets more meaning
from written mater-
ials, English or
Spanish, than
from verbal direc-
tions. . . .

Derives meaning from
visual clues and
pictures. . . .

Manifests ability
to perform motor
tasks very well. . .

Influenced by
his associates
or peers. . .

Sometimes can
work independ-
ently. . .

Sees relationships
among things and
qualities. . .; likes
many examples and
illustrations in
educational tasks. . .

Makes decisions after
carefully considering
all available informa-
tion. . .

BILINGUAL STUDENT NUMBER TWO

Spanish, respectively, to investigate the listening and reading capabilities of bilingual students, of Chicano and Puerto Rican background. Similar work has gone forward concerning the mathematical abilities of bilingual pupils. Provided a conceptual outlook and a common language, teachers can avail themselves of various instruments to probe cognitive style elements.

With respect to *Cultural Determinants*, observations of the effect of social groups on the meanings students assign to symbols are made. For instance, does the student talk about his family often? Would he rather work alone or in a group? Answers to the questions will indicate those cultural influences that are brought to bear upon the individual in the form of family, associates, and one's own individuality.

Concerning *Modalities of Inference*, illustrations of things to note are: (1) does the student often use words such as, "It's just like..., It's the same as..., But what if..." (Es como..., Es lo mismo como..."); (2) how neat and organized is his work? and (3) does the pupil deliberate in his thinking?

Numerous other techniques, such as self-assessment reports and interviews, can be utilized in focusing on the strengths of the bilingual child. Essential to the process described here is that teachers begin to communicate about the cognitive styles of their bilingual pupils and make humane and professional decisions that are sensitive to these students' educational needs.

VII Conclusion

This final section will give attention to some implications of cognitive style analysis for bilingual education. Not to be viewed as a panacea for all educational problems, cognitive style does offer exciting prospects for bilingual education and ESL personnel. These implications will take the form of a list comparing the positive and negative features of bilingual education and "The Educational Sciences."

Bilingual Education

1. Lacks a conceptual outlook and a common language for teachers to use in communication about their bilingual students.
2. Has been relegated to a "compensatory" status, representing a "deficit" theory of remediation.
3. Primarily concerned with the linguistic performance of the bilingual student in educational programs.
4. Lacks agreed upon assessment procedures that are sensitive to instruction and teacher oriented.

Educational Sciences

1. Offers a coherent conceptual framework for teachers with an attendant language. It calls upon teachers as principal agents in the process of instructing bilingual pupils.
2. Views the bilingual child as one engaged in the process of coming to know, by means of linguistic and nonlinguistic symbols, cultural influences and methods of reasoning. This represents a "difference" theory of strengths to which the educational system must adapt to insure success.
3. Concerns itself with the *total* bilingual child; focuses on strengths of the bilingual child to develop personalized educational programs.
4. Offers teachers a direction; invites them to discover ways in which bilingual students come to know, and emphasizes the important role of the competent teacher's human judgments.

BIBLIOGRAPHY

ASPIRA et al., v. Board of Education Consent Decree of August 29, 1974, Board of Education of the City of New York, 110 Livingston St., Brooklyn, N. Y.

Baecher, Richard E. *An Exploratory Study to Determine Levels of Educational Development, Reading Levels, and the Cognitive Styles of Mexican American and Puerto Rican American Students in Michigan.* Unpublished dissertation, University of Michigan, Ann Arbor, Michigan, 1973.

Berry, James, and Sutton, Thomas, *The Educational Sciences: A Bibliography with Commentary.* American Educational Sciences Association, 2480 Opdyke Rd., Bloomfield Hills, Michigan, 1973.

Bowman, Barbara; Burch, Betty; Hill, Joseph; Nunney, Derek; and Buttner, John, *Tip Personalized Educational Programs.* Pamphlet. East Lansing Public Schools, Mi., 1974.

Fitzpatrick, Joseph P. *Puerto Rican Americans: The Meaning of Migration to the Mainland.* Englewood Cliffs, New Jersey: Prentice-Hall, Inc., 1971.

Hill, Joseph E. "The Educational Sciences." *Pamphlet.* Bloomfield Hills, Michigan, Oakland Community College Press, 1973.

LaFontaine, Hernan, "Introduction to Bilingual Education." In *Urban, Social and Educational Issues,* edited by Leonard Golubchick and Barry Persky, Dubuque, Iowa: Kendall/Hunt Publishing Co., 1974, Chapter 5.

————, "Some Hard Questions About Bilingual Programs." *The New York Times*, Annual Education Section, Wed., January 15, 1975, p. 64.

Radike, Floyd, ed. *Handbook for Teacher Improvement Utilizing the Educational Sciences.* AESA, 2480 Opdyke Road, Bloomfield Hills, Michigan, 1973, Chapter 9.

Rivera, Luis, *A Proposed Approach to Implement Bilingual Education Programs, Research and Synthesis of Philosophical, Theoretical and Practical Implications.* The National Puerto Rican Development and Training Institute, Inc., New York, N. Y., 1973, Prologue.

Special Circular No. 32, Board of Education of the City of New York Division of Educational Planning and Support, November 8, 1974.

Steinberg, Lois, *Report on Bilingual Education: A Study of Programs for Pupils with English Language Difficulty in New York City Public Schools.* Department of Public Affairs, Community Service of New York, June, 1974, pp. iii-iv.

Vasquez, Jose, "Bilingual Education For New York State: The Pursuit Of The Ideal." *Keynote Speech of the 5th Annual Conference of New York State Administrators in Compensatory Education.* October 27-29th, Niagara Falls, N. Y., 1974, mimeographed paper.

A Brief Guide to Cognitive Style Mapping

I. SYMBOLS AND THEIR MEANINGS

Two types of symbols, theoretical (e.g., words and numbers) and qualitative (e.g., sensory, programmatic, and codes), are created and used by individuals to acquire knowledge and derive meaning from their environments and personal experiences. Theoretical symbols differ from qualitative symbols in that the theoretical symbols present to the awareness of the individual something different from that which the symbols are. Words and numbers are examples of theoretical symbols. Qualitative symbols are those symbols which present and then represent to the awareness of the individual that which the symbol is. (Feelings, commitments and values are some examples of the meanings conveyed by the qualitative symbols.)

T(VL)—Theoretical Visual Linguistics—ability to find meaning from words you see. A major in this area indicates someone who reads with a better than average degree of comprehension.

T(AL)—Theoretical Auditory Linguistics—ability to acquire meaning through hearing spoken words.

T(VQ)—Theoretical Visual Quantitative—ability to acquire meaning in terms of numerical symbols, relationships, and measurements.

T(AQ)—Theoretical Auditory Quantitative—ability to find meaning in terms of numerical symbols, relationships, and measurements that are spoken.

The five qualitative symbols associated with sensory stimuli are:

Q(A)—Qualitative Auditory—ability to perceive meaning through the sense of hearing. A major in this area indicates ability to distinguish between sounds, tones of music, and other purely sonic sensations.

Q(O)—Qualitative Olfactory—ability to perceive meaning through the sense of smell.

Q(S)—Qualitative Savory—ability to perceive meaning by the sense of taste. Chefs should have highly developed qualtitative olfactory and savory abilities.

Q(T)—Qualitative Tactile—ability to perceive meaning by the sense of touch, temperature. and pain.

Q(V)—Qualitative Visual—ability to perceive meaning through sight.

The qualitative symbols that are programmatic in nature are:

Q(PF)—Qualitative Proprioceptive (Fine)—ability to synthesize a number of symbolic mediations into a performance demanding monitoring of a complex task involving small, or fine, musculature (e.g., playing a musical instrument, typewriting); or into an immediate awareness of a possible set of interrelationships between symbolic mediations, i.e., dealing with "signs."

Q(PG)—Qualitative Proprioceptive (Gross)—ability to synthesize a number of symbolic mediations into a performance demanding monitoring of a complex task involving large, or gross, musculature (e.g., throwing a baseball, skiing).

Q(PDF)—Qualitative Proprioceptive Dextral (Fine)—a predominance of right-eyed, right-handed and right-footed tendencies (a typically right-handed person) while synthesizing a number of symbolic mediations into a performance demanding monitoring of a complex task involving small, or fine, musculature (e.g., writing right-handed).

Q(PDG)—Qualitative Proprioceptive Dextral (Gross)—a predominance of right-eyed, right-handed and right-footed tendencies (a typically right-handed person) while synthesizing a number of symbolic mediations into a performance demanding monitoring of a complex task involving large, or gross, musculature (e.g., throwing a baseball with the right hand).

Q(PKF)—Qualitative Proprioceptive Kinematics (Fine)—ability to synthesize a number of symbolic mediations into a performance demanding the use of fine musculature while monitoring a complex physical activity involving motion.

Q(PKG)—Qualitative Proprioceptive Kinematics (Gross)—ability to synthesize a number of symbolic mediations into a performance demanding the use of gross musculature while monitoring a complex physical activity involving motion.

Q(PSF)—Qualitative Proprioceptive Sinistral (Fine)—a predominance of left-eyed, left-handed and left-footed tendencies (a typically left-handed person) while synthesizing a number of symbolic mediations into a performance demanding monitoring of a complex task involving small, or fine, musculature (e.g., writing left-handed).

Q(PSG)—Qualitative Proprioceptive Sinistral (Gross)—a predominance of left-eyed, left-handed and left-footed tendencies (a typically left-handed person) while synthesizing a number of symbolic mediations into a performance demanding monitoring of a complex task involving large, or gross, musculature (e.g., throwing a baseball with the left hand).

Q(PTF)—Qualitative Proprioceptive Temporal (Fine)—ability to synthesize a number of symbolic mediations into a performance demanding the use of fine musculature while monitoring a complex physical activity involving timing.

Q(PTG)—Qualitative Proprioceptive Temporal (Gross)—ability to synthesize a number of symbolic mediations into a performance demanding the use of gross musculature while monitoring a complex physical activity involving timing.

The remaining ten qualitative symbols associated with cultural codes are defined as:

Q(CEM)—Qualitative Code Empathetic—sensitivity to the feelings of others; ability to put yourself in another person's place and see things from his point of view.

Q(CES)—Qualitative Code Esthetic—ability to enjoy the beauty of an object or an idea. Beauty in surroundings or a well-turned phrase are appreciated by a person possessing a major strength in this area.

Q(CET)—Qualitative Code Ethic—commitment to a set of values, a group of principles, obligations and/or duties. This commitment need not imply morality. Both a priest and a criminal may be committed to a set of values although the "values" may be decidely different.

Q(CH)—Qualitative Code Histrionic—ability to exhibit a deliberate behavior, or play a role to produce some particular effect on other persons. This type of person knows how to fulfill role expectations.

Q(CK)—Qualitative Code Kinesics—ability to understand, and to communicate by, non-linguistic functions such as facial expressions and motions of the body (e.g., smiles and gestures).

Q(CKH)—Qualitative Code Kinesthetic—ability to perform motor skills, or effect muscular coordination according to a recommended, or acceptable, form (e.g., bowling according to form, or golfing).

Q(CP)—Qualitative Code Proxemics—ability to judge the physical and social distance that the other person would permit, between oneself and that other person.

Q(CS)—Qualitative Code Synnoetics—personal knowledge of oneself.

Q(CT)—Qualitative Code Transactional—ability to maintain a positive communicative interaction which significantly influences the goals of the persons involved in that interaction (e.g., salesmanship).

Q(CTM)—Qualitative Code Temporal—ability to respond or behave according to time expectations imposed on an activity by members in the role-set associated with that activity.

II. CULTURAL DETERMINANTS

There are three cultural determinants of the meaning of symbols: 1) individuality (1), 2) associates (A), and 3) family (F). It is through these "determinants" that cultural influences are brought to bear by the individual on the meanings of symbols.

I—Individuality—Uses one's own interpretation as an influence on meanings of symbols.

A—Associates—Symbolic meanings are influenced by one' peer group.

F—Family—Influence of members of the family, or a few close personal friends, on the meanings of symbols.

III. MODALITIES OF INFERENCE

The third set of the cartesian product indicating cognitive style includes elements which indicate the individual's modality of inference, i.e., the form of inference he tends to use.

M— Magnitude—a form of "categorical reasoning" that utilizes norms or categorical classifications as the basis for accepting or rejecting an advanced hypothesis. Persons who need to define things in order to understand them reflect this modality.

D— Difference—This pattern suggests a tendency to reason in terms of one-to-one contrasts or comparisons of selected characteristics or measurements. Artists often posses this modality as do creative writers and musicians.

R— Relationship—this modality indicates the ability to synthesize a number of dimensions or incidents into a unified meaning, or through analysis of a situation to discover its component parts. Psychiatrists frequently employ the modality of relationship in the process of psychoanalyzing a client.

L— Appraisal—is the modality of inference employed by an individual who uses all three of the modalities noted above (**M, D, and R**), giving equal weight to each in his reasoning process. Individuals who employ this modality tend to analyze, question, or, in effect, appraise that which is under consideration in the process of drawing a probability conclusion.

K— Deductive—indicates deductive reasoning, or the form of logical proof used in geometry or that employed in syllogistic reasoning.

Chapter 41
Bilingual Education for Mexican American Children
Alfredo R. Flores*

Past educational practices designed to teach Mexican American children have been unsuccessful. There can be no other conclusion if one assesses the schools' performance by such evaluative indicators as drop-out rates, standardized achievement tests, grade retention figures, and other related measures. In addition to school related indicators there are the socio-economic-political indicators which reflect the fact that the Mexican American is on the bottom of the spectrum in income, unemployment, housing, and educational attainment. These depressing statistics direct attention to the dismal performance of the schools in meeting the needs of the Mexican American community.

A cursory examination into the educational practices pursued by the schools in teaching Mexican American children reveals a number of misguided efforts which may help to explain the dismal results that have evolved. An example that illustrates this point is the practice of teaching non-English-speaking children in a language foreign to them. This may sound like an isolated case but that has been the standard. Another practice pursued by schools is the failure to understand and incorporate the child's cultural heritage into everyday curricular activities. Implicit in this example is the inability to recognize differences in the value systems of culturally different children and the school's attempt to inculcate a different set of values both of which can lead to culture conflict. These methods presently employed to teach Mexican American children are contrary to the teaching and learning principles which dictate the integration of the child's language, experiences, and his cultural lifestyle in the teaching-learning process.

A strategy recommended to help overcome these problems is the implementation of a bilingual bicultural approach. Such a method would enhance the learning process for Mexican American children and legitimize the principle of cultural diversity. The schools could be receptive to this notion because of the significant influence of the movement currently in vogue which recognizes that alternative means have to be identified to educate culturally different children. The conventional programs based on "cultural deficits" have not worked and the concept of accountability requires a change in the approach followed which has proven to be ineffective.

Definitions

What is a bilingual bicultural education approach? It is a method that utilizes and encourages the use of two languages, one of which is English, both for instructional purposes and as a general means of communication. In addition, the culture of the child, including his value system is taken into consideration and is reflected in the regular curricular activities.

Who are the Mexican Americans? Mexican Americans, also known as Chicanos, are the people in the United States who trace their ancestry to Mexico. Some are recent arrivals and some trace their roots to the southwestern part of the United States during the 16th century, at the time when that area was a Spanish territory, before becoming Mexico and eventually the United States.

Goals of a Bilingual Program

The goals of a bilingual bicultural program approach are consistent with the democratic ideals as perceived by Ramirez (1972) who espouses cultural pluralism. According to this concept, people in a democratic society determine their values, their culture, and lifestyle. Differences in skin color, language, and culture are desireable and viewed as socially acceptable and as positive traits as opposed to negative ones. In accordance with this philosophy, the goals of a bilingual bicultural program are:
1. to develop the ability to communicate effectively in two language systems.
2. to develop the ability to acculturate into the dominant or a different culture.

*Dr. Alfredo R. Flores, Assistand Professor Early Childhood Education, University of Houston, Texas.

3. to develop the attitudes and the desire to maintain the first language and culture.

4. to develop a positive concept of self so that one can function effectively.

These goals are in addition to those global goals normally pursued by public school programs are specific to bilingual bicultural programs with the possible exception of number 4 which deals with self-concept. This goal is universally accepted and according to Nimnicht (1969) the culturally different child may need more halp with this aspect than the dominant culture child. The child that comes from a different socio-economic background or from a different culture is subject to being perceived in negative ways by society, teachers, and peer groups, as is indicated in research conducted by Rosenthal and Jacobson (1967). These negative perceptions contribute to feelings of rejection which can lead to a loss of self-image. For this reason, the development of a positive self-concept is a key goal in bilingual bicultural programs.

Developing individuals competent to effectively function in two languages is a worthwhile goal to pursue. The European system of education emphasized this goal with the end result that children are often not only bilingual but trilingual. Historically in the United States, the acquisition of a second language has not been advocated and for that reason monolingual education has become the standard. There are many reasons for encouraging bilingualism in all children, but the overriding one seems to be that as a result of learning a second language, a better grasp or understanding of the first language will come about.

The goal of developing the ability to acculturate into the dominant culture is a key one for the Mexican American child. For too long, schools have tried to assimilate culturally different children into the dominant culture of American society and have achieved little success. The apparent failure may be attributed to a host of reasons such as discrimination, economics, lack of opportunity, etc., but the underlying factor could very well be the inappropriateness of the goal itself. It is unrealistic to assume that Mexican Americans want to be mirror images of the lifestyle of the WASP American.

What do Mexican Americans want? They want their culture and language to be considered a part of the American lifestyle. They want to maintain their cultural heritage, their language, and values. Also they want to participate in the dominant cultural lifestyle when the situation demands so. Mexican Americans desire to be considered as truly bilingual (Spanish-English) and truly bicultural (Mexican American-dominant).

The ability to switch from one language to another and from one culture to another according to the dictates of the situation can be developed, particularly if initiated at an early age. However, the attitude and the desire to help children maintain their language and culture must be a specific goal which should be addressed in everyday instructional activities.

To be different was formerly equated with being inferior. Similiarities and homogeneity denoted positive traits. Such were the measuring yardsticks used to judge people. Mexican American children are brown, Spanish speaking and culturally different, hence, they were stereotyped even before stepping into a classroom. This stereotype included the following characteristics: slow, disadvantaged, non-verbal, and low-achieving. These perceptions that society formed about Mexican Americans helped to shape many of the doubts that ultimately led to the development of negative self-concepts. For these reasons, among others, bilingual bicultural programs should underscore the goal of developing healthy, positive self-concepts. It is imperative that every opportunity be seized to offer children a maximum chance to succeed.

Justification for a Bilingual Program

A bilingual bicultural approach can be justified by viewing it from three different perspectives. Historically the bilingual movement can be traced and one can observe a gradual evolution of progress which supports the validity of the approach. Also a legal basis has been established which provides for the necessary authority for the operation of such programs based on national concerns that eventually became translated into legislative and judicial actions. Finally the area of teaching and learning principles is surveyed which affirms the appropriateness of the approach.

Historically speaking as early as the 1820's American settlers in the Mexican state of Texas were teaching their children Spanish and English. English had been the first language of the American settlers but because they had immigrated to a Spanish speaking country and became Mexican citizens, instruction in Spanish became common. According to Barker (1925) Mexico's colonization law dictated that "...when a town was established a school must be maintained to teach the Spanish language" (p. 144). So Spanish was included in the curriculum. In Wisconsin, the first kindergarten established in the United States was German-speaking. Mrs. Karl Schurz founded it in Watertown in 1855 (Spodek, 1972). She had been trained under the principles developed by the father of the kindergarten movement Frederick Froebel. In 1899 the San Antonio Independent School District operated Saturday schools, according to Peralez (1976), to provide special intruction in Spanish, German, and English to non-English speaking children.

The United States Congress enacted the Bilingual Education Act in 1968 and this particular action provided the bilingual movement with the impetus needed. Not only was the legal basis established but funds became available for the operation of such programs. As a result of this law, the Office of Health, Education, and Welfare issued an Executive Memorandum requiring federally-funded school systems to provide assistance for language minority children. This edict indicated that "failure to provide such assistance, where needed, would be considered a violation of Title VI of the Civil Rights Act of 1964" (USCCR, 1975, p. 20). State legislatures followed congress' lead and passed similar legislation providing for bilingual education as a part of the regular school program. According to the United States Commission on Civil Rights (1975) states that took this action were Massachusetts, Texas Illinois, and New Jersey, making bilingual education compulsory.

In a much celebrated case the United States Supreme Court unanimously ruled in the Lau versus Nichols decision that "there is no equality of treatment merely by providing students with the same facilities, text books, teachers, and curriculum; for students who do not understand English are effectively foreclosed from any meaningful education" (USCCR, 1975, p. 21). This was landmark decision because it endorsed the Bilingual Education Act of 1968, the HEW Executive Memorandum, and state legislation mandating bilingual education, all in one swooping motion. Teitelbaum and Hiller (1976) state that this decision represents "the most important judicial bench mark for those who advocate bilingual education as a means toward achieving quality in education for language minority children" (p. 1).

Bilingual education can also be justified on an educational basis by taking learning and teaching principles into consideration. A learning principle that has long persisted and that has historically been recognized in education states that children learn best when their own experiential base is used as the medium of instruction. If this is indeed the case then it behooves teachers of Mexican American children to utilize the child's experiences as well as language in the daily curricular activities. The result will be a matching of children's language and cultural experiences with school content which will enhance learning.

Bilingual Education at the Early Childhood Level

A bilingual bicultural program approach can be implemented at the early childhood level. This can ensure maximum effectiveness since children at this age are more flexible and are not as inhibited as older children especially when it comes to learning another language. Teaching foreign languages to middle and secondary school children has been common in many public schools, however, the results have been dismal. There are a number of reasons for these poor results, among which are negative attitudes, biases, and age inappropriateness. An early childhood approach would overcome many of these problems.

A bilingual bicultural approach for linguistically different children should be initiated at an early age, certainly as soon as possible after age three. The reason for this is that these children in most cases know their first language and it is easier to maintain it when it is supported and reinforced in the school environment. In certain cases, particularly with middle class children, the first language is often dropped by age seven or eight. This is caused by interaction and association with English speaking peers only, in spite of the fact that Spanish may still be used at home. Even if the first language is not dropped entirely, its development has been hampered. A bilingual program started after the first language is dropped will not be as effective.

Young children are more open and receptive to language and cultural differences than are adolescents. To illustrate this fact the television program Sesame Street serves as a good example. Many children who watch that program have picked up the limited Spanish vocabulary and can recite numbers, colors, as well as names. The children also identify with the show's characters whether they have a black, brown or white face. These are valid reasons for beginning bilingual bicultural programs at the early childhood level.

According to Saville-Troike (1973) "at the age of three or four practically every child entering a foreign community learns to speak the new language rapidly and without a trace of an accent. This facility declines with age" (p. 19). Children have the capacity to learn languages and as they mature the ability diminishes. It is apparent then that the earlier a bilingual program is started the easier a second language is acquired.

Attitudes toward school are formed at an early age and these can either be negative or positive. Children who develop positive attitudes generally are the ones who succeed in school and these usually have a minimum of problems. These children are eager to learn and generally are well accepted by teachers and peers alike. On the other hand children who develop negative attitudes usually get poor grades, lack self-confidence and relate poorly to teachers and peers. A bilingual bicultural approach where children will have a chance to learn from one another and where differences are not looked down but appreciated may help in the acquisition of good attitudes. It is of the utmost importance then to make early school experiences as favorable as possible and the provision of a supportive approach like bilingual education for linguistically different children could be a means of achieving this goal.

Another important aspect of bilingual programs involves the formation of self-concepts which develop rapidly during the early years. Nimnicht, McAfee, and Meier (1969) cite studies which indicate that a kindergarten child's self-image is a good prediction of his reading ability in the third grade. If this is the case then the importance of an approach that will help children to acquire positive self-concepts becomes apparent. A bilingual program is especially helpful to linguistically different children because it gives them the chance to use those cultural experiences unique to them in addition to their language. The fact that the children's language and experiences are used in the program setting gives the children a feeling of acceptance which is a prerequisite for a good self-concept.

Early childhood teachers are more open and receptive toward innovative programs than are others in the field of education. This can be ascertained by observing the number of preschool models that have been implemented in the last ten years. These cover the range from developmentalist to behavioristic theory and early childhood teachers function well in all of these settings. The reasons why these teachers are more open and receptive stem from the type of training they receive and is also reflective of the age group they work with. A flexible characteristic that is descriptive of early childhood teachers is a necessity in the implementation of new educational approaches if these are to succeed. Children are very resilient people and this same attitude is apparent in their teachers, therefore, a logical reason for starting bilingual programs at the early childhood level.

Why a Bilingual Bicultural Approach for Mexican American Children?

The National Advisory Council on Bilingual Education (1975) recommends "that bilingual-multicultural education be promoted throughout the educational system as quality education for all students" (p. 9). While this may be a worthy goal, it should be recognized that neither the necessary financial resources or the appropriate attitudinal support exist for such an undertaking. It is for these reasons that the limited funds available for bilingual education be channeled to serve areas with a concentration of linguistically different children. In these areas it would be appropriate to include all children in the bilingual program regardless of language differences. The rationale for this being that a program that serves all children would tend to integrate rather than segregate children thus giving validity to the approach rather than treating it as a program for the "disadvantaged" or the "exceptional". Also the program would benefit all children and could serve as a bridge in promoting the ideals of bilingualism and biculturalism.

Mexican Americans comprise the largest group of linguistically different children in the United States and a bilingual bicultural approach would be advantageous to their education. This group is unique in that it has its own cultural lifestyle, language, and value system. It has resisted attempts to assimilate it into the majority culture and future attempts will probably meet with failure. The leadership in the Mexican American movement suggests instead the goal of acculturating into the dominant culture and see the advent of bilingual bicultural programs as the vehicle to accomplish that purpose.

When discussing the Mexican American Community it should be noted that is is not monolithic. Differences of all types abound. While many call these people the brown race, in reality the skin coloration ranges from light to dark. This is largely a result of the intermingling of the Indian with the Spanish people. Culturally there are Mexican Americans that are very traditional in their make-up and as Mexican as people from Mexico. Conversely, there are some that are atraditional and have assimilated totally into the American majority culture. Generally speaking, however, the Mexican Americans culturally are a composite of the Mexican, the Indian, and the Anglo. Language wise most are bilingual but there are a considerable number who speak Spanish only and a fewer number who are English-speaking only.

It can readily be seen that Mexican Americans are different from dominant culture Amerians. Failure to recognize these differences and to take them into consideration in educational activities can lead to culture conflict. This is a condition that affects school achievement, personal adjustment, and a loss of self-concept. Casavantes (1970), Justin (1970), and Espinosa (1971) have analyzed the culture conflict theory and confirm its negative affects.

Cultural differences that exist between and within groups can be handled easier through a bilingual program philosophy. Since the Mexican American holds to these differences, such an approach would be beneficial to him. Acceptance of his values, language, and cultural lifestyle and the incorporation of these elements into everyday instructional activities would help in making learning relevant to him. This is turn will develop positive self-concepts in children and can prevent culture conflict from occurring.

Opposition to Bilingual Education

To say that there is unanimity in the acceptance of bilingual education as a viable approach would be stretching the truth, for that is not the case. There are some who are opposed to it and for different reasons. One such reason is the requirement of a special bilingual teaching certificate which is a requirement in states where bilingual education is mandatory. There are many teachers who resent the thought of going back to college to take courses to qualify them for the certificate.

Bilingual education dictates the need for special competencies in addition to the generic ones in order to learn the specific skills and knowledge required in teaching bilingually. These competencies are in the area of culture and language and teachers are threatened by the thought of learning these. This is particularly true of monolingual teachers and many of them have banded together to fight the movement. However, it stands to reason that one is not born with inherent skills needed to teach bilingually, not even if one is bilingual. These skills are learned.

That bigotry and discrimination exist in these United States comes as no surprise. There are those who feel that ethnic, racial, and cultural differences are not desirable and instead there should be one language (English) and one cultural system (dominant). These persons decry cultural and language differences and question the patriotism of those who are different. Also many of these people feel that Spanish or any other language is inferior, so why learn it? The negative attitudes that exist clash with the goals of a bilingual bicultural program and where these feelings are strong, the conditions are not conducive for operating such a program.

Conclusion

Bilingual bicultural education as a viable alternative to monolingual monocultural education offers Mexican American children an opportunity for success. Certainly past attempts and well-meaning educators have been largely unsuccessful, and the fact that the children's language and culture, among other factors, have been denied should be given a large part of the blame. To be truly bilingual and bicultural is a lofty goal to work towards.

BIBLIOGRAPHY

Barker, E. *The life of Stephen F. Austin.* Nashville: Cokesbury Press, 1925.

Casavantes, E. J. *Variables which tend to affect (impede or retard) learning of the Mexican American student in American education.* August, 1970. (ERIC Document Reproduction Service No. ED 060 990)

Espinosa, M. *Cultural conflict in the classroom.* March, 1971. (ERIC Document Reproduction Service No. ED 054 669)

Justin, N. Culture conflict and Mexican American achievement. *School and Society,* 1970, 98, 27-28.

National Advisory Council on Bilingual Education. *Bilingual education: quality education for all children.* U. S. Office of Bilingual Education, HEW, November, 1975.

Nimnicht, G., McAfee, O., & Meier, J. *The new nursery school.* New York: General Learning Corporation, 1969.

Ramirez, M. & Castaneda, A. *Cultural democracy, bicognitive development and education.* New York: Acadmic Press, 1974.

Saville-Troike, M. *Bilingual children: a resource document.* Center for Applied Linguistics, Arlington, VA, 1973.

Spodek, B. *Teaching in the early years.* New Jersey: Prentice-Hall, 1972.

U. S. Commission on Civil Rights. *A better chance to learn: bilingual-bicultural education.* Clearinghouse Publication No. 51, May, 1975.

NOTES

1. Flores, A. R. A study of Mexican American and Anglo teacher's attitudes and behaviors toward Mexican American children (Doctoral dissertation, Northern Illinois University, 1974). *Dissertation Abstracts International,* February, 1975, 35, no. 8, 5188A.

2. Peralez, Alonzo, Bilingual Program Director, San Antonio Independent School District. Personal communication.

3. Teitlebaum, H. and Hiller, R. *Trends in bilingual education and the law.* Paper delivered at the Southwest Educational Development Laboratory Conference on Bilingual Education. Austin, Texas. June, 1976.

Chapter 42
Bilingual Special Education: Ahora
Nancy Ayala-Vásquez*

The Need for Bilingual Special Education

Bilingual Special Education is needed because special education was never designed to meet the needs of the ethno-linguistically different minority children. Special education was designed for a population, whose characteristics were those of English monolingual white children. These children's exceptionalities ranged from retardation to psychological abnormalities and physical handicaps (Kirk & Lord, eds., 1974; Krugman, 1948).

The nature of their exceptionalities demanded more attention. Society felt that unless special help was given to these children, they would never be able to be contributing members of society. This practice resulted in the exclusion of other exceptionalities whose characteristics were not as prominent: for example, giftedness. Gifted children were expected "to make it" in spite of any obstacle. In addition, this emphasis in the disabilities encouraged in the public, the fears and misconceptions that people have toward deviance. This fear of abnormalcy created an educational category for children who did not fit the established norms. Special education classes then became the obvious dumping ground for children who were deviant or different in an ethnolinguistic context (Tolliver, 1975).

Philosophical Differences

The differences between bilingual education and special education are the product of the theoretical base from which the philosophy of special education has been structured. The medical profession and psychology provided the information from which the educational system structured their program. This scientific information placed emphasis on the biological growth and development of humans. Any deviation from these fixed patterns of growth was treated as a loss that would affect the total capacities of the individual. Such losses created in the individual incapacitating disabilities mentally as well as physically (A Report of the AMA, 1964; Goodenough, 1949; Watson, 1953). The training and education given to them focused on their disabilities and not on their abilities. The extent of the disability in the individual created a comparable burden on society.

Bilingual education differs from special education in that the differences are seen as part of the uniqueness of each individual. These differences are mainly environmental and cultural. The exceptionalities are points in the continuum of normalcy where children differ from the average point where most children are going to be categorized. As such all exceptionalities need attention, because all the children are going to be different as well as the same. In this context, special education is viewed as a system by which all children are educated according to their potential, regardless of their race, ethnolinguistic background, physical ability and intellectual capacity. This definition has evolved along a concept of public education that maintains that children have the right to have an instructional program that takes into account their particular needs.

Responsibilities of the School Toward the Community

Each school system has the responsibility of providing a curriculum by which each child is provided with equal educational benefits. This curriculum and the benefits to be derived from it are determined by the value system of the society in general and by the community to which the children belong, in particular. The benefits of education are those skills provided to the individual which will allow him to become a full participant member of his community. As a participating member of his community he fulfills a role in different aspects of community life according to his ability. The failure of education to provide these benefits would strangle the individual from his community making him a burden to the state.

The American system of education is a barometer by which the socioeconomic and political climate can be

*Dr. Nancy Ayala-Vázquez, Professor of Education, City College of New York.

gauged. Since the era of the religious schools to the present, the public school system has been used to exert social influence in the shaping of opinions and values. Historically, the concept of American schooling has passed through several stages. The first stage was that schooling was a privilege for an elite group of people: the clergy. The second stage was that it was a democratic vehicle for the formulation of national values based on a homogeneous democratic society. Finally, in the current stage, education is the right of all children who are entitled to an equal education in a heterogeneous democratic society. As these concepts evolved, the norms for education continued to be those established by the value system of the white Anglo-middle-class American.

During the sixties, the educational value system was under a process of change to include minority groups. The concept of multiculture, multilingual education had begun to take hold. The Civil Rights movement, with the impact of the Desegregation Law of 1954, set a precedent in which the courts of law took a stronger stand regarding the rights of children. Until then, the courts recognized educators as the experts in determining what was best for the child. All educators do not agree on one theory of education or on any one educational policy; therefore, courts of law encountered many difficulties in rendering a verdict that could provide clear guidelines for education.

The implementation of Public Law 94-142 "Education for All Handicapped Children Act of 1975" is a milestone in the struggle of advocates, for the rights of *all* exceptional children to an education. This law is a great departure from the time in which the exceptional child was considered a curse, both to his parents and to himself. Originally, the two main priorities of the advocates for the exceptional child were: first, to have the public accept that exceptional children could happen in all races and socioeconomic levels; second, to have these children accepted in the public schools as an integral part of the system. When the exceptional children moved into the classroom, the inadequacies, biases, and attitudes within the system became evident. These inadequacies presented a definite problem. Would the system change so as to meet these special needs? The system did not of itself respond to the need. Other people who viewed this population as people who were capable human beings having potentiality, demanded that school officials see exceptional people in the same manner—as people with untapped resources and unmet needs. In recent years, the struggle of parents, lawyers, educators and other advocates has been concentrated in formulating protective laws that guarantee the exceptional child "a free and appropriate education" (PL 94-142) to meet their unique needs.

There is a parallel in the history of the conceptualization and implementation of bilingual education and special education. These educational policies have been in response to:

1. The needs of children;
2. The rights of children; and
3. The efforts of parents and other advocates of the rights of children to equality in education.

The education of minority children has been structured around a deficit model (Bereiter, 1965; Deutch, 1963; Hunt, 1968; Hurst, 1965; Jensen, 1969). This model had the mythical white middle-class as its norm. The deficit model of education has evolved under the influence of a particular English school of Anthropology led by Sir Edward Burnett Tyler, which placed culture in an hierarchical order, ranging from primitive to advanced. The method used to determine where a particular culture fitted was to compare that culture's norms and values with that of American society. If the culture was similar to the American one, then that culture was considered advanced. However, if it was different, then it was considered deviant, subhuman and primitive. Therefore, a large percentage of minority children in the school population have been classified as retarded, slow, disadvantaged, and culturally deprived. One particular group of children which have especially suffered under these labels have been the non-English speaking children (Calzoncit, 1970; Carter, 1971; Meisgiers, 1966; Riles, 1969).

In a study done by Mercer (1972), she found that there were disproportionately large numbers of blacks and Mexican-Americans labelled as mentally retarded, by community agencies. In her study she found 100 percent more blacks and 300 percent more Mexican-Americans in disproportion with the rest of the population. Many of these mislabelled individuals have been so labelled, because of inappropriate procedures.

Studies about language acquisition and second language learning in general have emphasized bilingualism as a deficit and a cause for retardation (Chander & Plakos, 1969), therefore, many non-English speaking children have been so labelled and classified as retarded (Dunn, 1968; Mercer, 1975; Riles, 1969; Tolliver, 1975; Vazquez, 1974; Warren et al., 1965). Recent studies have refuted this theory (Anastasi, 1953; Darcy, 1963).

Dunn (1968) questioned the need for special education for the mildly retarded, and criticized it as "discriminatory in view of the high percentage of minority children." Riles (1969) expressed the same concern as Dunn (1968) and Mercer (1972) did, as well. The established precedent of using special education classes as an exclusion technique (Fleishman Report, 1972; Education of Spanish Speaking Hearing, 1972) entails that extra caution be used in the structuring of guidelines for the assessment of the needs of the bilingual exceptional child. A clear definition of needs and of the characteristics of the population to be served will provide a better point of departure from which to structure service plans. The bilingual child couples his exceptionality with the added dimensions of language and cultural diversity. In most instances (Mercer, 1971; Bernal, 1972), the overlapping of dimensions creates an added difficulty in pinpointing clear-cut exceptionalities. An assessment of the needs should provide distinctive criteria from which to evaluate the underlying elements associated with language and culture. This criteria should help formulate distinctive categories separating the needs of exceptional children which are a direct result of exceptionality, from those which are cultural or linguistic (Baca, 1974).

With the renewed emphasis on bilingual education some of the issues in special education services for bilingual exceptional children have become more prominent. Some of the questions raised are:

1. Is special education necessary for bilingual children?
2. What kind of unique services can special education provide for bilingual children?
3. What kind of personnel is available for the bilingual children?
4. How are the bilingual children tested, labelled and classified?

The benefits of special education services for the bilingual child need to be categorized in the main areas of (1) curriculum, (2) instructional techniques, (3) testing, labelling and classification. The curriculum has to be based on skills needed for future job market needs and opportunities. Most of the present curriculum places emphasis on overcoming the children's handicaps to the exclusion of their abilities. The training for jobs does not correspond with existing job markets nor does it prepare them to function within their community.

There is a dearth of materials, techniques and curriculum designed for the bilingual exceptional children (Abad et al., 1974; Alexander, 1969). Most of the material available is not easily adaptable to specific needs of the individuals. Teachers need expertise in the following areas, to be able to adapt materials.

1. Teachers need to know about language acquisition skills.
2. Teachers need to know about different languages.
3. Teachers need to understand cultural differences.
4. Teachers need to know about variations within the language as it relates to countries, regions, as well as socioeconomic levels.
5. Teachers need to know about differences in cognitive styles, among individuals.
6. Teachers need to know about the significance of attitudes and life styles as they affect learning styles.

These variables influence and determine the attitudes of children toward school and their motivation. These attitudes and learning styles should determine the types of techniques needed and their use by the teachers and children. To enable the teachers to respond to these needs institutions of higher learning need to establish teacher-training programs for bilingual, special education teachers and provide in-service teacher training for the special education classroom teacher who is already in the field.

The needs for special bilingual education teachers are obvious. The bilingual teacher has within herself a resource to aid her in the teaching of bilingual children. The teacher's knowledge of the language and culture helps to bridge the communication gap between herself and the children. A common language provides a mutual ground from which to build. Teacher training programs for Bilingual Special Education teachers are practically non-existent. There is also a need to create and train for new professionals who can address the unique problems of the bilingual child. One of these new professionals is the "Bilingual Language Development/Impairment Specialist." This specialist needs language training in order to diagnose the bilingual child. The diagnostic language skills of this specialist include:

1. The language acquisition skills of the bilingual child (first and second language);
2. Language development;
3. Language impairment; and
4. Dominance and proficiency.

All specialists who are involved in work with bilingual children should have a working knowledge of the child's first language and child's culture. This knowledge will provide the base from which the specialist would be able to interpret behavior and to prescribe appropriate treatment in a culture relevant context.

Testing, Labelling and Classification

In addition to the usual problems in testing, the bilingual child brings the added dimensions of bilingualism. Bilingualism is defined as the use of two languages as a means of communication. But, since communication is contextual as well as informational, language then, should be viewed in context, that is, in its cultural aspects, economical aspects, social aspects, political aspects, and educational aspects. The bilingual person (Fishman's model) makes use of his language according to domains. Each domain has a set vocabulary which can overlap into more than one domain. The frequency of usage and the numbers of domains in which a language is used will determine an individual's dominant language. The dominant language will be one in which the person will be most fluent, comfortable, have a large vocabulary and better comprehension. A person could also be equally deficient in both languages (Fishman, 1964, 1971; Walker et al., 1975).

Before the exceptional bilingual child can be tested to determine his exceptionality, it is necessary to determine the range of his language competency; in what language he should be tested; which language should be the language of instruction and to what extent there is a developmental language handicap or language impairment (Brekke & Clark, 1974; Kirk, 1966). Currently available instruments in testing produce biased information (De Avila, 1971). This is because the instruments are culturally biased, since the norm population has usually been white, middle-class. This procedure does not take into account social and cultural differences (Altus, 1953; Cruickshank, 1972). The norms for bilingual children need to be established in a bilingual population as norms for this particular group and not as comparison to the already established norms for other groups (Anastasi, 1953; De Avila, 1974; Soeffing & Mercer, 1975). One of the criteria for the classification of mental retardation is the degree of social adaptation (AMA Conference on Mental Retardation, 1964).

Social adaptation is relevant in terms of appropriateness of behavior in the setting in which it occurs. Testing must be done by a bilingual person who, ideally should also be a member of the same cultural group as the child. A member of the same cultural group or a person knowledgeable in the culture would be more capable of assessing children according to the social adaptability in relevance to the child's culture. The interpretation of these criteria to the classroom teacher and other personnel would help define the treatment and program needed for the child. Learning characteristics and behavioral patterns of children are also culture and family related. Family life style and belief systems affect classroom learning situations. They are predeterminants of the attitudes and expectations of the children.

Role of the Parents

Most of the gains of the exceptional child in terms of acceptance, programs, research and other areas have been a direct result of the work of the parents. Parents are the best allies a teacher can have. Parental attitudes are going to influence children's motivation and attitudes toward school. Under the best of circumstances the school situation can be traumatic to children. Anxiety and stress can be exhibited in a negative overt behavior and loss of motivation. Parental involvement in the total program of the school will benefit both the school and the child in alleviating this trauma. Many aspects of the exceptional child program need to be continued at home. A knowledgeable parent can continue the treatment, or educational program. A hostile parent can sabotage the teacher's efforts, both at home and at school. The continuity at home of some of the classroom techniques would provide reinforcement of learning. This continuity would also help the child to strengthen his trust of the teacher. The parents' observation of the child of the use at home of newly learned skills provides needed criteria to evaluate the child's progress.

The bilingual parent is a resource for the teacher who can provide information in areas such as the language development, history and culture of the child.

Legal Resources Provided for Special Bilingual Education

The legal resources provided for Bilingual Special Education are quite numerous. The Bilingual Education Act of 1968 established bilingual education as a legal way of correcting previous inadequacies of the educational system. The failures of the system have been documented by Coleman (1966); Fleishman (1972); Silberman (1970) and Yarborough (1967). Congress enacted the Title VII Bilingual Education Act (ESEA) as amended in 1967. Section 702 of the act states:

In recognition of the special educational needs of the large numbers of children of limited Englsih speaking ability in the United States, Conress hereby declares it to be the policy of the United States to provide financial assistance to local educational agencies to develop and carry out new and imaginative elementary and secondary programs designed to meet these special educational needs. For the purposes of this title "children of limited English speaking ability" means those who come from environments where the dominant language is other than English.

The *Lau et al. v. Nichols et al.* (U.S.C. 9th Cir No. 72-6520) case of 1974 guaranteed a curriculum of equal benefits, for children whose language was other than English. The law guaranteed equal access to education, equal benefits and curriculum regardless of race, religion, sex or national origin. Public Law 94-142 mandates that the curriculum, the testing and the prescriptive diagnostic educational program be tailored to the unique needs of the individual, regardless of linguistic ability. The Local Education Agency (LEA) must provide adequate personnel capable of performing services in the child's dominant language. These laws have made inroads in the education of non-English speaking children. In the case of *Aspira v. The New York City Board of Education*, (U.S. District Court, S.D.N.Y. 72 Cir. 4002, consent decree) this principle was acknowledged as plans were made to meet the educational needs of the Hispanic child in the New York City school system.

Summary

A difference in language does not in itself constitute an exceptionality. The positive aspects of bilingualism need to be stressed (Lambert, 1955, 1956; Peal & Lambert, 1962; Pintner, 1937). Language learning is a stimulation of the brain. This stimulation would develop the brain giving the individual a new dimension from which to perceive his world. It would be advantageous to both English speaking monolingual children as well as non-English speaking children to have the knowledge and use of more than one language. The laws guarantee equal access to education, equal benefits and curriculum regardless of race, religion, sex or national origin. Special education is an integral part of public education and as such, it is part of the process of the democratization of the classroom.

SELECTED READINGS

Axline, Virginia, *Dibbs*. Boston: Houghton Mifflin, 1964.

Barsch, Dorothy, *One little boy*. New York: Julian Press, 1952.

Bettelheim, Bruno, *The children of the dream*. New York: Anon, 1957.

____, *The empty fortress*. New York: Free Press, 1967.

____, *Love is not enough*. New York: Anon Books, 1971.

Blatt, B. & Kaplan, F. *Christmas in Purgatory: A photographic essay on mental retardation*. Rockleigh, N. J.: Allyn & Bacon, 1966.

Buck, Pearl, *The child who never grew*. New York: John Day, 1950.

Coles, Robert, *Children of crisis: A study of courage and fear*. New York: Dell Publishing Co., Inc., 1967.

Green, Hannah, *I never promised you a rose garden*. New York: Holt, Rinehart & Winston, 1964.

Hershey, John, *The child buyer*. New York: Knopf, 1960.

Hunt, Nigel, *The world of Nigel Hunt: The diary of a mongoloid*. New York: Garrett, 1967.

Itard, J. & Gaspard, G. *The wild boy of Areyon*. New York: Appleton-Century-Crofts, 1962.

Kephart, N. C. *The slow learner in the classroom*. Columbus, Ohio: Merrill, 1960.

Keyes, Daniel, *Flowers for Algernon*. New York: Harcourt, Brown & World, 1959.

Killilea, Marie, *Karen*. Englewood Cliffs, N. J.: Prentice-Hall, 1963.

Neill, A. B. *Summerhill: A radical approach to child rearing*. New York: Hart Publishing Co., 1960.

Redl, Fritz & Winneman, David, *Children who hate*. New York: The Free Press, 1965.

Rubin, Theodore J. *Jordi, Lisa and David*. New York: Ballantine, 1971.

Trieschman, A. E., Whittaker, James & Brendtko, Larry K. *The other 23 hours*. Chicago: Aldine Publishing Co., 1969.

BIBLIOGRAPHY

Abad, V. et al. A model for delivery of mental health services to Spanish speaking minorities. *American Journal of Orthopsychiatry*, July, 1974, 44:4, 584-595.

Alexander, T. Retardation in intellectual development of lower class Puerto Rican children in New York City. Final Report. Washington Bureau of Education for the Handicapped (BR50359), May, 1969.

Altus, G. T. Wisc patterns of a selective sample of bilingual school children. *Journal of Genetic Psychology*, 1953, 83, 241-248.

Anastasi, A. & Cordova, F. A. Some effects of bilingualism upon the intelligence performance of Puerto Rican children in New York City. *Journal of Educational Psychology*, January, 1953, 44:1, 1-17.

Anastasi, A. & Cruz, A. Language development and non-verbal I.Q. of Puerto Rican pre-school children in New York City. *Journal of Abnormal and Social Psychology*, 1953, 48, 357-366.

Aspira of New York, Inc., et al. Plaintiffs against Board of Education of the City of New York, et al., defendants. United States District Court, Southern District of New York, 72 Cir. 4002, Consent Decree.

Bacca, M. L. M. Que esta sucediendo en haulas especiales bilinque? [What's going on in the bilingual special education classroom?] *Teaching Exceptional Children*, Fall, 1974, 7:25.

Bereiter, C. Academic instruction and pre-school children. In R. Corbin & M. Crosby (Eds.), *Language programs for the disadvantaged—The report of the NCTE task force on teaching English to the disadvantaged.* Champaign, Ill.: National Council of Teachers of English, 1965.

Bereiter, C. & Engelmann S. *Teaching disadvantaged children in the pre-school.* Englewood Cliffs, N. J.: Prentice-Hall, 1966.

Bernal, Jr., E. M. Assessing assessment instruments: A Chicano perspective. Paper presented at the Regional Training Program to Serve the Bilingual/Bicultural Exceptional Child, Montal Educational Associates, Sacramento, California, 1972.

Bilingual Education Act, 20 U.S.C. 880(b). Enacted January 2, 1968. PL 90-247, Section 702.

Brekke, B. & Clark, A. Observations of a Piagetian clinical interview on language acquisition. *Elementary English,* Fall, 1974, *51,* 291-294.

Calzoncit, N. Texans for the Educational Advancement of Mexican Americans: Special Education Committee Report, March 27, 1971, Mimeo.

Chandler, J. & Plakos, J. Spanish speaking pupils classified as educable mentally retarded. *Integrated Education,* 1969, 7, 28-33.

Coleman, S. et al. *Equality of educational opportunity* Washington, D. C.: Office of Education, HEW U.S. Government Printing Office, 1966.

Cruickshank, W. M. The right not to be labelled. In R. M. Segal (Ed.), *Advocacy for the legal and human rights of the mentally retarded.* Ann Arbor: University of Michigan Institute for the study of Mental Retardation and Related Disabilities, 1972.

Darcy, N. Bilingualism and the measurments of intelligence: Review of a decade of research. *Journal of Genetic Psychology,* 1963, *103.*

De Avila, E. A. Some cautionary notes on attempting to adapt I.Q. tests for use with minority children and a neopiagetian approach to intellectual assessment: Partial report of preliminary findings. Paper presented to Bay Area Bilingual Education League, San Francisco, California, 1971.

De Avila, E. A. & Havassy, B. Testing of minority children: A neopiagetian approach. *Today's Education,* November, 1974, 63:72, 5.

Deutch, M. The disadvantaged child and the learning processes. In A. H. Passow (Ed.), *Education in depressed areas.* New York: Columbia University Press, 1963.

Dunn, L. M. Spacial education for the mildly retarded: Is much of it justifiable? *Exceptional Children,* 1968, *35,* 5-22.

Education of the Spanish speaking. Hearings before the Civil Rights Oversight Subcommittee on the Judiciary, House of Representatives, Ninety-second Congress, Second Session on Reports of the U. S. Commission on Civil Rights. Serial No. 35. Congress of the U.S. Washington, D. C. House Committee on the Judiciary, January, 1972.

Fishman, J. et al. Guidelines for testing minority group children. *Journal of Social Issues,* 1964, *20, 129-145.*

Fishman, J., Cooper, R., & Ma, R. *Bilingualism in the Barrio,* Vol. 7. Bloomington, Indiana: Indiana University Press, 1971.

Fleischmann Commission Report. Part III: Children with language difficulties. A report of the New York State Commission on the Cost, Quality and Finances of Elementary and Secondary School, Vol. II, 1972, pp. 6-35.

Goodenough, F. L. *Mental testing, its history, principles and applications.* New York: Rinehart, 1949.

Hunt, J. McV. *Intelligence and experience.* New York: Ronald Press, 1961.

____, Towards the prevention of incompetence. In J. W. Carter (Ed.), *Research contributions from psychology to community health.* New York: Behavioral Publications, 1968.

Hurst, Jr., C. G. *Psychological correlates in dialectolalia.* Washington, D. C.: Howard University Communities Research Center, 1965.

Jensen, A. How much can we boast I.Q. and scholastic achievement? *Harvard Educational Review,* 1969, *39,* 1-123.

Kirk, S. A. *The diagnosis and remediation of psycholinguistic disability.* Urbana, Ill.: University of Illinois Press, 1966.

Kirk, S. A. & Lord, F. E. (Eds.). *Exceptional children: Educational resources and perspectives.* Boston: Houghton Mifflin Co., 1974.

Krugman, M. Orthopsychiatry and education. In L. G. Lowrey (Ed.), *Orthopsychiatry 1923-1948: Retrospect and Prospect.* New York: American Orthopsychiatry Association, 1948, pp. 248-262.

Lambert, W. E. Measurements of the linguistic dominance of bilinguals. *Journal of Abnormal and Social Psychology,* 1955, *50,* 197-200.

____, Developmental aspects of second-language acquisition. *Journal of Social Psychology,* 1956, *43, 83-104.*

Lau et al. V. Nichols et al. U.S.C. 9th Circuit No. 72-6520. January 21, 1974.

Meisgier, C. The doubly disadvantaged. Austin: The University of Texas, 1966.

Mental retardation: A handbook for the primary physician. A Report of the American Medical Association Conference on Mental Retardation, April 9-11, 1964.

Mercer, J. I.Q.: The lethal label. *Psychology Today,* 1972, *6,* 44-47.

———, Sociocultural factors in the education of black and Chicano children. Paper presented at the 10th Annual Conference on Civil Rights Educators and Students, NEA, Washington, D. C., January 18-20, 1972.

Naremore, R. C. & Dever, R. B. Language performance of educable mentally retarded and normal children at five age levels. *Journal of Speech and Hearing Research*, March, 1975, *18*, 22-95.

Newcomer, P. L. & Hammill, D. D. *Psycholinguistics in the schools*. Columbus, Ohio: Charles E. Merrill Co., 1976.

Peal, E. & Lambert, W. E. The relation of bilingualism to intelligence. *Psychological Monographs*, *1962, no. 546.*

Pintner, R. & Arsenian, G. The relation of bilingualism to verbal intelligence and to school adjustment. Journal of Educational Research, 1937, *31*, 255-263.

Public Law 94-142 (1975). Education for All Handicapped Children Act. Superintendent of Documents, U. S. Government Printing Office, Washington, D. C.

Riessman, R. *The culturally deprived child*. New York: Harper Brothers, 1962.

Riles, W. C. Education of inner city children: Challenges and opportunities. In President's Committee on Mental Retardation, Background Papers for the Conference on Problems of Education of Children in the Inner City. Washington, D.C.: P.C.M.R. 1969.

Silberman, C. E. *Crisis in the classroom*. New York: Random House, 1970.

Soeffing, M. Y • Mercer, J. R. The main way to know: New assessment techniques for mentally retarded and culturally different children. *Education and Training of the Mentally Retarded*, September, 1975, *10*, 110-116.

Tolliver, B. Discrimination against minority groups in special education. *Education and Training of the Mentally Retarded*, October, 975, *10*, 188-192.

United States Commission on Civil Rights Publication No. 51, May, 1975. A better chance to learn: Bilingual-bicultural education.

Walker, H. J. et al. Relationships between linguistic performance and memory deficits in retarded children.

Watson, R. I. A brief history of clinical psychology. *Psychology Bulletin*, 1953, *50*, 321-346.

Yarborough, R. Statement made at first session of the hearings before the special Subcommittee on Bilingual Education. Seante Committee on Labor and Public Welfare, Washington, D. C., May 18, 1967, pp. 1-2. Cited by T. Anderson & M. Boyer, *Bilingual schooling in the United States*, Vol. 1. Austin, Texas: Southwest Educational Development Laboratory, 1970, p. 6.

Chapter 43

Bilingual Special Education: Meeting the Needs of the Non-English-Speaking Mentally Retarded Child

Edward Rich*

Bilingual education and special education have both become areas of controversy in and of themselves. When the two disciplines are combined, in planning an educational program for the child with special needs who is predominantly non-English-speaking, we are faced with a multitude of theoretical and practical problems. The discussion which follows presents some of the issues related to the development and implementation of effective bilingual instructional programs for the child with special needs, particularly for the child identified as mentally retarded. Included in the presentation will be: (1) a brief definition of special education, followed by a discussion concerning the "labeling" controversy and the need for non-discriminatory assessment procedures which recognize and reflect linguistic and cultural differences; (2) the rationale for bilingual education, in general, and, more specifically, for bilingual special education for the mentally retarded; (3) the issue of special class placement vs. the "mainstreaming" approach, again with emphasis on the mentally retarded child; and (4) considerations basic to meeting the particular needs of the non-English-speaking mentally retarded child in planning a bilingual special education program.

I

Educators, today more than ever before, are stressing the need to understand and accept all children as they are. Rather than attempting to fit children into an educational mold, the modern-day conscientious teacher recognizes and responds to each child's individual differences, and endeavors to meet the diverse needs of all pupils. However, there are children who have handicaps which keep them from learning in the regular school situation, even when adequate attention is paid to individual differences and needs. Special education is provided for the child who differs "from the average or normal child in mental, physical, or social characteristics to such an extent that he requires a modification of school practices, or special educational services, in order to develop to his maximum capacity" (Kirk, 1962, pp. 4-5). Special education provides children with trained special educators, instructional programs utilizing specialized curricula and teaching techniques, and special instructional materials. Special education programs and services have been designed for children who demonstrate a need for special help in developing their physical, emotional, social, academic, and occupational competence, and who have traditionally been identified as: physically handicapped, mentally retarded, hearing handicapped, language impaired, speech disabled, visually handicapped, neurologically impaired, emotionally disturbed, socially maladjusted, and, more recently, learning disabled.

The use of such identifying labels has become a topic of much controversy in recent years, particularly for that group of children classified as mentally retarded. For those individuals who are truly mentally retarded, the label provides protection and special help. However, there are "others for whom the label...is a burden and a stigma, depriving them of an opportunity for a full education and plaguing them as they strive to find a place for themselves in adult society. A critical issue in mental retardation is that of distinguishing those for whom the label is a shield from those for whom it is an impediment" (Mercer, 1973, p. 197).

Historically, clinicians have been concerned with the possibility of mislabeling someone as retarded who is not really retarded. However, in recent years, there have been more and more claims made against the criteria used for labeling individuals as mentally retarded, the major target being the I.Q. test. When Binet developed his intelligence test, his aim was to include content which would be familiar to all persons. This is an impossible task in a society as diverse as ours. "Items and procedures used in intelligence tests have inevitably come to reflect the abilities and skills valued by the American 'core culture.' This 'core culture'

*Edward Rich, Project Director, ESEA Title VII Bilingual Program, Bureau for Children with Retarded Mental Development, New York City Board of Education.

consists mainly of the cultural patterns of that segment consisting of white, Anglo-Saxon Protestants whose social status today is predominantly middle and upper class" (Mercer, 1973, p. 13).

Not only may children belonging to various ethnic subcultures be mislabeled because otheir cultural backgrounds have not equipped them to handle standard I.Q. tests, contructed to reflect the dominant white, middle-class culture, but those whose native tongue is other than English are also handicapped by the language of administration of such tests, namely "standard" English. Zirkel (1972) points out that, in addition to the cultural factor, "such variables as the language...and extent of the verbal factor of such tests seem to significantly affect the performance of Spanish-speaking children" (p. 34). The need for valid criteria and careful screening can be seen in the testing results which led to a suit filed in behalf of nine Spanish-speaking Mexican-American children in the District Court of Northern California (Diana v. State Board of Education, 1970). According to their initial testing, their I.Q.'s placed them all in the mentally retarded range. When they were retested in Spanish, "all but one increased to above the cut-off score...used by the California School District to place children in the category of the educable mentally retarded or the educationally handicapped (Rivers et al, 1975, p. 238)." The results of the retesting certainly seem to corroborate arguments that testing procedures are prejudicial when they require a facility with the English language and that test items are culturally biased when they are geared toward the white, middle-class Anglo child.

Statistics regarding the placement of children in classes for the mentally retarded give further evidence of the need to change assessment techniques so that linguistic and cultural differences are taken into account. When the California State Department of Education analyzed the erhnic background of pupils assigned to special classes for the educable retarded, the results indicated that black and Spanish-American children "were seriously overrepresented. Even in 1971-72 they comprised 50.6 percent of the special class pupils as contrasted with only 25.3 percent in the total school population" (Dunn, 1973, p. 139). There are, of course, great variations in such statistical surveys. Mercer (1973), for example, found that in the city of Riverside, California, the rate of special class placement for Mexican-American children was four times larger than would be expected from their proportion in the student population. Whereas 11 percent of the sample student population were Mexican-Americans, 45.3 percent of the pupils placed in special classes were Mexican-Americans (pp. 112, 117). On the other hand, statistics reported by the United States Commission on Civil Rights (1976) indicated that in New York City the percentage of Hispanic background students in special classes for the mentally retarded (30 percent) was within only a few percentage points of what would be expected from their proportion (26.6 percent) in the student population (pp. 101, 104).

It is now recognized that poor performance on intelligence and other psychological tests by non-English-speaking children may simply reflect the linguistic and cultural bias of those tests. Such recognition extends to the federal legislative level: The new Education for All Handicapped Children Act (Public Law 94-142) requires that all methods used for testing and evaluation must be racially and culturally non-discriminatory, and must be in the primary language or "mode of communication" of the child. Furthermore, no one test may be the sole means of making a decision about an educational program. In addition to professional responsibility and moral obligation, educators now have a legal requirement to base their decisions as to whether or not children may be expected to profit from special education programs upon the results of extensive evaluations with appropriate instruments. Modifications in assessment procedures are needed which will not only utilize the child's linguistic and cultural background, but which will provide an accurate measure of his "adaptive behavior:" the "effectiveness with which the individual copes with the natural and social demands of his environment" (Mercer, 1973, p. 132). If a diagnosis of "mental retardation" is based solely on I.Q. and there is no concern for "evaluating other facets of behavior, then many persons from minority groups and lower socioeconomic status who are coping intelligently with social situations and interpersonal relations may be diagnosed as mentally retarded" (Mercer, 1973, p. 196).

While it certainly seems valid to "cease labeling children as mentally retarded unless a comprehensive assessment of mental ability, physical health, and adaptive behavior demonstrate[s] a handicap severe enough to justify the designation" (President's Committee on Mental Retardation, 1971, p. 21), most educators would not advocate either the dropping of all labels or the wholesale abandonment of special classes. Comprehensive and non-discriminatory assessment will help ensure that children are not stigmatized unnecessasrily, but "we do not want to rule out the possibility that there are minority and bilingual children who are handicapped.... We do not help a child learn when we insist that any problem she/he may have is due to the fact that English is his/her second language. There are minority and bilingual children who are mentally retarded" (Juarez, 1976, p. 11). It is for these non-English-speaking children that bilingual special education programs and services must be planned and implemented.

II

Bilingual-bicultural education provides the means whereby the non-English-speaking child is immediately launched "into a world of learning as opposed to a world of confusion and frustration; and...it creates for the child an atmosphere of personal identification, self-worth, and achievement" (NEA Reporter, 1974, p. 15). The non-English-speaking child who is provided with the opportunity to learn in his dominant language will experience success rather than failure in the school environment. "The use of the native language for classroom instruction allows the education of the child to continue uninterruptedly from home to school, permitting immediate progress in concept building rather than postposing development until a new language has been acquired" (Saville and Troike, 1971, p. 1). By accepting and using the language—and culture—that the child brings to school, we are "letting him know that he is valued as a worthwhile person with specific strengths and abilities" (Regents of the University of the State of New York, 1972, p. 7). One of our main tasks as educators, particularly special educators, is to build upon the strengths that children demonstrate. If children have handicaps, it becomes even more important to help them develop and enhance the strengths and abilities they have. In our attempts to meet their special needs, we must make every effort to take advantage of their special assets. If children speak a language other than English, we must help them develop that language and their ability to function in that language. If, instead, we consider the other language an additional handicap to successful learning, then in our attempt to ignore or negate the language competence they already have, we will prevent our students from progressing as rapidly as their intellectual capacity will allow. "Even more than for ...average youth, an educational program to foster the existing life-style and vernacular would seem to be justified for those who are less well endowed intellectually" (Dunn, 1973, p. 137).

If the goal of bilingual education is "to help non-English speakers become...all that they are capable of becoming" (Regents of the University of the State of New York, 1972, p. 3), then it is quite compatible with the goal of special education "to bring exceptional children and youth to the maximum of their developmental potential..." (Cruickshank and Johnson, 1958, p. 20). To make the most of his capacities, the mentally retarded child needs special training and guidance to help him develop the habits, attitudes, and skills which will enable him to live wisely and well in his environment. Classroom instruction in

an effective special education program for the mentally retarded is, therefore, oriented toward the practical goal of independent and productive living. However, without bilingual instruction, non-English-speaking mentally retarded children will be further handicapped by a language barrier in the classroom. Bilingual instruction, on the other hand, will help ensure that they will be able to learn and will be able to make the most of their capacities. If the purpose of special education is to give mentally retarded children essential skills which enable them to function productively in society, then bilingual special education is needed to give the same skills to mentally retarded children who do not speak the society's dominant language.

The actual benefits derived by mentally retarded children from their instructional program are predicated upon the students' active participation in the academic, functional, social, and vocational aspects of the special education curriculum. All aspects of the curriculum must be understandable and meaningful to the children if they are to profit from them. Language and cultural barriers limit the participation of non-English-speaking mentally retarded children and impede the optimum attainment of a meaningful educational experience. Non-English-speaking mentally retarded children need bilingual instructional programs and services which will create the necessary conditions for effective instruction and which will facilitate their successful participation in the special education program.

III

Although appropriate assessment procedures may be utilized and the need for bilingual special education programs and services recognized, we are faced with yet another dilemma which has become a matter of concern and controversy for special educators: Should children in need of special educational services be placed in special classes or should they be kept in the "mainstream" of education by placing them in regular classes? In recent years, general education has begun to adopt new approaches, including diagnostic and prescriptive teaching techniques, which are generally thought to enable more effective service for handicapped children, including the mentally retarded. It is proposed that many educable mentally retarded children can be helped to maximize their potentials if they are educated in an intellectually-integrated, rather than segregated, environment. In fact, the new Education for all Handicapped Children Act (Public Law 94-142) gives impetus to the mainstreaming concept by requiring that children be educated in the "least restrictive environment."

Children may be placed in special or separate classes, according to the law, only when it is impossible to work out a satisfactory placement in a regular class with supplementary aids and services. However, many educators, including those concerned with the linguistically- and culturally-different child, do not advocate the end of the special class. "One of the great achievements in public education in the last 20 years has been the development of special education programs, and we do not think that these should be abandoned hastily" (Mercer, 1972, p. 96).

There are pros and cons on both sides of the controversy. Arguments offered against special classes include the following: "evidence indicates limited value to the child placed in special classes; labels result in lowered self-concept; there are weaknesses and invalidities in noneducational classification systems; and protection is a poor preparation for the social reality students will face later on" (Smith and Neisworth, 1975, pp. 314-15). On the other hand, advocates of special class placement point out that in the mainstream, mentally retarded children, for example, cannot receive the specialized developmental curriculum which will prepare them for occupational competence and productive citizenship. Arguments in favor of special classes stress the greater opportunity for individualized instruction, the protection from academic failure and social rejection, the special training of the teacher, and the prevention of slowing down of "normal" students in regular classes (Smith and Neisworth, 1975, pp. 314-15). In a sociological study of Anglo and Chicano retardates, Henshel (1972) found that those of her Mexican-American subjects who were in special education programs "seemingly remained in class much longer than many of their normal counterparts. There might therefore have been a relationship between placement in Special Education and academic perserverance among Chicano retardates...the special programs possibly offered the students more individual attention, hence more encouragement..." (p. 108).

"Many objective observers agree that there are many sound considerations that recommend mainstreaming as a safeguard against simply using segregated special education as a means of getting large numbers of children...out of mind by getting them out of sight. But these essentially sympathetic commentators nevertheless express concern lest...mainstreaming will abolish special education classes altogether, not on the basis of sound pedagogical policy but in response to irresistible ideological pressure and in the belief that handicapped children will be readily accepted in regular classrooms" (Hechinger, 1976). As a matter of fact, research findings have shown that retarded children who are in regular classes tend to be rejected or ignored. "These findings should caution against wholesale integration into the educational mainstream of the mildly retarded...without careful attention to improving their acceptance in that setting" (Dunn, 1973, p. 150).

IV

There certainly seem to be valid arguments for recommending both mainstreaming and special class placement. Whichever approach is taken to provide for the special educational needs of mentally retarded children, we must not lose sight of non-English-speaking children. Bilingual-bicultural instruction must be included in the educational plan for these children. If the mainstreaming concept is advocated, the non-English-speaking child identified as mentally retarded would be placed in a regular bilingual education program, and provided with additional bilingual special educational resources. If the special class approach is implemented, the non-English-speaking mentally retarded child would be offered placement in a bilingual special education class. In both instances, the educational plan for the child would have to consider his needs (1) as a mentally retarded child and (2) as a non-English-speaking child. Because mentally retarded children do not learn as readily as their "normal" peers, particular attention must be paid to instructional practices which will facilitate their learning:

"1. Progress is from the known to the unknown, using concrete materials to foster understanding of more abstract facts.

"2. The child is helped to transfer known abilities from one situation to another, rather than being expected to make generalizations spontaneously.

"3. The teacher uses many repetitions in a variety of experiences.

"4. Learning is stimulated through exciting situations.

"5. Inhibitions are avoided by presenting one idea at a time and presenting learning situations by sequential steps.

"6. Learning is reinforced through using a variety of sense modalities—visual, vocal, auditory, kinesthetic." (Kirk, 1962, p. 121).

Oral language development, which is a major problem even for English-speaking mentally retarded children, becomes an essential element of the instructional program for non-English-speaking mentally retarded children. The language development problems associated with mental retardation serve to compound the language difficulties of "the Spanish-speaking child [who] has to learn English as a second language and then use this second language in his school work; while his out-of-school language is mainly Spanish... The result, therefore, for a large number of such children, is lack of sufficient mastery of any language" (Bransford, 1972, p. 6). These children, at first, may seem to be "getting by" in the monolingual English classroom, but there is evidence to indicate that "a language 'gap' can occur between the child's conversational grasp of English and the more complex English patterns he needs as a tool for education" (Hull and Hull, 1973, p. 330). In order to minimize these inequities in the child's language development, and to maximize language mastery, bilingual special education must provide a comprehensive program of first-language development, as well as a sequential and systematic program for teaching English-as-a-second-language.

Although this discussion has centered upon the non-English-speaking mentally retarded child, many of its contentions are valid for other non-English-speaking "exceptional" children. Bilingual-bicultural instruction for the child with special needs aims to create an environment that reduces linguistic and cultural barriers to learning, thereby promoting communication, participation, and academic achievement, so that these children may take full advantage of their special education experience.

REFERENCES

Bransford, Louis, "Mental Retardation and the Mexican American," a paper prepared for The Regional Training Program to Serve The Bilingual/Bicultural Exceptional Child, Sacramento, California, 1971.

Cruickshank, William M. "The Development of Education for Exceptional Children." In *Education of Exceptional Children and Youth*, edited by William M. Cruickshank and G. Orville Johnson. Englewood Cliffs: Prentice-Hall, Inc., 1958.

Dunn, Lloyd M. "Children with Mild General Learning Disabilities." In *Exceptional Children in the Schools*, edited by Lloyd M. Dunn. New York: Holt, Rinehart and Winston, Inc., 1973.

Hechinger, Fred M. "Bringing the Handicapped Into The Mainstream." In *The New York Times*, April 25, 1976, Section 12:15.

Henshel, Ann-Marie, *The Forgotten Ones*. Austin: University of Texas Press, 1972.

Hull, Forrest M.; and Hull, Mary E. "Children with Oral Communication Disabilities." In *Exceptional Children in the Schools*, edited by Lloyd M. Dunn. New York: Holt, Rinehart, and Winston, Inc., 1973.

Juarez, Manuela, "Special Education In The Bilingual Program," a paper presented at the Third National Conference on Multicultural Curriculum and Materials, San Francisco, 1975.

Kirk, Samuel A. *Educating Exceptional Children*. Boston: Houghton Mifflin Company, 1962.

Mercer, Jane, "IQ: The Lethal Label." *Psychology Today*, 1972, 6: 44-47, 95-97.

Mercer, Jane R. *Labeling The Mentally Retarded*. Berkeley: University of California Press, 1973.

NEA Reporter, "Bilingual Schooling Advocated For All Children." Washington, D. C.: National Education Association, February, 1974.

President's Committee on Mental Retardation. *A Very Special Child*. Washington, D. C.: U.S. Government Printing Office, 1971.

Regents of the University of the State of New York. *Bilingual Education*. Albany: The State Education Department, 1971.

Saville, M.; and Troike, R. *Handbook of Bilingual Education*. Washington, D. C.: Teachers of English to Speakers of Other Languages, 1971.

Smith, Robert M.; and Neisworth, John T. *The Exceptional Child, A Functional Approach*. New York: McGraw-Hill Book Company, 1975.

United States Commission on Civil Rights. *Puerto Ricans in the Continental United States: An Uncertain Future*. Washington, D. C.: U.S. Government Printing Office, 1976.

Zirkel, Perry Alan. "Spanish-Speaking Students and Standardized Tests." *Urban Review*, 1972, 516: 32-40.

Chapter 44
Innovative Approaches to Multi-Cultural Programming
K. Balasubramonian and C. Frederickson*

Although each individual is a scheme of his own, both novel and enigmatic, man both individually and in groups, lives in a variety of cultures and the cultures of man are in constant change. Given this setting of constant change and uncertainty, it is little wonder that man's effort to understand himself and justify any given course of action is fraught with conflict and frustration. To escape this predicament many groups prefer to avoid contact with others, or once having been placed in contiguity, may look upon different cultures as immoral or inferior, having been conditioned by the belief that a certain way must be best.

What is needed today is for Americans to change from their segmented views of the world, to become macroscopic rather than microscopic, and to learn to be both nation-minded and world-minded. Ethnocentrism must be replaced by the understanding that one particular nation's way is not in itself superior. No individual, nation, or ideology has a monopoly on rightness, liberty, and human dignity: In the words of Amos Comenius: "We are all citizens of one world... Let us have one end in view, the welfare of humanity."

From an historical point of view, the United States, celebrating its bi-centennial anniversary, is a young and dynamic society. It may be another two hundred years, if then, before a homogeneous "American Culture" emerges. Meanwhile, educators and students stand to gain from the acceptance of a sense of cultural diversity and pluralism, recognizing poly-ethnic differences instead of denying or ignoring their existence.

According to Frances Sussna, director of San Francisco's Multi-culture Institute:

In the past, educational institutions assumed that the most useful way to encourage American-ism was to ignore racial and ethnic distinctions, submerging them in an undifferentiated general curriculum.

There was an implication that the American ideal required us to strive to be "more American" by losing anything which distinguished us from a nondescript fictional prototype. This concept was disparaging and detrimental to all Americans.[1]

It is the contention of the authors that a well-planned multi-cultural program can benefit every child within the school setting. By initiating a culturally-responsive type of educational program, at least three general goals may be achieved:

1) Society would be unified by recognizing that the wholeness of a society is based upon the unique strengths of each of its parts;

2) Educators would become responsive to the cultural values and knowledgeable about the lifestyles of those they serve;

3) Students would be encouraged to develop positive self-concepts as well as to understand and appreciate the views of others.

In order to define the terms used with this paper, the writers refer to the 1974 report of the NEA Task Force on Bilingual-Multiculture Education, which describes bilingual education within the context of a multicultural curriculum as "a process which uses a pupil's primary language as the principal medium of instruction while teaching the language of the predominant culture in a well-organized program encompassing a multicultural curriculum."[2]

An ethnic group can be distinguished according to racial, religious, and/or national origins sharing a common and distinctive culture. It may also be defined as inherited interest groups which are continually recreated by new experiences, even after distinctive language, custom, and culture losses.[3] A more humanistic definition suggests that one belongs to an ethnic group in part involuntarily, in part by choice. Ethnicity is a "set of instincts, feelings, intimacies, expectations, patterns of emotion and behavior; a sense

---

*Dr. K. Balasubramonian, Coordinator of Field Services, Bilingual Education Service Center, Arlington Heights, Illinois. Dr. Charles Frederickson, Coordinator, Department of Research and Evaluation, Board of Education, Chicago.

of reality; a set of stories for individuals—and for the people as a whole—to live out."[4]

The term "Cultural pluralism" provides subsocietal separation to guarantee the continuance of the ethnic cultural tradition and the existence of the group without interfering with the carrying out of standard responsibilities to the national welfare.[5] An even more comprehensive theory, called "cultural democracy," is characterized as a pluralism of cultures within the same educational process. Proponents give three general reasons for this new approach.

1. Researchers have determined that permanent psychological damage often results when the student's cultural identity is denied or suppressed in school.
2. Students have been found to achieve better academically when teachers respond to their cultural identities positively, thus drawing on their strengths.
3. Each culture has a special contribution to make to the experience of all students in the educational process.

The Illinois Consultation, a statewide coalition of community leaders representing ethnic and minority groups, social scientists, public officials and educators at all levels, issued a position statement which contends:

> . . . Multiethnic studies should not be treated as a peripheral or "add-on" component of eduction; i.e., a fashion in thinking to which attention is paid only when a community group makes a demand on its schools. Accordingly, an 'integrative' approach is suggested whereby elementary and secondary schools would be encouraged to inject multiethnic curriculum content into established curricula, rather than to start separate studies programs on different ethnic/minority groups.[6]

The advantage of a multi-cultural program is that it can avoid the risk of ethnocentrism and provide for the self-worth of each individual in the student population. The school and teachers must pay close attention to cultural variations in interaction and coping, formal and informal patterns of communications, and disciplinary styles.

Staff members must possess intimate knowledge and understanding of the language and culture of the students, parents, and community with whom they are seeking to establish desirable working relationships. This knowledge and understanding can be brought about only by teachers who possess personal qualities of understanding, enthusiam, dedication, and the ability to identify with others, but who, in addition, have been prepared to transmit to others the knowledge, skills, and attitudes needed to create an enlightened citizenry capable of communication with speakers of other languages.[7] Staff members must seek to provide for all individual differences, emphasizing abilities to think creatively and objectively. Teachers should encourage self-definition and development as well as group-identification and acceptance of the contributions of various groups to society as a whole.[8] A multi-cultural curriculum is a systematic group of courses or sequence of subjects using textbooks, resource books, reference books, nontextual materials, teaching aids, audiovisual aids, manipulatives, and other instruction tools that are culturally appropriate, avoiding stereotyping and misconceptions. Instruction centers around the individual needs of students and, because of the wide range of abilities among children at all grade levels, the curriculum and approach are modified to meet varied needs.

Multicultural instruction and materials development utilize a comparative analysis, which serves many useful purposes. The comparative approach can guide the teacher in gathering, preparing, and presenting "culture fair" materials and it can provide the teacher with a sympathetic understanding of the difficulties students encounter as they struggle to learn new language features and to recognize similarities and differences in cultural areas.

Schacter describes a linguistic-based contrastive analysis, as follows:

> By contrastive analysis is meant the analysis of the similarities and differences between two or more languages. The value to the teacher stems from the fact that students tend to transfer the features of their native language to the language they are learning. From this it follows that features of the foreign language that are similar to features of the native language will present little difficulty, while features of the foreign language that are different from those of the native language still require some amount of attention on the teacher's part. A contrastive analysis, by specifying just which features the two languages have in common and which they do not, can thus alert the teacher to what in the foreign language really needs to be taught.[9]

On making cultural comparisons, Lado writes:

> We cannot hope to compare two cultures unless we have more accurate understanding of each of the cultures being compared. We must be able to eliminate the things we claim to do but actually don't do. We must be able to describe the things we do without being conscious of doing them, and we must make sure we are able to desribe practices accurately, not haphazardly or ideally. And we must be able to describe the situations in which we do what we do.[10]

Since language and culture are inextricably related,

appropriate curriculum materials should be developed for two major areas:

Language Development

first language
second languages and dialects
other languages
comparative linguistics

Cultural Development (Historical, geographical, economic, sociological, anthropological, political, religious, urban-rural considerations)

home culture
cultures represented in community
area studies
cross-cultural studies

Another possible way of looking at culture is through a structural analysis, based on Sapir's statement: "All cultural behavior is patterned."[11] This stress on structured systems for purposes of comparative cultural analyses is also expressed by anthropologists:

> Cultural anthropologists, during the last twenty-five years, have gradually moved from an atomistic definition of culture, describing it as a more or less haphazard collection of traits, to one which emphasizes pattern and configuration. Kluckholm and Kelly perhaps best express this modern concept of culture when they define it as 'all those historically created designs for living explicit and implicit, rational, irrational, and nonrational, which exist at any given time as potential guides for the behavior of men.' Traits, elements, or better, patterns of culture in this definition are organized or structured into a system or set of systems, which, because it is historically created, it is therefore open and subject to constant change.[12]

Benjamin Bloom suggests that the development of stimulating and reponsive environments is central in preparing all materials and methods of instruction. He believes that new methods of teaching and superbly produced materials can profoundly affect the instructional process and markedly change the intellectual and emotional climate of teaching and learning and that all effective education is "programmed" in some degree, sometimes by the learner himself.[13]

Lado points out that when the bilingual-bicultural child goes to a traditional school, he faces a different set of social and cultural patterns as well as a different language, which may cause adjustment problems.[14]

Increasing numbers of educators are realizing that today's schools must seek to provide innovative educational programs which meet students' individual needs, interests, abilities, and backgrounds rather than expecting students to accomodate to the traditional demands of the schools. It has always been considered society's role to help children obtain a more realistic understanding of himself and others and to learn what racial and ethnic identities mean and what they don't mean. If we assume that the schools are the most effective agent for transmitting this information, the basic question is *how* to go about it.

Josue M. Gonzalez lists five different tupes of programs presently in existence, presented in increasing order of conceptual sophistication:

Type A: ESL/Bilingual (Transitional)
Type B: Bilingual Maintenance
Type C: Bilingual/Bicultural (Maintenance)
Type D: Bilingual/Bicultural (Restorationist)
Type E: Culturally Pluralistic

The culturally Pluralistic Model, labeled the most comprehensive, is characterized as follows:

> ...The emphasis is not restricted to those students from a particular ethno-linguistic group. Instead, all students are involved in linguistically and culturally pluralistic schooling. The approach represents a philosophy which is diametrically opposed to that of the "melting pot" ideology. The underlying assumption is that all constituencies of education benefit from an active participation in and appreciation of each others' backgrounds.[15]

Within the framework of multilingual education, there are many possibilities for a multitude of programs and approaches, all of which require different strategy models. Atilana A. Valencia, says the following:

> It is conceivable that no one particular bilingual model is applicable for every geographical area . . . Yet, it there is commonality, (i.e. language) a bilingual model, with culturally relevant materials for urban and rural children, can be a valid proposition . . .

> The type of bilingual program, the instructional scheme, and the types of materials to use must be relevant to the level of first or second language comprehension and usage. It is conceivable that thinking, reasoning, recalling, and other cognitive processes can be developed through media of one or both languages.[16]

There are many types of bilingual education and many types of language situations with different linguistic cultural aims and objectives. A bilingual program for recent arrivals from Puerto Rico, for example, would differ from a bilingual program for second generation Mexican-Americans. What is needed, therefore, are descriptions of different types of bilingual alternatives to be adapted by local educators, considering the appropriate community, family and school contextual settings.

For Chicago, four basic instructional models may be selected by local schools as follows:

Team Teaching Model

The team-teaching model uses the services of two teachers who join efforts in providing their students with a full program of instruction. A teacher aide completes the team. The advantage of this model include the following:

1) more adequate provision for individualization and grouping of students
2) the richer language and cultural experiences that two teachers can provide.

Departmentalized Model

The departmentalized model is used mainly in seventh and eighth grades and in high school. A few elementary schools also use it for grades five and six. In this model the children go to different rooms for each subject. The students in the bilingual program are integrated with other students (as much as possible). They are divided into groups according to their language dominance and functioning level.

Self-Contained Model

The self-contained model features one teacher, one aide, and one group of students in one learning environment for the entire school day. Students in the bilingual program receive instruction in all subject areas from bilingual-bicultural teachers. This program model has the advantage of providing a comprehensive bilingual-bicultural education.

Integrated Full-Day Model

The integrated full-day model is a modified "pull out" approach in which pupils from several classes are given the opportunity of special instruction by a bilingual teacher. The special instruction, however, is not to exceed 50% of the total instructional time.

There are two kinds of models to be distinguished. Those described above are instructional models; in addition there are program models. The program model chosen depends on the needs and goals identified by the planning committee or group. Program models may be analyzed in terms of the treatment and use of the languages and cultures.

Following are three program models which correlate with the number of years a student is enrolled in a bilingual program: model one is used for first-year participants; model two, for second-year participants; and model three, for third-year participants.

Time allotments for linguistic balance vary from 70 percent of instruction in the first language and 30 percent in the second language during the first year, to a 60-40 ratio during the second year and a 50-50 balance ratio during the third year. Expectations also increase from a 70-75 percent predicted level of mastery during the first year, to 75-80 percent the second year and 80-85 percent during the third year. The following chart summarizes the long-range program expectations.

DISTRIBUTION OF LANGUAGE INSTRUCTION AND EXPECTED LEVELS OF ACCURACY

Time Allotment by Language of Instruction	Number of Years in Program		
	Model 1 1 year	Model 2 2 year	Model 3 3 year
Dominant language	70%	60%	50%
Second language	30%	40%	50%
Level of accuracy	70-75%	75-80%	80-85%

Before proceeding to develop a multilingual or multiethnic program, it must be determined if such a program will meet the needs and desires of the students and the community. Several factors must be considered:

Does the existing educational program completely meet the students' needs?

Do the students need an enrichment program to meet their cultural and linguistic needs?

Are the supervisors, administrators, and teachers sensitive to students' needs?

Are the staff and community committed to the philosophy of bilingual-bicultural education and willing to work to make the program successful?

In discussing the desirability of a multi-cultural program, it is recommended that parents of potential students and community members be involved. The first step is to draw up a list of the tasks or steps involved. Although several steps will occur concurrently, the checklist should be approximately chronological in order, with space for indicating which individual or group will be primarily responsible for performing each task, the proposed beginning, and estimated completion dates.

The following sample checklist of tasks can be used, with modifications, for most bilingual or multicultural education program:

1. Inform community of meaning and benefits of bilingual/multicultural education

2. Establish a program planning committee
3. Conduct a needs assessment of the community and student population
4. Identify the target population and establish program priorities
5. Develop and disseminate general program goals and performance objectives
6. Define the kind of program which is most appropriate within the local content
7. Establish criteria for selecting and grouping students
8. Choose the type of curriculum to meet program goals and objectives
9. Specify staff selection requirements
10. Develop an Evaluation Design
11. Plan a staff development program
12. Choose appropriate facilities and adapt as necessary
13. Set budget standards for the program
14. Recruit and hire program staff
15. Coordinate class programming procedures
16. Conduct staff preservice training to inform total staff of program
17. Select and order, or obtain, materials, supplies, and equipment
18. Plan specific program methodologies and behavioral objectives
19. Pretest, group, and schedule students
20. Begin instruction
21. Conduct inservice training of staff as an ongoing basis
22. Produce curricular materials to meet the individual needs of students
23. Continue community involvement, set up advisory council and provide special activities
24. Disseminate information on program
25. Evaluate periodically student progress, program effectiveness, and community response; modify as needed[17]

The tasks mentioned are not exclusive of all others, but are presented to provide an idea of the kinds of activities and especially, the recommended order in which to do them.

In order to determine exactly what the educational needs and problems are, program planning is necessary to decide what kind of bilingual or multicultural program will best serve the needs of the students, the desires of the parents and the community, and the personnel, financial, and physical resources of the school.

A planning committee is vital to the success of a bilingual program since, if properly established, it will represent all people directly affected by the program. Members should include school administrators, teachers, parents of potential students, representatives of the community, and — in the case of an upper level school program, students. The establishment of this committee will provide three major advantages:

The people whom the program is to serve will be able to express their attitudes, needs, and desires.

Crucial decisions will be made—and supported—by all involved groups.

Responsibility for the success of the program will be shared by all; hence, accountability will not be a threat to anyone.

If the planning committee performs its tasks—identifying needs and problems, designing a program to meet them, and helping marshal the resources for implementation—the chances for the program succeeding are high.

The planning committee should have specified responsibilities. These may include: participating in a needs assessment of the students; surveying the needs and problems of the community; studying the educational and other services already offered in the community; determining the advisability of a bilingual program within the local community; and participating in planning and organizing the bilingual program.

In order to determine which students need bilingual education, available statistical data, test scores, questionnaires, and interviews should be used.

Standards of performance for the specific content areas and skills should be established for particular ages and linguistic levels. At this point decisions can be made as to the degree of language dominance of students and whether the numbers warrant a program, the extent to which needs are already being met by existing programs, and the opportunities for enrichment activities provided by community groups.

If, after serious consideration and discussion of the identified needs, it is decided to develop a bilingual education program, the next step to be undertaken is that of planning a program that will best meet these needs. In doing this, several questions will have to be answered.

Who will participate in this program (staff and students)?

What are the specific goals?

What behavioral objectives will achieve the goals?

What activities will help to accomplish the objectives?

What staff development will be needed?

What education will the community be given in the rationale for bilingual-bicultural education so that they can provide support and assistance?

What type of program is planned?

Once it has identified the needs and problems of the students and proposed a solution, the planning committee is prepared to undertake the next series of tasks: establishing criteria for selecting and grouping students, developing a curriculum of study, determining staff selection criteria, planning a staff development program, choosing facilities and materials and, finally, planning a budget.

When the program is ready to be implemented, in addition to beginning instruction, five activities need to be carried out: testing students for placement in the program and diagnosis of individual needs; conducting inservice training for teachers in methods of instruction; involving the parents and community in operating the program; disseminating information about the program; and evaluating the students' achievements and the program's accomplishments.

Conclusion

In summary, what is advocated is recognition and support for the *right* of ethnic groups to maintain some degree of cultural difference and some degree of ethnic communality and to regard this cultural variation as essentially beneficial for society as a whole, realizing that it will ultimately strengthen, rather than weaken, the political solidarity of the nation. It is well stated in "A Statement of Policy and Proposed Action by the Regents of the University of the State of New York:"

A person living in a society whose language and culture differ from his own must be equipped to participate meaningfully in the mainstream of that society. It should not be necessary for him to sacrifice his rich native language and culture to achieve such participation.[18]

FOOTNOTES

[1]Frances Sussna, "Ethnic Studies Can Be Up Beat," *Today's Education;* January, 1973.

[2]National Education Association, *NEA Task Force Report on Bilingual-Multicultural Education;* 1974.

[3]Lorraine A Strasheim, "We're All Ethnics," *The Modern Language Journal* (Boulder, Col.: The National Fed. of Modern Language Teachers Association, Sept.-Oct., 1975). Note: See also studies of Moynihan, Glazer, and Handlin.

[4]Michael Novak, *The Rise of the Unmeltable Ethnics* (New York: The MacMillan Company,1972).

[5]Milton M. Gordon, Assimilation in American Life (New York: Oxford University Press, 1964).

[6]G. Roth, Statement on Multiethnic Education submitted to the Illinois State Board of Education (Chicago: Illinois Consultation on Ethnicity in Education, 1975).

[7]Mary Finocchiaro and Michael Bonomo, *The Foreign Language Learner* (New York: Regents Publishing Company, Inc., 1973).

[8]Frances Sussna, *Some Concepts of a Multi-Culture Curriculum* (San Francisco: Multi-Culture Institute, 1973).

[9]Paul Schacter, "Transformational Grammar and Contrastive Analysis," *Teaching English as a Second Language* (New York: McGraw-Hill Int. Book Company, 1972).

[10]Robert Lado, *Linguistics Across Cultures* (Ann Arbor: The University of Michigan Press, 1971).

[11]David G. Mandelbaum, "The Status of Linguistics as a Science," *Selected Writings of Edward Sapir* (Berkeley: University of California Press, 1949).

[12]Harry Hoijer, "The Relation of Language to Culture; *Anthropology Today* (Chicago: University of Chicago Press, 1953).

[13]Edgar Dale, *Building a Learning Environment* (Phi Delta Kappa Educational Foundation, 1972).

[14]Robert Lado, "Linguistic and Pedagogical Barriers," *Our Bilinguals* (El Paso, Texas: Second Annual Conference of Foreign Language Teachers, November, 1965).

[15]Josue M. Gonzalez, "Coming of Age in Bilingual/ Bicultural Education: A Historical Perspective," *Inequality in Education* (Harvard University: Center for Law and Education, February, 1975).

[16]Atilana A. Valencia, "*Bilingual-Bicultural* Education: A Prospective Model in Multicultural America," *TESOL Quarterly*, 1973.

[17]Adapted by the authors from Guidelines *for E.S.E.A. Title VII Programs* (Washington, D.C.: U.S. Office of Education, 1970).

[18]*Bilingual Education* (New York: A Statement of Policy and Proposed Action by the Regents of the University of the State of New York, August, 1972).

Chapter 45
Self-Determination Through Education: A Canadian Indian Example
June Deborah Wyatt *

Derived from the basis premise that Indians are a folk people, whites are urban people, and never the twain shall meet, have been such sterling insights as Indians are between two cultures, Indians are bicultural, Indians have lost their identity, and Indians are warriors... These slogans have come to be excuses for Indian failures. They are crutches by which young Indians have avoided the arduous task of thinking out the implications of the status of Indian people in the modern world.

Vine de Loria, in
Custer Died for Your Sins

Native Indians in North America are frequently characterized by non-natives as "caught between two cultures." Abundant evidence that the majority of Indians have neither "made it" in the "white man's world" nor live exactly as their ancestors did leads to the glib perception that Indians are members of neither world and hence caught between the two. Implicit in this line of reasoning is the perception that the identity of native people in the contemporary world is an either/or proposition: Either Indians must, in order to remain Indians, remain totally traditional or they must, in order to survive at all, become totally assimilated into "white" society.

Tracing the development of the Mt. Currie Indian Community School in the rural village of Mt. Currie, British Columbia, provides evidence that this view of the choices open to native people is simplistic and ignores vital processes of self-determination and identity formation; or as de Loria states it, "the arduous task of thinking out the implications of the status of Indian people in the modern world." The Mt. Currie community is not the first in Canada or the U.S. to develop an Indian-controlled school. Notable earlier projects have been initiated at Blue Quills and Hobbema in Alberta, James Smith in Saskatchewan, Nass River in British Columbia, Rae-Edzo in the North West Territories, and Rough Rock in Arizona. With the exception of Rough Rock, little is available to document the alternatives native people have had and the choices they have made in developing educational programs.[1]

In the Mt. Currie community, the locally elected All-Indian community school board 1) rejects the assumption of many radical educations—native and non-native—that an Indian-controlled school has to be entirely immersed in traditional Indian ways to maintain integrity and native identity; 2) feels the school should provide young people with salable skills on the job market; 3) is interested in innovation but is sensitive and responsive to many conservative parents who are hesitant about rapid change; 4) is sustaining a number of aspects of traditional life; 5) chooses to work within the structure of the school rather than attempt rapid transformations. I will show that this patient approach to change, which incorporates elements of both Indian and non-Indian society, contributes to the goal of cultural and educational autonomy.

Mt. Currie is a community of 1,200 native Indians located about 100 miles north of Vancouver in the British Columbia interior. Nearby is the non-Indian town of Pemberton, population 2,400. A locally elected, all-Indian school board has administered the Mt. Currie Community School (formerly a Department of Indian Affairs day school) since August, 1973. From September, 1972, to September, 1976, school enrollment has increased from 130 to 300. This reflects, in part, an expansion of the school to accommodate students in grades 8-12, all of whom previously had to leave the reserve. It also reflects the fact that a larger proportion of children below grade 8 now attend the school. In addition, a native teacher aide and native teacher education program as well as a native language and culture curriculum have been started. More and more, community members see the school as a viable alternative to the provincial system. However, a number of parents, either because they are not convinced that native people can run a school or because the physical facilities of the Mt. Currie school

*June Deborah Wyatt is director of the native teacher training program described in this article. She is also a member of the faculty of education at Simon Fraser University, B. C. Reprinted with permission from Phi Delta Kappa.

are sub-standard, continue to send their children to the provincial public school five miles away in Pemberton.

I will show that, in the process of creating an educational alternative to the previous white-controlled school program, a group of native people has synthesized aspects of the traditional and the contemporary. They maintain their culture and identity as Indians, not by returning to the past but by nurturing traditional elements which persist in the present. Without totally immersing themselves in non-Indian society, they have incorporated aspects which they identify as valuable. They prove that developing Indian identity does not require wholesale rejection of contemporary non-Indian institutions. They have "thought out the implications of the status of Indian people in the modern world" and have taken action which represents their view of what that status ought to be. They are strongly in favor of community involvement in and control of education and are taking steps, outlined below, to implement this approach.

Gaining control formerly held by the Department of Indian Affairs facilitates synthesizing the traditional and the contimporary. In the past, the government demanded that native people accept the culture and schools of the dominant society and reject their own culture. Political and cultural repression generated hatred and rejection, not assimilation, of much of non-native culture. Now native people are making demands of their own. They are demanding and getting control over decision making. With this control comes a new ease in integrating aspects of both cultures; freer to choose, native people find elements of non-native culture less threatening than before. They feel free to combine elements of both cultures and do so without weakening their own vitality and identity as Indians. They are engaged in a creative process of "culture building,"[2] which I shall describe.

Indian Control of Indian Education

As a group, native people, in part because of their unique status as wards of the federal government, have experienced powerlessness to a greater degree and for a longer period of time than any other group in Canadian history. For individual members of the board who were sent to residential schools as children, prohibited from speaking their native language and from practicing most of what they had learned at home, the powerlessness is something they have experienced in their own lifetimes—and it is strongly associated with school settings. Every aspect of community life reinforces the theme. The federal government regulated community life, with only token power allowed to the locally elected council.

In the autumn of 1972, the Mt. Currie board took the first step in reversing this trend in education by starting a class on the reserve for 20 junior and senior secondary students (grades 8-12). Some of these students had dropped out of the provincial school in the nearby town; others were on the verge of doing so. Most had poor academic records.

The class was deliberately given a native name, Tszil, in order to identify it with the community (the name refers to a mountain glacier visible from the village). No special curriculum was designed at the time. The most important feature was that the class was located on the reserve. Until this time students could attent the Department of Indian Affairs day school on the reserve for nursery, kindergarten, and grades 1-6 only.

The next decisive step was taken in February, 1973. The Mt. Currie board took over the administration of the day school in existence on the reserve since the 1930s. This followed the Department of Indian Affairs endorsement of the National Indian Brotherhood Policy Paper: *Indian Control of Indian Education*. The eight members of the board and its chief administrative officer, the secretary-treasurer, are chosen by the Band Council. The board is a subcommittee of the Band Council, to which it is directly responsible. This administration takeover gave the board the authority to determine curriculum, hire staff, draw up the educational budget, and make long-range plans for the schools' development. As a first step in training native professionals, six native teacher aides were hired.

In September, 1973, the board approached the Faculty of Education at Simon Fraser University and asked for assistance in setting up a native teacher education program on the reserve. Credit courses have been offered at Mt. Currie since July, 1974, and in July, 1975, eight experienced teacher aides began a teacher preparation program which is co-sponsored by the board and the university. Practice teaching is done in the Mt. Currie School; all additional coursework required for provincial teacher certification is also offered at Mt. Currie. In July, 1976 intensive work in curriculum development began. All university programming, as well as selection of students and staff, has involved joint planning and shared responsibility by the board and university personnel.

Each of the above developments comes as a result of a deeply rooted conviction that success for native children derives from local community control of educational processes. Radical educators, native and non-native, frequently assume that establishing native identity through education necessitates a wholesale rejection of non-native institutions in favor of traditional practices. At Mt. Currie, establishing the locus of educational control within the community has been the first and most critical step in reinforcing aspects of traditional community life. It *has* meant reducing the role the Department of Indian Affairs plays in the community, but it has *not* meant dismissing the value of a non-native institution: schools.

Traditional community life is also being reinforced without precipitously rejecting white society or becoming immersed in the past by reducing role specialization and the fragmentation it produces, narrowing the generation gap brought about by rapid change, counteracting depersonalization, and emphasizing traditional moral values.[3] The board seeks these goals at the same time that it models the school after contemporary formal educational patterns. Modeling is evident in the school curriculum and in the teacher training program. (Details are given in the last section of this article.)

In the past, teaching skills and values to children and playing an active role in community decision making were part of being an adult. Today these tasks tend to be done by specialists, and the board is working to counteract this. Older people are now called upon to include children in their work of gathering roots for baskets and in catching, cleaning, and drying fish. The board fights fragmentation by integrating education with other roles people play.

Just as teaching was an integral part of adulthood in the past, so too was decision making about subsistence, relationships with other groups, personal misconduct, and spiritual matters. Today most decisions are made by the Band Council, its subcommittees, and salaried administrators. Over the years the Department of Indian Affairs has prevented them from becoming autonomous, convincing most adults that participation would be futile.

Athough fragmentation and non-involvement are widespread, there are also signs of vigor. Decision making by consensus is highly valued. The board wishes to nurture and reinforce this type of decision-making process and in so doing reduce the fragmentation that has come to characterize community life.

Change and the Generation Gap

Rapid changes in technology, communication, and values have created a generation gap at Mt. Currie comparable to that in other sectors of society; but in some ways it is more evident here. In other sectors of society the generation gap is characterized by differences in style of communication; in Mt. Currie it is often characterized by the use of entirely different languages—English and the native language. Oral traditions no longer bind generations together as they did in the past. The wisdom of the elders is no longer necessasry for the material survival of the community.

For many years, Indian parents have not encouraged their children to learn the native language because it would have been a handicap in school. Many still feel that, for this reason, the language should not be taught. At first by prohibiting it and then by ignoring it, schools have made children ashamed of their culture—of their parents and grandparents. The board feels that restoring pride in and knowledge of native language and traditions is one way to narrow the generation gap and to initiate the dialogue necessary for continued community growth.

Depersonalization

Depersonalization is frequently identified as a hallmark of contemporary urban living. Mt. Currie and other rural communities have been able to sustain a way of life where neighbors are not strangers. Ties of friendship and kinship form a web of relationships traceable for generations. Perpetuating this aspect of community life has been a central motivation for maintaining a school in the community. It is a place where children and young adults feel secure and at home. Reinforcing close personal ties is an essential part of narrowing the generation gap and strengthening communal, as opposed to individualistic, values.

Traditional Moral Values

Contemporary society has been criticized because of the value placed on competition, individualism, and materialism. Community educators at Mt. Currie see these values emerging among their own children and hope to combat them by reinforcing traditional values, which stress commitment to the well-being of the group, care for fellow humans, and maintenance of the proper balance in relationships between humans and nature. In describing outstanding childhood experiences in the community, a number of adults in a class I taught on the reserve referred to the times when people worked together in building houses, the community hall, fishing, taking in the hay, and gathering firewood. Money was of minimal importance and all goods were shared and exchanged freely.

The same kind of cooperation on a familywide basis is evident today at fishing season when everyone in an extended family group works very long hours catching and preparing fish. The height of this activity is in late August and early September. Student teachers are developing curriculum materials in language arts and social studies which relate to these activities, and the school calendar has been modified so that children may accompany their parents.

A native language program and subsistence and crafts activities in the curriculum are as integral a part of self-definition and survival in today's world as they were in traditional society. The native language embodies unique aspects of local culture. Fluency in it widens the network of individuals sharing a unique perspective on the world and strengthens their identity. A subsistence activity like fishing which provides a major part of the local diet, is still most effectively conducted using traditional techniques and knowledge. The intent is not to restore these elements as museum pieces but to continue building on them and to integrate them with contemporary education.

Emphasis on the Contemporary

While reinforcing aspects of the traditional, the board also emphasizes formal schooling, curriculum development, and the training of skilled professionals—all of which are directly derived from an alien cultural tradition. Though innovations in these areas are being made at Mt. Currie, none fundamentally challenges the structure of conventional education. Decisions not to introduce radical change are based on a number of factors outlined in the introduction to this article. Parental sentiment has been especially important. Community members are convinced that eliminating schools is not the route to self-determination. They are well aware of economic realities of contemporary society—and of the survival skills schools provide. They are also aware of the limited chance of the school itself initiating and carrying out a process of economic revitalization in the community at large.

Coupled with their conservative approach to the institution of the school and its non-native curriculum is a relatively conventional set of expectations about teacher preparation.

Formal Schooling: Curriculum

Along with efforts to take some aspects of education out of the school and into the community is the conviction that formal schooling should still be at the core of education. The need for a structured curriculum has not been challenged, but modifications in the content of that curriculum have been made. Basic guidelines in curriculum set out by the British Columbia Department of Education are followed and supplemented with 1) classes in native language at all grade levels taught by native people trained by a linguist, 2) native songs and dances taught by community resource people, 3) social studies and literature curricula in secondary grades which focus on vital issues in contemporary native life. Work-study

programs providing outlets for student energies and at the same time involving them in the productive life of the community are also being considered. Large-scale projects in the community to which students could contribute would be ideal. However, the impetus for these must come from the community at large, not from the present administrative structure of the school. It would be impossible, given the personnel and resources currently available, to have the school serve as the fulcrum for community economic development. However, if overall coordinated community development is to proceed, economic growth must soon parallel growth in education programs.

Some of the students graduating from the Mt. Currie school will be able to use their skills to assist in economic development. Some may require further eduction outside the community before they are able to do this. The future holds many possibilities; nonetheless, economic projects which can be initiated independently of educational ones will be an asset.

Presently, the aim of the school is to provide students with an education which will enable them to have greater freedom of choice than they have had in the past. For some this will mean staying on the reserve; for others it will mean moving elsewhere. The board feels that providing a strong academic program is the best way to insure that students will be in a position to make choices.

Critics of contemporary schools might find this approach rather tame, especially coming from a group of people ill served by the conventional system. They would probably be surprised to learn that many parents in the community are wary of the teaching of the native language. Why this hesitancy? Why not a complete overhaul of the system? The parents at Mt. Currie want to be sure that their children will be successfully educated— that they will have social and economic security. Schools, in their conventional form, have provided this for other children; they want this success for their own children. They cannot affort the luxury of experimenting with many of the recent alternatives that reject structure and academic discipline; at the present time it is far too great a risk. This does not mean that innovation particularly appropriate to Mt. Currie will not develop—the adaptations in curriculum listed above show this has already begun—but it is a gradual process.

Formal Schooling: Preparing Teachers

Classroom experience is at the core of the Mt. Currie Teacher education program.* Applicants who had not

*Focusing training in the school is somewhat conventional in comparison to a number of recent programs for minority group teachers which provide a dual internship in school and community.

graduated from high school were admitted on the basis of four months of demonstrated ability as teacher aides in the Mt. Currie school. Upon completion of the program, they will earn British Columbia teaching certificates. The professional year involves six months of intensive practice teaching integrated with six months of coursework designed to enhance practical experience. All coursework and practice teaching take place at Mt. Currie—a significant departure from programs that divide the student teacher's time between the classroom and the university campus. A full-time resident supervisor helps provide continuity in programming.

Bringing the school and the community closer together and bringing the culture of the community into the school are goals the Mt. Currie program shares with other training programs for minority group teachers. Achieving this goal requires 1) that teachers be very familiar with the child's life outside the classroom, 2) that parental involvement in the school be encouraged, and 3) that curriculum materials which reflect the life of the community be developed.

The trainees in the Mt. Currie program are long-term residents of the community. Involvement with their families provides them with continued links to community activities. They are extremely knowledgeable about the home background of their students. Emphasis is placed on building on these informal contacts through parent interviews, school open house programs, and parental involvement as assistants in field trips and as resource persons for cultural activities.

Local Curriculum Materials

Throughout the program, standard coursework is linked closely to the community setting. All student teachers are taking linguistics courses, and considerable work has already been done in creating lesson material to teach the native language. Courses in literature and the social sciences are designed to draw on the student teachers' own cultural experiences. In a course in curriculum development, 18 study units focusing on the community were produced.

Training native teachers primarily in a school setting (as we are at Mt. Currie) need not subvert a community perspective on education. Creating links between school and community does not require that trainees do a comprehensive community internship. This has been necessary in community school settings where trainees have not grown up in the community. In addition, the community school, in which there are a number of vital interlocking roles—teacher, community resource person, community liaison worker—is designed to bring the life of the community into the school. To do

this it is necessary for the teacher trainee to learn to work with all of these individuals; it is neither necessary nor desirable that the trainee master all of their roles.[4]

Conclusion

In less than four years, the board at Mt. Currie has gone from a position of powerlessness to one of power and control based on the development of administrative, political, and educational skills. The board now handles all aspects of school administration and the school will soon be staffed by native teachers. A native curriculum is being developed. The student dropout rate is decreasing.

In the same period of time, eight individuals, some of whom had not completed high school, started out as teacher aides and are less than a year away from fulfilling requirements for British Columbia Department of Education teaching credentials. They will, moreover, have the added advantage of being able to teach their native language. Last June a small group of students made up the first graduates of Tszil; several years ago some were dropouts. At last year's Christmas concert, to the delight of parents, fifth-graders made up skits performed both in English and their native language.

Parents are increasingly in evidence at the school as volunteers and visitors. As such events occur more frequently, the message is becoming clearer: This is a school run by community people for community people.

The initial concern at Mt. Currie was that schools were not serving native needs. One response could have been to dismiss schools on the grounds that they were not Indian. This was not done. Neither, however, were they accepted just as they were. Rather, the people at Mt. Currie took an institution which was in many ways a reflection of the white man's world and are making it their own. They do not intend to allow schools to be a tool of cultural subjugation, but neither do they intend to forgo any of the benefits it provides white society. They do not consider that in making use of the skills white society has to offer they have been co-opted. Neither do they feel that in reinforcing and nurturing aspects of traditional life which are still a vital part of their culture they are turning back the clock.

Like colonized native peoples in other parts of the world, the people at Mt. Currie are

...engaged in a never-ending, ever-changing innovative process of culture building and affirming cultural identity.

They are also creating

...expressions of ethnic identity and group solidarity retained in part from precolonial traditions but reshaped, altered, and created anew, sometimes using selected elements of the dominant culture.[5]

Local control of decision making and greater freedom of choice have facilitated the combination of skills of white society with traditional knowledge and values. Aspects of traditional culture—language, music and dance, subsistence techniques, localized decision making by consensus, and values of harmony and cooperation—exist easily alongside a school curriculum and teacher education program taken from non-Indian society.

Freed from some of the pressures of the past to accept non-Indian culture without question, the native people at Mt. Currie are easily adapting aspects of this culture to their own needs. Sustained community control of the growth process should continue to promote an affirmation of a new cultural identity—one integrating the old and the new in a vital synthesis.

FOOTNOTES

[1] Donald Erickson and Henrietta Schwartz, *Community School at Rough Rock*, a report to the Office of Economic Opportunity, April, 1969.

[2] Robert Glauner, "Internal Colonialism and Ghetto Revolt," *Social Problems*, vol. 17, 1969, pp. 393-408.

[3] These features of traditional community life are noted and explored with reference to community education by Fred Newmann and Donald Oliver in "Education and Community," *Harvard Educational Review*, reprint series #3, 1969, pp. 1-46.

[4] For a fuller discussion of these issues, see Larry Cuban, "Teacher and Community," *Harvard Educational Review*, reprint series #3, 1969, pp. 63-82.

[5] Mina Caulfield Davis, "Culture and Imperialism," in Dell Hymes, ed., *Reinventing Anthropology* (New York: Random House, 1972).

Section V
Curriculum

Introduction by Maria Medina Swanson *

It is now more widely understood that there are as many issues involved in bilingual education as there are variables in the linguistic, cultural and academic needs of the bilingual or non-English speaking student. The following articles serve to reflect the growing views by educators that an educational solution to the needs of these students is an integrated curriculum which reflects and reinforces the home culture(s), builds linguistic competence in both languages, and develops skills in the cognitive and social domain. This perspective not only integrates content and process, but also serves to reiterate the interrelatedness of self-esteem/concept and academic performance.

Each author focuses on a particular aspect of this curriculum and provides suggestions for implementation. Christina Bratt Paulston, for example, describes some activities used by the English Language Institute to teach ESL to literate, educated adults. She emphasizes the tightly controlled language approach which facilitates movement from a mechanical stage to a free creative stage. As she covers the areas of speaking, reading, and writing, she points to culture and other factors affecting language use. Focusing also on language issues, Joshua Fishman expertly discusses from a global perspective the evolution of languages and their utilization. His conclusions on the perseverance of the multilingual nature of our world have obvious curriculum implications for all educational efforts.

In her article, Angela Carrasquillo evaluatively considers the factors and approaches for the teaching of reading in a bilingual classroom. Discussed are both reading methodologies and management approaches—their advantages and usage. Carrasquillo also brings out the importance of knowing the student and of providing relevant experiences and materials.

Jane M. Hornburger echoes these sentiments in her article, in which she describes the educational situation of the bilingual child and shows how multicultural literature and creative activities can strengthen self-identity while fostering self-expres-

sion and developing skills.

Skills students need to function in the adult world, especially math, are of primary concern to William M. Perel. In his article, he delineates a rationale for teaching non-segregated math classes. Perel also points to the benefits of training teachers in the discovery method.

Non-verbal communication is the topic of George Szekely's article on art education for the non-English-speaking student. Szekely addresses the monolingual teacher suggesting ways in which to transfer art processes and concepts to the teaching field.

Minerva Beatriz Rosario looks at the early childhood curriculum identifying ways in which music and movement activities can help teach and reinforce cognitive, affective and motor skills while integrating different areas of the curriculum.

Although self-esteem and culture are mentioned by most of these authors, these topics are brought into primary focus in the articles by Dr. Leona M. Foerster and H. Ned Seelye. Seelye's article serves to identify areas of cognitive and affective stress experienced by the bicultural child. He also provides background information on the nature of self-identity. Descriptions of programs and classroom activities to turn culture conflict into cultural integration are also included.

Foerster's article takes a programmatic approach delineating the major components of a multicultural curriculum, their interrelationship and skills needed by students and teachers.

These articles will not only serve to provide useful implementation strategies, but help direct research and teacher training in the field of bilingual multicultural education.

*Dr. Maria Medina Swanson, Director, Bilingual Education Service Center, Arlington Heights, Illinois.

Chapter 46
Will Foreign Languages Still Be Taught In The Year 2000?
Joshua A. Fishman*

The year 2000! The year 2000! The younger one is, the more the number has a mystical and utopian quality about it, one that inspires the altruistic and millennial inclinations that we all harbor. The older one is, the more it merely implies another illusion, another impossible dream, another sad and dreary let down of the kind we have all experienced. In reality, of course, the year 2000 is neither the one nor the other. It is what we will make of it—neither more, nor less. Given the inevitable inaccuracy in post-dating the birth of Christ, the year 2000 will not even really be the year 2000. So much for revealing my own psychological age and UQ (utopianism quotient)!

The question posed by the title of this article is not even meant to be taken seriously. If it were, we could merely answer yes and let it go at that. What is really of interest is not whether mankind will continue to speak and teach a huge array of mother tongues for interaction with kith and kin and other intimates, and whether it will continue to speak and teach a rather small number of other tongues for interaction with those who are physically and psychologically more removed, but, rather, whom it will define as being in the one category or the other (and when), and which other tongues will be involved.

Yes, I do assume that most vernacular mother tongues are here to stay. Those that are protected by their own political establishments certainly are, and most of the others, that have no political power to back them, have learned or are learning to utilize modern social institutions and media on behalf of the sentimental, ideological, moral, esthetic, religious, or purely customary power with which they are associated. Of course, among the vernaculars without political power some will wax and others will wane, and still others (the ones that are most exposed to participatory social change guided by power structures related to other vernaculars) will vanish. However, new vernaculars are also being born out of pidgins round the world. All in all, therefore, I foresee only a small possible diminution in the total number of mother tongues by the year 2000 or by other foreseeable dates. Frisian- and Catalan- and Breton- and Basque- and Yiddish-speaking mothers are likely to continue to feel and believe that their mother tongues are as good and as beautiful and as inimitable—at least for everyday use with their children, husbands, and grandmothers—as do mothers that speak Albanian, Afrikans, or Hebrew. And the latter are likely to continue to believe that their mother tongues, for these same functions of intimacy, are every bit as good as French and English and Russian.

Dichotomous Distinctions

Thus far we have made three dichotomous distinctions: mother tongues vs. other tongues, non-political vs. political power and intimacy functions vs. status/distance functions. However, in reality, more refined distinctions need to be made, and additional dimensions need to be considered if the language situation of the world in the year 2000 is to be fully appreciated and if the language teaching consequences thereof are to be accurately gauged. Nevertheless, let us hang on to our three dimensions as long as we can. They still have heuristic value, even if they are not exhaustively or exclusively productive.

Just as speakers of politically unprotected languages (not to mention speakers of politically threatened ones) must come to a *modus vivendi* with the political establishment that surrounds them, so must small political establishments recognize larger ones. Such recognition needs arise in connection with education, work, commerce, travel, military experience, and inter-group contact of whatever kind, whether free or forced. There are, of course, societies whose bilingualism is fully indigenized and internalized—and these should be a lesson and a light to us all—but, by and large, second language learning, whether societal or individual, involves a we-they distinction. The first question, therefore, is whose language is to be dominant in we-they interactions, and the second, and

*Dr. Joshua Fishman, Professor of Sociology, Yeshiva University. Reprinted with permission of the author and Hispania Magazine, December, 1974.

more interesting one, into which, if any, internal function should "their" language be admitted if it turns out to be the dominant one for intergroup purposes? In this latter connection I foresee a long-term trend toward greater mutual toleration than would have seemed likely in 1900, when many nationalist movements were still at the white heat stage.

More and more politically unestablished and unprotected vernaculars are being admitted into at least primary (or early primary) school function in the western world, and I would expect that tendency to continue there and also to become more common, within the limits of feasibility, in other parts of the world with modernizing and consolidating minorities. The better known cases of Landsmal (Nynorsk), Frisian, Irish, Catalan, Lappish, Valdostian, and Romanish have their less well-known but equally numerous and revealing counterparts in Southern and Eastern Europe, Canada, the U.S.A., Latin America, and elsewhere. Indeed, I do not expect that the pressures for similar recognition for Basque, Breton, Occitan, and the like to disappear by the year 2000. Rather, I expect them to be increasingly admitted into the elementary school of one type or another, in one form or another, very much as is and will be the case with vernacular forms of Arabic and of the more sizeable sedentary and concentrated African and Asian populations without political establishments that are primarily their own. Often such recognition carries with it a modicum of further momentum into local governmental institutions and local mass media. However, it is really quite instructive to note the extent to which the latter half of the 20th century has witnessed the tapering off of secessionist movements and their satisfaction, instead, with a modicum of localized cultural autonomy. Of course, different parts of the world are at different stages in this accommodation process. While one part has cooled off, others are still boiling and steaming. Nevertheless, all in all, I would expect more vernaculars to be used/taught in the early elementary grades in the year 2000 than is the case today. Even Israel is timidly experimenting in this direction, and even with its Jewish population! The result, however, will be that speakers of non-state languages will more often be taught two languages at school rather than one—the language of their intimacy and the language of their functional polity.

Shifting Sun

Oddly enough, the same will also be true for almost all speakers of mother tongues that correspond to small and intermediate polities. These are learning languages of more powerful regional and/or international intergroup contact (and will continue to do so increasingly). Indeed, for some reason this is a more conflicted process than it is for them to permit their own minorities a modicum of self-dignity. The latter they can write off as petty nonsense (conveniently forgetting that they themselves once struggled for the same privilege). The former is a blow to their *amour propre*. Some have themselves only recently established their political and cultural autonomy. It is hard for them to admit that another language—however useful—should be made part and parcel of everyone's post-primary education when their own language has only so recently been admitted to academic respectability. For others, who recently basked in the sunlight of regional or international splendor, it is hard to admit that the fickle sun has shifted to others now and that they themselves must now do what they formerly glibly advised others to do: learn a language of wider currency and functional generality. Nevertheless, hard though it may be, I expect this trend to continue. France may be among the last to submit, for the pill is hardest to swallow in her case. Nevertheless, she will do it, as have Germany, Spain, Italy, and Japan, and find her self-image untarnished in the end, for true culture will (in France) still and always be only French.

Will I really come to an end without mentioning English, the linguistic *eminence grise*, at all? Will it continue to spread as a second language the world over, as a benevolent bonus or creeping cancer of modernity? Perhaps, particularly since Russians and Chinese and Arabs (even "Francophone" Arabs) are increasingly inclined toward it, rather than toward each others' regionally dominant languages. Perhaps, because it is not dependent on either overt political or cultural control for its spread, but rather on less threatening commercial and technological expertise and efficiency. Nevertheless, *sic transit gloria mundi*. The mid-19th century could not foresee the end of French dominance as the international language of culture and diplomacy, but it came with the political and economic downgrading of certain centers and the upgrading of others during the past century. English may enjoy a longer or shorter period of basking in the international sun. The fact that we cannot now foresee the end of its sway does not mean that it is greater or stronger or nobler than any of the other imperial languages of the past. Indeed, among sedentary populations other tongues have displaced each other much more rapidly than have mother tongues, and when they have receded, far fewer tears have been shed.

In the meantime, during its heyday, the major negative impact of English is on the anglos themselves. Unlike linguistically less-favored populations, they have little need to learn other languages or to learn them well. They are even too thick-skinned to be embarrassed by the ridicule of Francophones. They simply go elsewhere for their vacations! Surely they are paying a high price for the linguistic dominance that they have in the world of know-how and consumerism. The non-state peoples are grateful for minimal recognition of their mother tongues, but they often (and increasingly) learn both a national/regional language and an international one as well. The small state, intermediate state, and even large state peoples often (and increasingly) learn a wider regional or international language as well as their own. Indeed, all in all, there is more language teaching today (i.e., more languages being taught more widely)—and there will be even more in the year 2000—than ever before in world history. Even corners of the anglo world have had to swallow their pride (e.g. in Canada, in the Philippines, in South Africa, in Puerto Rico). But the anglo heartland continues to speak only to God and, as is well-known in the U.S.A. and in Great Britain, God has always spoken English when He was serious. However, if God were to become fickle and begin to speak Russian or Chinese in his more efficient undertakings, anglos too might begin to discover the broadening impact of bilingualism.

Fate of Fraternity

And, finally, we come to consider the fraternity of mankind: the real question of questions and, certainly, the one underlying the title of this paper. Are we not all becoming more alike? Do we not realize more fully with each passing decade the danger and folly of ethnocentrism? Does not both capitalist pragmatism and communist ideology require and lead to one language for us all? Perhaps, but not by the year 2000, and, if ever, not as a mother tongue and therefore, not as the vehicle of our deepest feelings, our most sensitive creativity, our most human humanity. The unity of mankind is a unity of fate and not a unity of face; it is a unity of ultimate interdependence, not of ultimate identity. It is true that modern technology and modern ideology lead everywhere in similar directions with respect to behavior and life styles. However, modernity is just one stripe in the cloak of many colors that every society wears. Other stripes are of treasured traditional, regional, local, and even class-derived vintage and, as a result, societal multilingualism will not merely linger on in backward corners of the globe, but it will defend and advance itself via modern methods and media (rather than merely giving in to such), and will do so within the very heartland of modernity per se.

The new ethnicity movements in the U.S.A., and similar movements already in existence (and others yet to come) in Great Britain, France, Spain, Germany, Italy, and the Soviet Union, will help to clarify the need of modern man for unique societal intimacy and intimate societal uniqueness: in his food and dress; in his music and poetry, in his art and artifacts in his celebrating and mourning, in his dying and giving birth. Thus, by the year 2000, with the continued cooling off of conflicted, exclusivistic, and ideologized ethnicity (nationalism) in most parts of the globe, it may become clearer even to intellectuals (who are always the last to understand reality since they are so convinced that it is merely their task to create it) that the fraternity of mankind requires a recognition and acceptance of mankind's diversity and of the creative use thereof. Thus, it is the dialectic between uniformation and diversification which must be seen not only as the true foundation for sharply increased foreign language teaching by the year 2000 but additionally as the true foundation for much of what is most challenging and creative in modern society (local, regional, and international) the world over.

Overall, therefore, the cut-and-dried yes that we originally gave as an answer to the question in the title of this paper is, in reality, a very resounding yes. Isn't the world getting smaller all the time? Exactly, and that is the chief reason that more, rather than less, foreign language teaching will be done in the year 2000. Almost regardless of the size and power of mother tongue speech communities these are being admitted into elementary instruction. Again, almost regardless of the power and size of mother tongue speech communities, one or more larger and more powerful languages are being required in upper elementary, secondary, and tertiary education. Both of these trends taken together lead to more rather than less foreign language teaching. Both of these trends together also indicate that diversification and uniformation in language and culture are concomitant tendencies in modern times. The smaller world, the brave new world, will be neither entirely the one nor the other. It will, indeed, require foreign language teaching in order to be one world, and even in order to exist to and beyond the year 2000!

The problem of modern man is not that he does not love, but that he must integrate a larger number of loves than ever before: love for himself, love for his family, love for his neighbor nearby, and love for neighbors at successive distances. Most of these loves bring with them an additional language. Ultimately modern man will be sufficiently mature to fully demonstrate the parable that to know another is to love him, to love him is to know him, and nothing is more centrally identified with us or with others than the languages we speak best and most. The language teacher's potential contribution to the future of mankind is a fateful one indeed. Would that we will all be equal to the task ahead or, failing that, that we will not permit our personal failings to color our societal goals and perspectives. (MAP/*materiales en marcha*, December, 1973)

. . . I am going to rough and unknown regions but I will reach my journey's end. . .

Chapter 47
Self-Identity and the Bicultural Classroom
H. Ned Seelye*

Children who grow up with a foot in two different cultures have a unique opportunity to view objectively what in most people is a conditioned reflex beyond easy scrutiny. Biculturalism is not without its stresses, for cross-cultural contact inevitably provokes cross-cultural conflict. In focusing on stress, this article risks the appearance—at once depressing and negative—of not acknowledging the rich potential inherent in being bicultural. This appearance would be grossly inaccurate. Nonetheless, tension is produced by intimacy with disparate cultures and it can be dynamic or destructive.

To the extent we prescribe the same aspirin for *all* the maladies that cultural differences produce, Jimmy the Greek would give us low odds on our patient survival rate. The odds will improve when we make a more exact diagnosis of the problem and prescribe a more appropriately specific medicant. Culture problems fall into a number of areas. Some concern adults, others, children. In some, people of one or another ethnic background are involved in different ways. Some problems call for skill development, others require affective treatment. This article will focus on both affective and cognitive stress centering on how bicultural youths perceive themselves.[1]

Social Marginality and Conflict Integration

It takes two to tango and it takes two to miscommunicate. Bilingual students are exposed to the trails, trivia, heroes, and villains of *both* Latin America and the U.S. The challenge is for them to *integrate* what they hear. I studied Mexican history in Mexico and U.S. history in the U.S. Only after several hours of history lectures about the U.S. Southwest did I realize that my U.S. teacher was talking about the same historical period that my Mexican teacher had addressed previously. In the area of overlap, there were two completely different histories!

Bilingual teachers have three choices: they can ignore the problems of integrating two separate world-views and ways of doing things—and leave the student to his own recourses; they can take regional and partisan positions and "sell" the slanted version of one country or the other; or they can help students deal with the effects of cultural conditioning.

Because of the ambiguous and conflicting messages that a bilingual child experiences, it is essential that bilingual teachers be both sympathetic *and* accepting of the child's idiosyncratic presence. Bilingual teachers who show sympathetic disposition to *both* cultures avoid exacerbating the student's own identity dilemma. Cultural premises can be challenged, when appropriate, by playing either the role of loyal oppositon or Devil's Advocate—as long as the tone of sympathetic playfulness comes through.

The reality of the bilingual classroom forces us to deal with the student's cultural heritage vis a vis U.S. cultures. The twain hath met. It is the bilingual teacher's role to interpret both cultures honestly and sympathetically and to help students who are *between* cultures avoid schizophrenia, diarrhea, and assorted nervous tics. I am writing this paper ten thousand feet up in the Andes mountains, where Spanish-speaking teachers confront classrooms of Quichua-speaking children. The survivors—both children and teachers—are those who can function biculturally. (Since one cannot function within a society without being able to communicate with its inhabitants, bilinguality is a prerequisite of biculturalism.) But to be bicultural is to be marginal. Bicultural people are absolutely essential to society, but are regarded, in many situations, as marginal nonetheless, since a bicultural person's communicative patterns differ from mainstream members of either culture, and since he cannot be counted on to have the values of one culture to the exclusion of the values of the other culture in those areas where they contrast.

How to help a kid feel good about himself, his family, his cultural roots while he is exposed to the kind of feedback that regards him as a sociological problem? How to help him keep the respect of his monocultural relatives while at the same time helping

*H. Ned Seelye, Chairman of the Board of International Resource Development Inc., (Chicago), and formerly Illinois State Directory of Bilingual Bicultural Education.

him win friends and influence people in the U.S.? How to help him find his own way to integrate conflicting values and social behavior? How to show him that you think he's neat!

Classroom activities can be provided to afford explicit help in integrating conflicting values. There are a number of cognitive things that can be done to highlight these conflicts (see Seelye, 1974), but there is no pat way to dispatch the confusion that accompanies the ensuing conflict. Tender-loving-care seems to be the response that inspires most confidence. Uvaldo Palomares' technique of the magic circle may bring some of these affective confusions to light for subsequent discussion. For high school children, value clarification exercises may make the problem easier to deal with (see, for example, Casteel and Hallman, 1974).

One can escape being culturally different by forfeiting one of the two cultures—and there is always considerable pressure on economically and politically subservient groups to make this sacrifice—but trading one brand of monoculturalism for another seems an unnecessarily palid business. Besides, to go from monocultural Y to monocultural X requires passing through a state of biculturalism, and that is where the action is. To the extent a culture group is also physically distinguishable from "mainstream" people then "escape" from being regarded as different is often impossible. Bilingual teachers are ideally suited to get their students to sing of the poetry and freedom of being a "marginal" bilingual. The French intellectual André Malraux argues that we, the world, are between cultures. Just as the fall of Rome ended one era, the end of European colonization (circa 1950) ended another. We are now living in the *interim* between a colonial era and a "decolonial" era, he says. David S. Hoopes, director of the Society for Intercultural Education, Traning and Research, refers to the potential of the bilingual person to "mediate" between cultures. Perhaps marginal, interim, bicultural man can put his mediating imprint on the next, more compassionate, era.

It is the expectation of most people in the U.S. that the child's efforts wil be amply rewarded when he loses the "annoying" vestiges of a "foreign" culture and becomes an All-American. The realization of this expectation would be as tragic for the intellectual development of the U.S. as for the child. In becoming All-American the child is expected, like Judas, to deny his past associations and allegiances, rather than to build on them: the Chicano first-grader, suffering through reading in a language he does not yet know so that in high school he can suffer through Spanish I, a language he was made to forget. If mainstream, dominant people get what they think they want — the

extinction of minority cultures — and this is a world-wide phenomenon, they will inherit the bitter irony of rootless uniculture, with its attendant alienation and commerce in headache remedies. Given the world-wide practice of immigration for employment (e.g., the German need for Italian workers), "foreigners" can be expected to be present in any developed country for some time.

To the extent that parents want Juanito to be a little replica of themselves, talking, acting, and thinking as they do, they are consigned to disappointment. The culture of the parents was a seasoned reponse to the conditions in which they lived. Often, they lived an agrarian, pre-industrial life that bears little resemblance to present urban life in Mexico City or San Juan. It was often a life lived before there were many opportunities for the occupation of the son to differ substantially from that of the father; it was a pre-women's liberation life that relegated the opinions of the daughter to be those of the mother, and later, perhaps, to those of the mother-in-law; it was life where social classes "knew their place." It was a life enriched by folk art, strong beliefs, and wise adages. And the culture worked, witness the very existence of children from that cultural parentage in our classrooms. But it was a culture that is largely dysfunctional in post-agrarian societies. That this is so is seen in the daily Latin American drama where thousands of rural people flock to the cities in hope of a better life. A hope generally not realized in their generation. At any rate, it was the culture of another generation, and the prerogative—and necessity—of each generation is to modify the rules of the game.

Nor are children home free who emigrate from an urban culture outside the U.S. While the urban cultures of London, Buenos Aires, Mexico City, and Los Angeles probably have more in common with each other than any does with the peasant classes in their respective countries, there are still important differences among them. Each culture is a response to present needs seen through the many-colored but distorted prism of its own unique past experiences.

No, the culture of bilingual children cannot be precisely that of the parents. To be so would be to sacrifice the experience and independence of the children for the expediency of the status quo.

The Origin of One's Sense of Identity

Before we look at ways to strengthen self-identity and improve self-esteem in bilingual children, let us examine how one's self-identity emerges.

Non-human life forms evolve behavioral characteristics that are largely determined by genetic selection brought about through the interaction of the species with forces that selectively favor the propagation of certain genes. In Homo Sapiens, it is man's *culture*—not his genes—that evolves to meet the exigencies of changing life conditions. Culture is the principal adaptive mechanism humans use to cope with life's circumstances. When these circumstances change, the adaptive mechanism must also change if the individuals concerned are to continue as healthy organisms. To the extent survival of a society is threatened by behavior that has become dysfunctional through an overly rigid and specific response to mutant circumstances, then those dysfunctional cultural aspects become a liability to the group. In H. Sapiens, there are no sub-species to evolve different genetic directions; there are only sub-cultures that are tools, not living organisms, to help man adapt to his environment.

Were culture seen simply as an adaptive tool, to use or discard as needed, then culture change would not evoke the emotional trauma associated with its occurrence. The culture of man, besides being pragmatically adaptive, also provides the vehicle for aesthetic and moral satisfaction. Thus, culture change induces anxiety in the gratification of the most subjective of basic needs, the psychological. Were epistemological inquiry into the nature of beauty and truth cross-cultural, "future shock" would be greatly diminished. Unfortunately, cultures define beauty and truth as ethnocentrically as any other topic. Hall (1976) argues that man must learn to separate his perception of self from the cultural extensions of his self that he fabricates in response to adaptive pressures. These cultural responses can easily lose their functionality as circumstances change. The bicultural person is an outgrowth of adaptive needs. From these, in turn, must be identified those belief forms that have cross-cultural validity in satisfying aesthetic and moralistic needs.

A child begins life with a genetic, chemical, neurological base that will be affected by age, disease, and nutrition. Physical anthropologists have not discovered *any* gene present in one race or ethnic group that is not found in other races or ethnic groups as well. Given populations have a higher frequency of certain genes than have other populations, but humans share the same gene pool, dipping into it to greater or lesser extent with regard to specific genes.

Nutrition varies widely from population to population. To the extent that we are eating better food than our parents, our in-born genetic program acts out its development without debilitating hinderances. We are what we eat, some say. A child with an extra Y chromosome, Down's Syndrome, will never have the intellectual capacity to be a nuclear physicist regardless of what he eats, but a genetically-abled genius will never realize his potential if his first few years are spent in belly-swollen malnutrition. It is also unrealistic to expect a child from a ghetto environment, where his parents have been unable to resolve the essential problems of food and roof, to come to class disposed to reach for academic excellence per se. It takes a lot of teacher skill to so motivate the child. Some character traits appear to be present at birth, for children of the same parents and raised in the same home often display different traits such as aggressiveness, passivity, and strength, that persist throughout life.

No matter how smart your mother was, or how much vitamin D-enriched milk you drink, you are not going to be a nuclear physicist if you are born—and stay—in a Kapauku Papuan village in New Guinea. Nor are you going to design a suspension bridge (a Pigmy invention) if you live in the Sahara Desert. One realizes potentials within a cultural setting. It is no genetic accident that different cultures experience a flurry of meritorious production in the arts—a Golden Age—at infrequent but discernable periods in their history. It is a *cultural* accident. Facilities for intellectual development in modern Latin America, as reflected by preferred governmental scholarships, go to bright children who want to become engineers, not poets. The intellectual capacity for both is there in the gene pool, but cultural elements engender one at the expense of the other. (Some would say that poets thrive in adversity.)

When we think of ourselves, it is in relation to some basic inherited urges, to past experience and to our present condition. We see ourselves *in relation to* our environment. The way we perceive this relationship depends on the looking glass we use. Our in-born intelligence, our group-intelligence (the wisdom of the tribe), our language system, and the particular situations in which we find ourselves are the major determinants of how we see ourselves.

The brilliant neanderthal who invented the wheel did not see movement the same way his neighbors, the Flintstones, did, although they adopted his/her insight readily enough. Individual intelligence is the source of the folk wisdom of a people. Alan W. Watts (1968) has observed that "the stereotyped attitudes of a culture are always a parody of the insights of its more gifted members." Bilingual children will develop different world-views because—but not *only* because—of differences in intelligence.

The collective wisdom of one's culture influences one's concept of self in such basic matters as whether we see ourselves as subject and the rest of the world as object (Western thought), or whether we se ourselves at one with the world, a pattern of energy interacting with all things and getting our form from this interaction (Eastern thought). Do we have an identity independent of our interaction with others and with nature? Social psychologists would say no. As products of Western thought, however, we rebel against the notion that we are not captains of our ship. But does the realization that our self is inseparable from its environment take away any of our uniqueness? Who has had the same genetic combination? Who has had the same experience in life? The possibilities for human uniqueness are infinite in spite of our dependence on "...circumstances beyond our control."

A big step in liberating ourselves from the caprices of cultural conditioning is taken when we soberly perceive the immense importance it plays in the determination of our self concept. In discovering this concept of self, the bilingual person does not deny the influence of one or another culture on his character—he accepts that he is a product of all his experiences. The Spanish philosopher Jose Ortega y Gassett expresed the interaction of self and culture in this way: *Yo soy yo y mis circunstancias*. Once one knows how the game of life is played, and that it is a game—complete with arbitrary rules and plaster of Paris incentives—one is free to take a more sporting attitude toward the human scene.

Teachers can help their students develop insight into the part cultural conditioning plays in the formation of their own identity by having them talk about the extent they want to enjoy the company of family and friends, and how much, on the other hand, they want to march to the tune of a different drum beat. Whose drum beat? What type of person are they describing? Are they comfortable with the description? A puzzle in the interrelatedness of self identity and societal feedback that may intrigue older students focuses on a literary dilemma: Is Sancho Panza immortal because Miguel de Cervantes Saavedra, or does Cervantes owe his immortality to Sancho Panza?

For adult members of mainstream U.S. culture, there is an excellent video-tape series for use in a two-day workshop (by a trained director) to bring the viewer into conscious awareness that his values are culturally conditioned and that subtle manifestations of these conditioned values can be observed in common everyday behavior. Some fourteen different sequences appear on the video-tape, and each sequence illustrates one U.S. cultural pattern through six brief episodes. Each episode, lasting from a few seconds to three or four minutes, shows an American interacting with a "contrast-American." The contrast-American plays the part of someone who has values that differ from those of the American. Because of the resultant misunderstandings, the detection of mainstream values is made pedagogically easier than it would otherwise be. Even so, in some of the episodes the conversation seems so "natural" that one is hard pressed to detect any "subtle manifestations of a culturally conditioned

value." These tapes were developed with a grant from the Bilingual Department of the Illinois Office of Education for use in schools with bilingual programs. The tape is aimed at U.S. teachers, administrators, and other school staff who interact with children, parents, and teachers of a different cultural background. The setting and roles reflect those found in a multicultural school. One result of the tape is that mainstream Americans understand themselves better as people who—like everyone—have culturally conditioned values. Another result is that they have an *explicit* understanding of fourteen of these values. (For further information concerning this tape, contact Dr. Alfred J. Kraemer, Human Resources Research Organization, 300 North Washington Street, Alexandria, Virginia 22314.)

Diverse Models For Adjusting to Bicultural Conditioning

Still, a powerful predictor of behavior is knowledge of a person's cultural background when subcultural variables such as age, sex, social class, and place of residence are taken into consideration. If one is the product of cultural conditioning, then bicultural people are the product of two *contrasting* forms of cultural conditioning. Who are we when we are between cultures? What moral principles do we hold?

Looking at the behavior of people who have attempted to "make peace" with disparate cultural systems, molding conflicting experience into an integrated sense of self, it is clear that there are many different ways to accomplish this. The models that other people provide can help students see where they are vis á vis the process of biculturation. These models can also help students judge the usefulness of different forms of adaptation for their own lives.

Real-life models cover a wide range: Amish farmers following the customs of rural farmers of two centuries ago—even though their descendants who remained in Germany no longer share that culture; Eskimo fishermen who return home after years of medical treatment in sanatoriums in urban Canada, never to mention anything that happened during those "foreign" years; nativistic South Sea Islanders who create a glorious, ancient culture the way they imagine it to have been; the person who changed his name from Hipólito Pérez Ramos to Hal Rome, and says he's of Italian descent if anyone asks; the angry militant who rejects *all* cultural values; the Buddhist Bodhisattva, who sees life as a game where one avoids confusion of social role with self identity; the person who neatly compartmentalizes values into separate boxes, one for each culture; and so on.

Eight divergent ways in which individuals respond

to situations of marginality or uprootedness were identified in an unfunded proposal written a quarter of a century ago by Donald T. Campbell, the social psychologist, from descriptions found then in the social science literature: (1) To become an agent of change through a personal and creative deployment of innovation; (2) To have one's ego damaged, as characterized by neurotic indecisiveness, aimlessness, schizoid withdrawal, self-deprecation, cynicism, and destructiveness; (3) To convert a relativism of values into a stable standard of reference and a way of life; (4) To adapt to situations by focusing on the interplay between role and reference group, letting one's behavior be guided by several discrete "generalized others;" (5) To retain one's first cultural goals (e.g., money) while abandoning the culturally prescribed means of achieving them; (6) To reestablish an orthodoxy, often more rigid that the "natural born" variety, characterized, perhaps, by a reactionary return to the parental culture or in the return to the ghetto; (7) To rigidly over-conform to the second culture, and in anti-egalitarian, anti-lower-class attitudes on the part of the socially mobile; (8) To adopt, in concert with other uprooted persons, a novel orthodoxy, differing from and probably hostile to all of the traditional cultures whose contact may have produced the marginality.

Cultural relativism can be discussed in a classroom from several perspectives: if you wanted people to think you were brave, and you were in culture A, what would you do? What ideas do you have that you would be willing to hurt someone else to keep? If someone from culture B came to your house for dinner and ate his spaghetti with his fingers, what would you do? What if it were against your beliefs to eat any kind of meat and you had not eaten anything all day and you were invited to a friend's home for dinner and all they served was steak and potatoes?

If a student can find "kindred spirits" among the school staff, perhaps someone of the same ethnic background, his attempts to find suitable models for emulation will be aided. But teachers should not make the mistake of thinking that they are all things to all students. Bicultural teachers can bring to the student's attention a wide range of models found in literature (see Marquardt, 1969, for suggestions) or in examples of people living in the community. Students can be given the assignment of interviewing different people in their family or community who are bicultural to see how they describe their attempts at integrating cultural differences. There is no *right* way to become bicultural, but there are ways that are healthier than others. The healthier ways use all experience as a springbroad to greater awareness of the interrelatedness of self and the universe; they do not deny experience. Examples of how others have

worked out the problem let students know they are not alone and they let them know there are many ways to accomplish cultural integration. By projecting his own concerns into some one else's problem, the student can retain privacy while effecting definitional clarity of his own frustrations.

The Individual and the Group

A factor to be considered consciously by a bilingual child is to what extent he receives satisfaction from group endeavor rather than from individual accomplishment. Each society has people of every ilk, but some societies are oriented around one relationship more than another. In the U.S., for example, the Protestant Ethic, the frontier spirit, laissez-faire, high class and geographic mobility, and the large size of the country have produced a lot of Captain Marvels who change the rest of the world to suit themselves by shouting, *"SHAZAM!"* In Mexico, on the other hand, the extended family often affords the setting within which one achieves psychological sastisfaction. In socialist or communist countries a major attempt is being made to have individuals sublimate their own cravings into societal priorities so that the good of the group has more psychological force than drives toward individualization.

All societal institutions pit the group against the individual, but some societies do it with more efficiency than others. A person who is highly ego-centered can expect frustration in a society whose institutions are based too efficiently on subordinating individual interest to group goals. Likewise, a person who feels comfortable in working for the good of the many will experience distress in a society where he is expected to contribute as a individual, without aid of family, friends, or work cohorts.

One semantic trap to avoid in a discussion of ego is the following continuum popular among Western psychologists:

strong ego . . . . weak ego

This falsely implies a positive value on "strong ego" and a negative value on "weak ego." An antidotal continuum might be the following:

weak sense of universe . . . . strong sense of universe

Here, strong ego is synonymous with weak sense of universe.

Espressing values

A bilingual child's search for identity necessarily will have to examine the feedback he receives from people of diverse cultural conditionings. He will observe many people of both cultures confusing the symbol with the value it represents. To the extent that a person associates the absence of a particular symbol, say a handshake, with an absence of the value it represents, respect and friendship, then that person's vulnerability to culture shock is considerably increased.

There are many ways to express basic values, and these ways usually differ in form or distribution from culture to culture. A child may begin to identify self by saying, "I am a person who always shakes hands with friends when we stop to talk," but he will want to consider, as he becomes bicultural, to identify himself more generally as a person who always observes the conventional responses to show respect and friendship. It is helpful in developing a sense of self to separate values from the diverse ways to express them. This is not to say that we are concerned with philosophic ends rather than with means, for we never arrive at ends— we spend all our time with means. Psychological values, on the other hand, are actualized through behavior. Some thinkers, B. F. Skinner, for example, would say that we get our values from our behavior. The "bicultural self," however, would probably not say, "I behave differently depending on where I am;" he might say instead, "I express myself in different ways depending on where I am." The former statement lacks the personality integration of the latter. A good example of how personality integration occurs on a daily basis is our juggling of roles: mother, wife, husband, cab driver, scout leader, etc.

Importance of Cognitive Success

It is hard to feel good about yourself if everyone except your mother is telling you what a dud you are. From the age of six to 18 or 22, a dud is anybody in school who gets below a B, or, depending on the neighborhood, a C. Successful school experiences are like jolts of energy that recharge the batteries of self esteem. Bilingual program efforts to strengthen pupils' self esteem *must* include skill development. One of the concluding observations made by Lieberman, Yalom, and Miles (1973) in their study of encounter groups is:

"The participant must be able to carry something out of the group experience that is more than a simple affective state. He must carry with him some framework, though by no means necessarily well-formulated, which will enable him to transfer learning from the group to his outside life and to continue experimenting with new types of adaptive behavior... Most small groups will spontaneously evolve into a social unit which provides the affective aspects of the intensive group experience; the leader's function is to prevent any potential obstruction of the evolution of the intensive experience, and in addition to be a spokesman for tomorrow as he encourages group

members to reflect on their experiences and to package them cognitively so that they can be transported into the future" (p. 439).

Success in the "non-cultural" cognitive areas of the curriculum will bolster a healthy sense of self-esteem. So in a real sense, the math or gym teachers are aiding the cause of self-identity when they ply their trade to get kids to do things they could not do before.

Two common mistakes usually accompany cognitive skill development in bilingual programs. The more common of the two is to falsely assume that the learning style of the "average" Anglo child, as embodied in course syllabi, will snugly fit the Latino child if only it is translated into Spanish. The other mistake is to falsely assume that most Spanish-speaking children share the same learning style, even if it is seen as differing from the Anglo. The trick—and it does not matter what ethnic group you happen to be teaching—is to be prepared to help a student learn concepts and skills in the best way for him/her. One can expect nearly as much variance within ethnic groups as between them.

Messages From the Dominant Culture

Since much, if not all, of our sense of self comes from the feedback of others, it is essential that members of the dominant culture experience a more positive stance with regard to the "foreign" background of the bicultural child. An excellent way of accomplishing this is to include "mainstream" children in portions of the bilingual program, especially to learn the language and culture of the "minority" children. In areas where the "transitional" nature of bilingual education makes this difficult to do, efforts expended in convincing local administrators and board members that it is worthwhile to use local funds to accomplish the integration of mainstream children can reap excellent rewards. It is not enough for a child to feel positive about his background—his feeling must be reinforced by those whose opinion he values.

Some people value bilingualism only as a desired condition of people of non-English background, while expecting children and adults from the dominant culture to remain monolingual. This view negates the worth *per se* of bilingualism and would limit its utility to that of a remedial, communicative tool for discourse with the dominant culture. The self-esteem of the "minority" bicultural child is enhanced by the presence of teachers, administrators, and peers of the mainstream culture who are fluent in the language and customs of the minority ethnic group. It is also positively affected by the presence of bilingual bicultural models from the minority culture as well. It is easier for a child to see the value of bilingualism and biculturalism if it is sought after by people from all cultural backgrounds.

Culturally General or Specific Texts?

Motivation to learn can be enhanced if the student finds in his instructional materials people and problems with which he can identify. A student booklet developed by the Peace Corps in Ecuador, entitled, "Ñucanchi Mundoca Cashnami" ("This Is How Our World Is"), contains a graphic of a Quechua woman nursing her child, of corn growing, of a carpenter at work, etc. It was made expressly for Quichua-speaking *otaveleño* children to learn about the world around them through images that really belong to their world. The book has been a success—among *otaveleños*. When the book was tried with Quichua-speaking children of other tribes, the pictures provoked laughter—the corn was all right but the headdress of the woman looked wierd and the long braid of the carpenter struck them as even wierder. The bilingual teachers were faced with a dilemma: to publish different editions for each subcultural division of the Quechua world, or to broaden the child's world by including graphics of many different Quichua-speaking people at the expense of total relevance. The latter decision was made by the Peace Corps and the results are encouraging. In the case of the excellent SCDC materials developed by Ralph Robinett *et al* in Florida, the decision was made to publish three versions of their materials: a Mexican version for the Southwest, a Cuban-Puerto Rican version for the East, and a version for use in areas such as Illinois where there is a mixture of Mexicans, Puerto Ricans, Cubans, and other Hispanic nationalities. The economics of the situation heavily weighs the decision. No one in the U.S., for example, is getting out versions of their materials that would allow a Guatemalan or Argentine child to immediately relate to them. However, to unduly shrink the world a child is exposed to would duplicate the error of previous textbook writers and illustrators who thought the world was populated solely by WASPS. In deciding how culturally specific to make instructional materials, some compromise can be healthy.

National vs. Ethnic Origin

There is one area where the pedagogic response must be culturally specific: when the objective is positive reinforcement of one's national or ethnic origin. Ironically, one of the least potent ingredients of self-identity in monolinguals is a sense of being part of a national political system. There are only a few occasions yearly when nationality is given ritualistic observance. Other than during an election year, or celebrations such as Independence Day or birthdays for deceased statesmen, one hardly thinks of one's "national" identity. Much more powerful are subnational identities such as family, city, region, or roles such as woman, teenager, Mormon, or high school teacher. Nationality becomes significant by contrast with another nationality in much the same way that ethnocentrism comes into relief when its basic premises are challenged by an outsider from a different value system. Governments often play upon this reality by making much ado about some political problem involving "outsiders," while at the same time muting criticism of internal affairs. Territorial disputes, for example, are bombastic occasions to sound the drums of national identity.

Looked at from the perspective of nationality, ethnic identity is often a thorn in its side. Ethnic factions often have strong regional and social class connotations and are frequently hostile to the national concept: witness Ireland, the Basques and Cataláns of Spain, the Brittanies of France, the Ukrainians of Russia, the Yucatán Mayas of Mexico, the Colorados of Ecuador, etc.

Focusing on a national level of identity can obscure important ethnic differences within any one nationality. Likewise, a narrower focus on ethnic background can overlook importantly shared attitudes and behavior. One blond, blue-eyed, prospective bilingual teacher was berated by an ethnically conscious community worker who claimed, with much feeling and some sarcasm, that Puerto Rican students would not be able to identify with her. There are however, Puerto Ricans of all types of backgrounds, and this prospective teacher happened to be one of them. It is common to hear Spanish-speaking activists in the U.S. refer with pride to the Indian side of their backgound. This is a healthy sign of self-acceptance as long as the other sides of their ethnic background are not being denied in a nativistic attempt to forget that there are no "pure" races. The "raza cósmica" that Jose Vasconcelos speaks of is a mixed, mestizo "race."

Of the two, ethnic background is more significant that nationality *if* the person is residing within the country of birth. Where I lived for several years in Italy, people were first Vicentini, second from Veneto, thirdly from Northern Italy, and only fourthly Italian. When we go abroad, however, national identity assumes greater importance—the Vicentino is Italian, the Alabaman in Mexico is a *yanqui*, and the Welshman in France is an *anglais*. One of the characteristics of living in a second country is that one finds oneself dealing frequently with what was hitherto an infrequent concept of self-identity—nationality. One is generally, by consequence, ill equipped to deal with the national aspect of one's identity except in contrast to behavior of a different nationality. The effort is often tiring, but a positive sense of both ethnicity and nationality enhance self-esteem.

Whether an event provokes a behavior change in its participants depends on the situation in which it occurs. For example, when five men talking in a room are joined by a woman colleague, this will have greater perceived significance than when the men are joined by a male colleague. The extent to which this particular event disrupts the group dynamics varies widely from culture to culture. It is precisely this variance that increases cross-cultural fatigue.

The bilingual teacher may be more effective in buttressing the self-esteem of a child when ethnic identities are not lost in the national conglomerate. Bilingual children need help in seeing the forest (the nation) as well as the trees (the subcultural entities). (An excellent guide to help Americans abroad understand and interpret mainstream U.S. culture was prepared for college-educated adults by Edward Stewart, 1971.)

The Glorious Past vs. the Troublesome Present

In the context of strengthening self-identity, there are differences of opinion concerning the utility of acquainting children with the historic past versus the contemporary life. Do we teach about the Aztecs or about Mexico's leading heart specialists? (Often, from a child's perspective, anything older than five years is "ancient" history.) Both ancient and recent happenings have their place in bilingual programs, but serve different funtions. Knowledge of one's ethnic and/or national background serves to provide a sense of one's own continuity with the past and provides the feeling (some would say illusion) that the traditional ways are being retained, if only via memory. The Jivaro Indians of Ecuador are doing just this in their bilingual programs through transcriptions of stories told by old shamans. This is especially important where an awareness of continuity is threatened by loss of language or by a sudden, drastic change in what one does or how one looks. Knowledge of historic and anthropological accomplishments can instill pride in one's background and give one a sense of cultural roots. Examples taken from contemporary life, on the other hand, have a more immediate appeal to youth; they aremore a call to action. For some students of mathematical aptitude, modern mathematicians like Einstein may be more effective models than ancient giants like Aristotle.

Rapid culture change breeds alienation if the change is imposed by outside forces. It is common for cultures to experience a confrontation-depression-revival syndrome, the whole process taking about a hundred years, as a result of contact with a culture perceived to be dominant. Bilingual teachers can help combat this particular source of alienation by helping insure that control of the direction of bilingual eduation is principally influenced by those most affected, including parents and students. Alienation is reduced when one thinks of himself as choosing the "best" of the second culture; the potential for alienation increases when one adopts wholesale a different way of life in place of one's own.

This paper has discussed some of the stresses routinely experienced by bicultural youth, including social marginality, identity crisis, value ambiguity, provincial school curricula, and negative feedback from the dominant culture that occasionally degenerates into "racial" discrimination. The result is energy-draining.

It is difficult for monocultural, mainstream educators to scratch more than the surface in helping bicultural children realize their creative potential. This will remain true as long as teachers, current curriculum and curricula developers remain monocultural in experience and outlook. Everyday role changes manifest a subcultural flexibility that can aid both monocultural and bicultural educators to develop insight into the process of biculturation.

Throughout biculturalism, children need to experience and internalize individual self-determination in their efforts to integrate diverse systems. The difficulties involved in integrating two differing value systems are not resolved by either having an individual accept "cultural pluralism" or by having him live in a society that enthusiastically accepts it. The critical integration in this process is a personal, psychological one that can be helped by teachers who themselves understand the process explicitly. At present, this understanding is intuitive and fragmentary.

SELECTED REFERENCES

Casteel, J. Doyle, and Clemens Hallman, *Cross-Cultural Inquiry: Value Clarification Exercises.* Gainesville: University of Florida (Center for Latin American Studies), 1974.

Cole, Michael, Joseph A. Glick, and Donald W. Sharp, *The Cultural Context of Learning and Thinking: An Exploration in Experimental Psychology.* New York: Basic Books, 1971.

Goodenough, Ward Hunt, *Cooperation in Change.* New York: Russell Sage Foundation, 1963.

Hall, Edward T. *Beyond Culture.* New York: Doubleday, 1975.

Jessor, Richard, Theodore D. Graves, Robert C. Hanson, and Shirley L. Jessor, *Society, Personality, and Deviant Behavior: A Study of a Triethnic Community*. New York: Holt, Rinehart and Winston, 1968.

Lieberman, Morton, A., Irvin D. Yalom, and Matthew B. Miles, *Encounter Groups: First Facts*. New York: Basic Books, Inc., 1973.

Marquardt, William F. "Creating Empathy through Literature between the Members of the Mainstream Culture and the Disadvantaged Learners of the Minority Cultures." *Florida FL Reporter*, vol. 7, i (Spring/Summer 1969): (Special anthology issue entitled *Linguistic-Cultural Differences and American Education*.)

Padilla, Amado M., and Rene A. Ruiz, *Latino Mental Health: A Review of Literature*. Washington, D.C.: Superintendent of Documents, U.S. Government Printing Office (# 1724-00317), 1973.

Seelye, H. Ned, *Teaching Culture: Strategies for Foreign Language Educators*. Skokie, Ill.: National Textbook Co., 1974.

Seelye, H. Ned, and V. Lynn Tyler, eds. *Intercultural Communicator Resources*. Provo, Utah: Language and Intercultural Research Center, Brigham Young University, 1977.

Skinner, B. F. *Beyond Freedom and Dignity*. New York: Knopf, 1972.

Stewart, Edward C. *American Cultural Patterns: A Cross-Cultural Perspective*, Pittsburgh: University of Pittsburgh (Regional Council for International Education), 1971.

Wallace, Anthony F. C. *Culture and Personality*. New York: Random House, 1963.

Watts, Alan W. *Psychotherapy East and West*. New York: Ballantine, 1969.

FOOTNOTE

[1] The author acknowledges the extensive input on the subject of this paper provided by Jacqueline H. Wasilewski (University of Southern California, Washington Education Center), and thanks the following for critiquing an earlier draft of this paper: Judy Guskin (Illinois Bilingual Education Service Center), Brian E. Bethke, Romeo C. Gatan, and Judith J. Ratas (all three from the Bilingual Education Department of the Illinois Office of Education).

Chapter 48
Components of A Multicultural Curriculum
Leona M. Foerster*

Multicultural education, a product of the seventies, appears to be a trend that cannot be ignored. Multicultural programs are springing up across the country in response to the needs of a society which is exceedingly diverse. These programs, although related to the ethnic studies programs of the sixties, go beyond the study of one or more racial or cutural groups. Instead, the major goal of multicultural education is to enable students to interact successfully with others in our society despite great differences in heritage, family patterns, life styles, value sets, and so on. Multicultural education is education for cultural pluralism. It compares and contrasts all people across racial and ethnic lines in a non-judgmental atmosphere. Diversity is examined across cultures, studying the strengths and contributions of all peoples to the greater society. Further, multicultural education helps students view cultural differences as positive and promotes cultural pluralism as the ideal posture for society.

American education faces a legacy of a curriculum which is monocultural in character. Historically, American society has operated within the "melting pot" framework. As a society, we were willing—even grateful—for immigrants from other lands to till the fields and staff the factories of a budding nation. Founding fathers such as Thomas Jefferson and Benjamin Franklin had value sets which included the provision for education to produce intelligent citizens and to build within the neophyte nation a strong, prideful identity. In order to accomplish the latter, it fell to the institution of education to fuse persons with diverse backgrounds into a united whole over a period of time—the birth of the melting pot. To be a "good American," in this sense, meant to speak English only and to adhere to traditional Anglo values and life styles.

The melting pot theory is no longer tenable. Rather than a melting pot, as a nation we are more like a salad bowl. The posture of cultural pluralism views present day society realistically and recognizes the identity of subcultural groups within the larger society. It allows or perhaps even encourages these groups to retain their identity without denying them full participation in society (as has happened in the past). Flowing from the orientation of cultural pluralism is the belief that a person can be a Mexican American, or a Hopi or an Asian American, retaining certain cultural and linguistic differences which set that group aside from mainstream America and yet be a "good American."

It is time for the monocultural curriculum of the past to give way to the multicultural curriculum of the present and future. Multicultural education is an answer to the serious educational problem of making school experiences meaningful for students whose racial, ethnic, cultural, socioeconomic and religious backgrounds differ from those of mainstream students. But it is not for these students alone. Multicultural education is for all students and provides a culturally pluralistic approach to building curricula relevant for all.

As often happens with new terms which are added to educational jargon, there appears to be some confusion as to the nature and major components of a viable multicultural curriculum. The introduction to this article was an effort to pin down the nature of multicultural education. The remainder of the article will attempt to break down this curriculum into managable parts which can be examined closely and which will offer guidelines or keystones to persons who are curious about or interested in building a curriculum in multicultural education appropriate for their educational setting.

From this writer's point of view, there are four basic components of a multicultural curriculum. These are (1) self concept; (2) prideful identity; (3) valuing of others; and (4) skills development. It is obvious at the outset that there is a mixture of the cognitive and affective domains within each component. Thus multicultural education is comprised of a careful blend of content and process which requires commitment on the part of the teacher for implementation and success. Each of the components will be examined in turn. A discussion of the role of the teacher in implementing a multicultural curriculum will conclude the article.

*Dr. Leona Foerster, Professor, Texas Tech University, Lubbock, Texas.

Any curriculum worthy of implementation in a school setting must deal with the self concept of the child. A multicultural curriculum is no different from any other curriculum in that respect. Yet unfortunately, far too many educational programs neglect the self concept and assume that somehow the teacher will see to it that experiences which will enhance the self are provided for each child.

The development of positive feelings of self are bound up in both content and process—*what* is taught and *how* it is taught. The younger the child and/or the more negative feelings of self which he has, the greater will be the attention which must be given to self concept. Typically, economically disadvantaged youngsters, many of whom represent ethnic or racial minorities, come to school with warped perceptions of self. These children present the greatest challenges to the teacher in terms of modifying existing negative or distorted perceptions.

Providing content and using processes which will help each child build a prideful identity (component #2) will contribute greatly to helping pupils build positive self concepts. Certainly skills development (component #4) is extremely important to self concept, also. Unless children are equipped with the skills prerequisite for success in school, they will fall into the failure syndrome with the concomitant damage to self concept which generally occurs. A more complete discussion of components #2 and #4 will follow shortly. Let it suffice to state here that all four components are interwoven as the curriculum is implemented and can be separated from one another for closer scrutiny only in a limited and artificial manner.

Self awareness activities help the child see himself/herself as unique from others. Discussions which help pupils explore feelings may be used. Dramatic activities such as role playing and puppetry can provide opportunities for self discovery. Children's literature may be useful, too. Expressive activities such as writing, art, movement, and the like provide needed outlets for self-expression. Positive feelings of self accrue as children are engaged productively in a variety of activities which provide enough of a challenge to be stimulating but not overwhelming. A backlog of successful experiences will enable students to deal with failure realistically and to use failure experiences as stepping stones to personal growth.

The quality and quantity of the teacher's interactions with students also play a role in self concept. The teacher who treats each child with respect and shows with actions that he/she truly values the uniqueness of each, will go a long way in helping pupils develop positive self concepts.

The second component, building a prideful identity, is intertwined with self concept. Whereas the latter helps the child see himself/herself as a worthy individual, prideful identity will enable the child to perceive himself as a member of a worthy group. Prideful identity involves helping the child identify with his heritage and build positive feelings for that heritage. It is here, perhaps, that ethnic studies should be mentioned.

It is important to note that the multicultural curriculum should not be equated with ethnic studies. The two are not the same and perhaps some clarification is in order as confusion seems to exist in the minds of some concerning the relationship of the two. Whereas ethnic studies focus upon one or more ethnic/racial groups and provide an in-depth study of the group(s) involved, multicultural education purports to provide relevant cross-cultural experiences for all pupils. Thus multicultural education is broader in scope and purpose than ethnic studies. However, if the building of prideful identity is a valid component of the multicultural curriculum, of necessity this curriculum must draw from the content of ethnic studies to build pride in heritage.

Perhaps an example will make this more lucid. If a Native American child, let's say a Navajo, is to become a fully fuctioning person, he needs to feel good not only about himself, but also about the group of which he is a member. He must come to feel that it is "good" to be a Navajo. This is accomplished in various ways.

First of all, he must feel that others in his environment feel that Navajos are worthy people. In the school setting, this would mean that the actions of teachers and others in positions of authority would indicate that they have positive feelings toward Navajos. In addition, the child would need to expand his knowledge of the history and culture of his people. Appreciation and valuing of one's culture and heritage rest upon a sound knowledge base. Thus, for the Navajo child, a culturally relevant curriculum would include such topics as Navajo history, legends, religion, medicine, language, and other aspects of culture appropriate for the age and experience of the child. In addition, the physical environment of the classroom—indeed the school—should reflect his culture. From the content and processes of a curriculum designed to reflect the child's culture should come the appreciation and valuing of heritage so important for building prideful identity.

As the first component, self concept, seems to flow naturally into the second, prideful identity, so the second appears to flow naturally into the third, valuing of others. It has been postulated that before an individual can accept, appreciate and value others, first he must accept, appreciate and value himself—both as an individual and as a member of a group. The multicultural curriculum would be incomplete without attention to interpersonal relations. Given the culturally pluralistic nature of society, and the reality that students will be living among and working with diverse peoples, valuing of others regardless of the differences in culture, life styles, value sets and so on, will be essential for full and successful participation in tomorrow's world (not to mention today's).

To reach the level of valuing others, various elements are involved. First the child will need to develop sensitivity to the differences in others. He/she will need to gain knowledge of human diversity relating both to heredity and environment, to acquire understanding of cultural differences and begin to make non-judgmental cross-cultural comparisons. In addition, if the purposes of the multicultural curriculum are to be served, the child will need to learn about the contributions which the many subcultural groups comprising American society have made and are continuing to make to that society in order to move that child toward appreciating and, finally, valuing others. Although the terms *appreciating* and *valuing* may be considered synonyms, the latter term seems to be stronger, perhaps involving a greater intensity of feelings hence the distinction made in this paper.

The first three components of a multicultural curriculum are woefully incomplete without the last, the skills component. As this component is quite complex, perhaps for clarity an explanation of what is meant by "skills" as used in this paper is in order. Various categories of skills may be considered. One category may include academic skills such as communication and mathematical skills. These skills are essential for success in school and consequently may determine to a great measure the range of career alternatives open to the individual upon completion of formal schooling. Equally important are skills in the social domain which are important for success in interpersonal relations. Society demands successful relations between its members. Full participation in society is built upon the individual's ability to get along with others in a variety of contexts. Certainly other categories of skills are important, too. Various psychomotor skills are given attention at each level of education. Skills in areas such as music, art, drama, movement, and the like should not be neglected either.

Skills development does indeed relate to the first three components and simply cannot be left out of any viable curriculum for today's students. As pupils proceed through the grades, increasingly greater demands are placed upon them in terms of acquisition and use of a wide range of skills. The pupil who has not mastered basic reading skills simply will be unable to utilize most of the learning materials written for his grade level. Until that student is helped to fill these learning gaps, he/she will be greatly limited in the ability to work independently, use reference materials, and complete assigned tasks successfully. Opportunity to build a sense of competence will be restricted indeed.

It is to be expected that no student will exhibit the same degree of proficiency in all skill areas. But strengths can help the pupil overcome weaknesses without damage to the self concept. Nevertheless, success in school by and large is dependent upon acquisition of a hierarchy of skills within certain time constraints. Greatest pressures are faced by the pupil in the area of communication skills. When skills development lags or is thwarted, the student is placed at an extreme disadvantage in the school setting. As feelings of anxiety, frustration and hopelessness build, the integrity of the self is threatened. As a result, students frequently elect to drop out of school rather than face feelings of failure and defeat daily at school. Thus, it cannot be stressed too much that a multicultural curriculum *must* provide for equipping students with the skills upon which success in school is built.

The teacher is the key to the successful implementation of any curriculum. If the multicultural curriculum is to provide a viable alternative in the form of a more effective means of educating pupils, the teacher must have understanding of and commitment ot multicultural education. The teacher must have a sincere interest in each child and respect for his uniqueness. He/she must understand and value the heritage of every child in order to help each pupil build positive feelings toward self and his/her culture. Diagnostic-prescriptive teaching which lends to individualization of instruction is a must if pupils are to acquire important skills and to apply these skills successfully in a variety of experiences both in and out of school. The teacher's skill in interpersonal relations is an important factor, too. If he/she is to facilitate the social growth of students, the teacher must be well acquainted with group dynamics and be able to develop a warm, nurturing emotional climate in the classroom. Finally, the success of the multicultural curriculum is highly contingent upon the teacher's sensitivity to capitalizing upon as many opportunities as possible to provide culturally relevant experiences for all pupils in an environment which reflects the diversity which they bring from home. Certainly the successful implementation of the multicultural curriculum will offer a challenge for all teachers.

In summary, the four basic components of a multicultural curriculum are (1) self concept; (2) prideful identity; (3) valuing of others; and (4) skills development. Each contributes uniquely to building a curriculum relevant for all pupils. It should be emphasized again that multicultural education is not just another program for the "disadvantaged." It is not solely for America's ethnic and racial minorities. Multicultural education offers an alternative which reflects the pluralistic nature of society and promotes cultural pluralism. Certainly it's high time for American education to react responsively and realistically to the nature and needs of the society it serves.

Chapter 49
Educational Activities and Practical Implications for the Classroom
Christina Bratt Paulston*

The major part of my educational activities in TESOL concerns the English Language Institute of the University of Pittsburgh. ELI, Pitt is an intensive English training program, one of twenty CIEP (Consortium of Intensive English Programs, National Association of Foreign Student Affairs) members. The major objectives of ELI and other similar centers is to prepare adult foreign students for academic life in the United States. All of our activities are influenced by the fact that in six months we have to enable a student who comes to us with barely one word of English to do academic work. With such pressure of time, maximum efficiency of learning becomes the all overruling criterion. None of us at the Institute doubt that there are other successful ways of teaching languages, but we are also reasonably certain that for our situation with adult, literate, academically oriented students our ways work best. It should, however, be pointed out they are not the ways we would teach children or semi-literate immigrants or slow high school students. A detailed account of our methods of teaching can be found in Paulston and Bruder, *Teaching English as a Second Language: Techniques and Procedures* and Paulston and Bruder, *From Substitution to Substance*.

A final comment by way of explanation. The staff of ELI cooperates intensely in all aspects of the program, and so invariably as director of ELI, my own educational activities are so closely linked with those of my staff's that I prefer to discuss the experimental activities of the ELI staff rather than just my own. The following discussion is organized according to the language skill involved in the activity.

A. Speaking

1. Mary Bruder's *MMC: Developing Communicative Competence in English,* which I mentioned previously, is based on the conceptual framework of language teaching which I outlined in two articles "A Classification of Structural Pattern Drills" and "The Sequencing of Structural Pattern Drills."[2] It no longer can be considered experimental (an Ohio State dissertation[3] established the efficacy of the conceptual framework), but I would very briefly like to expound on its basic principles.

The text is our basic grammar text. The students are first exposed to the patterns they are to learn for each lesson in natural context (dialogues). Next follow one or more mechanical drills like the following for fluency practice, the purpose of which is for the students to learn the formal aspect of the pattern:

when/where
Model: The runner has to run when the batter hits.
 The coach stands where the batter can see him.

1. M1 Rep: John saw the game when he was in Chicago.
    Sub: Bill
      went to
      the theater
      New York
  S: Bill saw the game when he was in Chicago.
    Bill went to the game when he was in Chicago.
    Bill went to the theater when he was in Chicago.
    Bill went to the theater when he was in New York.
                              cont.

2. M1 Rep: I told him where he could find his friend.
    Sub: get a good meal
      get a bus
      make a phone call
      get a bus schedule
  S: I told him where he could get a good meal.
    I told him where he could get a bus.
    I told him where he could make a phone call.
    I told him where he could get a bus schedule.
                              cont.

GENERALIZATION
When introduces clauses referring to a time; *where* intoduces clauses referring to a place. Do not confuse these with question words—the word order is the same as in statements.

*Dr. Christina Bratt Paulston, Professor, Department of General Linguistics, University of Pittsburg.

Wh Question   Where *can he* get tickets?
Clause: I don't know where *he can* get tickets.

Use Present or Present Perfect tense following *when* to express future time:
He'll come when he *has* time.
He'll come when he *has written* the paper.

In contrast to *while* (duration of action), *when* usually refers to an action at a point of time.

While I was watching TV, the earthquake struck.
I was watching TV *when* the earthquake struck.[4]

Next the target patterns (or target pattern and previously learned patterns) are contrasted for functional discrimination, i.e., the difficulty of, say, the present progressive lies not in learning the form of it but when and when not to use it, in the functional aspect:
M1
T: It happened while I was watching the game.
    She broke her leg while she was skiing.
    I had an accident while I was driving home from school.
    The child ran in front of the car while John was coming down the street.
    The boat sank while we were sailing down the river.

S: I was watching the game when it happened.
    She was skiing when she broke her leg.
    I was driving home from school when I had an accident.
    John was coming down the street when the child ran in front of the car.
    We were sailing down the river when the boat sank. [5]

Next follow meaningful drills. In the mechanical and mechanical-testing drills there is only one correct answer possible and those drills are usually conducted chorally. In the meaningful drills the response may be correctly expressed in more than one way and they are therefore not suitable for choral drill. There still is a right answer and the student is supplied with the necessary information for answering, like in this drill:
M2
T: She fell during the party.
    She fell during the trip.
    She fell during our vacation.
    She fell during my visit.

She fell during the storm.
She fell during the game. cont.

S: She fell while (we were at the party) (they were having a party) (she was on her way to the party).
    She fell while (we were on a trip) (she was taking a trip). [6]

These drills are followed by communicative drills in which the student adds *new* information to the classroom, he communicates something of his own:

T: Imagine your favorite | place / time. What's it like?

S: (It's a place where there is not pollution.) (It's a time when there are no tests or homework or English classes.)

What were you doing when | the typhoon hit? / the men landed on the moon?

What were you doing/thinking while | the men were walking on the moon? / you were waiting for news of ( )?[7]

All of the structural patterns which are studied follow such an MMC sequence. There is minimum emphasis on the mechanical drills (much of that work is done in the language laboratory) although we do believe firmly in their necessity, however brief. The major emphasis is on the communicative aspects of the activity, during which incidentally the students are rarely interrupted with corrections unless they would produce a serious mistake on the very target pattern, and much of the correction is by unsolicited peer teaching.

2. Our concern for teaching communicative competence has led to the very recent publication of two complementary texts: Kettering's *Developing Communicative Competence: Interaction Activities in English as a Second Language*[8] and Paulston, Britton, Brunetti, and Hoover's *Developing Communicative Competence: Role plays in English as a Second Language,*[9] with which we have experimented very successfully in the Institute during the last year. We believe that learning specific sounds and patterns through drills does not necessarily entail the ability to use them, and our students need practice in using the linguistic forms for the social purpose of language. There is experimental evidence that this is a necessary step in efficient language learning so we incorporate it in the teaching process.

There is one set of procedures which holds for all the communicative interaction activities, and which I cannot emphasize strongly enough. There should be *no* correction from the teacher during these activities. If the basic teaching point is getting meaning across, the students have achieved the objectives of the exercise if they succeed in doing so. It is inhibiting, hampering and frustrating beyond belief to be consistently checked and corrected when one is struggling with ideas in another language. On the other hand, the teacher helps with vocabulary, grammar and pronunciation, when the students ask him as they frequently do. The students should very early on be taught phrases for talking themselves out of trouble: phrases like "How do you say this in English?", "Is that right?", "What's the word for the thing that . . .?" are very useful to know. What we do in the Institute is that the teacher writes down the worst horrors he hears, and then the class spends five or ten minutes after the exercise in a friendly post-mortem. We concentrate on clearing up idiom and vocabulary confusion, and it is elementary psychology but nevertheless effective to point out *good* word choices and expressions too.

a. There are three basic types of activities in Kettering's *Interaction Activities:* social formulas and dialogues, community oriented tasks, and problem solving activities. The social formulas and dialogues in the unit on "Establishing and Maintaining Social Relations" covers such speech encounters as greetings, parting introductions, excuses, compliments, complaints, hiding feelings, etc. It is very difficult to lie, to complain, and to turn someone down for a date in another language, and our students need to be taught how to do this in an appropriate manner. These are exercises deliberately designed to develop communicative competence as in this section on "Excuses and Apologies":

Excuses and Apologies[10]
(abbreviated)

I. Phrases
  A. Formal
   1. Excuse me, please   Of course.
      Pardon me.   Certainly.
      I'm very sorry.
      I'm sorry.
      I beg your pardon.
   2. Excuse me for being late.
                                 That's quite alright.
      I'm sorry I'm late.
      Excuse me for a moment please.
                                 Think nothing of it.
      I'm sorry I forgot to $\begin{cases} \text{call.} \\ \text{come.} \end{cases}$

I'm sorry I didn't $\begin{cases} \text{answer your letter.} \\ \text{inform you.} \end{cases}$
I'm sorry, but I must leave early.

  B. Informal
   1. Sorry I'm late.   It's O.K.

      Sorry I forgot to $\begin{cases} \text{call.} \\ \text{write.} \\ \text{come.} \quad \text{Don't worry.} \\ \text{tell you.} \quad \text{Sure.} \end{cases}$
      Just a minute. I'll be right back.
                                         It's alright.

II. Dialogues

  A. Formal
   1. A: Miss Larson?
      B: Yes?
      A: Please excuse me for losing my temper in class yesterday.
      B: That's quite alright. Was something troubling you?
      A: Yes. I had just gotten a letter from a friend of mine and I guess I was more upset than I thought.

  B. Informal
   1. A: How was your vacation, Maria?
      B: I had such a good time, I hated to come back.
      A: Did you get my postcard?
      B: Yes, thanks. And I meant to write to you too but I was just so busy! I'm sorry.
      A: That's O.K. I knew you probably didn't have much time.
   2. A: I'm glad you're here! Sorry I'm so late.
      B: Don't worry. The bus hasn't come yet.
      A: I was just walking out the door and the phone rang. It was my mother and . . . well, you know how my mother talks!
      B: I'm surprised you aren't later!

III. Situations

  A. Structured
   1. A: How was your vacation?
      B: Great. Hey, thanks for the postcards.
      A: Sure. But I didn't get any from you!
      B:
  B. Semi-Structured
   1. A: Hey, where were you last night?
      B: I was waiting for you to call to tell me what the address was.
      A:
      B:

2. A: What'd you get so angry at me for this morning?

   B:

   A:

   B:

C. Unstructured

1. You're in class and suddenly you don't feel well.

2. You are at a friend's house for dinner. You must leaver early to study for a test for the next day.

3. You told Fred you would come over to study with him last night, but you forgot. He sees you and asks you why you didn't come.

In all of these activities, there is a progression from tightly controlled language use, where the student is learning the social formulas to a situation where he can use them. The phrases and the dialogues lend themselves well to work in the language laboratory, but it is important that the teacher spends some time in the initial presentation of the section in explaining the meaning, the connotations, and the sorts of situations in which one would use the various expressions, an introductory mixture of Emily Post and sociolinguistics as it were. Note Section IB. In all of these encounters, the students are taught a formal and an informal way for apologizing, saying thank you, etc. I doubt that one can systematically teach style variation in all areas of language, but we *can* teach our students to be sensitive to levels of style so that noting such levels becomes part of their language learning strategies.

Community Oriented Tasks are sets of exercises which compel the student to interact with native speakers outside the classroom. The teaching point here is twofold: (1) communicative participation in the community in what Stevick would call "real" situations and (2) (and this is what assures their success) the collection of highly relevant and needed information. Here is an example:

The Bank[11]

1. What is a checking account? A savings account?
2. Can you take money out of a savings account at any time?
3. What is interest? What bank gives the highest interest rate in Oakland? What is 'compounding' of interest? What is the difference between interest compounded daily, monthly, quarterly, bi-annually, annually? Which gives you the most money?
4. What does 'withdrawal' mean? 'Deposit?'
5. What is 24 hour banking? Does the Oakland Pittsburgh National Bank (next to the Book Center) have 24 hour banking?
6. How do you open an account?

7. If you take out a loan, do you want a high interest rate or a low interest rate? Why?
8. There are three types of checking accounts:
   a. minimum balance
   b. 10¢ a check
   c. free checking
   What are the differences between these three kinds? Advantages and disadvantages?
9. What happens if you 'overdraw?'
10. What other services do banks provide besides the above?

*(All place names must be changed to local names.) The assignment is handed out in class, and the topic explained in general terms. Then it is up to the students to find the answers outside of class. After a reasonable amount of time, they report their findings to the rest of the class. An alternative to oral reports is to have them act out their answers in a role play, like this one:

Role Playing: The Bank[12]

SITUATION: Alfred Newman has just moved to Pittsburgh and has gone to the Pittsburgh National Bank to open both a checking account and a savings account. He must answer questions asked by a bank employee who types out the information. He has a check for $5000 which he wants to put in the savings account and his first pay check for $289.35 with which he will open the checking account.

ROLES: Alfred Newman—young man who has just moved to Pittsburgh.

Tilda Thompson—bank employee.

USEFUL EXPRESSIONS:

Alfred "I just moved to Pittsburgh."

"I would like to open a bank account."

"I have two checks to deposit."

Tilda "Good morning. May I halp you?"

"I need your name, address, etc."

"Let me have your checks and I'll deposit them for you and bring your receipts."

"What type of checking account do you want?"

Information Necessary To Open Bank Accounts:

A. Checking Account
   1. Name, address, phone number.
   2. Occupation and employer.
   3. Individual or joint (with wife, parent, etc.) account.
   4. Type
      a. Regular—no minimum balance, free checks.
      b. Deluxe—personalized checks, service

charge for each check deducted from balance each month (10¢/check). $300 minimum balance.

B. Savings Account
1-3 Same as for a checking account.
4. Social Security Number.
5. Pays 5% a year interest.

The role play should then be followed by a discussion session where the students may ask questions on matters that seem unclear to them. It is absolutely vital that the topic is relevant to the student needs. An automobile exercise is of no use to students who have no intention of driving or buying a car, but it is one of our most successful exercises with those students who do.

Problem solving activities are just what they sound like; the students are presented with a problem and some alternative solutions from which they have to choose one. The following exercise from Kettering contains directions for use as well:

A Camping Trip[13]

You are going on a three day camping trip up in the mountains. You will carry *everything* you need for the three days on your back. Since you are going into the mountains, it will be cold. This kind of trip is called a pack trip because you walk and carry everything you take with you on your back in a bag called a 'pack'. You have decided that you can't carry more than 25 pounds on your back comfortably. You made a list of things you want to take with you but they add up to more than 25 pounds. Now you have to read your list and include only the most important items. Remember they cannot add up to more than 25 pounds including the pack. Also remember that you will not see anyone for the three days and must include everything you need in order to survive.

You must come to a decision in your groups (and be sure you add up weights so they don't total more than 25 pounds). You must be able also to tell why you chose each item. There is no one correct list although certain items must be included on each list. When you have finished your list, choose a representative from your group to present your list to the other groups. You may challenge or be challenged by another group to tell why you chose an item so be sure you can justify each item.

If you don't understand the meaning of any item, you may ask your instructor.

LIST:
6 lb. sleeping bag
3 lb. pack
1 lb. pillow
6 oz. small book to record what you see
8 oz. swimming suit
4 oz. dish soap
4 oz. toothpaste
2 oz. tooth brush
1 lb. pot to cook in
1 lb. flashlight
1 lb. rain jacket
3 lb. extra pair of shoes
6 lb. water container (full of water)
4 lb. camera
6 lb. 3-day supply of food
12 oz. plate, fork, knife, spoon
12 oz. insect repellent
2 lb. extra set of clothing
3 lb. fishing pole
6 oz. towel
1 oz. matches

16 ounces = 1 pound; oz. = ounce; lb. = pound

I used this exercise when I taught in Sweden in 1974, and it was my first successful effort at getting my students to talk freely. They protested at once that one should not go alone into the mountains, laughed aloud at the notion of a swimming suit, pointed out to me who had not thought of it that you don't need any insect repellent when it is cold in the mountains because then there are no insects. My quiet Swedes became positively talkative, and it illustrates a basic principle of these exercises; the closer you can come to the students' interests and prior experience, the more successful the exercise will be. Being Swedes, all of my students had been on camping trips, and they knew what they were talking about.

As a final remark on these activities, I'd like to qualify an earlier point. I said that the teacher should not correct, but you normally get a lot of peer teaching and correction in these activities, and that is as it should be. It may seem like correction, but actually the students only help when some one gets stuck or if they don't understand. The emphasis is on putting meaning across, not on linguistic forms.

b. The *Role plays* contain exercises where the student is assigned a fictitious role from which he has to improvise some kind of behavior towards the other role characters in the exercise. I am not considering the acting out of set dialogues or plays as role play, nor the acting out of dialogues and plays written by the students themselves. In some role plays, as the one on opening a bank account above, the student may simply be assigned the role of playing himself but then you have a simulated situation rather than real role play. The two basic requirements for role play, as I see it, is improvisation and fictitious roles.

Role play can be very simple and the improvisation highly controlled, or it can be very elaborate. It is primarily a matter of student proficiency which one chooses. Certainly role play can be used in beginning classes.

The format of a role play consists of three basic parts: the situation, the roles, and useful expressions. Occasionally a section on background knowledge is needed for advanced role play. The *Situation* sets the scene and the plot, i.e. explains the situation and describes the task or action to be accomplished—again the task can be very simple, such as a telephone call, or very elaborate as settling a complex business deal. The situation is a good place to include specific cultural information if that is part of the objectives of a given role play.

The *Roles* section assigns the roles, the list of characters. The roles should all have fictitious names; it aids the willing suspension of disbelief. Here one needs to include such information as personality, experience, status, personal problems and desires, and the like. A role can be very simple, merely a skeleton name and status, or quite elaborate.

In *Useful Expressions* we put the linguistic information, primarily expressions, phrases, and technical vocabulary (an efficient way to teach vocabulary) but certainly grammar patterns which are necessary also fit in here, e.g. wh-questions for an interview situation. We try to incorporate as much socio-linguistic information as possible in this section. In one role play about a car accident, the wife of one driver is angry with both the police and with the young boy who hit their car. It can be useful to know how to express anger with a policeman in an acceptable manner, and in this section we deliberately try to incorporate style and mood variation in language.

Background Knowledge is occasionally an essential section. It is no good at all to ask students to act out roles which demand a general knowledge they don't have. In order to act out a school board meeting on open classrooms, a town meeting on local industrial pollution, or a newspaper interview on the problems of the aged, the students must have subject matter information prior to the role play. It need not be complicated at all, a short reading assignment, a lecture by the teacher or, always appreciated, a guest lecture, a film, etc. But some source of knowledge is necessary, or the role play won't come off.

Here is an example of a roleplay:

The Grocery Store Accident

I SITUATION

Robert is doing his weekly grocery shopping. It is Saturday morning and the store is very crowded. As he takes a bottle of pancake syrup off the shelf, a number of the bottles are upset and fall to the floor—breaking two of them.

II ROLE ASSSIGNMENTS

Robert—a college student who is in a hurry. He has syrup all over his jeans, socks, and shoes. Obviously upset, he is no mood for comments from anyone.

Mrs. Kelso—a middle-aged woman whose suede shoes were splattered with syrup. She accuses Robert of clumsiness and feels he should buy her a new pair of shoes.

Mr. Benson—the store manager, who feels Robert should pay for the two broken bottles of syrup.

Willy—a stock boy, who, at first, thinks the entire incident is very funny, but then, complains because he has to clean up the mess.

III USEFUL EXPRESSIONS

Robert (to Mr. Benson)	"Oh, my God!"
	"I don't believe this happened to me!"
	"It was an accident. I'm sorry."
	"If you'd stack the bottles correctly."
	"Why should I pay for them? It wasn't my fault."
(to Mrs. Kelso)	"I'm sorry ma'am."
	"I think it will wash off."
	"It could happen to anybody. Why should I buy you new shoes?"
Mrs. Kelso	"If you'd pay attention to what you're doing, things like this wouldn't happen."
	"Just look at my brand new shoes. They're ruined."
	"I expect you to buy a new pair for me, young man."
Mr. Benson (to Robert)	"You're going to have to pay for these (the bottles of syrup), fella."
	"I lose money when things like this happen."
(to Willy)	"Get a mop and clean this mess up."
Willy	"Man are you a mess!"
	"I'm getting tired of cleaning up after people."
	"Some people. Why don't you be more careful?"

Students Not Participating Must Decide Whether Or Not Robert Should Pay For Mrs. Kelso's Shoes And The Broken Bottles Of Syrup.[14]

In some role plays, not all players know the task or

strategy of the other players, and the actual role play is preceded by "secret" group work. I'll finish this section on role plays by telling you about one that our students do, written by Dale Britton. It is a courtroom scene; some students have been charged with violations such as screaming and hollering in front of the university dormitory at 2:00 A.M., kicking dogs, or turning over park benches—all actual suits, by the way. Some students are counsel for the defense, others for the prosecution, and the rest are witnesses. They then go into group work planning their defense and prosecution, respectively, of their various cases, but no group knows what the others are planning. They get a lot of legal information, not at all useless for foreign students, in the process. The day I visited a class doing this role play, the young man charged with screaming and hollering claimed in his defense that he had been attacked by two men, who tried to kidnap him while he was on his way home from the Computer Center, where he had been working, and that he had screamed for help. Subsequent witnesses brought out the fact that he was the son of wealthy parents and a man of staid and studious character. An eye-witness attested to having seen two men fleeing as the police officer approached to make the arrest. The witnesses were subjected to a very tough grilling by the counsel for the prosecution—incidentally a very shy Thai student who rarely spoke in class—but to no avail. The witnesses could not be shaken, and they improvised right along to meet the many questions, designed on the spot to trip them up. The judge's verdict of not guilty was greeted with cheers by the class.

I hope you get the same feeling I had in watching these students, that they were having great fun and that they were very pleased with themselves in being able to follow and handle unexpected arguments in a language they were far from fluent in. As they were struggling with the language in proper court procedure—they knew more about it than I did—they were also processing rules and beliefs of our judiciary system which are basic to our cultural values.

It may seem strange that an Institute for which efficient learning holds such priority would waste students' time on what may look like nothing more than games. On the contrary, we would argue that this is efficient learning, and that all the study of English skills is a waste of time if we don't also teach our students how to function in our culture with those skills.[15]

3. We have experimented for some time now with a sound-symbol approach to teaching pronunciation, basically the same as that used by Allen, Allen and Shute.[16] As a result we teach spelling with pronunciation rather than with writing. After Allen,[17] each vowel sound is labelled with a number, and we have found this system remarkably helpful for the

students. A part of a sample lesson from the still experimental materials of Vernick and Nesgoda will serve to demonstrate:

Practice these words. All of the underlined letters have the #1 sound.

Examples: #1 up nut

Say:

up	nut	dumb	mud	u-
us	cut	but	pun	-u-

General Rules

Common Spellings:

In *monosyllabic words* the #1 sound is represented by:

  1. *u* in initial and medial position—except before *r* or *y*.

Examples: *u*

  #1 up

    nut

In *polysyllabic words* the #1 sound is represented by:

  1. *u* in initial or medial position before [CC][1]— except when the first [C] = R.

Examples: *u*

  #1 under

    summer

Listen as the 2 lists of words are pronounced.

A	B	
nut	note	Sight words -o[C]e
bun	bone	
cup	cope	

In which column would you put the words *some* and *come*?

On the basis of spelling, you might put these words in column B. But because they are pronounced more like the words in A, they belong there.

Some, come and the other words below are SIGHT WORDS because they are pronounced differently from most words which have the spelling -o[C]e. In these SIGHT WORDS, the letter *o* has the #1 sound. The final letter *e* is silent.

LOOK AND LISTEN:

      some   come   done

      none   one[1]   love

(Additional SIGHT WORDS can be found at the end of the lesson.)

General Rule

The letter *e* in final position is usually silent.

EXAMPLES: some come done

---

[1][CC] may represent a double consonant letter such as in the word "summer," or two different consonants as in the word "public."

[1]The letter *o* in the word "one" = /w+#1/sounds.

Listen carefully to the sounds of the underlined letters as the words in columns A and B are pronounced.

A	B	
n<u>u</u>t	n<u>o</u>t	**Sight words**
c<u>u</u>t	c<u>o</u>t	o-
<u>u</u>p	<u>o</u>dd	-o-

Where would you put the words *of, son* and *from?*
*On the basis of spelling, you might put these words
in column B. But because they are pronounced more
like the words in column A, they belong there. Of,
son,* and *from* are SIGHT WORDS because they
are pronounced differently from most words spelled with *o.*

In these SIGHT WORDS, the letter *o* has the #1 sound.

LOOK AND LISTEN: *of*   s<u>o</u>n   fr<u>o</u>m   m<u>o</u>ney
                                M<u>o</u>nday   w<u>o</u>n   m<u>o</u>nth   <u>o</u>ther

SUMMARY REVIEW
Sounds for *o:*
Lesson 1:

#0	<u>o</u>n	(common spelling)
	m<u>o</u>m ❊	(common spelling)

Lesson 2:

#1	<u>o</u>f	(sight word)
	s<u>o</u>n ❊	(sight word)
		18

B. Reading

Our reading program, under the direction of Lois
Wilson, is probably the aspect of the program we
continue to experiment the most with. We are at
present involved in developing a reading series but it
would take me too far astray to discuss it in detail. But I
can mention some aspects of the program which may
not be part of the conventional approach.

An integral part of the reading program is teaching
advanced grammatical patterns (which the students
have not yet studied for productive use) for receptive
use, for decoding only. We put great emphasis on
vocabulary acquisition, having become convinced
over the years that our students' poor reading is directly
related to their poor vocabulary. There is never any
reading aloud; reading aloud is recoding, not decoding,
and if anything interferes with the reading process. Of
course there is no translation. Of comprehension
questions, we put the major emphasis on *before-*
questions, in West's terms, and spend very little
classtime on police-type comprehension questions.
Instead we prefer to spend time on discussions of the
rhetorical principles by which authors organize their
writing and exercises designed to facilitate such
comprehension. On the intermediate level, the reading
and writing activities are immediately coordinated by
type of writing, like comparison, classification,
analysis, etc. But the basic problem is one we all share,

making sure the students really do their reading;
ultimately, we believe, one learns reading by reading.

C. Writing

Another project I am involved in with ELI staff
Robert Henderson, Mary Call and Patricia Furey
concerns the production of a set of materials of
controlled composition according to the same
principles of MMC: 1) the pattern is presented in a
model paragraph, 2) the grammatical explanation
states the formal rule and the functional explication
followed by 3) some fairly tightly controlled exercises
with a minimum opportunity for making mistakes
while the students first learn the pattern through 4)
some fairly imaginative ones to 5) a free composition
on a similar topic to the model. Again, a sample lesson
may be helpful:
Model Paragraph

The Ashtray Caper

Detective Leroy Schmidt is trying to solve one of the
most puzzling crimes he has ever encountered. Last
night a diamond-studded ashtray worth at least two
million dollars was stolen from the office of Mr. B. J.
Mitchell, on the twenty-fifth floor of his company's
headquarters. Schmidt thinks that it *might have been*
an inside job, since it is impossible to enter the office
without passing the security guards. Mr. Mitchell,
however, says that the thieves *could have come in*
through an open window by using a helicopter or a
very long ladder. His secretary is very upset, because
she *should have closed* and *locked* the windows. She
told Detective Schmidt that she *would have closed*
them before she left, but forgot when one of the guards
invited her to dinner. The police believe that the guard
might have tricked the secretary, but Schmidt points
out that it *would have been* easier for him just to walk
into the office through the door. The guard thinks Mr.
Mitchell *must have taken* the ashtray himself. What do
you think?
Explanation

                    Modal + *have* + past participle
The modal auxiliary verbs *may* and *might* (possibility)
and *must* (probability) are sometimes used to talk
about something in the past, by combining the modal
with *have* and the past participle of the main verb.
  Example:
    Did Daniel call you last night?
    I don't know. He *might have called* while I was
    outside.
    Gloria got a very good grade on the test last week.
    She *must have studied* a lot.
Other modal verbs in this construction (*could have,*

should have, would have) are used to tell about something that probably did *not* happen in the past.

Example:

He *should have worked* yesterday.

This sentence indicates that he probably did not work.

I *could have answered* that question if I had studied.

This sentence indicates that I could not answer the question because I did not study.

Step 1

Read this paragraph about all the bills that Mrs. Ramirez must pay for utilities:

The end of March is very near, and Mrs. Ramiriz has several bills which she should pay before the end of the month. She owes about $10 for water, $20 for gas, $15 for electricity, and $10 for telephone service. If she can pay them before the month is over, she will save about ten percent on each one, but she doesn't expect to receive another pay check until April 15. She might be able to borrow a little money from her brother, but he is out of town (he must know she needs some cash). With the money she has in the house, she can pay some of the bills, but then she will have to find cheap food for her family to eat, and she doesn't want to do that. So she has to wait and pay a little extra later.

Assignment: Now it is April; write a paragraph about the bills that Mrs. Ramirez had to pay last month, but didn't. Change all the verbs to the correct past tense forms. Begin:

The end of March *was* very near, and Mrs. Ramiriz had several bills which she *should have paid* before the end of the month. . .

Step 2

Read the Model Paragraph about the ashtray caper, and then write a similar story about a ruby-covered candlestick that was stolen from the dining room of Mrs. Hilda Vandersnoot last night. Try to use the modal construction *could have, might have, must have, should have* and *would have.* Underline these verbs before showing your paper to your teacher.

Step 3

Write an original paragraph about an athletic team (baseball, football, soccer, or basketball) which has just finished a very poor season, and tell how they could have played better. Try to use the modal auxiliary verbs, and underline them before you show your paper to your teacher.[19]

These are materials designed to be a compensatory program for junior high school students from Hispanic background who still have some difficulties with English.

Students are assigned to specific patterns as they make mistakes in their regular course work. We have attempted to program these materials for individual pacing. The sample lesson only includes one exercise of each type but in the materials there are several exercises of each type, and the notion is that if a student completes a meaningful exercise correctly, he then proceeds to an imaginary. However, if he still makes many mistakes, he goes over the grammatical explanation again and then writes another meaningful exercise which must be correct before he is allowed to go on. Similar procedures are followed for the imaginary exercises. In this fashion the students receive as much aid as they need from the materials while they are allowed to progress at their own pace. The approach is an adaptation of Paulston and Dykstra.[20]

Amy Troyani and I have also during the last two years worked out a similar approach for teaching written English to young children. The following exercise has been prepared for the bilingual education program at the LaMar Center, Edinburgh, Texas.

First, the children listen to a record which tells the story of the three bears in Spanish. Next they listen to it told in English. Then they work through a sequence of exercises like the following on possessives. Notice the progression from mechanical through meaningful to imaginative activity:

1. DIRECTIONS

Make some sentences using the information in the boxes.

Be sure to use each choice in Box A and Box C only once.

Be sure that every sentence contains one item from each box.

A	B	C
Papa's cereal Baby's bowl Papa's bowl Mama's bowl Baby's cereal	is	big too hot just right blue little

1. Papa's cereal is too hot.
2.
3.
4.
5.

2. DIRECTIONS

Complete these sentences.
1. *Papa's* hair is brown.
2. I see _____ books on the floor.

3. _____ dog is very big.

4. _____ desk is in the last row.

5. I don't know _____ brother.

3. DIRECTIONS

Describe some things for us.

1. Tell us about something that belongs to Dalia. *Dalia's dress is blue.*

2. Tell us about something that belongs to the boy.

_____ .

3. Tell us about something that belongs to Mrs. Martin.

_____ .

4. Tell us about something that belongs to the policeman.

_____ .

5. Tell us about something that belongs to Jose.

_____ .

6. Tell us about something that belongs to the teacher.

_____ .[21]

FOOTNOTES

[1]This paper was written for the *UNESCO Meeting of Experts on the diversification of methods and techniques for teaching a second language, September, 1975,* and follows the specifications given. The wording of the quotation is taken from the letter of invitation.

[2]C. B. Paulston, "Structural Pattern Drills: A Classification," *Foreign Language Annals.* 4:2 (December, 1970), 187-193 and "The Sequencing of Structural Pattern Drills," *TESOL Quarterly,* 5:3 (September, 1971), 197-208.

[3]E. G. Joiner, "Communicative Versus Non-Communicative Language Practice in the Teaching of Beginning College French: A Comparison of Two Treatments." Unpublished Ph.D. dissertation, Ohio State University, 1974.

[4]Bruder, *MMC,* 350.

[5]Bruder, *MMC,* 351.

[6]Bruder, *MMC,* 352.

[7]Bruder, *MMC,* 352.

[8]Judy Kettering, *Developing Communicative Competence: Interaction Activities in English as a Second Language.* Pittsburgh, Pa.: University Center for International Studies, 1975.

[9]C. B. Paulston, D. Britton, B. Brunetti, and J. Hoover, *Developing Communicative Competence: Role plays in English as a Second Language.* Pittsburgh, Pa.: University Center for International Studies, 1975.

[10]Kettering, 22 ff.

[11]Kettering, 45.

[12]Paulston *et al,* 6.

[13]Kettering, 54.

[14]Paulston *et al,* 23.

[15]The previous discussion on inter-action activities and role play is based on a paper by C. B. Paulston, "Developing Communicative Competence: Goals, Procedures and Techniques," Washington, D. C.: TESOL, 1974.

[16]R. Allen, V. Allen and M. Shute, *English Sounds and Their Spellings.* New York: Thomas Y. Crowell, 1966.

[17]Robert Allen, "On the Use of Numbers in a Pronunciation Key," NAFSA Studies and Papers No. I, April, 1958.

[18]Judy Vernick and John Nesgoda, *Symbol to Sound.* Pittsburgh, Pa.: English Language Institute, Ms.

[19]C. B. Paulston, R. Henderson, P. Furey and M. Call, *Write On: A Program of Controlled Composition.* Barrons, in preparation.

[20]C. B. Paulston and G. Dykstra, *Controlled Composition in English as a Second Language.* New York: Regents, 1973.

[21]Amy Troyani, Ms. no title, Pittsburgh, Pa.: English Language Institute, University of Pittsburgh, in preparation.

Chapter 50
Using Literature With Bilingual Children
Jane M. Hornburger*

Her name is Maria. She is nine years old and speaks Spanish. There are nearly three million other American pupils like Maria.

Spanish-speaking children make up the largest number of non-English speaking students. According to the U.S. Office of Education, in 1968 there were 2,002,776 Spanish surnamed students enrolled in elementary and secondary schools in the United States. The two major ethnic groups represented by this number are Mexican-Americans and Puerto Ricans.

The 1970 government census certified more than 10 million Spanish-speaking persons in the United States. This ethnic count was composed of Mexican-Americans, Puerto Ricans, Cubans, and Latinos. The Mexican-American grouping included Spanish Americans, Latin Americans, and Chicanos. Among these Spanish-speaking groups were six million Mexican-Americans, two million Puerto Ricans, one million Cubans, and the remaining million Latinos are from other Spanish-speaking countries (Rodriguez, 1970).

The Changing Scene

Before 1965 most Mexican-Americans were concentrated in the five southwest states of Arizona, California, Colorado, New Mexico and Texas. The Cubans lived in Florida and Metropolitan New York, while the Puerto Ricans inhabited New England and the Middle Atlantic states. Between 1965-1970 thousands of Mexican-Americans migrated to Wisconsin, Indiana, Ohio and Illinois—Chicago alone is estimated to have 400,000 Spanish-speaking residents. As a result of the migration, Utah, Kansas, and neighboring states now have large concentrations of Mexican-Americans. It was understandable that these shifts would affect the population makeup of various cities.

By 1970, eighty percent of the Spanish-speaking population lived in urban areas. More than a million Puerto Ricans lived in the metropolitan New York area with 250,000 in New York City alone. Many thousands also lived in Bridgeport, Chicago, Philadelphia, Newark, Hoboken and Paterson. As a rule, the highest concentrations of Mexican-Americans were found in cities of the west and southwest. More than 700,000 lived in Los Angeles and the number in Mexico City even surpassed this figure.

Although this chapter focuses upon the Puerto Ricans and Mexican-Americans, it should be noted that next to the Spanish speakers, the American Indians constitute the largest group of non-English speakers in America. In 1970 there were more than 200,000 Indian children between the ages of six and eighteen in public or Bureau of Indian Affairs schools. However, the increasing Spanish-speaking population in the urban areas gives rise to justifiable emphasis. This continuing flow of non-English-speaking children has placed a heavier burden upon inner-city schools and the task of providing equal educational opportunities has become more difficult.

It was expected that both teachers and students would be faced with certain problems attendant to the aforementioned educational situation. What are some of the teacher-learning problems inherent in this special kind of educational setting? What are these children like? What kinds of experience have they had?

A Profile of Bilingual Children

What is bilingualism and who are bilingual children? Malkoc and Roberts (1970) say that bilingualism "refers to facility in the use of two languages, ranging from a minimal knowledge of either language to a high level of proficiency in both" (p. 721). Ching (1976) gives her well-rounded definition as follows:

...When bilingualism is used in its broadest sense, it is considered without qualification as to the degree of difference between the two languages or systems known; it is immaterial whether the two systems are languages, dialects of the same language, or varieties of the same dialect. Thus, a bilingual's achievement may be limited to one aspect of a language, a dialect, or variety of a

*Dr. Jane Hornburger, Professor of Education, Boston University.

dialect, such as understanding, speaking, reading, writing; or he may have varying degrees of ability in all aspects.

The teacher in a classroom of bilinguals is likely to encounter children who show great variety in their patterns of linguistic competency. Some may speak very little English while others may speak English almost as well as their mother tongue (p. 1).

By this definition, then, surely the many Spanish-speaking children in the nation's schools qualify as bilinguals. Our bilingual students have the same educational needs as Anglo or monolingual children, but many factors stemming from their home life or familial backgrounds may often impede their academic progress. Consider the following factors as possible influences on these children's learning.

Mexican American

- Dropout rate is more than twice the national average.
- The average number of school years completed is 7.1.
- In Texas 39 percent of the Chicano population have less than fifth-grade education.
- In California more than 50 percent of Chicano high school students drop out between grades ten and eleven.
- Less than half of one percent of the college students enrolled on the seven campuses of the University of California are Chicano.
- In 1969, of 83,053 in five major colleges in the southwest, only 600 Spanish surnamed students were graduated (Nova & Sancho, 1975, p. 113).

Puerto Rican Americans

- In New York City, Puerto Rican-American pupils account for 22.8 percent of the total school population.
- Seventy percent of them became school dropouts.
- Fifteen percent of Puerto Rican youth who are 25 years of age graduate from high school.
- Puerto Rican youngsters are lowest in reading, highest in dropouts, and weakest in academic preparation of all pupils in New York State (Baecher, 1976, p. 141).

American Indians

- In 1960, sixty percent of adult Indians had less than an eight-grade education.

- Today the Indian dropout rate is more than twice the national average and in some school districts is 80 or 90 percent.
- In an all-Indian public school near Ponca City, Oklahoma, 87 percent have dropped out by the sixth grade.
- In Minneapolis, where more than 10,000 Indians live, the Indian dropout rate is more than 60 percent.
- In Washington, Muckleshoot children are automatically retained an extra year in first grade; and the Nooksack Indians automatically are placed in slow-learner classes (Kobrick, 1972, p. 56).

It is conceivable that children who have experienced some of the above situations may have suffered rejection and crushed spirits, but what is worse is the school's inability or unwillingness to adjust to their needs. The evidence indicating the school's failure to help these children cope with the dominant culture is also discouraging. This serious situation is lamented by La Fontaine (1976), who asserts:

It is nothing less than tragic to realize that there are still thousands of students in our schools in the United States who, for all intent and purposes, are not participating in any meaningful way in the learning process. In many schools a child whose native language is not English must try to function and to learn entirely in English even though his skills in that language may be virtually nonexistent. It is not difficult to understand why a child, forced to operate under such a handicap, falls behind and is not successful academically. If, indeed, he does learn and does achieve in English, most often it has been at the expense of his home language, his cultural heritage and his very identity (p. 132).

The plight of a large number of America's students is tragically clear. In most cases we have adequate supplies; we have more professional expertise than ever before and yet this dismal picture recurs year after year. Why does it persist? Why do so many children fail to achieve academically and eventually drop out of school?

Continuing Problems

The real tragedy in the education of bilingual students is indicated in their low achievement records and their high dropout rates. These are indications that the schools are not as effective as they could be in meeting the needs of this group of youngsters. Kobrick (1972) believes that:

One reason schools are failing in their responsibility to these children is that they offer only one curriculum, only one way of doing things, designed to meet the needs of only one group of children. If a child does not fit the mold, so much the worse for him. It is the child who must change to meet the needs of the school (p. 56).

Such has often been the case where bilingual children were concerned. Rodriguez (1970), chief of the Spanish-Speaking and Mexican Affairs Unit of USOE, cogently summarized the recent historical educational experiences of these children:

A recurring pattern of the educational difficulties of the Spanish-speaking began developing by 1965. The basic problem was the inability of the school to cope with the language and cultural assets of the Spanish-speaking youngster. Many of these young people came to school speaking Spanish with a limited or non-existent communication skill in English, and frequently the youngster was functionally non-communicative in both languages. Yet here was a child with a high potential of becoming a bilingual member of society. The general approach of the school was to place the youngster in a class called English as a Second Language in order to teach him sufficient English to enable him to learn in the English-dominated classroom environment. As a means of hastening his acquisition of English, speaking Spanish was forbidden at school. The result was that the Spanish-speaking child might spend more than two years learning English isolated from the rest of his classmates for a large part of the school day. The inevitable happened: the youngster was caught in a language and culture conflict between his home and the school. He began to doubt his identity as a member of a family with a treasured language and culture, and to suspect the motives of the school in insisting that he reject his linguistic and cultural diversity in order to meet the standards of the system. He dropped behind his classmates because he was taught little subject matter—just English (p. 726).

It is not difficult to see why these children soon become disenchanted with school. Could this be one of the reasons why the dropout rate is so high? Isolating bilingual children from their peers and depriving them of their language is robbing them of two of the most effective means of learning. This is a disarming procedure and it is psychologically unwholesome.

Kobrick (1972) further explains the language problem:

The effects of this treatment on a child are immediate and deep. Language and the culture it carries is at the heart of a youngster's concept of himself. For a young child especially,..."language carries all the meanings and overtones of home,

family, and love; it is the instrument of his thinking and feeling, his gateway to the world."...and so when a child enters a school that appears to reject the only words he can use, "he is adversely affected in every aspect of his being."

With English the sole medium of instruction, the child is asked to carry an impossible burden at a time when he can barely understand or speak, let alone read or write, language. Children are immediately retarded in their school work. For many this situation becomes hopeless, and they drop out of school. In other cases, believing the school system offers no meaningful program, parents may fail to send their children to school at all (p. 56).

A second factor associated with the problems bilingual students face has been negative teacher attitude. The research of Risk (1970) and others has clearly indicated that teacher attitude is the most influential determinant of student achievement. "Learning can be facilitated or impeded on the basis of interaction between teacher and student" (Hornburger, 1976, p. 21). Negative or uninformed teacher attitudes can be very counterproductive where bilingual students are concerned. When youngsters feel that they are not accepted because of their language, they begin to develop negative feelings about themselves—after all, our language is the means by which we perceive ourselves and our world.

Sometimes the teachers who teach English as a second language to our Spanish-speaking students do not themselves speak Spanish. Kobrick (1972) believes that this is doing an injustice to children and quotes the following example of a little girl's experience with such a teacher:

Sitting in a classroom and staring at words on a blackboard that were to me as foreign as Egyptian hieroglyphics is one of my early recollections of school. The teacher had come up to my desk and bent over, putting her face close to mine. "My name is Mrs. Newman," she said, as if the exaggerated mouthing of her words would make me understand their meaning. I nodded "yes" because I felt that was what she wanted me to do. But she just threw up her hands in despair and touched her fingers to her head to signify to the class I was dense. From that day on school became an ordeal I was forced to endure (p. 56).

Negative teacher attitudes certainly are not conducive to effective learning of a second language and what is worse is the fact that the result is often viewed as failure on the part of the student when it really should be considered a failure on the part of the school. Because bilingual children do not always understand our language is no reason to assume that they are dense. Kocher (1974) believes that "we judge people by their way of speaking often without any other cues" (p. 483). She affirms that "we must alert ourselves to prejudice against any child for the language he or she brings to school" (p. 484). Bilingual students should be helped to understand that they are advantaged rather than disadvantaged, and that no language is superior to another in its potential for expression.

Another problem bilingual children have had to cope with was the school subject curriculum. As a rule the textbooks they had to use offered little or no support for their personal identity. Often these were not relevant, and the illustrations in picture books did not relate to minority children. When they did, it was in a negative, stereotypical manner. Speaking of the Mexican-American child and the Anglo curriculum, Rodriguez (1970) said:

> He found little or nothing in the school curriculum and books that would help him identify with his own role in his country. ...Probably one of the most destructive aspects of the bilingual, bicultural child's educational experience was the general attitude of the school toward its responsibility for developing an educational program to meet his needs (p. 727).

Some school curriculums may actually discourage academic progress for most bilingual children as implied by Ortego (1971):

> The high dropout rate cannot be blamed on a lack of emphasis on education in the home. ... "There appears to be little difference between Mexican-American families and other families with respect to the amount of emphasis on education that the child experiences in his home." Moreover, "these children experience the same high degree of encouragement and assistance at home as do their classmates." The inescapable conclusion is that the academic failures of many Mexican-American youngsters are the result of inadequate school programs rather than the consequence of low achievement or aspiration levels of their families (p. 63).

There are many indications that schools are becoming more receptive to cultural diversity, and this holds out the promise that they will eventually adjust their curriculums to meet the needs of bilingual children.

Teaching Strategies

Teachers have always affirmed the importance of accepting children for what they are, and using their background and experience as springboards to further learning. With no group can this idea be more beneficial than with bilingual children, for doing so can help to erase the fear of a new learning experience or a strange educational setting. In some cases this may help a child to make the transition from a family orientation to an independent self orientation. Ching (1976) believes the teacher of bilingual children should become acquainted with their cultures and help these youngsters develop their own personal values without negatively affecting their self-concepts in the process (p. 3).

In her booklet, *Reading and the Bilingual Child*, she outlines the following special needs:

1. Cultural Values
   It is especially important that the teacher of bilingual children develop sensitivities to the cultural values of the children he teaches.
   - Level of Aspiration
     The child should be helped to set goals which are within his grasp but which also are rewarding in terms of effortful achievement.
   - Value Orientation
     Certain fairly standard values held by society in general may not be held by the child in his culture.
   - Socialization
     Children may come from environments in which some practical amenities necessary for harmonious interaction with others or for appropriate behavior in school may not have been acquired.
2. Sense of Personal Worth
   The teacher of bilingual children must provide a program which gives them opportunities to feel secure and accepted, to receive peer recognition, and to achieve success. A happy, relaxed atmosphere—one in which children are free to converse, to enjoy and share experiences, to use language to make mistakes and correct them—is especially important.
3. Language
   - Experiential-Conceptual-Informational Background
     Many bilingual children fail to comprehend what they read in school because they lack the experience to help them acquire meaningful concepts.
   - Auditory Discrimination
     Because bilingual children have been exposed to a system of speech sounds which is at considerable variance with English, they may have difficulty in comprehending the speech of others and may give a unique sound to English words.

- Vocabulary Development
  The bilingual child's vocabulary may be inadequate because concepts he has developed may have labels or names which are unique to his own culture. The bilingual child who has a restricted English vocabulary must be provided with a variety of meaningful experiences where new English words and their meanings are presented in many interesting ways.
- Syntax
  The syntactical structure with which bilingual children are familiar is often quite different from that which they hear or try to read in school. Both the order and complexity of textbook sentences, as well as those the teacher used in the classroom may be overwhelming to them. Therefore, it is necessary to provide many opportunities for these youngsters to hear and use English in various situations such as listening to stories, singing songs, chanting poems, participating in short plays (without memorizing lines), role play and choral reading (pp. 2-6).

Through activities such as the above, the teachers may easily adapt the curriculum to individual student needs and aid in the development of skills needed for rewarding school experiences.

By integrating children's literature into the curriculum, the teacher will be able to provide a wide range of creative activities which stimulate learning in every area. One of the greatest potentials of literature is its ability to present role models for the young readers. Bilingual children will want to read and hear about people and situations they can relate to, and literature will be a never-ending source of worthy role models for them. Many Mexican-American children will feel pride in reading Ruth Franchere's *Cesar Chavez* (Crowell) and Puerto Rican children will enjoy Pura Belpre's *Santiago* (Warne) and Martha Alexander's *Sabrina* (Dial). Byrd Baylar's *Before You Came This Way* (Dutton) will furnish wholesome reading for Native-American children.

The vocabularies and experiential backgrounds of bilingual children may often be limited; here again, literature will offer many exciting vicarious experiences which strengthen their self-identity and add new dimensions to their lives. In addition to providing role models and broadening their backgrounds, literature books offer many opportunities for developing the skills children need for success in the content areas—through creative activities which naturally arise from their experiences with books and poetry.

It is a good idea to use the kind of activities that allow *all* children to achieve success; this will avoid embarrassment for those children who are less gifted than others in certain academic areas. Puppetry is especially useful in this respect for it gives the shy child an opportunity to speak his/her thoughts through "someone else." In literature children may present their messages through a book character they admire. Choral reading is also good for this purpose since it not only aids in oral expression but gives children an in-group feeling and permits them to "speak out" through the protection of a group. Some types of choral reading also enable certain children to assume the role of leader if desired. Singing folk songs and chanting poems together are also good activities for bilingual children; in this kind of situation they are able to benefit from the English word sounds their Anglo classmates say. This will provide the experience they need with clear enunciation of words. Short skits and plays also offer opportunities for speaking as well as creative dramatics and role play. Many times when children read or hear a story read, they may want to act out the entire story or certain parts of it. Learning lines to stories and plays is not recommended as this would place an added burden on the children and add to any existing insecurity. Spontaneous acting out of stories and poems, however, is recommended and children should always be encouraged to do so, but not forced.

Role playing a short story or certain scenes from it is a good activity for bilingual as well as monolingual children. This activity is not only useful in the area of social studies but it also aids in oral expression and gives children practice in speaking before a group. Another value of role play is the fact that it gives children the opportunity to relate to characters they like and at the same time take sides on certain issues which may affect their lives and communities.

Children's literature makes opportunities for *every* child in a class to participate in ways that are satisfying to him or her. Some children may prefer to construct dioramas and paint murals relating to stories and they should be encouraged to do this. Others may wish to perform experiments or make collections after reading or listening to trade books on magnets, ants butterflies and shells. This is a good way to integrate science with the language arts/reading areas because children will need to label certain objects and possibly write short paragraphs about their projects.

Another valuable activity involving children's books is "you read to me; I'll read to you." This is done by having a Spanish-speaking child read portions of a book to a non-Spanish-speaking child and vice versa. Some children's books are written in Spanish and English and are particularly good for this purpose, but this activity does not have to be limited to such books.

Children may select the portions of a book that they would like to read to each other. Several word games can be designed through children's books also. For instance, after students have been exposed to a good number of books, they may be asked to fill in blanks where there is a color in the title of the book, such as *Hans Brinker and the _____ Skates, Island of the _____ Dolphin, The Rabbit Who Wanted _____ Wings,* and _____ *Eggs and Ham.* To aid in spelling, simple, scrambled word games might be created from short book titles such as *Little Toot, Charlotte's Web,* and *Peter Rabbit.* It is a good idea to make sure children know the books that you plan to use in these games; this will assure enjoyable learning rather than adding to the frustrations which some children may already be experiencing.

Bilingual children need to experience success in many areas; they need to feel accepted by their teacher and their peers. Often, peer acceptance comes as a result of demonstrated competency. Literature will give the bilingual child an opportunity to demonstrate his/her competency. Through children's literature the teacher is able to change cultural differences into cultural advantages, and this is the key to academic success for bilingual children.

REFERENCES

Baecher, Richard E. The challenge of the ASPIRA decree. In Golubchick and Persky (Eds.), *Urban social and educational issues.* Dubuque, Iowa: Kendall Hunt Publishing Co., 1976.

Ching, Doris C. *Reading and the bilingual child.* Newark, Delaware: International Reading Association, 1976.

Hornburger, Jane M. Teaching reading by way of literature. In Golubchick and Persky (Eds.), *Innovations in education.* Dubuque, Iowa: Kendall Hunt Publishing Co., 1975.

Kobrick, Jeffrey W. The compelling case for bilingual education. *Saturday Review,* 1972, 55, 54-58.

Kocher, Margaret, If you care.... *Elementary English,* 1974, 483-87.

LaFontaine, Hernan, Introduction to bilingual education. In Golubchick and Persky (Eds.), *Urban, social and educational issues.* Kendall Hunt Publishing Co., 1976.

Malkoc, Maria, & Roberts, Hood, Bilingual education: a special report from CAL/ERIC. *English Journal,* 1970, 59, 721-6.

Nova, Alfonso R., & Sancho, Anthony R. Bilingual education: una hierba buena. *Claremont Conference Yearbook,* 1975, 113-17.

Ortego, Phillip D. Schools for Mexican Americans: between two cultures. *Saturday Review,* 1971, 54, 62-64+.

Risk, Ray C. Student social class and teacher expectations: the self-fulfilling prophesy in ghetto education. *Harvard Education Review,* 1970, 40, 411-51.

Rodriguez, Armando, The necessity for bilingual education. *Wilson Library Bulletin,* 1970, 44, 724-30.

SPECIAL REFERENCES

Text that contains recipes on Chicano cookery; also an excellent text for use in all other areas of this design: *Information and Materials to Teach the Cultural Heritage of the Mexican American Child.* Dissemination Center for Bilingual Education, Austin, Texas, 1972.

Text that contains prose, fiction, and poetry written by and about the Chicano experience: Philip Ortego. *We Are Chicanos.* New York: Washington Square Press, 1973.

Gordo is a syndicated comic strip that appears in major Sunday editions of Southwestern and Western newspapers. If not available, Mexican comic books are available through the bilingual dissemination centers which are listed below.

Text which contains a variety of poetic styles and poetic themes related to the Chicano experience: Victor Ochoa. *Nation-child Plumaroja.* San Diego: Toltecas and Aztlan Publications, 1972. (Centro Cultural de la Raza, San Diego, California 92101).

Anthologies of Chicano plays are available through the Commission for Mexican American Affairs, 1514 Buena Vista Street, San Antonio, Texas 78207. The Commission provides a free catalog containing lists of books, posters, films, magazines, journals, and pins related to the Chicano experience.

Record companies do record Chicano *corridos.* Check through a record shop for addresses.

Dissemination Centers

Elementary school level centers:
Bilingual Education Services
P.O. Box 669 or
1508 Oxley Street
South Pasadena, California 91030
Dissemination Center for Bilingual Bicultural
Education
6504 Tractor Lane
Austin, Texas 78721
Secondary school level centers:

Commission for Mexican American Affairs
1514 Buena Vista Street
San Antonio, Texas 78207

Quinto Sol Publications, Inc.
P.O. Box 9275
Berkeley, California 94709

Chapter 51
Integrated Reading Approaches for Bilingual Learners
Angela Carrasquillo*

Why Teach Reading?

As a major mode of communication that is considered of great value in education, reading instruction plays an important role in the school curriculum. Smith (1971) defined reading as an act of communication in which information is transferred from a transmitter to a receiver. Success in school depends to a large degree on rapid development of reading skills. The reading program must develop independent readers who can think critically and distinguish facts from opinions. It must develop readers who can enjoy reading and can get personal improvement and satisfaction.

It is common to hear bilingual educators asking which is the best method or approach to teach reading to bilingual learners. There is not one bilingual reading method. Approaches, techniques and methods vary, depending on the nature of the group, the initiative of the teacher and the level of the student. Many factors need to be considered in selecting reading approaches.

Acquisition of reading skills is perhaps the most important aspect of learning, since the success in learning other academic subjects depends on these skills. Sequential development of reading skills is especially important for the teacher to help bilingual children acquire the basic reading skills that make it possible for them to succeed in learning to read and to gain independence in reading. Areas of skill development should include vocabulary (word meaning) and word recognition skills, including contextual, phonetic and structural analysis; and comprehension skills, including critical reading.

Teaching reading in the child's native language first is highly recommended in bilingual programs. Modiano (1966) has provided data to support what has become a general conclusion that children learn to read more successfully in their native tongue than they do in a different language. Therefore, the native language is viewed as an asset, and the child's present language development can be used to further his progress in his two languages. It is also assumed that an oral-aural English program should precede reading in English for the non-English child, since development of oral

English skills greatly facilitates the acquisition of reading skills. As Thonis (1970) noted, there is a positive transfer of skills to the task of learning to read in the second language on the part of those who are literate in their native tongue.

Bilingual-bicultural education works more specifically with instructional adaptation than any other discipline. Light (1974) observed that adjustments were necessary for the acceptance of the multi-cultural educational approach—involving grouping of non-English speaking children; grouping political strength of minority groups; and acknowledgment of the dismal record of traditional approaches to the education of culturally different children.

The three instructional approaches to be discussed in this article—whole group, small group, and individualized reading—should be integral parts of every bilingual reading program. These three modes work very well together, although it takes a great deal of time and effort to put together a balanced and meaningful program. This author has not seen bilingual reading programs suggesting the use or integration of three approaches. Most of the bilingual specialists' perceptions have been in favor or against one or another. Although one approach may be better than another for the acquisition of a specific skill, its effectiveness will depend on the teacher's knowledge and ability of that particular approach. The teacher of bilingual childrn must recognize the fact that not one particular reading approach or single combination of approaches will guarantee that the bilingual child learns to read. The teachers must be knowledgeable about a variety of reading approaches and procedures that will enable him or her to select and utilize effectively the appropriate ones.

*Dr. Angela Carrasquillo is an assistant professor in the Bilingual Education Program at Fordham University, Lincoln Center, New York City.

Bilingual Reading Approaches

The following factors are most important in selecting and development bilingual reading approaches.

1. *Preferred mode of Learning*

Children are obviously different in their individual ways of learning. As Spache (1973) noted, social factors such as education, cultural interests, income level, family stability and vocational adjustment all affect the child's purposes and uses of the reading process. Educators are responsible for identifying and determining the child's preferred style of learning. To accomplish this goal, the students need the opportunity to try different approaches and methods, ask questions, share ideas, react to situations, and test or try out ideas or the ideas of other people. The classroom instructional setting should fulfill the child's social and psychological needs. Students will enthusiastically study and learn when a balanced reading program is given in which their interests and needs are met. The success or failure of the developmental process of reading for a bilingual child depends on the sensitivity of the teacher toward the student's environment, his/her culture, and socioeconomic level.

2. *Variety of Reading Experiences*

The traditional monolingual English curriculum has apparently failed to meet the educational needs of the children from different language backgrounds. Bilingual reading programs offer them the opportunity to meet their educational needs before their self-concepts and probabilities for success can be destroyed in a setting in which they cannot understand.

Broadening reading experiences and stimulating recreational reading is important for the bilingual child to improve his attitude toward reading and to induce him to read for pleasure. Such experiences might include listening centers which expose children to good books; a film viewing center with filmstrips related to good stories in children's literature; an attractive library area filled with good books on the children's reading levels; a regular story-telling time by pupils and teacher; individual or group projects on stories; individual record-keeping of books read by the children with panel discussions on them; and general discussions on books in reading clubs.

3. *Relevance and Suitability*

It is essential to adapt reading to the developmental needs of the child. A positive self-image is one of the most important aspects of early learning. It is important that the manner in which reading is taught does not cause children to feel defeated and unsure of themselves. The whole group, small group, or individualized instructional settings may be used to stress important skills for bilingual children such as visual discrimination, auditory discrimination, sounds of letters and letter combinations, and word attack since there are some skills that can be stressed better in one specific learning mode.

4. *Grouping*

Different reading approaches must be used in the classroom. Grouping students by interests, needs, and abilities will increase their motivation to learn to read. Approaches like basal readers, phonemic reading, linguistic, language experience, one-to-one sound symbols, and perceptual discrimination should be seen as part of broader approaches like the whole group, small group and individualized instruction. The grouping should not be fixed but rather should be flexible to provide students with different learning experiences to meet their needs. Particular groups should be formed because the students in that group have something in common. They may function at approximately the same level, or they may have difficulties acquiring the same skill. The criterion for grouping depends on the nature of the lesson.

Whole Group Instruction

In this instructional setting or approach the entire class is taught a particular reading skill, or the group participates in one reading activity. The whole group instruction approach has the following advantages, especially at the beginning of a bilingual reading program: 1) It helps beginning readers or newly arrived students to learn how to participate as a member of the class; 2) It helps and encourages verbal participation by the more timid or non-verbal students of the class; 3) It helps the teacher assess the overall range of abilities in reading in one particular class as a whole, since the entire group is exposed to the same reading materials; 4) Children exposed to others may interact with children who possess a variety of abilities.

Let us consider one way to use the whole group approach to beginners of reading in a second language; 1) Select a story or a selection that is not too long or too complex and is in accord with the child's interests; 2) Prepare or select drawings or pictures related to the story to motivate the children to read the story. Discuss some of the drawings with the children to develop an on going interest through the story; 3) Read the story aloud and clearly while students listen and look at their own copies for understanding. Help students get the meaning with the use of pictures, gestures, dramatizations, and context clues. 4) Ask comprehension questions throughout the reading to make sure the children are understanding the story. 5) Reread the story, pausing at new words and hard-to-understand phrases. 6) Have a good picture, drawing or topic sentence to end the story. 7) Have individual children and different rows of children read parts of the story aloud. Use specific and interesting questions to gain the attention of the whole group. 8) Students should read the story silently to answer oral or written comprehension exercises 9) Have follow-up language or specific reading skills activities planned for the independent or small group.

In the whole group approach the teacher may assign tasks, review informatin, give directives, correct assignments and use group activities in which the children would learn from one another. Each child has an opportunity to contribute without being unduly singled out, and errors are not overemphasized.

Phonics, vocabulary, study and comprehension skills might be stressed using the whole group approach. When mechanical reading skills are emphasized, this approach might be also used. Since the bilingual learner is working with two languages at the same time, reviewing and reinforcement of language skills may be developed through a whole group setting. Language arts lessons would be presented to the entire group, since language experience, grammar, and morphology are essential to successful reading. In developing these activities, the teacher should develop appropriate cultural content to bilingual children. There are two reading approaches in which the use of the whole group instructional setting is appropriate. These are the language experience approach and the linguistic or phonics approach.

The Language Experience Approach

The rationale of this mode is that instruction must be related to the experiences of the learner. As the name indicates, language and child experience are used in combined equality. The child dictates from his own experiences those things of interest to him and which he may wish to share with others. The teacher writes down what the child relates, and the child perceives that what he says is important and can be written down and read. The content of what the child reads represents concepts that are part of his culture and are meaningful and important to him and the whole group. Through the child's own view of reality at home and at school, he can think about people, places, and things with which he is familiar. His thoughts can be expressed using printed words and can be written by his teacher or by him. First, the bilingual child learns to read only what he has thought about, has said, and has heard. Later he can learn to read what others have thought about and have written. This method can effectively be incorporated in the whole group approach since each child brings a variety of experiences which are similar and different to others in

his class. These experiences can be used to encourage appreciation of the relationship between oral and written language. By this method the child sees his thoughts and the thoughts of others take another form (writing) which can come back to him in the process of reading. This technique may be particularly effective with bilingual learners, since learning to read in the new language presents a variety of new skills to be learned for beginning reading, as well as a transfer of previously learned skills for those who have learned to read in their native language. The emphasis is on helping every child to acquire vocabulary for the things he or she is learning.

The Linguistic Approach

Phonic instruction is also taught with the whole group. Through the development of linguistic skills the child will be guided to see the pattern structure of the language rather than simple facts without meaning. For example, repetition of a variety of sounds and words in groups helps the child gain confidence in these skills when he participates as part of the group. This method is particularly effective for bilingual learners, since reading in a new language or beginning reading in their own language is a new experience which needs the support and reinforcement of peer group activities. Workbook exercises may be utilized in these sessions in which phonetic clues could be used for helping the child to recognize and pronounce words. After these introductory lessons, the follow-up activities will be in a small group situation and with individual children as well. Phonic instruction should be of the kind where the child gets the sound *after* hearing and seeing it in a word. For the bilingual learner the word is meaningless if it is presented in isolation. Phonics are taught through group games and activities, especially those involving vocabulary building and/or sight words as well as drills for audio, and visual discrimination. Each child has an opportunity without being directly singled out, and individual errors are not over emphasized. The whole group instruction setting should be used occasionally but must be practiced at least once a week, since it has the advantages of children working together as well as encouraging the socialization of bilingual-bicultural children.

Small Group Instruction

A small group differs from a whole group in that a small group is a subset of the whole and its members have some diagnosed reading problems in common. The members of the group can often self-correct and help each other to some extent. In the whole group setting, the teacher may find that some students are having difficulties with the rhythm and intonation of the written language or perhaps with comprehension. The teacher thus has to work with these students either in small groups or individually.

In planning for the small group, the teacher must identify the problem or problems shared by the group. Some activities which can be used with small groups are those that allow each child to take an active role and at the same time allow the teacher to evaluate the child's progress—a difficult task in a whole group setting. In the small group setting children are more likely to speak up and ask questions, thus being able to participate without being lost in the group. There are pupils who are shy in a large classroom but can work effectively when they are in a small group. The following are advantages of this approach: 1) The teacher may provide activities which are relevant to the needs of each particular group of students; 2) The pupils in any given group still share the advantages of group interaction and support of the peer group; 3) The children will not be constantly compared to more capable students; 4) Capable students may be incorporated into a slower group to help the others and to build up his or her own self-image; 5) The teacher may better assess the progress of each small group according to improvement in particular reading skills. Using the small group setting, the teacher may group children according to their needs. For example, all children who have difficulty with initial consonants, common in bilingual children, may work in an activity which deals with initial consonants.

Basal Readers

Basal readers and supplementary reading materials should be used in a small group instructional setting. Basal readers provide the student with a sequential series of reading experiences; an orderly sequence of skill building; a defined plan of action for developing and extending these skills; content that is geared to grade levels and controlled in vocabulary and concept level; and a variety of content. On the negative side basal readers may contain content that is completely middle-class Anglo-oriented, content that is irrelevant to the experiential, cultural background and values of the bilingual child. Basal readers may also contain speech patterns unfamiliar to the child, and content so controlled by vocabulary as to make it uninteresting. Basal readers when not used selectively by the teacher may fail to take individual differences into consideration. The teacher can adopt a basal reader to fulfill the needs of the bilingual student by choosing only what is pertinent at the time and filling in any gaps by other methods and materials. If basal readers present only the middle-class stereotype, the teacher

can make efforts to replace it with different ethnic and environmental facts through pictures, slides, and even reading content. Even though many specialists have deplored the use of basal readers, its success depends on the teacher's ability. Teachers can select selections and avoid or substitute others. While the basal reader's workbook is effective in emphasizing specific skills, it should be noted that not all groups should have to do the same amount of exercises. Each group may work similar or different exercises, depending on the group level and teacher's objective. After the completion of the exercises, the various groups may meet together to discuss these exercises. In other instances, the teacher should develop other exercises, depending on the student's needs.

A basal reading program should be carefully selected for bilingual learners. Factors to be considered in selection include content's relevance to children; phonological and structural patterns used; vocabulary controlled; and variety of exercises and activities.

Individualized Instruction

Individualized instruction implies a specific instructional procedure adapted to the learning style and personality of each individual. We may define individual instruction as a classroom organization which provides for the effective learning activities and experiences of each class member. The student works on a particular task on his own without the teacher, or the teacher works with one student on a one-to-one basis.

This approach is highly recommended since the child may work at his own rhythm. There are more opportunities for diagnostic devices; the child is provided with more satisfaction. The teacher has the opportunity to understand and respect the values, traditions and cultural heritage of the student. Age, growth, culture, cognitive potential, environment, interests and personal philosophies all differ in each individual. A student through varied teaching methods and learning styles must be allowd to become a self-directed learner and critical, creative thinker. In an individualized classroom, the teacher should direct the child into his/her individual learning style and need, since the culmination of any reading program is individualization. Individualization should be provided for the student who needs regular one-to-one instruction, and the student who merely needs occasional individual help. A teacher may give a whole group lesson on a particular skill, then, in order to reinforce that skill, the teacher can provide individualized exercises to meet an individual student's different levels of competency in the skill.

With the use of the tape recorder a student may

practice a specific skill—for example, the pronunciation of a new vocabulary word. Have a set of pictures divided according to the initial letters. In the front of the picture write the initial letter and on the back the complete word. Prepare a worksheet for each letter with fill-in sentences using the given vocabulary. Have a tape recording of the words in sequential order according to corresponding numbers on the pictures. The student listens to the first tape several times. A second tape is played which gives the word in mixed order. The student has to write the number of the picture of the word he/she has heard. The teacher can then assess the student's auditory discrimination of the words. The student does the written work; then he reads his answers into the tape recorder. The teacher plays back the tape and assesses his oral and reading mastery of material. In addition to testing each individual, the teacher can listen to the tapes at home and can determine which student needs more practice with particular sounds or vocabulary skills.

Individualized reading is not a commercially prepackaged kit of materials nor a series of books. It provides for the possible utilization of the thousands of varied children's books which free the child from the closed structure of the basal readers or the linguistic oriented programs. The main task of the teacher is to obtain a large cultural collection of easy-to-read books on a variety of subjects that are of interest and appropriate reading level for children of a given class. The child may share the content of these books with other students or can be helped by an advanced reader. After reading an interesting book, the student might continue working individually in order to: 1) prepare or ask his own questions; 2) interview other students; 3) write reports on what he has learned; 4) read his report to the whole or small group.

The teacher must devote some time to talking directly with the student. The conference is a short period of time spent with each child, listening to him read and talking with him about the individual reading tasks the student is performing. It provides the teacher with a variety of facts concerning each child's needs and interests. It provides a means for checking on errors and on comprehension. It is also a time for guidance and evaluation. It is a time for listening and noting the child's reactions, his/her likes, dislikes, fears and judges and his self-concept. By an informal examination of a pupil's previous work with the whole class, small class written notes, homework assignments, the bilingual student's individual needs can be determined.

SELECTED REFERENCES

Aukerman, Robert Co. *Approaches to Beginning Reading.* New York: John Wiley and Sons, 1971.

Kobrick, Jeffrey W. "The Compelling Case for Bilingual Education," *Teaching the Bilingual*, edited by Frank J. Piarlosi. Tucson, Arizona: The University of Arizona Press, 1974, pp. 169-178.

Light, Richard L. "Issues in Teacher Preparation for Cross Cultural Education." Paper presented at the Third Annual International Conference on Bilingual Education, New York City, May, 1974, ERIC.

Modiano, Nancy, "The Most Effective Language of Instruction for Beginning Reading: A Field Study," *Teaching the Bilingual*, edited by Frank J. Piarlosi, Tucson, Arizona: The University of Arizona Press, 1974, pp. 139-166.

Smith, Frank, *Understanding Reading.* New York: Holt, Rinehart and Winston, 1971.

Spache, George D. and Spache, Evelyn B. *Reading in the Elementary School.* Boston: Allyn and Bacon, 1973.

Chapter 52
Mathematics In Bicultural Education
William M. Perel*

One phenomenon which makes the United States nearly unique among the nations of the world is the diversity of national, cultural, and linguistic backgrounds of its people. While this diversity is a source of strength for our country, it also imposes obligations and problems on our schools, at all levels.

Recently considerable attention has been focused on the language problems of Chicano and Puerto Rican children and some attempt has been made to provide instruction in the Spanish language. Certainly, students who do not understand English cannot be expected to react positively to instruction in English and can hardly be expected to demonstrate acquired knowledge and skills in a language unknown to them. At one time students in public school were punished for speaking Spanish, even when they knew no English and even those teachers able to teach in Spanish were prohibited from doing so. For the most part such regulations have now been changed, although a shortage of teachers able to use Spanish effectively in the classroom remains.

Less attention has been given to the linguistic problems of other groups. Most Americans who are foreign born have already passed through the public school system and their children are experiencing little in the way of linguistic difficulty. However, many native born Americans speak and understand various kinds of non-standard English. Although their difficulty is less obvious, they also experience problems in understanding the teacher and the teacher experiences difficulty in understanding them. Of course, we may hope that all students will acquire some skill in standard English, since it is in this language that the scientific and technical literature is most commonly available to our citizens. Attacks upon standard English on the grounds that it is the language of the middle class or that it is "white English," while accurate, are also counter productive.

Perhaps more important and certainly even more neglected are the different cultural and moral values which some children bring with them to the public schools. If such children are competent in standard English, cultural differences are likely to go unnoticed, in spite of the problems which such differences are likely to create.

It is unfortunate that a common solution to almost every educational problem is a pretense that no problem exists. If a school fails to teach Black children to read and write standard English, it can decide that standard English is neither necessary nor important for such children and begin to teach them Black English, a dialect which they presumably already know. Colleges and universities have begun to do the same thing and Black English has become a specialty within the field of linguistics. Black English can and should be studied. It is a language with its own grammar and is not a random selection of words and phrases as some may suppose. A very learned Black professor once gave a lecture on this subject to a lay audience, speaking Oxford English except when presenting examples of the Black dialect. During the question period, a Black mother, who had not been fooled by the rhetoric, made the following point. "I am glad to know that what I have been speaking all my life qualifies as a language and has been found worthy of study by professors. But I want my son to learn to speak the way you speak. He already knows how to speak the way his parents and neighbors speak." The professor had no answer to give her.

If a school administration finds that standardized test scores in reading and mathematics are falling, especially among minority group children, it can claim that test scores do not measure anything anyway. However, when such scores are high, the same administration will point to them with pride.

Sometimes an unconscious prejudice operates, a prejudice just as real as if it were conscious. What is the school preparing the student to do with his or her life? If to remain in a Black ghetto, Black English may be sufficient, and perhaps little mathematics will be required. But the school should not close off opportunities for a fuller and richer life, as well as opportunities to make a larger contribution to the cultural, scientific, intellectual, and even political life of the nation.

*Dr. William Perel, Professor of Mathematics, Wichita State University, Wichita, Kansas.

The problem of cultural differences among students presents a dilemma to the schools. Two extreme approaches are possible, and both are to be avoided. One approach is to insist that all students learn and operate within the language and the culture of the socially and educationally dominant group, whatever their background and culture and without any transition. The other extreme is to give up trying to teach the student to accommodate to the dominant culture and concentrate instead on the values of the culture which he brings with him and perhaps to help him to be happy in or adapt to the culture into which he was born.

If the first approach is used, as it is very commonly, many children fail to learn, are unhappy and unsuccessful in school, and drop out of school as soon as the law allows them to do so. All of the radio and television commercials urging students to remain in school ("Don't be a Drop-Out," etc.) fail and will continue to fail because they do not address the question of cause. What has the student dropped out of and why? What is the Black, or Spanish speaking, or other minority culture student to do with the WASP figures of American history? Can such a student relate easily to George Washington, Abraham Lincoln, and Franklin Roosevelt? Can such a student relate to the writers studied in literature, or to their characters? Of course, there are aspects of history and there is literature which would bridge the gap, but are these aspects mentioned, let alone stressed in the average classroom?

The second approach is equally unfortunate, because it provides a second class education, which even the children and their sometimes uneducated parents are learning to recognize as such. The question whether Black English (or Spanish) is "better" or "worse" in some abstract sense than standard English is irrelevant. So is the question of which culture is superior. Immigrant children often learned to speak English in school and Italian, Polish, or whatever at home. The maintenance of diverse cultures within the United States has enriched American life. However, economic success and the upward economic mobility of which Americans boast absolutely requires skill in standard English and some knowledge of and adaptation to the dominant culture. It is not that the middle class American culture and language is superior to other languages and cultures, but that these are dominant. In other countries, other languages and cultures are dominant and Americans who seek to travel, live, or work in other countries soon learn that it is they who must adjust.

An important goal of education is to teach children what they need to know in order to operate successfully as adults in this country, within whatever limitations of native ability exist. This goal includes competence in standard English and an understanding of the dominant culture. Without these, higher education and the professions are likely to be forever closed to certain segments of our citizenry. Institutions of higher learning are making great efforts to attract and retain students from minority groups and to provide them with whatever they may need in the way of remediation, but such efforts are not very successful, because it is usually too late. Whatever name is given to remediation, the student knows what it is and it cannot help his or her self image. The place for our greatest effort is the elementary school.

To accomplish this stated goal, it is not necessary to deride either the language or the culture which the student brings to the school. On the contrary, positive aspects of both need to be emphasized and teachers may need special skill and training in this area. Children must not be made to feel that they are inferior because they are different. Children (and adults) tend to perform somewhere near the level of expectation. It is neither necessary nor desirable to require that a child forget his Spanish in order to learn English. It is also neither necessary nor desirable for the child to become alienated from the culture in which he or she was born and nurtured and to which the child returns at the end of the school day. If handled properly, some instruction in minority languages and cultures may well enrich the education of middle class children while at the same time improving the self image of minority children. But educators must not lose sight of the goal, stated above.

Many approaches can and should be used. But one important and very neglected approach to the problem is a much greater emphasis on mathematics at all levels, but most especially in the elementary school.

Mathematics is an important discipline, even more important then most teachers realize. Many high school graduates find careers closed to them, because they cannot overcome both a dislike and an incompetence in mathematics. Any pretense that mathematics is the province of the white middle class child must be refuted and eliminated. Such an attitude is racist and should be recognized for what it is. Children (and their teachers) need to learn that mathematical activity has been carried on successfully within all cultures. Oriental children need to know of the great accomplishments of Chinese and Japanese mathematicians of the past and present. Indian children need to know of the great mathematics done by the Mayans in the Oaxaca valley of Mexico, centuries ago. Black children need to know that mathematics was done in Africa thousands of years ago. In fact, an abacus dated at 8000 BC was found in the Congo a number of years ago. Black mathematicians exist within American university faculties, although not in great numbers. But their existence needs to be called to the attention of Black children. However great the failures of our schools in teaching reading and writing to minority children, the failure in mathematics is more universal and more enormous.

Mathematics is acultural. It is not identified with any particular culture or group. An important principle of education is that what is to be learned should be related to the background and present knowledge and/or experience of the student. But what if the student's background experiences are unpleasant. When American history is studied, Black children learn that their ancestors were slaves and American Indian children learn that their ancestors lost more battles than they won. Texas Chicanos learn that Mexicans did not fight particularly successfully either in the war for Texan independence nor in the Mexican-American War. It is doubtful if they ever learn that the battle at the Alamo was a Mexican victory. If sociology is studied, Black children learn that their poeple commit several times as many crimes per capita as do white people. Most literature studies again emphasizes negative aspects of minority cultures or ignores them altogether. Many movies also emphasize negative aspects or pretend that minority groups do not exist. The very abstractness of mathematics, which is supposed to make it so difficult to learn, also manages to avoid all of these negative aspects. Mathematics can and should be related to the background of students, but it can be related to every possible culture, as well. Certainly, the study of mathematics cannot be used either to lower a child's self image or to negate the value of any culture or group.

Mathematics is a subject or discipline of high prestige. It does not matter whether or not this status is justified by any attribute inherent in the subject. But attitudes of the students themselves and of their teachers and others towards them is what is important here. Black children are now expected to do well in athletics and Black young people have shown their skill on high school, college, and professional football and basketball teams. Blacks and Chicanos are expected to do well in music and dancing. Many also assume these children possess skill in arts and crafts. But programs in music, athletics, and arts and crafts are often established in order to disguise failures in traditional academic disciplines, including especially mathematics.

All American children, but most especially Black children are bombarded with athletics. Role models in professional sports are readily available. Television often portrays Black professional athletes giving instruction to ghetto children. It is natural for such children to aspire to professional athletic careers, with all the money and glamour which such careers promise. Some may even achieve successful careers, but most will not. It is tragic that in some fields it is possible to have a successful career and life with mediocre talent, whereas in others such as athletics, music, and the theater, mediocrity means starvation.

The relative Blackness of athletic teams and the whiteness of advanced mathematics classes in a typical, integrated American high school is well known. What is not so readily admitted is the pressure put upon Black males and also Chicanos to excel in sports, perhaps as compensation for academic failure. Athletic success does nothing to correct the notion that Blacks and Chicanos cannot learn mathematics or other academic subjects. Such notions are held by the children themselves and their teachers.

Even modest success in mathematics, on the other hand, cannot but improve the self-image of students. And it will raise the level of academic expectation on the part of both teachers and students. Black men have demonstrated success in the "Three M's," Muscles, Music, and Ministry. It is time to include a fourth 'M', Mathematics. When teachers and the public school establishment sees Black children performing well in mathematics, they can no longer pretend that Black males must be and can be no more than "Dumb, Black Jocks."

Of course, in the average public school within the United States, the language of instruction is and will continue to be English, even in mathematics. Mathematics is much more verbal than the average mathematically ignorant person supposes, and it cannot be pretended that the student who does not understand English will experience no difficulty in handling mathematics instruction in the English language. However, there is a language of numbers which is universal or nearly so. There is no reason that the Spanish speaking pupil cannot learn to recognize, to write, and to manipulate numbers as easily as one whose native language is English.

It is often argued that minority children are not interested in mathematics or academics in general. Instead they are interested in athletics, music, and a study of their particular cultural heritage. This appears to be a self fulfilling prophecy, as well as an excuse for the failures of the education establishment. It is also part of the challenge. Concentration on mathematics is one of many ways to meet the challenge.

While a study of different languages and cultures can enrich the academic life of the white majority students as well as support the egos of the cultural and linguistic minority students, too great a concentration on differences can be divisive. It tends to emphasize differences, while ignoring the even more important ways in which we are alike. One often hears Chicanos and Italian-Americans talk of the life they led as children in the ghettos to which their parents were confined. Sometimes their descriptions sound so pleasant that one might feel that life in a ghetto is superior to life in a suburb. But such persons are usually residents of the suburbs, having left the ghetto behind as soon as they were able. Such talk should not lead to a confusion of issues. They are talking of family background, parents, brothers and sisters, and friends. They do need to remember from whence they came. But they also want to know where they are going. And where they want to go is to the mainstream of American life.

If the schools teach of the poverty life styles of the ghetto and barrio, majority attitudes are reinforced. "They like living in slums." "They like doing 'stoop labor.' They are used to it." "They would ruin nice houses, if they lived in nice houses."

A young Black writer who grew up in Mississippi reports that he and his fellows believed that white men were superior to Black men in athletic ability. After all, the heros of professional and college sports were white. He and his friends assumed that white men and boys possessed some innate superiority in athletic ability. In fact, their highest praise for one of their fellows was that "he runs like a white boy." That was forty-five years ago and the myth of white superiority in athletics has been dispelled. Perhaps, it has even been reversed.

Today a minority child is not likely to have contact with scientists, engineers, and mathematicians. Through television he sees minority athletes, not only in broadcasts of sporting events but on talk shows as well. Within his own neighborhood he may see minority ministers, social workers, or an occasional physician after whom he may see to model himself. His horizons need to be broadened. Just as the child of nearly half a century ago believed that white men were superior to Black men in athletics, so it is natural for the minority lad of today to believe that science and mathematics are for someone else.

It is alleged that public school teachers are white and middle class. It is further alleged that even those who were neither became white and received middle class status along with their teaching certificates. One can find considerable evidence to support such conclusions, even though they are obviously not completely valid. The problem is that prospective teachers need special training if they are to cope with the problems which they are to face. For the most part, they are not getting it.

Teachers must know what is to be taught. Subject matter mastery on the part of the teacher cannot be ignored, even in the fact of the importance of other facets of teacher education. Certainly, teachers in the elementary schools need to know a great deal more about mathematics than most of them do. The Committee on the Undergrade Program in Mathematics (CUPM) of the Mathematical Association of America has made an exhaustive study of the problem and recommends twelve semester hours of specially designed mathematics courses for prospective elementary school teachers. Such a proposal seems fairly modest since mathematics is such an important part of the elementary school curriculum and twelve hours represents less than ten percent of the teacher's bachelors degree. Yet, almost no teacher training institution requires this much and many states require no mathematics courses whatever for elementary school teacher certification. This situation is a national scandal and disgrace. Not even during the height of the sputnik hysteria when there was supposedly so much emphasis (some would say over-emphasis) on science and mathematics was there any great change in mathematics certification requirements for elementary school teachers. The curriculum was changed drastically, and not entirely for the better, but the same teachers with little or no background and interest in mathematics were supposed to accommodate themselves to the change.

Minority students do not need a different sort of mathematics than do other students. In the October 1976 issue of the *American Mathematical Monthly*, in an article entitled "Mathematics and Sex," John Ernest proposes that mathematics classes especially for females be established. It is true that mathematical disability is more common among minority students and possibly more common among female students, but this fact does not justify separate classes. No study has shown that the nature of mathematical disability is in any way related to race, sex, or cultural background. It is remarkable that even in ancient times and in diverse parts of the world, students of mathematics made the very same kinds of mistakes. Consequently, there is no justification and no academic purpose to be served by the establishment of separate classes on the basis of race or sex. To separate students on the basis of race used to be called segregation, and was condemned. Even students with linguistic disabilities can surely learn mathematics in the same classroom with the majority of their fellow students if they are able to handle other disciplines in integrated classrooms.

Project SEED (Special Elementary Education for the Disadvantaged) was established in Oakland, California, in response to a felt need for improving the success of minority students in mathematics. Since its beginning, the Project has been tried successfully with Blacks in California and Kansas, with Chicanos in California and Texas and even with Eskimos in Nome, Alaska. Dr. William Johntz, the founder of the Project, has demonstrated its possibilities even on the floor of the California legislature.

The Project uses the Discovery Method of teaching mathematics, primarily in grade school, but also in junior and senior high schools. The mathematics is abstract. Persons not trained or interested in mathematics are likely to view abstract mathematics as more difficult than that with which they are familiar. For this reason, junior high schools teach algebra (x's and y's) to the better students and "general mathematics," which is supposed to be "practical" and "concrete" to the poorer student. But this notion is mistaken. Practical or concrete mathematics at that level is likely to be highly verbal, thus imposing linguistic and reading disability difficulties on poorer students and especially such applications are often far from culture free, with problems which refer to the number of tiles needed for a patio in a ranch house, for example. The pictures, if any, typically show white anglo males working with mathematics. Such pictures and cultural content are rarely to be found among the x's and y's of algebra. Anyone who has taught mathematics at any level knows the difficulty students (all students) have with what are called "word problems" or "thought problems" in the public school and "applications" in colleges and universities. Students who read poorly can still learn to manipulate the x's and y's, but they cannot do "story problems."

But the most important component of the Project is not the content, but the Method. The Discovery Method demands that the students discover for themselves the mathematical relationships which form the content of the program, under the guide of a teacher, or course. Students enjoy and remember what they discover for themselves. Knowledge gained in mathematics is important for its own sake, of course, but the improved self image which accomplishment in mathematics brings to the students affects their performance positively in other parts of the curriculum, as well.

The scarcity of teachers at the elementary level who are qualified to use the Discovery Method required Project SEED to bring professional mathematicians, usually on a volunteer basis, into the elementary schools. While such persons typically have had neither training nor experience in teaching elementary school children, they experienced no difficulty. Unfortunately, no program can survive indefinitely on a volunteer basis. What is needed is more and better trained teachers, to provide better instruction, in smaller classes. The cost is high, but so is the cost of continuing to permit cultural minorities to pass through our public schools without becoming acculturated and without having acquired the necessary skills to operate within the dominant culture of the United States.

It cannot be pretended that concentration on mathematics education alone will solve all of the educational problems experienced by cultural minorities. However, mathematics is a part of the general culture of the civilized world. Surely no group should be deprived of that most universal part of our national culture. More important is the fringe benefit of greater self esteem and expectation which success in mathematics can bring to those who have been made to feel inferior because of their differences in language and culture. Most important is the extent to which competence in mathematics will open doors to careers and professional opportunities denied to the mathematical incompetent.

Other approaches to the educational problems of cultural minorities should not be neglected. But it is mathematics that has been most often neglected and its particular role and possible contribution to the education of cultural minorities needs to be emphasized.

BIBLIOGRAPHY

Anderson, T. "Bilingual elementary schooling: a report to Texas educators." *Florida FL Reporter*, 1963, *34*, 6, 25.

Bull, W. "The use of vernacular languages in fundamental education." In D. Hymes, *Language in Culture and Society*. New York: Harper and Row, 1964.

Camejo, Antoni, *Documents of the Chicano Struggle*. New York: Pathfinder, 1971.

Fishman, J. A. "The American dilemmas of publicly subsidized pluralism." *School and Society*, 1959, 87, 264-267.

Fishman, Joshua, A., Robert L. Cooper, Roxana Ma, et. al. *Bilingualism in the Barrio*. Bloomington (Ind.): Language Science Monographs, Indiana University, 1971.

Gordon, Milton M. *Assimilation in American Life*. New York: Oxford University Press, 1964.

MacNamara, John, "Bilingualism and thought." *(Georgetown University) Monograph Series on Language and Linguistics*, 1970a, 24-25.

Perel and Vairo: *Urban Education: Problems and Prospects,* David McKay, New York, 1969.

Chapter 53
Art As A Communication System
George Szekely*

The non-English speaking child feels abandoned in a classroom without a means of communication. Children who do not know our language are often shy and embarrassed about what they feel is a disability. They frequently avoid the teacher's direct glances, and most attempts to speak at them in an idiom which they do not comprehend are unsuccessful. Facial expressions reveal embarrassment and inadequacy.

Many teachers consider the ability to speak the English language as crucial. The inability to do so is often looked upon as a sign of not being intelligent. In the face of the child's bewilderment with English, the teacher may continue with frustrating monologues often alienating the child completely. Our entire body is a communicator as well as a receiver of information. As communication is disrupted it acts as a line of defense which often visibly signals the scars of frustration in its inability to complete communication function. The NES child becomes suspicious, angry, disappointed with himself and others when he is not able to partake in conversations.

Here is an example of how this dilemma can be solved by turning a disability into an asset as was demonstrated by a great artist to a public including thousands of enthusiastic witnesses:

Pablo Cassals, the renowned cellist, was also one of the world's greatest music educators. The Masterwork Series, filmed for public broadcast television, presented some of the mannerisms of this great teacher-musician and has inspired us in the teaching of art. Cassals, with a limited English vocabulary, had a rich understanding of the language of music. He was fully in command of the communicative possibilities of his medium and used the entire range of musical means available to him in his discourse. As one listens and observes the flow of music among participants, it is common to see the master hum, pluck, tap, sing, as well as play, his message to his students. Communication is received by listening and the response is through the sounds of his selection.

Do we, in the art teaching profession, communicate to our students through the language of art? The art class can become a special place where visual experiences are communicated between student and teacher. This packet is intended to build an awareness of the unique nature of art as a nonverbal communicator, especially useful in teaching the non-English speaking child.

Since I have considerable experience in teaching art to a non-English speaking population in the elementary schools of New York City, this writer frequently had the opportunity to explore the non-verbal nature of art. There are over 140,000 non-English speaking children in New York City alone and the current approaches of teaching art through reliance on the English language are inadequate for them. In this manual for the art teacher of the non-English speaking child, we have defined the specific channels available and delineated the skills the art teacher should possess for successful nonverbal communication.

Communication channels are described in detail as to their nature and purpose. Throughout its pages the present chapter sets up a correlation between the work of the artist, the creative process, and nonverbal art teaching. The objective is to show how teachers especially trained in nonverbal communications can successfully plan and carry out the various necessary functions in this process.

While art teachers may be highly competent in their fields, most often they have not receivced special training with reference to the non-English speaking child. It would be highly impractical to expect a teacher to learn a second or third language, or to wait for the student to learn English thus wasting valuable teaching time. An alternate "language" *is* available. Art in its visual nature has the full capacity of functioning as an expressive system for verbal communication. In re-training art people, we are dealing with a population already familiar with some of the possibilities of this type of non-verbal idiom through their specialized training and their own art experiences.

*Dr. George Szekely, Assistant Professor, Art Education, College of Staten Island, City University of New York.

The artist talks to himself as he works, as well as to his colleagues; all communications are implied in art conversations. The resulting artworks become records of the dialogue between the artist and the world. Steps along the way are descriptions of the artist's thinking and planning.

Before entering school, children have perceived a variety of manipulative and visual experiences. Upon entering school, they are confronted with a new emphasis on reading and verbal skills. Many children have not succeeded in adjusting to school because of their inability to conform to the literal demands of the environment. The non-English speaking student faces an even harsher reality in a setting where intelligence is directly correlated with reading and writing performance.

The art teacher himself is also adversely affected by the norm, but in order to succeed, yields many of the special qualities he has gained as a result of his art experiences. The teacher who is educated and experienced in visual thinking is forced by the school into verbal compliance. Written lesson plans are the expected format; supervisors often frown upon plans in terms of sketches or diagrams. In the written plan, the teacher decides what to say and not what he will do to make the lesson "visible." A step-by-step objective is asked for, prescribing the outcome of each lesson. This is incongruous with the art process where steps are not always sequential, logical, or predictable. Sharing the art experience with the NES child leads to a new understanding of the art teacher's role as a "partner" in the creative journey.

After a short span of time, few visual communication skills remain with the art teacher. Those that remain are supportive to the importance of the verbal system. Visual communication has been understood to mean visual aids. When visual aids are employed in teaching, they are only supporting verbal communication. They thus become mere illustrations of what is being presented verbally. Without an explanation, there is no guarantee that understanding occurs. Proper visual understanding can only be assured if all relevant propositions are stated visibly.

Studies in nonverbal communication, for example those of Suzanne Loss, have customarily focused on the appearance and behavior of students and teachers. While the facial expressions and body movements' studies are important, they are only segments of the nonverbal interactions in the art room. Art teachers communicate themselves, as well as extensions of themselves, through the arrangement and selection of art materials, art spaces, and art processes.

To implement communication channels, one has to consider art teaching as an art process. The artist painstakingly selects his canvas size, shape, feel, and color before the brush ever strikes the canvas. With these preliminary considerations having been made, much of the painting has already been done. In teaching non-English speaking children, similar preparations have to be afforded before the child enters the art room. Spaces, areas and objects must be defined to facilitate communication.

Artworks can be perceived as a result of dialogue. The artist involved in creating engages in a series of transactions with his world. The art teacher who uses this method, is prepared for a dialogue with the non-English speaking child—an exchange of views through the language of art. The dialogic format used conducts transactions with materials, spaces and art processes stimulating questions, directions and replies. This visual dialogue, unspoken, represents a real communion between individuals and these visual forms.

The creative behavior of the artist-teacher is perceivable in both his art performance as well as in the treatment he administers to his general environment. A close analogy can be formed between the teacher's handling of spaces, objects, his engagement with the work of others, and his own art workings. As art teachers become more aware of how they create in and outside the classroom, they can become better facilitators in transmitting the information using each of the described means. This new awareness may permit a purposeful environmental structuring as well as plans for appropriate art processes.

The distinguishing elements of our approach, versus the traditional consideration given to nonverbal communication are the following: This program

1) makes use of the art teacher's training, background and inherent feeling for the language of art;

2) is designed and implemented as a full-fledged communication system of its own and not a support to verbal interaction;

3) views art as a social process rather than a solitary struggle to create, a social process into which other participants may enter; and

4) pursues art teaching no longer as aiming towards a specific product—the solution of which is predetermined by the teacher—but as a set of questions and experiments to be worked out in collaboration with the students.

In employing this method with non-English speaking students, it is not vision alone that the art teacher must hope to affect, but the whole being. Art communication for the student attempts to involve the art teacher in the human relations aspects of communications. The ideal use and implementation of this methodology is not simply for relaying art information to be mastered, but a genuine concern through sharing via art.

We shall now discuss how non-English speaking children can be given art instruction in public schools, and how their verbal handicap can be turned into a factual and psychological advantage for the teaching of art.

The Channels of a Non-verbal Communication System

Art Education for NES Children

Communication—Channels One and Two encompass the material and space preparation in the design of a communication environment by the art teacher.

Communication—Channels Three and Four develop communication strategies using the movements and actions related to the making, as well as the appreciation of art works.

According to our system, based on experience and common sense, channels One and Two call for the teacher to perform creatively in the selection, arrangement, and display of materials; but the teacher communicates in an indirect manner—the true content of the lesson is embedded in the materials, objects, and spaces themselves. Appropriate materials, objects, and spaces are chosen for their art communication properties. Similarly, the teacher performs creatively in developing the structure for movements and actions used in Channels Three and Four, but the movements and actions chosen must be those related to the making and appreciation of art works.

Channel One: Materials

Channel One is based on the practice of careful material selection in the planning of a piece. Paintings, for example, begin well before the brush stroke actually touches the canvas. Important selections regarding the outcome are made by the painter. Similarly, materials are also selected by the art teacher; such choices have great importance in the outcome of children's work. Selected materials can elicit certain responses from children, while discouraging others. The painter decides on brushes, paints, and canvasses according to texture, size and shape—each decision influencing the work's direction.

The art teacher's decisions must be equally deliberate; children respond in different ways to materials, depending upon their size, shape, familiarity, or availability. Usually the painter arranges his canvas, paints, and brushes with care; e.g., canvas can be shaped, draped, stretched, or rolled according

to the perceived outcome. By the same token, the teacher's planning has to envision possible results in order for materials to communicate successfully.

In Channel One, the art teacher not only selects materials and objects to be used in the work, but also arranges and displays the selection. Through the arrangement of the materials (codification), the student receives information about the lesson. The selection process both determines and is determined by the objectives of the lesson that is to be taught.

Thus, Channel One covers the materials and objects of the art process. This includes a large array of materials available to the teacher in various sizes, shapes, colors, and textures. Also, communication possibilities exist with reference to combination, placement, juxtaposition, and amount of the materials.

Such materials communicate to the student by their very nature: feeling, shape, size, smoothness, hardness, etc. Therefore, the teacher selects materials according to aspects of size, shape, texture and color. Our instructor first selects materials that most clearly express the concept of idea to be communicated. Then the teacher determines the most effective placement of the materials chosen. (Materials should be displayed so as to clarify the concept—if there is any possible ambiguity.) As a rule, materials should be displayed so as to eliminate the possibility of detracting from the message.

Materials chosen should be considered for their aesthetic appeal. They should invite touch, manipulation and rearrangement through their colors, shapes and textures.

The arrangement or placement of the materials should also communicate a style or technique to be used. The combination and sequencing of the materials should imply what is to be accomplished and how it is to be done. (To use a very primitive example—a blackboard with well-known, but incomplete words on it invites completion, if chalk is nearby.)

Materials displayed may also be presented altered from their known, original state. This may invite action of the type that will restore the original state. This action may, in turn, lead to creation; i.e., re-creation leading to creation.

The teacher is not limited in Channel One to conventional art supplies. A large variety of materials, which may not be traditionally considered as school art materials, may be used to carry art messages. In fact, the more familiar the object, the greater the chance that the student will know how to use it.

Classroom surfaces themselves can be among the possibilities of materials used for art communication. Walls, floors, ceilings, and desks suggest processes that can be used in conjunction with other types of materials and objects.

Channel Two: Space

Channel Two involves the *preparation of spaces* and environments for art processes and communication of these processes. Classroom space can direct student attention to art "investigations" in the classroom. They can direct movement to the work, or suggest the amount and types of movements to be performed. Spaces can provoke interest in themselves, or in the activities and materials contained in them. Classroom space is flexible and may contain different "visual clues;" thus, the teacher who is interested in creativity should keep the space flexible but well structured with familiar symbols.

In planning the space, the teacher should diagram placement and order of materials, objects, and movements to be used. Space can be structured to reflect movements and steps an art problem involves; space arrangements can define the number of participants; space can be structured to manifest feelings and moods that may underline a solution to a problem; and arrangement of space can define the scale and size of the work.

In planning an expressive space, one is shaping the art work itself: space can describe or emphasize neighboring spaces; the level of organization in spaces can directly influence the nature and intensity of the product; or space can be shaped and densified to give greater or less visual clarification of the problem. Arrangement of space can also aim at any or all of the following: movement, light, and direction. The amount of expressiveness depends, of course, on the message—how it necessitates an expressive environment for its understanding.

The art teacher must be aware of the communicating factors of a space—such as its size, density, light, and texture. It must be decided what materials and objects are to fill the space (how Channels One and Two are to be combined). It also must be decided how a space becomes an environment, how the space is to serve as a communicator or an artist's inspiration, and how the space will motivate individual or group interest in an art problem.

Art room appearances and arrangements present particular atmospheres which communicate by having the student anticipate what will confront him in the room with regard to work and people. If there is a special arrangement, the student anticipates a new goal or process. The pupil also anticipates new functions of even the same materials and objects in the room. (For example, canvasses on easels with open jars of paint beside them may signal the student to begin painting; the same scene with closed jars of paint means wait for the teacher to give directions. Easels and canvasses stacked near a door may suggest that they are to be moved somewhere.) Thus, function is defined by objects in a space—more specifically by *how* they are arranged in a space.

Art-related movements can be arranged through the manipulation of classroom spaces—using barriers or other physical arrangements regulating movement. The movement itself can be constricted or made to flow with greater speed. Rows of work tables, for example, make one aware of a rigid system. This directs attention to a specific way of doing things. An open room, on the other hand, without much furniture, makes the occupants aware of the available space and induces interaction of movement and work.

While a rigid system entailing rows or work tables presents one set of problems, open arrangements may bring about other problems. An open space invites decoration, a "filling in" of the space, even its transformation. An open space not carefully structured may invite a number of individual choices—generally a freer, more open approach to art works. The teacher must work harder at channeling and developing aesthetic sensitivity rather than being concerned with activities which are ramifications of other human endeavors.

Channel Three: Teacher Performance

Channel Three refers to communicative acts which can be used to elicit creative responses. It involves the art teacher himself, rather than the materials and objects—or the spaces in which the materials and objects are arranged. It concerns the art teacher performing creatively. It involves the teacher directly inspiring creative acts.

In Channel Three, the art teacher performs along with the students. Materials and objects are still used to elicit action and excite. The teacher may join in. Spaces are still structured so that action is suggested. Again, the teacher can directly join in the action.

In Channel Three, the teacher plans movements and activities. In a sense, the teacher is choreographed into these movements, and interactions are structured. Some interactions may be aleatoric, others more sequentially planned. Students can draw directly on the art teacher's work, or the art teacher can freely draw on the work of students—without the student feeling criticized or competitive.

In Channel Three, the teacher's movements and actions around the room are used to exemplify the artistic method and illustrate various possibilities with regard to the piece under consideration. The art teacher freely ventures into student "territory" and shares in the solution of art problems. Rather than students being an audience to a performance (as in the case of lecture-demonstration) very often creative actions are planned which involve both the teacher and the students. Art techniques are acquired by the students, as the teacher and learners share in trying to solve some problems.

In Channel Three, the non-English speaking child should have a clear perception of the art problem and processes. The problem to be solved should instruct as well as involve the non-English speaking child. The structure should be clear enough so that the teacher's actions do not confuse the student. The objects, materials, spaces and environments should have enough familiarity so that students know what the teacher is doing and why he is doing it. All this involves careful planning.

Care in planning includes design of a problem that visually requires the teacher and students. In Channel Three, problems are designed so that the students will feel comfortable in sharing work surfaces, materials and process; unlike in Channels One and Two, here the problems are resolved jointly through the cooperation of the group.

But the student must not be alienated by a display of complicated materials, or dazzled by the teacher as a performer. In the art teacher's performance, the processes and techniques should be simple in order for ideas and concepts to be clearly communicable. In other words, enough frustration should be "built-in" or structured so that students feel a need to call upon the teacher for assistance. Then, the students and teachers share in solving the problem (rather than the teacher merely *demonstrating* what is to be done).

During the process of the group sharing in a solution to an art problem, communications take place. The teacher communicates feelings, attitudes, and other nonverbal aspects of behavior by

(a) smiling, nodding, and patting,

(b) spontaneously reacting to something a student has done,

(c) carefully examining work,

(d) comparing two different solutions to a problem,

(e) completing something that is almost, but not quite, finished, and

(f) obtaining a sample of a similar solution from a different class.

It might also be best, in Channel Three, to emphasize abstract art rather than realistic representations of subject matter. Demonstrations of artistic ability could deal with arrangements, creative manipulations, visual thinking, and ways of working out problems. In this way, the students can immediately respond and share in the activity, rather than being an "audience" to a demonstration. The initial forces set into motion by the structuring of materials, objects, and spaces are not supported by creative actions of the art teacher, but with minimal assistance the students should then perceive possible solutions to the art problem.

Thus, Channel Three involves the teacher as a creative artist with the students as well as the invisible architect of the structured materials, objects, and spaces. The students call upon the teacher for assistance, and directly observe the creative behavior of the art teacher as an artist. Let us now proceed to Channel Four.

Channel Four: Evaluation

Channel Four deals with appraisal and evaluation. Students are taught nonverbally to compare and judge. Let us touch upon some of these ways.

First, students are afforded a visual and tactile review of an art problem. Channel Four is designed to include a series of fact-finding exercises focusing attention on the details, design, media, and technique used in the production of a work.

Photographs and Photostats

Photographs and photostats permit reworkings of a problem. Reproduction helps the eye focus sequentially on the process, seeing details not readily available at a glance. In addition, the teacher and students can trace and draw over a photostat or Xerox copy.

The evaluation process encourages reproduction mechanically through photostats, reproductions, film, slides, photographs and tracings. Reproduction leads to the understanding of complex elements and their relationships that compete for attention. In reproducing or approximating, details are simulated. If the students are involved in this reproduction, it is even better; the physical involvement provides interest and the time necessary for art evaluation. Tracings may be used to collect visual data from the art work or its reproductions. With each tracing, there is a residual product such as a collection of shapes, lines, or colors. Seeing the elements removed from the original work allows for visual comparisons.

In Channel Four, as in previous channels, it is recommended that the group process be used in examining the products. Many more nonverbal communications are possible in the group process. Nods of approval are frequent; eyes light up; children make exclamations; children shake each other's hands as visual discoveries are exchanged.

Estimating

In the re-evaluation process, the artist may make visual "estimates" and comparisons. The students may test their estimates by tearing or cutting facsimiles and placing them on the original work. Colors and lines may similarly be examined by matching strings, wires, and paint swatches alongside similar qualities in an art work.

A Puzzle Approach

Reproductions may be cut or torn apart and the pieces reassembled. This process encourages consideration of the work's design, how pieces fit into a total scheme that makes up an individual art work. The disassembling may be guided by a number of qualities displayed in the work—the major divisions of color, light, or spaces.

Coloring Book Approach

"Coloring over" a projection or reproduction of the art work clarifies understandings that otherwise may be disregarded visually. This process may cover subject and details but clarify major movements and reveal structure. In attempting to re-diagram an art work, one is not only remaking the surface of the work, but develops an understanding of the underlying work and its creator. In attempting to duplicate the artist's steps, one reverses the art process of continuously elaborating on an idea. The result is a sense of a "peeling away" layers of the artist's experience and understandings. In the coloring process, close attention must be paid to selecting materials and processes that approximate the original works.

Art works under evaluation may serve to stimulate individual judgments and appreciations. Students, at this time, have the opportunity to record their perceptions and reactions through several means.

Visual Note-Taking

Art appreciation performed nonverbally needs a means of eliciting reactions to the work which may be "voiced" visually. This process in evaluation moves away from the work, steps back from direct manipulations to recording, diagramming or sketching. The drawings visually clarify as well as represent individual reactions. Through the sharing of individual responses between the teacher and the student, personal judgments are formulated. Visual notes attempt to make evaluative thinking visible, reminding the participants that a great deal of decision making in the arts is a visual phenomena.

The art products need not necessarily be hung or shown by the teacher. The teacher can structure the room so that the students will know they are to select the best works. For example, picture hooks may be installed in a row with paintings available in the corner. The teacher may hand one and employ the necessary body language to encourage other choices for display.

The artist's involvement in work-related evaluations is not primarily to pass judgment but is a learning experience directed at helping to improve his own productions. A third type of evaluation concerns itself with the application of evaluative learnings to new art works.

The Application Process

The findings of visual investigations from previous art works may serve as a direct basis for new art productions. Another approach may be using photographs of previous art works to inspire new production. The photographs may serve as records of what has already been done and may also provide a means of comparisons.

The difference in size between a photograph and the original art work adds a different dimension to the goal of Channel Four—affording a visual and tactile review of an art problem. First, students manipulate a representation of the original art work and there is a different tactile sensation. Secondly, students perceive the art details in a different perspective. Thirdly, students have to fit the art works into a new "gestalt" creating additional problems and possibilities.

As stated before, Xerox copies of the art works can also be made, and using these Xerox copies, students can attempt further corrections and elaborations. In order to set forth new ideas, the students are forced to re-examine past compositions. With each new step, there is a re-tracing and re-diagramming of the original work's direction.

Evaluation and sorting of opinions have traditionally been the most verbal and language-oriented procedures in art teaching. In this system the model used is not the critic of art but the artist himself—thus enabling visual considerations by using art processes. When the artist is used as a model there occurs a union between the making of art and the appreciating or criticism of same.

The project approach not only facilitates evaluation, but for the non-English speaking child, this is an important aid to socialization, and an escape from verbal and psychological isolation.

Comparisons

When the student is helped to develop personal taste he is exposed to the responses of the artist-teacher as well as other participants. He is encouraged to make selections and to become aware of the selections of others.

Works can be hung, exhibited or collected in portfolios—allowing for sortings and comparisons. Comparisons can be suggested between children's own work, between the work of the children and that of the teacher, or between the work of the teacher and that of other adult artists.

A Gallery Approach

In a critical examination of the work, the artist may visually diagram or extract from the work's structure information he may further employ in art production. The student needs similar opportunities of selection.

As a cue or signal that appraisal and evaluation are taking place, paintings, slides, film, or photographs may be displayed as in a museum or gallery. The environment is carefully planned so students know that finished or almost finished works are now being displayed.

Thus a great variety of actions and procedures can combine the four Channels to constitute a vast repertory of possibilities to offer art instruction and evaluation virtually without the use of verbal language, by widening the scope of communicative instruction methods.

Recommendations

Generally, the success of the nonverbal system has shown its viability as an alternate to verbal art teaching. The translation of art instruction into verbal communication of other languages is not necessary when the nonverbal system is available. This approach demands continuous creative involvement of the art teacher—not just sideline directions, but creativity in the most direct manner.

Therefore the following recommendations for the use of a nonverbal system are of major importance:

1) Art teachers in cities which traditionally have been the centers of changing populations should receive instruction in the use of art as a potentially universal language capable of cross-cultural communications. The nonverbal system developed in this study could be a main source for training future art teachers in the communicative use of art.

2) In such a program, the nonverbal system may be integrated into a comprehensive art methods curriculum. Field-based learning experiences of art education should be a follow-up to nonverbal system training. As teacher training institutions search to expose future art teachers to the full realities of urban schools, efforts should be made to incorporate learning experiences regarding the non-English speaking child.

In the training of future art teachers, educators must emphasize the preparation of artist-teachers, the best potential users of the nonverbal system. This would mean an emphasis on the special communicative abilities the student learns in studio art. Future art teachers should be aware of their communicative abilities as artists, and how art education methods can best focus on and employ these non-verbal communication skills. Art and art education must be the comprehensive guides to the teaching approaches of the future art teacher.

3) On the elementary school level, future classroom teachers (as well as paraprofessionals) may be recipients of instruction in nonverbal art systems. Since these professionals may spend more time with the non-English speaking child than the art specialist, this could insure that art communications would continue. The nonverbal system using art as its tool may form the basis of an inter-disciplinary type of classroom instruction where other subject areas may be taught to some extent through art communication.

4) In-service education for art teachers presently employed, and facing the problems of working effectively with the non-English speaking child, should receive nonverbal system instruction as well. The art package has been so developed that its instruction and resources can be incorporated into course work or supervised independent study. Graduate art education may effectively serve those presently teaching by the inclusion of this type of special training.

5) In the school system, the non-English speaking child should be assured of the continued benefits of art instruction. With the current emphasis on bilingual education (retaining the child's first language and enriching it with the second), the same concern is needed for retaining the child's art education while enriching it with a new art language.

A child who can visually communicate and who is visually literate is well-prepared for his environment. Bilingual education and the nonverbal system must jointly become an integral part of all non-English speaking children's education. A child in a new culture must be prepared in more than just its new verbal language. The non-English speaking child has to be readied for our new culture with an explicit emphasis on visual communication.

6) In schools with large non-English speaking populations, art must gain its proper importance. It should not be used only in a supportive role to language and reading studies. Art in these schools is to be made useful for the non-English speaking child's exploration into his new environment. It should be employed from the onset as a means to allow shared perceptions with fellow students and teachers. It is to be used in establishing positive ties with the new school and new surroundings. Art studies should be used immediately to reduce the pressure and emphasis placed on reading

and language demands which magnify the child's inabilities. Let us turn the education of NEW children from a nightmare into a thrilling experience.

REFERENCES

Arnheim, R. *Art and Visual Perception*. Berkeley: University of California Press, 1969.

Barlund, D. C. *Interpersonal Communications*. Boston: Houghton Mifflin Company, 1968.

Bennis, W., & Benne, K. D. *Planning of Change* (2nd ed.). New York: Holt, Rinehart and Winston, 1969.

Birdwhistell, R. *Introduction to Kinesics*. Louisville: University of Louisville, 1955.

Brigental, D. & Love, K. L. Perception of Contradictory Meanings Conveyed by Verbal/Non-Verbal Channels. *Journal of Personality and Social Psychology*, 1970, *16*(4), 84-92.

Broudy, H. S. *Enlightened Cherishing: An Essay on Aesthetic Education*. Chicago, University of Illinois Press, 1972.

Common Council for American Unity. *Around the World in New York: A guide to the City's Nationality Groups*. New York: Common Council for American Unity, 1950.

Debes, J. *Communication with Visuals*. Rochester, New York: Eastman Kodak Company, 1969.

Debes, J. *Some Semantics of Visual Communication*. Fourth Conference on Visual Literacy. Cincinnati, Ohio, 1971.

Dodson, D. W. Changing Population Patterns in New York City, *Trends in Metropolitan New York and Implications for Education*. Working Paper No. 1. New York City: College Teacher Education Conference, April 17, 1959.

Eisner, E. *Educating Artistic Vision*. New York: McMillan Press, 1972.

Ekman, P. E., Sorensen, R., & Frieson, Pan Cultural Elements in Facial Displays of Emotion. *Science*, April 4, 1969, *64*(3875), 86-88.

Evans, T. P. *An Exploratory Study of Verbal and Nonverbal Behaviors of Biology Teachers and Their Relationships To Selected Personality Traits*. Unpublished Dissertation. Columbus: The Ohio State University, 1968.

Fast, J. *Body Language*. New York: M. Evans Co., 1971.

Feldman, E. B. *Art as Image and Idea*. Englewood Cliffs, New Jersey: Prentice Hall, 1967.

Franscecky, R. B. *Visual Literacy and the Teaching of the Disadvantaged*. Cincinnati: University of Cincinnati, 1970.

Franscecky, R. B. & Debes, J. *Visual Literacy, A Way to Learn, A Way to Teach*. Washington, D. C.: Association for Educational Communications and Technology, March, 1972.

French, R. *A Study of Communication Events and Teacher Behavior*, Verbal and Non-Verbal. Minneapolis, Minn.: American Educational Research Association, 1970. (ERIC Document Reproduction Service No. ED 041 827)

Gaitskell, C. D. and Hurwitz, A. *Children and Their Art: Methods for Elementary School Art*. New York: Harcourt, Brace and Jovanovich, Inc., 1970.

Galloway, C. M. *Teaching is Communication, Nonverbal Language in the Classroom*. Washington, D. C.: Association for Student Teaching, 1970.

Gibb, J. R. Socio-psychological Aspects of Teaching and Learning, Nelson B. Henry (Ed.). *The Dynamics of Instructional Groups*, 59th Yearbook, National Society for the Study of Education. University of Chicago Press, 1960.

Grant, B. M. & Hennings, D. *Nonverbal Activity*. New York: Teachers College Press, 1971.

Haber, R. N. How We Remember What We See. *Scientific American*, 1970, *222*(5), 104-115.

Hall, E. T. *Hidden Dimension*. New York: Doubleday and Company, 1959.

Halpin, A. W. Muted Language. *School Review*, *68*(1), Spring, 1960, 85-104.

Heger, H. K. *Verbal and Nonverbal Classroom Communication: The Development of an Observation Instrument*. Minneapolis, Minn.: Annual Meeting of the American Educational Research Association, 1970. (ERIC Document Reproduction Service No. ED 040 957)

Hinkle, J. E. *Evaluation and Nonverbal Techniques*. Fort Collins, Colorado: Colorado State University, May, 1969. (ERIC Document Reproduction Service No. ED 033 412)

Jourard S. *Disclosing Man to Himself*. Princeton, N. J.: Van Nostrand Reinhold, 1968.

Kees, W. & Ruesch, J. *Nonverbal Communication*. Berkeley: University of California Press, 1956.

Kendall, P. Evaluating an Experimental Program in Medical Education. Matthew B. Miles (Ed.), *Innovations in Education*. New York: Teachers College Press, 1964, 343-360.

Knobler, N. *The Visual Dialogue*. New York: Holt, Rinehart and Winston, 1972.

Lanzetta, J. T., & Kelch, R. Encoding and Decoding of Nonverbal Affects in Humans. *Journal of Personality and Social Psychology*, 1970, *16*(1), 12-19.

Loss, S. P. *Analysis of Physical Nonverbal Components of Interaction in Home Economics Classrooms*. Unpublished Doctoral Dissertation, Pennsylvania State University, 1973.

Lowenfeld, V. & Brittain, W. L. *Creative and Mental*

Growth. (5th ed.). London: Collier-Macmillan Ltd., 1970.

Miles, Matthew B. (ed.) *Innovations in Education.* New York: Teachers College Press, 1964.

Munro, T. *Art Education-Its Philosophy and Psychology.* New York: Bobbs-Merrill Company, Inc., 1956.

Pancrazio, S. B. & Johnson, W. D. *Comparison of Three Teacher Training Approaches in Nonverbal Behaviors Which Encourage Classroom Interaction.* New York City: Annual Meeting of the American Educational Research Association, 1971. (ERIC Document Reproduction Service No. ED 049 198)

Parkinson, R. Gaining Visual Literacy Through Inservice Training. *Audiovisual Instruction, 1969, 14*(8).

Read, H. *Education Through Art.* London: Faber and Faber, 1970.

Scheflen, A. E. Human Communication. *Behavioral Science,* 1969, *13*(5), 28-34.

Silverman, R. H. *The Uses of Art in Compensatory Education Projects.* Chicago University Press, 1966.

Smith, V. O. A Concept of Teaching. In B. O. Smith & R. H. Ennis (Eds.), *Language and Concepts in Education.* Chicago: Rand McNally Company, 1961, 98-106.

Chapter 54
Reinforcing Bilingual-Bicultural Early Childhood Instruction with Music and Movement Activities
Minerva Benitez Rosario*

In recent years there has been a trend towards the creation of educational programs that take into consideration the diverse ethnic make up of the various groups within this society. The language, culture and distinct identity of these groups should be maintained. The existence of bilingual-bicultural programs is a step forward in recognizing the needs of different ethnic groups.

These programs recognize the fact that non English speaking children do have a language in which they may continue learning. The culture and language of the child are used to strengthen learning. Bilingual education gives "children the opportunity to become fully articulate and literate and broadly educated in two languages and sensitive to two cultures" (Andersson, 1970). Bilingual education programs allow the children to feel pride in their culture and heritage and in being able to communicate in two languages. This in turn helps the development of a positive self image in a child.

Children coming to bilingual classes may do so with quite diverse language and cultural backgrounds. There may be varying levels of bilingualism as well as differing abilities and backgrounds amongst the children attending bilingual programs. The teacher must consider all of this when planning curiculum and when searching for suitable materials to reinforce language learning and cognitive skills. Hence, the consideration of music and movement activities as a means to convey and strengthen learning in a bilingual education classroom.

The education of young children through music and movement is not often thought to be particularly related to bilingual education instruction. However, through music and movement activities, exciting and most challenging teacher experiences may be provided that will help children acquire skills necessary to learning in all curriculum areas. Not only are so many skills reinforced through this medium but the teacher may accomplish what is an essential part of bilingual-bicultural education, the development of pride in oneself and a positive self image.

Following is an attempt to show how music and movement, with their universal qualities, would be excellent, enjoyable vehicles for teaching children of different language backgrounds. A description will follow showing how music and movement activities not only reinforce language and learning skills that may be transferable to other curriculum areas, but with them the teacher may provide a program that will help the development of the "whole" child, physically, emotionally, socially, and intellectually.

Physical Growth and Development

Whether monolingual, bilingual or multilingual, children are naturally active and full of energy. Sitting still is indeed a very difficult task for them. This energy and spontaneity can be channelled to more creative directions in an educational program that makes use of music and movement. Most children living in the cities receive exercise while playing in the streets. Working parents have few opportunities to take their children to parks or places where they can run and play freely. The dangers of the streets stop many parents from allowing their children to play outdoors without their supervision, so these children receive little, if any, exercise and physical activity. It is therefore up to the school to provide a program giving enough opportunities for children to exercise and develop physically.

A movement program may provide activities that will help the development of large and small muscles. Activities involving locomotor and nonlocomotor movements will allow the children to develop better body coordination while moving through space. Children will not feel as restricted when provided with opportunities to move about freely and explore space with their bodies. Body movement is a most important language of expression for the young child. Children use their bodies to communicate their thoughts, feelings, moods, and experiences. The child who is non English speaking is encouraged to participate through

*Dr. Minerva Rosario, Assistant Professor, Early Childhood Education Program, Eugenio Mariá de Hostos Community College, City University of New York.

music and movement activities. Singing games, finger plays, playing rhythm instruments, all provide a means of helping a child develop physically since they exercise their small and large muscles and develop manipulative skills when performing these exercises.

Emotional and Social Development

Emotionally, these activities help to free children of tensions and worries and provide a natural, healthier outlet for aggressive feelings. As a child gains control of his body he also gains self confidence and respect for his achievement. A child entering a bilingual classroom may need even more encouragement than most. This is expecially true if the child is not truly bilingual but is learning English as a second language and may have recently arrived in this country. The teacher must provide encouragement and help develop in him the feeling of achievement so important to his emotional development. A child's ability to conquer a particular motor task, to play games and sing songs that are part of his culture, to play an instrument, to create a dance, gives him feelings of accomplishment or achievement that are important in the development of a positive self concept. This is vital in the learning process since it may lead to more confidence when attacking problems or participating in activities in other areas. The child's learning accomplishments help develop in him a self confidence that may be transferred to other classroom activities. Among the many benefits to children attending bilingual programs is the development of a better self concept, being proud and positive about oneself and one's abilities. A child's feeling of success in these activities fosters this essential part of a bilingual program.

Not only do these activities help a child feel comfortable, relaxed and welcome in the classroom, but they help him relate to others and socialize. Children are encouraged to participate and their attitudes towards each other greatly improve when they share enjoyable experiences. Singing, dancing and moving together gives children opportunities to partake in group activities. They work together, relate to each other, learn to lead, to follow and take turns. This is all essential to their social development.

Intellectual Development

Cognitive skills may be reinforced or developed through these activities. Instruction given in both languages will not only develop positive attitudes in children about speaking both languages but will facilitate the learning of both. Children will participate successfully because they understand and are able to follow the instructions given. Verbal comprehension is enhanced, new vocabulary may be developed for both languages being taught as well as problem-solving and decision making skills.

The Curriculum

Bilingual teachers should use music and movement in their classrooms. Teaching in two languages will be enhanced when the lessons include such enjoyable experiences and a great deal can be learned about different cultures through their music and dances. No special training or large amounts of money are needed. The teacher can make use of the child's experiences to create activities. The teacher should base selection of the activities upon the needs, characteristics, abilities, levels, and interests of the children. Preplanning must take place so the teacher may examine how the class will benefit from the activities. How these activities will be incorporated into the program and how instruction in both languages is to be given is up to the individual teacher. Special time may be set aside for everyday activities in music and movement or these could very well be integrated with the rest of the curriculum to make learning more pleasurable and enjoyable in these areas.

Music and movement activities provide an exciting way of making concepts and words become a part of the child. Interpreting words, phonics lessons, dramatizing stories and rhymes through movement can help the child to better understand and adds another dimension to the Language Arts program. Singing can be a most enjoyable way of learning another language. The rhythm and flow in a song make the pronunciation of unfamiliar words a much easier task. Children become more conscious of numbers and mathematics lessons are strengthened when they keep time and count beats in dance movement. Finger plays and songs may reinforce math skills like counting, subtracting, adding. Spatial awareness is gained through movement, horizontal and vertical space may be explored. The Social Studies area can be made more interesting and exciting when children study the music, instruments and dances of the different cultures. They may learn new songs and act out scenes from each culture they are studying and in the different languages they are learning. Different countries have their own birthday songs, holiday songs, folk songs, that may contribute to study about particular cultures and languages. The child may participate in specific activities that will help reinforce science concepts, such as interpreting natural phenomena through movement. Snow falling, lightning striking, the wind, the rain cycle, all lend themselves to dramatization through movement. These are only a few examples of how music and physical activities may be used to reinforce learning in the different curriculum areas.

Suggestions for Activities

Directions for the following activities may be given in either language being studied. The teacher may evaluate the child's understanding of the language by observing if he or she was able to perform the particular tasks required.

1. To help children relax and make free movements with their bodies, let them dance to a fast, exciting record. This activity will allow exposure to music from many cultures, for example, African, Latin, Oriental.

2. To have the children exercise their body parts, the teacher may play a record and have the children isolate parts of their body (for example, the hips, head, shoulder, etc.) moving these parts in as many ways as possible while keeping time to the music.

3. Moving to the beat of rhythm instruments (drum, tone block, guiro, bongoes) may provide a way for the teacher to introduce various instruments from different cultures to the class. As the instrument is played, the player may increase or decrease the tempo and the children match the tempo with locomotor and body movements.

4. Pantomiming or acting out words and stories with action and no words. A child may choose a word or story and try to act it out through movements. The others try to guess. Feelings (sad, angry, happy, afraid, hurt, pain), animal movements (elephant, lion, snake, monkey, bird, turtle), and games (hop scotch, jacks, baseball, basketball, football) easily lend themselves to interpretation through movement.

5. In group pantomime the child may work together with the group as well as individually. Groups may dramatize scenes with movement and no speech. Playground, family, school, beach scenes may all be used for group pantomime.

6. Stories and rhymes from various cultures may be acted out through movement and speech.

7. Finger plays and songs may be taught. These reinforce language, math, and other skills.

8. The teacher may provide experiences with action songs or singing games.

9. Making up songs or adding own verses to familiar tunes allows for creativity and language development through music.

10. Dancing with scarves, balls, sticks, hoops, balloons, ropes, the children will respond creatively to rhythm.

11. Have the children create and record their own dances. They may combine body and locomotor movements counting the beats necessary for each and creating a definite sequence of movements.

12. Have the children perform simple dances typical to a specific culture.

Conclusion

Creativity on the teacher's part may lead him or her to think of many different ways music and movement activities may be used to bring about a better understanding and appreciation of both cultures and both languages in a bilingual program as well as providing more exciting lessons in all areas of the curriculum.

BIBLIOGRAPHY

Bilingual Education

Andersson, Theodore and Boyer, Mildred, *Bilingual Schooling in the United States.* Volumes I and II. Southwest Educational Development Laboratory, Austin, Texas. January, 1970.

Saville, Muriel and Troike, Rudolph, *A Handbook of Bilingual Education.* Teachers of English to Speakers of Other Languages, Washington, D. C. 1974.

Saville, Muriel and Troike, Rudolph, *Bilingual Children: A Resource Document.* Center for Applied Linguistics, Arlington, Virginia. August, 1973.

Music and Movement

Andrews, Gladys, *Creative Rhythmic Movement for Children.* Prentice-Hall, Inc. Englewood Cliffs, New Jersey, 1954.

Bentley, William G. *Learning to Move and Moving to Learn.* Citation Press, New York, 1970.

Dauer, Victor P. *Essential Movement Experiences for Preschool and Primary Children.* Burgess Publishing Co. Minnesota, 1970.

McCall, Adeline, *This is Music.* (For Kindergarten and Nursery School) Allyn and Bacon, Inc. 1966.

Miller, Mary and Zajan, Paula, *Finger Play.* G. Schirmer. New York, 1955.

Murray, Ruth Lovell, *Dance in Elementary Education.* Harper and Row Publishers. New York, 1975.

Sheehy, Emma, *Children Discover Music and Dance.* Teachers College Press. New York, 1968.

Section VI
Staff Development

Introduction by Lourdes Travieso*

The section on Staff Development offers six papers representing the views of persons involved in different aspects of bilingual training.

Each program described in the articles reflects an overriding concern to prepare highly skilled and competent individuals to serve in bilingual-bicultural settings. Furthermore, there is a serious attempt to synthesize bodies of knowledge in the areas of language development, community studies, and pedagogy in order to create significant models for training personnel. The papers describe unique and innovative training approaches and, therefore increase our body of information and sources of successful models. Through the evidence presented in the subsequent pages, it becomes clear that new modes of training and of delivering services are imperative if we are to assist bilingual-bicultural persons achieve acceptance of themselves and their identity—whether that be in a classroom or in a social service agency such as a hospital.

Theodore Andersson's "The Role of the Teacher in a Bilingual-Bicultural Community" stresses the importance of teachers having a thorough knowledge of the community and the role of the home in shaping language, culture, and values in order to assist young children make an easier transition in the classroom. He urges cross-cultural understanding by utilizing the heretofore untapped resources of the community.

Bernice Williams, in "A Community Resource: The Bilingual Paraprofessional" builds a strong case for the inclusion of the bilingual paraprofessional as an integral member of the teaching team to facilitate communications between the school and the home and to ease the transition into the school by providing familiar role models in the classroom.

Valles-Fallis in "Training the Bilingual Teacher: The Case for Language Development," demonstrates effectively that language training modalities for native Spanish speakers must be restructured in order to expand their skills in the standard native language, and to individualize programs to accomplish these ends.

Elliot Glass and Nancy Liberti describe an innovative approach for native Spanish speakers as well as non-Spanish speaking persons to increase their knowledge of Spanish through a career oriented course called, "Spanish for Hospital Personnel." Extensive use of video-tape is used to practice the technical aspects of vocabulary needed to function in hospitals. Video-Tape enables students to view themselves and their professional settings in a new perspective and enhance their professional commitments in a bilingual setting.

Margarita Mir de Cid's article, "Bilingual Teacher Training in Higher Education," highlights the need for a comprehensive design for bilingual teacher training that includes early field experiences for the preservice student as well as a competency-based design that will allow for flexibility and mastery of specific competencies.

Richard Beacher's article, "Multicultural Bilingual Inservice Teacher Education," couches bilingual education in a broader context—that of multicultural education and the concomitant enrichment that may result if viewed from this perspective. He focuses on the examination of "teaching styles" and its implication in multicultural bilingual education.

For all of us seeking new insights into approaches for staff development, these papers provide us with valuable information and experience.

*Dr. Lourdes Travieso, Director, Bilingual Teacher Corps, New York City Board of Education.

Chapter 55
The Role of the Teacher in a Bilingual Bicultural Community
Theodore Andersson*

Let us imagine a specific case.** You are a kindergarten or first-grade teacher in a bilingual bicultural community. And I am Juanito or, more imaginatively, Mariquita, aged five or six, just home after my first day at school. My parents ask me how things have gone. I may well answer as a little Anglo child once did under similar circumstances: "It was a complete waste of time. The teacher didn't even teach me how to read." I often ponder these words and their covert reproach of our easy-going instructional system.

I am also reminded of another childish story. A colleague of mine was taking a six-year old niece on a ride in the country. When he stopped for gas, the station attendant asked the little girl where she was from. "From Lone Oak," she answered.—"Oh, that's just a little widening in the road up there a piece, isn't it?"—"Yes, that's right, all right," she answered, "but that's not *all* right." Out of the mouths of babes...

I report these anecdotes not only for their humor but also to draw some conclusions from them.

In this article I will discuss the role of the teacher of Spanish or Portuguese in a bilingual bicultural community. We cannot properly do this without also considering the roles of the schoolchild, of his family, and of the community.

Let us begin with Juanito and Mariquita (or Joaozinho and Mariazinha), whom I shall now refer to in the third person. They have presumably been born into a Spanish-speaking or Portuguese-speaking family and community and have done the major part of their preschool learning in their home language. I shall first consider the phenomenon of preschool learning and then the role of the home language in school.

One of the fields of most intensive study and research today is that of early child development. Linguists, psychologists, sociologists, anthropologists, home economists, and teachers are all busy subjecting the human infant to microscopic scrutiny in an effort to understand all forms of learning, but especially language acquisition.

As one example of early childhood research let me cite Burton White's Preschool Project at Harvard. White started by studying children between birth and age six, both exceptionally able children, whom he called "A's," and exceptionally unable—but not abnormal or handicapped—children, whom he called "C's." Soon White discovered that the three-year-old A's seemed more competent that the six-year-old C's. "White came to conclude that most of the qualities that distinguish six-year-old A's, such as the ability to use other people as a resource, are achieved by age three, or as White puts it in slight hyperbole: 'It's all over by age three. Kids can start to lose potential after their first birthday and it's hard to turn them around after age three.' "[1]

Even more striking are the discoveries of Dr. Glenn Doman, Director of the Institutes for the Achievement of Human Potential, in Philadelphia, who works with brain-damaged children. In a paper presented to a Conference on Child Language in Chicago in November 1971 he writes:

When you are confronted with a brain-injured two-year-old who is no further advanced than a newborn babe—who gives no evidence of being able to see or hear, let alone crawl or raise his head—teaching him to read isn't the first thing you think about. What you think about is how to get through to him, by any method, on any level.

Young Tommy was such a child. His eyes wouldn't follow you, or follow a light, or work together. A loud noise wouldn't make him start. You could pinch him and get no reaction. In fact, the first time we ever got a reaction out of Tommy was when we stuck pins in him: he smiled. It was a great moment, for us and for him. We had established contact.

*Dr. Theodore Andersson, Professor, The University of Texas at Austin. Reprinted with permission of the author and Hispana Magazine (December, 1974).

**Based on a paper presented to the Connecticut Chapter of the American Association of Teachers of Spanish and Portuguese at the Central Connecticut State College in New Britain on October 13, 1973.

That was when Tommy was two. By the time he was four he was reading, and thereby hangs a tale. Let me tell it to you just as it happened, because we didn't set out to teach him to read, it just happened along the way, as part of our overall problem of establishing communication.[2]

And in a book titled *How to Teach Your Baby to Read: The Gentle Revolution* he summarizes his views on early reading by asserting that "Children can read words when they are one year old, sentences when they are two, and whole books when they are three years old—And they love it."[3]

Another striking example of this potential of very young children is provided by Dr. Ragnhild Söderbergh, a linguist in the University of Stockholm. In a book titled *Reading in Early Childhood*[4] she describes in detail her success in teaching her daughter to read Swedish between ages two years four months and three years and a half, using the Doman method. Another teacher, this one from Great Britain, who has written a book to report her successful teaching of reading to her own two daughters at ages two and three as well as other young children is Felicity Hughes. Her book, *Reading and Writing Before School*,[5] exudes the same enthusiastic acceptance of the evidence of direct experience and observation as do the other writings on this subject. In a book called *The Case for Early Reading*, George L. Stevens and R. C. Orem[6] have drawn together the various evidence for the children's early reading potential.

These recent findings merely confirm the insights of earlier observers of young children. For example, Maria Montessori has written that "Only a child under three can construct the mechanism of language, and he can speak any number of languages if they are in his environment at birth."[7] Allport[8] and Kluver[9] have studied children's amazing powers of memory, called "inventory memory" or "eidetic imagery," powers which enable children to reexperience a sensory stimulus in precise and vivid detail. And the late Soviet poet of childhood, Kornei Chukovsky, has described charmingly the imagination of young children in a little book titled *From Two to Five*,[10] which he considers the best years for learning. Let me give three of his examples of children's imaginative expression, cleverly reinvented in English by the translator, Miriam Morton:

(1) When Lialia was two and a half years old, a man whom she did not know asked her: "Would you like to be my daughter?" She answered haughtily: "I'm mother's and no other's."

(2) It cheered me to hear a three-year-old little girl mutter in her sleep: "Mom, cover my hind leg."

(3) And finally, "When it is day here it is night in America. Serves them right, those capitalists!"

My first conclusion, then, drawn from these various pieces of evidence is that the teacher in a bilingual bicultural community—as indeed in any other kind of community— needs to understand the extraordinary learning potential of the preschool child, especially before the age of three. How to make best of this understanding we shall see later.

Let us now turn to the function of the non-English home language in the learning process. Assuming that Juanito and Mariquita have done most of their preschool learning in Spanish, we may safely conclude that Spanish is not only their best learning medium, but also their natural, spontaneous means of expression. This means that you as their kindergarten or first-grade teacher will want to welcome them to school in their own language, guide them in such a way as to minimize the shock of leaving home and going to school, and so teach them that their preschool learning will not be interrupted but rather intensified. In a word, you will endeavor in your use of language to play the role of a bilingual bicultural teacher—a relatively new role in American education.

There are no hard and fast rules to guide the teacher in the use of two languages in teaching but there are certain common sense principles to observe. Maintaining for a moment our assumption that Juanito and Mariquita—as well as Lupita, Pepito, Panchita, Jesusito, and all the rest of those beautiful children— use Spanish easily and English with difficulty or not at all, you and I—from now on I shall align myself with you as teachers—you and I must welcome the children just as they are, linguistically and in all other ways, too. The language they bring to school is an essential part of them, of their families, and of their community and must be respected without the slightest reservation. It will be easier for us to meet Juanito/Joãozinho and Mariquita/Mariazinha on their own ground if, in addition to being bilingual (in English and Portuguese/Spanish), we are bidialectal (in the local as well as in the so-called standard form of Spanish/Portuguese). If we are not bilingual and/or bidialectal, we must have acquired through direct contact or reading or both an understanding of, and full respect for, the local forms of the language and of those who speak it. Without this understanding and respect, we will inevitably help to scuttle a bilingual program.

The question is often asked, "How should English and the home language be used in the teaching process?" What I have said so far suggests that for children dominant in the home language this home language should be the principal teaching medium in the early stages and English should be introduced only very gradually. An interesting experiment which I believe would have a good chance of succeeding would be to do all of the teaching in the non-English language in kindergarten and the first grade and then gradually introduce English. This kind of home-school language-switch programs has been successfully conducted in French in the English-speaking St. Lambert School, near Montreal, under the supervision of Wallace E. Lambert of McGill University and a team of psychologists.[11] It would have to be conducted with all the rigor of the St. Lambert Experiment, and the teachers especially would have to be selected with great care. In such a project Mariquita and Juanito would appear to have all the advantage, which would be a good reversal of the usual situation. Johnny and Polly, having the greater cultural security, would probably enjoy the challenge of having to make a special effort and might well learn as much from Joãozinho/Juanito and Mariazinha/Mariquita as from their native Portuguese- or Spanish-speaking teachers. It would of course be quite impossible to reverse the situation and do all of the teaching in English because of the social insecurity felt by Mariazinha/Mariquita, Joãozinho/Juanito, their parents, and the non-English-speaking segment of the community.

In my opinion non-English-speaking children should learn to read in their home language first, without the delaying tactics known as "reading readiness." The reading program in Spanish/Portuguese can serve as a reading readiness program for English once the elements of English have been mastered audiolingually. The relative regularity of the Portuguese/Spanish writing systems gives them a gread advantage over English for the beginning reader. The results obtained by Doman, Söderbergh, and others also suggest the advantage of preschool reading over waiting until grades one and two. And I have a hunch that if everyone around the two- or three-year-old child shared his reading with the young child approximately as much as he shares his talking, most children would learn to read without very much instruction. Naturally, certain precautions, such as providing very large characters, would have to be observed. Attention should be called to large signs outdoors, which should be read aloud. Children can be read to practically from birth and should be allowed to follow the large print and pictures in children's books as parents, grandparents, or older siblings read to them. Objects around the house can be labeled in large colored (not necessarily capital) letters. And, above all, mothers, especially, can respond to infants' desire to read, using the Doman or Söderbergh techniques.

For *oral* instruction, either of the two basic techniques may be used, depending on the local situation. One is the team-teaching method exemplified by the Dade County Bilingual Program and described by Gaarder[12] and Gaarder and Richardson.[13] The other has been called "free alternation" by William F. Mackey in his excellent description of the program of the John F. Kennedy School in Berlin, *Bilingual Education in a Binational School*.[14] In this system the bilingual teacher alternates freely between two languages.

So far we have been considering the human and educational needs of Juanito/Joãozinho and Mariquita/Mariazinha in the kindergarten or first grade and have been taking Johnny and Polly for granted. This is natural, for most of the social, economic, and educational pressures fall on the Spanish- or Portuguese-speaking segments of our bilingual bicultural communities. It is they who in the past have been expected to adjust to the dominant culture while the members of the Anglo culture have made relatively little effort to understand the non-English cultures or to help Mariquita/Mariazinha and Juanito/Joãozinho make the necessary adjustment comfortably. Polly and Johnny don't have to learn Spanish or Portuguese if they don't want to or if their parents don't care whether they do or not. They don't even have to understand Juanito and Mariquita, but the latter *do* have to learn to understand Johnny and Polly. The big question is whether the learning process is going to be comfortable or uncomfortable. It is of course the teacher who is in the position to stimulate the learning on both sides and to make it pleasurable. With a display of trust and affection he or she can instill in Juanito and Mariquita the confidence and sense of pride needed to learn. And knowing what is that makes children tick, he or she can also stimulate in Johnny and Polly the kind of curiosity which will make the learning of Spanish or Portuguese irresistible.

But it is high time that we move out of the classroom. By describing the role of the teacher in the classroom as that of an agent of cross-cultural understanding, I have already suggested his or her principal role in the community. The teacher's most natural contact with the community is through the parents of the pupils, but there are also ways in which the teacher can inform and influence large segments of the community. Let us consider in order the teacher's relations to the parents and then to the community at large.

It would be ideal if a teacher enjoyed a personal acquaintance with the parents and families of his or her pupils even before welcoming the children to class, but this is usually a practical impossibility. But a serious realization by the teacher of his responsibility to parents will help him or her to seize every opportunity to meet and get acquainted with parents. For example, parents can be encouraged to bring their children to school the first few days and to deliver them personally into the charge of their teacher. The teacher who can greet the parents in their own language is in a good position to build a sense of trust from the beginning. A standing invitation to parents to visit school at any time will deepen their feeling that the school belongs to them. I have seen only one school in which I was conscious of such a relationship among parents, school board members, teachers, and children, and that was the Rough Rock Navajo Demonstration School in Chinle, Arizona, a school that is operated by the Navajo community. Here one can see one or more of the school board elders visiting at almost any time, community artists and craftsmen working in the school studios and workshops, and a Navajo grandmother telling an old folktale in Navajo in the middle of one of the classrooms. I also remember the Las Cruces, New Mexico bilingual program for the fact that much of the teaching material and equipment had been made by parents, thus increasing their sense of involvement and their children's pride and pleasure when they could say, "My father made these blocks" or "My mother made this beanbag." A teacher who is perpetually conscious of the children's homes will also seek occasions to write notes of commendation or suggestion concerning Juanito's or Mariquita's work at school or will have the children take samples of their work home to show the family. Still another means of bringing the school and the home closer together is to guide the children in the preparation of a periodic newsletter containing samples of the children's handwriting, drawing, stories, and poems. An idea which to my knowledge has not yet been implemented is to invite interested family members to submit poems, stories, anecdotes, memories of early childhood, traditional folktales, and the like, for publication in the newsletter.

Since the teacher's time for visiting families is necessarily limited, many school districts have one or more specially designated and often specially trained visiting teachers who do nothing else. This is one way to extend bilingual bicultural education into the home, where it can teach preschool children. For example, a home-visiting teacher is one of three features of a Home-Oriented Preschool Educational Laboratory in West Virginia which could rather handily be adapted to a bilingual program in rural areas. The other two are a daily TV lesson beamed into the homes and a weekly visit by a mobile classroom unit. Still another idea which is gaining ground is the training of schoolage children to tutor younger preschool brothers and sisters at home.

In this communication between the home and the school the teacher of Spanish or Portuguese plays an essential role. We have seen that an understanding of the learning potential of infants, of the role of the home language, and of the principles of cross-cultural appreciation are all essential if the teacher is to exercise a leadership role.

And finally, by means of talks to public meetings,

radio and TV appearances, attendance at educational meetings, a Spanish or Portuguese teacher can inform and influence large segments of the community, whose support in the final analysis is essential if a bilingual bicultural program is to progress.

The teacher of Spanish or Portuguese in a bilingual bicultural community can, then, depending on his or her personality, experience, and perceptiveness, play a decisive role in the classroom, in the homes of the children, and in the community at large. In the classroom the teacher or teaching team is forging a new role in American education, built on a new understanding, an understanding of what has gone into the child's preschool learning, an understanding of the role of the home language as a continuous medium for learning, and above all an understanding of the value of the home culture. The teacher can greatly increase his effectiveness by directly or indirectly extending his efforts into the home and tapping the enormous educational resources represented by the various members of the extended family and especially capitalizing on the great learning potential of the young preschool children. And finally the bilingual bicultural teacher can exercise a leadership role in the community by helping to explain persuasively the complexities of cross-cultural understanding and cooperation, upon which the dream of bilingual bicultural education depends.

NOTES

[1] *Carnegie Quarterly*, Carnegie Corporation of New York, 21, No. 3 (Summer 1973), 6.

[2] Glenn J. Doman and Daniel Melcher, "How Brain-Injured Children Learn to Read," in Theodore Andersson and William F. Mackey, editors, *Bilingualism in Early Childhood: Proceedings of a Conference on Child Language* (Rowley, Massachusetts: Newbury House Publishers, forthcoming).

[3] Glenn J. Doman, *How to Teach Your Baby to Read: The Gentle Revolution* (New York: Random House, 1964), p. 1.

[4] Ragnhild Söderbergh, *Reading in Early Childhood: A Linguistic Study of a Swedish Preschool Child's Gradual Acquisition of Reading Ability* (Stockholm: Almqvist Wiksell, 1971).

[5] Felicity Huges, *Reading and Writing Before School*, with an introduction by Glenn Doman (New York: St. Martin's Press, 1971).

[6] George L. Stevens and R. C. Orem, *The Case for Early Reading* (St. Louis, Missouri: Warren H. Green, Inc., 1968).

[7]Maria Montessori, *Education for a New World* (Adyar, Madras, India: Kalakshetra Publications, third impression, 1959), p. 40.

[8]Gordon W. Allport, "Eidetic Imagery," *British Journal of Psychology* 15 (1924), 99-120.

[9]Heinrich Kluver, "Eidetic Imagery," in C. A. Murchison, editor, *A Handbook of Child Psychology*, second ed. Worcester, Massachusetts: Clark University Press, 1933), pp. 699-722.

[10]Kornei Chukovsky, *From Two to Five*, translated and edited by Miriam Morton, foreward by Frances Sayers. (Berkeley and Los Angeles: University of California Press, 1966).

[11]Wallace E. Lambert and G. Richard Tucker, *Bilingual Education of Children: The St. Lambert Experiment (Rowley, Massachusetts: Newbury House Publishers, 1972).

[12]A. Bruce Gaarder, "Organization of the Bilingual School," *Jounal of Social Issues* 33, No. 2 (1972), 10-20.

[13]A. Bruce Gaarder and Mabel W. Richardson, "Two Patterns of Bilingual Education in Dade County, Florida" in Thomas e. Bird, editor, *Foreign Language Learning: Research and Development: An Assessment*, Reports of the Working committees of the 1968 Northeast Conference on the Teaching of Foreign Languages (Menasha, Wisconsin: George Banta Co., Inc., 1968), pp. 32-44.

[14]William F. Mackey, *Bilingual Education in a Binational School: A Study of Equal Language Maintenance Through Free Alternation* (Rowley, Massachusetts: Newbury House Publishers, 1972).

[15]*Summative Evaluation of the Home Oriented Preschool Education Program: Summary Report*, Division of Research and Evaluation, Appalachia Educational Laboratory, Inc., Charleston, West Virginia, December 1971.

Chapter 56
Multicultural Bilingual In-service Teacher Education
Richard E. Baecher*

Inservice teacher education (ISTE) in the United States represents a huge investment in the formal and informal process of assisting educators grow as people and as professionals. Joyce *et al.* (1976, p. 2) estimate as many as a quarter of a million individuals participate as instructors in some aspect of inservice staff training. This is one instructor for every eight teachers. Yet, many people feel the effort is a dismal failure. Professionals and nonprofessionals are discontented with ISTE; there is little agreement about defining and carrying out ISTE; finally, many individuals involved in staff development agree that its major problems are structural.**

Among the more urgent structural problems confronting ISTE is "multicultural education," or that sort of education which values and cares for cultural pluralism. In recent years, educators have shown increasing concern in preserving the heritages of ethnic groups in the United States and adapting instruction to the community and the child as they are, instead of neglecting and ignoring cultural, lingual, and individual differences. Multicultural education, especially in the context of a bilingual educational setting employing two languages as modes of instruction, creates enormous inservice needs. These range from providing accurate and relevant knowledge pertaining to the ethnic background and contemporary life-styles of various subcultural groups to meeting these groups' real and concrete needs. The emerging role of the educator, then, is one of being a model of multiculturalism, thereby presenting an alternative to current forms of inservice teacher education.

The objective of my article is to formulate some basic assumptions of multicultural bilingual education as presently understood in Fordham University's bilingual teacher training program. A second objective is to explore the concept of teaching style as defined in the Educational Sciences and its relationship to the substantive aspects of inservice teacher education.

The purpose of the article is to increase our understanding of multicultural bilingual education, a relatively undeveloped area, and to recommend further investigation of the conceptual framework of teaching style in connection with multicultural bilingual staff development.

The Soundness of Multicultural Bilingual Education

Multicultural bilingual education offers a relatively untried and sound approach to instructing students. The American Association of Colleges for Teacher Education (1973) summarized the central theme of pluralism in education:

> Multicultural education is education which values cultural pluralism. Multicultural education rejects the view that schools should seek to melt away cultural differences or the view that schools should merely tolerate cultural pluralism. To endorse cultural pluralism is to endorse the principle that there is no one model American. To endorse cultural pluralism is to understand and appreciate the differences that exist among the nation's citizens. It is to see these differences as a positive force in the continuing development of a society which professes a wholesome respect for the intrinsic worth of every individual.

This policy statement attests strongly to the need and viability of multicultural education.

Complementing this endorsement are the following postulates that form the basis of Fordham University's bilingual inservice teacher education program. They indicate the conceptual focus of multicultural bilingual education as currently understood by the staff charged with the preparation of bilingual teachers.

Each bilingual person is unique. No two bilingual persons mediate meaning in exactly the same way. Whereas one may seek meaning through reliance upon listening in his/her home language, another may prefer to read for information, either in English or the native

---

*Dr. Richard Baecher, School of Education, Fordham University at Lincoln Center, New York, New York.

**Joyce *et al*, view the structure of ISTE as four interacting subsystems: (1) The governance system, (2) the substantive system, (3) the delivery system, and (4) the modal system. My paper addresses the substantive system, or the content and process of ISTE.

language, respectively. One bilingual individual may be successful in educational tasks in cooperation with peers; another may function well independently. Furthermore, one bilingual student may reason in terms of categories while another thinks in contrasts and/or relationships. No two bilingual persons, therefore, are exactly alike.

Cognitive ability is universal among human beings. Each individual, because of one's social nature, derives meaning from his/her own personal experiences and environment. Beginning at birth and continuing well into school age, the individual is capable of conceiving and perceiving meaning through the use of various types of symbols. Children from different ethnic backgrounds, e.g., Hispanic, Italian, Chinese, manifest this cognitive ability through their mother tongue and other symbols reflective of their feelings, commitments, and values.

The ability to understand others and to express one's self in another language represents an asset in the educational development of the individual. There are millions of children of primary school age in the United States who already possess competence in another language. It is wasteful to remain oblivious to conditions that cause language loss in these children. Rather, it is beneficial to foster the maintenance and development of this rich language resource. Multicultural bilingual education can contribute to this end.

Bilingual education must be defined in the context of a multicultural curriculum. Bilingual education is an instructional process that uses a pupil's predominant language as the principal mode of instruction while teaching the language of the majority culture in a well-organized program encompassing a multicultural curriculum. An enrichment to all students, bilingual education enables minority pupils to use their language and culture as a base from which they can develop abilities and acquire knowledge in the English language. It enables majority students to share learning experiences and to achieve a richness in learning that might not otherwise be possible. Multicultural bilingual education, in other words, is reciprocal bilingual education.

The term "bilingual" refers to persons who demonstrate abilities in two languages. Bilingualism does not necessasrily mean equilingualism. Most bilingual persons manifest different degrees of abilities, not only in the two languages generally, but also in the skills in each language. One may understand and speak Language A with native-like proficiency, yet be illiterate in A while being literate in Language B, through speaking and understanding B with far less than native-like proficiency. Moreover, bilingual people tend to assign their two languages to specific domains. For instance, Language A may be the language of the family, home and church; language B may be the language of school, work and the media.

These assumptions express the theoretical framework of multicultural bilingual education as it continues to evolve at Fordham University. They describe the beliefs held by the staff in their efforts to meet the concrete needs of teachers of bilingual pupils. They are indicative of the soundness of this approach to inservice teacher education. The next section explores in greater detail the emerging role of teachers engaged in bilingual education.

Teaching Style Within a Multicultural Bilingual Context

The need to explore "teaching style" as part of the emergent role of the teacher of multiculturalism is adequately stated in the following observation:

> The heart of the educational process is in the interaction between teacher and student. It is through this interaction that the school system makes its major impact upon the child. The way the teacher interacts with the student is a major determinant of the quality of education the child receives (U. S. Commission of Civil Rights, 1973, p. 7).

The role of the teacher as a model of multiculturalism and in providing equal educational opportunity is crucial. The teacher directs classroom instruction in which students engage for five to six hours daily. The teacher presents curriculum and plans experiences for the pupils. It is the teacher who is responsible for helping and assessing the students. Effective teachers, then, are of paramount importance in delivering multicultural bilingual services.

The conceptual outlook identified as "teaching style" can logically clarify the teaching process implied in multicultural bilingual education. It provides a common language whereby educators can communicate among themselves pertaining to problems that directly affect their roles as teachers of multicultural education.

Teaching style is one of the Educational Sciences being developed by Hill and his associates (1972). Hill suggests there are seven educational sciences. Each includes its own factural descriptions, concepts, and principles. These sciences are:

1. Symbols and their meanings.
2. Cultural determinants of the meanings of symbols.
3. Modalities of inference.
4. Educational memory.
5. Cognitive styles of individuals.
6. Student, teaching, administrative, and counseling styles.
7. Systemic analysis decision making.

It is not my aim to examine each of the educational sciences in depth. Instead, only that material included in the sixth educational science, particularly teaching style, that is pertinent to multicultural bilingual education will be considered. For a more detailed description of the educational sciences, the reader should consult the bibliography by Berry, Sutton and Mc Beth (1975), Hill (1975), Baecher (1976), and other materials noted in the reference list.

Teachers with highly similar interests and philosophical orientations may exhibit teaching styles that are significantly different. For example, one teacher may assign high priority to the individual student's well-being in a particular situation, and another teacher may give greater emphasis to an instructional method in a similar context. The educational science of teaching style identifies the different behaviors that are evident among teachers, thereby providing greater clarity of the role-set of teachers.

Teaching style refers to an individual's mode of behavior in the performance of his/her tasks as a teacher. Teaching style is represented by a cartesian product of three sets of information pertaining to: (1) demeanor, (2) emphasis, and (3) symbolic modes of presentation, or communication.

DEMEANOR x EMPHASIS x SYMBOLIC MODE

The *Demeanor Set* of teaching style, or the posture that is characteristically employed by a teacher, includes three elements: (1) Predominant (Pap), meaning a relatively *fixed* style of teaching, whether it is authoritarian or permissive, (2) Adjustive or "Switcher" (Sap), referring to the teacher's tendency to use a students's cognitive style as a point of departure and then moving that student in directions that will enable him (the student) to accommodate the teaching style which the teacher wishes to employ, and (3) Flexible (Bap), implying that the teacher employs a style that would appear to be "best" for the pupil's cognitive style.

These three demeanor classifications can occur as either a major orientation in one element (50-99th percentile range) with minor orientations in the other two (26-49th percentile range), or two major orientations with a minor in the remaining element. Each of these elements is subscripted as *authoritarian* (a) or *permissive* (p). Hill (1974) defines the authoritarian type as an individual who respects the wishes and decisions of persons in superordinate positions relative to one's own, and expects his wishes and decisions to be respected when he assumes the superordinate role. A permissive individual is one who does not exercise this "respect," and does not expect it to be exercised by others regarding his role.

The *Emphasis Set* of teaching style, or the relative strength accorded the elements of a social system, includes the following: (1) Persons (PN), e.g., *students* involved in instruction, (2) Processes (PS), e.g., a *method of instruction* that employs two languages, and (3) Properties (PT), such as media, facilities, desks. This set indicates the way in which a teacher assigns priorities to the elements of a social system within which he/she is working.

The *Symbolic Mode of Communication* refers to an individual's tendency to rely on qualitative and/or theoretical symbols, or a combination of both termed reciprocity. This set of teaching style includes three elements: (1) Theoretical Predominant (TP), or the teacher who usually employs words and numbers to convey meaning, either in English or the student's native language, respectively, (2) Reciprocity (RP), meaning the teacher who employs theoretical symbols (lectures, explanations) half the time, and for the other half, brings into play the qualitative symbol (talking about experiences, using visual aids and pictures), and (3) Qualitative Predominant (QP), meaning greater use of visual aids and other activities such as the student's performance involving qualitative symbols.*

Teaching style, then, is a cartesian product of demeanor, emphasis, and symbolic mode. The orientations in the demeanor set are combined with those of the emphasis and symbolic mode set to form profiles indicating the teaching style of an individual. By way of illustration, suppose a bilingual teacher's teaching style was mapped as follows:

DEMEANOR		EMPHASIS		SYMBOLIC MODE
Ba	x	PS PN'	x	TPe RP'

This teacher tends to present material and concepts primarily by means of theoretical symbols (TP)-words and explanations-mostly in English (e), with some occasional use of qualitative symbols, as indicated by the condition of reciprocity (RP'). Normally using a style "best" and suitable for the student (Ba), this teacher is *process* oriented (PS) with some consideration of the persons involved in instruction (PN'). This teaching style profile translates to the individual's perception and understanding of his/her role to others. Since the sets of teaching style include

*Hill (1972) defines two types of symbols, theoretical (e.g., words and numbers) and qualitative (e.g., sensory programmatic, codes). Theoretical symbols differ from their qualitative symbols in that the theoretical symbols present to the awareness of the individual something different from that which the symbols are. Qualitative symbols are those symbols which present and then represent to the awareness of the individual that which the symbol is. (Feelings, commitments and values are some examples of the meanings conveyed by the qualitative symbols.)

monomial and binomial elements, it shoud be noted that the maximum number of profiles in an actual teaching style is: 4 x 4 x 4 = 64 profiles. No "best" teaching style is assumed by the educational science of teaching style because of the plurality of profiles that are possible in the context of multicultural bilingual education.

Teaching style can clarify the emerging role of the teacher of multicultural education by providing a necessary common language. Teaching style addresses the content aspects of multicultural education. More important, by indicating the orientations that a teacher may have towards the elements of a social system that is the classroom, teaching style defines the instructional process in a manner that is open and systematic.

Summary and Recommendations

My objective was to formulate some essential assumptions of multicultural bilingual education as currently understood in Fordham University's bilingual teacher training program. Five postulates were briefly described in the hope that they might add to the national thrust towards multicultural education.

Another objective was to explore the educational science of teaching style as a systematic framework to clarify the emerging role of the educator who is engaging in multicultural bilingual inservice education. I recommend that such a common language be studied further for its implications in delivering multicultural education to students in our school system.

REFERENCES

Alatis, James E. and Twaddell, Kristie. *English As A Second Language in Bilingual Education: Selected TESOL Papers.* Washington, D. C.: Teachers of English to Speakers of Other Languages, 1976.

American Association of Colleges for Teacher Education. "No One Model American." *Journal of Teacher Education,* 24 (1973): p. 264.

Baecher, Richard E. "Bilingual Children and Educational Cognitive Style Analysis." In Antonio Simoes, Jr., editor, *The Bilingual Child: Research and Analysis of Existing Educational Themes.* New York: Academic Press, Inc. 1976.

Berry, James J.; Sutton, Thomas J.; and McBeth, Lloyd S. *The Educational Sciences: A Bibliography With Commentary.* The American Educational Sciences Association, Bloomfield Hills, Mi., 2nd Edition, 1975.

Blanco, George M. "La Preparación de Profesores Bilingues." In R. Troike and N. Modiano (eds.), *Proceedings of the First Inter-American Conference on Bilingual Education.* Center for Applied Linguistics: Arlington, Va., 1975.

Center for Applied Linguistics. *Guidelines for the Preparation And Certification Of Teachers Of Bilingual-Bicultural Education.* 1611 North Kent Street, Arlington, Va., November, 1974.

Dissemination Center for Bilingual Bicultural Education. *Teacher Training Bibliography: An Annotated Listing of Materials for Bilingual Bicultural Teacher Education.* 6504 Tracor Lane, Austin, Texas, January, 1975.

Garcia, Ricardo, *Learning in Two Languages.* Bloomington, Indiana: The Phi Delta Kappa Educational Foundation, 1976.

Hill, Joseph E. *The Educational Sciences.* Bloomfield Hills, Mich.: Oakland Community College Press, 1972.

Hill, Joseph E. *The Educational Sciences.* Bloomfield Hills, Mich.: Oakland Community College, 1974.

Hill, Joseph, E. "The Educational Science of Memory: Function x Concern x Condition." *The Educational Scientist* 1 (1975): 3-12.

John-Steiner, Vera and Cooper, Elizabeth, "Recent Trends in Bilingual Education." ERIC Clearinghouse on Urban Education, Teachers College, Columbia University, August, 1976.

Joyce, Bruce R.: Howey, Kenneth R.; Yarger, Sam J. "Issues to Face." *Report I. Inservice Teacher Education,* Palo Alto, California, June, 1976.

Lipson, Paul, *Influence of Educational Cognitive Style and Teaching Style on Grading Practices in a Junior High School.* Unpublished dissertation, Detroit, Mich., 1974.

Mc Adam, Glenn, *Personalizing Instruction through the Educational Sciences of Cognitive Style and Teaching Style.* Unpublished dissertation, Wayne State University, Detroit, Mich., 1971.

National Conference of EPDA Bilingual Education Project Directors. *Preparation and Certification of Teachers of Bilingual Bicultural Education.* Center for Applied Linguistics, 1975. ERIC 115-118.

National School Public Relations Association. *Inservice Education: Current Trends in School Policies and Programs.* 1801 N. Moore St., Arlington, Va., 1975.

Ogletree, Earl L. and Garcia, David, *Education of the Spanish-Speaking Urban Child: A Book of Readings.* Springfield, Illinois: Charles C. Thomas, 1975.

Perry, Harold, *Matching Cognitive, Actual, and Preferred Teaching Styles of Inner-City Elementary*

Teachers and Paraprofessionals. Unpublished dissertation, Detroit, Mich., 1975.

Ramirez, Manuel and Cantaneda, Alfredo, *Cultural Democracy, Bicognitive Development and Education.* New York: Academic Press, 1974.

Rivera, Luis, *A Proposed Approach to Implement Bilingual Education Programs, Research and Synthesis of Philosophical, Theoretical and Practical Implications.* The National Puerto Rican Development and Training Institute, Inc., New York, N. Y., 1973.

U. S. Commission on Civil Rights. *Teachers and Stu-*
dents, Report V, Mexican American Education Study. Washington, D. C.: GPO, 1973.

Valencia, Atilano, *Bilingual-Bicultural Education For The Spanish-English Bilingual.* Berkeley, California: BABEL Productions, 1976.

Wyett, Jerry, *A Pilot Study to Analyze Cognitive Style and Teaching Style with Reference to Selected Strata of the Defined Educational Sciences.* Unpublished dissertation, Detroit, Mich., 1967.

Zintz, Miles, *Education Across Cultures.* Second edition, Dubuque, Iowa: Kendall-Hunt Publishing Co., 1969.

Chapter 57
Training the Bilingual Teacher: The Case for Language Development
Guadalupe Valdés Fallis*

A short time ago, at the beginning of the 1975-76 academic year to be exact, a medium-sized southwestern university was faced with the following problem: it had received ten fellowships which were to support ten Mexican-American students through doctoral studies in bilingual education. It was assumed that these students would be "Spanish-speaking;" but since interview and selection procedures were typical of these programs in general, it turned out that while these young persons could communicate superficially in Spanish, the majority of them were completely incapable of teaching classes in this language in the variety of subjects which make up the ordinary elementary school curriculum. Several of the fellows felt that they could read in Spanish with some degree of comfort, but most confessed that they could not read at all, could not spell correctly, and very few even dared to attempt a conversation in Spanish on topics of general academic interest.

Very briefly, each one of these doctoral students, veteran teachers of bilingual education programs, was simply English dominant. The question was: What could be done with these students? What methods, courses, etc., were available that would result in the needed fluency for these teachers (all of whom, to the person, were committed to language maintenance programs in bilingual education)? The southwestern university had no answers. The college of education was not equipped to take on such a task and its efforts were limited to teaching a number of "bilingual methods" courses in both English *and* Spanish. On the other hand, the department of Spanish had not ever before been faced with such a practical problem. Like universities all over the United States, this department was designed around the teaching of Spanish to non-speakers, that is, as a foreign language and around the production of the traditional Spanish major. Courses therefore included: beginning and intermediate Spanish for non-speakers, advanced conversation, advanced grammar and composition, and principally some ten or more courses in Latin American peninsular literature. The only concession made to the fact that this university was surrounded by native speakers of

the Spanish language was a two-semester course (Spanish 213-214) entitled Spanish for Spanish-speaking students, with which Mexican-American students could fulfill their language requirement and not compete with the beginning non-speaking students.

It was evident when faced with the problem of placing the ten doctoral students mentioned above, that there was not even a single course which could provide these students with the overall development in the language which they so desperately needed. The course designed for undergraduate native-speaking students was not at all well-defined. It generally depended on the specific instructor of the course, whether the emphasis would be placed on teaching traditional grammatical terminology, teaching a standard dialect, or the teaching of basic reading and writing skills. At the same time the course in advanced conversation used a text designed to elicit ordinary speech for traveling, ordering meals, etc., at a level already mastered by all of these doctoral students. The advanced grammar and composition course, on the other hand, was aimed at future teachers of the Spanish language as a foreign language. Thus the emphasis was placed on a review of traditional grammar and on perfecting elementary skills in the area of written Spanish. Indeed it was soon apparent that while many of the courses in literature or even in linguistics would help, they simply were not designed for the task at hand. Everyone agreed that the undergraduate course for native-speakers could be recommended only for those doctoral students who could not read and write at all, but to this day (with a new crop of fellows in the wings) the question is still being pondered.

The purpose of this article then is to center the attention of those concerned with the training of bilingual teachers on this problem: the problem of the language development and language growth of the

*Dr. Guadalupe Valdés Fallis, Professor of Foreign Languages, New Mexico State University.

English dominant, Spanish-speaking student who hopes to increase his total command of the Spanish language for the purpose of functioning in that language at a level equivalent to that of most educated Latin Americans. I will therefore examine the two principal existing approaches in teaching ethnic students their mother tongue. I will examine the time-honored emphasis on the teaching of traditional grammar, the new-found interest in teaching ethnic students the "standard" dialect of their mother tongue, and finally I will compare each of these approaches and its results with that of a program in language development which would have as its principal objective the overall growth in proficiency by the student.

The Teaching of Traditional Grammar

Despite recent advances in the theory of language acquisition and generative grammar, etc., for most language teachers the question: "What does it mean to *know* a language?" is best answered by the time-honored view that to *know* a language is to *know consciously* and *express verbally* exactly how it functions within a system of traditional grammar. Thus, it is not unusual to find that a teacher of the Spanish language will often complain that a fluent native-speaking student of the language in a particular class knows less Spanish that an English-speaking monolingual (with perhaps two semesters' study in the language) simply because the native speaker cannot verbalize exactly how he is using his language. It is not sufficient for the instructor to observe that the native-speaker will never confuse *ser* and *estar*, always observes the rules of verb/subject agreement, noun/adjective agreement, etc. If the native speaker cannot list the rules verbatim, he is told that he does not *know* his language. In many cases instructors go so far as to say that third-semester English monlinguals studying Spanish will "write" more competently than Spanish-speaking students in the same class. When questioned further it turns out that the elaborateness of well-formed sentences produced by the Spanish-speaking students cannot be matched by the former group, it is only that "writing" to some instructors means *spelling* and not *composition*. Thus, when faced with designing a course for these Spanish-speaking students, it is not unusual for a department or for a lone instructor, given that responsibility, to decide that what this student needs is a text in traditional grammar which from the very beginning will teach him what every item in his language is known as to the traditional grammarian. Instruction then is devoted to endless definitions of articles, adjectives, nouns, verbs, etc., and testing involves rote recognition of parts of speech,

listings of verb paradigms (which are often clearly a part of these speakers' everyday language) and verbalizations of rules and more rules and exceptions to the exceptions. Whatever writing is done is limited. The student is given little credit for the skills he brings with him, and at the end, success is achieved if these students manage to resemble as far as possible the products of the traditional intermediate courses for non-speakers. Indeed they are well on their way to becoming more and more like all other traditional Spanish "majors," the principal product of such departments.

Unfortunately it does not occur to these instructors or to these departments that while such a grounding in traditional grammar is essential, at this time, for those persons going on to major in the language and perhaps going on to teach traditional grammar themselves, it is of little value for those students who are simply taking a course in order to develop their existing limited skills. If these students can be offered a means by which they can develop their total language skills (speaking, understanding, reading and writing), and in addition to that learn to recognize the niceties of its structure well and good. But if one must choose between learning how to recognize what one does when one uses *ser* vs *estar* or the preterite vs the imperfect and being able to read comfortably in the language (due to extended and varied practice,) then the choice is clear. Minority Spanish-speaking students who do not want to be Spanish majors, but who want to maintain and build on their existing skills are not being aided in the process by simply being made to talk about areas in which they never or seldom err. They will and do learn what is taught them—but seen against an entire lifetime, as perhaps the only opportunity to "study" Spanish formally, it can be a tragic waste. Progress will only be made if departments of language will stop looking at each course as having to prepare the student for the courses which follow. In other words, simply because there may be a course in advanced grammar at the junior level, this does not mean that every course at the sophomore level need be taught as if the student were going on to this specific advanced course. Perspective majors can very easily be told which courses must be taken prior to enrolling in the required grammar sequence. Other courses can and must exist which offer students other alternatives.

The Teaching of the Standard Dialect as a Second Dialect

I have mentioned elsewhere (Valdés-Fallis, 1975, 1976) that for some time the foreign language teaching profession has not concerned itself with teaching ethnic students their mother tongue. But even today the newly awakened interest which arose in the wake of the civil rights movement and the current emphasis on cultural pluralism is still largely concerned with correcting the damage that has been done at home. Indeed if the language teacher is concerned at all with the oral proficiency of these students it is only to point out that this oral language is different and therefore inferior to the "standard" dialect of the language. Sadly enough, the precedents already well-established within the English-profession by Kochman (1974), Sledd (1969, 1972), Shuy (1971, 1973), Stewart (1970), Goodman (1976), and Underwood (1974) concerning second-dialect teaching and dialect eradication have had little or no impact on these departments. Indeed it would seem that the profession, and especially departments of Spanish are laboring under the following delusions (Which have already been widely discussed within the English teaching profession):

1. That bidialectalism is a desirable end in itself, in that, in order to be truly quality Spanish-speaking persons, U. S. Hispanos must speak like Spaniards or Latin Americans who have both power and social prestige in their own countries. (In other words they must sound like upper-class Madrileños or Bonairenses.)

2. That it is possible to "teach" a second dialect in a classroom setting. And,

3. That dialect differences are numerous and serious.

I will not repeat here the arguments which I have put forth elsewhere (Valdés-Fallis, 1976) concerning the problems underlying each of the above assumptions. Suffice it to say, that there is no evidence whatsoever that a given dialect is inferior or superior to any other. Prestige comes not from the dialect itself but from the social position of its speakers. In the case of Mexican-American students for example, it is a well know fact that they are not going to enjoy a wide acceptance in Mexico by the upper classes, regardless of what dialect of Spanish they speak. On the other hand, a large number of Mexican citizens and Latin American citizens speak a dialect which (with a few exceptions) is identical to that spoken by U.S. Hispanos. If bidialectalism is desirable, it is not desirable because the native-dialect is unsuitable or inferior. It is desirable because, for the Spanish-speaking student, it can theoretically offer a wider range of experiences in his lifetime.

The arguments put forth by the CCC in its very vital issue entitled "Student's Right to Their Own Language," (1974) are as valid for Spanish and every other minority language as they are for English. Unfortunately it will take some time before members of any of these professions come to realize that edited written language necessarily differs from the spoken language. Indeed instruction must involve teaching the student where written and spoken language differ, but it would seem important for instructors to be aware of the fact that both the prestige variant of a given language and its non-prestige variants differ from the standard edited form.

My own personal objections to making the teaching of the standard dialect as a second dialect the principal thrust of the Spanish-teaching profession in the teaching of U. S. Hispanos has to do with three principal factors:

1. We do not know for a fact that a second dialect can be taught. We know that it can be learned, but up to this point, it has not been demonstrated that it can successfully be taught in a classroom setting. Indeed, both Shuy (1971, 1973) and Stewart (1969, 1970) have made clear the fact that quasi-foreign language methods can be confusing and ineffectual, simply because bidialectalism implies dialect appropriateness and it is difficult to create (in a classroom setting) the various contexts within which each dialect would be considered naturally appropriate.

2. While there has been much talk concerning the importance of self-image to the extent that elementary schools throughout the country are being made aware that to demand English of a non-English-speaking child when he enters school may make him feel that there is something seriously wrong with either himself, his parents, his background, or his language, there has been less talk concerning what happens to, for example, a Chicano student who is very clearly made to feel that his dialect of Spanish is simply not the "right" one. If we *are* concerned with language maintenance among ethnic minorities (and perhaps that is open to question), then we must be concerned with the fact that minority students do not become convinced that the mother tongue they bring with them is not worth maintaining.

3. Second dialect teaching as a principal thrust within a language teaching program does little to encourage and promote overall growth in the language as a whole. This is not to say that dialect differences would not be mentioned. This simply means that in the same way that a student who learns grammatical terminology exclusively during a semester, the student who learns standard dialect equivalents for each of his "non-standard" forms exclusively has added little to his ability in speaking, understanding reading and writing. With very few exceptions, he is exactly where he was before in terms of functional potential.

In the final section of this paper, I will attempt to further clarify the above point.

Three Instructional Options and the Linguistic Characteristics of the English-Dominant, Spanish-Speaking Bilingual

In this section, I will discuss the two instructional options already mentioned as well as a third option: the total language development program. While I will be using examples from the U. S. Hispano experience, the parallels will be obvious for the teaching of most other "minority" languages in the United States.

Figure I (adapted from Clyne, 1967) represents the relative Spanish and English language proficiency of the English-dominant, Spanish-speaking student. Because of his English-language, public school education, the secondary school-age bilingual is, with very few exceptions, English dominant. His Spanish vocabulary is restricted to the home, neighborhood, and perhaps church domain; while his English vocabulary encompasses his intellectual and abstract thought, his interaction with the majority culture (the working world, the media, etc.). Because he is bilingual, this type of student has a large area of overlap; that is, of vocabulary which the bilingual may have trouble identifying as belonging to only one of his languages. Thus he may use a series of loan words, loan translations, etc., fully convinced that they are truly Spanish items. As a member of a bilingual speech community his Spanish contains a large number of integrated borrowings which are in fact part of the Spanish variant that his community speaks. This contrasts with spontaneous transfer or interference (which is not the norm in his community) but which is characteristic of all persons whose languages are in contact.

In addition, the Spanish dialect or variant of this speaker is characterized by a number of features which are not found in the standard dialect of the Spanish language, that is, in edited written Spanish. It is important to notice, however, that the dialect or variant of this student shares many features with the same standard Spanish. Contrary to popular opinion, there is no one-to-one correspondence between Chicano or Puerto Rican Spanish and written edited Spanish. There are no "non-standard" translations for all standard Spanish sentences, and it is quite impossible to give non-standard equivalences for mathematical, geographical, or sociological terminology. Indeed, depending upon the register in use by a particular Chicano or Puerto Rican speaker, the most formal to the most informal within his own specific variety, most of his utterances may be quite identical with the written edited language.

Figure II represents the first instructional option discussed above, the teaching of traditional grammar. As can be seen in the diagram, the overall proficiency in English and Spanish remains the same. In essence, what the student learns to do is to speak about the Spanish that he already speaks. In many cases he may learn rules for using tenses or moods which may not be

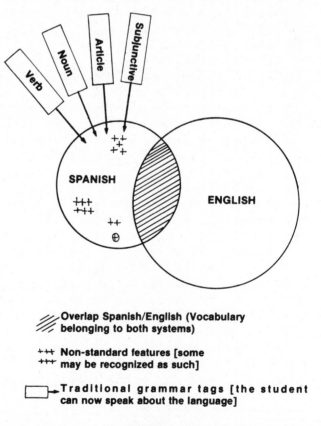

Overlap Spanish/English (Vocabulary belonging to both systems)

+++ Non-standard features [some
+++ may be recognized as such]

Traditional grammar tags [the student can now speak about the language]

FIGURE II
INSTRUCTIONAL OPTION A: THE TEACHING OF TRADITIONAL GRAMMAR

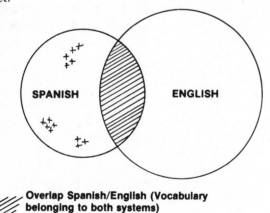

Overlap Spanish/English (Vocabulary belonging to both systems)

+++ Non-standard features

FIGURE I
THE ENGLISH—DOMINANT U. S. BILINGUAL

characteristic of his spoken dialect at all. Possibly such instruction may make clear to him the fact that certain items (say the radical-changing verbs) are regularized in his dialect and not in the standard. Very clearly then, if one seeks to provide instruction which will provide growth in all areas of the Spanish language experience, such instruction is not an ideal choice.

Instruction which has as its central purpose the eradication or correction of non-standard features as well as the eradication of the items brought about by the overlap of the two languages would resemble that depicted by Figure III. Very obviously the general use of competence in the Spanish language remains the same. Instruction is designed so that the student can identify each and every one of his non-standard features and hopefully remember them long enough to pass an examination at the end of the semester. If the student is fortunate, he will also receive instruction in spelling and reading in addition to tedious explanations based upon traditional grammar. In the best of cases, the above student will be able to take his place among Spanish majors, and teach the language as a foreign language or even as a second dialect, having been well versed in all the current "errors." But seldom will he feel that he has in fact gained much in his overall knowledge and fluency.

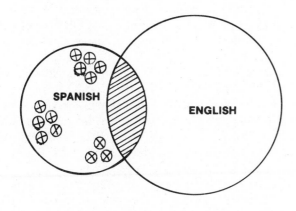

/// Overlap (Student memorized long lists of stigma-tized "anglicisms"); RESULT: Student guards against integrated forms but cannot guard him-self against spontaneous interference

⊕⊕ Each type of non-standard feature is analyzed
⊕⊕ and corrected

FIGURE III
INSTRUCTIONAL OPTION B: TEACHING STANDARD FEATURES FOR ALL NON-STANDARD FEATURES (TEACHING THE STANDARD DIALECT AS A SECOND DIALECT)

It is evident, moreover, that second dialect instruction cannot really help the student guard himself against every incidence of spontaneous interference. Using word lists, drills, etc., such instruction may make some headway against the commonly recognized integrated forms used by such bilingual speakers, but it cannot create two perfect monolingual speakers out of a bilingual speaker. His two languages are and will be in contact, and until such time as his weaker language grows and is strengthened to the degree that he is not "at a loss for words" in this language, he will continue to spontaneously create terms when he needs them. Indeed this may and does happen to even so-called "balanced" bilinguals.

In essence then, instruction dedicated to the goals depicted in Figure III seem dubious at best, and for the Spanish-teaching profession to put its eggs into this one basket in the light of what we have learned in the past decade about the second dialect teaching is criminally incompetent. For all the beautiful materials we can produce, for all the *asinas* we may change to *así*, and the *puedmos* to *pòdemos*, etc., we will not have solved the problem of the bilingual speaker who wants to increase his total command of his first language.

Figure IV represents a third instructional option. Within such instruction the primary objective is the development of the Spanish language to resemble the development of the English language as a whole. Attention is devoted to increasing oral command of the language, to writing (orthography), to composition, to creative use of the language, to reading skills, and to exposure to numerous topics and domains which are normally handled by the student in his dominant language. If non-standard features are mentioned at all, they are mentioned as variants which, while existing in the spoken language, are never written except when consciously imitating such specific speech patterns. Examples of such items are *tavía, pa, sía, bia visto*, etc. The aim of the instruction as a whole is to develop total command of the first language, including a mastery of edited, written Spanish.

Very obviously, such an aim is a difficult one, and very certainly as inaccessible in the majority of departments of Spanish in the U. S. as it was in the specific southwestern university of which I spoke above. Such instruction would take time, effort, planning, and above all, an individualization of requirements and activities to suit the specific capabilities of each student. For some students, who are simply receptive bilinguals, the process would be long and hard. But for others, a carefully designed program could build upon existing skills and move forward. The questions are: How long would it take? How much would it cost? Who would be qualified for such a program? and What would have to be eliminated in order to bring such instruction about?

I confess that I do not have clear-cut answers to all of these questions. I am convinced, however, that they must be answered. If the profession can be convinced that instruction does not have to begin with remodeling the inner Spanish core of the bilingual student before proceeding to develop the language in general, they *will* be answered. In past decades, a number of applied linguists have found ways to increase the effectiveness of language training programs for non-speakers. If they have been able to produce competent communicating personnel for various functions, certainly it is not beyond us to produce qualified bilingual teachers who

can in fact bring about minority language maintenance in this country. We need only stop to think that there are other reasons for teaching language than those in which we have involved ourselves in the past. We must examine the student before us and his needs and then design our programs and our materials. We cannot continue to insist that students become assembly-line products of an outdated and perhaps irrelevant machine.

REFERENCES

Clyne, Michael G. 1967. Transference and triggering. The Hague: Martinus Nijhoff.

Goodman, Kenneth S. 1976. Reading: A psycholinguistic guessing game. Current topics in language, ed. by N. A. Johnson. 370-383. Cambridge, Mass.: Winthrop Publishers.

Kochman, Thomas, 1974. Standard English revisited or who's kidding/cheating who(m). F.F.L.R 12. 31-44. 96.

Shuy, Roger, 1971. Social dialects: Teaching vs. learning. F.F.L.R. 9. 28-33, 55.

Shuy, Roger, 1973. Some useful myths in social dialectology. F.F.L.R. 11. 17-20, 55.

Sledd, James, 1969. Bi-dialectalism: The linguistics of white supremacy. English Journal. 58. 1307-1315.

Sledd, James, 1971. Doublespeak: Dialectology in the service of big brother. College English. 33. 439-57.

Stewart, William A. 1969. Language teaching problems in Appalachia. F.F.L.R. 7. 58-59, 161.

Stewart, William A. 1970. Foreign language teaching methods in quasi-foreign language situations. Teaching standard English in the inner city, ed. by R. W. Fasold and R. Shuy, 1-19. Washington, D. C.: Center for Applied Linguistics.

Students' right to their own language. 1974. Journal of the conference on college compositions and communication. 25. 1-32.

Underwood, Gary R. 1974. Bidialectal freshman handbooks—the next flim-flam. F.F.L.R. 12. 45-48, 97, 99.

Valdés-Fallis, Guadalupe, 1975. Teaching Spanish to the Spanish-speaking: Classroom strategies. System. 3. 54-62.

Valdés-Fallis, Guadalupe, 1976. Pedagogical implications of teaching Spanish to the Spanish-speaking. Teaching Spanish to the Spanish-speaking: Theory and practice, ed. by G. Valdés-Fallis and R. García-Mora, 5-27. San Antonio, Texas: Trinity University.

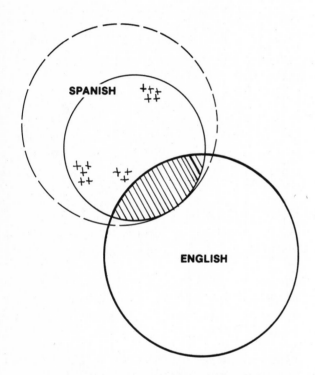

SPANISH

ENGLISH

- - - - Spanish area expanded to approximate English area (Growth takes place in speaking, understanding, reading and writing)

"Anglicisms" are not "corrected." While the overlap area expands, Spanish vocabulary exceeds the vocabulary of the overlap area significantly; Spontaneous interference will continue to occur

++ Non-standard features are not "corrected;" Standard features far exceed non-standard features; All growth has taken place in the standard language

FIGURE IV
INSTRUCTIONAL OPTION C: DEVELOPING PROFICIENCY TO APPROXIMATE ENGLISH PROFICIENCY

Chapter 58
Bilingual Teacher Training In Higher Education
Margarita Mir de Cid*

The Rationale

The Spanish speaking population in the United States is between nine and twelve milltion people, according to Isidro Lucas (1973). It is composed of Mexican Americans, Puerto Ricans, Cubans, Dominicans, and of representatives of each of the South American republics. Mexicans are mostly in the Southwest; Puerto Ricans in New York, New Jersey and Chicago; Cubans are concentrated in New Jersey and Florida, especially; Central and South Americans reside in all states.

In North America, bilingual education began as a political phenomenon and not as a pedagogical advancement. Bilingual education began long before the Bilingual Education Act of 1967, Title VII of ESEA today. Yet, it has been only ten years since national policies and federal funds have been committed to strengthen the cause of bilingualism throughout the country. Recent Supreme Court and several lower federal court decisions have been guidelines to programs which will help non-English speaking children to meet their needs, educationally deprived because as they did not understand English well or did not know it at all, students were, as Justice William Douglas (1975) said, "effectively foreclosed from any meaningful education." Thousands of children have been flooding our country for several decades while the melting pot mentality in the school systems did not allow for a development on immigrant bilingualism. In an age of colonialism, of American imperialsim and authoritarianism, even English dialects were looked as lack of linguistic maturity. The society had English monolinguism as a predominant cultural value. New York City, which has the largest school system of the United States, had a 2.7 percent (*Bilingual Education in New York*, 1975) of Spanish professional personnel in positions facing Ibero Americans demands. The so-called Fleischmann Commission Report stated that only in the state of New York there were 94,800 Puerto Ricans with serious deficiencies in English.

After the Consent Decree between ASPIRA of New York, Inc., *et al.*, and the Board of Educatin of the City of New York, *et al.*, students from Spanish origin were given an exam in order to evaluate their needs for bilingual education. In January, 1975, the *New York Teacher* published an article which said that the Board of Education had estimated that 3,000 bilingual teachers would be needed for September. The New York Times on January 26 of the same year specified that only 1,500 had been certified. The United Federation of Teachers opposed to bilingual education perhaps, among other things, because it represents the interests of a very high percentage of the Anglo teachers who mainly control the school system in New York City, and would not agree that bilingual teachers replace many of them in order to support children's needs. We have witnessed how "the most complex bureaucratic machine in the world," (Glazer and Moynihan, 1970) had to accept the gradual, social, and political pressures changing the balance of former processes. It was logical, yet hard. Results of researchers done in both sociolinguistics and psycholinguistics arenas were obvious and specific. Findings of studies as well as critical thinking on educational research had brought the need to prepare personnel for this bilingual education in a pluristic society. The ethnocide concept is over in really educated minds. More and more the public within a cultural population is aware of its rights to maintain one's linguistic and cultural heritage while adhering to the social norms and standard responsibilities of the nation one lives in. This is why bilingual education besides being a pedagogical process is also a sociological movement.

Since language is inextricably bounded to culture, bilingualism and biculturalism move together. "Culture," says Eduards Seda, "is not biologically transmitted—it is transmitted by learning (enculturation and interpersonal conditioning). Culture determines one's humanity and one's identity."

*Dr. Margarita Mir de Cid is Assistant Professor of the School of Education of Brooklyn College, C.U.N.Y., and Chairman of the Advisory Council of the Regional Cross-Cultural Training and Resource Center, 110 Livingston Street, Brooklyn, N. Y.

A culture is imparted and acquired by direct, frequent, and varied participation and experiences outside the learner's awareness. As cultures reside in people, the teaching of culture is not just the teaching of folklore, history, and artistic expression in a classroom. Resides in and is transmitted by people on a day to day basis through a culturally meaningful curriculum with a staff and activities meaningful to students. The process of schooling must be congruent with the total cultural experience of the child. With this philosophy, a bilingual teacher *makes culture* in the school. This is a process and must not be confused with teaching biculturalism, which is an untenable construct.

Higher education institutions understand today the rationale behind the respect for diversity and have begun preparing Hispanics for survival. Crossland's study (1971) stresses that a college degree can be essential because "social and economical mobility, increasingly appears to be dependent upon academic credentials. Hence, the educationally disenfranchised are persuaded with good reason—that they are denied access to equitable reward status and social participation," if they can not get into a college. The Consent Decree established a precedent which other groups may choose to follow, and represents a recognition on the part of the Board of Education that bilingual education is the necessary and appropriate educational program for children with English language difficulties. Social justice for minority groups can be attainable when institutions of higher learning offer both programs and economic support to prepare Latinos, among other careers, as teachers, counselors, and administrators. Especially right now there is a dire need for bilingual teachers, suitable trained ones for the challenge of Latin American children and youth. Reviewing carefully what the Deputy Chancellor of New York City, Dr. Bernard Gifford, wrote in September 20, 1976, we can point out again the need of Spanish bilingual teachers.

	1960-61	1964-65	1975-75	1975-76	1976-77
Pupil Ethnicity					
Hispanic	15.6%	17.9%	28.0%	28.9%	29.3%

When Blacks are 36.8 percent and "Other," 33.9 percent, the Latino Americans in New York City schools are almost 30 percent. And we know several areas in the Bronx and Brooklyn boroughs demanding more bilingual teachers in order that schools in different districts establish the programs which the law enforces. This is the bilingual reality confronting us. This is one of our community's expectations. The Board of Education has indicated its intention to voluntarily extend the benefits of bilingual education to all children in need of it. Truly bilingual teachers can

serve as appropriate role models for children. It is now to colleges and universities to prepare these teachers and to expand bilingual programs to a graduate level.

The Preparation

The Center of Applied Linguistics at Arlington, Virginia, has suggested some *Guidelines for the Preparation and Certification of Teachers of Bilingual-Bicultural Education* (January, 1975). These guidelines emphasize personal qualities, attitudes, skills, experiences, and knowledge rather than courses and credit hours. There is a cardinal principle observed throughout the guidelines; that the teacher of bilingual-bicultural education should have the same quality academic preparation as any other teacher of subjects at comparable levels. We wish to strongly stress that, as a teacher is not adequately qualified to teach language because he knows well his mother tongue or vernacular, a bilingual teacher is not one just because he knows a second language. This second, target language needs to be mastered in order to communicate in both languages, appreciate both cultures, and function easily in either one. In other words: because you know a language it does not mean you know how to teach it. And because you know two languages, it does not mean you can be a bilingual teacher. You need to be a teacher first, and second, you ought to move easily in both languages and cultures.

Several university programs offer today a teacher education preparation for bilingual teachers. They are planned—according to *A Comprehensive Design for Bilingual-Bicultural Education*—"to produce teachers skilled in teaching two languages to students who have no background in or knowledge of one of the languages" and who need language skills in both in order to move in both languages; to produce teachers sensitive to the unique educational needs of bilingual bicultural students and their families," "to serve in line and staff positions at all levels," "to improve staff understanding of the philosophy behind bilingual education;" to improve skills in bilingual class management; to have classroom teachers with great understanding of the student's native language skills because that is an important factor in his personality development.

Good teaching is a personal matter. It's a personal discovery of how to provide meaning to the learners, using one's self as instrument. In order to achieve this, prospective teachers need to be aware that there is much more than subject matter and teaching techniques. Bilingual practitioners must make non-English speaking children behave differently as a result of teaching. Teachers-to-be ought to work in the field—in the schools where bilingual programs are held—from the very beginning of their careers, developing in the pre-service training the competencies that will be utilized gradually in any bilingual program. Three essential competencies are that he should demonstrate ability to apply knowledge of professional content to appropriate bilingual teaching learning situations; that he should demonstrate personal growth and development and those personal/professional qualities which enable establishment of effective relationships with bilingual students, parents and others, in culturally diverse settings that he should demonstrate ability to provide a satisfying and constructive learning environment in which the principles of individual differences are applied effectively with bilingual individuals and bilingual groups.

In order to attain these competencies the program of the preparation and education of teachers must include situations and activities that enable the future teacher to see and interpret what goes on in a bilingual classroom which is an everchanging arena of human situations. He needs to understand the behavior of children; to have a knowledge of the process of developing positive self-images; to interpret situations with the right set of attitudes.

Most beginning teachers are very concerned with the maintenance of discipline and class control that facilitates learning. These skills of classroom management are important during the learning process in order to reinforce changes in the behavior of bilingual children. And as in order to understand others we need to understand us first, the self-awareness of how to manage and accept ourselves is a must. Specific human relations behavior lead to the sense of wholeness described in the Gestalt theory. Martin Buker speaks of this unexpressable uniqueness when he writes of the global "thou" in his book, *I, Thou*. The trainee can observe himself through snapshots taken by the College supervisor and through videotaped teaching while he proceeds in his human relation training and teaching. There is no competence without love and prospective bilingual teachers need to commit themselves much more sincerely to the non-English speaking children because they can't easily adapt themselves to many school situations as others. The bilingual teachers are in loco parents "to make children and youth grow in the cognitive, affective and psychomotor domains; to help them perform better in school and society."

Schools of Education committed to the training of bilingual teachers through a pre-service development of competencies' perspective will deal with bilingual programs in the schools. The trainees shall visit, work and participate in operating bilingual classrooms for several hours weekly, according to the stage in the educational sequence and thus will receive supervised experiences with children and youth progressively, with parents and the community at large. It is wonderful to see how many college instructors work with clinical students in a variety of on and off campus activities. The university staff has to be genuinely interested and experienced in Bilingual Education and committed to its philosophy. The knowledge, skills and attitudes of the prospective bilingual teacher—that is, his competencies—need to be identified and explained thoroughly to each trainee so that he is aware of what is expected from him, aware of his acts, reflecting the key roles, responsibilities and functions of the bilingual teacher. The study of references, site visits, observational reports, review of instructional bilingual resources, preparation of lessons in simulated and real situations and attendance to workshops and seminars need to be included in their preparation. Bilingual faculty will assess each bilingual student's performance utilizing one or more instruments such as examinations, logs, research papers, supervision, observation, conferences, video-tapes and any independent study experience. Assessment will take place in the college classroom in the bilingual school setting and in conference with the prospective teacher. Each competence will be assessed according to established criteria on which the bilingual teacher has been made aware of. And only in this way we will get from bilingual teacher training programs the overall goals we intend to accomplish:

● to improve bilingual prospective teachers' proficiency in listening, speaking, reading, and writing in both their native and the target language;
● to provide the schools with the personnel who will maintain the appropriate instructional program to bilingual-bicultural students;
● to make them aware they are responsible for the improvement of each bilingual student—achievement in the basic subject area using their native and second languages;
● to develop in them competency to assist each bilingual student in developing a positive self-image and helping him to achieve realistic goals with increasing self-direction and self-confidence because they themselves have also grown in this direction;
● to improve the skills of the prospective bilingual teachers which will enable them to adapt bilingual existing material and create new ones to meet the needs of bilingual bicultural students;
● to provide the bilingual trainees with knowledge and appreciation of their ethnic history and courage so that, in turn, they encourage their actual and future students with such appreciation and teach them how to live in a pluralistic democratic society;
● to improve the dialogue and cooperation of several

ethnic groups in the schools and communities where they will be working as bilingual teachers;

● to update the curriculum of the schools in order to meet the special needs of the bilingual pupils they teach and educate.

A great partnership between local colleges and universities with schools and districts is the cooperative venture in bilingual teacher education focusing the improvement of instruction, the teaching-pedagogy; the whole range of supervisory field experiences from micro-teaching to "practicum" and/or internship; and the offering of courses for prospective and in-service teachers related to development of bilingual curriculum, teacher-training procedures, research and bilingual evaluation techniques.

We assume that each university has determined the most suitable program for its students and is trying to respond to the challenge of increasing the number of teachers prepared to implement the quality bilingual education which will guarantee permanency of the programs. We find ourselves in perilous times. As school people, we have a piece of action. And bilingual educators can take a responsible leadership in bringing about constructive changes in teaching to our Hispanics, improving their standards of behavior, their attitudes towards school, and opportunities for a better schooling in future years. Teachers in bilingual programs can do that for Latinos, not only by teaching but also by *being*. Being humane to them. Because teachers establish important relationships in the life of any child. Mutual respect and caring encourages and motivates learning, develops a positive self-image, promotes a dialogue that avoids and helps in possible school and family-life conflicts. Bilingual teachers can prevent drop-outs, can make children proud of their values, culture, and origin. These educators can teach human relation values in depth, that is, respect for others who are different from oneself in terms of sex, skin color, language patterns, religious beliefs, economic status, and educational background.

This is why the preparation of these competent, understanding teachers is not easy. They need good ears to hear *The Other America* (Harrington, 1962) presenting their unmet demands; children from *Slums and Suburbs* (Conant, 1961) asking for educational equalities; pupils represented in *The Culturally Deprived* (1962) longing for cognitive training, affective education, psychomotor direction. These boys and girls need to be taught how to study and how to think; how to live and how to be themselves. This target population is asking for connections, says Masters (1970), between "life like it is" in the school, in the Hispanic family, in the community they live in. Willing to be something other than traditional, bilingual educators ought to teach in relation to the needs of these children and of society today. In this way they will be agents of change for the improvement of IberoAmericans. They have had enough of obsolete years of schooling! We agree with Margaret Mead (1970) when she states they need "experiential knowledge, without which no meaningful plans can be made. It is only with the direct participation of the young who have that knowledge, that we can build a viable future."

This is why we insist again on the necessity for a competency-based, field-centered program for the preparation of teachers, performing from the very beginning of their undergraduate education in the real world of schools. Only a clinical student facing simultaneously both pedagogical and cultural components of a bilingual teacher education program in different college, schools, and community activities can demonstrate the needed competencies to be what she/he is expected to be and to be certified as having met the required levels of competency. Students are able to pretest and demonstrate whether they have a skill *before* instruction begins and to design instructional strategies and procedures for acquiring these skills. Students are forced to become accountable in a CBTE program which respects the individual talents, interest, and needs. When students know the criteria for satisfactory performance, they are more receptive to its program and its components. They even develop an attitude of continual search and discovery. When the prospective bilingual teachers finish the educational sequence they need to be adequately trained as practitioners to cope with the ability to teach and understand Hispanic children. They will be no carbon copies. They have learned to be themselves, to use themselves, to give themselves, to be responsible to their ideals, and to guide humanistically children and young in a democratic culturally pluralistic society.

Time alone will tell how much bilingual education was not only challenged but challenging. By the way, I am a teacher educator, a member of this profession, besides being a bilingual teacher trainer. If I weren't both, I would not care so much!

BIBLIOGRAPHY

ASPIRA of New York, Inc., *et al.*, Plaintiffs, against Board of Education of the City of New York, *et al.*, Defendants. 72 Civ-4002, U.S. District Court Southern District of New York.

Banks, James, Editor, *Teaching Ethnic Studies*. Washington, D. C., 43rd Yearbook of the National Council for the Social Studies, 1973.

"Bilingual Education in New York," *Introduction to*

Bilingual Education. New York, Anaya Las Americas Publishing Company, 1975.

"College Programs," *Spanish Bilingual Directory* (New York City). Bilingual Resource Center, Title III ESEA, 110 Livingston Street, New York, 1974.

Conant, James B., *Slums and Suburbs: A Commentary on Schools in Metropolitan Areas.* New York: McGraw Hill Book Co., 1961.

       The Culturally Deprived. New York, Harper and Brothers, 1962.

Department of Government Funded Programs of the Board of Education of the City of Chicago, *A Comprehensive Design for Bilingual-Bicultural Education.* Chicago, 1975.

Crossland, Fred E., *Minority Access to College.* New York, Shocken Books, 1971.

Federal Interagency Committee on Education, "Task Force Report on Higher Education and Chicanos, Puerto Ricans and American Indians." Washington, D. C., April, 1973.

"Fleischmann Commission Report," a report from the New York State Commission on the Cost, Quality, and Finance of Elementary and Secondary Schools, Part III, Vol. II (n. D. on the copy distributed by the Bilingual Resource Center, New York).

Gifford, Bernard R., "New York City Schools are Being Bludgeoned," *The New York Times,* September 20, 1976.

Glazer, Nathan and Danial Moynihan, *Beyond the Melting Pot,* Cambridge, Mass., M.I.T. Press, second edition, 1970.

Harrington, Michael, *The Other America: Poverty in the United States.* New York, Macmillan Co., 1962.

Justice William Douglas, quoted in *Bilingual-Bicultural Education.* Chicago, Illinois, Board of Education, 1975, p. 13.

Lucas, Isidro, "Multi-National Spanish Speaking Communities in the Midwest," U.S. Department of Health, Education, and Welfare, Region 5, Chicago. 1973.

Machotka, Otakar, *The Unconscious in Social Relations.* New York, Philosophical Library, Inc., 1964.

Masters, Nicholas, "Politics and Power Related to Educating Teachers," *Teacher Education: Future Directions.* Margaret Lindsey, Ed. A report of The Fiftieth Anniversary Conference of the Association for Student Teaching. Washington, D. C., 1970.

Mead, Margaret, *Culture and Commitment.* Garden City, N. Y., Natural History Press, 1970.

Regents of the University of the State of New York *Bilingual Education: A Statement of Policy and Proposed Action,* Albany, N. Y. The State Education Department, 1972.

Seeley, H. Ned., ed. *Teaching Cultural Concepts in Spanish Classes,* Springfield, Illinois: Office of the Superintendent of Public Instruction, 1972.

Zintz, Miles V. Education Across Culture. Iowa: William C. Brown, Co., Publishers, 1963.

Chapter 59
A Community Resource:
The Bilingual Paraprofessional
Bernice Williams*

In our society, language is the primary means by which the home indoctrinates the child into its culture. In the process of acquiring speech, the child gains an increased understanding of his culture as well as an extension of his experiential world. Within this framework of reference, a natural continuation of the language patterns of the home is obtained.

The bilingual child's language is a representation of his immediate environment; his speech is a reflection of his home, his neighborhood, and his community. His language is intimate and personal, and it operates as a useful tool in communicating his desires and needs to his peers, to his family, and to his neighbors. In the establishment and maintenance of his contacts with his surroundings, the bilingual child's mode of expression serves him well.

Upon entering school, a bilingual child may be confronted with very different language models, formal and informal, if he is not English dominant. What is considered correct usage in the classroom may be at variance with his expressive mode. This dilemma may induce a restructuring of the child's value system, and a questioning of the culture of his community. Prior to his school experience, he may have viewed his community as a continuous source of gratification.

If the child is asked to reject his language within the school culture, the school threatens his self-image and increases the distance between the school and the community. Care must be taken to avoid this situation, if effective working relationships between the school and the home are to be realized.

Educators generally agree that the language of some bilingual children differs from the language of instruction, whatever the curriculum model may be. Communication of ideas is essential for progress and development; for communication to be effective, the ideas presented must be understood by the receiver as well as the sender. If, in the process of sending and receiving messages, the cycle is interrupted by faulty perception of word forms, there is no occurrence of enlightenment. In the cases of some bilingual children, the channels of communication may be disturbed.

How to cope with this divergence in language systems while preserving a relationship with the school community may result in a quandary for the school. How does the school maintain a balance, accepting the child's linguistic system within the framework of the school without negating the child's culture and reducing his self-concept?

Should not the school reexamine its structure with relationship to the school community, and its utilization of community resources? Should not the school explore in depth its community resources?

In existence within the school system is a compensatory program that offers a linkage with the child's culture; namely, the paraprofessional program. The typical paraprofessional is a resident of the school community; she is representative of its lifestyles and experiences. Very often, the paraprofessional has children attending the school where she is employed; she may become active in the Parent-Teacher Association (PTA), as a consequence. On the whole, she is familiar with the customs and mores of the community, and may be quite familiar with the parents. Within this context, she serves as a "cultural bridge with the child" (Bowman, Klopf, 1968).

Research is needed to determine the nature of this avenue for increased communication within the school community. In a larger sense, perhaps the solution to the problem of how to extend home-school dialogue may lie within the community. In order for such dialogue to be meaningful, the school must demonstrate genuine acceptance of the partnership role of the community in the education of its children. The paraprofessional talks the language of the community; her role in the school setting may suggest alternative approaches to the seemingly ever-present communications problem.

The Paraprofessional: A School-Community Liaison

Many of the paraprofessionals employed by the schools are bilingual; many of the children attending urban schools are bilingual. In the main, both groups

*Dr. Bernice Williams, Instructor, St. John's University, Queens, New York.

reside in similar areas and share similar cultures. An exploration of the bilingual paraprofessional's linguistic system and lifestyle might suggest implications for the school system, trying to strengthen school-community ties.

To a large extent, the inclusion of the paraprofessionals in the school setting was a step towards involvement of the school community in the educational scene. A considered advantage of the paraprofessional program is that it offered a new dimension "—by having adults who go into the community every day—" (Morine, Morine, 1970). When teacher-paraprofessinal teams "include persons from the community served, there is closeness to the lives of the students themselves which enriches and enlivens the school climate" (Bowman, Klopf and Joy, 1969). The paraprofessional, as a school-community liaison, brings the environment of the community into the classroom; her experiences and lifestyles are in closer proximity to the culture of the children. Moreover, the addition of other adults to the classroom offers a partial solution to the need for greater individualization of instruction, utilizing the concept of differentiated staffing.

On the whole, the paraprofessionals can help to lessen the gap between the school and the community. They bring to the school a picture of the community it serves. And, indirectly, they take the message to the community that it, too, is involved in the education of its children. Furthermore, the bilingual paraprofessionals are able to relate to the children in a positive fashion; they speak the same language. The bilingual paraprofessional, as a school-community liaison, may be the connecting link in lessening the divergence in the language of instruction and the language of the bilingual child.

Commonality of Language

In the case of the bilingual child, the bilingual paraprofessional could function as a translator, to help bridge the gap between the child's language and the language of the majority. As a community person, the paraprofessional could be considered as part of the child's experiential background, both possessing similar culture styles. This commonality of backgrounds may well include understanding of the idiomatic structure of the bilingual child's language. Dialects may be better understood and interpreted. A common ground may be reached with the child, and "immediate gratification" may be offered to him as he seeks to improve his academic standing (Janowitz, 1969). Indeed, much of the paraprofessional's time is spent "talking quietly with children" (Institute, 1970), and opportunities for such close interactions are abundant in the school setting.

In addition to the informal role of translator, the bilingual paraprofessional represents a physical symbol of identification for the bilingual child. Her presence in the school may lessen the child's possible feelings of alienation, and might conceivably affect other intangibles, such as self-image, self-pride, and self-respect.

In effect, the bilingual paraprofessional symbolizes adaptability to the school culture; she serves as a demonstration of participation in both cultures. The paraprofessional, in her quest for upward mobility, has accepted a role within the school system, while continuing the community lifestyle. Concomitant with the obligatory training associated with the school, college attendance is encouraged via the career ladder aspects of her position.

Conclusion

Better knowledge of the community's linguistic systems may foster greater home-school communication. Understanding the role of the bilingual paraprofessional might well lead to greater understanding of the community speech patterns, and possibly lessen the gap between school speech and community speech. If, in the educational process, children have difficulty in understanding what's being taught because of linguistic differences, then the school is not fulfilling its obligation to the community, the education of its children.

Specifically, if the problem of bilingualism exists within the school system, might not the bilingual paraprofessional supply clues as to how to approach that problem? The bilingual paraprofessional is a part of the school setting as well as part of the school community; her dual role can certainly be utilized with reference to the instructional system.

While great strides have been made in bilingual and bicultural education, not all children have bilingual/TESOL training. We must continue to try to serve them, utilizing all of our resources. Prominent among these resources is the bilingual paraprofessional. The paraprofessional is often referred to as "another pair of hands," and regarded as a helper from the community. Let's extend that role definition to include the rest of her—her culture, her language, her intimate knowledge of the community.

Suggested Tasks For The Bilingual Paraprofessional

1. Function as community liaison in the interpretation of the goals of bilingual education.
2. Serve as a resource person in the school, a representative of culture of the bilingual population.
3. Suggest approaches to education related to the culture of the community.

4. Participate in workshops for parents.
5. Develop materials for parental workshops.
6. Set up displays relating to culture of the school community.
7. Participate in assembly programs, highlighting aspects of the culture of the bilingual population of the school community.
8. Interpret philosophy of the school to bilingual pupils.
9. Provide support—cognitive and affective—to pupils as they seek to achieve school-related goals.
10. Demonstrate awareness of bilingual and ESL concepts in the teaching-learning situation.
11. Provide remedial and oral written skills in the language of the learner.
12. Engage in a variety of activities to foster oral communication on the part of the bilingual child.
13. Keep abreast of advances in bilingual/bicultural education.

BIBLIOGRAPHY

Bowman, Garda W. and Klopf, Gordon, *New Careers in the American School*. Bank Street College of Education for the Office of Economic Opportunity, 1968, 10.

Morine, Harold and Morine, Greta, *A Primer for Inner City Schools*. New York: McGraw Hill, 1970, 14.

Bowman, Garda W.; Klopf, Gordon; and Adena, Joy, *A Learning Team: Teacher and Auxiliary*. New York: Bank Street College of Education, 1969, IX.

Janowitz, Morris, *Institution Building in Urban Education*. New York: Russell Sage Foundation, 1969, 91.

Institute for Educational Development, *An In-Depth Study of Paraprofessionals*. A Study for the Board of Education of New York City, December, 1970, 80.

Chapter 60

Video Tape: A Means to Develop the Bilingual Professional In The Community College

Elliot S. Glass and Nancy Liberti*

Almost all of the publicity related to bilingualism has been directed toward the development of bilingual skills in non-English speaking children in the elementary and secondary schools, and indeed this is primarily what bilingualism is all about.

Nevertheless, there is an area of bilingual language training that has gone almost completely unrecognized: the teaching of language skills to Spanish speaking and non-Spanish speaking career-minded students and professionals working in bilingual settings. Much of this work has gone on at two year colleges. The two year college, with its close contact with the surrounding community has helped to set into motion a national trend in higher education: the development of second language courses for career-oriented students and professionals. Even the most prestigious colleges and universities are now offering courses such as "Spanish for Medical Professionals," "Spanish for Social Workers," "Spanish for Teachers," "Business French," "Business and Technical German," etc. In some universities, these courses are beginning to replace the traditional literature courses and are being offered in two and three semester sequences.

Despite this shift in emphasis, most universities, with the exception of Hostos College, seem to feel that bilingual training should be completed before the student enters the college or university. Foreign language departments, however, have always felt that career-oriented courses should be developed to enable the professional to deal effectively with the non-English speaking citizens.

Since the bilingual professionals and paraprofessionals provide valuable information and services, which enable the non-English speaking citizen or resident to fully utilize the public institutions, they often serve as the only conduits through which the non-English speakers gain access to the democratic process.

Because of a high birth rate, a liberalized immigration policy, and a relatively unchecked illegal immigration, the number of non-English speaking people in the United States will continue its upward trend for at least the next decade. Teachers, social workers, doctors, lawyers, clergymen and civil servants will have to acquire a proficiency in a second language to effectively meet the challenge ahead. Even today a casual perusal of the want ads reminds us that in many industries and public service areas bilingual skills are on par with professional abilities. Today's professional men and women are becoming more and more aware that bilingualism is not just for children. The bilingual professional is better equipped to meet the demands of the job market and the requirements of a society that advocates equal rights and opportunities for all of its citizens.

The Queensborough Experience

For the last two and one half years the Department of Foreign Languages and Literatures at Queensborough Community College has been using a video tape oriented method to improve the bilingual skills of Spanish speaking students and provide a degree of professional proficiency in Spanish to English speaking students.

The following paragraphs outline the various ways in which video tape was used as a primary teaching device in our "Spanish for Hospital Personnel" course.** The method described, however, may be applied to any career oriented language course which services native speakers and non-native speakers of a second language.

I Live Situation Tapes

The students view video tapes recorded on location: in an emergency room, in a general ward, in a clinic, in a doctor's office, and in a V.D. clinic.[1] In these tapes, which have been done in a documentary style, all of the professionals and the patients are Spanish speaking people. Each unrehearsed video tape lasts

*Dr. Elliot Glass is chairman of the Department of Foreign Languages and Literatures at Queensborough Community College. Professor Nancy Liberti also teaches Spanish at Queensborough Community College of the City University of New York.

**Ninety percent of the students who registered for the course have had at least some high school Spanish. As of the Fall 1976 semester the course has been divided into two courses; one for those who have had some formal Spanish and one for those who have had no formal Spanish.

approximately 7 minutes. While most of these tapes have not been altered, some minor edits have been made so that students might be exposed to useful commands and statements such as "¡cálmese!" (calm down), "¡no se preocupe!" (don't worry), "no es nada serio" (it is nothing serious), and "le voy a poner una injección para aliviar el dolor" (I'm going to give you a shop to alleviate the pain).

The Spanish speaking students have indicated that this type of tape provides them with useful technical vocabulary such as "entablillado de yeso" (a cast), "prueba de orina" (urine specimen), and "haga girar el tobillo" (rotate your ankle). On two of the tapes the Spanish speaking students noted that some of the patients disliked being addressed with the "tú" form. This was particularly true with those patients who were not from the Caribbean. Most of the Spanish speaking students were unfamiliar with the "usted" form especially in the commands, and, thus, this kind of tape helped to point to a grammar area which had to be covered.

The non-Spanish speaking studends have stated that they like this style of video reporting because they are able to focus on patients' remarks, the commands used by the professional, as well as the technical vocabulary.

After the tape has been played twice, a vocabulary sheet is circulated. The tape is then played again and after this third playing the students are asked questions related to the vocabulary and the content.

II Role Playing Tape 1: Two Spanish Speaking Students

The Spanish speaking students play the role of both the patient and the professional. The students are given a minimal amount of information such as where they are and what the problem is (emergency room/heart attack). What follows is usually a ten minute dialogue or exchange. In this kind of tape words such as "norsa" (nurse), "lonche" (lunch), "empushar" (to push) crop up and the instructor is able to point out the more standard variants: "enfermera" (nurse), "almuerzo" (lunch), and "empujar" (to push). It is here that the Spanish speaking students are able to really put to the test their ability to handle a specific or technical vocabulary.

In many instances, the students would substitute English words without being cognizant of the switch even when watching the tape for a second or third time. Almost invariably the non-Spanish speaking students become aware of the substitution before the Spanish speaking students. This type of tape is excellent for building the technical vocabulary of the Spanish speaking students and it provides the non-Spanish speaking students with more exposure to Spanish as it is

spoken in the streets of many major North American cities. It is this "street Spanish" which these professionals will undoubtedly hear frequently while in the process of carrying out their duties.

In an effort to expose the students to as many dialects and phonetic peculiarities as possible, instructors, friends, and students not enrolled in the class are often asked to play the role of the patient. During the past two years, members of the "Spanish for Hospital Personnel" class have been able to hear Colombians, Ecuadorians, Cubans, Puerto Ricans, Spaniards, Peruvians, Argentinians, Chileans, and Venezuelans and as a result they know that "Cómo e_tá u_té" means "¿Cómo está usted?," that "Xicardo ba a comeʃ" means "Ricardo va a comer" (Richard is going to eat), and that "Jo no se, pero vos sabes" means "yo no se, peru tú sabes" (I don't know, but you know).

Unlike the first type of tape, questions on content, vocabulary, and phonetic peculiarities follow each tape. Both content and vocabulary recall have been particularly good among the Spanish speaking students. Course evaluations written at the end of the semester reveal that this type of tape did more than build vocabulary. One student remarked, "The tapes made me see myself as a professional who possessed a great skill (speaking Spanish). I was never really aware of the importance of speaking Spanish. I was really proud of my home language and thankful that my parents always spoke to me in Spanish." This kind of response was quite common among native speakers.

The non-Spanish speaking students were particularly pleased with this kind of tape because they now learned the meaning of words and phrases that they had heard in the hospital but had not been able to find in standard dictionaries.

III Role Playing Tape 2: One Spanish Speaking Student and One Non-Spanish Speaking Student

At Queensborough the "Spanish for Hospital Personnel" course has usually attracted an equal number of Spanish and non-Spanish speaking students so that this role playing tape has never been difficult to produce. First the Spanish speaking students play the role of the patients and the non-Spanish speaking students play the role of the professionals; then the roles are reversed. As in *Role Playing Tape 1* the students are given a minimal amount of information and they are asked to act out the situation. At the end of the tape questions related to content and vocabulary are asked.

In their course evaluations the non-Spanish speaking students have indicated that this taping experience has helped them to gain confidence in their ability to get their ideas across in Spanish; they began to see themselves as being able to effectively carry out their professional duties in a second language. Many students were surprised to see that they took on "another personality" when they spoke the second language: gestures, facial expression, body posture, and voice tone all seemed to undergo some alteration. One non-Spanish speaking student remarked, "With each new tape, I became more accustomed to my new self. And now everytime I speak Spanish to a patient, I get a mental picture of how I looked on the tape...it's a challenge now and even fun. The tapes helped me to not feel funny speaking Spanish. I know the grammar but I always used to feel silly trying to put the words together...Now I see I can give commands and be effective on my job."

For the Spanish speaking students this type of tape gives them an opportunity to employ their new vocabulary words and to practice the "usted" commands.

IV Role Playing Tape 3: Two Non-Spanish Speaking Students

In this type of tape one student plays the role of the professional and the other the role of the patient; the roles are then reversed. As in the other role playing tapes minimal information is given and students are asked to act out a situation. This kind of tape is used only after the non-Spanish speaking students have been exposed to numerous other tapes and have mastered the major part of the vocabulary required for the course. It is here, just as it was for the Spanish speaking students in their *Role Playing 1* tape, that the non-Spanish speaking students show their weaknesses in formulating subjunctive sentences, e. g., "Quiero que usted va a la clínica" instead of "Quiero que usted vaya a la clínica" (I want you to go to the clinic), and it now at the close of the course that the formulation of such subjunctive sentences is reviewed.

Concluding Remarks

After two years of using video tape in this career oriented language course, it is possible to make the following observations:
(1) Students who participate in the making of the tape tend to have greater immediate and long range recall than those who were merely spectators.

(2) Usually Spanish speaking students are quick to learn all of the standard Spanish words and phrases, the correct use of the subjunctive, and the "usted" commands.
(3) Non-Spanish speaking students tend to learn the "street Spanish" and forget the more standard forms; they are generally quick to learn the "tú" form commands and the correct use of the subjunctive.
(4) All students tend to quickly assimilate the technical vocabulary and tend to have a good recall for dialect and phonetic peculiarities.
(5) The preferred tape for the Spanish speaking students was most often *Role Playing 1: Two Spanish Speaking Students*.
(6) The preferred tape for the non-Spoanish speaking students was usually *Role Playing 2: One Spanish Speaking Student and One Non-Spanish Speaking Student*.

Video Tape has enabled the students to view themselves and their world (professional) in a new light. As a teaching tool it has provided them an opportunity to "replay" and correct their errors while at the same time it has supplied them with the technical language necessary to effectively carry out their professional commitments.

As a result of the use of this video tape program, we at Queensborough Community College are pleased to report that there has been a significant improvement in the bilingual abilities of both the Spanish speaking and the non-Spanish speaking students. They have become more proficient in handling the language used in a professional environment.

This improvement in the language facility of the students plus their specific vocational training, together, will make them more competitive in today's business world.

In addition, and probably more important, the bilingual professional can serve as a much needed liaison between the school and the community.

FOOTNOTES

[1] The video equipment used is a 3400 Sony Rover Portapack and a portable monitor.

Section VII
Evaluation and Language Assessment

Introduction by Protrase E. Woodford*

The effective evaluation of skills, academic aptitude and achievement is a difficult process. Extreme care must be taken in the creation of instruments to ensure that they are valid (that they measure what they purport to measure) and that they are reliable (that they render consistent results).

Difficult are the design and development of such measures for monolingual, relatively homogeneous populations. Consider how much more difficult the process becomes when the target population is "bilingual" and "bilingual" includes individuals ranging from those monolingual in language A to those monolingual in language B; literate in one, or both, or neither of the languages at issue.

Who is unaware of the frightening misuse of "intelligence" tests designed for middle-class English speakers being administered to non-English or limited English speeches with test results being used to classify children as "slow" or worse?

One initial reaction to such blatant misuse of tests and abuse of individuals was a condemnation of all testing in bilingual education.

Practitioners and administrators found themselves between Scylla and Charybdis. On the one hand they would condemn the use of tests in their programs and with their students because all or most of the tests were "culturally biased," "normed on an inappropriate reference group" or unsuitable for some other reason. On the other hand results on the same instruments, if they indicated an educational deficit for their students, vis a vis the majority population, were regularly cited in support of requests for new programs and services to overcome the deficit.

Administrators wanted measures that could quickly, efficiently and economically provide needed information for decision making:

- A test to determine whether or not children should be placed in a "bilingual" or mainstream class
- A test to determine when a child was ready to cope with an English medium class
- Tests to indicate level of performance in mathematics and other subject areas for children whose language skills were differentially developed across two or more languages and/or dialects—so that they could be "placed" appropriately.

The practitioners, the classroom teachers, have had their own measurement needs. They want to know what each child's strengths and weaknesses are so that they may help to maintain or increase the strengths, overcome the weaknesses and meet the needs of each individual.

Another group with great interest in measurement and evaluation consists of the money disbursers; the federal and state agencies who distribute funds for bilingual programs and who require "objective" evidence of need and progress in order to justify the assignment of monies.

Narrative reports and observational data are difficult to interpret, cumbersome to deal with and virtually impossible to use for purposes of comparison. Preference is usually for data in a neatly quantifiable form. If post-test scores are higher than pretest scores, then there has been gain. (It may be that the "gain" is within the standard error of measurement and therefore of no significance.) If the Spanish score is higher than the English score then the student is "Spanish dominant" and is placed in a bilingual program. (The two measures may not be parallel in content or in level of difficulty. Indeed the lower score on the English test may be reflective of greater proficiency than the higher score in Spanish.)

The theoreticians, the psychometricians and linguists, search for the measures that will provide complete, detailed information, free of cultural or any other bias. They are not overly concerned with the practical problems of time and cost, tester training, reporting time and the myriad other issues

*Dr. Protrase Woodford, Director, Language Programs and Test Development, Educational Testing Service, Princeton, N. J.

that must be faced in the field.

The five papers presented here deal with both theory and practice. Perry Zirkel provides an overview of the state of the measurement art in bilingual education. He identifies major areas in bilingual education where measurement instruments or procedures exist or are needed and he identifies instruments and measurement resources.

De Avila and Havassy emphasize "the failure of the testing industry to consider fully the cultural and linguistic differences of minority children when constructing psychological "tests." The pitfalls of translation, of assuming common cultural backgrounds, experiences and responses and the inappropriateness of IQ tests used with linguistic minorities are well illustrated.

Alternative procedures for needs assessment and program evaluation are explored and described, in particular an assessment model, derived from the work of Piaget and tried out in the Southwest with Mexican American children.

The paper by Tilis, Weichun and Cumbo describes the causes behind and the development of the Language Assessment Battery (LAB) created and used by the City of New York in response to a Consent Decree entered into between the N.Y.C. Board of Education and Aspira of New York. The paper presents a detailed description of the test battery per se, the "rationale purpose and use of the LAB" and of the statistical properties of the tests.

Whereas the Tilis, Weichun, Cumbo paper deals with a specific measurement need in a Spanish/English bilingual context, Brisk, Chu-Chang and Loritz deal with the problem of diagnosing and assessing the English language skills of non-native speakers. In this instance primarily Chinese and to a lesser degree, Spanish-speaking students, are discussed. Six instruments and/or procedures designed to evaluate the four traditional language skills plus "appropriate language use" were developed and administered to samples of Chinese and Spanish speakers. The results of the study and their implications for language teaching are discussed.

Roger Shuy attacks the entire notion of language dominance tests. He questions the accuracy of the administrative decisions based on such tests and the overall value of such instruments in the educational process. He advocates abandonment of dominance tests (which he considers "administrative tests") and recommends that programs "...simply diagnose (the) language ability of individual children and prescribe programs for their individual needs."

A number of theoretical considerations in language acquisition are explored in this paper as are their implications for the diagnosis, assessment and evaluation of language ability.

Different points of view, different needs and different experiences are reflected in the papers herein presented.

No definitive answers are given to all the complex questions that arise nor are any panaceas offered. Recognizing how little has been done to improve assessment in bilingual education these five papers can only aid in focusing our attention on the issues and clarifying them for us.

Chapter 61
Evaluation and Testing in Bilingual Programs
Perry A. Zirkel*

Introduction

The number of bilingual programs in public schools in the United States has increased steadily since their rebirth in the early 1960's. The federal funding of Title VII of ESEA, which was enacted in 1967, alone accounts for over 400 such programs across the nation. The amount of professional literature dealing with bilingual education has similarly sky-rocketed. However, rather than leading the way or at least keeping pace, the quantity and quality of evaluation data and testing instruments relating to bilingual programs has lagged far behind.

The general neglect of the measurement aspect of bilingual education is reflected in staff training materials. For example, an informal review of a sample of tests (Andersson & Boyer, 1969; Fishman, 1976; John & Horner, 1971; Ortega, 1975; Van Maltitz, 1975) which are available in the field of bilingual education reveals only one (John & Horner, 1971, pp. 142-163) with a chapter, albeit of limited length, on testing and evaluation. Similarly, despite the recent boom in university training programs in bilingual education (Dissemination Center, 1975b), the number of native specialists in the measurement area is still negligible.

Evaluation Results

The task of evaluating bilingual programs has consumed millions of dollars and has yet to yield psychometrically solid and practically generalizable results. Recognizing the deserved criticism of its unproductive local evaluation efforts, the U.S. Office of Education has launched a nationwide evaluation of bilingual education (Capitol Publications, 1977). Research data from other sources (e.g., UNESCO, 1953) suffer from deficiencies in design instrumentation; differences in temporal, cultural, and socioeconomic conditions; and limitations in scope and duration (Engle, 1975; Venezky, 1970). The incompleteness and inconclusiveness of the findings are further clouded by the wide range of philosophical and programmatic views of bilingual education.

Test Instruments

The linguistic and cultural limitations of the standardized instruments used for testing and evaluation in the bilingual field have been abundantly documented (e.g., Mendoza-Friedman, 1973; Mercer, 1972; Zirkel, 1972) and legally recognized (Oakland & Laosa, 1976). Yet the remedies to these problems remain more as rhetoric than reality. The steps taken thus far have resulted in limited progress, more due to insufficient degree than incorrect direction. Modification of existing instruments and practices has not gone beyond—and often has not reached—the level of mere translation. The use of native-speaking paraprofessionals as interpreters for school psychologists conducting individual assessments with standardized I.Q. instruments often creates more problems than it solves. Typically done on little more than an ad hoc basis without specific training or preparation, this practice can serve to intensify communication and rapport difficulties as well as to reinforce the stigmatically subordinate position of the native language and culture.

Similarly, the translation of the directions of standardized instruments can add to the linguistic confusion and "psychological insulation" (Anastasi & Cordova, 1953) often experienced by Spanish-speaking and other non-English-dominant students. The further step of translating test items as well as directions frequently ignores differences in dialect and inevitably involves differences in word difficulty and cultural content. When the test instrument used language as the end as well as the means—that is, when it is designed to measure oral or written communication skills, such as auditory dissemination or reading blends—the problems become as formidable as translating poetry from one language to another. The ultimate step of developing linguistically and culturally customized instruments remains largely,

*Dr. Perry A. Zirkel, Co-Director of the Division of Curriculum & Foundations, College of Education, University of Hartford.

although not entirely (BABEL, 1972) a distant goal. At the opposite extreme, merely translating the directions of a standardized instrument can be a complicated and consuming task; Finch (1971) reports that it took almost a year to develop the Spanish directions of the *Test of Basic Experiences*, notwithstanding a court order to do so in half that amount of time.

Overview of Problems and Progress

The remaining part of this article will provide an overview of the current state of the art in this area, including its progress as well as its problems. This overview will identify illustrative instruments, resource materials, and research issues for each of the three major target areas of bilingual education programs: linguistic, cognitive, and affective. For the sake of focus, each of these illustrative items will be discussed in terms of Spanish-English bilingual programs, which constitute the principal part though certainly not the entire range of such programs.

Linguistic Area

The linguistic aspect of bilingual programs can be analyzed into two subareas: language dominance and language proficiency. Language dominance refers in this context to the comparison of English and Spanish language skills. For screening and placement purposes, such instruments are typically used to classify pupils into such categories as Spanish dominant, balanced bilingual, and English dominant. Given limited resources, most programs focus their attention on the Spanish-dominant pupils, seeking to move them to full bilingualism or English dominance, depending on whether the goal of the program is maintenance or transition, respectively.

Annotated listings of the growing number of language dominance and proficiency instruments are available (e.g., Language Dominance, 1976; Zirkel, 1976). These reviews reveal that the earlier language dominance instruments, like Hoffman's *Bilingual Background Schedule*, lent themselves to research purposes, but that there has been a recent trend toward developing parallel Spanish-English instruments specific to the needs of bilingual programs. Examples of such instruments are the *James Language Dominance Test*, which is commercially available, and the *Language Assessment Battery*, a more comprehensive instrument developed by the New York City Board of Education in response to the *Aspira* consent decree. Neither instrument is as yet accompanied by extensive psychometric data.

Research in this area (e.g., Fishman et al., 1971; Fishman, 1976) reveals language dominance to be a rather complex phenomenon affected by social as well as educational factors. A neglected segment of the dominance continuum in terms of placement and progress in bilingual programs is that of the "alingual" child, the pupil who is neither dominant nor proficient in either language.

Language proficiency also refers to skills in Spanish and English but separately rather than comparatively. Thus, it overlaps with language dominance. Language proficiency instruments in English specifically for non-native pupils are relatively numerous as a result of English as a Second Language program. Examples of aural and oral instruments in English, respectively, are the *Linguistic Capacity Index*, which was produced by an educational institution, and the *Bilingual Syntax Measure, (BSM)* which is available from a commercial publisher. *BSM* is also available of Spanish as is BABEL's *Spanish Test of Oral Proficiency*. Tests of written language skills overlap with the cognitive area, since they are often seen as representing academic achievement.

Cognitive Area

Annotated listings of test instruments for Spanish-speaking students designed to assess ability in reading, other areas of academic achievement, and mental ability are also available (Dissemination Center, 1975a; Erlich, 1973; National Consortia, 1971; Pruebas en Uso, 1971; Rosen & Horne, 1971). The use of standardized tests in English for Spanish-speaking students has, as already mentioned, been a cause of controversy. The translation of some of these tests for research purposes has revealed their inherent language barrier. For example, a study by Cruz et al. (1975) showed that Spanish-speaking youngsters scored significantly higher on a Spanish translation than the English version of the verbal subtests of the *Metropolitan Readiness Test*.

Test instruments in Spanish are available from the lands of origin of Spanish-speaking students (e.g., Pruebas en Uso, 1971). Their accompanying normative data, although not directly applicable to these pupils' milieu in the U.S., provide at least a peripheral point of reference. Other Spanish instruments have been developed for use in the United States. The *Inter-American Series* is probably the most widely used in bilingual programs because of its parallel Spanish and English forms (National Consortia, 1971) which, unfortunately, is its only outstanding feature (BABEL, 1972).

A major movement growing out of the BABEL (1972) Bilingual/Bicultural Testing and Assessment Workshop was in the direction of criterion-referenced instruments in Spanish. As a result, the BABEL organization has produced *Prueba de lectura*, a CRT series designed to measure reading proficiency in Spanish, and Science Research Associates has published a similar but more extensive instrument called *SOBER-Espanol* (System for Objectives-Based Evaluation of Reading in Spanish). Further, the Spanish Curriculum Development Center in Miami has produced criterion-referenced assessment packages to accompany its curriculum materials in Spanish.

Affective Area

The annotated bibliographies of test instruments compiled by the Dissemination Center for Bilingual/Bicultural Education (1975a) and its predecessor, the National Consortia for Bilingual Education (1971), include extensive entries not only for the linguistic and cognitive areas, but also for the affective area. The affective area is perhaps more prominent in bilingual education projects than in mainstream programs. The enhancement of cultural attitudes and self-concept are central to the use of the native language and culture in bilingual programs. Examples of instruments in these two areas respectively are the *Cultural Attitude Scales,* which is a commercially available series of Anglo, Black-American, Mexican-American, and Puerto Rican modular measures, and the *Primary Self Concept Scale,* another commercially available instrument apparently directed at Mexican-American pupils. Both instruments are orally presented in Spanish and English in relation to pictorial stimuli as an attempt to minimize language and literacy problems in their administration.

Other affective instrumentation and research in the bilingual area focus on such constructs as locus of control, learning style, parent attitudes, and sociometric interaction. As an example of research in this area, Jackson & Coscia (1974) found statistically significant differences between the teacher-student interactions of Mexican-Americans and Anglo students, respectively.

Conclusion

The field of evaluation and testing in relation to bilingual programs is still in its infancy, but is ready for and needful of rapid and rigorous growth. Bilingual instrumentation and its uses for pupil diagnosis, program evaluation, and empirical research must be improved intensively and extensively on a collaborative and committed basis if bilingual education is to move in a deserving direction. Developments to date constitute a foundation for making widespread progress possible. Efforts to develop test instruments and research data have extended across the linguistic, cognitive, and affective

dimensions of bilingual programs and beyond to their community (Zirkel, 1973) and curricular components (Puerto Rican Congress, 1976). The time for training bilingual/bicultural measurement specialists and developing correspondingly authentic measurement materials is now. ¡Ya es tarde!

SELECTED BIBLIOGRAPHY

Anastasi, Anne; and Cordova, F. "Some Effects of Bilingualism Upon Intelligence Test Performance of Puerto Rican Children in New York City," *Journal of Educational Psychology*, 1953, 44:1-19.

Andersson, Theodore; and Boyer, Mildred, *Bilingual Schooling in the United States.* New York: St. John's University Press, 1969.

BABEL, *Bilingual Testing and Assessment.* Berkeley, California: Bay Area Bilingual Education League, 1972.

Capitol Publications, "Newsnotes: Fed Scrutinizes Effectiveness of Bilingual Education in U.S.," *Phi Delta Kappan*, 1977, 58:441.

Cruz, Sylvia et al. "A Study of the Language Factor in Administering the MRT to Spanish-Speaking Students," *Integrated Education*, 1975, 13:43-44.

Dissemination Center for Bilingual Education, *Evaluation Instruments for Bilingual Education: An Annotated Bibliography.* Austin, Texas: Dissemination Center for Bilingual Education, 1975(a).

—————,*Guide to Teacher Education Programs for Bilingual Bicultural Education in U.S. Colleges and Universities.* Austin, Texas: Dissemination Center for Bilingual Education, 1975(b).

Engle, Patricia Lee, "Language Medium in Early School Years for Minority Language Groups," *Review of Educational Research*, 1975, 45:283-325.

Erlich, Alan, Tests in Spanish and Other Languages and Nonverbal Tests for Children in Bilingual Programs. New York: Hunter College, Bilingual Education Applied Research Unit, (1973). (mimeo)

Finch, F. L. Various Ways to Develop a Bilingual Examinacion. Paper presented at the Annual Meeting of Teachers of English to Speakers of Other Languages, New Orleans, March, 1971.

Fishman, Joshua A. *Bilingual Education: An International Sociological Perspective.* Rowley, Mass: Newbury House Press, 1976.

Fishman, Joshua et al. *Bilingualism in the Barrio.* Bloomington: University of Indiana Publications, 1971.

Jackson, Gregg; and Coscia, Cecilia, "The Inequality of Educational Opportunity in the Southwest: An Observed Study of Ethnically Mixed Classrooms," *American Educational Research Journal*, 1974, 11:219-299.

John, Vera P., and Horner, Vivian, M. *Early Childhood Bilingual Education*. New York: Modern Language Association of America, 1971.

"Language Dominance Measures," in *Non-Biased Asessment of Minority Group Children: With Bias Toward None*. Lexington: University of Kentucky, CORRC, 1976.

Mendoza-Friedman, Minerva, "Spanish Bilingual Students and Intelligence Testing," *Changing Education*, 1973, 5:25-28.

Mercer, Jane, "IQ: The Lethal Label," *Education Digest*, 1973, 38:17-20.

National Consortia for Bilingual Education. *Tests in Use in Title VII Bilingual Education Projects*. Forth Worth, Texas: National Consortia for Bilingual Education, 1971.

Oakland, Thomas; and Laosa, Luis, "Professional, Legislative and Judicial Influences on Psycho Educational Assessment Practices in Schools," in *Non-Biased Assessment of Minority Group Children: With Bias Toward None*, Lexington: University of Kentucky, CORRC, 1976.

Ortega, Luis (ed.), *Introduction to Bilingual Education*. New York: Las Americas Publishing Co., 1975.

Pruebas en Uso: Catalogo General, Hato Ray, Puerto Rico: Departmento de Instruccion Publica, Oficina de Evaluacion, 1971.

Puerto Rican Congress of New Jersey, *Evaluation Echoes: A Teacher's Guide for Selection Bilingual Education Materials*. Trenton: Puerto Rican Congress of New Jersey, 1976.

Rosen, Pamela; and Horne, Eleanor, "Tests for Spanish-Speaking Children: An Annotated Bibliography," *Head Start Test Collection Reports*, Princeton: Educational Testing Service, August, 1971.

UNESCO, *The Use of Vernacular Language in Education*. Monographs of Fundamental Education No. 8. Paris: UNESCO, 1953. (o.p.)

Van Maltitz, Frances W. *Living and Learning in Two Languages*. New York: McGraw-Hill, 1975.

Venezky, Richard, "Non Standard Language and Reading," *Elementary English*, 1970, 67:334-345.

Zirkel, Perry A. "Spanish-Speaking Students and Standardized Tests," *Urban Research*, 1972, 5:32-40 (reprinted in *Educational Yearbook*. New York: MacMillan, 1973).

———, "An Educational Survey of Spanish-Speaking Parents," *Journal of Integrated Education*, 1973, 11:23-26.

———, "The Whys and Ways of Testing Bilinguality Before Teaching Bilingually," *Elementary School Journal*, 1976, 76:3-16.

Chapter 62
Problems in Assessing Language Ability in Bilingual Education Programs

Roger W. Shuy*

Several recent efforts at determining which children in a school system need special English language services have led to a clarification of the goals of language assessment in bilingual education programs. Two major reasons seem to exist for measuring such children's language ability:

1. To make a binary cut decision as to whether a child goes to a bilingual education program or whether he goes to the regular monolingual classroom.

2. To assess the specific language abilities of an individual child in order to determine what sort of educational program to give him.

The first of these is, in reality, an administrative test. That is, its purpose suits administrative needs rather than pedagogical ones. It helps determine how many children are in a given program but it offers no hint as to what to do about teaching them. The second is prescriptive and individualistic. It presumes to measure a child's stage of ability in such a way that the results will aid the teacher to select appropriate materials and strategies for individual children.

In their haste to implement bilingual education legislation and mandates, schools often confuse these two types of assessments. The so-called language dominance tests are often used as administrative tests to determine, as quickly and efficiently as possible, which language should be used to instruct a child. If he appears to be dominant in English, he is sent to the regular monolingual classroom. If it is determined that he is dominant in some other language, he is placed in the appropriate bilingual program. The major thrusts of the dominance test, then, is administrative. Through a series of questions, an administrative but not a diagnostic decision is made. The child is placed but not necessarily analyzed.

With good reason, teachers are beginning to question the value of the dominance test. At a conference of the National Education Association, in fact, it was concluded that dominance tests were only inferior and partial language ability tests and that if the schools are to put such effort into assessment efforts, they should provide the teachers with something useful for their classroom, not just a simple, binary, non-diagnostic instrument like the dominance test.

Linguists join the classroom teacher in their complaint, arguing that the concept of dominance, at least as it is now being used, is unrealistic and simplistic. Dominance can only be measured in some sort of realistic context. Thus a speaker with only minimal knowledge of French could easily be assessed as dominant in French if the measurement were taken in a Paris taxicab. In order to determine dominance, one must specify, in detail where, under what circumstances, and to what extent the language is used, all in relationship to other contexts. Are children dominant in Spanish in their home? At school? On the playground? With their grandparents? By what criteria, quantitative or qualitative, can one such context be said to be more important than another.

Efforts to carry out the bilingual legislation requirement for an administrative decision include the New York City *Language Assessment Battery*, the Chicago Public Schools' *Short Test of Linguistic Ability*, the *James Dominance Test* and many others. These measurements do not profess to be individually diagnostic. They offer only to determine whether a child needs to have bilingual education or whether he does not. How the threshold is determined for such decision making is, at best, arbitrary and, at worst, dangerous.

New York City may serve as a case in point. There the *Language Assessment Battery* was developed in response to the school system's interpretation of the Aspira Consent Decree. A set of questions, largely related to the pronunciation, grammar and vocabulary of English and Spanish was developed. The questions were normed on a population of 15,000 Anglo New York children. By administrative decision it was decided that the score earned by the lower 10 percent of the Anglo children would serve as the threshold of acceptability for the New York Puerto Rican children. When reviewed by the federal district judge, the 10 percent threshold cut-off point was challenged and when the city school system was unable to offer

*Roger Shuy, Georgetown University and Center for Applied Linguistics.

satisfactory evidence to support the decision, the cut-off point was arbitrarily moved up to 20 percent. Naturally, there was no more reason to use the 20 percent figure than the 10 percent one, but, barring any other criterion upon which to operate, the federal judge decided upon 20 percent as a more acceptable figure.

In general, there has been no adequate way to establish the administrative decision required by bilingual legislation. Dominance tests are flawed linguistically and pedagogically and measurements developed in response to local legislation have been equally arbitrary and inefficient.

The conclusion seems clear: rather than developing or using extant administrative tests, why not simply diagnose language ability of individual children and prescribe programs for their individual needs?

In order to determine whether any test is valid, one compares the claims of the test against the instrument itself. The most critical question to ask of any test is whether it measures the right things. This is frequently referred to as *content validity*. If the test is a test of language ability, for example, one looks for the measures of language ability which are known to exist in the knowledge base of the content area. Thus the most critical question to ask in assessing a test's validity is: "Is the item a valid indicator of the subject being measured?" The research fallacy here is a common one. Correlation is not causation. For example, even though it might be shown that eating habits correlate with income, there is no reason to believe that eating habits cause income chances.

The first question to be asked of the procedure used by most schools, than, concerns the content validity of the language questions. This should be followed by the question of methodology.

What should a language diagnosis measure? The O.C.R. Guidelines clearly point out that a language test should determine the relative skills that a child has in English and in the other language to which he has significant exposure. These guidelines also specify that the test must be individual and that the results of the assessment must justify the educational program to which the child is assigned.

Many tests of language proficiency exist but few are designed for school aged bilingual children and even fewer were designed for language other than English. Many schools have found the existing instruments not useful and many, like the Chicago schools, have adopted procedures unique to their district, whether or not they have validity or reliability.

The specific wording of *Lau* vs. *Nichols*, the Consent Decree entered in *Aspira of New York* vs. *Board of Education of the City of New York*, and many other pieces of legislation includes the phrase,

"effective participation in the classroom." That is, assessment is to be made by the schools to determine in which language the child can most effectively participate in the classroom. Traditionally, education has taken the quickest and presumably easiest route to such an assessment. Often the child is asked questions involving the pronunciation or grammar of English. The assumption is, for example, that if a Spanish speaking child can distinguish *choose* from *shoes*, he can effectively participate in the classroom.

I would disagree with such a definition of "effective participation," as far as language is concerned. This is not to demean the importance of pronunciation or precise grammar, but linguists argue that the *functional use* of language is more critical for effective participation than are the language forms *per se*. They would argue, for example, that the child's ability to seek clarification from his teacher when he does not understand something is more functional in school than native-English-like pronunciation or grammar. The focus on uses of language underlies much of language learning, but little of language teaching and none of language assessment.

We know that by the age of six, a child has acquired most of what he needs to know about the pronunciation of his native language. By age ten he has acquired almost all of what he will need to know about the grammar of his native language. We also know that these language functions such as seeking clarification, requesting, interrupting, getting a turn, refusing, condoling, etc., are learned much later and, in some cases, not at all. A model of native language learning is displayed as follows:

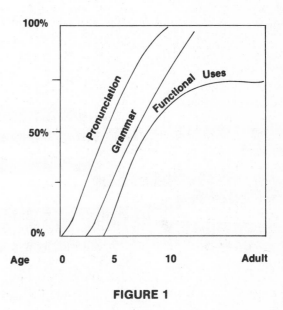

FIGURE 1

In this theory of language acquisition, the earliest learned characteristics, pronunciation and grammar, are learned primarily to implement the functional use of language. Many adults never learn all of the possible language functions effectively (condoling, for example); thus, this learned curve never reaches 100 percent.

If a school system is to have content validity in a language test, then, it must decide what "effective participation" means, then find the best ways to assess it. This must be done with a linguistic sophistication about what matters most in language learning. If one has any doubts that language functions are more crucial than pronunciation, one should simply ask oneself which child is in the better shape: the ten year old who can seek clarification when he doesn't know the answer but whose pronunciation is foreign versus the ten year old whose pronunciation is very English-sounding but administer and score but it is difficult to measure in

Once it is established that there is a clear understanding of what matters most, the language test maker must next worry about how to test for it. In the past five decades, there have been at least five general approaches to language assessment which establish a continuum from most to least formalized.

1. *Discrete-point tests*. These are the usual first impressions which people have of language tests. The widely used Test of English as a Foreign Language (TOEFL) is a clear example. Such tests usually have multiple choice items, each item probing the knowledge of a particular fact about language. Such tests can measure some of the language skills which a child has but only if we are willing to assume that the skill of language can be isolated and shrunk into a small component for measurement purposes. The problem of such tests is in how to select representative items. In any language test, a severe problem arises when language is measured outside of its naturally occurring context. Language is always used in a specific situation, at a specific time with different participants for different purposes. This principle is clearly set forth in the Lau Remedies. Contextual factors heavily influence both language form and usage; language ability is, however, almost always assessed out of context, yielding, at best, an approximate indication of such ability. Probably the major reason why such tests remain popular is that they are easy to administer, score, and cross compare test results.

2. *Integrative tests*. These are similar to discrete-point tests in many ways, but they do not isolate from natural context quite as much and they do not shrink the questions into such small components for measurement. A good example of this type is the often used listening comprehension test where paragraphs of running text are used to elicit responses to specific

questions of content. Attention is also given to the formal properties of the response used by the child. In this way, such integrative tests attempt to give a more global picture of language ability. Alternative methods include dictation questions where the child listens or reads, then repeats as close to verbatim as possible and the "cloze" procudure where ten to twenty percent of the words are omitted and the student must fill them in.

Like discrete point tests, integrative tests are easy to administer and score but is is difficult to measure in natural contexts with such assessments, and it is not exactly clear what they measure.

3. *Direct Rating Methods*. To increase content validity, current work is underway to have a trained observer rate a speaker's use of language. The Foreign Service Institute of Washington, D. C. has used this procedure for many years. Usually a speaker spends about thirty minutes with two observers, at least one of whom is a native speaker. Conversation topics which are introduced are similar to on-the-job situations. Under such conditions, it is possible to assess a full range of pertinent skills. This method tends to get fairly good natural context language (within limits, of course). The major drawbacks are in the amount of time and individual attention required and the degree of reliability among observers. It is generally regarded, however, as having the highest degree of content validity of all known testing procedures.

4. *Self-Report Ratings*. Although such procedures are common in survey work or in census collections, they are not well regarded in testing circles. The major assumption here is that the speaker can accurately monitor how well he performs and that he is willing to be honest. Such tests are easy to develop, to administer and to score but their content validity is highly questionable. It is also clear that young children cannot rate their own ability. Parental ratings of their own children's language ability has been shown to be only about 40 percent accurate.

5. *Direct Observation*. Although this procedure is used extensively in many areas, its application to language testing is relatively new. It requires that an assessor observe children using language in day to day situations (a process by which *all* aspects of how the school district assesses language levels including instruments, category definitions, video-tape instruction, the environment in which language is assessed, and ultimate face-to-face contact between teacher and child). It is highly desirable to measure language use in natural context, since language behavior is observed, not artificially elicited. The problem here is in determining first just exactly what behaviors are desired and valued and then to decide exactly how they will be measured. This method is better for measuring how children produce language

than for how they understand it, since one could only infer the latter.

Of the above approaches, the schools have relied most heavily, by far, on the discrete-point test. Education consistently places a high premium on the visible, quantifiable surface aspects of its work. In the teaching of language, it is considerably easier to measure accuracy in pronunciation or vocabulary than in meaning, despite the fact that most specialists would agree that the major thrust of language is to get at meaning. The typical evaluation points in language measurement may be described as an iceberg with the visible features above the water line but the more critical ones below:

more quantifiable and testable

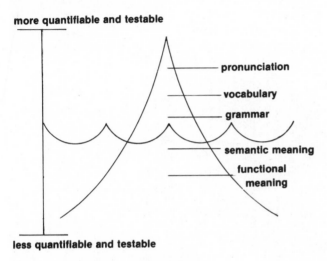

less quantifiable and testable

FIGURE 2

What typically happens in the measurement of language learning ability as well as reading ability is that the more visible, highly recurring features (pronunciation, vocabulary and sometimes grammar) are measured and quantified throughout the learning program without regard for their interrelationships with the other accompanying measurement points. These features are measurable because their inventory is reasonable to assess and because we know what they are. They are not measured because of what we are certain they will tell us about language learning ability. Because such features recur, they are easily quantifiable, thus lending an air of scientific respectability. When couched as test questions such features become discrete-point test items and it is assumed that by knowing the answer to such questions, one evidences significant ability in the gestalt of which it is a small part.

The schools have shied away from direct rating methods from fear of time and cost. One-on-one test situations are expensive and require expert test takers. Most schools want the advantage of the results of such an approach without a financial commitment to it.

Self report data have been used by the schools in their efforts to find an inexpensive way to make their required binary, administrative decisions. The results, however, have been highly questionable. For example, in one large midwestern school system such a survey yields a list of such languages as Indian (there are hundreds of American Indian languages and many languages in India), Belgian (Dutch? French? German?), Austrian (German is spoken in Austria), Chinese (Mandarin or Cantonese?) and, believe it or not, African. It is difficult to tell whether the problem is the child's ability to communicate his language or the teacher's ability to record it. But something usually goes wrong and such data are not to be trusted.

It seems odd that the simple observation of language use should be the last approach resorted to in the schools. Behavior is observed and recorded in other areas without too much difficulty. If we want to measure how well the janitor and the school secretary are doing we usually evaluate their performance. It would probably not occur to us to give them a discrete-point test on the use of the screwdriver or the typewriter. But with children, schools seem to be less interested in measuring what the children know than we are in solving administrative requirements.

There are a few ways that a dominance test can be helpful in the task of instruction. A dominance test is really only a small part of an ability test. It assumes that the context of testing is generalizable and that the test event itself is accurate and fair. If a visitor from a distant planet were to administer a dominance test to me while I was touring in France, he might determine that I was dominant in French. Although my French is atrocious, I could be deemed French dominant in such a case. I always speak French in French taxicabs. But of what use would such information be to anyone? What would be useful would be an analysis of my abilities in French. The ability test can provide the information required for an administrative decision but the administrative test cannot provide the information required for a teaching decision. It would appear that some schools are interested in placement but not in learning.

The concluding pleas of a paper such as this are probably obvious but it may be useful to summarize them.

1. Of the two kinds of tests currently being developed, administrative tests and ability tests, only the latter should be used. What the learning situation requires is that we discover the childrens' language ability in order to know how to place, diagnose and teach them. Any effort to do this which yields only binary, administrative results is wasteful of teacher and student time.

2. Any assessment of language ability should contain

content valid questions. Care should be taken to insure that the test measures validly what it claims to measure and that reliability is not confused with validity.
3. Research must be carried out to determine better ways of discovering and measuring what really matters in language learning.
4. Methods of measuring language ability in natural language contexts must be developed and perfected. Discrete-point testing in language must be abandoned as soon as possible in favor of more accurate and realistic strategies.

This is a tall order for language instruction. At present, there is no natural predisposition toward research in the schools and no full understanding of the dangers of current practice. It is time for a unified front to be established by those who fear that inaccurate or unfair language assessment will bring harm to all of bilingual education.

Chapter 63
The Testing of Minority Children –
A Neo Piagetian Approach
Edward A. DeAvila and Barbara Havassy*

The National Education Association, the popular press, the courts, civil rights organizations, state and federal agencies, and others have pointed to the failure of the test-publishing industry to consider fully the cultural and linguistic differences of minority children when constructing psychological tests. Test publishers have responded by translating existing intelligence and nationally normed achievement tests into other languages such as Spanish, adjusting norms for ethnic subgroups, and attempting to construct culture-free tests. Each approach involves distinct problems. Moreover, in our opinion, the tests as they are currently designed are of little use to anybody.

Translating existing intelligence or achievement tests for non-English-speaking children often creates problems. First, regional differences within a language make it difficult to use a single translation in a standardized testing situation where examiner and examinee are permitted virtually no interaction. Thus, while *toston* means a quarter or a half dollar to a Chicano, it means a portion of banana squashed and fried to a Puerto Rican.

Second, monolingual translations are inappropriate because the language familiar to non-English-speaking children is often a combination of two languages as in the case of Tex-Mex. Third, many non-English-speaking children have never learned to read in their spoken language. For example, many Chicano children speak Spanish but have had no instruction in reading Spanish.

Another major response of the testing industry to criticism has been to establish or to propose establishment of regional and ethnic norms. Such a practice leads to lower expectations for minorities, which in turn may lower childrn's aspirations to succeed. Furthermore, ethnic norms do not take into considertion the complex reasons *why* minority children on the average score lower than Anglo American children on IQ tests. Ethnic norms are potentially dangerous from the social perspective because they provide a basis for invidious comparisons between racial groups. The tendency is to assume that lower scores are indicative of lower potential, thereby contributing to the self-fulfilling prophecy of lower expectations for minority children and reinforcing the genetic-inferiority argument advanced by Arthur Jensen and others.

In addition, if test publishers and users are willing to establish ethnic norms, they should also establish norms based on sex differences. To take into account both sex and all the ethnic subgroups in the United States would require an almost infinite set of norm tables. From the practical point alone, this is absurd. One might wonder what norms a publisher would use for a set of male/female twins who had a Mexican father and a Hungarian mother.

The testing industry has also responded to criticism of conventional IQ tests by attempting to create culture-free tests. Such tests are difficult to construct, and many question whether they achieve their goal of being free of cultural bias. Tests of mental ability and/or achievement attempt to determine the ability of a child to manipulate certain elements of a problem into a predetermined solution. It is difficult to conceive of test elements equally familiar to children of all ethnic or cultural groups, especially when test developers are members of a group themselves.

In a large number of frequently used IQ and achievement tests, cultural influences on items cause the tests to measure something other than that for which they were designed. Thus, aside from what many tests set out to measure, to a large extent they also measure—

Socialization

Certain test items are actually measures of the child's family value system. In tests marketed in the United States, the referent value system is, generally, that of the Anglo American middle class.

*Dr. Edward A. DeAvila, Director of Educational Planning and Research, Bilingual Children's Television. Dr. Barbara Havassey, Langley Porter Neuropsychiatric Institute, University of California, San Francisco. Reprinted with permission from Today's Education, November-December, 1974.

This characteristic is particularly evident in the comprehension scale of one of the major individually administered IQ tests. The test presents questions very much like this one provided by the publisher as typical, but not authentic, item from the test: "What should you do if you see someone forget his book when he leaves his seat in a restaurant?" This type of question has little or nothing to do with a child's ability to process, manipulate, and/or code information. The answers depend almost exclusively on whether a child has been socialized under the particular ethical system implied by the question.

Productivity or Level of Aspiration

Many tests confuse what they hope to measure with a measure of productivity or level of aspiration. For example, in a large number of tests, the child who produces the most responses receives a higher score than the one who stops responding after only a few attempts. The assumption underlying this type of test is that all subjects will produce as many responses as they are able, in other words, that they all have the same level of aspiration.

Timed tests also confuse the measurement of ability with the measurement of aspiration. In timed tests, which constitute the majority of published group tests, the tester asks children to work quickly, quietly, and efficiently. Little regard is given to children who are not motivated to work in that manner. For the purpose of boosting statistical reliability, tests are constructed in such a way that children are asked a large number of questions which vary only a little in content.

A similar problem involves tests which sequence items in order of increasing difficulty. In these, children encounter increasing levels of failure and frustration. For those who start out fearfully, as do most children unfamiliar with the social demands of the school or test situation, the first indication of failure or difficulty discourages them from continuing.

Experience or Specific Learning

Tests that require answers of fact assume that all children taking the test will have had about the same exposure to the facts being tested. Any number of examples involving vocabulary bear out the spuriousness of this assumption. It is impossible to determine whether minority children miss a test item because they have never been exposed to the word or because they lack the capacity to understand the word. Problems of this type are found in virtually any test of mental ability which uses a score on a vocabulary subtest to infer ultimate capability.

One of the most widely used individually administered intelligence tests is full of examples of the importance of specific experience on test results. For example, the child is asked questions of vocabulary which bear directly on past experience or exposure to the words being tested.

Now let us consider the validity and utility of the IQ score. Forgetting for a moment standardized achievement tests, the original justification for the use of the IQ test was that the scores statistically predict mental retardation and low school achievement. Yet in 1971, sociologist Jane Mercer found that of adults who scored below 79 on an individually administered IQ test (and who would have been labeled mentally retarded had they been schoolchildren), 84 percent had completed eight grades or more in school, 83 percent had held a job, 80 percent were financially independent, and almost 100 percent could do their own shopping and travel alone. In other words, even at the task for which experts agree the IQ test is best suited—screening for mental retardation—the IQ measure probably has a dubious real-life validity.

In addition to its traditional use as an indicator of mental retardation, many educators and politicians have come to consider the IQ test to be a useful instrument for teachers, school districts, and state and federal agencies. Indeed, many states mandate that districts administer IQ tests several times as a child goes through the school system. But do the results really help the teacher do a better job?

Let us consider a typical example. A teacher suspects that a child has a severe learning disability and asks the school psychologist to test the child. After the psychologist gives an individually administered test in which the child scores an IQ of 87, the psychologist writes up an extensive report of impressions of the child's performance and potential. Upon receiving the report, the teacher responds in surprise, "But I knew all that. I want to know how I can reach this child." Thus, neither psychologist nor teacher is any wiser despite considerable time and expense administering and evaluating the IQ test.

While few psychologists would agree that educational decisions affecting a child's life should be made just on the basis of an IQ score, the fact remains that such decisions are made by educators who, through personal fiat, supported by state mandate, ignore both individual subscale profiles and psychologists' admonitions for the sake of practical expediency. The result is, of course, a form of default institutional racism.

Thus, while much of the controversy surrounding the IQ tests and minority children focuses on whether the IQ model is a valid one, a more practical question concerns the general utility of the information the test produces. In order to answer, one must consider who is asking the question and why. Within the educational system, there are qualitative differences in the type of information needed, depending on the source of the need. To a large extent, much of the confusion surrounding the issue of whether to test stems from failure to consider these differences.

Several levels within the educational system require information traditionally obtained through IQ testing: the funding level which involves federal and state agencies; the local level, which involves district personnel and school principals; and the school level, which involves classroom teacher, paraprofessional and parents.

Federal and state funding agencies expect IQ tests to supply them with information cocerning statewide or districtwide needs for the purpose of allocating funds and information concerning program effectiveness. There would seem to be far better ways of meeting the first need than trying to infer specific needs from an omnibus assessment based on so poorly understood a concept as IQ Assessment procedures which can evaluate whether specific educational programs are needed in specific areas such as science would be more useful. Such procedures exist, and these allow direct inference from test performance to program need.

The second need—that of knowing about the effectiveness of particular programs—has become particularly demanding recently in light of accountability and evaluation/audit requirements. In response, these federal and state agencies have often mandated that IQ and standardized achievement tests be administered to evaluate programs.

Actually, program evaluations can be made through a variety of procedures, none of which necessarily has anything to do with IQ or standardized achievement tests. For example, a reasonable assessment can be made by interviewing administrators, teachers, parents, and children as to their perceptions of program effectiveness and by testing specific program objectives and reporting changes in group scores without reference to individual scores.

Local school district personnel require information about the needs of children and the effectiveness of programs in the same way as do the federal and state agencies. However, since needs assessments are usually conducted at the state level, local officers tend to rely on the state-provided information rather than to conduct expensive research on their own.

Ideally, evaluation of individual programs should center around collection of data dealing directly with program objectives and activities. However, instruments of evaluation often have little to do with the actual program; IQ or nationally normed achievement tests are used, providing scores which often have little in the way of information about effectiveness of individual programs and program components.

The last to be considered in the educational hierarchy are, unfortunately, classroom teachers and what they need to assist the learner. How can teachers translate numerical IQ scores into curriculum or instructional prescriptions? This question is particularly perplexing because teachers cannot rely on absolute point differences on IQ scores. For example, if a teacher wanted to know what should be done differently for children with scores of 92 and 100, the answer would have to be "nothing" because these scores are functionally equivalent. They are both within the "normal" range, i.e., within one standard deviation of the mean. However, when the same eight-point difference is between IQ scores of 84 and 92, there is a different implication. The score of 84 is approximately one standard deviation below the mean and is, in some states, considered to indicate that a child is in the "retarded" or "slow learner" category. In this case, the eight points which separate the 84 and 92 scores would necessitate different recommendations for the children involved.

In many cases, the same criticisms apply to achievement tests that provide collapsed or summary achievement scores. What educational distinctions and decisions can teachers make about children with reading grade equivalency scores of 3.2 versus 3.6 and 3.6 versus 4.0? Neither the IQ score nor the collapsed achievement score provides enough information on which to base sound daily educational decisions.

These issues have brought us to consider an alternative assessment model which derives from the work of Jean Piaget. We have been working with Juan Pascual-Leone of York University, Toronto, in developing a neo-Piagetian procedure, which has been tested with approximately 1,100 Mexican American and other children in four Southwestern states. Children were tested using standardized tests of school achievement, IQ, and four Piaget-derived measures developed individually and jointly by De Avila and Pascual-Leone over the past 10 years.

The goals of this reasearch were:

1. To test interrelations among the four neo-Piagetian measures in a sample of primarily Mexican American children who live in different areas and come from different socioeconomic backgrounds

2. To examine the psychometric properties of these neo-Piagetian measures

3. To examine the relation between the developmental level as assessed by the neo-Piagetian procedures and IQ as assessed by standardized measures

4. To examine sex differences in performances on the tests.

Results of this research have shown that:

1. These measures exhibit a developmental progression of performance scores across age in accordance with Piaget's theory of cognitive development.

2. Performance of the primarily Mexican American sample is developmentally appropriate and within the limits of expected levels of cognitive development for given chronological ages.

3. There are no meaningful differences between the sexes.

4. Scores of children taking the tests in English, Spanish, or bilingually showed no appreciable differnces.

5. There were no ethnic group differences on the neo-Piagetian measures of cognitive development at the New Mexico location, the only place where direct ethnic group comparisons could be made. There were, however, consistent ethnic group differences on the IQ measures (Otis-Lennon Mental Ability Test) and on the achievement measure (Comprehensive Tests of Basic Skills) always in favor of Anglo Americans.

These results have several implications. First, as this was a field study, further work is needed with greater control over such variables as language background, ethnicity, and achievement. With such controls, the nature of the relationship between neo-Piagetian measures and traditional measures of capacity and achievement can be assessed with greater precision. Second, results of this study indicate that the relationship between cognitive development and school achievement, especially of Mexican American children, must be more closely examined. Third, the failure to find a difference between Mexican American and Anglo American children on the neo-Piagetian measures leads us to adopt the position that Mexican American children develop cognitively the same as Anglo American children. It appears, however, that cognitive development in Mexican American children and perhaps others is not in itself a sufficient condition to engender a level of school achievement equivalent to that of middleclass children.

Failure of Mexican American children to achieve in school and to perform well on traditional capacity and achievement measures must be attributed to reasons other than alleged cognitive inferiority. Some reasons for poor performance, we feel, lie in the design characteristics of curriculum and other classroom materials, language usage, and the situational contexts or givens used in both testing and presenting curriculum. Culturally biased in favor of particular groups, they put all children at a distinct disadvantage.

While these findings are of importance in understanding the cognitive development of Mexican American children, the more basic question remains: How can the classroom teacher use the information provided by the neo-Piagetian approach on a regular day-by-day basis?

In an attempt to generate test information which directly fulfills informational/instructional needs within the schools, we have designed a computerized system which deals with information needs of the three levels of school personnel discussed previously. At the administrative level, this system provides group statistical data for program evaluation and needs assessment and, at the teacher level, provides classroom recommendations rather than scores.

This system simultaneously takes into account achievement and developmental scores for both the individual child and the child's referent group. It thus becomes possible to determine all of the possible test outcomes and, thereby, to design individual computerized program prescriptions for each child tested. Workshops are then held with the teachers involved to discuss the implementation of these prescriptions. A copy of these recommendations can also be sent to the home so that parents are aware of what the teacher is trying to accomplish with the child and can, with guidance from the teacher, participate in the child's education.

This system, called Program Assessment Pupil Instruction (PAPI), was tested successfully in the same four states where data were gathered for the above described research.

It should be noted that the PAPI system is designed so that a child's peer or referent group can be designated in numerous ways, such as grade, sex, or program group.

Thus far we have tested the PAPI system by working directly with classroom teachers, by explaining the computer printouts, by listening to suggestions, and by continuously refining our approach.

Chapter 64
On Language Testing: The Development of the Language Assessment Battery

Howard S. Tilis, William Weichun, and Richard F. Cumbo*

Introduction

The purpose of this article is to present to the reader some of the practical and technical problems inherent in the development of a test in two languages. At the initiation of the project described in these pages there were very few individuals or institutions who had any significant experience in the development of tests in two language. As described below, there were many conceptual problems to be faced before any progress could take place. We believe it is important to share our experiences in the development of the Language Assessment Battery (LAB) so that others wishing to embark on such a task would have the benefits of already existing insights. It is also important for all using the LAB to know the nature in which it was constructed so they can use it with greater confidence.

Historical Development of Language Assessment Battery

The Language Assessment Battery is a product of a Consent Decree (72 Civ. 4002) entered into between the Board of Education of the City of New York, et al., and ASPIRA of New York, Inc., et al. on August 29, 1974. The suit was instituted in September, 1972 on behalf of children born in Puerto Rico or of parents recently arrived from there. The basis of the complaint was that the children speak little or no English; that the schools these children attend provide predominantly English language instruction, and consequently there is lowered educational achievement and test score; poorer rates of promotion and production. These consequences, it was argued, would lead to concomitant problems for college entrance, employment, civic participation, and the quality of life in general. It was argued that the continued practice of predominate English language instruction to children who are basically Spanish speaking is a violation of the Fourteenth Amendment of the Constitution of the United States which provides for equal protection and due process.

In order to implement the Consent Decree the problem of identification and classification of Spanish speaking and Spanish surnamed children had to be solved. The Decree specifies that an "—improved method of classifying shall be designed among other things, to identify those children whose English language deficiencies prevent them from effectively participating in the learning process, and who can more effectively participate (in the learning process) in Spanish. Such improved methods will identify the children according to their ability to speak, read, write and comprehend English and Spanish (72 Civ. 4002)." The above quote specifies that both expressive and receptive skills must be assessed and that there were no published instrumentation to adequately perform the task. Consequently, with the mandate for improved assessment of "effectiveness in English and Spanish" the Office of Educational Evaluation was commissioned to develop a Language Assessment Battery (LAB).

Problems of assessment of bilingual children was something the testing industry and others interested in assessment did not give much attention to until the January, 1974 unanimous supreme court decision in *Lau* V. *Nichols* 414 U. S. 563. This monumental decision in favor of bilingual education forced measurement experts to direct their attention to this important problem. At this point in time of the supreme court decision, commercial testing companies had not invested their energies and resources into the development of tests for bilingual pupils. As a result, bilingual programs used already existing tests by merely translating them or they filled the psychometric void by developing their own tests. The tests available or developed were very limited in terms of their applicability, grade levels, norms, and content (De Avila & Duncan, 1976).

Consequently, the problem faced by NYC was in reality a unique one. The Consent Decree mandates that we take a new look at the manner in which bilingual students are assessed. What follows in the remainder of

---

*All authors are currently employed by the Board of Education, City of New York in the Office of Educational Evaluation, Language Assessment Unit.

this paper is a description of the development of the Language Assessment Battery (LAB). The LAB was developed by the Board of Education of the City of New York in order to comply with the mandate of the Consent Decree.

Description of Language Assessment Battery

The LAB was designed to assess reading, writing, listening comprehension and speaking in English and Spanish for children in grades Kindergarten through twelve (K-12). The areas to be tested by the LAB are defined as follows:

: 1) Reading—the recognition of the morphological, syntactical structure and comprehension of English and Spanish in graphic form.

2) Writing—the recognition of the grammatical signals of the language in graphic form.

3) Listening comprehension—the recognition of what one hears.

4) Speaking—the ability to orally produce and connect grammatical structures.

The LAB (English and Spanish) has three levels; level I is designed for use with grades K - 2, level II is to be used with grades 3 - 6, and level III is for grades 7 - 12.

Level I (grades K - 2) is individually administered. This level is comprised of;

Test 1. Listening and Speaking (20 test items).

Test 2. Reading (10 test items).

Test 3. Writing (10 test items).

Level I (English and Spanish) takes approximately 5-10 minutes per child to administer.

Level II (grades 3-6) has a total of 92 items. Test 1, 2 and 3 are group administered and Test 4 is individually administered.

Test 1. Listening (30 test items)—approximately 8 minutes to administer.

Test 2. Reading (28 test items)—approximately 20 minutes to administer.

Test 3. Writing (28 test items)—approximately 8 minutes to administer.

Test 4. Speaking (14 test items)—approximately 5 minutes to administer.

Level III (grades 7-12) has a total of 92 items. Test 1, 2 and 3 are group administered and Test 4 is individually administered.

Test 1. Listening (30 test items)—approximately 8 minutes to administer.

Test 2. Reading (28 test items)—approximately 20 minutes to administer.

Test 3. Writing (28 test items)—approximately 8 minutes to administer.

Test 4. Speaking (14 test items)—approximately 5 minutes to administer.

National, Purpose and Usage of LAB

The purpose of the Language Assessment Battery, as used by the New York City Public Schools, is classification. It is the intent of the LAB to classify a child's "effectiveness" in English and Spanish.

Figure 1 below is a conceptualization of the classification testing process.

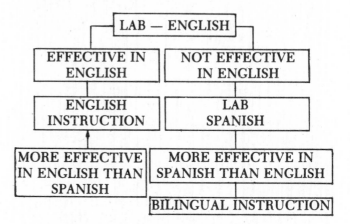

FIGURE 1. CONCEPTUALIZATION OF TESTING AND INSTRUCTIONAL DECISION—MAKING PROCESS.

The model indicates that the child is first tested with the LAB-English and a decision is made as to whether the child is "effective" in that language. If it is found that a child is effective the testing is stopped, if, however, it is found the child is not effective the child is tested with the LAB-Spanish and a comparative judgment is made as to whether the child is more effective in English or Spanish.

The problem of test development in relation to the Consent Decree revolves around an interpretation of the phrase "effectively participating in the learning process." What does it mean when one states that a particular child is "effectively participating?" Does it mean that the child is at the lower end of a continuum (if effective participation could be viewed as going from least to most)? Is a child who receives a score of 95 more effectively participating than a child who receives a score of 65? Is a child who receives a score of 50 effectively participating? In brief, what are the variables which make-up effective participation? At what point on a continuum is one effective or not effective?

Effective participation looked at through the tunnel of language, which the Consent Decree necessitates, is misleading. The problem really is whether one can equate "linguistic effectiveness" with the concept of "effectively participating in the learning process." It would seem that linguistic effectiveness, as measured by the LAB, is but one of many aspects of "effective participation." Effective participation may be conceived as the interaction of many variables; as the interaction of personal and situational factors. The individual child is a multidimensional being. In any learning situation a child has certain dimensions of personality which he brings to the environment (i.e. linguistic capabilities). These personal dimensions interact with situational variables (i.e. culture, peer relationships, classroom structure, teacher personality, etc.). Consequently, in testing for comparative linguistic effectiveness, one can not "automatically" conclude that one can or cannot "effectively participate in the learning process." What the process conceptualized in Figure 1 above does enable one to do, is make a "relative" judgment as to comparative effectiveness in English and Spanish language skills. In using the LAB-English and Spanish, as outlined in this paper, one may conclude that the child seems to be more effective on one language as opposed to the other.

From the above discussion, one may readily glean the process of dual decision-making. Each step in the process is intended to further refine a "class", so that children who have little or no English language skills and are more effective in Spanish are selected for bilingual instruction.

There are many problems inherent in a decision making model such as this, but the most difficult conceptual problem is that of a "cutting score" to determine effectiveness in English. A "cutting score" is that point which functions to dichotomize groups. In the instance of the LAB-English it is that score above which children are considered "effective" in English, and below which one is not considered effective in English.

The Consent Decree mandates that a child's effectiveness in the learning process first be determined in English. This legal requirement, then, dictates the logic of the decision-making model utilized. An assessment of the child's ability to function would have to be made and compared to a group who is already "effectively" functioning in English. This logic would then necessitate the use of a monolingual English norm group. The norm or standardization group is composed of individuals who are not hampered from participating in the instructional process because of English language handicaps. They may, however, not be effectively participating for reasons other than language deficits (i.e. discipline, intellectual, family, etc.).

Theoretically, since the concept of "effectiveness" is so closely linked to mastery, one would expect the lowest score achieved by the norm group to be that point below which one is not effective. Thus, the proportion of items answered correctly by the target population in comparison to the norm group, would be one measure of effectiveness in English language functioning. This model is seeking "perfection" in an environment marred by less than perfect measuring instruments. The model as suggested by Meskauskas (1976), requires an alternative approach to "construct a decision model which takes into account factors that introduce measurement error—the deficiencies of the examination and the functioning of random processes of various types (p. 143)." Since the extent of the measurement error was not known at the time of initial use, the cutting score was set by the court at the twentieth percentile. It is our judgment that this point is more than sufficient to allow for any random measurement errors which may occur.

Item Analysis Program

The development of the Language Assessment Battery—English and Spanish, had three separate item analyses studies performed. An item analysis is intended to provide statistical information on how each item functions. Item analysis provides the following information; the percentage of students who pass each item (item difficulty) and whether the test items can differentiate between the top and bottom 27 percent of the norming group (item discrimination).

The initial item analysis study was completed in March, 1975 for the LAB-English. Following is the number of test items used in each level of the test:

	Level II	Level III
Reading	130 items	100 items
Writing	40 items	70 items
Listening	113 items	128 items
Speaking	40 items	40 items
	323 items	338 items

There were a total of 20 schools, representative of the New York Public Schools who participated in this pilot study. There were approximately 7500 children in grade levels K - 12 who participated in the pilot study. On the average then there were approximately 500 children per grade level who were included in the pilot testing program. The data were analyzed basically for item difficulty and appropriateness of item content. Items with difficulty levels below .60 were excluded. Based on the results of this item analysis a version of the LAB-English was produced and ready for use in April 1975.

Based on the March, 1975 item analysis the April, 1975 LAB-English had the following number of items:

	Level II	Level III
Reading	58 items	59 items
Writing	26 items	26 items
Listening	89 items	89 items
Speaking	40 items	40 items
	213 items	214 items

The above version of the LAB-English was subjected to a new item analysis for grades 5 and 8. The number of students was approximately 350 at grade 5 and 550 at grade 8. Again item difficulties and item discrimination indices were computed. Note that no item analysis was performed at Level I because the decision was already reached to change the test format.

The 1975 LAB-Spanish had the following number of items at each level of the test.

Level I had a total of 40 individually administered items.

	Level II	Level III
Reading	58 items	59 items
Writing	28 items	26 items
Listening	78 items	90 items
Speaking	40 items	40 items
	204 items	215 items

Similarly, item analyses were performed for pupils in grades 1, 5 and 8. The Ns for each grade level approximated 300 students.

Based on the above analyses, the 1976 LAB-English and Spanish was developed.

The 1976 LAB-English and Spanish, Levels I, II and III were also item analyzed. The LAB-English was item analyzed for grades K - 12 using a monolingual English speaking population. The LAB-Spanish was item analyzed using a population of students who were Spanish dominant. The Ns ranged from 350 to over 1000 students per grade level for grades K - 12.

As can be gleaned from the above, at each of the stages of item analysis, the total number of items was reduced. The test items which remained at each stage of development were considered to be the best functioning items. That is, for the purposes of the use of the LAB in the New York City Public Schools, those items with average difficulties of .60-95 were retained for both English and Spanish LABs. The inclusion of these items in the 1976 LAB thus corresponds to the objectives set.

Standardization Program

From the point of view of the development of the Language Assessment Battery, one of the most critical stages was the theoretical/philosophical issues concerning separate norm groups for the LAB-English and LAB-Spanish. The utility of a test for a particular use, can only be highlighted by reference to the tests' validity and norming process. A test whose stated purposes correspond with yours is said to be valid. However, a test may be valid for your purposes, in terms of its item content, but not suited for your use because the norm group composition is not appropriate. A norm refers to that group to which the scores of your subjects will be compared. Norms are the statistics or values describing the performance of one or more groups on a test. In terms of the LAB, raw scores were transformed to percentile ranks and stanines. The percentile rank refers to the performance of students in the norm group (i.e. it is that raw score at which a certain percentage of the norming group fill).

The norms are only relevant if the characteristics of your group are consonant with that of the norming population. As discussed above, in the case of the LAB decision making model, a child must be evaluated in terms of one's ability to "effectively function in the learning process in English." This then would mean that the target population (i.e. Spanish speaking and Spanish surnamed children) should be *compared* to a group who are not hampered from effectively participating in the learning process because of English language deficiencies. In terms of the above reasoning the norm group was composed of children who were monolingual English from grade levels K - 12.

The monolingual English norming population was selected on the basis of school buildings. The initial selection of school buildings was made on the basis of the percentage of monolingual English speaking children (i.e. Black and Other) in the building. *Community School Profiles 1973-74 of the Board of Education of the City of New York was used.* An initial sample of 464 elementary and junior high/intermediate schools and 65 high schools, who met the above criteria, were selected. Each of the above schools had a composite composition of at least 75 percent Black and Other. This initial sample was considered to be monolingual English and not prevented from effectively participating in the learning process because of English language deficits.

The next step in the sampling process was to randomly select three samples of 45 schools each (15 elementary, 15 junior high/intermediate and 15 high schools). Following this procedure means, by grade level, based on the city-wide reading test was computed for each of the three separate samples. The next step in the sampling process was the comparison of the means of the city-wide reading test of each of the three independent samples with the city-wide means at various grade levels. The sample with the mean that was closest to that of the city-wide mean became the primary sample and the one which was used.

The sampling procedures for the selection of schools for the norming of the LAB-Spanish was the same as above. The initial selection of schools was based on approximately 100 schools which had over 70 percent Spanish population. The remaining procedures for the selection of the sample were eventually selected to participate in this study were those children who can read and write Spanish as well as speak and comprehend. Any answer sheet which did not have all of sections complete were eliminated.

The final number of children, by grade level, used in the English and Spanish norming study are presented in the table below:

Grade	English Sample	Spanish Sample
K	795	344
1	923	432
2	925	465
3	835	258
4	953	306
5	941	361
6	959	368
7	1191	741
8	1176	668
9	1017	702
10	1013	944
11	986	681
12	818	451
	12,532	6,721

Reliability of LAB

Presented below are the split-half reliabilities corrected for length by the Spearman-Brown formula for each of the subtests averaged across the grade levels for both LAB-English and Spanish. As is evident, the reliabilities are all over .80 for the subtests (except speaking, which approaches .80). The reliability, as would be expected, for all items taken together is close to or above .90.

Reliabilities of the magnitude reported above when looked at in conjunction with the standard error of measurement (SEm) for total score indicates that the LAB is quite good for making decisions concerning effectiveness. The SEm for Level I does not exceed two raw score points and for Levels II and III does not exceed three raw score points. Thus, the LAB seems to measure (whatever it is that it does measure) with a high degree of precision. The variation of 2-3 raw score points is quite small in relation to the range of possible scores.

SPLIT-HALF RELIABILITIES FOR SUBTESTS AND TOTAL SCORES

LEVEL I

	English	Spanish
Listening & Speaking	.85	.81
Reading	.83	.94
Writing	.81	.90
Total	.89	.94

LEVEL II & III

	English		Spanish	
	L II	L III	L II	L III
Listening	.87	.79	.87	.78
Reading	.86	.86	.93	.81
Writing	.88	.84	.90	.88
Speaking	.69	.76	.78	.77
Total	.94	.92	.96	.94

Future Developments

Efforts will be made to continually improve the Language Assessment Battery. A number of studies are currently in progress or in the planning stages to meet this end.

A study of criterion related validity is currently in its beginning stages. Briefly, a research effort is underway to define children's classroom behavior, across a number of dimensions, in order to determine how these behaviors are related to LAB percentile ranks. A comparability study is also underway which will provide comparable scores for LAB-English and Spanish. A number of school districts across the country are participating. In addition, data has been collected and is now being processed which will provide both Fall and Spring norms for the LAB-English and Spanish.

As you can see, work is progressing at a rapid pace in our continuing efforts to improve the LAB.

REFERENCES

Board of Education, City of New York, Community School Profiles, 1973-1974.

Board of Education, City of New York, Language Assessment Battery (LAB), English, 1976.

Board of Education, City of New York, Language Assessment Battery (LAB), Spanish, 1976.

Consent Decree, August 29, 1974, Entered in case of ASPIRA of New York et al., vs. Board of Education of the City of New York, et al., Southern District of New York, Docket No. 72 Civ. 4002.

De Avila, E. A. and Duncan, S. E. "A few thoughts about Language Assessment: The Lau decision reconsidered." Paper presented at the conference on research on Policy Implications of the Task Force Report of the United States Office of Civil Rights, Southwest Educational Laboratory, Austin, Texas, June 17-18, 1976.

Lau vs. Nichols 414 U. S. 563, 1974.

Meskauskes, J. A., Evaluation Models for Critérion Referenced Testing: Views regarding Mastery and Standard-Setting. *Review of Educational Research, p. 46, 133-158.*

Chapter 65

Summary of a Language Skills Assessment of Chinese Bilingual Students

Maria Estella Brisk, Mae Chu-Chang, and Donald L. Loritz*

With the advent of Bilingual Education Act, many studies and research have been carried out, mainly on Indo-European minorities, specifically the Hispanic population. However, little research so far has been done on the largest non-Indo-European minority population in the U. S., the Chinese population. In many ways this study summarized here represents a first attempt at a systematic study of English language skills in this direction. The language barrier is the greatest difficulty faced by Chinese children and adults alike. The Chinese language is orthographically, structurally, phonologically, and pragmatically very different from the English language. Certain features in English are not distinctive in Chinese, e.g. the plural concept. On the other hand, certain Chinese features are not distinctive in English, e.g. the tonal system. From the point of view of educators and ESL instructors, it would be most illuminating to study such a group whose native language is extremely different from English. This will expose many linguistic features which are taken for granted by native English speakers but difficult for ESL students. We have been careful, however, to include a group of Spanish students in many of our tests, as Spanish is similar to English in many respects. Comparing and contrasting the Chinese and the Spanish groups highlights the similarity and diversity of ESL students of differing background. Many of our finding and many of the methods used in this study should be widely applicable to all language groups.

The study consisted of six tests designed to cover five general areas of language abilities i.e. listening, speaking, reading, writing and appropriate language use. In the absence of existing diagnostic methods which are culturally and linguistically appropriate for use with bilingual students of diverse backgrounds, the major task confronting us in this study was the development of suitable methodologies.

A maximum of forty Chinese students participaed in this project. The age range was 14 to 22. All of them were of lower SES. In our sample 29 percent of them first learned English after arriving in the U. S., 47 percent first learned English in a Hong Kong English school, 25 percent first learned English in a Hong Kong Chinese school. Such information was obtained from an attitudinal questionnaire given to the student. The attitudinal data have been factor analysed with the date from our diagnostic tests.

Cloze Tests

In recent studies (Tucker, 1974; Oller, 1973) cloze procedures have been found to yield global estimates of learners' second language reading skills which agree well with results obtained by more elaborate tests. To assess first and second language reading skills, four cloze passages were prepared, two Chinese and two English. One English and one Chinese passage were selected from original language passages, each was then translated into the other language by the researchers. Every 5th word was deleted in the Chinese passages and every 9th word was deleted in the English passages. Students' mean Z-scores were computed and used as indices of students' first and second language reading skills.

As with all tests used, the object was to secure relative scores within the population of Chinese bilingual students. Tests standardized on different populations (e.g. Spanish bilingual students) would not have provided information meaningful to our objective of assessing the idiosyncratic structure of Chinese students' English language skills.

Thirty-five Chinese students took the Cloze tests in two sessions, eight students were absent from the second session.

The correlation between the two English passages was high, so was the correlation between the two Chinese passages. These correlations indicate that each test was a reliable index of language-specific reading ability despite the varying content of the passages.

*Dr. Maria Brisk, Director, Bilingual Program, Boston University; Mae Chu-Chang and Donald L. Loritz are graduate students at Boston University.

Word Recognition Tests

A second assessment of Chinese students' reading skills investigated their immediate recall of tachistoscopically presented word lists. The stimulus word-lists were projected on a screen, and the students were instructed to select from a response list those words which had appeared in the stimulus word list. Response lists were so constructed that incorrect response words were homographs (visual distractor), homonyms (phonological distractor), or synonyms (semantic distractor) for stimulus words. In recent studies (Conrad, 1972) native English speakers are found to respond phonologically. Because written Chinese is ideographic, it was hypothetically possible that Chinese students would respond more frequently to homographs, the visual distractors. This test was conducted using both Chinese and English stimuli.

Twenty-two Chinese students and sixteen Spanish students participated in this experiment.

As indicated above, the subjects could respond to the stimuli utilizing either a visual, a phonological or a semantic strategy. The main results showed that a different response strategy was used in the first language task (Chinese students in the Chinese Word Recognition Test), as opposed to the second language task (Chinese students in the English Word Recognition test and Spanish students in the English Word Recognition Test). In the first language task a predominantly phonological strategy was used by the Chinese, and in the second language task a predominantly visual strategy was used by both Chinese and Spanish. However, within group error analyses (one-way ANOVAs and Tukey comparisons) showed that the Chinese subjects made significantly more visual responses than phonological responses, whereas the Spanish students' visual and phonological responses were not significantly different.

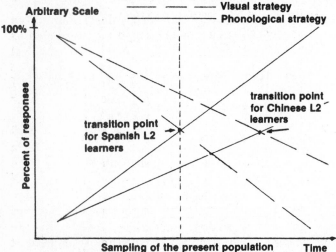

FIG. 1 A MODEL OF READING FOR SECOND LANGUAGE LEARNERS

A two-stage model of reading is proposed for second language learners (See fig. 1). Both the Chinese and the Spanish students begin with a visual strategy in recognizing English words. However, as the students acquire knowledge of the sound system of the English language, a predominantly phonological strategy develops. In the present study the sample of subjects is probably at a hypothetical point A where the Spanish subjects are just beginning to change to a phonological strategy but the Chinese subjects are still firmly attached to a visual strategy. The Chinese group probably remains at the visual stage longer, partially because the strategies they used when they began to read Chinese characters were predominantly visual (Van & Zian, 1962).

Vowel-Length

Listening skills were assessed with respect to two aspects of English phonology which were observationally difficult for Chinese students: appropriate English pre-consonantal vowel-lengthening and a decoupling of lexicon and English suprasegmental fundamental frequency contours.

Post-vocalic voicing distinctions do not exist in Cantonese, all final stops being grossly characterizable as 'unvoiced.' In English, the difference between minimal pairs such as 'shot' and 'shod' is primarily cued by the greater length of the vowel before voiced consonants. The ability to make this distinction was therefore taken as a critical index of the students' English listening skill which was independent of their ability to disambiguate heard words on the basis of syntactic or non-linguistic context.

There were three parts to this test. In the first part, students were to identify which of a minimal pair such as 'shot'/'shod' was spoken, given tape-recorded stimuli such as:

1) Uncle Bill shot Rod's horse.
or,
2) Uncle Bill shod Rod's horse.

In the second part, the final consonant burst was spliced from tape-recorded stimuli such as:

1) Uncle Bill's horse was sho(t).
or,
2) Uncle Bill's horse was sho(d).

In the third part, students had to select the presented minimal pair element given one of four stimulus types:

1) Uncle Bill shot Todd's horse.
2) Uncle Bill shot Dodd's horse.
3) Uncle Bill shod Dodd's horse.
4) Uncle Bill shod Todd's horse.

Thus, in part one, all possible cues to final consonant identification were available. In part two all cues except vowel length and the (unanalyzed) formant transition cues were excised. In part three, the vowel-length cue was set in competition with the pre-vocalic cues of the following word.

Twenty-eight Cantonese and fifteen Spanish bilingual high-school students participated in this test. Control data was collected from twelve native adult speakers of English.

The principal results are presented in Fig. 2.

As can be seen from Fig. 2, both groups performed significantly worse on this feature than the English control group. The better performance of the Spanish speakers might be explained by the fact that Spanish possesses regular differences in vowel-length akin to the English feature tested here. Spanish speakers' chance performance on test sentences of the type:

Uncle Bill shot Dodd's horse.

might be explained by the fact that Spanish intervocalic consonants also undergo a phonological transformation of the manner feature (e.g. /t/ /d/, /d/ /d/) which would tend to decrease the value they place upon the vowel-length feature in such environments.

Two major types of conclusions might be drawn from these results. The poor performance of the Cantonese students appears to reflect a problem also evidenced in their characteristic 'staccato' accent. Their tendency to pronounce 'sawed' as 'sought' seems to be grounded in their inability to perceptually identify three values of vowel-length (corresponding to English 'sought', 'sawed', and 'saw').

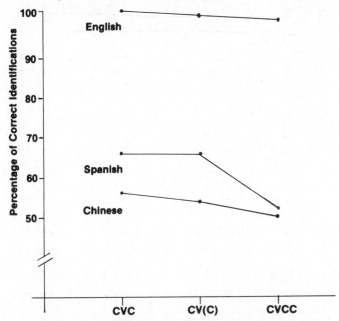

FIGURE 2 PERCENT CORRECT IDENTIFICATION OF VOICED-VOICELESS DISTINCTION BY THREE GROUPS IN THREE CONTEXTS: CVC: UNCLE BILL SHOD/SHOT ROD'S HORSE. CV(C): UNCLE BILL'S HORSE WAS SHO(D)/SHO(T). CVCC: UNCLE BILL SHOD/SHOT TODD'S/DODD'S HORSE.

It may also be argued that this difficulty is an instance of interference since Cantonese has only two values of syllabic vowel length (corresponding to English 'sought' and 'saw'). The superior performance of the Spanish students would seem to support this conclusion.

English Stress/Juncture

A second test of English speech perception required the students to make binary classifications of English nominal-compound/adjective-noun phrase 'minimal pairs' excised from four different, tape-recorded, English intonational contours:

1) Not Buckingham Palace, the White House!
2) Not the green house, the white house!
3) Buckingham Palace, the White House,....
4) the red Ford, the White house,....

where types 3 and 4 were recited with prosodic contours appropriate to a boring list.

These four intonational contours correspond to four distinctive and canonical tones of Chinese. Perception of the contours as cues to English stress and/or juncture would lead to a different binary grouping of the four stimulus types than perception of the contours as lexical features after the Chinese model. Individual students' performances were scored according to the correlation of their judgements with those of a control group of native English speakers. Again, the objective of this test was to secure an estimate of the students' listening skill which would be independent of syntactic and extra-linguistic cues. And again, the feature investigated is one which observation and contrastive analysis identify as a unique and significant problem for Chinese English learners: appropriate usage of English fundamental frequency.

Nineteen Cantonese bilingual high school students participated in this study. Nine native English speakers served as controls.

Presentation of the materials described above resulted in responses which could be interpreted as same-different judgement among the four intonational contours studied. Factor-analytic techniques were employed to arrive at a graphical representation of how the Chinese and English subjects 'clustered' or categorized these four stimuli (Fig. 3).

Fig. 3 shows that the Chinese students clearly divided the four contours into a 'high-tone' group and a 'low-tone' group. The English controls divided the same contours into a clearly-defined 'moving-tone' group and a more poorly-defined 'level-tone' group. Subsequent stepwise- and multiple-regression analyses of the responses of each group further supported the conclusion that the Chinese students were not responding to English stress or juncture cues but were performing this task as if English were a tonal language like Chinese.

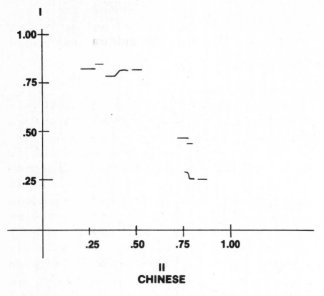

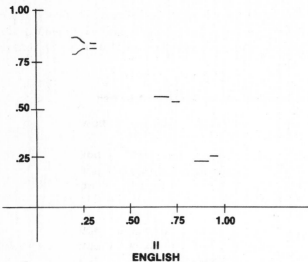

FIGURE 3 FACTOR LOADINGS FOR FOUR ENGLISH "TONES" AFTER VARIMAX ROTATION.

Dictation-Repetition Test

Data was also collected on students' listening and written syntactic skills through the use of a repetition-dictation test. A passage of diverse syntactic structures was constructed and tape-recorded with response intervals after each sentence. By presenting the passages sentence-by-sentence rather than word-by-word (as in most classical dictation procedures), a kind of repetition-imitation design is incorporated. Such techniques have been investigated by several researchers. Swain, Dumas and Naiman (1974) have concluded that the technique 'taps both comprehension and production skills.' As such it was

hoped that the procedure could provide information about the students' active command of several observably difficult aspects of English syntax.

Twenty-one Chinese high school bilingual students took part in this test.

Results were obtained by arranging the students' responses to each item according to the format of Table 1.

Table 1 gives the actual results from the last sentence of the passage. The columnar arrangement of responses effectively highlights areas of greatest phonological, morphological, and syntactic difficulty. For example, phonological confusion is indicated by substitutions of 'He' or 'This' for 'These.' The patterns of errors revealed by the columnar analysis of results are not nearly so readily apparent when dictation-repetition tests can provide the teacher with valuable summary diagnostic information.

Communicative Competance

A last test procedure was designed to assess students' pragmatic competance in English. Administered to a subset of our sample population, it represents an attempt to assess students' ability to use their second language, not simply in a linguistically 'correct' fashion, but in socially appropriate ways. Despite its obvious practical importance, this language ability has just begun to be systematically studied. In this test, students were asked to respond, both in their first and second languages to situations calling for speech acts which could be generically classified as 'requests.' Students were asked to put themselves in the position of a character in a situation characterized by verbal description and an artist-drawn picture. For example, one picture depicted a student asking for an extension on a paper. Taking the student's role, the subject was asked 'What do you say' and his request for an extension was recorded. The subject was then informed that his (first) request was turned down, and he was invited to present another request (first escalation). This second request was also turned down and a 'second escalation' was elicited. The obtained data provided a sample of the range of requesting strategies and politeness formulas the subject had at his command in his first and second language.

Six Chinese students, five Spanish students and five English native speakers were interviewed and taped for analysis of their 'everyday' speech, in English as well as in their native language.

Each request was coded as to whether it was a question, or a statement; whether the subject used 'can/will', 'would/could', 'may/might' or 'please' as politeness markers. The first and second escalations were coded as to whether the request was grammatically more complex, the same or less complex as compared with the previous request. The requests were coded the same way for length, number of reasons give, 'obliqueness' and general impression of 'politeness.'

It was found that the greatest number of statements was used by the Chinese group. The English native speakers used the greatest number of questions. This may be explained by the lack of the question-inversion form in Chinese. An interesting result was that the native English speakers would not use the word 'can' in requesting, they invariably used 'could' or an equivalent word in subjunctive form. The second language groups (Chinese as well as Spanish) used the word 'can' almost one-third of the time. This could be attributed to the fact that 'can you...' form is heavily taught as a request form in current ESL materials. Therefore, it is important for ESL curriculum writers to design materials that are relevant to actual language use. All Chinese students recognized the word 'could' but considered it as the past tense of 'can', no one regarded it as a 'politeness marker.' There were also some socio-cultural differences between Chinese, Spanish and English speakers in how much they would persist in making, much less 'escalating' their requests after having met with repeated refusals.

Conclusions

The most important conclusions to be drawn from these studies relate to the development of new diagnostic and pedagogic methodologies appropriate to the unique linguistic and cultural heritages of bilingual students.

Diagnostic Methods:

Modern linguistic theory and psycholinguistic research have developed many detailed models and methods for describing and evaluating language behavior. In the studies summarized above, we attempted to either adapt traditional ESL diagnostic techniques to recent theory or to modify psycholinguistic research techniques for educational application. Unless we are to be satisfied with simple answers to the complex task of language learning, much further study by teachers and researchers will be necessary. That study will entail detailed investigations of phonology, morphology, syntax, semantics, and pragmatics with specific reference to the cultural-linguistic background of the bilingual student. It is our belief that the procedures we have employed in the present study can provide useful models for further study.

18.	These	are		questions	which	we		can't	answer	now.
01	These		the	question	which		was		answered	now
03	This			question				can not be	answer	now
06	These	are	the	question		is	not	to	be set	out
07										
08	This	one		question						
11	These	are		question			to	be	answer	now
13	He		the	question			was		answer	it now
14	This	are	the	question				can't	answer	now
15	This	are	the	question	which	we		couldn't	answer	now
16	These	are	the	question		we		want	to	asked
17	This		a	question		we		can't	answer	now
18	This			question						
20	This	are		question						
23	This		a	question	which					
25	He	said								
26	Do	you has	any	question	to	ask				
27	These	are		question				couldn't be	answer	now
28	This			questions	would	be		president	answer	now
29	There	are	be a	question				to	answer	now
33	These	are		questions	which	we		can't	answer	about
34	These	are		question	which				answer	it's aloud

TABLE 1. STUDENTS' RESPONSES TO ITEM 18 OF THE DICTATION-REPETITION TEST

Pedagogic Methods:

Our findings have given rise to several specific recommendations for the teaching and learning of English in Chinese bilingual classes. For example, Chinese pronunciation of English might be improved by paying greater and explicit attention to such non-obvious aspects of English as vowel-length and variations of intonation. We have suggested trying to introduce English reading through the use of rebus reading materials in an attempt to decouple visual and phonological reading strategies. Such methods can be and should be tested and elaborated in the bilingual classroom.

REFERENCES

Conrad, R. 1972. Speech and reading. In Kavanagh, J. F. & Mattingly, I. G. (Eds.) *Language by Ear and by Eye*. Cambridge: MIT Press.

Oller, J. W. Jr. 1973. Cloze tests of second language proficiency and what they measure. *Language Learning, 23*, 105-118.

Tucker, G. R. 1974. The Cloze test: a measure of English proficiency. *The Modern Language Journal, 239-241.*

Swain, M., Dumas, G. & Naiman, N. 1974. *Alternatives to spontaneous speech: elicited translation and imitation as indicators of second language competence. Working Papers on Bilingualism #3,* 68-79.

Van, Y. Y. & Zian, C. T. 1962. *(Acta Psychologica Sinica), 3,* 219-230.